CLASSICAL SOLAR RETURNS

J. Lee Lehman, Ph.D.

4880 Lower Valley Road, Atglen, Pennsylvania 19310

LEE LEHMAN IS THE AUTHOR of *The Ultimate Asteroid Book* (Schiffer, 1988), *Essential Dignities* (Schiffer, 1989), *The Book of Rulerships* (Schiffer, 1992), *Classical Astrology for Modern Living* (Schiffer, 1996), *The Martial Art of Horary Astrology* (Schiffer, 2002), *Astrology of Sustainability* (Schiffer 2011), *Traditional Medical Astrology* (Schiffer 2011) and a translation from the French of *Papus' Astrology for Initiates*.

Type set in Souvenir Lt BT

Astrological Charts produced in Sirius 1.1

ISBN: 978-0-7643-4100-7
Printed in the United States of America

Schiffer Books are available at special discounts for bulk purchases for sales promotions or premiums. Special editions, including personalized covers, corporate imprints, and excerpts can be created in large quantities for special needs. For more information contact the publisher:

Published by Schiffer Publishing Ltd.
4880 Lower Valley Road
Atglen, PA 19310
Phone: (610) 593-1777; Fax: (610) 593-2002
E-mail: Info@schifferbooks.com

For the largest selection of fine reference books on this and related subjects, please visit our website at

www.schifferbooks.com

We are always looking for people to write books on new and related subjects. If you have an idea for a book please contact us at the above address.

This book may be purchased from the publisher. Please try your bookstore first. You may write for a free catalog.

In Europe, Schiffer books are distributed by
Bushwood Books
6 Marksbury Ave.
Kew Gardens
Surrey TW9 4JF England
Phone: 44 (0) 20 8392 8585; Fax: 44 (0) 20 8392 9876
E-mail: info@bushwoodbooks.co.uk
Website: www.bushwoodbooks.co.uk

Classical Solar Returns

List of Charts, Tables and Figures

Preface

"Toto, I've a feeling we're not in Kansas any more."
— Dorothy, in *The Wizard of Oz* (1939)

THE WHOLE PROCESS OF DELINEATING SOLAR RETURNS HAS BECOME TOO COMPLEX. This has actually been true for several decades, and was the reason that, before I became a classical astrologer, I had stopped using solar returns with my clients.

What happened to this technique? It has a singularly simple definition, namely: a chart drawn for the time when the position of the Sun is exactly the same as the position of the Sun at a person's birth. What happened was modern life! Several historical factors converged which created greater complexity, further complicated by certain trends within astrology itself since the 1800s.

Briefly put, these factors are:

- **Location.** While people have always traveled, the ease of travel has increased to the point that mass mobility for leisure means that many people can choose to be someplace else for their birthdays. Furthermore, virtually all astrologers have access to astrology software that will not only compute the solar return for any location, but also make examining multiple choices of location easy.

- **Residence.** Large numbers of people no longer reside in their place of birth, or even nearby.

- **Precession.** In the 19th century, Western astrologers became more aware of Vedic astrology and its sidereal orientation, thus leading Western astrologers to reconsider the possible importance of precession within the lifetime.

- **Confusion of technique.** Astrologers as a group have often been most reluctant to reject multiple variations, and so prefer to allow *all* possibilities, evidently for fear of missing some valuable piece of information. The result is that predictability becomes lost when too many variations produce conflicting results.

When I began to study solar returns in earnest almost twenty-five years ago, this was the situation that confronted me. Beyond the usual question of house systems, different astrologers were advocating completely different methods. The major variations boiled down to six possible solar return charts because there were two sets of variables:

1. Whether the chart should be calculated using precession or not.
2. Whether the birthplace, residence, or actual location coordinates should be used.

I did what probably a lot of other astrologers did: I asked a number of people with good birth times to tell me about significant years that they had experienced, and then I went looking to find the events in the charts, computing all six variations. And as, during this time period, I had several opportunities to travel on or around my birthday, I personally sampled the question of whether the actual location served to produce a different result than the residence or the natal would.

The result was chaos. Almost always I would *see* something interesting in *one* of the charts, just not the same one from year to year. It was so tantalizing and so frustrating at the same time! So I simply threw up my hands in disgust, and went on to other methods that were working more consistently.

In the meantime, I became steeped in traditional horary. My horary background taught me the dangers of multiple choice options for prediction. Simply put, when you have multiple possibilities for the rulership of a house, each ruler can produce a different scenario — and a different answer. In a horary, this is disastrous, so successful horary method must include a protocol for selecting the appropriate significator to use.

In natal, several different alternatives may be real because a year isn't just a single event or scenario, as a horary is. The challenge with natal is to have a way to distinguish between the major theme(s) for the year, and the minor ones. Simply dumping one technique on top of another doesn't accomplish this.

The solar return itself is a technique that shares something vital with horary, namely, its relatively short duration. The reason for being restrictive in horary about possible options is that a horary covers a limited span of time and emphasizes the trend of events *if* no major conscious decisions take place. There's actually little time for learning with a horary. One might argue that, while a year is enough time for *some* learning and development, it is still not a huge amount of time when compared with the entire life. Thus, one might hypothesize that a solar return might be interpreted as intermediate between natal, with its great mandate for choice and change, and horary, which gives a quick answer to a single question. The solar return is the map of change for the year. But a year can pass unnoticed, or it may present a sudden change which shifts the flow of life entirely.

I would only come back to solar returns personally years later, after I had begun to study classical: and specifically because of a wonderful gift I received from Clara Darr. Sadly, Clara was going blind, and she sold her astrological library. I bought a piece of it: the classical part. One book of that, Gadbury's work on King Charles II, would factor heavily in my thinking. As I began to study this work, I realized that here was a clearly defined method for working with solar returns that did not have the problem of six multiple-choice charts for each year. In reproducing this method and extending it, I found my own solar return niche, and then I discovered that this particular lineage had never died, but was still practiced in many European schools, albeit with variations.

This in turn raised other, deeply troubling issues. While all of a sudden, I was a great enthusiast of solar returns, my method fundamentally disagreed with that of many colleagues — even many friends. But I feel that we cannot progress as a craft without addressing these more difficult issues. This is something I will defer until after Chapter 1, which presents a history of the application of solar return charts, so that we can understand how we have gotten to our particular place. Chapter 2 introduces the method through examples, and in Chapters 3-12, we will examine how this system operates in practice. We shall summarize our results in Chapter 13.

I would ask in the meantime that the reader suspend judgment about variations presented from what you already know. I realize that most of my readers use solar returns. You probably already have your own theories, and I can pretty well predict: you will agree with some of what I say, but not all!

My goal is not to convince you that I'm right, but to present a clear view of the method I have adopted, along with the invitation to explore with me some fundamental methodological questions. As a foreshadowing of our upcoming discussions in Chapter 13, I think that much of the present confusion has resulted from people approaching the technique with different goals in mind. Astrologers are using solar returns for different purposes, and so consequently they emphasize different aspects of the methods. Unfortunately, without a clear, forthright discussion of these different purposes and viewpoints, all the discussion collapses down into a cacophony of different voices, thus confusing beginners as well as everybody else.

Any history of solar returns in the 20th century is necessarily incomplete. The reason for this is a lack of publishing continuity. In the last century, many astrological works were self-published, and also many small publishing houses did not last past the death of the founder. Because there has not been great interest in collecting astrological material through regular library channels, it is simply impossible to trace and research material. If anything, the plethora of self-published material in the age of e-books threatens to make this even more true for the 21st century. It is unknown how well that material will remain available as electronic formats morph and authors die.

Nonetheless, in this irregular atmosphere, many astrologers were incredibly innovative. Without formal lineages, or continuity of teaching method, it can be difficult to trace the history of ideas. As a result, I will surely make errors when I arrive at the 20th century in Chapter 1. But I do not want to use these facts as an excuse not to try to work through this period. Hopefully, those who follow will find this a useful exercise to build upon.

However, I do not want to leave these preliminary matters without expressing the opinion that what is *not* okay with this material is to accrete blithely all the variations, and attempt to include all of them in your technique. Ultimately, this method will fail — and its failure can actually be seen in the pages of some of the modern works on solar returns.

There are techniques that predict, and there are those that don't. In astrology, there is no virtue to a technique that cannot predict. It is one thing to leave room for free will: it is another to leave so much room that fate is left unaccounted. Prediction is merely a statement of what could well happen if the Native doesn't change the outcome by applying free will. Prediction does not preclude free will: it addresses its absence.

One way to understand our job as astrologers is to frame it within the Serenity Prayer of Reinhold Niebuhr (1892-1971):

> *God grant me the serenity to accept the things I cannot change; courage to change the things I can; and wisdom to know the difference.*

Oftentimes, astrologers have slanted their methods to one extreme or the other, either addressing fate without free will, or free will without fate. Yet, it is in defining the parameters of these two old friends that we discharge our responsibility to promulgate the best method that we can. If our methods don't allow us to address this balance, then why bother with them at all?

When I was challenged to teach method at Kepler College, I found that I was forced to reconsider all of astrological method in light of several basic questions:

- What is the historical foundation of a technique? In which culture did it originate, using what assumptions? When, where, and why were the major variations laid down?
- What is the stated purpose of a technique? What information does it attempt to convey? What other techniques either duplicate the same information, or supplement it?

- Do methodological variations also produce differences in what information is conveyed? Do the variations increase or decrease the predictability of the technique?
- How universal is the technique? Is it something which can be applied in many situations, or only in specific ones?

Put succinctly, when there are many more methodologies that could be applied to a delineation than there is time available, on what basis is one technique chosen over another? And also, how much time can be devoted to variations on the same technique? It is these practical factors that must force us to choose.

From a teaching standpoint, the more I thought about it, the more that I realized there is a value to presenting just such a controversial technique precisely in order to illustrate this issue of choice. In actuality, we don't often have *choice* modeled to us. Instead, we are immersed in a sea of methodologies, with lots of possibilities, but little thought to *why* the student might want to choose one technique over another.

Consider one basic type of client session: the yearly update. There is roughly an hour to go over the high and low points of the year ahead. How do you do it?

Most certainly, you'll want to cover the transits. But which ones? Chances are, you'll highlight the biggies: the hard aspects of the Outers to the Inners, the age-specific transits like Saturn square Saturn, perhaps the progressed lunation cycle. Maybe eclipses. But what else?

Maybe you want to use the secondaries, or the solar arcs, or the solar return, lunar returns, or tertiaries. But how do you choose from within this list? If you cover all of them, you will run out of time — and you may get contradictory results. How do you choose from among these methods which do, at least in theory, cover much of the same ground?

My own approach has been to limit this second list only to solar returns, because I am looking for one specific function out of the solar return: the function of significance. I do not break up the solar year into smaller increments to find predictive moments. In my client work, I have never been asked to do so, because the discussion tends to focus on major themes for the year, not specifics.

My query for solar returns is more traditionally based: I want to know if this is going to be a memorable year. In a given decade, the odds are, you will only actually remember one or two years. And further, you are at least as likely to remember a year for "bad" reasons as for "good" ones. Therefore, I want to know if this is going to be one of those memorable years, and, if so, is it good or bad?

My job as an astrologer is very different in those two sets of circumstances. Suppose the Native shows superior earning power in only two years in this decade: and next year is one of those years. Wouldn't some preparation be a good thing? But if this is going to be an average year, then the Native is not going to be called upon to step out terribly much. Life proceeds largely on autopilot, with the transits then showing the distractions from the norm.

Many astrologers seem to be concerned that if they don't use several overlapping techniques, such as secondaries and solar arcs, they will somehow miss important points. My opinion is that the important points will too likely be drowned out by the less important glut of information that so easily results from too many similar methods. I am reminded of a conversation with Batya Stark some years ago. I had asked her about the Uranian system of examining the multiple transiting planetary pictures that occur in a single day. Her comment was: you can see the pictures alright, but how do you tell the difference between the ones you personally experience, and the ones you see on the nightly news? Too much information can drown out the important with the merely mundane.

Many astrologers are very quick to declare that they are looking for confirmation in multiple methods: that it is good to see the same perspective from different angles. Many of us have had fascinating experiences along the way to such confirmations. But just as frequently, we have been confounded by conflicting indicators. More than any other factor, I have seen beginners in a method simply stopped when the dissonance between two arguments becomes too great.

And this is where I must comment on our current mundane astrology as a driving force behind this book. There are in fact many books that have been written on solar returns: why do I believe the community needs one more?

It is *not* because there are no good books on the subject! There are good books from the classical period (pre-1700), and there are good books from the modern period (19th-21st centuries). The problem, as I see it, is this: From now until 2043, Pluto is in Saturn's signs. In *Astrology of Sustainability*, I talked about how this impacts our experiences. Much of life gets stripped down to the Saturnian bare bones, the essence. That it is precisely this sojourn in Capricorn and then Aquarius (the one time in the zodiac when consecutive signs have the same ruler) that ideas cannot simply be thrown around: they must be broken down, digested, understood, and applied — or discarded.[1]

The primary growth in astrology, as well as current New Age philosophies, has occurred while Pluto transited Virgo, Libra, Scorpio, and Sagittarius: signs of Mercury, Venus, Mars, and Jupiter. While people's tempers may have gotten a little frayed under Pluto in Scorpio, *none* of these Pluto signs presented a mandate for paring down technique. They all provided the ground for expansion of ideas and concepts. They allowed us to generate the astrological equivalent of derivatives. Why? In an expansionary period, everything works — or seems to. People experience their lives as a series of opportunities. It seems that there are few limitations. Surely, any style of astrological interpretation which hints of fate cannot possibly be right!

Along comes Pluto in Capricorn, and the bubble has burst. Suddenly, not only does the economy crash, but so does this sense of possibility. Several scenarios come to mind. A person is suddenly laid off, and has to look for a job with a much lower salary, while paying a mortgage (or two!) on a house that is no longer worth even the balance on the first mortgage. That's a different world. Or one discovers that one's parents had learned about reverse mortgages, and suddenly that inheritance that was counted upon to cancel the children's debts turns into a debt itself, as the heirs find that their parents' reverse mortgage was calculated on property values *before* the real estate crash. Or, how about that decision from thirty years ago made by a parent or relative to buy their apartment? Now the heir discovers that the monthly maintenance fee continues to be owed, at an exorbitant rate for a non-inhabited place, in which the co-op association can block a sale because it doesn't want the co-op dumped at a fire sale price.

While the Great Recession may temporarily ease, there is no question that there are many people who will be feeling the effects of that Pluto Ingress into Capricorn for years, if not decades to come. The effects take the form of reduced assets, increased debt, reduced retirement expectations, and reduced life styles. Many twenty- and thirty-somethings cannot find paying jobs, and find themselves forced to live with their parents. Many of these people are likely to never recoup the losses they are experiencing now in their lifetime financial pathways. Resource issues of peak oil, infrastructure, pure water, and safe food are just a few of the factors that we are likely to see on center stage over the period of Pluto in Capricorn.[2] For reasons that I explain in *Sustainability*, I expect the 2010s to be remembered as the Decade of Denial, in which almost everyone still acts as if they can turn back the clock to the period before 2005.

It is precisely we astrologers who can understand that Pluto in Sagittarius is not coming back. But following the consequences of this simple conclusion demands a level of courage and foresight that prior Pluto passages did not require. But then, this is truly the "hitting bottom" phase of the Pluto cycle. How must we respond? It is because of *this* question, that I believe this book is not merely necessary, but that it is the beginning of a conscious approach as to how we can adjust our thinking to the new reality.

As we shall see in Chapter 1, while traditional astrology[3] had its variations, the fact that astrology was part of the Liberal Arts and embedded in university settings meant that a large number of historical astrologers shared the same philosophical and intellectual framework with their colleagues. While some disagreements remained, new proposals or elaborations were embedded into existing theory and technique. It was only after the 1600s that astrology, jettisoned from its academic moorings, no longer had such a common philosophical basis among its practitioners. What flourished were many more lineages and schools, disconnected from other schools, and sometimes even hostile to the others.

Unfortunately, one of the biggest things lost when astrology was booted out of the academy is what academicians call the critical apparatus. From our standpoint, there are two components to this which are absolutely necessary if astrology is to remain a vibrant discipline over multiple generations to come:

- **The acknowledgment of sources.** If I get an idea from another person, it is only proper that I acknowledge the source. Beyond the fact that theft of ideas is something that every author must shun (even if we can never totally eliminate unconscious elements of this), the failure to cite sources specifically results in broken lineages, and in people not understanding the context in which astrological ideas have been developed.
- **The discrimination of theories and ideas.** There is dry thought as well as wet thought, and dry technique as well as wet technique. In *Traditional Medical Astrology*, I discussed the ancient element and temperament types.[4] Basically, wet thinking makes connections between things, whereas dry thinking makes distinctions. Both modes are necessary to any complete system, and neither mode is superior, just as it would be improper to think of *Yin* as superior to *Yang* in Chinese medicine and philosophy. In just the same way, a complete dominance of one at the expense of the other is generally a derangement. In astrology throughout the 20th century, there was a general preference for wet thinking, in which any idea is welcomed, and is simply thrown in the pot with all the other existing ideas. No serious attempt to distinguish differences in techniques is made.

What I am suggesting here is that wet thinking is more prevalent in an expansionary period, whereas dry thinking will predominate in a contractionary period. Again, this is not a value judgment. It's like saying that breathing in is better than breathing out. Without both, you die. Without both equally, you die. But that simple fact does not negate the human observation that most people seem to prefer the breathing in phase — the expansionary phase — over the contractionary one.

When Pluto went into Capricorn, we went crashing from an expansionary period to a contractionary one. Not only was this psychologically unwelcome, but it was downright unfamiliar. Sagittarius, the last of the Fire signs, ruled by Jupiter, is about as expansionary as it's possible to be. Capricorn, the last of the Earth signs, and ruled by Saturn, is about as contractionary as it's possible to be. Thus, the phase shift we have just experienced is as severe as it can be. And we are creatures of habit: we don't want to change, especially *this* change.

So we do the human thing: we resist. It is this drag or inertia which I discuss in *Sustainability* as being partly responsible for why one of the primary functions of Pluto in any sign is cleaning up the messes of Pluto in the previous sign.

We did get a preview of this when Neptune made the same Ingress, in 1984-1985. This corresponded to the transition between the first and second terms of Ronald Reagan, surely one of the United States' most optimistic presidents ever. Reagan was elected by a landslide over Jimmy Carter, who can be classified as one of our more Saturnian presidents ever. (Here, you can see Saturn's exaltation of his sun sign, Libra.) Carter had the audacity to respond to the Arab Oil Embargo by suggesting that Americans should cut their dependency on foreign oil! No, no, no! Neptune's sign touches on how we instinctively think and feel the world works.[5] Rationing during Neptune in Sagittarius? Unthinkable! Then, the Iranian students had the temerity to embarrass President Carter when the U.S. embassy was overrun. In swoops Reagan, the hostages are freed without anyone stopping to contemplate *how*, and trickle-down economics became king, possibly one of the most perfect statements of Sagittarius economics until the development of derivatives.

Reagan's speeches were an unending litany of "tax and spend liberals," while the size of the government ballooned under his administration. He walked what he said was his opponent's walk — and *nobody seemed to notice*. As Neptune slipped into Capricorn, his economic theories collapsed. But we may ask the obvious question: why didn't President Reagan's polemics change when Neptune went into Capricorn? The answer is simple: *nobody likes this transition*. This is the most wrenching transition in the entire zodiac. Fire-Jupiter to Earth-Saturn. The party's over! Now who wants to be the town crier for this state of affairs?

The entire Reagan Era has come down to us embedded as Neptune in Sagittarius amber. More than a Saturn cycle later, early Pluto in Capricorn Republicans are still evoking Reagan as if the budgets were balanced and government was shrinking!

Now: if your clientele happens to be the super-rich, then they can probably manage to keep that Pluto in Sagittarius feeling going for at least another seven years. But what can you do when your clients *aren't* that rich, *know* they are worth less now than they were in 2008, and are rightly worried about their future? What do you tell them?

This is where I say something truly radical: the astrology you already know may not still work with Pluto in Capricorn. You can ignore this statement at your peril. Understand: I am not making this assertion as a polemic in favor of classical astrology. I am not

saying that any *style* of astrology — whether traditional, modern, esoteric, psychological, evolutionary, or cosmobiological — is fated to shrink or disappear. My assertion is actually much more technical (remember, I'm a Virgo). You are likely to find that *any* specific technique you use needs tightening up: the rules need to be more precise to maintain accuracy.

Put more prosaically, life is easier in expansionary times when we appear to encounter fewer, smaller obstacles. This means that our craft does not need to be so precise in these times. We can be more positive in our predictions, and less inclined to dwell on negative outcomes. A mediocre year can be seen as mildly positive. In general, we are rewarded for being a bit over-optimistic, *because that is how life is experienced by most people*. People reasonably *expect* their lives to improve. They could operate under the premise of those most maligned and parodied (yet immensely popular) books of self-help affirmations: every day in every way, things are getting better and better!

In contractionary times, the reverse is true. Mediocre is now mildly negative – or worse. It takes more positive indicators for a year to be truly positive financially. So where does this leave astrological method? If we don't have a way to adjust our technique to account for more challenging times, then we will just be spinning false positives that will be of no practical help to our clients.

This is a topic I alluded to in *Traditional Medical Astrology*. There, my subject was about the kinds of diseases that people have in any particular era change, and that our astrology must be able to adapt to these demographic changes. In both these cases, I am making what is in effect an ecological or sociological statement: astrology cannot be practiced in a cultural vacuum where societal limitations play no part in how astrology is understood and interpreted.

How has your astrology changed since Pluto went into Capricorn? I can tell you that mine has, even though, as a classical astrologer, you might expect that I was already more "fate-driven" in outlook than the average astrologer. One has to adjust to the probabilities of outcome, whether that means using the same techniques with a tighter interpretation, or by consciously adopting techniques that feature more restrictive results.

Either way, we are past the point where we can reasonably expect to simply gather more and more and more technique. In the mid-20th century, a conscious shift to the *invention* of astrological techniques occurred, as astrologers like Edward Johndro and Ronald Davison (who we shall revisit in Chapter 1) set out to create new techniques for what they considered new times. This is yet another expression of expansionary times. Now, as we enter contractionary ones, we need to make sure that these techniques are really giving us the bang for our reduced bucks.

So: a recurring theme of this book is the exploration of how to assimilate, understand, simplify, and produce a leaner, meaner technique. As such, I hope this work will provide insight into how to apply this process to other systems as well. Happy hunting!

Preface Endnotes

1. Lehman, J. Lee. *Astrology of Sustainability: The Challenge of Pluto in Capricorn.* Atglen, PA: Schiffer Press, 2011.

2. See especially, Lehman, 2011, Chapter 9.

3. You will note that I am using the words "traditional" and "classical" pretty interchangeably. I give a fuller explanation of the reasons and history behind this equation in: Lehman, J. Lee. *Traditional Medical Astrology.* Atglen, PA: Schiffer Press, 2011, p 2.

4. Lehman, J. Lee. *Traditional Medical Astrology.* Atglen, PA: Schiffer Press, 2011.

5. See the important work on this subject: Barker, Stan. *The Signs of the Times: The Neptune Factor and America's Destiny.* Llewellyn's Popular Astrology Series. 1st ed. St. Paul, Minn., U.S.A.: Llewellyn Publications, 1984.

Acknowledgments

THIS WORK BRINGS TO A CLOSE A TRILOGY OF BOOKS I HAVE WRITTEN IN JUST OVER A YEAR AND A HALF. Superficially, they have nothing in common, since *Astrology of Sustainability* was about mundane, *Traditional Medical Astrology* was about medical, with a mixture of natal, horary, and electional, and this one is purely natal. While the topics are different, writing so intensely and continuously brought topics together in my mind, at least. While I plan to continue writing, future books will probably not appear at such a close interval.

These all fall within what I see as my personal mission and mandate: producing works for practitioners, not merely historical discussions of techniques. I do not reject techniques because they were discovered before or after a particular date. However, my rejection of a technique because its methodology doesn't "fit" with the rest of the delineation does reflect my belief that lineages matter.

For example: what does one do with out-of-sign aspects? Lilly used them.[1] But he wasn't the first: Abraham ibn Ezra did as well.[2] Ibn Ezra admitted that this was not the practice of the ancients, but he took exception. So here we have a classical precedence, and a fairly early one in the Arabic period. Yet many modern astrologers, Jungians, for example, deny the validity of the out-of-sign aspect.

Who is right? The answer may well be: it depends on the system being used. It might be in the symbolical/mythical/psychological usage of the Jungians, the out-of-sign aspect doesn't work, but in classical horary, it does.

I could not have created this threesome of books without the encouragement, not to mention, editorial skills, of my partner Maggie Meister, who continues to work tirelessly to make all my books more readable to you, gentle reader.

Many astrologers and astrology students have provided help, even if they didn't know that they were helping eventually to gestate this book. Foremost have been several different groups of students – the students at Kepler College, at Avalon School of Astrology, at the Midwest School of Astrology, and at the Academy of Astrology near Amsterdam. I would also thank all the astrologers who have attended intensives that I have given, for their comments and reactions to the material. They have been most helpful. And I would like to thank my clients for being my guinea pigs, with the hope that these experiments proved useful to them.

This book, compared to my other works, has provided some specific challenges. It truly is easier to write about authors long dead than to have to critically evaluate colleagues and friends. Hopefully, I am not creating enemies here, but engaging people in a discussion of techniques.

Again, I would also like to thank David and Fei Cochrane of Cosmic Patterns Software. All charts shown here were generated by their program Sirius, either version 1.1 or 1.2. Appendix F owes its creation to the robust search capabilities of Solar Fire, for which I thank Esoteric Technologies, Graham Dawson, and Stephanie Johnson.

Finally, I would like to thank my publisher, Pete Schiffer, and my editor, Doug Congdon-Martin, for all their assistance, support, ideas, and encouragement.

Acknowledgment Endnotes

1. For example, Lilly, William. *Christian Astrology Modestly Treated of in Three Books : The First Containing the Use of an Ephemeris, the Erecting of a Scheam of Heaven, Nature of the Twelve Signs of the Zodiack, of the Planets, with a Most Easie Introduction to the Whole Art of Astrology : The Second, by a Most Methodicall Way, Instructeth the Student How to Judge or Resolve All Manner of Questions Contingent Unto Man, Viz., of Health, Sicknesse, Riches, Marriage ... : The Third Containes an Exact Method Whereby to Judge Upon Nativities*. London: Printed by John Macock, 1647, p 152, 386, 401, 471.

2. Ibn Ezra, Abraham ben Meèir, Raphael Levy, and Francisco Cantera. *The Beginning of Wisdom; an Astrological Treatise*. Baltimore, Md., London,: The Johns Hopkins press; H. Milford Oxford university press; [etc.], 1939., p 209.

1

The History of Solar Returns

SOLAR RETURNS, WHICH WERE ALSO CALLED REVOLUTIONS UNTIL THE 17TH CENTURY, ARE A TECHNIQUE FOR UNDERSTANDING THE LIFE BY BREAKING IT DOWN INTO ONE-YEAR SEGMENTS, AND STUDYING EACH SUCH TIME SLICE, WHETHER INDIVIDUALLY OR SUCCESSIVELY. Using the time period of a year already implies the importance of the Sun to its understanding, because the interval itself is defined in terms of the Sun: it takes a year for the solar cycle to complete.

The very idea of the return of the Sun to the same place it was a year ago is a statement of faith in a primary agricultural cycle. If this year Spring begins in March, it better not begin next year in October! A solar year is understood as a regular unit, an expression of order in nature and the divine that is virtually axiomatic.

We can understand the earliest references to the solar return as impersonal: they were simply the expression of the repetition of seasons, experienced by human, animal, or plant alike. This early working out of the solar cycle by humans was the movement to create the calendar: the time-keeping that virtually every human society craved to keep human activity in sync with the seasons.

Repetitive observations over time led to the approximation of 360, and then 365, days as the length of the year – along with the increasingly sophisticated assessment that even 365 was not completely accurate. (Remember leap years?) As civilizations devoted regular observation to these affairs, they learned that the two great time-keepers, the Sun and the Moon, could not be easily integrated into a single calendar: the number of days in a lunar month varies somewhat, and there isn't a fixed number of lunar months in a year. Thus, a civilization had to pick whether to have a solar-based calendar, a lunar one, or a hybrid soli-lunar type. Each had advantages and disadvantages, and each had consequences.[1]

But it is impossible to conceive of a "personal" solar return until there was a personal Sun upon which to base it. Thus, it was not possible to conceive of a solar return before there was a personal nativity, and that means no earlier than the 5th century BCE.[2] While astrology was alive and well long before that date, it was functioning as the Heavenly Writing: the communication between the gods and men, not a system for delineation of an individual person's fate.

For our purposes here, I will follow the development of the technique of solar returns historically, by discussing its development during the standard historical periods of astrology. In most of my works, I simply stop discussing the development of technique at about the year 1700, which is a pretty good cut-off date for the classical period. The reason that I have not done so here is that developments of the late 20th century have raised some fundamental philosophical questions about the nature of what is being done when a solar return is studied: and these philosophical issues deserve serious discussion quite apart from the issues raised by the more specific lineage-based techniques of modern astrology.

The Hellenistic Period

Were there Hellenistic solar returns? James Holden thinks not.[3] Again, we are confronted with the issue of personal vs. impersonal returns. The quintessential impersonal return is what we call the Aries Ingress: the return of the *transiting* or *mundane* Sun to the position we note as being the beginning of Spring.[4] Holden argues that Ptolemy did develop the concept of the New Moon of the Year. Yet Ptolemy's Book II, Chapter 10 is so tantalizingly close to a statement of an Aries Ingress chart![5] We know that virtually all subsequent authors in the traditional period refer to the series of cardinal ingresses in a mundane context as revolutions of the world, with the solar revolution as the personal version, so we have to consider that the development of either in the Hellenistic period would at least represent a point of origin for the technique. It would not be the slightest bit surprising to see the mundane version of the method appearing before the personal version could be developed.

In Book II, Ptolemy refers to the New Moon of the Year as the New Moon closest to the Vernal Equinox. In the Robbins' translation, we see:

> To be sure, one could not conceive what starting-point to
> assume in a circle [i.e., the zodiac], as a general proposition; but
> in the circle through the middle of the zodiac one would properly

take as the only beginnings the points determined by the equator and the tropics, that is, the two equinoxes and the two solstices. Even then, however, one would still be at a loss which of the four to prefer. Indeed, in a circle, absolutely considered, no one of them takes the lead, as would be the case if there were one starting-point, but those who have written on these matters have made use of each of the four, in various ways assuming some one as the starting-point, as they were led by their own arguments and by the natural characteristics of the four points. This is not strange, for each of these parts has some special claim to being reasonably considered the starting-point and the new year.[6]

After going through a discussion about why each of the cardinal points could have primacy, he continues:

> It seems more proper and natural to me, however, to employ the four starting-points for investigations which deal with the year, observing the syzygies of the sun and moon at new and full moon which most nearly precede them, and among these in particular the conjunctions at which eclipses take place, so that from the starting-point in Aries we may conjecture what the spring will be like, from that in Cancer the summer, from that in Libra the autumn, and from that in Capricorn the winter. For the sun creates the general qualities and conditions of the seasons, by means of which even those who are totally ignorant of astrology can foretell the future.[7]

So near – and so far! What else this is near to is the Babylonian definition of the months. In their calendar, which was then taken over by the Jews, the first month of Spring, *Nisan*, was defined as the first appearance of the Moon following the first new moon of Spring.[8] Was Ptolemy's choice of the lunation *before* the Babylonian one a deliberate departure? It is, perhaps, unfortunate on two counts: that it really isn't Spring yet, and also because the last month of the year was the one that would be duplicated to add an intercalary month, so that is an especially strange choice.

What is not strange about this idea, either of Ptolemy or his Babylonian forebears, is that both recognize the *two* Lights as primal, and thus, such a system of New Moons associated with cardinal points incorporates elements of both systems, thereby maintaining the soli-lunar balance.

This section of Ptolemy is Book II, which is on mundane matters. It is Books III and IV which relate to nativities. Here, at the very end of Book IV, in a section on the **chronocrators**, or Time Lords, Ptolemy discusses the sign ingresses of the planets, especially those which happen to be Time Lords when the ingress occurs. He says:

> *And if the same planets are lords of both the times and the ingresses, the nature of the predicted event is made excessive and unalloyed, whether it incline to the good or to the bad; all the more so if they govern the species of the cause not only because they are chronocrators, but also because they ruled it originally in the nativity.*[9]

Again, this isn't a solar return, and this isn't the use of an Aries Ingress in a personal capacity, but it is what we might call a pre-figuring or prerequisite to the development of the concept.

The Arabic Period

It is to this period that we turn for the development of both the Aries Ingress and the solar revolution. But there are definite technical problems. A calendar based on computing the first day of Spring or Summer merely has to get the day right, which is easy enough to establish by **siting stones**. An Aries Ingress *chart* has to get the minute right – or close. That is much harder to establish correctly.

The Arabs were hampered by the **epicyclic** mathematical astronomy they inherited from the Greeks, which produced fair approximations at the gross level, but lacked considerable precision

at the fine level – and calculating an Aries Ingress *time* requires precision.

Arabic astronomy and astrology was well-supported from the 8th century CE, the production of *zīj*, or treatises containing astronomical calculations and tables, were a prominent output.[10] Arabic work in this area was hampered by two considerations:

- The precision limitations of naked eye astronomy, which made it easy to work at the level of the calendar, but harder to work at the level of the four minute precision that would represent an average degree on the Ascendant.
- The limitations of mapping planetary movement of elliptical orbits by a series of circles within circles of the epicyclic theory, which ultimately resulted in the periodic insertion of empirical data to "save the phenomenon."

It was not for lack of trying that the Arabs were not successful in conquering these limitations. The Arabs also benefited from the activities of the Indian astronomers and their observations. As early as the end of the 9th century, the astronomer al-Battānī mentioned the use of observation tubes, rather like telescopes without the lenses, which allowed the observer a more precise view of the sky without light pollution, and also, over the next century, the construction of large instruments, which was the best way to get precision in this time.[11] By the 11th century, it was clear to the Arabic astronomers that they were unable to resolve the problems they inherited from Ptolemaic astronomy, and that new methods would be necessary.[12] When this work was begun systematically in the 9th century, the seven hundred year gap since Ptolemy showed clear variations, and the Arabic astronomers approached this problem not merely as an exercise in creating a fudge factor, but a total re-examination of the process. Lest this be thought to be terribly esoteric from the standpoint of Aries Ingresses and solar returns, let me state that what the astronomers tackled was the definition of the solar year, and the discrepancy between the **tropical year** (return to a seasonal point, like Spring) and the **sidereal year** (return to a conjunction to a star) – and in so examining Ptolemy, these 9th century astronomers challenged whether Ptolemy's numbers should be considered reliable at all, or whether it was necessary to go back to Hipparchus.[13] If something as basic as the solar constant is questioned, then any calculations based upon precision of this constant are open to question – thus, this is critical to the calculation of Aries Ingresses and solar revolutions. The work in which this challenge was issued was called the *Book on the Solar Year*.

It seems odd that the solar orbit would be such a challenge, especially since the Sun is the one body that lacks latitude, meaning, that the plane of the Sun-Earth orbit is *defined* as zero degrees ecliptic latitude. However, it has been long known that the daily motion of the Sun is not constant. The mathematics of this inequality was still being addressed by the great 9th century astronomer Thābit b. Qurra.[14]

The 10th century astronomer al-Battānī produced the "Sabian Tables," the tables and treatise which was translated into Latin, and thus to the Medieval West, under the author name of Albategni or Albatenius.[15] Even so, a century later the great astronomer al-Bīrūnī (973-1050) was still grappling with the precession constant and solar motion.[16] al-Bīrūnī mentioned the astrology of both the Aries Ingress and personal solar revolutions, not just the astronomy behind such calculations.[17]

Thus, we can see of Arabic astronomy that:

- While they all studied Ptolemy, they did so *critically*. When obvious errors cropped up, they were not afraid to correct him.
- Programs of direct sky observation were necessary to correct Ptolemy's and later equations.
- The development of trigonometric functions such as sines and cosines made the mathematization of astronomical functions *even* more complete.

Masha'allah (740-785) wrote *The Revolution of the Years of the World*, which has been recently translated into English by James Holden.[18] I discussed this work on the Aries Ingress in *Astrology of Sustainability*.[19] As noted, the Aries Ingress is the mundane version of what in nativities is the solar revolution or return; however the sophistication of the mathematical astronomy needed to correctly achieve each is different. We have already noted that the Arabic astronomers put a great deal of work into studying solar motion. As Holden notes in his translation of Morinus, which we shall revisit shortly in the section on the Early Modern Period, the issue was bad enough from an accuracy standpoint to be producing the possibility of errors in the Ingress charts of several hours, even when Morinus had access to the considerably more accurate Rudolphine Tables, based on Kepler's equations rather than the Medieval geocentric epicyclic equations.[20]

Clearly, we have the somewhat embarrassing fact that a mundane method of considerable interest to astrologers developed in a period where the calculations could not be accurate. What do we make of this? First, this kind of error is only completely comprehensible in hindsight. So we know that what they said, they said in earnest.

It may not be clear to the reader why this problem is more pronounced for the Aries Ingress mundane method compared to solar revolutions. The reason is that the problem that had not been solved concerned the solar constant – the fact that the speed of the Sun isn't quite constant from day to day *within* a solar year. This is a very difficult problem to solve. The upshot is that an "error of more than a quarter of the sky" could be present at an Ingress – *and this error could not be measured by their technologies, and thus compensated for*.[21] However, a solar return did not require an exact measurement between tropical and sidereal solar years, and thus, was strictly comparative – the error in the Sun of a solar return would be about the same as the error in the nativity, and thus *relative* to each other, the solar return would be reasonably accurate.[22]

We see a number of references to Aries Ingress and revolutions in the Medieval Arabic astrologers. In the *Centiloquy of Hermes Trismegistus*, a compilation of aphorisms of Arabic origin, the Aries Ingress is referred to in aphorisms 70 and 77; and the solar revolution in aphorism 94.[23]

David Juste recently produced a critical work on an early Latin volume (10th century; two centuries before the bulk of the translations) of Arabic material. In this work, one of the manuscripts, the *Quicumque*, includes the revolutions of the planets as one of its subjects. The problem is that the exact authorship and transmission of this material is not clear.[24]

The foundational work from the Arabic period has to be Abū Ma'shar's *On Solar Revolutions*, recently available in English translation.[25] In this work, Abū Ma'shar outlined the system for working with **profections** and solar returns together, where the profected Ascendant and its ruler are used in the solar return much like the equivalents in the nativity: as sensitive points which emphasize the importance of the particular solar return, and its likelihood of bringing results. I examined profections in their Medieval interpretation in *Classical Astrology for Modern Living*: in that context, they are understood as a system of directing by moving the chart one house per year.[26] In their earlier Hellenistic incarnation they are a system for directing the chart by one sign each year – these two systems were formally equivalent under the system of whole sign houses. The addition of profections to the solar return delineation is to help to focus attention on particularly important years: years where the themes "pile up," by being evident in all the various charts indicated.

In Abū Ma'shar's assessment, the sign of the profection (that is to say, of the profected Ascendant), is even more important than sign on the solar return Ascendant. What you are attempting to verify is whether the profected Ascendant and solar return Ascendant are free from affliction and dignified, in which case there is the potential for a very good year.[27] Difficulties with these placements can mean

difficulties for the year. How good or bad the year will be is essentially a process of summing up the good and bad arguments for these two derivative charts, relative to the nativity. Ideally, benevolent planets which are well dignified and angular will predominate in these charts, with the malefics well dignified and not so emphasized. Abū Ma'shar would also assess the charts relative to the quality of the Arabic parts.

Abū Ma'shar also incorporated the full Hellenistic system of **_handing over_**, a concept which mostly dropped out of overt discussion in Medieval astrology, but which is important to understanding why something like profections or solar returns could be vitally important in the first place. Here's the gist of the argument.

How is one unit of time different from another? Today, I am in a car accident, something that didn't happen to me yesterday, and which doesn't happen tomorrow either. So far, this could simply be a transit. But suppose instead I am looking at a longer unit of time than a day – a time period in which I am accident-prone? Maybe I don't have accidents three days in a row, but for a period of six months or a year, I'm in several accidents? How does this work? Within the system of yearly profections, with each year, the profected Ascendant is handed off to a new ruler. A planet in that new house can result in yet another hand-off to that planet.

Whenever one is directing a chart, whether through profections, primaries, or solar arcs, when there is a change of sign or house, the affairs of the body, cusp, or point being studied are "handed off" from the old ruler to the new ruler. While there were some variations in how this process of handing over was understood in the Hellenistic period, when even the changing of Terms could result in a handing over, the important concept is that when a body or cusp changes sign, there is also a change of ruling planet.

The difference between how this happens in a solar return or a direction is that, in the direction, the handing over is part of a continuous process of movement. A solar return is a discontinuous process: a new chart is drawn up for each year that doesn't morph or convert from the old chart to the new one: although one might argue that there is a period of time when the effect of the old solar return wanes, while the effect of the new one emerges. But we shall re-examine this question of when a solar return takes effect as we examine the modern delineation of solar returns.

In the 150 aphorisms of Almansor, we have an early reference to the fortunate significance of the solar return chart being similar in form to the radix – a cycle which occurs every thirty-three years, as we shall see in detail in Chapter 2. (Almansor did not indicate any knowledge of that cycle.)[28] Almansor refers to the Aries Ingress in Aphorisms 84 and 144.[29]

The Medieval Latin Period

The mega-source for the transmission of Arabic material into the Latin West is Bonatti, whose massive work preserved much of Arabic astrological learning in an extremely comprehensive and detailed reference.

Bonatti's section on revolutions is Treatise 8, which comprises about 300 pages in translation.[30] This Treatise begins with the Aries Ingress, then quickly introduces the natal technique of solar revolutions. However, most of the first fifty chapters are devoted to mundane matters. Although the calculation for the **Lord of the Year** is said to be for either technique.

The Lord of the Year is the planet powerful enough to determine the outcome of the year. One begins with the Ruler of the Ascendant, and like the calculations for the *Hyleg* in medical, one examines the possible candidates, and then either verifies them as meeting the rules, or goes to the next most plausible candidate until a Ruler is declared.

- The preferred Lord of the Year would be the Ruler of the Ascendant. And this will be so, if the Ruler of the Ascendant is not combust or retrograde. It must also be within 4 degrees conjunct the Ascendant.
- Combustion or retrogradation destroys any possible Lord of the Revolution, so if either condition holds, it is necessary to check the next possible candidate, which in this case, would be the Exaltation Ruler of the Ascendant, then the **Sect Light** (the Sun if it's a day chart, or the Moon if a night chart) if the Sect Light disposes the Ascendant, then the Term Ruler of the Ascendant, then the Triplicity ruler of the Ascendant, then the Lord of the 10th (if conjunct the 10th) and if not, the Exaltation Ruler of the 10th, or either Light, if it disposes the 10th, then the Term ruler of the 10th, then the Triplicity ruler of the 10th; and if none of that works, then repeat the process for the 7th, then the 4th, then the 11th, then the 9th, then the 5th, then the 3rd. I might add parenthetically that going past the 10th is likely to produce a weakened Ruler anyway![31]
- If none of these machinations produce a suitable result, then consider:
  - The Ruler of the Ascendant
  - The Exaltation Ruler of the Ascendant
  - The Sect Light
  - The Almuten of the Ascendant

  If any of these are angular and conjunct the angle, then they could be used as the Ruler of the Year.[32]

Not surprisingly, again using the Hyleg calculation as a guide, if you have to go past the 1st and the 10th in the computation, that Lord of the Year will not be considered as strong.[33] Bonatti's iterations for the calculation of this point are very detailed, and further suggest someone deep in the method – who has encountered those frustrations we all endure when the definition doesn't encompass the chart we have before us. By contrast, the method of Omar of Tiberius (Umur Muhammed ibn al-Farrukhan at-Tabari, d. 816-817) was to use the first planet to change sign, change orientality, or arrive at the position of the Moon or the Ascendant.[34]

Were this an Aries or other Ingress, then the next step would be to calculate the Significator of the King, but we shall omit that consideration, as it doesn't apply to natal revolutions.[35]

If the above doesn't sound clear, Bonatti then gives a fifty-four step system to calculate this placement![36]

The reason for going to all this trouble is simple: if the Lord of the Year is well placed, then it is a good year. Well placed means in the 1st, or a house friendly to the 1st (5th and 9th). But one predicts the reverse if the Ruler of the Year is in a bad house with respect to the Ascendant (6th, 7th and 12th). Even though Bonatti had laid down provisions to reduce or eliminate the possibility of a Lord of the Year being combust or retrograde, he still mentioned how retrogradation would weaken the Lord of the Year.[37]

Although this is a *solar* revolution, Bonatti does consider that the Sect Light (the Sun in a day chart, or the Moon in a night chart) must be considered, along with the condition of the Ascendant and its ruler. One is examining the placement for aspects to the benefic or malefics, and, in the case of looking for problems, those are given by combustion, retrogradation, or **besiegement** – the placement of a body between two malefics.[38]

Mars and Saturn above the horizon (*i.e.*, in the 12th through 7th houses) are capable of more mischief than when they are below the horizon, and even more so if they dispose each other. The benefics are capable of greater deeds when they are above the horizon.[39]

The Early Modern Period

Jerome Cardan

The great Renaissance polymath Jerome Cardan (1501-1576) not only wrote on many things astrological, but on virtually every other field of human knowledge at the time. Unfortunately, his work, *Book on Revolutions*, is not yet translated into English. Pieces of Cardan's method have been available in English for over three centuries, because a selection of his aphorisms were translated by William Lilly in 1675, and that included aphorisms on solar returns.[40] These appear to follow closely upon Arabic method and that of Bonatti.

Jean-Baptiste Morin

What is not always appreciated by English-speaking astrologers is how very much Jean-Baptiste Morin (1583-1656, known also as Morinus) was a reformer. It is important that we contextualize this period of reform, which also included John Gadbury, who we will feature prominently in many of the following chapters. Patrick Curry has discussed the 17th century and its astrology at length in *Prophesy and Power*.[41] At the beginning of the 17th century, astrology was still taught at most European universities. At the end of the century, this was no longer true. In between, astrology reached what might well have been the apotheosis of its social relevance during the English Civil War, when astrological broadsides and almanacs focused public opinion for and against the Crown.

And that was the point. The Civil War with its beheading of the sitting monarch, Charles I, terrified the rest of Europe. So the experience of astrologers in this century was strange indeed. Morin could be present at the birth of Louis XIV in 1638; and yet the Sun King, once installed, would try to ban the publication of almanacs with astrological content – something also tried unsuccessfully by Frederick the Great of Prussia (1712-1786).

Morin the reformer abandoned the Terms and Faces, and produced a lineage that transmitted into modern astrology, especially in French, German, and Spanish-speaking areas through Sindbad (Friedrich Schwickert, 1857-1930), Henri Selva (1861-1952?), and Adolph Weiss (b. 1888).

Morin began where most of his contemporaries would do the same: by declaring the combination of primary directions and solar revolutions to be the ideal combination for working with the chart over time, although Morin emphasized the ultimate primacy of the natal chart.[42]

James Holden, Morin's translator, notes that, unfortunately, Morin's presentation of solar returns still suffers from calculational errors, which, as we have already reviewed in the earlier period, were more profound for the Aries Ingress method than for an individual return.[43]

Morin is significant in evidently being the first astrologer to compute solar returns for the actual location of the Native – a point about which he was *very* specific.[44] We should add that this is probably the case that Morin was the first person to *deliberately* do this, because it is entirely possible that astrologers before him working with tables of houses found it easier to use the local table of houses for someone born elsewhere, than to work out the different longitude and latitude for someone born in a distant place.

Morin's method also stripped out the use of the Hellenistic Lots, or Arabic Parts, as a primary delineation method. In Bonatti's work, this was so important that his Treatise 8 on Revolutions is divided into two parts, the second being the interpretation of the Parts in return charts.

Morin addresses the question, can a solar return produce something not already seen in the Nativity? Morin says *no*, there must at least be the *potential* for anything portended by the solar return given in the nativity. Thus, if a nativity denies marriage, a solar return cannot bring it.[45]

Morin covers the lunar returns, while rejecting doing the quarters of the lunar returns. He does address the issue of whether the quarters for the solar return should be done, as was done for mundane ingresses of all four cardinal points.[46]

Between Morin and Gadbury, whom we shall shortly consider, we have a wealth of worked out chart examples – something necessary to truly understand the method in application. We shall consider this method more specifically in the next chapter, but for now, I shall outline some of the important general considerations of Morin's methods.

William Lilly

William Lilly (1602-1681) discussed return charts beginning on page 734, Chapter 172 of his monumental work, *Christian Astrology*. Lilly, while younger than Morin, was more conservative in his astrological method. He begins by giving an explanation about how to compute the solar return. On interpretation, Lilly suggests the following:

- First, he calculated the chart and then presented it as a separate chart. But then, in that era of square charts, it's hard to imagine any other format.
- Next he compares the solar return chart with the birth chart, looking for "agreement" by the cusps of the compared houses, their rulers, and principal significators. Agreement would mean being of the same Triplicity (element).
- The Lord of the Ascendant free from combustion and dignified, this is a good thing, as is also the same condition of the Lord of the house that the Sun is in, as well as a dignified Moon.
- The sign of the Ascendant of the revolution square or opposite that of the Nativity, or the Ascendant being a cusp of a bad house in the nativity brings losses.
- The ascending sign reversed relative to the Radix brings quarrels and contentions, and yet the desire for marriage.
- Danger occurs when the solar return Ascendant is either afflicted by the revolutional malefics, or by the Radix positions of any body acting as a malefic.
- Opposite disposition to the Nativity produces an ill result, *even if that means that the revolution planets are therefore dignified.*[47]

Joseph Blagrave

Joseph Blagrave (1610-1682) practiced astrological medicine, but also wrote *Blagrave's Introduction to Astrology in Three Parts*.

In the natal section, he discussed solar returns, and he characterized the delineation as follows. He computed the chart for the revolution, and then he took the five Radix **hylegical points** (i.e., the points which could be **hyleg** – Sun, Moon, Ascendant, Part of Fortune, and Midheaven), and looked for aspects to them from the solar return planets – and read those aspects as if they were primary directions. He also looked for aspects from the solar return planets to the Radix house cusps, interpreting hard aspects (including the conjunction) as malefic, and soft aspects as benefic. Thus, we can see that Blagrave was essentially applying directional rules to the solar return: he was not really treating it as an independent entity.[48]

John Gadbury

John Gadbury (1627-1704), who, like Morin, was a reformer, discussed solar returns at length in his work on natal method, *Genethlialogia*, Chapter 32, as well as in several short worked out volumes. This book of Gadbury's was published in the same year as Morin's massive work. If we include his published delineations, his may actually be the most extensive. Thus, it is interesting that the two most reform-minded astrologers wrote the most on this topic, at least from a natal perspective.

There are thus four extensive works from the classical period:

- Abū Ma'shar's, where solar returns are entwined with Hellenistic profections.
- Bonatti's, whose work on mundane is foundational to the extent that the Aries Ingress is an analogous chart to the solar return.
- Morin's, who introduces the complexity of the relocated solar return, while also discussing lunar returns for timing.
- Gadbury's, which with the *Genethlialogia* and several example volumes, provides a practical, worked out model for the use of solar returns that can operate in a stand-alone fashion, not just integrated with other techniques.

The 18th-19th Centuries

In the *Textbook of Astrology* by A. J. Pearce (1840-1923), the author recognized the solar revolution as a symbolical chart, and noted its significance was not especially great if it differed fundamentally in interpretation from the primary directions of the same time period. He also specified that the chart should be drawn for the place of birth, but that a second version for the place of residence was appropriate should the residence be a considerable distance away.[49]

Pearce noted the following items in interpreting the solar return chart:

- Pearce referred to it as "symbolical." The question is: what did he mean by that? He clearly drew the revolution chart as a chart, not simply as a set of transits relative to the natal. The probable meaning is given in Davison as those systems in which the positions of the angles and planets are given through the addition of a fixed or variable increment, based upon actual motion.[50] On this basis, I would question Pearce's interpretation, because the year of time elapsed between returns introduces a radically different time interval to that used in primaries, secondaries, or solar arcs.
- He cited Zadkiel I (Pearce was Zadkiel III) on the significance of angularity in a solar return chart, especially if aspecting the Sun or the Moon.
- Pearce notes that the approximate Ascendant recurs every thirty three years – this for the birth location, of course.
- The Ascendant opposite the natal position is considered unfortunate.
- Jupiter or Venus rising or culminating is favorable.
- Pearce lists the most important consideration to be the house placement of the Sun.
- Next in importance is the Moon position when in the 10th and aspecting the Sun or other body.
- Next in importance is a recapitulation of a planetary placement at

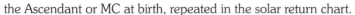

the Ascendant or MC at birth, repeated in the solar return chart.

- The degree of natal Saturn, Mars or Uranus as the ascending degree means danger to the affairs of the house where that body is posited natally.
- Venus or Jupiter at the Ascendant or MC gives a good year.
- The Sun square or opposite Saturn gives either danger or reverses to the father.
- The Moon in hard aspect to Saturn in the solar return gives illness or accident.
- The location of Venus natally as the solar return Ascendant gives romance, marriage, and increase in one's family, or business advancement.
- Venus and/or Jupiter rising for the solar return is a good year both for health and business.

20th Century Astrology

Alexandre Volguine

While often neglected in English-language writings, one of the most influential works on solar returns was that of Alexandre Volguine (1903-1976), first published in 1937. Beginning as such books needed to in those days with the method for calculating the solar return by hand, Volguine then wastes no time in stating that the solar return must be computed for the actual location of the Native at the time of the return, and not using the ancient system of calculating the chart for the birthplace. Volguine unfortunately then decided to use the chart of Helena Blavatsky to illustrate his point: about as bad a choice as humanly possible, because Blavatsky's data is so dirty that not even the *year* of birth is undisputed.

Having advocated for the place of the return, Volguine's analysis of it features a cookbook approach to comparing the positions of the solar return houses with the natal houses, the placements of the solar return planets by house, and the aspects of the planets in the solar return.

For timing, Volguine took all the aspects within the day of the solar return, and proportioned the 24 hours of ephemeris time into the appropriate ratio to be the equivalent of 365 days of time.[51]

Ronald Davison

This survey of modern approaches to solar returns has been ordered by date of publication, which, with respect to our next author, presents some anomalies. Ronald Davison (1914-1985), an eminent member of the British astrological community, had published most of his works in the 1950s and 1960s – but not so his book on solar returns, which was only published in 1990, five years after his death. However, as the person who took over editorship of the *Quarterly* from Charles C.E.O. Carter, Davison's ideas had a ready voice within the astrological community long before his widow made the manuscript available for publication.

Davison was quite capable of some radical departures: and this is illustrated nicely as early as page 19, when he states that a figure cast for the return of the Sun to the natal Moon placement – an Annual Moon chart – is at least as effective as a solar return.[52] This chart has been all but ignored by most astrologers: but those who have tried it have found it to be a very remarkable chart. He actually mentions quite a number of possible return charts: a monthly return to the natal lunar position, plus 30 degrees for each successive month; and a synodic return, where the return is to the angular separation of the Sun and Moon, which is repeated every month. By citing the Church of Light for this idea, he suggests a lineage which may go back through Thomas Burgoyne to the Hermetic Brotherhood of Luxor, a 19th century occult group that was somewhat competitive with the Theosophical Society. With planetary returns as a general case, and the solar return as merely one particular, he was one of the people who trail-blazed for the solar return as part of a larger group of possible returns.

Davison gives H.S. Green credit in an article in the 1902 edition of *Modern Astrology* for the idea of using the precessed Sun position for the solar return. The precessed solar return was likewise adopted by Cyril Fagan, one of the early 20th century Western siderealists. He also credited Alan Leo in the *Progressed Horoscope*, for proposing a solar return to the position of the progressed Sun, a technique still being advocated recently in the work of Zipporah Dobyns.[53]

Then, were this not enough, Davison mentions converse returns, both to the natal and progressed positions. At this point, I stopped wondering why he had not published this work within his lifetime. However, Davison does state that it is important to lay out *all* the possible methods of calculation, so that the student may *choose* the desired method. The problem, as we will see, is that many if not most students of astrology, will not *choose*, but will slavishly accumulate all possible variations, producing a cloud of similar techniques, resulting in nothing but foggy weather.

Davison states that the solar return chart should be viewed as a stand-alone chart.[54] He suggests that an important year will be shown by planets within a degree or two of the solar return Ascendant or MC. Were this idea rigorously followed, then the student might well have a pretty robust system for making the choices Davison admitted were necessary. After the chart had been viewed as a stand-alone, the relationship of the solar return to the natal was studied.

Davison developed a series of ideas for particular configurations that would tend to denote certain significations within the year, such as:

- Marriage
- Birth of children
- Change of residence
- Change of occupation
- Travel
- Financial fluctuations
- Bereavement
- Illness
- Accidents
- Marriage of son or daughter
- Birth of grandchild
- Divorce[55]

This sounds great – except that, viewing his data, he himself was not able to use the various solar return options to sort out repeating patterns, where one of the calculations consistently worked better. Unfortunately, this means that the reader never does achieve any sense of clarification about which system is giving an accurate and reliable means of forecasting. There is simply too much clutter.

The book turns into a techniques festival, as Davison covered all possible variations in method: again, with no synthesis. But we must ask: as a posthumous volume, had Davison never published it because he was unhappy with what he had produced? We'll never know. It nonetheless remains a compendium of possible variants in return methods.

Ray Merriman

In Ray Merriman's (1946-) presentation of solar returns, originally published in 1977, emphasis is laid on two points:

- The usefulness of relocating the solar return to the actual location of the Native as a method to improve the effectiveness of the solar return.
- The development of daily timing strategies for predicting when the overall themes promised by the chart will manifest using a "one degree per day angular progression method."[56]

Ray's approach is clear: as he considers the solar return to be defined as an event, the event must be taking place where the person actually is located who is experiencing the event. As a result, within this definition, the only valid solar return can be the one for the location of the Native at that time.[57]

This approach of Merriman's is a complete break with the traditional approaches – but it is far too well thought-out simply to be dismissed on historical grounds. Merriman's approach contains several underlying assumptions that must be addressed:

- He assumes that the solar return is an independent chart, and thus, must be interpreted as such.
- *Because* it is an independent chart, he emphasizes that only using the actual coordinates of the Native makes any sense.
- Merriman presents such a very specific timetable regarding the actual time of the solar return and what should be done, in terms of meditation, and planned events, that this approach can be easily classified as a form of magical invocation.

James Eshelman

It was not too much later that the Western siderealist and occultist, Jim Eshelman (1954-), published an influential work on solar returns. Being a siderealist, it is hardly surprising that he advocated the idea of using precessed solar returns in 1985. It is curious that, while his use of the western sidereal zodiac itself had little impact on tropical astrologers, the one concept that should have had a hit was the use of a precessed Sun position – but translated into tropical coordinates! It is perhaps a sad testimony to the history of astrological ideas that the single factor of using a precessed Sun position was so neatly excised from its original context. Once so excised, its interpretation became increasingly out of context, as many astrologers forgot (or never knew) the source of the idea.[58]

Mary Shea

One of the very influential works on solar returns in the 1990s was that by Mary Fortier Shea (1947-), who uses tropical unprecessed solar returns using the Placidus house system for the location in which the solar return actually occurs. In other words, Shea follows the Merriman system pretty closely, at least as far as structure of the return is concerned. She mentions the possibility of calculating the solar return for the birth location, but rejects its primary efficacy, stating that the use of the birth location strips the interpretation of the free will of choosing to be in another location at the time of the return.

Shea states the rationale behind the relocated solar return forcefully: *"We cannot underestimate the power of the mind in this process. The relocated solar return is like a vision, intention or affirmation. It is a statement concerning what you think you can and will handle and also what you hope to manifest in the highest sense."*[59]

Shea notes that relocation has no effect on progressions or solar arcs – that it is only the solar return that can reflect these changes in free will. Actually, it is entirely possible to develop a system of solar arcs or progressions with a relocated Ascendant. She also discusses the issue of what period of time the solar return rules, noting the frequency of an issue three months before the solar return that may focus energy and attention on the themes of the new return, but noting its primary impact beginning about one month in advance, with the old one still in force but declining a month after the new return.

She also states that the solar return shows more of the psychological and spiritual growth issues than actual events: *"Events are not crucial to the growth process and are therefore harder to predict."*[60]

For timing techniques, she nominates:

- Progressing the solar return Moon
- Transits to the angles and other house cusps of the nativity
- Transits to the angles and other house cusps of the solar return[61]

However, this rather begs the question. If, as she states, the solar return is a map primarily to the psychology of the year, then why worry about timing mechanisms at all?

Bernadette Brady

Bernadette Brady (1950-) covered solar returns in less detail than some of the other systems she discussed in *The Eagle and the*

Lark, but in sufficient detail for our purposes here. Brady began by referring to any kind of return as a personalized cycle. This departure in terminology is a very useful one, because it gives a good context for understanding the return process generally.[62] Brady made the undocumented statement that return charts were first done in the sidereal zodiac, but she herself used unprecessed returns.

What follows is a series of practical observations about how to read return charts in general, with examples given for both the solar and the lunar return. Like most of her predecessors, she recommended reading the chart as a stand-alone, emphasizing the importance when the return planet (generally the Sun) conjoins an angle. She considered the 8th and the 12th houses malefic, and the 5th and 9th houses benefic. She noted that one should look for the major themes and the tightest orbs.[63]

Brady advocated using the location where the Native is at the moment of the return, and then relocating *this* solar return as the person moves during the year. The implication of this system is that perhaps traveling to a "better" location for a solar return doesn't accomplish that much, if the chart snaps back to the residence location (or any series of intermediate locations) as soon as one changes location. So by this logic, unless one is truly able to stay away from home for a year, relocation on the day of the return doesn't mean that much.

I have yet to see a really insightful discussion of this very point. Merriman's logic is that the solar return is an *event*, which means that any relocation of that event is secondary. Brady's interpretation is that the return is a personal *cycle*, and so the location is driven by where the person is at any point in time. These two positions are not easily reconciled, but more unfortunately, little attempt has been made to reconcile them.

Celeste Teal

Celeste Teal's books have emerged as more recent re-statements of modern astrological technique: her section on solar returns occurs in her book, *Predicting Events with Astrology*.[64] Teal states that secondary progressions (the other major technique of that volume) are of more significance. This no doubt reflects on the usage of many modern astrologers, although we know of course that secondaries were only invented a couple of centuries ago.

Teal first hedges on whether to use precessed or unprecessed charts: then she decides to use both. Then she adds converse returns, thereby generating four different solar returns – and she hasn't even addressed the question of the location for the chart! But lest the reader feel that this is still inadequate, Teal reminds us that there are also the lunar returns!

I have to confess that by this stage, I was embarrassed. Perhaps this is my horary training showing, but when I see a method that gleefully generates four different charts to serve the same function, I have to question how predictive any of them can be on a regular basis, because otherwise, why would you need all four? *If you need this many multiple choices, then none of them is giving you enough information for prediction, and you are just throwing in random events in the hopes that one of them will be explanatory after the fact.* You might as well throw in the towel, and admit that you have no method. Here, Teal clearly forgot Davison's admonition about *choosing* a tree from within the forest.

The existence of a lot of multiple choice in method like this, where several charts are allowed rather than having to make the hard choice and decide which is the right technique, simply guarantees a system in which ambiguity and confusion is preferred over any kind of prediction whatsoever. What do you do when the converse unprecessed solar return says you will have a great year financially, but the regular precessed says you will lose money? How do you rate the relative importance of each? If you don't have a system for comparing, and for selecting the method amongst conflicting arguments, then you have wishful thinking, not method.

Lynn Bell

Still later, we have the work on solar returns by Lynn Bell.[65] This work, part of the Centre for Psychological Astrology series of workshop transcripts, shares with the other works in that series the immediacy of the audience as part of the picture. But this format makes it hard to study a topic systematically, because the flow is broken constantly by questions. Accordingly, one cannot get as strong a flavor for Bell's system, compared to either Shea or Merriman, but what Bell expresses seems to be a strong psychological touchstone upon a layer of Eshelman and Merriman, but with a strong layer of Volguine: hardly surprising, since she has lived in Paris for many years.

Ciro Discepolo

The approach to solar returns among European astrologers has not always been the same as among American ones. A good example of this difference can be seen in the work of Ciro Discepolo (1948-). Unfortunately, most of his work is not available in English, but his work, *Transits and Solar Returns*, is an interesting one. Like most modern astrologers, he advocates picking a location for the solar return, which he refers to as Aimed Solar Returns. He further states that it is impossible to properly read the solar return without the use of transits, and that the worst houses for prominent placements in the solar return are the 1st, 6th, and 12th houses, which produce consistently bad years.[66]

Not present is any discussion about converse solar returns or precession. He presents the concept of an index of risk, and includes a lengthy discussion of examples, most of them negative in nature. This is in part because Discepolo takes a position that negative events are more common than positive ones. The difficulty with this work is that the index of risk is used, but not rigorously defined. This makes it difficult to reproduce his model and test it with one's own data.

Anthony Louis

We shall end with Anthony Louis, who combines both 20th century astrology with classical. In fact, one of his stated objectives is to reinvigorate Volguine's method for English audiences, rightly pointing out that Volguine stands within the tradition of Morin, although not purely so.[67] Louis has also worked on the Morin translation project, although not the volume on solar returns.[68] Louis presents an excellent historical overview, as well as an extensive number of chart examples.

Ok, So...

Our brief view of the history of this technique puts us in the uncomfortable position where, if we are intellectually honest, we will have no choice but to conclude that not all authors can be right. What can we do?

We shall take up this question in greater detail in the next chapter, as well as in Chapter 13. For now, let me mention one interpretive idea, and that relates to the question of fate and free will: which actually may well be the crux of the matter.

Here's the problem. If all the different variations on the solar return chart are equally "true," then we are confronted with the same challenge that made me run away from this method for a decade: which one of them to believe in any one year? While we like to believe that looking at the chart from multiple directions and techniques serves to fortify our conclusions by showing the same theme from multiple perspectives, this shotgun approach is just as likely to show completely different options. When the latter happens instead of the former, the student becomes confused and despondent – and also, too frequently the student concludes that that she or he must be at fault.

A couple of thoughts here. Having worked with two Vedic astrologers, Dennis Harness and Gary Gomes, and one modern astrologer, Karen Hamaker-Zondag, on horary/prasna interpretation, we found there were overlaps (thus leading to the ideal situation that doing this was complementary rather than confusing) *only if* each astrologer worked within his or her tradition. In other words, what worked to produce interesting results was not *combining* methods, but producing independent analyses, which were then compared. What did *not* work was taking an aphorism from one school and attempting to apply it in a delineation set up within a completely different tradition.

Thus, I would now say more specifically that the problem that I have with the Davison and Teal material is that both authors purported to use multiple different charts for the same purposes, rather than sorting out a hierarchy of when to apply each, and for what purpose. If you don't believe me, try this on your own chart for a few years, and you will see how very confusing it is to have multiple charts showing different results with no way to decide which one to believe.

If we are going to allow for multiple variations, then I propose that *each chart used must serve a different purpose*. If that is the case, then we have a framework in which to understand the inevitable variations between the charts.

My thinking on this matter has been very much affected by Rob Hand's review of Neoplatonic ideas. When Rob became interested in classical astrology, he immediately undertook a theoretical analysis of why classical astrology seems so much more fate-driven than modern astrology. In understanding how the ancient astrologers understood the concepts of fate and free will, he created a space in which both traditional and modern astrologies could be understood – and even used together.

Rob's main point was that the philosophers understood that not all "fate" is actually the same. There is the fate that the gods assign particular humans – as Oedipus was going to end up marrying his mother. Then there is fate caused by ignorance, such as if I crash my car into another car, not having first bothered to learn how to drive. The former is not changeable, but the latter is.[69] What most astrologers

would agree upon is that traditional methods show fate more clearly, while modern astrology emphasizes free will. But in reality, *completely* free will is practically mythical, because it ignores the individual's past, and it also assumes that *all choices are equally easy*.

Let me explain what this means. If you, Gentle Reader, have ever been to an astrology conference, you probably saw that the nametags were printed with spaces to allow you to put your Sun, Moon, and Ascendant signs along the bottom of the nametag. Now, at each conference some mischievous astrologers decide to assume another chart, so up on the nametag goes Scorpio/Scorpio/Scorpio. We will assume that *everyone* at such a conference would know what to do to mimic a Triple Scorpio for a weekend. (Granted, the modern astrologers will play the part more Plutonically, while the classicists would play Mars.) But how *easy* is it to assume this part? The answer is largely determined by how much of a dissonance there is between the Triple Scorpio actor's chart and the Triple Scorpio persona. Assuming a part or persona that does not come naturally actually requires a lot of continuous work. One finds oneself constantly having to think about one's role rather than what is going on. While this is a fascinating exercise for a weekend, it makes the point – the exercise of free will is really the exercise of the willingness to be conscious in *every* moment – something most humans actually find difficult to do. Thus, we begin to intuit that the limit to free will is often precisely our own inertia.

But this also gives us ideas about how fate and free will work together. Some time ago, I realized that the easiest way to conceive of this idea in horary is to understand that *every* horary implicitly begins with the phrase, "If things continue as they are now..." We can see this very clearly in Lilly's famous stolen fish horary.[70] Lilly has an order of fish stolen, and the chart said he wouldn't get them back. Lilly didn't like that answer, so he took matters into his own hands – in other words, he did not allow things to continue as they were then. As a result of relying on himself (and using electional astrology) and not the authorities, Lilly found the thief – and recovered part of his fish. It is possible sometimes to reverse engineer a horary from the standpoint: what would I have to do to get the result I want? This is the exercise of free will.

It has become commonplace to assume that there is more room for the exercise of free will in the nativity – but I'm not entirely sure this is true. The theory of more options is that a person has a whole lifetime to make choices. Entirely true. But it is also true that one's expectations and choices are affected by one's gender, age, ethnic background, social group, and cultural matrix. The exercise of free will is much easier when the person is younger – things, people, and ideas accumulate like baggage, and many is the older person who is very fond of his or her creature comforts. The exercise of free will is much easier in times of peace and economic plenty.

So let us begin to organize our thoughts around this hypothesis: doing the solar return for the birthplace is like doing the Aries Ingress for the capital of the country – for our birthplace is each of our individual capitals. This is the chart that shows our fate. One unique feature of the birthplace location is that we can run the entire lifetime of solar return charts for the individual in question, and they will have a meaning, regardless of *where* that individual goes during her or his life.

The residence and the actual location of the solar return show something about the matrix of free will that the person has. The residence can be understood as the reservoir of free will to this point. *This* is where the Native has settled at *this* time in his or her life. Since the awareness of relocational astrology really dawned in the astrological community in the late 19th century, the idea of relocating the birthchart to one's residence location is an idea that has been generally accepted. However, even though it is accepted, there are few astrologers who would use the relocated chart in place of the birthchart. Rather, the tendency is to use the relocated chart to see the interaction of the Native and the place where the Native resides, *within the greater field of the birthchart*. If this is true of

natal interpretation, then it would be consistent within solar return interpretation as well.

Finally, the location of the Native at the moment of the actual solar return is a potential focal point of energy – but the danger is that, once the Native returns to his or her usual location, the residence location will swamp the effect of the solar return moment.

I would argue that Ray Merriman has understood this danger, because he is very clear in his book about the need to engage in what we could call a series of secular rituals that are probably best understood as sympathetic magic. The purpose of creating a field of sympathetic magic is obvious: by doing so, the Native *fixes* both the actual time *and place* to maximize its effect for the coming year. Granted, Ray states the primacy of the event location because of seeing the solar return as an independent event – but his methodology surrounding it suggests that a bit more is actually going on with his method.

Under the hypothesis I am proposing, we thus have a place for three of the solar return variations. However, there is no history of tropical astrologers adopting sidereal calculations apart from this idea for the solar return. For all of the Arabic period forward, tropical astrologers certainly *knew* about the two systems; they simply never *chose* to mix them. It was only in the late 19th century with the involvement of astrologers in the Theosophical Society that this kind of mixing occurred.

There is also no history of converse directions, progressions, or returns prior to the 20th century. So I suggest that both precessed and converse be eliminated as extraneous, or until such time as the proponents of these methods can clearly demonstrate *what* these variations are showing that is different from the usual methods, and *how* such variations contribute to the accuracy of prediction by looking *forward*, not through accuracy in hindsight.

Please notice that I am referring to this as a hypothesis. In actuality, I think some of the ideas proposed in the 20th century have their merits, but they may be pointing to differences in application.

For example, Mary Shea's work has consistently shown a stronger spiritual dimension than Ray Merriman's. This doesn't negate either approach, but it does suggest that, rather than indiscriminately combining the methods, there would be more potential information if each method were considered separately, according to the goals of the practitioner.

However, before we proceed, there is a conceptual problem in some of these modern methods that we need to consider, and that's the question of when the solar return takes effect. There does seem to be a developing consensus among modern astrologers that the new solar return does begin to take effect before the birthday. Or at least, the opinion seems to be that the effect of the current solar return attenuates, and that it is not an instantaneous cross-over from one solar return to the next. But we have seen two primary theories of when the new solar return begins to manifest: about a month earlier than the actual solar return in Merriman, and about 90 days in advance according to Mary Shea.

If the solar return manifests in advance of the time of the solar return, how can any location except the birthplace location have meaning? Prior to the solar return taking effect, no other location actually has any meaning, because the Native has not yet manifested a free will choice of the location.

At this point, we shall delve into a more detailed classical consideration of solar returns, and how to obtain information from them. This is the topic of Chapter 2.

Chapter 1 Endnotes

1. For further information about the development of early calendar systems, see Rochberg-Halton, F. "Calendars: Ancient Near East." *The Anchor Bible Dictionary*. Ed. D.N. Freedman. 6 vols. New York: Doubleday, 1992, pp 810-14, and Hannah, Robert. *Greek and Roman Calendars : Constructions of Time in the Classical World*. London: Duckworth, 2005.

2. The source given for the earliest nativities is: Rochberg, Francesca. *Babylonian Horoscopes*. Transactions of the American Philosophical Society, V. 88, Pt. 1. Philadelphia: American Philosophical Society, 1998.

3. Morin, Jean Baptiste. *Astrologia Gallica : Book Twenty-Three, Revolutions*. Trans. James H. Holden. Tempe, AZ: American Federation of Astrologers, 2002, 2003, p 6, footnote 2.

4. We may note here that in the tropical system, this point wasn't always defined as zero degrees Aries: there was a slippage in the degree of the vernal point before there was complete understanding of the difference between tropical and sidereal reckoning. See for instance: Neugebauer, O. *The Exact Sciences in Antiquity*. 2d ed. Providence, RI: Brown University Press, 1957.

5. Ptolemy, and Frank Egleston Robbins. *Tetrabiblos*. The Loeb Classical Library. Cambridge, MA: Harvard University Press, 1940, pp 194-201.

6. Ptolemy, *Tetrabiblos*, pp 195-197

7. Ptolemy, *Tetrabiblos*, pp 197-199.

8. A good source on calendar systems is: Rochberg-Halton, F. "Calendars: Ancient Near East," pp. 810-14.

9. Ptolemy, *Tetrabiblos*, p 457.

10. Morelon, Régis, "General Survey of Arabic Astronomy," pp 1-19 *in* Rashid, Roshdi, and Régis Morelon. *Encyclopedia of the History of Arabic Science*. London ; New York: Routledge, 1996.

11. Morelon, pp 9-10.

12. Morelon, Régis, "Eastern Arabic Astronomy between the eighth and eleventh centuries," pp 20-57 *in* Rashid, Roshdi, and Régis Morelon, 1996.

13. Morelon, p 29.

14. Morelon, pp 34-37.

15. Morelon, p 46-47.

16. Al-Biruni, Muhammad ibn Ahmad, and Robert Ramsay Wright. *The Book of Instruction in the Elements of the Art of Astrology*. London,: Luzac & Co., 1934, pp 88-91.

17. Al-Biruni, pp 322-323.

18. Masha'allah. *Six Astrological Treatises by Masha'allah*. Trans. James H. Holden. Tempe, AZ: American Federation of Astrologers, 2009.

19. Lehman, 2011a, Chapter 1.

20. Morin, Holden, footnote 3 on page 7; also for the Rudolphine Tables themselves see: Kepler, Johannes, Tycho Brahe, and Jean Baptiste Morin. *Tabulæ Rudolphinæ, or, the Rudolphine Tables Supputated to the Meridian of Uraniburge*. London: [s.n.], 1675.

21. Morin, Holden, p 7, footnote 3.

22. I have observed that some astrologers seem to believe that the calculation of the solar return requires an exceptionally accurate birthtime. While I think all astrologers would agree that the more accurate the birthtime, the more ideal, the point of the calculation is as follows. If the birthtime is wrong by, say, eight minutes, then the solar returns will likewise be wrong by eight minutes, because the solar degree will be wrong by that amount, and it will continue to be wrong by the same amount each year. Eight minutes would be, on average, 2 degrees on the Ascendant or any other house cusp, and almost unmeasurable on the planetary positions. Most of the time, that 2 degrees will not produce a major change in delineation, although, over the course of the life, that is certainly within the range where an astrologer observing would detect a consistently early or late pattern to events, concluding that a rectification would be appropriate.

23. Holden, James Herschel. *Five Medieval Astrologers*. Scottsdale, AZ: American Federation of Astrologers, 2008, pp 102, 103, and 105. While the name would evoke a Hellenistic source, this was not the case.

24. Juste, David. *Les Alchandreana Primitifs : Étude Sur Les Plus Anciens Traités Astrologiques Latins D'origine Arabe (Xe Siècle)*. Leiden: Brill, 2007, p 56.

25. Abū Ma'shar. *On Solar Revolutions*. Trans. Benjamin N. Dykes. Persian Nativities. Vol. III. Minneapolis, MN: Cazimi Press, 2010.

26. Lehman, J. Lee. *Classical Astrology for Modern Living : From Ptolemy to Psychology & Back Again*. Atglen, Pa.: Schiffer Press, 1996, Chapter 14.

27. Abū Ma'shar, pp 74-75.

28. Holden, *Five Medieval Astrologers*, p 137, aphorism 64.

29. Holden, *Five Medieval Astrologers*, p 139 and 147.

30. Bonatti, Guido. *The Book of Astronomy by Guido Bonatti*. Trans. Benjamin N. Dykes. Golden Valley, MN: Cazimi Press, 2007, pp 815-1105.

31. Bonatti (Dykes), pp 818-823.

32. Bonatti (Dykes), pp 823-824

33. Bonatti (Dykes), p 823.

34. Tiberius, Omar of. *Three Books on Nativities*. Trans. Robert Hand. Berkeley Springs, WV: Golden Hind Press, 1995, p 54.

35. Bonatti (Dykes), pp 830-833.

36. Bonatti (Dykes), pp 824-830.

37. Bonatti (Dykes), pp 837-838.

38. Bonatti (Dykes), pp 849-852.

39. Bonatti (Dykes), pp 857-859.

40. Bonatti, Guido, and Jerome Cardan. *The Astrologer's Guide*. Trans. Henry Coley and William Lilly. London: Regulus Publishing Co., Ltd, 1986.

41. Curry, Patrick. *Prophecy and Power : Astrology in Early Modern England*. Princeton, N.J.: Princeton University Press, 1989.

42. Morin (Holden), p x.

43. Morin (Holden), see footnotes 1-3 on page 7.

44. Morin (Holden), p 9.

45. Morin (Holden), p 23.

46. Morin (Holden), pp 88-93.

47. Lilly, William. *Christian Astrology*, pp 736-737.

48. Blagrave, Joseph. *Blagrave's Introduction to Astrology in Three Parts* London: Printed by E. Tyler and R. Holt for Obadiah Blagrave, 1682, pp 296-297.

49. Pearce, Alfred John. *The Text-Book of Astrology*. Washington, DC: American Federation of Astrologers, 1879, 1970, Chapter 26, pp 215-222.

50. Davison, Ronald C. *Cycles of Destiny. Understanding Return Charts*. Wellingborough: Aquarian, 1990, p 13.

51. Volguine, p 104.

52. Davison, p 19.

53. Davison, p 27.

54. Davison, p 41.

55. Davison, Chapter 5.

56. Merriman, Raymond Allen. *The "New" Solar Return Book of Prediction*. W. Bloomfield, MI: Seek-It Publications, 2000, p 16.

57. Merriman, p 18.

58. Eshelman, James A. *Interpreting Solar Returns*. San Diego, Calif.: ACS Publications, 1985.

59. Shea, Mary Fortier. *Planets in Solar Returns : Yearly Cycles of Transformation and Growth*. Glenelg, MD: Twin Stars, Unlimited, 1998, Chapter 1.

60. Shea, Chapter 1.

61. Shea, Chapter 13.

62. Brady, Bernadette. *The Eagle and the Lark : A Textbook of Predictive Astrology.* York Beach, ME: S. Weiser, 1992, p 244.

63. Brady, p 245.

64. Teal, Celeste. *Predicting Events with Astrology.* 1st ed. St. Paul, MN: Llewellyn Publications, 1999.

65. Bell, Lynn. *Cycles of Light : Exploring the Mysteries of Solar Returns.* London: Centre for Psychological Astrology Press, 2005.

66. Discepolo, Ciro. *Transits and Solar Returns.* Napoli: Ricerca '90, 2007, pp 6-14.

67. Louis, Anthony. *The Art of Forecasting Using Solar Returns.* Bournemouth: The Wessex Astrologer, 2008.

68. Morin, Jean Baptiste. *Astrologia Gallica : Book Eighteen, the Strengths of the Planets.* Trans. Anthony Louis LaBruzza. Tempe, AZ: American Federation of Astrologers, 2004.

69. Rob has spoken and written on this in many places, but one good source is: Hand, Robert. Towards a Post-Modern Astrology. http://www.astro.com/astrology/in_postmodern_e.htm, 2005.

70. Lilly, *Christian Astrology*, pp 397-399.

2

Classical Application of Solar Returns

ONE OF THE HARDEST THINGS ABOUT LEARNING METHODOLOGY FROM MULTIPLE SOURCES IS TRYING TO PARSE THE VARIOUS APPROACHES. As we have seen, the modern era has produced an uncritical acceptance of multiple methods that really do not work together, presumably out of a reluctance to reject any one source.

This is exactly what produces bad method in horary – and I have begun to doubt that it can ever produce good method in any other endeavor either. Let me explain.

Because horary is recognized as being results oriented – the point is to get the correct answer – many astrological students understand that horary may require a fairly rigid application of rules. Whether teaching at Kepler College or privately, I have always stressed to my students that problems will arise if they attempt to take horary rules from different times and traditions and simply "pile them on," as if the point was to produce as many arguments as possible. It is of the utmost importance for clarity that each person or thing represented in a horary have a single significator – because it is only possible then to find the single outcome which represents the answer to the question. Multiple methods will result in confusion, because each method introduces the possibility of a contradictory result, as there is no assurance at all that the different significators of the second, third, or fourth method will produce the same results. This is even true within a single tradition, if more than one method is given.[1] I discussed this in The *Martial Art of Horary Astrology*, but I also acknowledged that my emphasis about this matter was not ever stressed by a prior author.[2]

In natal work, it's much easier to believe that the more techniques, the more comprehensive the understanding. We say, people make choices, and have a lifetime to live out many different components of their charts. If different methods produce contradictory results, then we can argue that people do in fact adopt contradictory approaches. I can be conservative about money, but liberal about sexual mores. But while this is true, it's also important that the astrologer always bear in mind that two different astrological methods may not be producing a more comprehensive picture, but instead a more confusing one. This is why we must always approach our learning with a critical eye.

A Dangerous Year

When a person has a dangerous solar return year, the choices begin to narrow down. How much choice does one have? If the classical method was mostly to use the birth location, while many modern astrologers would use the location of the solar return, what does this say about choice? As a first assessment of this question, see Chart 1, which is an example from my own past history, the year I had my first concussion.

We have not yet systematically stepped through the classical rules for solar returns, but I think we studied enough in the last chapter to make my point. *As a chart,* this return shows danger. The **partile** conjunction of Saturn and the South Node is dangerous, located in the 12th house of self-undoing in the natal location, with the Moon-Jupiter bracketing the 8th house cusp. It is further enhanced by the partile square of the Saturn-South Node to Pluto, located in the 4th house. The Moon and Saturn are in mutual reception, and Saturn in Detriment. We have seen repeatedly, and based on Bonatti, that malefics in dignity are less malefic, but malefics in debility are even more so. This suggests that I was capable of doing something stupid that would be dangerous to my life. This was true. What happened was that I was Treasurer of a student group at Rutgers, where I was attending graduate school. We were holding a dance, and some teenagers came into the dance, and stole the cash box. My Midwestern small-town instincts, combined with my Mars-Pluto rising rashness, stupidly told me to chase them, and I did, resulting in my getting my head smashed in by teenagers much more accustomed to street-fighting than I was. But my tactic at least resulted in delaying them long enough for them to be captured and arrested.

As a starting position, let us assert that the natal location of the solar return shows the Native's fate for the year, and in this case, my fate was to be stupid. Let us hypothesize that the relocated solar return shows something of the extent that free will can affect fate, and here, because my solar return occurred in New Brunswick, where I was living, that issue of free will is collapsed into one chart. My natal mean North Node is zero Aquarius, so the placement of the South Node on the locational Ascendant shows there's not much chance my stupidity will be averted. In fact, it was the cultural difference between my Midwestern upbringing and my Metro New York location that directly exacerbated the incident. The Venus-Uranus conjunction in the 4th house of the New Brunswick chart, along with the Moon-Jupiter conjunction close to the 7th house cusp shows danger in a public place (the student union building).

The natal location shows the danger more prominently; the locational chart shows the circumstances. Notice that we are not reading the two charts as interchangeable in the sense that we are attempting to just get confirmation from them – or even consonance. *Attempting to read two different charts for the same purpose will simply result in confusion when they don't perfectly agree – which they won't.* Oftentimes, we can fudge our way through ignoring the contradictions by choosing to see the dissonances as representing additional details. But frankly, the more negative the fate, the more those rationalizations will drop out.

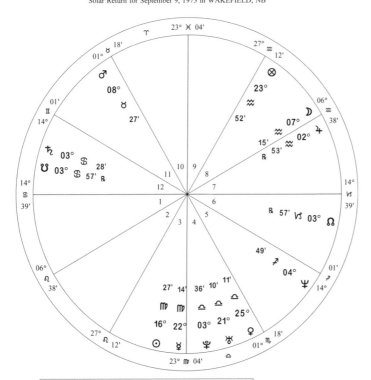
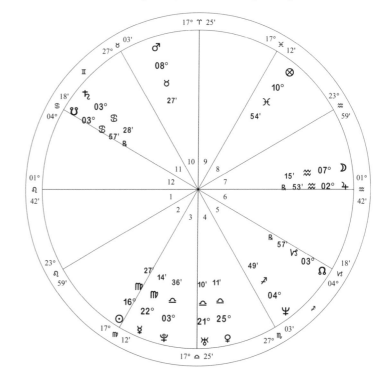

J. Lee Lehman
WAKEFIELD, NB
Time Zone: 0 hours West

September 9, 1973
42 N 16 96W52'12"
Tropical Regiomontanus

6:49:19 AM
Standard Time

Solar Return for September 9, 1973 in WAKEFIELD, NB

J. Lee Lehman
New Brunswick, New Jersey
Time Zone: 5 hours West

September 9, 1973
40N29'10" 74W27'08"
Tropical Regiomontanus

2:49:19 AM
Daylight Saving Time

Solar Return for September 9, 1973 in New Brunswick, New Jersey

Example 2-1. Solar returns for Lee Lehman, 1973. Birth location is Wakefield, Nebraska; location of return is New Brunswick, NJ.

A Disappointing Year

Let's also consider an historical example, in this case from Jean-Baptiste Morin. In his work, *Astrologia gallica*, he gives a number of examples from his own life. Here we apply one of them.

We will also show these two charts in a modern calculation, both to demonstrate the kinds of typical error functions we previously discussed in Chapter 1, and also because it is often difficult for the modern eye to see as much in the traditional square format as the more familiar round one.

So first, let's sort out what makes this solar return notable, and see how we would apply it to an actual example.

As we begin to study solar returns, we do two things:

- We examine the solar return as a chart in its own right
- We also compare to the nativity

As a separate chart, almost the first thing that greets us is the Sun right on the Descendant. It is actually closer in our computation than in Morin's own. The 7th house represents two primary factors in charts, whether natal or solar returns: partnerships (especially the marriage partner), and quarrels as well as open enemies. Here, the presence of the Sun so close to the angle means that this will be a public (angular) year with regard to one or the other. And with the Moon, Saturn, and Jupiter angular, this actually will be a very public year.

Why didn't I count Mars? I didn't forget him! In his discussion of his 39th solar return, Morin showed that he used the Medieval **5 degree rule** (or 7/5/3 degree variation; we cannot tell), in that he referred to the Sun being in the 9th, despite technically being a degree past in the 8th.[5] In the 5 degree rule, a planet up to five degrees on the cadent side of a house is "called back" to the prior house, as a planet within 5 degrees of the Ascendant on the 12th house side can be considered angular. In the case of this solar return we are

examining, Mars counts as being in the 2nd house despite actually being placed in the 1st.

At any rate, the more angular the number of planets, the more public the life in that year. Morin's one natal angular planet was Mars, which would suggest his more combative side to be the public part – and judging from his own description of his solar returns, I would have to say that this was true!

What Morin thought most notable about this solar return chart was the number of squares and oppositions between the three superiors, Saturn, Jupiter, and Mars, with each other, and also with the Part of Fortune. For our purposes, the Part of Fortune does not appear to be part of the group, but please observe that in Morin's calculation of this chart, he used the daytime formula for the Part of Fortune, which placed it at 26 Gemini 22. We might add that these hard aspects fall pretty close to his nodal axis natally. Clearly, something confrontational was afoot.

And it was. In this part of the 17th century, one of the great problems in navigational astronomy was how to measure longitude.[6] The significance of this may be somewhat lost on the modern reader, but consider: the Age of Exploration had European ships sailing all around the globe. Sailors could calculate latitude fairly easily, *but not longitude*. As a result, sea captains often had no idea how close to land they were. This is a tremendous problem, and there were several prizes that had been announced, to encourage the enterprising astronomical engineers to figure this out. Morin was one of many to try his hand at this: and he believed he had discovered a creditable answer to the problem. In the style of the Medieval *Quaestio Disputata*, Morin presented a public demonstration of his ideas with the appearance that he had triumphed, only to be confronted with a written rejection some ten days later which Morin felt was politically motivated and prompted by his enemies.

In addition to the squares and oppositions we have already mentioned, Morin noted that his 12th house natal cluster of planets (as translator Holden notes, he did not use the word "stellium")

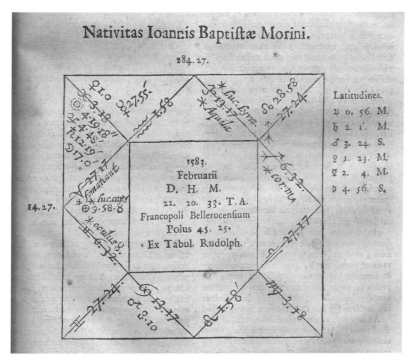

Example 2-2. Morinus' version of his natal chart.[3]

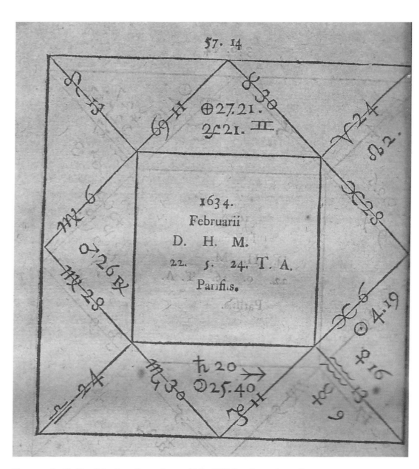

Example 2-3a. Morinus' version of his 1634 solar return.[4]

Jean Baptiste Morin
Beaujeu, France
Time Zone: 0 hours West

February 23, 1583
46 N 09 4 E 36
Tropical Regiomontanus
NATAL CHART

8:33 AM
Local Mean Time

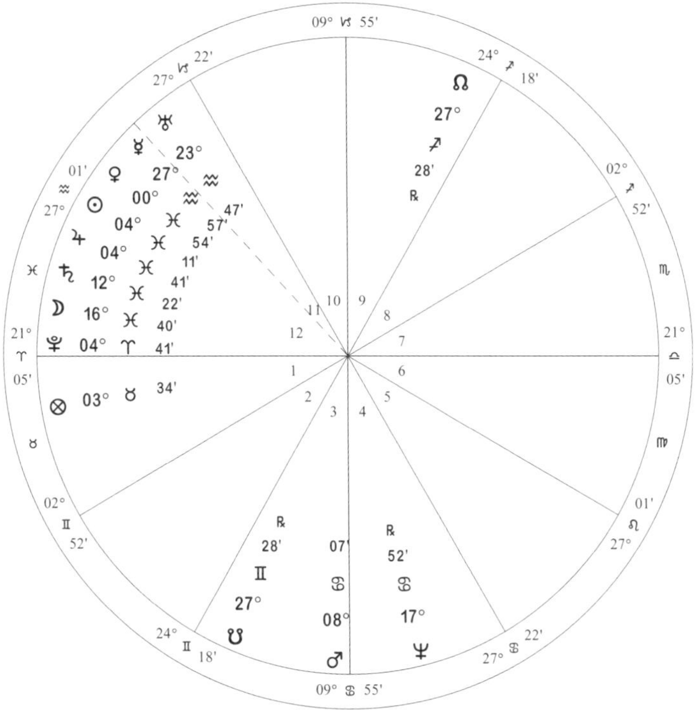

Jean Baptiste Morin
Beaujeu, France
Time Zone: 0 hours West

February 22, 1634
46 N 09 4 E 36
Tropical Regiomontanus
Solar Return for February 22, 1634 in Beaujeu, France

5:37 PM
Local Mean Time

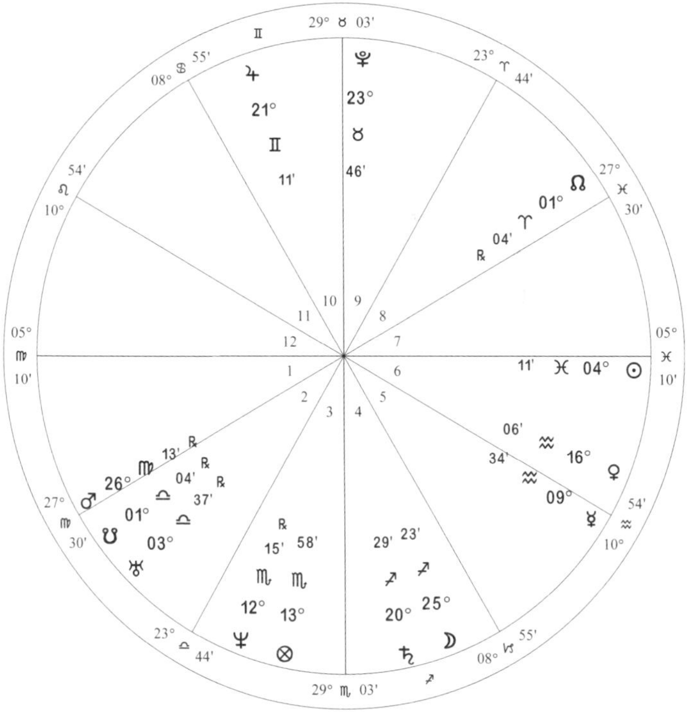

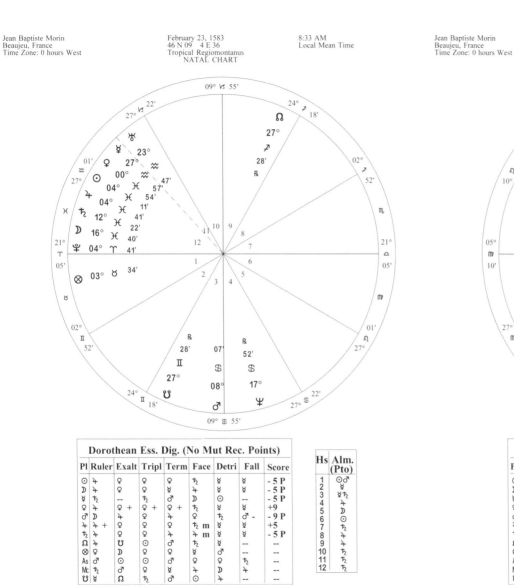

Dorothean Ess. Dig. (No Mut Rec. Points)

Pl	Ruler	Exalt	Tripl	Term	Face	Detri	Fall	Score
☉	♃	♀	♀	♀	♄	☿	☿	- 5 P
☽	♃	♀	♀	☿	♃	☿	☿	- 5 P
☿	♄	--	♄	♂	☽	☉	--	- 5 P
♀	♃	♀ +	♀ +	♀ +	♄	☿	☿	+9
♂	☽	♃	♀	♃	♀	♄	♂ -	- 9 P
♃	♃ +	♀	♀	♀	♄ m	☿	☿	+5
♄	♃	♀	♀	♃	♃ m	☿	☿	- 5 P
☊	♃	☋	☉	♂	♄	☿	--	--
⊗	♀	☽	♀	♀	☿	♂	--	--
As	♂	☉	☉	♂	♀	♀	♄	--
Mc	♄	♂	♀	☿	♃	☽	♃	--
☋	☿	☊	♄	♂	☉	♃	--	--

Hs	Alm. (Pto)
1	☉♂
2	☿
3	☿♄
4	♃
5	☽
6	☉
7	♄
8	♃
9	♃
10	♄
11	♄
12	♄

Dorothean Ess. Dig. (No Mut Rec. Points)

Pl	Ruler	Exalt	Tripl	Term	Face	Detri	Fall	Score
☉	♃	♀	♂	♀	♄	☿	☿	- 5 P
☽	♃	☋	♃	♂	♄	☿	--	- 5 P
☿	♄	--	☿ +	☿ +	♀ m	☉	--	+5
♀	♄	--	☿	♀ +	☿ m	☉	--	+2
♂	☿	☿	☽	♂ +	☿	♃	♀	+2
♃	☿	☊	☿	♄	☉	♃ -	--	- 10 P
♄	♃	☋	♃	♄ +	♄ +	☿	--	+3
☊	♂	☉	♃	♃	♂	♀	♄	--
⊗	♂	--	♂	♃	☉	♀	☽	--
As	☿	☿	☽	☿	☉	♃	♀	--
Mc	♀	☽	☽	♂	♄	♂	--	--
☋	♀	♄	☿	♄	☽	♂	☉	--

Hs	Alm. (Pto)
1	☿
2	☿
3	☿♀
4	♂
5	♄
6	☿
7	♀
8	♃
9	♂
10	☽
11	♃
12	☉

Example 2-3b. Morin nativity and the solar return for 1634 recalculated in a modern format.

was mostly to be found in the 7th house of the solar return, thus linking secret enemies to open enemies as a major theme for this solar return.[7]

That this was a major year for him, we can see by simply listing some of the characteristics of the solar return:

- The Sun conjunct an angle
- The solar return Moon square natal Moon by sign
- Mercury in the same sign in the solar return
- Solar return Mars sextile radix Mars by sign
- Solar return Jupiter square radix Jupiter by sign
- Solar return Saturn square radix Saturn by wide orb

All in all, that's representing a lot of conflict, and a lot of action, between the solar return and the natal planets.

Patterns in Consecutive Solar Returns

But before we continue with more examples, I want to return to some issues that I originally raised in reviewing Mary Shea's book: that there are patterns within solar returns, when you examine them consecutively. This will also afford us the opportunity to see how consecutive solar returns form patterns which themselves may then be interpreted. To accomplish this, I have chosen to examine the chart of Theodore Roosevelt, from 1898-1908. This eleven year time span encompasses his public career, from New York State Governor, to President of the United States.

Theodore, known to the public as Teddy, also known as TR, is our one example of "B" data in this book, where the time of birth is from a biography. However, that time is cited from a contemporary account of a friend of the family, so we have to assume it has the accuracy of many A recordings.

In 1898, Teddy was already forty years old. He was the product of an old wealthy family, by American standards, from the period when New York was New Amsterdam. A sickly child, he was educated at home until he attended Harvard, then Columbia Law School. By the age of forty, he had already been married twice, which we will examine in Chapter 3. The romance that led to his first marriage began at age nineteen. For the moment, let me just mention that age 19 in the solar return cycle is a nodal year. TR's natal Moon was in Cancer: thus, at age nineteen, his solar return Moon was likewise in Cancer. In general, aspects between the Sun and the Moon will generally repeat every nineteen years.

The New Moon Solar Return – It doesn't Always Happen!

To give an illustration of this process, let's consider TR's solar returns for 1867, 1886, and 1905. These three years were his New Moon years, which we can also use to illustrate yet another idea, which is the New Moon solar return.

In 1867, at age nine, TR had his first New Moon solar return. Quite honestly, a New Moon in the years of childhood is often not much of a big deal – everything is already new! TR's biographer Brands barely mentions this year. However, the lunar position comes close to repeating every nineteen years. As the solar position is by definition fixed, i.e., at the natal Sun position, this means that if you are examining an aspect *between* the Sun and Moon, that aspect will roughly repeat every nineteen years. In the 1867 example, the Moon is just under 8 degrees past the Sun – barely combust.

Nineteen years later was 1886. We shall examine this chart in more detail in Chapter 3, but it was a very significant year for TR: he lost the election for mayor of New York, he married his second wife, he suffered a major financial loss on his North Dakota cattle ranch which ended his career as a cattle rancher, and finally, his eldest son was born. That's quite a year! TR's natal Moon was in Cancer; here by definition, since he was a Sun in Scorpio, any New Moon would mean that the Moon was in Fall. Thus, one would not assume that the event of the New Moon would necessarily or primarily be pleasant. However, all these events did conspire to be a new beginning. TR had had his interest piqued in cattle ranching,

Theodore Roosevelt
New York, New York
Time Zone: 0 hours West

October 27, 1858
40N42'51" 74W00'23"
Tropical Regiomontanus
NATAL CHART

7:45 PM
Local Mean Time

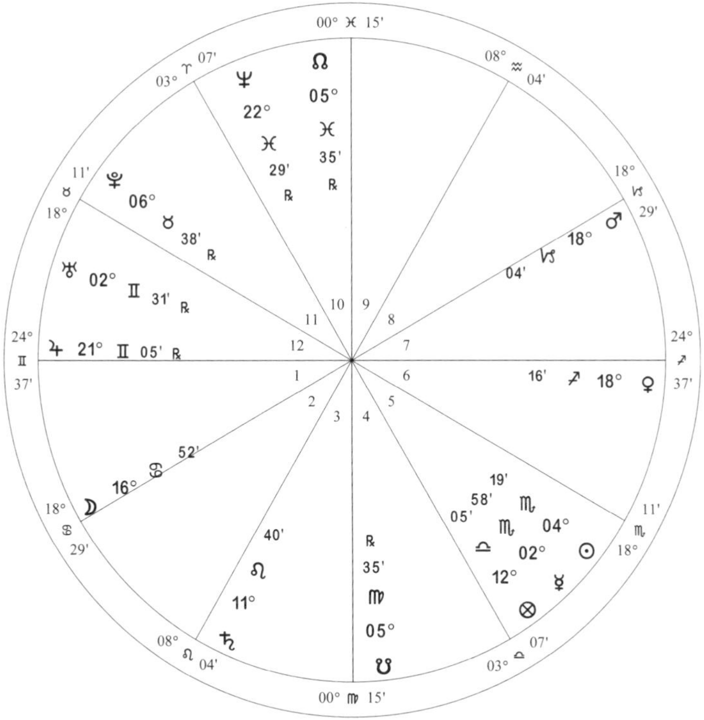

Dorothean Ess. Dig. (No Mut Rec. Points)								
Pl	Ruler	Exalt	Tripl	Term	Face	Detri	Fall	Score
☉	♂	--	♂	♂	♂	♀	☽	- 5 P
☽	☽ +	♃	♂ m	☿	☿	♄	♂	+5
☿	♂	--	♂	♂	♂	♀	☽	- 5 P
♀	♃	☋	♃	☿	☽	☿	--	- 5 P
♂	♄	♂ +	☽ m	♃	♂ +	☽	♃	+5
♃	☿	☊	☿	♄	☉	♃ -	--	- 10 P
♄	☉	--	♃	☿	♃	♄ -	--	- 10 P
☊	♃	♀	♂	♀	♄	☿	☿	--
⊗	♀	♄	☿	♃	♄	♂	☉	--
As	☿	☊	☿	♄	☉	♃	--	--
Mc	♃	♀	♂	♀	♄	☿	☿	--
☋	☿	☿	☽	☿	☉	♃	♀	--

Hs	Alm. (Pto)
1	☿
2	☽
3	☉
4	☿
5	♄
6	♂
7	♃
8	♂♄
9	☿♄
10	♀
11	♂
12	☽

Example 2-4. Theodore Roosevelt nativity

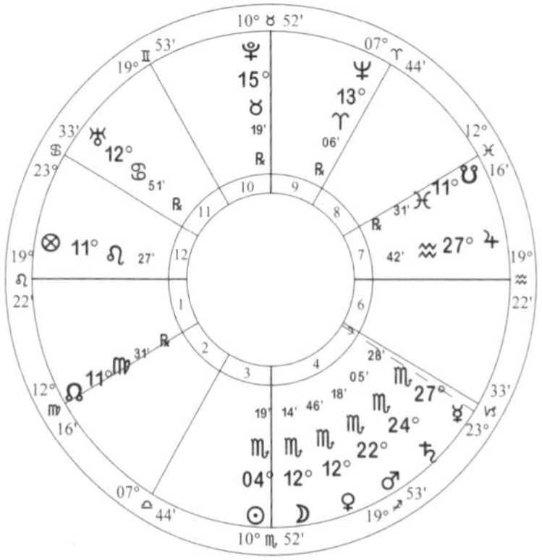

Theodore Roosevelt
October 28, 1867
12:09:25 AM
New York, New York
Solar Return for October 28, 1867 in New York, New York

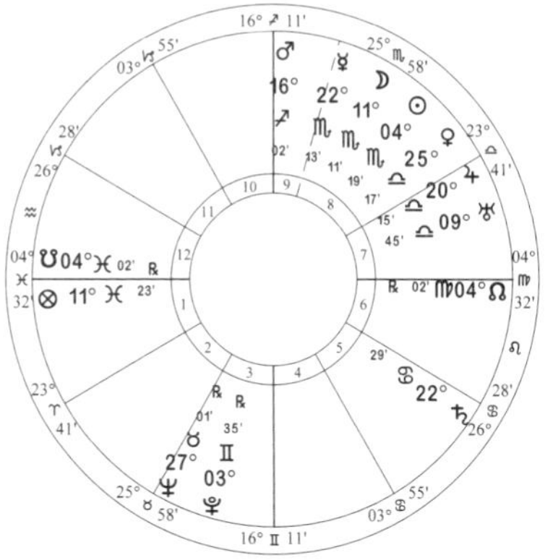

Theodore Roosevelt
October 27, 1886
2:31:41 PM
New York, New York
Solar Return for October 27, 1886 in New York, New York

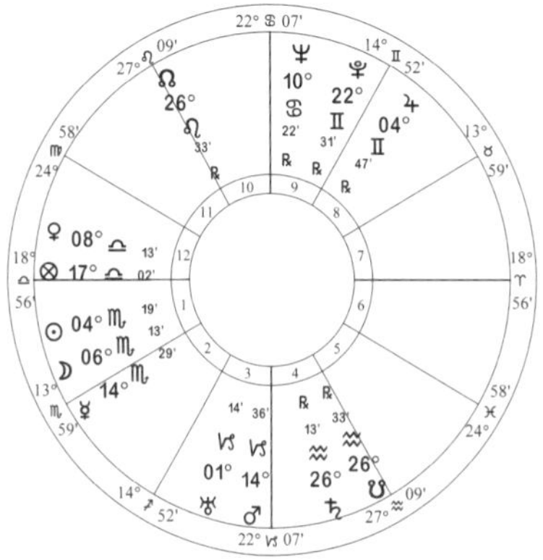

Theodore Roosevelt
October 28, 1905
5:07:16 AM
New York, New York
Solar Return for October 28, 1905 in New York, New York

Example 2-5. Theodore Roosevelt New Moon solar returns for 1867, 1886, and 1905

but he really got involved after his first wife died. His second wife was a woman he had known before he met his first wife, but they had evidently had a falling out. Thus, both the marriage *and* the "death" of the cattle ranch coincided to a new direction combined.

In 1886, the Moon was seven degrees past the Sun: in other words, in the New Moon phase. In 1905, the Moon was two degrees past the Sun. In 1886, the conjunction was in the 8th. In 1905, the conjunction was in the 1st. TR was originally elected to the vice presidency, but only a few months after taking office President McKinley was assassinated. So TR became president initially as a result of this tragedy. It was only through the 1904 election that he was elected president in his own right. Thus, we see him coming into his own in this year, and how better to do it than by being elected and re-elected at the same time?

We shall concern ourselves with the 1905 chart shortly. But we want to begin to examine roughly a decade of his life with 1898. In 1898, TR had turned forty. As we saw in *Astrology of Sustainability*, the first part of 1898 was the time of the Spanish-American War.[8] In 1897, as Assistant Secretary of the Navy, TR had done everything possible to bolster naval preparedness. When the Maine was sunk, and the US began the war, TR resigned his naval job in order to enlist as a soldier, finding his way to Lieutenant Colonel of the Rough Riders. In precisely one battle, he so distinguished himself for his courage that, when the war ended so quickly, he was out in time to run for Governor of New York in the same year.

Theodore Roosevelt – Solar Returns 1898-1908

Up to this point in his political career, TR had held a number of jobs, both elected and appointed. He had been a New York State Assemblyman; he had been a Police Commissioner; he had held two federal government jobs. He had written a number of books, and far more articles. He had campaigned across the country as an attack dog for the Republicans. He was a known quantity and excellent copy, being as colorful as he was. And now he was a war hero, even if the war was a very short one.

Teddy's 1898 solar return occurred just shortly before the election, so the election certainly was writ large in the return. How do we enter this solar return and interpret it?

Let's begin with the Sun. First, let's observe how the Sun changes positions in sequential years. Roughly, it moves diurnally (i.e., from Ascendant to the MC to the Descendant to the IC to the Ascendant again) roughly one quadrant per year. In 1898, TR's Sun was in the 9th. In 1899, the Sun was in the 6th. In 1900, it was in the 3rd. In 1901, it was in the 1st. In 1902, it was in the 10th. In 1903, the Sun was in the 6th. In 1904, it was in the 4th. Notice that this motion is not precise in the sense of being exactly three houses per year, but it's clear that the Sun will not be in the same house or even nearly so in sequential years, unless we are doing a chart for the polar regions.

It *is* possible to have the Moon in the same house in consecutive years, something not possible for the Sun, because of the approximate quadrant effect. But having the Moon in the same sign in consecutive years is worth noting. The same quadrant effect would also mitigate having the Ascendant in the same sign in two consecutive years.

It is possible to have Venus in the same sign in consecutive years: as an inferior planet, it cannot stray too far from the Sun. But because Venus can easily be two houses away from the Sun, it is possible (if rare) to have Venus in the same house in consecutive years. There is a well known eight year cycle for Venus, which has five synodic cycles embedded in it. The eight year cycle shows strongly here, as the ages that are divisible by eight all show Venus in its natal sign. In other examples, there could be some exceptions, especially if natal Venus is early or late in a sign.

Mars is not in the same sign in consecutive years because of the length of its sidereal cycle. The outer superiors may, because of the length of theirs. It's very common for Saturn on out to be in the same sign for several years or more, depending upon the planet. Most astrologers also recognize the shorter Jupiter cycle of approximately 12 years.

Recall that we already noted the reoccurrence of the approximate natal angles at ages 33 and 66, but these are not the only possible times when the Sun returns to its natal house placement. Morin comments in his delineation of his 33rd revolution how similar it was to his nativity, and he notes the same similarity in Cardan's description of his 34th without evidently being aware of the pattern of return symmetry that makes this so, generally.

But there are some general conclusions that we can draw about these lifetime solar return patterns, if the Native lives long enough to experience the full sequences.

- The Sun moves in a regular sequence from quadrant to quadrant. The Sun is never in the same house in consecutive returns.
- One specific interpretation of the MC/IC quadruplicity is regarding fixed signs. It is very difficult to get action to move forward in a year with fixed signs on the cusp of the area of interest. Accordingly, if this is something like moving house (which would be an Ascendant or 4th house matter), one of these runs of fixed signs could make that process difficult. Similarly, if your client wants to start a new business (which as an owner is at least partially a 10th house matter), a run of cardinal signs on the MC could mean the possibility of several years to get the business started.
- Inferior planets will more frequently repeat their natal signs, because of their proximity to the Sun. Superior planets will repeat according to their own synodic period.
- In consecutive years, the Moon or inferior planets can be in the same sign.

Add to these ideas the whole emphasis on planets in their natal positions being more significant, and we now have a basis to study Theodore Roosevelt's life from 1898-1908.

However, before we do so, let's go back to his natal chart to try to understand this. TR was born into a wealthy family. This fact alone, you cannot get from the chart, as the natal chart will show how he does *relative* to his starting place in life, whether he exceeds the expectations of his parents, or the reverse, or ends up in just about the same place. He's got the Moon in Cancer in rulership right on the 2nd house cusp. Financially, he will get a lot, but he will also spend a lot. Moon associated with the 2nd house is cash flow. The essential dignity raises the amount of cash flow! Jupiter on his Ascendant means he wants more, always more, but with Jupiter in Detriment, it's hard for him to be realistic or practical about his desires.

What I have just said translates to Teddy having absolutely no sense about money. And he didn't. Teddy was what we would now call a trust baby: someone in a wealthy family where in each generation, only a small number of relatives actually invested and maintained the wealth that the family collectively inherited; the others were more or less isolated from the process, living off a portion of the wealth rather than generating it. In the old parlance, South Node in the 4th would be an indication of wasting the patrimony, which is another way to say he would spend more than he would earn.

However, let's examine his Moon-Mars opposition, with both of them dignified. There are a number of interpretations possible, From a classical perspective, this combination is described for the two bodies lacking dignity, and then the definitions are attenuated to compensate for the dignity, so to speak. What did I just say? This combination is considered pretty nasty, because it's argumentative, quarrelsome, a scold, harsh-tongued, completely lacking in empathy, a harsh critic, rash, malicious, treacherous, and unable to just have an idle conversation without suddenly lashing out. Ouch! How do we attenuate *that*? And furthermore, sitting right on the 2nd-8th, it would really argue for spending beyond his means – which he regularly did.

Here is this sickly boy with asthma, which was variously attributed to Mercury,[9] Jupiter,[10] or Venus,[11] with Jupiter in Detriment in Gemini right at the Ascendant, but with Mars ruling his 6th. The weakness he was showing as a boy was coming from his 1st house (vitality) not his 6th house (illness). That Jupiter was square Neptune, meaning, both an affliction to his vitality (through Jupiter being conjunct his Ascendant, and this, affecting vitality), and a difficulty in diagnosing what was actually wrong with him (Neptune producing confusion or misdirection).

So what was wrong with him? Here is this boy with this amazingly tight Moon-Mars, who *needed* an outlet for this energy: and what parent is going to put up with an arrogant kid with an aggressive streak that just doesn't quit? A Moon-Mars opposition just doesn't work in polite company, and especially so when, as a child, one is by definition in a weak or submissive position. Furthermore, he was short and needed eyeglasses, so he was not the ideal specimen for athletic achievement.

It was only as a teen and then as an adult where he could find ways to use this opposition, whether through trips into the wilderness, cattle ranching, hunting, or other such manly activities. He *had* to test himself, he *had* to take himself to the brink. Later, when as Assistant Secretary of the Navy, he did everything possible to set the pieces up for the Spanish-American War, he *had* to enlist to actually fight in that war, rather than to help run it from a desk.

His biographer Brands actually gives a stunning picture of TR's Moon-Mars when he says of him:

> Roosevelt didn't easily abide ambiguity; it made him nervous and uncomfortable. And when he was uncomfortable, he tended to lash out."[12]

Theodore Roosevelt – 1898 Solar Return

- The Moon square its radix position
- Mercury in its radix sign
- Venus in its radix sign
- Mars opposite its radix sign
- Jupiter trine its radix sign
- Saturn trine its radix sign

TR himself in this solar return was ruled by Saturn, ruler of the SR-Ascendant. Saturn has dignity by mixed Triplicity: not extremely strong, but not bad either. Two indicators in this chart show his recent soldiering, and how this had affected his reputation. First, Mars ruled the MC, his honor and reputation: and Mars was angular in the 7th house. And Mars was **Co-Almuten** of the Ascendant. As we shall see repeatedly when we examine the charts of athletes, Mars in its Detriment or Fall is actually a very powerful Mars – for competing or fighting.[13]

In 1898, the New York State Republicans were recovering from a financial scandal that neutralized their more usual moral advantage against the Tammany Hall machine. And who should come along and be available, but the hero of the hour, who further had a history with the New York City Police Commission of fighting corruption? The United States has a long history of electing military generals or heroes, such as George Washington, Andrew Jackson, U.S. Grant, and in our era, Dwight Eisenhower. TR's attack dog role in the Republican Party, shown here by Mars in Cancer (an interesting amalgam of his natal Moon-Mars opposition if ever there was one) was precisely what they needed and wanted. Teddy won the governorship, but by a nose.

Most of his 1898 solar return applies to the aftermath of the election: his first year as governor. And here is where we see the difficulty. Mars is all over this chart: it's angular in the 7th house, it's ruling the 10th, it's ruling the Sun and Mercury, it's Co-Almuten of

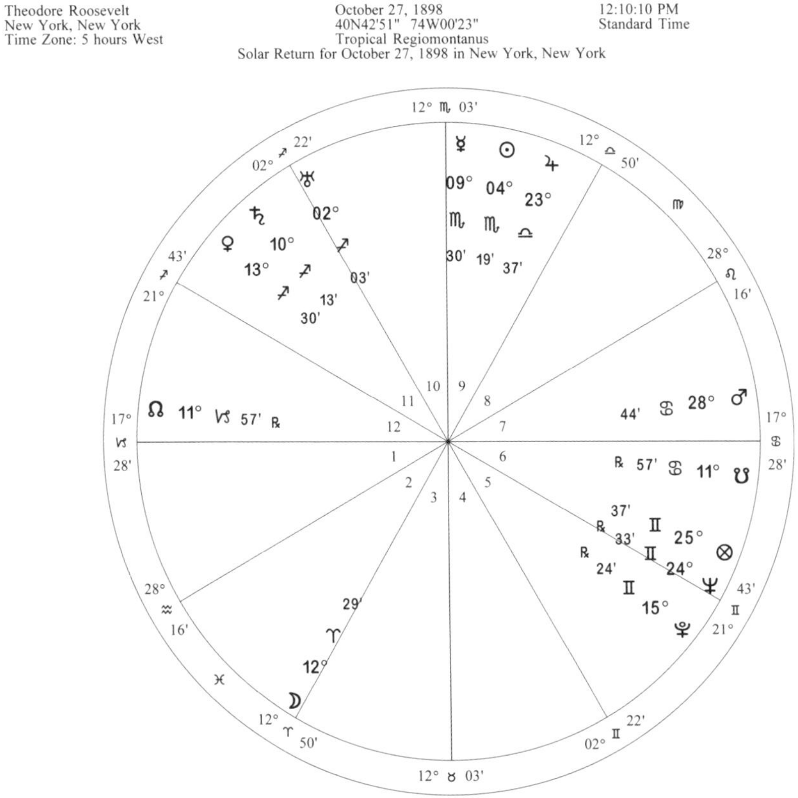
Theodore Roosevelt
New York, New York
Time Zone: 5 hours West
October 27, 1898
40N42'51" 74W00'23"
Tropical Regiomontanus
Solar Return for October 27, 1898 in New York, New York
12:10:10 PM
Standard Time

Dorothean Ess. Dig. (No Mut Rec. Points)								
Pl	Ruler	Exalt	Tripl	Term	Face	Detri	Fall	Score
☉	♂	--	♀ m	♂	♂	♀	☽	- 5 P
☽	♂ m	☉	☉	♀	☉	♀	♄	- 5 P
☿	♂	--	♀	♃ m	♂	♀	☽	- 5 P
♀	♃ m	☋	☉ m	♀ +	☽	☿	--	+2
♂	☽ m	♃	♀	♄	☽	♄	♂ -	- 9 P
♃	♀ m	♄	♄	☿ m	♃ +	♂	☉	+1
♄	♃	☋	☉	♀	☽	☿	--	- 5 P
☊	♄	♂	♀	☿	♂	☽	♃	--
⊗	☿	☊	♄	♂	☉	♃	--	--
As	♄	♂	♀	♃	♂	☽	♃	--
Mc	♂	--	♀	♃	☉	♀	☽	--
☋	☽	♃	♀	♃	☿	♄	♂	--

Hs	Alm. (Pto)
1	♂♄
2	♄
3	☉
4	♀
5	☿
6	☿♄
7	☽
8	☉
9	♄
10	♂
11	♃
12	♃

Example 2-6. Theodore Roosevelt solar return for 1898

the Ascendant, and the Moon is in Aries, disposed by it. He had just literally left the military after some months of exactly the kind of martial activity that he craved, and here he is, back in civilian life, governor of a large state, having been elected with very little personal agenda of his own save political advancement, and what is the man to do?

And realistically, Roosevelt was elected by a Republican machine that wasn't a lot weaker than the more infamous Democratic one. His 1898 chart looks like he was still spoiling for a fight: this is a very belligerent solar return in the life history of a very belligerent man. So he fought the machine. But he was also forty years old: he picked his battles, rather than attempting an all-out assault on every decision, every appointment, and every action.

The extent of the Mars focus in this solar return also impacted one of his first legislative initiatives: a corporate tax on monopolies. The corporations howled. TR did not back down. While his fiscal policy may not have been comprehensive, if it included a fight, Governor Roosevelt was up for it.

In the Summer of 1899, a reunion of the Rough Riders brought large crowds out to meet his train as he traveled across the county: his star was rising.

Theodore Roosevelt – 1899 Solar Return

- SR-Sun in the 6th house
- SR-Mercury in the radix sign
- SR-Saturn trine radix Saturn
- SR-Mars even more dignified than radix Mars
- SR-Venus in Detriment

By this time, there were quite a few Republicans who thought that TR would be an excellent addition to the 1900 national ticket: as Vice President. From Teddy's standpoint, the drawback was obvious: the Vice President had no job description to speak of except

Theodore Roosevelt
New York, New York
Time Zone: 5 hours West

October 27, 1899
40N42'51" 74W00'23"
Tropical Regiomontanus

6:07:54 PM
Standard Time

Solar Return for October 27, 1899 in New York, New York

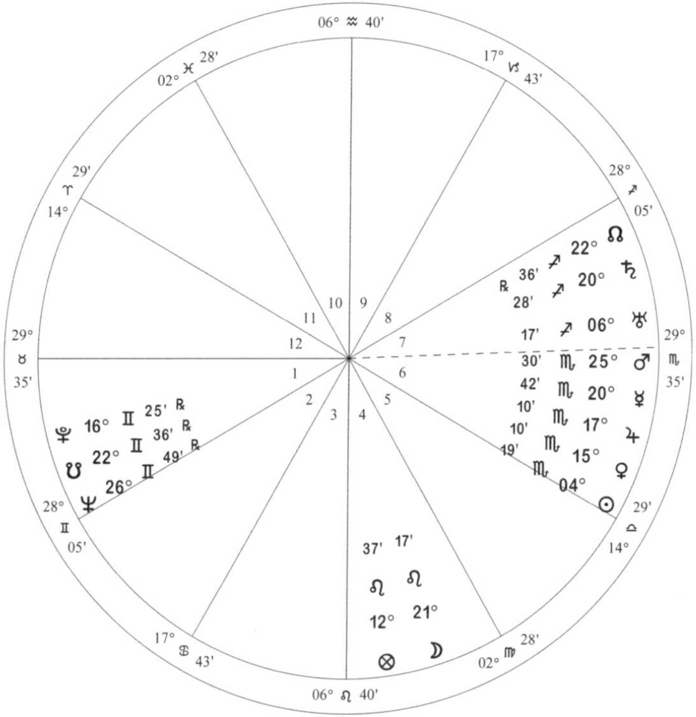

Dorothean Ess. Dig. (No Mut Rec. Points)								
Pl	Ruler	Exalt	Tripl	Term	Face	Detri	Fall	Score
☉	♂	--	♂	♂	♂	♀	☽	- 5 P
☽	☉	--	♃	♃	♂	♄	--	- 5 P
☿	♂	--	♂	♀	♀	♀	☽	- 5 P
♀	♂	--	♂	♀ +	☉	♀ -	☽	- 3
♂	♂ +	--	♂ +	☿	♀	♀	☽	+8
♃	♂	--	♂	♀	☉	♀	☽	- 5 P
♄	♃	☋	♃	♄ +	♄ +	☿	--	+3
☊	♃	☋	♃	♄	♄	☿	--	--
⊗	☉	--	♃	☿	♃	♄	--	--
As	♀	☽	☽	♂	♄	♂	--	--
Mc	♄	--	☿	☿	♀	☉	--	--
☋	☿	☊	☿	♄	☉	♃	--	--

Hs	Alm. (Pto)
1	☽
2	☿
3	☽
4	☉
5	☿
6	♀♄
7	♂
8	♃
9	♂♄
10	☿♄
11	♀
12	☉♂

Example 2-7. Theodore Roosevelt solar return for 1899

being a backup. It also hardly had decent pay. The question was whether taking this job would help him be the presidential candidate in 1904, when McKinley's two terms would be over. During this time, the nominating convention chose the Vice President, not the presidential candidate. As McKinley was making noises about jettisoning his current Vice President, it became more and more likely that TR could get the nomination if he wanted it. The question was: did he want it?

Meanwhile, the boss of the New York State Republican party found himself liking the idea of kicking Roosevelt upstairs onto the national ticket, thereby relieving a thorn in his side without appearing ungrateful, which would look bad to the voters. The bottom line was: the people liked TR, but the big Republican donors didn't. What to do?

Teddy had a fairly angular solar return, with Pluto, the Nodes, Saturn, Uranus, the Moon, and Part of Fortune all angular. And he certainly was in the public eye. With Leo Moon for the year, perhaps in the end, he couldn't resist the comparative honor of being nominated by a national convention. Despite some doubts about whether it was really the right path for him, he accepted the nomination for Vice President.

Theodore Roosevelt – 1900 Solar Return

- SR-Sun in the 3rd house conjunct the IC
- SR-Mercury in the radix sign
- SR-Venus in Fall and Triplicity
- SR-Saturn in rulership
- SR-Jupiter opposite radix Jupiter, but in rulership

We have just seen three consecutive years in which Mercury was in the same sign as the radix. Actually, this is not unusual, because of Mercury's constant geocentric proximity to the Sun. Once again, the nomination and most of the campaign season fell under the prior solar return; the last couple of weeks of the campaign fell under the new solar return.

TR's job, again, was attack dog, as McKinley preferred to stay in the White House, rather than actually campaign. TR did his job to perfection, and this was what he loved anyway – a good fight. But soon the fight was over, and he found himself the understudy – with not much to do, because the Senate typically didn't meet during Spring and Summer. Here the meaning of the angles becomes clear. The Mars at the Ascendant shows exactly his bellicose nature. But then, the prominent angle is the IC: at the end of March, he and his family trooped back to their Oyster Bay home, planning to stay there (and out of sight) until October – essentially, his next birthday.

But that's not quite how everything worked. McKinley had followed tradition in ignoring his Vice President. But Leon Czolgosz did not ignore McKinley. An anarchist, he decided that shooting McKinley was the right thing to do – and he did so on September 6, 1901. McKinley didn't die immediately, but of infection from the wound. Roosevelt became President on September 14, 1901, just before the age of 44.

Theodore Roosevelt – 1901 Solar Return

- SR-Sun in the 1st house
- SR-Mercury in the radix sign
- SR-Venus in the radix sign (this was the solar return "Venus return" that occurs roughly every eight years)
- SR-Jupiter debilitated like the radix Jupiter, but in a different sign
- The Moon exalted

If the first few couple of months of Roosevelt's administration were devoted to protestations of continuity and consultation with Congress, by his next solar return, he was coming into his own. But at the beginning of the 20th century, the U.S. presidency was not the

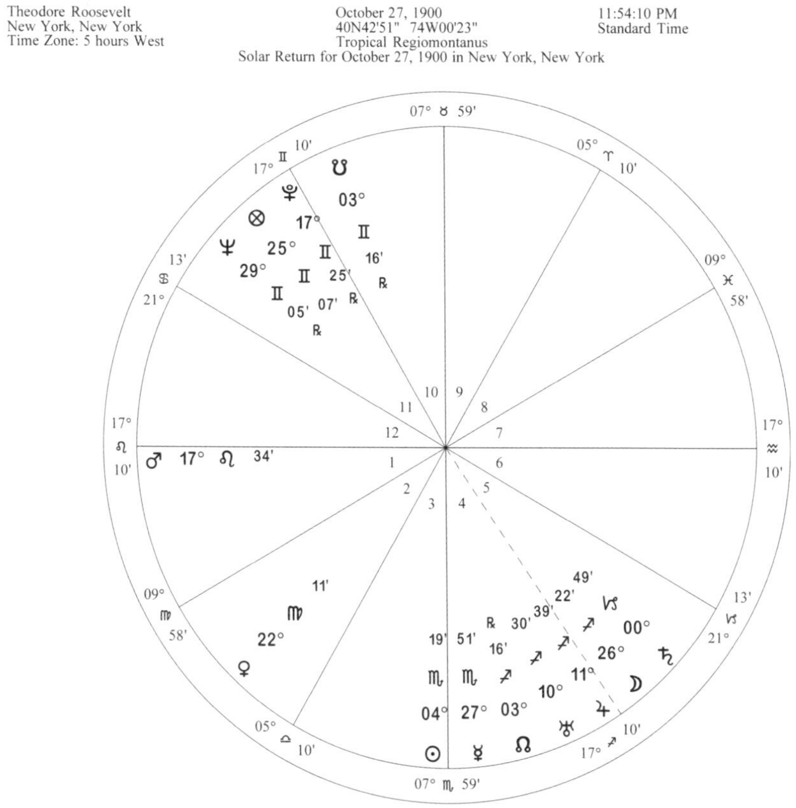

Theodore Roosevelt
New York, New York
Time Zone: 5 hours West
October 27, 1900
40N42'51" 74W00'23"
Tropical Regiomontanus
11:54:10 PM
Standard Time
Solar Return for October 27, 1900 in New York, New York

Dorothean Ess. Dig. (No Mut Rec. Points)

Pl	Ruler	Exalt	Tripl	Term	Face	Detri	Fall	Score
☉	♂ m	--	♂	♂	♂	♀	☽	- 5 P
☽	♃	☋	♃	♂	♄	☿	--	- 5 P
☿	♂	--	♂	♄	♀ m	♀	☽	- 5 P
♀	☿	☿	☽	♄ m	☿ m	♃	♀ -	- 9 P
♂	☉ m	--	♃	♀	♃	♄	--	- 5 P
♃	♃ +	☋	♃ +	♀	☽	☿	--	+8
♄	♄ +	♂	☽	♀ m	♃	☽	♃	+5
☊	♃	☋	♃	♃	☿	☿	--	--
⊗	☿	☊	☿	♂	☉	♃	--	--
As	☉	--	♃	♀	♃	♄	--	--
Mc	♀	☽	☽	♀	☿	♂	--	--
☋	☿	☊	☿	☿	♃	♃	--	--

Hs	Alm. (Pto)
1	☉
2	☿
3	♄
4	♂
5	♃
6	♂
7	♄
8	♃
9	♂
10	☽♀
11	☿
12	☽

Example 2-8. Theodore Roosevelt solar return for 1900

Theodore Roosevelt
New York, New York
Time Zone: 5 hours West

October 28, 1901
40N42'51" 74W00'23"
Tropical Regiomontanus
Solar Return for October 28, 1901 in New York, New York

5:49:51 AM
Standard Time

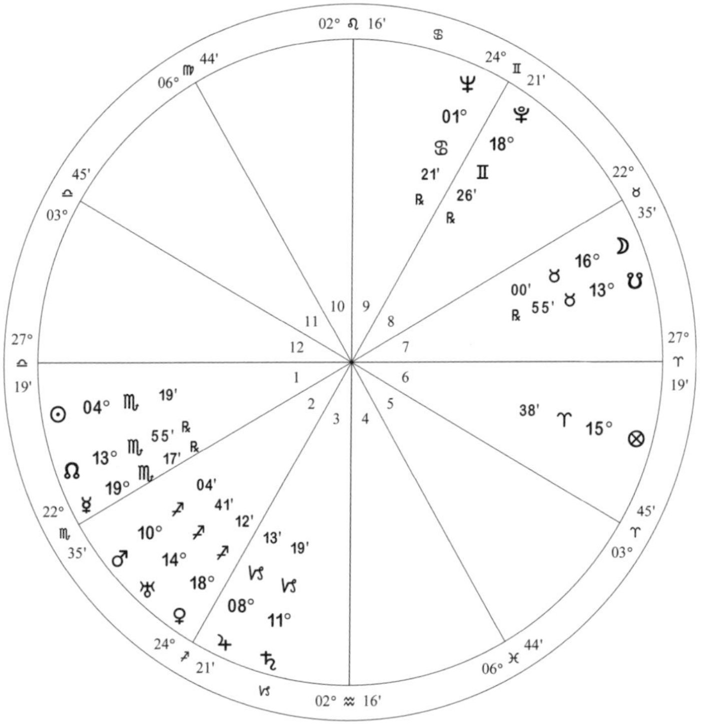

Dorothean Ess. Dig. (No Mut Rec. Points)								
Pl	Ruler	Exalt	Tripl	Term	Face	Detri	Fall	Score
☉	♂	--	♂	♂	♂	♀	☽	- 5 P
☽	♀	☽ +	☽ +	♃	☽ +	♂	--	+8
☿	♂	--	♂	♀ m	☉	♀	☽	- 5 P
♀	♃	☋	♃	☿ m	☽	☿	--	- 5 P
♂	♃	☋	♃	♀	☽	☿	--	- 5 P
♃	♄	♂	☽	☿	♃ +	☽	♃ -	- 3
♄	♄ +	♂	☽	☿	♂	☽	♃	+5
☊	♂	--	♂	♃	☉	♀	☽	--
⊗	♂	☉	♃	☿	☉	♀	♄	--
As	♀	♄	☿	☊	♃	♂	☉	--
Mc	☉	--	♃	♄	♄	♄	--	--
☋	♀	☽	☽	☿	☽	♂	--	--

Hs	Alm. (Pto)
1	♀
2	♂
3	♃
4	♄
5	♀
6	♂
7	♂
8	☽
9	☿
10	☉
11	☿
12	♄

Example 2-9. Theodore Roosevelt solar return for 1901

imperial version – much more power resided with Congress than is the case today. TR consulted regularly with the top members of Congress, but he did have control over the cabinet. In the Winter of 1902, he began to challenge the Trusts – megacorporations that had developed in an era when what puny teeth the Sherman Antitrust Act had were being pulled out by the Supreme Court. But his goal was not to dismantle *all* trusts, only those whose business principles involved deception, or other mean-spirited approaches. He emphatically did not object to trusts run on what he considered to be high moral principles.

His 1901 solar return with the Sun in the 1st house shows that TR simply regarded this period as a time when he had come into his own. He was comfortable in his own skin, so to speak. This solar return has the flavor, if not the precision, of a Full Moon solar return. Please note that it is entirely possible for a person to not have any solar New Moons or Full Moons, depending upon the precision of the orb one requires to define it. TR's position on trusts looks *very* similar to his attitudes when he was Civil Service Commissioner or Police Commissioner: he had a low tolerance for those persons or institutions that did not operate for the public good, and he considered it a moral failing.

So how do we see all of this in a chart? Since Hellenistic times, Mercury has been known as the planet of traders and commerce. Mercury was in TR's radix sign, once again. The Moon was opposite Mercury, and the opposition is pretty close to the 2nd-8th cusp; more-so with Mercury. There are two oppositions in that year: that one, and Venus partile opposite Pluto, which unequivocally is in the 2nd-8th house. The houses suggest the financial issues at stake, and Venus-Pluto the subject: money and plutocrats. And of course Venus ruled the Ascendant: Roosevelt dug in against the plutocrats. And we have observed how this was the solar return/Venus return, where Venus returns to its natal placement roughly every eight years, making Venus, representing TR, even *stronger*.

One of his earlier bill signings was of the Reclamation Act of 1902, a conservation bill. Here we see a Jupiter-Saturn conjunction in *earth*, trine the Moon in Earth, for a bill which was designed to help reclaim *land*. It's worth mentioning that Roosevelt's interest in the land was as a *user*: he was not a preservationist, and he certainly believed in development. He could see setting aside a location, such as Yosemite, for its natural beauty, but he would be perfectly happy with the development of the next valley over.

Theodore Roosevelt – 1902 Solar Return

- SR-Sun in the 10th house
- SR-Jupiter trine the radix Jupiter
- SR-Saturn dignified

As usual, Teddy's birthday fell late during the election cycle, and this year the issue was coal. If you ever heard the Weavers sing, "I owe my soul to the company store," they were singing about the coal mines. In that industry, the mine operators owned everything: the miners lived in their houses, and shopped in their stores. They set the price for the coal the miners brought to the surface, and then weighed it in scales that may or may not have been accurate. Everything about the miners' lives kept them down. The miners had run out of patience and had gone on strike.

In 1902 coal was *the* fuel for nearly everything from the factories to home heating. The internal combustion engine had not become big enough to drive fuel use toward petroleum yet. The strike meant that a cold winter would literally kill people – and the population was running out of patience. Roosevelt brokered an arbitration that eventually awarded the miners a 10% pay increase, but no union representation. It was a decision close enough to middle ground to seem like a really good solution at the time.

Roosevelt's 1902 solar return does not have the same resonance with the radix that the 1901 had – but it is still a very powerful chart.

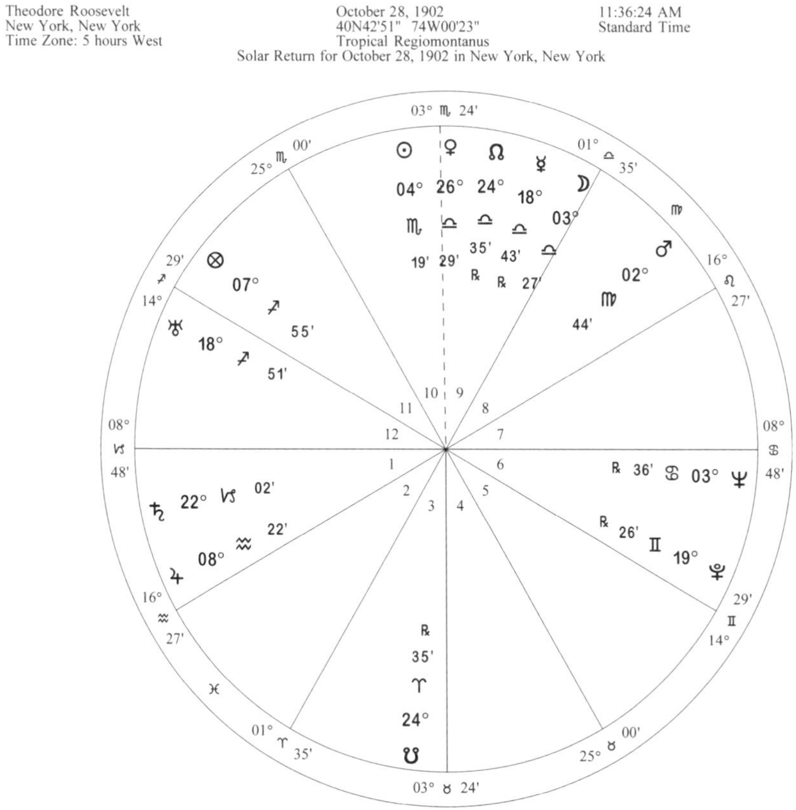

Theodore Roosevelt
New York, New York
Time Zone: 5 hours West

October 28, 1902
40N42'51" 74W00'23"
Tropical Regiomontanus
Solar Return for October 28, 1902 in New York, New York

11:36:24 AM
Standard Time

Example 2-10. Theodore Roosevelt solar return for 1902

Theodore Roosevelt
New York, New York
Time Zone: 5 hours West

October 28, 1903
40N42'51" 74W00'23"
Tropical Regiomontanus
Solar Return for October 28, 1903 in New York, New York

5:23:53 PM
Standard Time

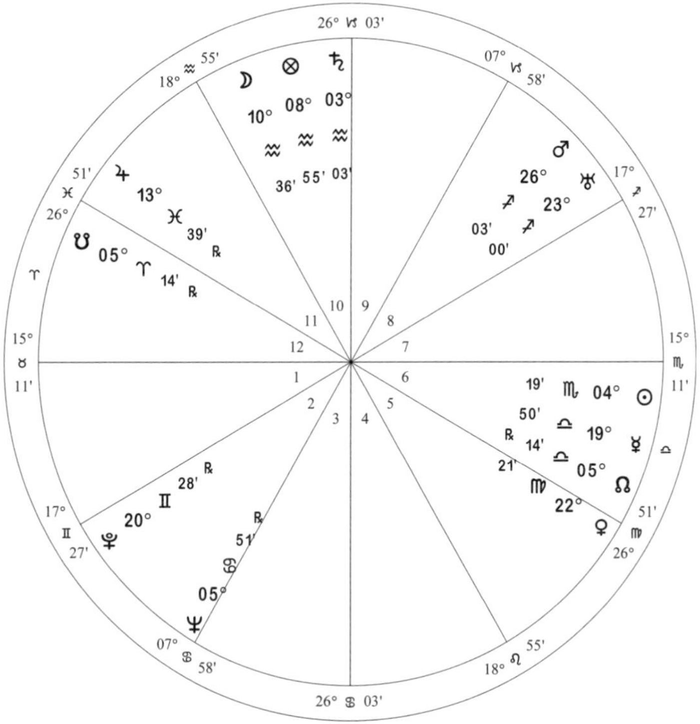

Dorothean Ess. Dig. (No Mut Rec. Points)								
Pl	Ruler	Exalt	Tripl	Term	Face	Detri	Fall	Score
☉	♂	--	♂	♂	♂	♀	☽	- 5 P
☽	♄	--	☿	☿	☿	☉	--	- 5 P
☿	♀ m	♄	☿ +	☿ +	♄	♂	☉	+5
♀	☿ m	☿	☽	♄	☿	♃	♀ -	- 9 P
♂	♃	☋	♃ m	♂ +	♄	☿	--	+2
♃	♃ +	♀	♂ m	♃ +	♃ +	☿	☿	+8
♄	♄ +	--	☿	♄ +	♀	☉	--	+7
☊	♀	♄	☿	♄	☽	♂	☉	--
⊗	♄	--	☿	☿	♀	☉	--	--
As	♀	☽	☽	♃	☽	♂	--	--
Mc	♄	♂	☽	♄	☉	☽	♃	--
☋	♂	☉	♃	♃	♂	♀	♄	--

Hs	Alm. (Pto)
1	☽
2	☿
3	♃
4	☽
5	☉
6	☿
7	♂
8	♃
9	♄
10	♄
11	♄
12	♃

Example 2-11. Theodore Roosevelt solar return for 1903

Saturn in Capricorn, in rulership, is in and rules the 1st house. The Sun is in the 10th – and by this time, TR was past his learning curve as President, even if there were a fair number of opponents who still tried to think about him as the accidental President. I would describe the transition from the Sun in the 1st to the Sun in the 10th in consecutive solar returns as being the process of coming into your own, and then manifesting it in the world. In 1901, Roosevelt was saying that he was adhering to McKinley's policies, and that this was continuity. By the following year, TR was following his own course completely.

In 1902, with the Sun in the 10th, Mars, ruler of the 10th, was in the 8th, dignified by participating Triplicity in Virgo. The 8th house? The financial sector. Mars? The Coal industry – any *energy* source.

Theodore Roosevelt – 1903 Solar Return

- SR-Sun in the 6th house
- SR-Venus in Fall
- SR-Jupiter square the radix Jupiter and dignified
- SR-Saturn dignified

Notice that a couple of angular Sun placements in a row don't guarantee that it stays that way. This was TR's first cadent Sun year as President. His 10th still looks quite strong, with the Moon, Fortuna, and Saturn there, with Saturn dignified and disposing all that.

He spent a large portion of the year traveling, especially in the American West, which served to assuage his lust for adventure, but also served to put him in front of a lot of ordinary citizens. It was also in this period that the United States concluded its negotiations with the newly minted Panamanian government for lease rights to build the Panama Canal.

In mundane astrology, it's usual to consider the 9th house for foreign affairs, but the United States has long had a special relationship with its neighbors, Canada to the North, and the Monroe Doctrine in general for all of the Americas. Over this point, I am really struck with Neptune in his solar return at the 3rd house cusp, especially partile at the ***Bendings***. On the one hand, Saturn ruling the 9th for foreign affairs would be interpreted as foreign affairs going well for Roosevelt, and hence, the United States. On the other hand, the amount of bribery, underhandedness, and deception involved in the independence movement of Panama from Columbia after Columbia rejected the U.S. proposal for the Canal lease (presumably expecting to get more money) does make one powerfully attracted to that Neptune!

As TR went into the 1904 campaign, his personal opinion was that the securing of the Canal route was the greatest accomplishment of his presidency, but many of his fellow Republicans disagreed. While he was never popular in the more moneyed portion of his party, the Senator who most clearly represented this more conservative branch died of typhoid fever in early 1904, which meant that Roosevelt had little opposition for renomination. The tradition of a sitting President not campaigning kept him off the campaign trail for the first time in twenty years.

Theodore Roosevelt – 1904 Solar Return

- SR-Sun in the 4th house
- SR-Mercury in the radix sign
- SR-Venus in the radix sign (not the 8 year return)
- SR-Jupiter dignified by Triplicity
- SR-Saturn dignified
- SR-Nodal reversal by sign

Roosevelt won by a landslide. Looking back on his solar return charts that we have examined, 1899-1900 had all fixed angles; 1901-1902 had fixed MC/IC and cardinal Ascendant/Descendant; 1903-1904 and 1907-1908 had fixed Ascendant/Descendant and

Theodore Roosevelt
New York, New York
Time Zone: 5 hours West

October 27, 1904
40N42'51" 74W00'23"
Tropical Regiomontanus
Solar Return for October 27, 1904 in New York, New York

11:22:32 PM
Standard Time

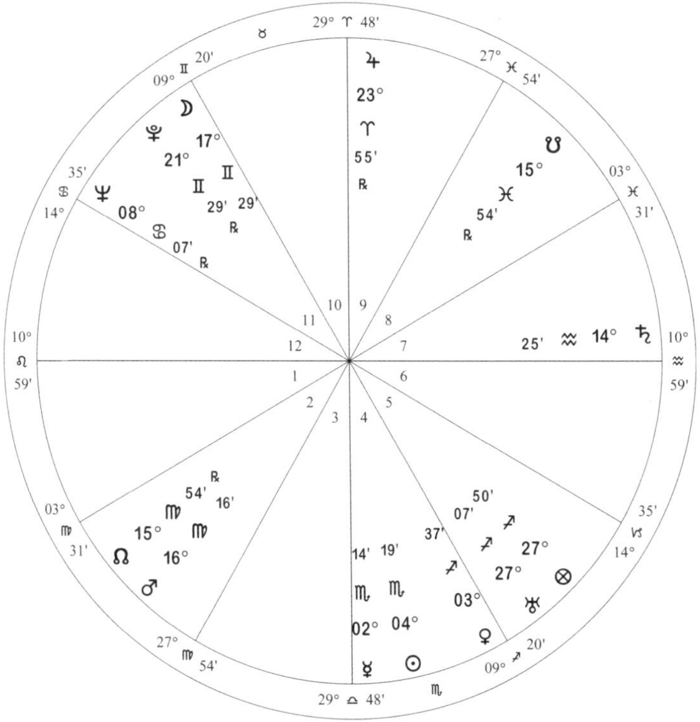

Pl	Ruler	Exalt	Tripl	Term	Face	Detri	Fall	Score
☉	♂	--	♂	♂	♂	♀	☽	- 5 P
☽	☿	☊	☿	♀	♂	♃	--	- 5 P
☿	♂ m	--	♂	♂	♂	♀	☽	- 5 P
♀	♃	☋	♃	♃	☿	☿	--	- 5 P
♂	☿ m	☿	☽	♃ m	♀	♃	♀	- 5 P
♃	♂	☉	♃ +	♂ m	♀	♀	♄	+3
♄	♄ +	--	☿	♀	☿	☉	--	+5
☊	☿	☿	☽	♃	♀	♃	♀	--
⊗	♃	☋ +	♃	♂	♄	☿	--	--
As	☉	--	♃	☿	♃	♄	--	--
Mc	♂	☉	♃	♄	♀	♀	♄	--
☋	♃	♀	♂	☿	♃	☿	☿	--

Dorothean Ess. Dig. (No Mut Rec. Points)

Hs	Alm. (Pto)
1	☉
2	☿
3	☿
4	♀
5	♃
6	♂♄
7	☿
8	♀
9	♃
10	♂
11	☿
12	☽

Example 2-12. Theodore Roosevelt solar return for 1904

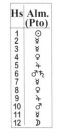

cardinal MC/IC. These kind of mini-patterns are not at all unusual in solar returns. The same astronomy that results in the Sun progressing through the quadrants diurnally each solar return also means that the Ascending sign changes roughly four signs as well, outside the polar regions. Under certain conditions, these quadruplicity patterns can actually last for five or more years in a row: when this happens, the change can be a disruptive year. Here, with two sequentially, there's hardly an effect when the change does occur, but when it stays the same, there is one more component of continuity from year to year.

Right after the election, TR announced that he would count his three-and-a-half years of fulfilling McKinley's term as his first term, and so accordingly, following custom, he would not run again. This was an incredibly *dumb* statement! It is a well-known phenomenon in American politics that there comes a point during any presidency when the members of Congress begin to perceive that they potentially have a longer future in Washington than the President does. Until this point, the President tends to act as policy head; after this point, the President is a "lame duck," as party members find it easier to disagree with the President without any political penalty. So here was Roosevelt, unpopular in his own party to begin with, coming off a landslide victory which should have sent a message within his party ranks, potentially still able to run one more time, because his "first" term wasn't *his*, but McKinley's – and he just threw all his advantage away. What came over him?

TR had boasted of being the best-read President since Jefferson; he had to have known better. Perhaps it was the twenty-nine degrees on the MC/IC, a placement that is a harbinger of change, about being just barely still in the old and feeling the new coming on. Perhaps it was the Sun in the 4th, that most private of angles. And perhaps it was Jupiter, ruling the 9th, and in the 9th in Triplicity. TR prided himself as being a man of his word; it is documented that he had been discussing this very question with his close political friends for some time, and his strong sense of righteousness prevented him from not speaking what he was thinking about this. Whatever it was, he made his job harder by his frankness.

But not all his job. Shortly after his election, he issued the Roosevelt Corollary to the Monroe Doctrine, which more directly addressed the ability of the US to further its interests by force. Returning to our 3rd-9th question of the prior year, isn't it interesting that both the ruler of the 3rd and the 9th in this solar return is disposed by *Mars*? This was, after all the President with the motto: "Speak softly and carry a big stick."

In 1905, TR got to try his hand at international mediation, as he was asked to be the mediator between Japan and Russia in their war. After much back and forth, an accord was reached. This emphasis for the year on foreign policy could coincide with the dignified Jupiter ruling the 9th and placed in the 9th: foreign affairs.

Theodore Roosevelt – 1905 Solar Return

- SR-Sun in the 1st house
- SR-New Moon chart
- SR-Mercury in the radix sign
- SR-Venus dignified
- SR-Mars in the radix sign
- SR-Jupiter in the radix sign
- SR-Saturn dignified
- SR-Nodal reversal by sign

Some of the harmonics of the return sequence are age related. For example, approximately every twelve years, Jupiter will be in the radix sign, because that is the approximate length of the Jupiter cycle. But other factors, such as the solar return New Moon, if it happens during the life at all, needn't happen at any particular age but, if it does happen, it can be expected to repeat every 19 years from then. We already discussed the effect of this solar return New Moon for TR in 1886. Now we see it again.

This New Moon occurred at age 47 – hardly a decrepit age, but maybe not the easiest for a new direction. The new direction that he took seemed to take a little while to put together, but here was the gist of his problem. It's easy to say that TR was from the progressive wing of the Republican Party, but what did that mean? The major fight within the Republican Party in the late 19ᵗʰ century was concerning the patronage system and the extent to which it ruled politics. In 1884 a faction of Republicans who were labeled Mugwumps refused to support the Republican candidate against Democrat Grover Cleveland , who then won the election. While TR had a lifetime of service with the goal of clean government, he did not support the Mugwumps. Similarly, he had acted in his first term as president against a trust – but not all trusts. TR was at heart, a Republican – and he recognized that the complexity of modern life and manufacture required concentrated capital. He wanted the trusts to act for the public good and, as long as they did, he had no objection to their size. But in his second term, Roosevelt would exercise his vision for the future of the United States based on another kind of trust: the public trust, as his interest in conservation would come to the fore. As I discussed in *Astrology of Sustainability*, the conservationism of TR's era was much different than environmentalism is now. This idea of the Pluto in Gemini era was to *manage* natural resources, not necessarily to *preserve* them. This was the conservation of a man who was as big a game hunter as any of his generation, a man who would never have conceived of taking pictures of big game instead of shooting them. TR's issues cut across the usual party ideological lines. And it is this way of thinking that really seems to come forward precisely with this solar New Moon in the 1ˢᵗ: not as a radically new way of thinking, but as a change in emphasis and priority.

This solar year had a great amount of planetary emphasis, whether through planets being in their radix signs or, if not, in their dignities. And I can't help wondering whether the nodal reversal (i.e.,

Example 2-13. Theodore Roosevelt solar return for 1905

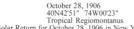

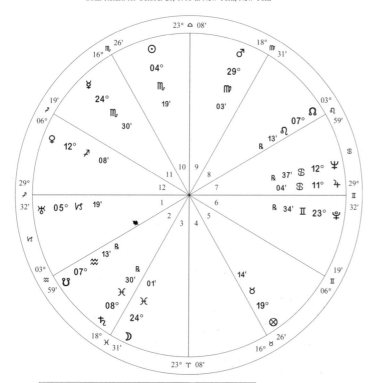

Theodore Roosevelt
New York, New York
Time Zone: 5 hours West

October 28, 1906
40N42'51" 74W00'23"
Tropical Regiomontanus
Solar Return for October 28, 1906 in New York, New York

10:57:19 AM
Standard Time

Dorothean Ess. Dig. (No Mut Rec. Points)								
Pl	**Ruler**	**Exalt**	**Tripl**	**Term**	**Face**	**Detri**	**Fall**	**Score**
☉	♂	--	♀ m	♂	♂	♀	☽	- 5 P
☽	♃ m	♀	♀	♂	♂	☿	☿	- 5 P
☿	♂ m	--	♀	☿ +	♀	♀	☽	+2
♀	♃	☋	☉ m	♀ +	☽	☿	--	+2
♂	☿ m	☿	♀	♂ +	☿	♃	♀	+2
♃	☽ m	♃ +	♀	♃ +	☿	♄	♂	+6
♄	♃	♀	♀	♃	♄ +	☿	☿	+1
☊	☉	--	☉	☿	♄	♄	--	--
⊗	♀	☽	♀	♃	☽	♂	--	--
As	♃	☋	☉	♂	♄	☿	--	--
Mc	♀	♄	♄	☿	♃	♂	☉	--
☋	♄	--	♄	☿	♀	☉	--	--

Hs	Alm. (Pto)
1	♃
2	♄
3	♃
4	☉♂
5	♀
6	☿
7	☿
8	☉
9	☿
10	♄
11	♂
12	♃

Example 2-14. Theodore Roosevelt solar return for 1906

the North Node in the radix South Node sign and vice versa) may not also have contributed to this new/old way of thinking.

Roosevelt could envision the need for oversight to achieve the public good far more strongly than could most Republicans. Thus, he tended not to be a union buster, He tended to abhor secret business deals, and encouraged legislation that banned secret price fixing. But being for regulation at all put him right up against the conservative wing of the Republican Party – which was substantial. The fundamental congressional wrangling of the year was precisely over railroad regulation and rates, which TR narrowly won. It was also the year that he managed to get regulation of the meat packing industry enacted, even if the form was less rigorous than he had preferred.

Theodore Roosevelt – 1906 Solar Return

- SR-Sun in the 10th house
- SR-Moon trine the radix Moon sign
- SR-Mercury in the radix sign
- SR-Venus in the radix sign
- SR-Mars dignified at 29 degrees
- SR-Jupiter in the radix sign
- SR-Ascendant at 29 degrees

Because the Sun "moves" roughly one quadrant per year in the solar return sequence, that means that every four years, there is a quadrant return, so to speak. This isn't necessarily precise by house, but within the U.S. presidential cycle, it sets up a certain symmetry between terms in office, since the term length is also four years. Thus, we see the progression from the Sun in the 1st to the Sun in the 10th here in 1905-1906, just as we did in 1901-1902.

What is different this time, however, was the 29 degrees rising, with Mars partile square the SR-Ascendant. Furthermore, the Moon is coming to oppose Mars, with both Moon and Mars having dignity by Triplicity. Further, the Moon is translating the Light from Pluto to Mars. There was an incident in his presidency that year which has the look of Mars-Pluto: there was a shooting incident involving soldiers and a group of townsfolk, but what complicated matters was that the solders were black and the townspeople were white. TR dishonorably discharged three companies because the innocent men would not testify against the guilty men. This then blew up into a national scandal while Roosevelt exercised another component of this solar return: the Jupiter-Neptune in the 7th.

Jupiter-Neptune is often indicative of strong religious belief, but this is a solar return and not a natal placement. Here, we may note that the conjunction occurred in the 7th house, and that the chart has quite a bit of water to it. Roosevelt started spending more time with his wife this year. Not only did they purchase a getaway house where they could escape from Washington, but Roosevelt did something no president had done before: he left the Untied States while in office, sailing on a battleship with his wife down to Panama, to inspect the developing canal.

As for the 29 degrees rising, one interpretation is: matters being taken to extremes. This is not necessarily dangerous, so much as testing an idea by trying to examine its most extreme consequences. For example, in this period, the United States had retained political and business interests in Cuba following the Spanish-American War: the war that had made Roosevelt a hero, and thus, ultimately, president. The political situation in Cuba by 1906-1907 had deteriorated to the point that there was an armed insurrection. Roosevelt sent Taft, his Secretary of War, to assess the situation, negotiate if possible, and recommend troops if all else failed. After extensive attempts at mediation, Taft recommended troops.

TR had always been one to call a spade a spade, even going so far at one point as to recommend changes to the language. But here, confronted with the reality of intervention, he specifically admonished Taft not to use the term, but to say that the troops were being sent to protect American interests. By engaging in this linguistic legerdemain, Roosevelt got around Congress's powers to declare war, and established the presidential precedent of interventions without congressional approval that became the norm in the 20th century. But it was a complete violation of his personal principle of plain speaking.

The myth that I think of for 29 degrees rising in a solar return is Wotan in Wagner's Ring Cycle. Wotan is king of the gods – but in this mythology, the gods are subject to laws, just as humans are: they are powerful, but not omnipotent. Wotan is bound by the oaths he makes, and while he may try to wheedle his way around them, eventually, the twilight of the gods occurs when the inconsistencies and downright incompatibilities of his oaths eventually become dominant. Twenty-nine degrees rising means that it's time to pay the price for inconsistent and incompatible oaths, beliefs, or actions. It's a time when the consequences of prior action taken comes home to roost.

Plain speaking on the surface sounds wonderful: but it doesn't leave room for the white lie that may be the most compassionate choice in a particular moment. Any absolute has the ability to be inappropriate under some circumstances. Roosevelt came to what he needed as a policy only by abandoning the absolutist nature of one of his own personal principles: this, in a year of Jupiter-Neptune. What was the cost of this to him? We'll never know.

Another possible meaning of the 29th degree is given by one other incident of this year: the curtailment of the power of the president to place federal land into forest reserves. This practice had begun with a law in 1891, and Roosevelt's predecessors collectively had set aside 50 million acres. Roosevelt set aside 150 million. The forest industries were furious. They curtailed the power of the president by attaching the curtailment to an agriculture bill that TR could not veto, so his hands were tied; thus, the 29 degree Mars ruled the 4th house (land), and his power to conserve land ended in this year.

Theodore Roosevelt
New York, New York
Time Zone: 5 hours West

October 28, 1907
40N42'51" 74W00'23"
Tropical Regiomontanus
Solar Return for October 28, 1907 in New York, New York

4:54:31 PM
Standard Time

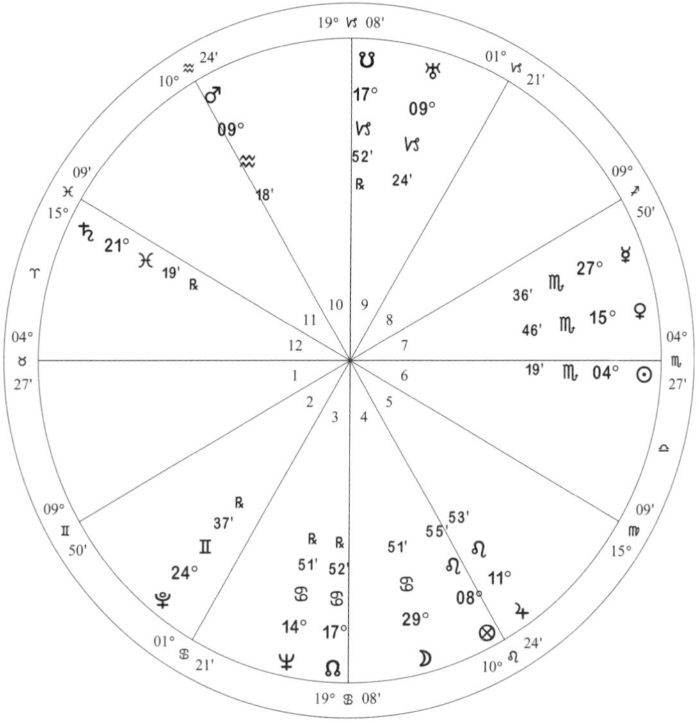

Pl	Ruler	Exalt	Tripl	Term	Face	Detri	Fall	Score
☉	♂	--	♂	♂	♂	♀	☽	- 5 P
☽	☽ +	♃	♂	♄	☽ +	♄	♂	+6
☿	♂	--	♂ m	♄	♀	♀	☽	- 5 P
♀	♂	--	♂	♀ +	☉	♀ -	☽	- 3
♂	♄	--	☿ m	☿	♀	☉	--	- 5 P
♃	☉	--	♃ +	☿	♃ +	♄	--	+4
♄	♃	♀	♂	♂	♂	☿	☿	- 5 P
☊	☽	♃	♂	☿	☿	♄	♂	--
⊗	☉	--	♃	☿	♄	♄	--	--
As	♀	☽	☽	♀	☿	♂	--	--
Mc	♄	♂	☽	♂	♂	☽	♃	--
☋	♄	♂	☽	♃	♂	☽	♃	--

Dorothean Ess. Dig. (No Mut Rec. Points)

Hs	Alm. (Pto)
1	☽♀
2	☿
3	☽
4	☽
5	☉
6	☿
7	♂
8	♃
9	♄
10	♂
11	☿
12	♃

Example 2-15. Theodore Roosevelt solar return for 1907

Theodore Roosevelt – 1907 Solar Return

- SR-Sun partile conjunct the 7th house cusp
- SR-Moon in the radix sign, but 29 degrees
- SR-Mercury in the radix sign
- SR-Venus in Detriment
- SR-Jupiter in dignity

In 1906, Roosevelt's Ascendant was 29 degrees; here in 1907 it was the Moon at that degree. With the South Node conjunct the MC, this was TR's hardest year to date. It was hard not because his popularity evaporated, but because the issues for the year began with financial matters – matters that Roosevelt flat out did not understand. While prudence required him to side with the bankers, he wasn't very happy about it, but it did prevent a panic from catching hold.

The other issue for the year that occupied his attention was finding his replacement. In 1907, the sitting President was not the *de facto* party chief the way things are today. The state party bosses considered the sitting President almost as the enemy. Thus, it was highly unusual for Roosevelt to successfully push the candidacy of William Howard Taft, his Secretary of War. But Roosevelt had achieved his success himself as often by appealing directly to the people rather than through the bosses. So campaign for Taft he did. His reason was that he wanted to see another progressive Republican President like himself; he did not want to allow the conservative wing of the party to prevail.

While Teddy was pretty successful in passing the baton, the problem was that TR did not clearly see the ways in which he and Taft didn't agree. Here, we see the ruler of the 10th in the 12th, as well as the South Node at the 10th: this is a pretty good case of being careful what you ask for! It's not that Taft was lying or misrepresenting: he simply had a legalistic mind which approached problems in a far different way than TR, and further, he didn't have TR's martial side. However, TR's disappointment with Taft would lead to a split in the party in 1912, which allowed the Democrats to win. That was a story which benefited TR's younger cousin Franklin Delano Roosevelt, and it's a story we shall tell in Chapter 12. But for now, the ruler of the 10th in the 12th would signify bad judgment about leadership.

Theodore Roosevelt – 1908 Solar Return

- SR-Sun was in the 4th house
- SR-Mercury in the radix sign
- SR-Venus in Fall
- SR-Mars in Detriment
- SR-Jupiter in Detriment
- SR-Saturn in Detriment

For most of the first half of this solar return, Roosevelt truly was a lame duck. The election had taken place just before his birthday, but he would continue as president until March 1909. It is amazing how much debility this chart has: but this has to be the symbol for his return to private life after a very public eight years. For someone who enjoyed the limelight as much as he did, this has to have been a major transition, and not an entirely pleasant one. One indicator of the amount of debility, and especially of Mars, ruling the 10th, was that when Congress during this period did anything he didn't like, he no longer felt the need to be tactful: he spoke out with no restrictions whatsoever, politics be damned. As we shall see in Chapter 8, the Mars in Detriment is a very competitive Mars, and now TR could finally admit to being annoyed by Congress.

But the Mars opposite Saturn, both in Detriment and in the 3rd-9th axis had another meaning, because practically as soon as his presidency ended, TR was boarding a ship with his son Kermit for an African safari, while his wife took the younger children to Italy. Observe the 1st-7th house axis: TR and Edith, his wife. Teddy is the Sun: this is *him*, doing what *he* wants. Whenever the Sun represents the Native in a solar return, that person experiences it as positive,

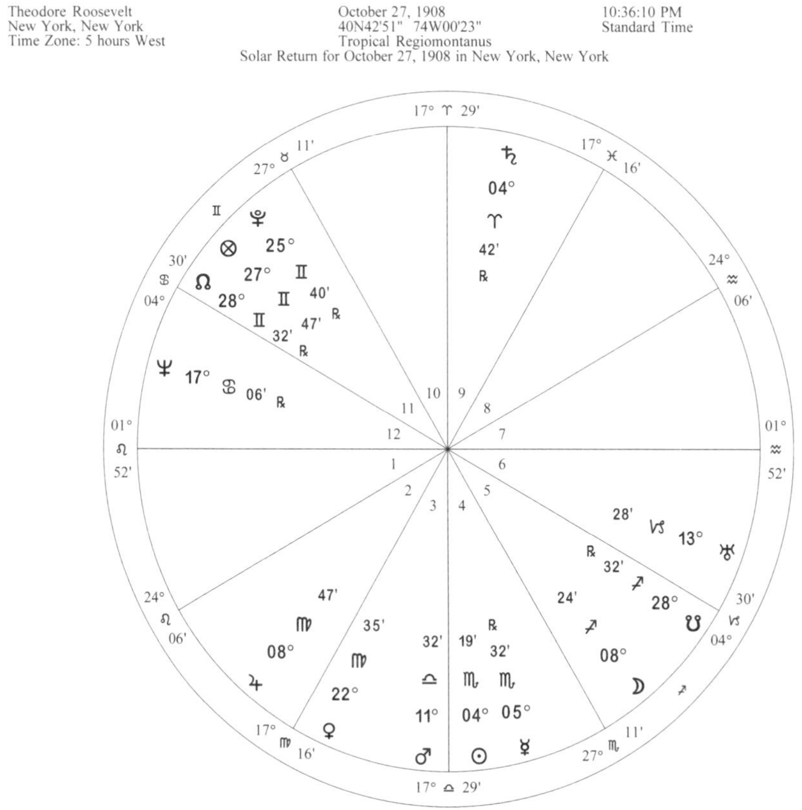
Theodore Roosevelt
New York, New York
Time Zone: 5 hours West
October 27, 1908
40N42'51" 74W00'23"
Tropical Regiomontanus
10:36:10 PM
Standard Time
Solar Return for October 27, 1908 in New York, New York

Dorothean Ess. Dig. (No Mut Rec. Points)								
Pl	Ruler	Exalt	Tripl	Term	Face	Detri	Fall	Score
☉	♂	--	♂	♂	♂	♀	☽	- 5 P
☽	♃	☋	♃ m	♀	☿	☿	--	- 5 P
☿	♂	--	♂ m	♂	♂	♀	☽	- 5 P
♀	☿	☿	☽	♄	☿	♃	♀ -	- 9 P
♂	♀	♄	☿ m	♃	♄ m	♂ -	☉	- 10 P
♃	☿	☿	☽ m	♀	☉	♃ -	♀	- 10 P
♄	♂	☉	♃	♃	♂ m	♀	♄ -	- 9 P
☊	☿	☊ +	☿	♂	☉	♃	--	--
⊗	☿	☊	☿	♂	☉	♃	--	--
As	☉	--	♃	♄	♄	♄	--	--
Mc	♂	☉	♃	☿	☉	♀	♄	--
☋	♃	☋	♃	♂	♄	☿	--	--

Hs	Alm. (Pto)
1	☉
2	☉♃
3	☿
4	♀♄
5	♂
6	♄
7	♄
8	♄
9	♃
10	☉♂
11	☽
12	☽

Example 2-16. Theodore Roosevelt solar return for 1908

and actually as being *exactly* the way he or she wants to be. This trip took over a year to plan. This was TR, the mighty hunter, the manly man. Meanwhile, Edith was Saturn in Aries: doing something she didn't want to do, and responsible for the younger children besides. *She* was looking forward to time with her husband at the end of eight years in a fish bowl. *He* was looking forward to adventure.

I have noted that the Sun ruling a house or in a house in the solar return acts as a benefic regardless of its actual dignity *as long as* it applies to the Native. If TR's peregrine Sun applies to him, it's a good thing. If it applies to somebody else, then it's a peregrine planet. So, note that the Sun also ruled the 2nd. Before going, Roosevelt had lined up a profitable contract with Scribners for a monthly serialized set of articles from his adventure, carefully labeled science, which would then be combined into a book. The finances were handled: the cost of the trip was paid for by Andrew Carnegie, even when the venture had substantial cost overruns.

So we shall leave Teddy and his son Kermit slogging through Africa. We shall discuss other years of his life in subsequent chapters, including his unsuccessful run for president in 1912 in Chapter 8. Let's review some of the ideas we have applied, so that we will have them in hand for subsequent chapters. Then, we can address some additional questions that this example did *not* answer.

- The return of any planet to its natal sign brings a resonance with that planet that makes its application feel very comfortable in that year. In other words, if the natal Mercury is in Taurus, any year that SR-Mercury is in Taurus will feel intellectually comfortable.
- The house positions of both Sun and Moon seem to show a lot about the focus of the Native in that year. Angular placement of the Sun really does argue for a more public experience.
- The Sun has certain unique properties in a solar return *precisely because* it is the planet that by definition must be in its radix sign. So when the Sun shows something about the Native, the Sun is a

positive influence being in its radix sign. However, the people in the solar return shown by any house with Leo on the cusp would be interpreted as being of the nature of the condition of that Sun.
- Unless a radix planet is in Detriment or Fall, having a planet in dignity is a positive influence in that solar return.
- The solar return, here shown almost exclusively for the birth location, is interpreted as a chart in its own right, but it is also referenced to the nativity in order to see resonance patterns, whether by sign recapitulation, or aspect mirrors.

The biggest question that we have not been able to address is: when does the solar return take effect? Authors in both the traditional period and the modern period have often suggested that the effects begin perhaps a month before the actual birthday, possibly as a kind of transition to the new chart, with others suggesting specific events possible even earlier.

The issue of transition is also complicated by the Hellenistic idea of **apoklima**: the intrinsically difficult twelfth part "behind" a cusp or body. This is the theory behind the observation that the month before the birthday can be a difficult time.

The reason we could not answer this with TR is that his birthday fell during the Autumn campaign season in an era before accurate polling systems had developed. There was simply no way to measure a "before and after" effect. In several of our examples, we will have a chance to address this question. It may also be possible to do this using sports figures, because almost all sports are seasonal in nature, and so some sports players will have their birthdays fall so that they will have one solar return per sports season, whereas others will have two. For example, in U.S. professional baseball, play currently runs from the beginning of April until the beginning of October, when the playoffs begin.

So: take a player like Mark Teixeira, the first baseman for the New York Yankees. Mark is a perennial slow starter each season in his batting statistics. Is the reason for the slow start because he was born on April 11, 1980, and thus, that the season starts in his *apoklima*? Or is this an effect of the change in solar returns? I would argue that it is more likely the *apoklima* effect, because he starts slowly after a great season, where arguably, this little piece of the old solar return should still be great!

Professional tennis would provide another good test, for this reason. The Grand Slam events of tennis are held at the same point in the calendar each year: in January, May, July and September. But this brings up an interesting possibility for studying tennis players. Now, it is usual to think of the tennis season as running from January with the Australian Open, to October with the U.S. Open. This annual cycle is used to note the very rare event of winning all four tournaments in a single season. But many tennis players will actually be playing in two personal seasons, as their birthdays will usually fall somewhere in this nine month time period. The challenge of performing so consistently through two consecutive solar returns is truly remarkable.

But before we proceed, please remain aware that the majority of each of our subjects' lives will not be found in these pages. This is not to say that the majority of years are meaningless: simply, that they are largely indistinguishable.

Suppose I decide to go to a university for a degree. For two, three, four, five, six years – my attention is focused on what I'm learning. I take good courses; I take bad courses, but probably I take more average courses. I have good days, bad says, sick days, tired days. In the end, I get out with my degree, and in my solar return, *that* year may show as an accomplishment – but really, it was impossible without all the work leading up to it. And yet, those years may well show largely as succedent or cadent placements – but working like crazy in the background. Then, when it's over, through the rites and rituals of graduation, suddenly I have a new and improved status in the world.

If we look at figure skaters, they all spend years and years learning their craft – just as I learned my craft at university. Parents embark on the task of raising children, and all those years don't stand out in a public fashion for others to see. So much of one's life passes in those private moments: happy, sad, poignant, achingly beautiful, or unbelievably horrible – but too ineffable for the world to see. These periods of private life may not show in the solar returns – at least in a fashion for those of us trying to peep into the life to observe. And furthermore, years without great themes are not a tragedy – life lived without huge plots and subplots is not a life that must stifle joy and satisfaction.

Over the next series of chapters, I will continue to lead you to examples of how to interpret solar returns by type of theme. But life is messy, and multiple themes may occur within a year. People whose lives are primarily private will not necessarily experience events in the same way as famous people in the public *eye*.

Please remember our starting hypothesis: that the solar return computed for the birth location represents the fate for the year, while the relocated versions (actual or residential) represent the extent of free will available given the planetary positions of the year. Each successive solar return is a new set of positions, apart from the Sun itself. It is in this difference between birth place and relocation that we also can understand the difference between what was called the essential and accidental dignities. While these concepts do not precisely map, they are close enough to add a layer of understanding. The signs and degrees of the planets, their aspects, and their essential dignities will be the same in any solar return calculated for any point on Earth in a given year. So if this year, your Sun is square Pluto and trine Mars, that will be true anywhere. What can vary is *which* houses those planets are in, or, in the case of the Sun and Mars, which houses, they rule. Whether the Sun aspects the Ascendant, Part of Fortune, or MC can vary.

And let's be honest. *If you want to travel to improve the look of your solar return, you must be prepared to work extra hard to actualize choice over unconscious destiny. If your life is exceedingly* busy, and you are spending eighteen hours a day ferrying the kids, working at your job, cooking meals, taking classes, walking the dog, and caring for your parents, you most likely don't have time for free will. Free will and choice require enough composure, leisure, and energy to stop and think, evaluate your situation and alternatives, and spend that extra hour to two researching options. It is this leisure side to it that always made free will easier for the rich – something that may seem woefully unfair. It seems rather like the adage that you have to have money to make money.

In this book, I will primarily discuss solar returns for the birth location. We will return to this question at the end, but part of my point is this: if you are about to embark on this work, please run your own lifetime solar returns. We never outgrow our birth location, even if we choose to add layers on top. And beginning to understand your solar returns as a process – not isolated points – helps you, your family, or your clients to understand planning in a profound way unavailable otherwise.

When I work with clients, I seldom do so without looking at a minimum of six solar returns at a time. I need to know where things are going, and not just in the next year. Could Theodore Roosevelt have reached his potential in a single year? Or Einstein? Or Mozart? The study of the lifetime this way gives us our mile-markers, but also the organic matrix in which a single year occurs. Choices cannot be made well in ignorance. The lifetime solar returns are there to study anytime.

Chapter 2 Endnotes

1. For example, William Lilly gives up to three or four possible significators each for the man and the woman in a question of marriage, *Christian Astrology*, pp 304-305. There is no way that these multiple choice methods will produce consistently the same result in practice, and it is exactly this kind of either/or which will completely frustrate students and clients alike.

2. Lehman, J. Lee. *Martial Art of Horary Astrology*. Atglen, PA: Schiffer Press., 2002, p 94.

3. Morin (1664), p 197.

4. Morin (1661), p 642

5. Morin (Holden), p 47.

6. The story of this saga is retold in: Sobel, Dava. *Longitude : The True Story of a Lone Genius Who Solved the Greatest Scientific Problem of His Time*. New York: Walker, 1995.

7. The story of this solar return is given in Morin (Holden), pp 49-51.

8. Lehman, *Astrology of Sustainability*, pp 119-128.

9. Partridge, John. *Mikropanastron, or, an Astrological Vade Mecum Briefly Teaching the Whole Art of Astrology, Viz. Questions, Nativities, with All Its Parts, and the Whole Doctrine of Elections, Never So Comprised, nor Compiled before, So That the Young Student May Learn as Much Here as in the Great Volumes of Guido, Haly or Origanus*. Printed for William Bromwich ... London, 1679, p 17.

10. Partridge, p 12

11. Saunders, Richard. *The Astrological Judgment and Practice of Physick, Deduced from the Position of the Heavens at the Decumbiture of the Sick Person, &C*. London: Thomas Sawbridge, 1677, p 20.

12. Brands, H. W. *T. R.: The Last Romantic*. New York, NY: Basic Books, 1997, p 177.

13. Brady, Bernadette and J. Lee Lehman. "Twelfth century castle besiegement in sport." *The Astrological Journal*, 39(3): 27-44, 1998.

3

Solar Returns for Romance and Relationship

LILLY AND MORINUS HAD IT MUCH EASIER WHEN IT CAME TO THE AFFAIRS OF THIS CHAPTER. In their day, intimate relationships were supposed to lead to marriage very quickly before things heated up too much, and marriage was the only alternative to celibacy that the Christian churches would recognize. Of course, none of this stopped prostitution, but that wasn't discussed in polite company, or even much in astrology books.

Let's begin by considering how the ancients would have viewed relationships through a solar return, and then proceed to translate this into our cultural context. Lilly states that when the sign of the radix Descendant is the sign of the solar return Ascendant, then the Native either has thoughts of marriage, or will marry.[1]

But our best source on revolutional theory from the late classical period is Gadbury. Thus, in the *Genethlialogia*, he gives the following delineation of the seventh house in a revolution (in part, citing Argolus):

> *You may enquire from this House in a Revolution, of the Natives marriage, of the Condition of his Wife, (or if it be a Woman,*

her Husband) the Agreement or Disagreement between them, &c. And herein you may observe these Rules.

> *1. When the Lord of the Ascendant shall be in conjunction with the Lord of the seventh, in the seventh, fifth, or eleventh houses, the Native (if capable) may marry in that year. In sextile or trine from good Houses, the same.[2]*

> *2. Venus in the Radix in the dignities of Jupiter, and Jupiter in the dignities of Venus in the Revolution, discerns many pleasures and delights with Women, and sometimes it portends Matrimony in that year; and Venus in the Revolution in the place of Jupiter in the Radix, denotes the same.*

> *3. The Lord of the Radix, and Revolution in the seventh House, the Ascendant in the radical place of Venus, and the Lord of the seventh (by [primary] Direction) to the Lord of the Ascendant; all these are ample Testimonies of Marriage in that year unto the Native, if capable.*

4. When Jupiter, Venus and Moon, or Fortuna, shall be in the seventh House, it shews a propensity in the Native to marriage in that year. The Lord of the seventh with Jupiter, Venus or Lord of the Ascendant, the same.

5. The Ascendant of the Revolution, the radical place of Venus; Venus in a Revolution in her own dignities; Venus in Conjunction of Moon in the dignities of Jupiter; all these denote marriage, or a great propensity thereunto in the Native that year.

6. If Venus in a Revolutional Figure, the Moon, and Lord of the seventh House shall be free from the afflictions of the Infortunes, and strong and potent, by reason of their accidental and essential positions; it discerns the good state of the Native's Wife in that year.

7. Venus occidental of the Sun in the Revolutions, and in conjunction of unfortunate Stars, or in their evil Aspect, threatens the death of the Native's Wife or Sweet-heart in that year.

8. If in a Revolution Venus shall be afflicted of the South Node, the Wife of the Native will be subject to many infirmities of Body and Mind; she may also prove Meretricious.

9. Mercury in opposition to the seventh House of a Revolution, signifies great danger of the Natives Wife in that year; and manifest mischief to the Natives publick Enemies.

10. The Moon and Venus, or Lord of the seventh House of a Revolution in evil Aspect of Saturn or Mars, denotes much evil to the Wife of the Native in that year.

11. If Saturn being in the seventh House of a Nativity, shall be found in the seventh of a Revolution, it threatens the death of the

Natives Wife in that year. Mars and the Dragon's Tayl so posited, doth denote little less.

12. Saturn or Mars evilly posited in the seventh or fourth Houses of a Revolution, threatens death to the Natives Wife. The Lord of the seventh infortunated of Saturn or Mars, Sine auxilio Jovus, without the friendly Beams of Jove, denoted very much evil unto the Natives Wife; but not death.

13. Mercury afflicted of the Malevolents in the seventh House of a Revolution, portends much hurt to the Natives Wife. But Venus afflicted in a Revolution, always denotes evil unto the Wife. The like of Moon.

14. The Lord of the seventh Combust in the fourth, or any other way infortunated, denotes much danger unto the life of the Natives Wife. If Combust in the second or eighth, judge the same.

15. The Moon and Venus in the seventh House, in a watry Signe with Mars, or in a Quartile or Opposition of him, denotes evil to befal the Mother or Wife of the Native in that year. Venus and the Moon in the Ascendant, in Opposition or Quartile of Saturn, denotes the same.

16. When Venus, the seventh House, and Lord of the seventh, and the Moon shall in a Revolution be free from the Malignity of the Infortunes, the Wife of the Native will live free from any of the before-named evils.

17. For the private Enemies of the Native, observe this general rule: If the Lord of the Ascendant or Moon shall be afflicted by the Quartile or Opposition of the Lord of the seventh, the Native in that year shall be mischiefed by his private Enemies; chiefly

if the Lord of the seventh be better fortified then the Lord of the Ascendant: but if the Lord of the Ascendant be strongest, the Native shall overcome his Enemies."[3]

So this is the theory. Notice that the aphorisms fall into roughly two types. First, there are the arguments of marriage. This approximates benefics associated with the 7th house, especially Venus, marking a year to marry. Then, there are the arguments that the marriage partner is obnoxious or in danger for the year. Malefics associated with the 7th house result in problems for the spouse, with the degree of difficulty escalating according to how severe the malefic influence is.

Understood in this light, we can expect to be able to extend these ideas to our more complex relationship patterns, where "it's complicated" has become a descriptor for our world in which marriage may not be considered desirable, where divorce rates exceed 50%, where gender may not be a defining criterion for a partner, and where monogamy may not be assumed.

On the other hand, it's not that everybody in history ever followed the official script anyway. We shall examine:

- Buzz Aldrin's first and third marriages
- Marie Curie's marriage and widowhood
- Mary Shelley's "It's complicated"
- Dorothy Hammill's three marriages
- Eleanor Roosevelt's marriage, discovery of her husband's affair, and subsequent relationship
- Theodore Roosevelt's two wives
- Percy Shelley's "It's *very* complicated"

Two of Buzz Aldrin's Marriages

The astronaut Buzz Aldrin's nativity shows two different influences regarding marriage: the ruler of his seventh house is

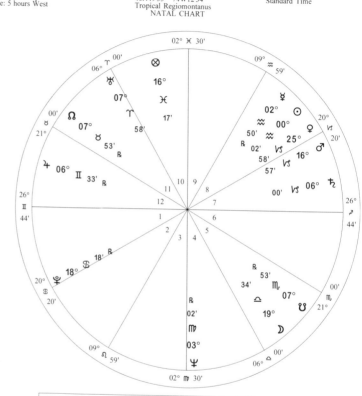

Edward "Buzz" Aldrin
Montclair, New Jersey
Time Zone: 5 hours West

January 20, 1930
40N49'33" 74W12'34"
Tropical Regiomontanus
NATAL CHART

2:17 PM
Standard Time

Example 3-1. Buzz Aldrin nativity

Edward "Buzz" Aldrin
Montclair, New Jersey
Time Zone: 5 hours West

January 20, 1954
40N49'33" 74W12'34"
Tropical Regiomontanus
Solar Return for January 20, 1954 in Montclair, New Jersey

9:55:04 AM
Standard Time

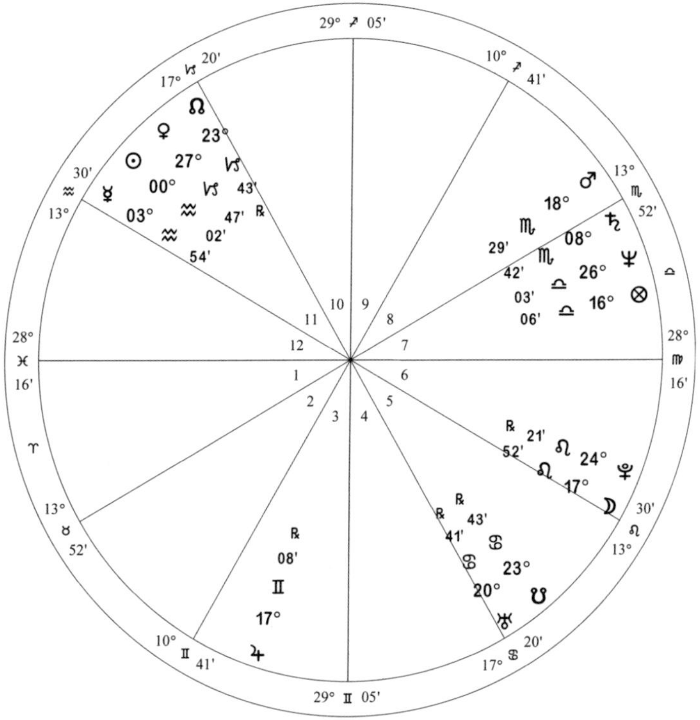

Dorothean Ess. Dig. (No Mut Rec. Points)								
Pl	Ruler	Exalt	Tripl	Term	Face	Detri	Fall	Score
☉	♄	--	♄	♄	♀ m	☉ -	--	- 10 P
☽	☉	--	☉	♀	♃	♄	--	- 5 P
☿	♄	--	♄	♄	♀	☉	--	- 5 P
♀	♄	♂	♀ +	♄	☉ m	☽	♃	+3
♂	♂ +	--	♀	♀	☉	♀	☽	+5
♃	☿	☊	♄	♀	♂	♃ -	--	- 10 P
♄	♂	--	♀	♃	♂	♀	☽	- 5 P
☊	♄	♂	♀	♂	☉	☽	♃	--
⊗	♀	♄	♄	♃	♄	♂	☉	--
As	♃	♀	♀	♄	♂	☿	☿	--
Mc	♃	☋	☉	♂	♄	☿	--	--
☋	☽	♃	♀	♀	☽	♄	♂	--

Hs	Alm. (Pto)
1	♃
2	♀
3	☿
4	☿
5	☽
6	☉
7	☿
8	♂
9	♃
10	♃
11	♂♄
12	♄

Example 3-1a. Buzz Aldrin relationship solar return for 1954

Edward "Buzz" Aldrin
Montclair, New Jersey
Time Zone: 5 hours West

January 20, 1975
40N49'33" 74W12'34"
Tropical Regiomontanus
Solar Return for January 20, 1975 in Montclair, New Jersey

12:20:14 PM
Standard Time

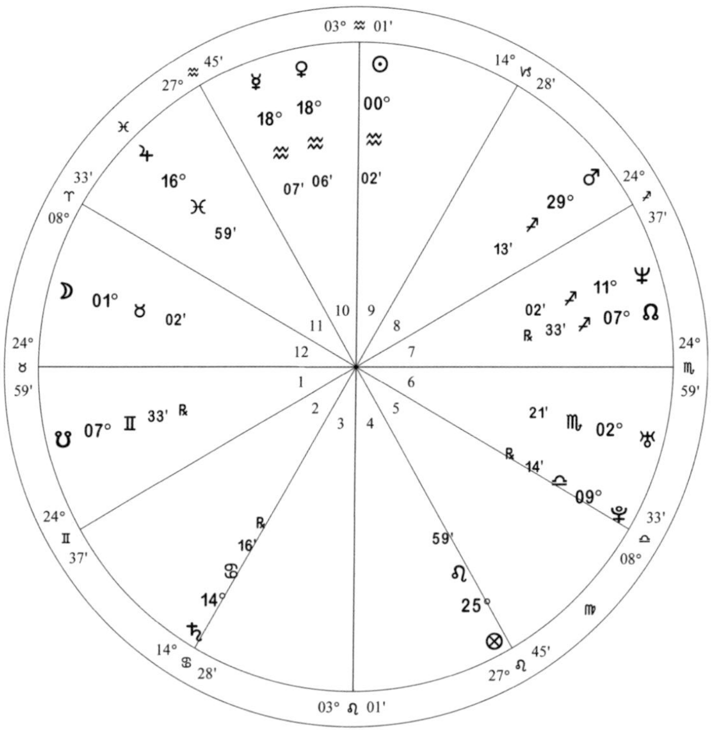

Dorothean Ess. Dig. (No Mut Rec. Points)								
Pl	Ruler	Exalt	Tripl	Term	Face	Detri	Fall	Score
☉	♄	--	♄	♄	♀	☉ -	--	- 10 P
☽	♀	☽ +	♀	♀	☿	♂	--	+4
☿	♄	--	♄	♀	☿ +	☉	--	+1
♀	♄	--	♄ m	♀ +	☿	☉	--	+2
♂	♃	☋	☉	♂ +	♄	☿	--	+2
♃	♃ +	♀	♀	☿	♃ +	☿	☿	+6
♄	☽	♃	♀ m	☿	☿	♄ -	♂	- 10 P
☊	♃	☋	☉	♃	☿	☿	--	--
⊗	☉	--	☉	♂	♂	♄	--	--
As	♀	☽	♀	♄	♄	♂	--	--
Mc	♄	--	♄	♄	♀	☉	--	--
☋	☿	☊	♄	♃	♃	♃	--	--

Hs	Alm. (Pto)
1	♀
2	☿♄
3	☽
4	☉
5	☉
6	♀♄
7	♂
8	♃
9	♂♄
10	♄
11	♄
12	☉

Example 3-1b. Buzz Aldrin relationship solar return for 1975

Edward "Buzz" Aldrin
Montclair, New Jersey
Time Zone: 5 hours West

January 20, 1988
40N49'33" 74W12'34"
Tropical Regiomontanus
Solar Return for January 20, 1988 in Montclair, New Jersey

4:08:15 PM
Standard Time

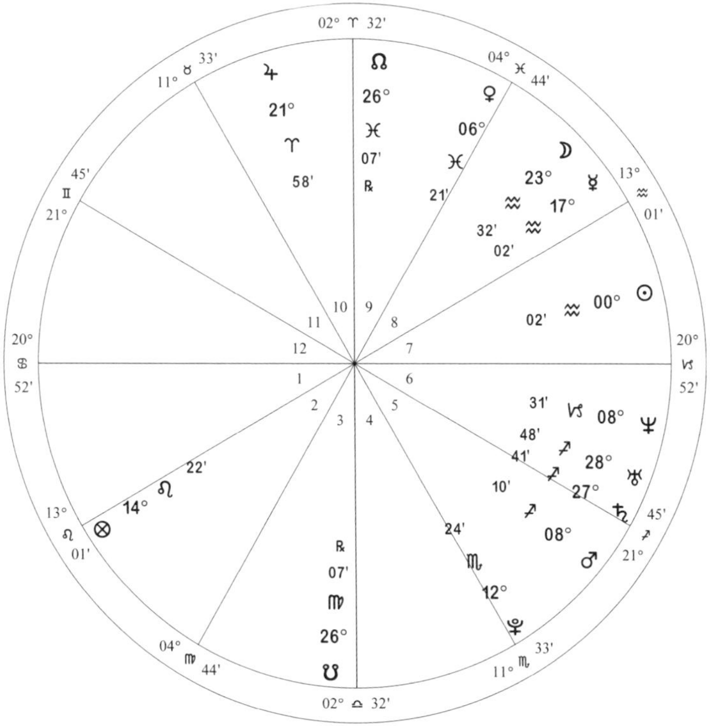

Dorothean Ess. Dig. (No Mut Rec. Points)								
Pl	Ruler	Exalt	Tripl	Term	Face	Detri	Fall	Score
☉	♄	--	♄ m	♄	♀	☉ -	--	- 10 P
☽	♄	--	♄	♃	☽ +	☉	--	+1
☿	♄	--	♄	♀	☿ +	☉	--	+1
♀	♃	♀ +	♀ +	♀ +	♄	☿	☿	+9
♂	♃ m	☋	☉	♀	☿	☿	--	- 5 P
♃	♂ m	☉	☉	♂	♀	♀	♄	- 5 P
♄	♃	☋	☉ m	♂	♄ +	☿	--	+1
☊	♃	♀	♀	♄	♂	☿	☿	--
⊗	☉	--	☉	♀	♃	♄	--	--
As	☽	♃	♀	♀	☽	♄	♂	--
Mc	♂	☉	☉	♃	♂	♀	♄	--
☋	☿	☿	♀	♂	☿	♃	♀	--

Hs	Alm. (Pto)
1	☽
2	☉
3	☿
4	♄
5	♂
6	♃
7	♂
8	♄
9	♀
10	☉
11	♀
12	☿♄

Example 3-1c. Buzz Aldrin relationship solar return for 1988

Jupiter in Gemini, and Saturn is in his seventh house, in Capricorn. If we interpret this as more than one spouse, then the two are clearly quite different.

In 1954, for his first marriage, Jupiter, radix ruler of his seventh, was once again in Gemini. And it ruled his SR-Ascendant. Like his natal placement, it was retrograde. The Part of Fortune was in the 7th, and it's ruled by Venus, which has Triplicity in the sign of Capricorn. Furthermore, Neptune is in the 7th: no doubt this felt like love for sure! After flying combat missions in Korea, there was no doubt a huge appeal to getting back to normal. Buzz had a fertile sign on his Ascendant and on his 5th house cusp that year, setting up for a typical 1950s family. And that is exactly how things worked out, as they had three children.

The only negative one can see in the chart is the 7th house ruler combust, which would tend to make his wife Joan invisible. But that again fit with the cultural patterns of the period. Life was supposed to be about Buzz.

After the trip to the Moon on Apollo 11, Buzz had some difficulty finding something to do with the rest of his life, and into that void went alcohol, and their marriage dissolved. This is shown in the divorce solar return of 1975. Gadbury and other traditional sources don't mention divorce, but one assumes that this would match the model for the years of tribulation with the spouse. What we see is the the baleful fixed star Algol on the Ascendant – already a pretty good hint of a miserable year. The South Node was in the 1st house, further adding to his misery. Buzz described this period in his autobiography, and he pretty much accepts responsibility for creating the conditions that led to the divorce. The Venus-Mercury partile conjunction in Aquarius does describe him as emotionally aloof, and this is especially important, given that Venus in the return was his ruling planet. His wife Joan is described through Mars: she was willing to stand up for her rights. This chart doesn't so much suggest that Joan had suddenly metamorphosed into a monster – Buzz had some genuine problems going on. This isn't a clash as much as a

Edward "Buzz" Aldrin
Montclair, New Jersey
Time Zone: 5 hours West

January 20, 2011
40N49'33" 74W12'34"
Tropical Regiomontanus
Solar Return for January 20, 2011 in Montclair, New Jersey

6:02:30 AM
Standard Time

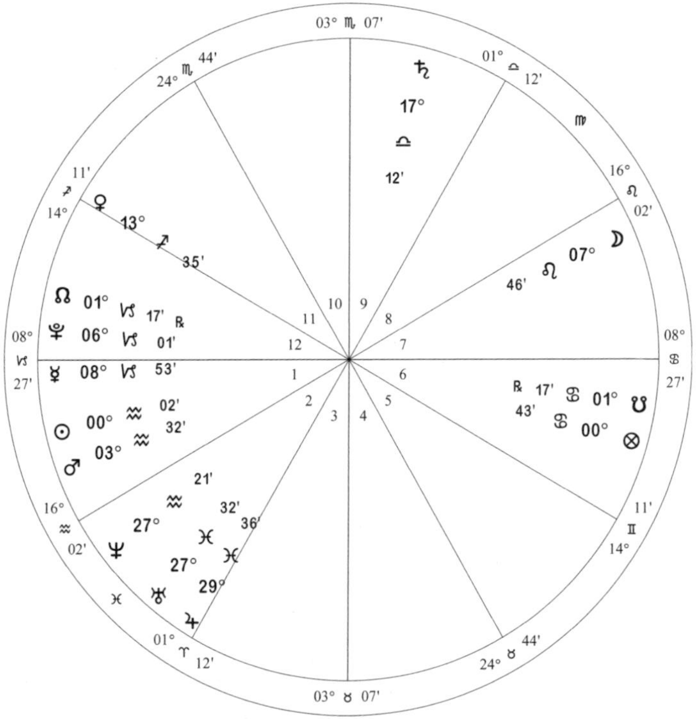

Dorothean Ess. Dig. (No Mut Rec. Points)								
Pl	Ruler	Exalt	Tripl	Term	Face	Detri	Fall	Score
☉	♄	--	☿	♄	♀	☉ -	--	- 10 P
☽	☉	--	♃	☿	♄	♄	--	- 5 P
☿	♄	♂	☽	☿ +	♃	☽	♃	+2
♀	♃	☋	♃	♀ +	☽	☿	--	+2
♂	♄	--	☿	♄	♀	☉	--	- 5 P
♃	♃ +	♀	♂	♄ m	♂	☿	☿	+5
♄	♀	♄ +	☿	♃ m	♄ +	♂	☉	+5
☊	♄	♂	☽	♀	♃	☽	♃	--
⊗	☽	♃	♂	♂	♀	♄	♂	--
As	♄	♂	☽	☿	♃	☽	♃	--
Mc	♂	--	♂	♂	♂	♀	☽	--
☋	☽	♃	♂	♂	♀	♄	♂	--

Hs	Alm. (Pto)
1	♄
2	♄
3	♂
4	☽♀
5	☽
6	☿
7	♃
8	☉
9	♄
10	♂
11	♂
12	♃

Example 3-1D. Buzz Aldrin relationship solar return for 2011

collapse. With the Sun square Moon in the 12th, Buzz was his own worst enemy: in his own opinion at the time, he didn't need help! At 29 degrees Sagittarius, Joan is locked out: she's not interacting with the rest of the chart, but her condition is about to improve.

By 1988, after several rounds of going back and forth with the alcoholism, another transitional marriage and other girlfriends, Buzz tried marriage again. This time, they were both older: in Buzz's solar return, Lois is ruled by Saturn in Sagittarius, thus in Triplicity, and Buzz is ruled by the Moon in Aquarius, disposed by that very same Saturn. Saturn is in Buzz's radix 7th house, in Capricorn. Moon and Saturn, the rulers of 1st and 7th, are coming together by sextile: not a complete match to Gadbury's aphorism 1, but close. Here, the houses are not quite as strong as one would like.

The presence of the Part of Fortune at the 2nd house is very suggestive, because this marriage was exceptionally good for Buzz, and on the level of fortune as well. Lois came from a very rich Arizona family, but one that lost most of its wealth just after they were married. However, Lois and her daughter encouraged Buzz to market *himself*, and he went on to enjoy a new career as a public speaker.

In 2011, Buzz filed for divorce from Lois, citing irreconcilable differences. In his solar return for the year, not one single planet (except the Sun, of course) is in its natal sign: quite simply, in 2011, he *wasn't* the man she married. The Moon ruled the 7th house and was opposite Mars, in the 7th-1st axis, creating conflict, a theme echoed by solar return Pluto square natal Uranus. The solar return Pluto conjunct the Ascendant from the 12th house side could represent pent-up resentments that finally came to the surface.

Marie Curie, in Marriage and Widowhood

Marie Curie really did find the perfect husband. Pierre was as much of a workaholic as she was, and their scientific passions were quite similar. Pierre clearly had no difficulty in having a wife

Marie Curie
Warsaw, Poland
Time Zone: 0 hours West

November 7, 1867
52 N 15 21 E 00
Tropical Regiomontanus
NATAL CHART

10:36 AM
Standard Time

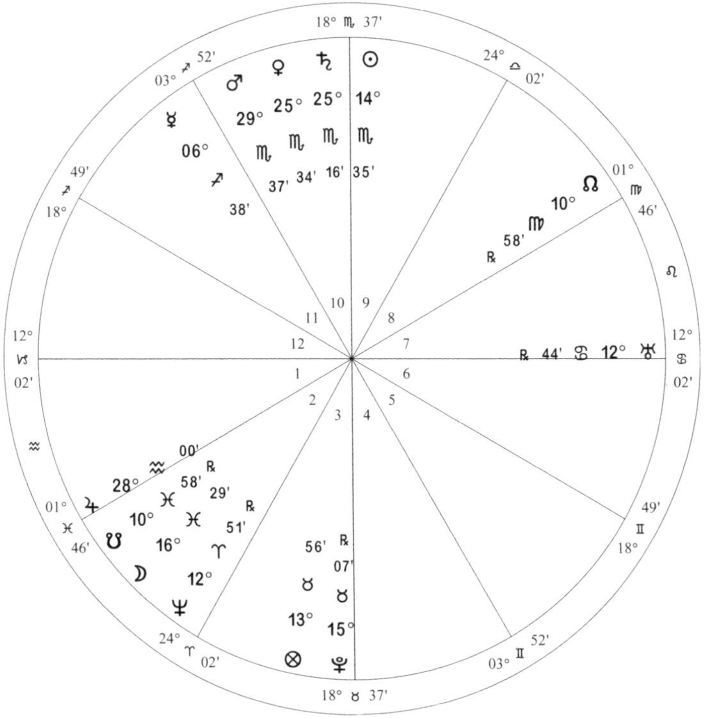

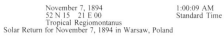

Dorothean Ess. Dig. (No Mut Rec. Points)								
Pl	Ruler	Exalt	Tripl	Term	Face	Detri	Fall	Score
☉	♂	--	♀	♀	☉ +	♀	☽	+1
☽	♃	♀	♀	☿	♃ m	☿	☿	- 5 P
☿	♃	☋	☉	♃	☿ +	☿ -	--	- 4
♀	♂	--	♀ +	☿	♀ +	♀ -	☽	- 1
♂	♂ +	--	♀	♄	♀	♀	☽	+5
♃	♄	--	♄	♂	☽ m	☉	--	- 5 P
♄	♂	--	♀	☿	♀	♀	☽	- 5 P
☊	☿	☿	♀	♀	♀	♃	♀	--
⊗	♀	☽	♀	☿	☽	♂	--	--
As	♄	♂	♀	♃	♂	☽	♃	--
Mc	♂	--	♀	♀	☉	♀	☽	--
☋	♃	♀	♀	♃	♃	☿	☿	--

Hs	Alm. (Pto)
1	♂♄
2	♀
3	☉♂
4	♀
5	☿
6	☿
7	♃
8	☿
9	♄
10	♂
11	♃
12	♃

Example 3-2. Marie Curie nativity

Marie Curie
Warsaw, Poland
Time Zone: 1 hr 24 min East

November 7, 1894
52 N 15 21 E 00
Tropical Regiomontanus
Solar Return for November 7, 1894 in Warsaw, Poland

1:00:09 AM
Standard Time

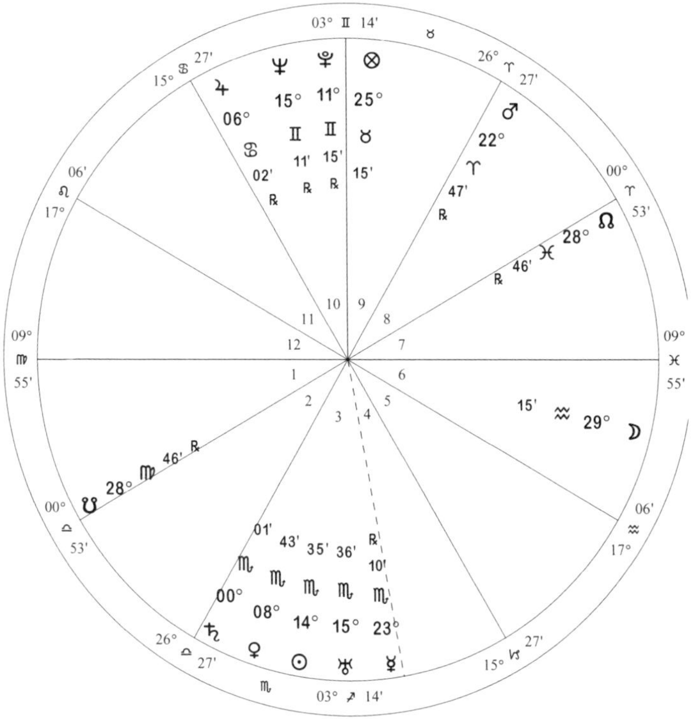

Dorothean Ess. Dig. (No Mut Rec. Points)								
Pl	Ruler	Exalt	Tripl	Term	Face	Detri	Fall	Score
☉	♂	--	♂	♀	☉ +	♀	☽	+1
☽	♄	--	☿	♂	☽ +	☉	--	+1
☿	♂	--	♂	☿ +	♀	♀	☽	+2
♀	♂	--	♂	♃	♂ m	♀ -	☽	- 10 P
♂	♂ +	☉	♃ m	♂ +	♀ m	♀	♄	+7
♃	☽	♃ +	♂ m	♃ +	♀	♄	♂	+6
♄	♂	--	♂	♂	♂	♀	☽	- 5 P
☊	♃	♀	♂	♄	♂	☿	☿	--
⊗	♀	☽	☽	♄	♄	♂	--	--
As	☿	☿	☽	♀	☉	♃	♀	--
Mc	☿	☊	☿	☿	♃	♃	--	--
☋	☿	☿	☽	♂	☿	♃	♀	--

Hs	Alm. (Pto)
1	☿
2	♄
3	♀
4	♃
5	♂♄
6	♄
7	♃
8	♂
9	♂
10	☿
11	☽
12	☉

Example 3-2a. Marie Curie relationship solar return for 1894

Marie Curie
Warsaw, Poland
Time Zone: 1 hr 24 min East

November 7, 1905
52 N 15 21 E 00
Tropical Regiomontanus
Solar Return for November 7, 1905 in Warsaw, Poland

5:05:25 PM
Standard Time

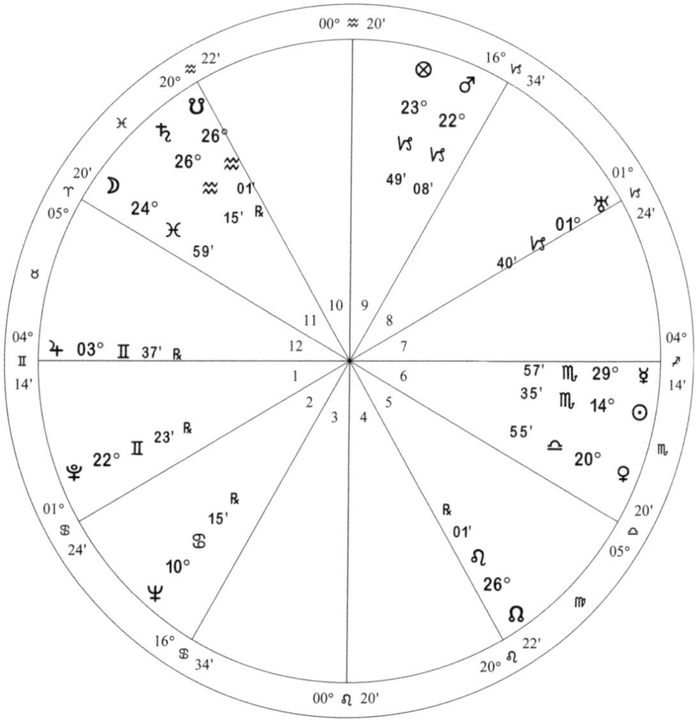

Pl	Ruler	Exalt	Tripl	Term	Face	Detri	Fall	Score
☉	♂	--	♂	♀	☉ +	♀	☽	+1
☽	♃	♀	♂ m	♂	♂	☿	☿	- 5 P
☿	♂	--	♂	♄	♀	♀	☽	- 5 P
♀	♀ +	♄	☿	☿	♃	♂	☉	+5
♂	♄	♂ +	☽ m	♂ +	☉	☽	♃	+6
♃	☿	☊	☿	☿	♃ +	♃ -	--	- 4
♄	♄ +	--	☿	♂	☽	☉	--	+5
☊	☉	--	♃	♂	♂	♄	--	--
⊗	♄	♂	☽	♂	☉	☽	♃	--
As	☿	☊	☿	☿	♃	♃	--	--
Mc	♄	--	☿	♄	♀	☉	--	--
☋	♄	--	☿	♂	☽	☉	--	--

Dorothean Ess. Dig. (No Mut Rec. Points)

Hs	Alm. (Pto)
1	☿
2	☽
3	☽
4	☉
5	☉♃
6	♄
7	♃
8	♄
9	♂♄
10	♄
11	♄
12	♂

Example 3-2b. Marie Curie relationship solar return for 1905

as brilliant as he was. His teaching position gave him the lab space that she needed and he was willing to share it. They became perfect collaborators, and after his death, the Sorbonne gave her his teaching slot, making her the first female professor there. His father continued to help her raise their children after Pierre's death.

Marie's natal chart has Uranus on the 7th – and this was a highly unusual marriage for the time, since Pierre did not hold to the traditional paternalistic ideals. Marie's solar return for the year of marriage shows Jupiter ruling the 7th – a benefic in Cancer, its exaltation no less! With that Jupiter in the 10th, we see the circumstances of their marriage perfectly: they were work partners as well as romantic partners. Furthermore, Jupiter was sextile the Ascendant: this was a very easy relationship.

The theme of beneficence is even continued by comparing the chart to the radix: SR-Moon was right on her natal Jupiter, with radix Jupiter Almuten of her 7th house cusp. Thus, in the year of marriage, the same planet lined up as ruler of the 7th, and in both cases, that planet was dignified, even more so in the solar return.

The year of her widowhood, once again Jupiter showed up ruling the 7th – but this time in Detriment and retrograde at the Ascendant. SR-Uranus was right on the 8th house cusp, showing a death theme from a sudden accident. Unfortunately, Neptune in the husband's 8th (the radix 7th) shows distraction related to his death, if death there would be in that year. And he was distracted: he died crossing the street, where he was run over in a traffic accident. In addition, Saturn was partile conjunct the South Node.

Mary Godwin Shelley's "Modern" Relationship Lifestyle

It is our modern prejudice that leads us sometimes to the erroneous conclusion that fear of pregnancy had a major impact on sexual patterns of our predecessors. No doubt this was true to a degree. But Shakespeare's sonnets are enough to convince us that our ancestors were just as sexually driven as we are.

Mary Godwin's parents are two of the people we have to thank for our "modern" ideas about love. They were, in their time, two of the great advocates of free love. What this meant was that both Mary Wollstonecraft and William Godwin had written on how marriage had become a prison for women especially. Wollstonecraft had had a child by another man before she met Godwin, and, to her, this was simply her right to express her passion, just as she expected to be able to express her reason. But in the end, she decided to marry Godwin. Godwin himself had also spoken of freedom – but he ended up marrying not once, but twice. Wollstonecraft had been the love of his life – and he raised *both* of Wollstonecraft's children as his own.

So along comes Percy. Young, brash, a man with prospects for inheritance, and a belief in the Wollstonecraft-Godwin philosophy of free love – who could resist? So he was married to someone else! Just a social convention! Off she goes to the Continent with Percy and her stepsister Claire Clairmont for a trip which only ended when the money did. Back to England they came, with Mary pregnant, then miscarrying, then pregnant again, where they continued to live together until Percy's wife committed suicide three years later. And then they married each other. While there were no more marriages for either of them, Percy did not know the meaning of the word *monogamous*. Mary, it appears, did. But Percy would drown less than six years into the marriage, and Mary would spend the rest of her life as a widow.

These first two charts – Mary's nativity, and the solar return for 1813 when she became sexually active – raise the issue of rectifying her chart by moving the Ascendant forward about one degree. In the nativity, would it make more sense to see Venus ruler of the 5th than Mercury? During the nine years of their sexual relationship, Mary gave birth to four children, and had at least two miscarriages. She was clearly of average or higher than average fertility. Virgo is considered a barren sign. But we could also argue that the barrenness

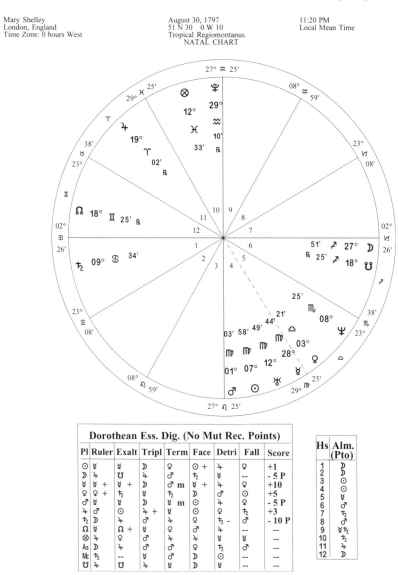

Mary Shelley
London, England
Time Zone: 0 hours West

August 30, 1797
51 N 30 0 W 10
Tropical Regiomontanus
NATAL CHART

11:20 PM
Local Mean Time

Dorothean Ess. Dig. (No Mut Rec. Points)								
Pl	Ruler	Exalt	Tripl	Term	Face	Detri	Fall	Score
☉	☿	☿	☽	♀	☉ +	♃	♀	+1
☽	♃	☋	♃	♂ m	♄	☿ +	♃	- 5 P
☿	☿ +	☿ +	☽	♂ m	☿ +	♃	♀	+10
♀	♀ +	♄	☿	♄	☽	♂	☉	+5
♂	☿	☿	☽	♂ m	♂	♃	♀	- 5 P
♃	♂	☉	♃ +	☿	☉	♀	♄	+3
♄	☽	♃	♀	♂	♃	♀	♂	- 10 P
☊	♀	☽	☿	♂	♃	♂	--	--
⊗	♃	♀ +	♂	♃	♃	☿	--	--
As	☽	♃	♂	♂	♀	♄	♂	--
Mc	♄	--	♂	♂	☽	☉	--	--
☋	♃	☿	♃	♃	☿	☽	--	--

Hs	Alm. (Pto)
1	☽
2	☽
3	☉
4	☿
5	☿
6	♂
7	♄
8	☿
9	♄
10	♄
11	♃
12	☽

Example 3-3. Mary Godwin Shelley nativity

Mary Shelley
London, England
Time Zone: 0 hours West

August 31, 1813
51 N 30 0 W 10
Tropical Regiomontanus
Solar Return for August 31, 1813 in London, England

8:12:06 PM
Local Mean Time

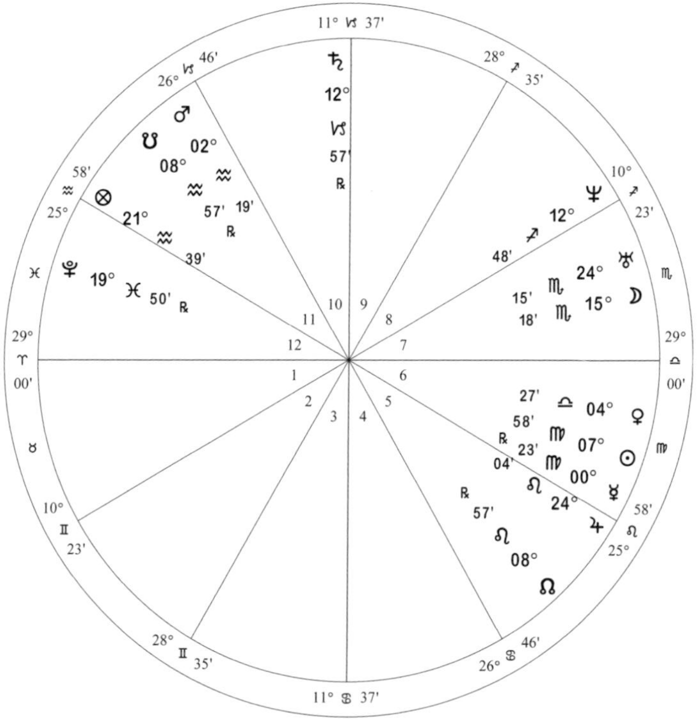

Dorothean Ess. Dig. (No Mut Rec. Points)

Pl	Ruler	Exalt	Tripl	Term	Face	Detri	Fall	Score
☉	☿	☿	☽	♀	☉ +	♃	♀	+1
☽	♂	--	♂	♀	☉	♀	☽ -	- 9 P
☿	☿ +	☿ +	☽	☿ +	☉	♃	♀	+11
♀	♀ +	♄	☿	♄	☽	♂	☉	+5
♂	♄	--	☿	♄	♀	☉	--	- 5 P
♃	☉	--	♃ +	♃ +	♂	♄	--	+5
♄	♄ +	♂	☽	♃	♂	☽	♃	+5
☊	☉	--	♃	☿	♄	♄	--	--
⊗	♄	--	☿	♃	☽	☉	--	--
As	♂	☉	♃	♄	♀	♀	♄	--
Mc	♄	♂	☽	☿	♂	☽	♃	--
☋	♄	--	☿	☿	♀	☉	--	--

Hs	Alm. (Pto)
1	♂
2	☿
3	☿
4	♃
5	☽
6	☉
7	♀
8	♃
9	♃
10	♂♄
11	♄
12	♄

Example 3-3a. Mary Godwin Shelley relationship solar return for 1813

Mary Shelley
London, England
Time Zone: 0 hours West

August 31, 1816
51 N 30 0 W 10
Tropical Regiomontanus
Solar Return for August 31, 1816 in London, England

1:36:16 PM
Local Mean Time

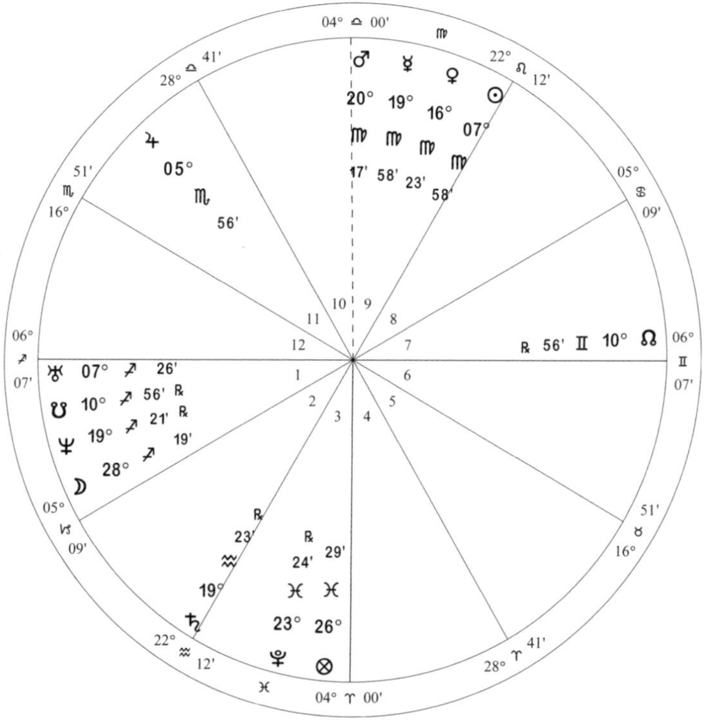

Dorothean Ess. Dig. (No Mut Rec. Points)

Pl	Ruler	Exalt	Tripl	Term	Face	Detri	Fall	Score
☉	☿	☿	♀	♀	☉ +	♃	♀	+1
☽	♃	☋	☉	♂	♄	☿	--	- 5 P
☿	☿ +	☿ +	♀	♄	♀	♃	♀	+9
♀	☿	☿	♀ +	♃	♀ +	♃	♀ -	+0
♂	☿	☿	♀	♄	☿	♃	♀	- 5 P
♃	♂	--	♀	♂	♂	♀	☽	- 5 P
♄	♄ +	--	♄ +	♀	☿	☉	--	+8
☊	☿	☊ +	♄	♃	♂	♃	--	--
⊗	♃	♀	♀	♄	♂	☿	☿	--
As	♃	☋	☉	♃	☿	☿	--	--
Mc	♀	♄	♄	♄	☽	♂	☉	--
☋	♃	☋	☉	♀	☽	☿	--	--

Hs	Alm. (Pto)
1	♃
2	♀♄
3	♄
4	☉
5	☉
6	♀
7	☿
8	☽
9	☉
10	♄
11	♄
12	♂

Example 3-3b. Mary Godwin Shelley relationship solar return for 1816

Mary Shelley
London, England
Time Zone: 0 hours West

August 31, 1821
51 N 30 0 W 10
Tropical Regiomontanus
Solar Return for August 31, 1821 in London, England

6:29:03 PM
Local Mean Time

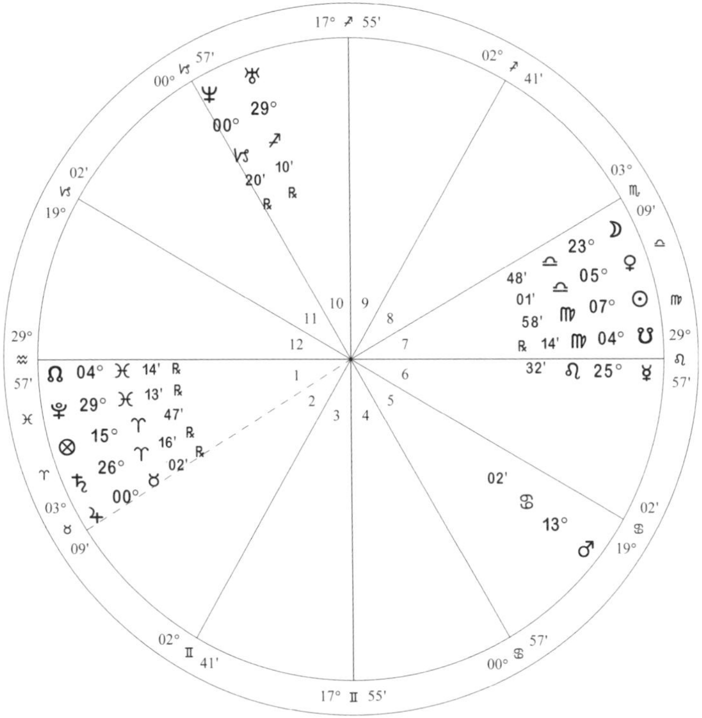

Dorothean Ess. Dig. (No Mut Rec. Points)								
Pl	Ruler	Exalt	Tripl	Term	Face	Detri	Fall	Score
☉	☿ m	☿	♀	♀	☉ +	♃	♀	+1
☽	♀	♄	♄	☿	♃	♂	☉	- 5 P
☿	☉ m	--	☉	♂ m	♂ m	♄	--	- 5 P
♀	♀ +	♄	♄	♄	☽	♂	☉	+5
♂	☽	♃	♀	☿ m	☿ m	♄	♂ -	- 9 P
♃	♀	☽	♀	♀	☿	♂	--	- 5 P
♄	♂	☉	☉	♄ +	♀	♀	♄ -	- 2
☊	♃	♀	♀	♀	♄	☿	☿	--
⊗	♂	☉	☉	☿	☉	♀	♄	--
As	♄	--	♄	♂	☽	☉	--	--
Mc	♃	☋	☉	☿	☽	☿	--	--
☋	☿	☿	♀	☿	☉	♃	♀	--

Hs	Alm. (Pto)
1	♄
2	♀
3	☿
4	☿
5	☽
6	☽
7	☉
8	♂
9	♃
10	♃
11	♀♄
12	♂

Example 3-3c. Mary Godwin Shelley relationship solar return for 1821

was in the final result, namely, the single surviving child. In either case, the 5th house Venus square Saturn would explain how, with at least six pregnancies, she only had one child who attained adulthood.

In the 1813 solar return, the idea of a zero degrees Taurus Ascendant for the onset of sexuality seems more appropriate to me than a 29 Aries one. But in either case, the comparison of these two charts reminds us that the idea of "sweet sixteen" actually has an astrological explanation, because Venus returns to approximately its natal position every eight years. So, at sixteen everyone has this natal bloom, so to speak – and Mary made the most of hers. Mary's Venus in Libra was a strong Venus indeed.

We also see Mercury in its radix sign. Percy very much supported Mary's writing, and their joint writing was something that they designed their household to fulfill. They often worked together in the same room.

The other remarkable feature of this 1813 chart is Saturn conjunct the MC. This Saturn ruled the 10th, which is normally the mother. But Saturn's natural rulership is of the father – and as the sole surviving parent, William Godwin filled both roles to a certain extent. And he was scandalized by the affair. The very idea – these children doing what he *said*, not what he had come to *believe* later in life! The nerve! Later, after her widowhood, he would resume being one of her greatest supporters, but this was not an easy year between William and Mary.

The year 1816 was a chaotic one. Not only was it the year of The Marriage, but also the year that Percy's first wife committed suicide, as did Mary's half-sister Fanny Imlay, the other child of Mary Wollstonecraft. So Uranus conjunct Mary's Ascendant in the solar return seems absolutely appropriate.

The solar return Moon was her natal Moon: the nineteen-year cycle we discussed in chapter 2. We can see also that the nodal axis is very close to the radix one. But SR-Neptune was closer. No doubt to Mary *certain* things really seemed to be falling into place, with Mercury and Mars also in their natal signs. But of course, everything was in a different house placement. The 1st house in this solar return generally looks as chaotic as the year was. That natal Moon and Mercury recapitulation may well have been what kept Mary going through the year.

Apart from the number of planets and points back in their natal signs, there isn't an indication of *marriage* per se. The 7th house ruler Mercury is dignified and in its radix sign, but it's also partile square Neptune. It is possible that we don't get a clear read because, for Mary and Percy, being married didn't fundamentally change much. It's also possible that the two suicides just a couple of months before simply put a pall over all the events going on.

The chart for 1821 we shall examine again in Chapter 11, when we discuss the topic of death. For this is the solar return under which Mary almost died from a miscarriage, and a few weeks later, Percy did die from drowning. We will only discuss it here from the standpoint of the 7th house analysis under Gadbury's rules.

Here, the argument of the 29 degrees rising is apt. So maybe we should think of this as a bookend with the 1813 chart for the onset of Mary's sexual activity, which also had 29 degrees rising. We may also note Uranus and Pluto both at 29 degrees and square each other: we can think of Mary's own angles as acting rather like a lightening rod to capture the energy of that square.

Saturn is Mary's ruler, and it is both in Fall and **imbecilic**. The Fall is not unlike the radix Saturn in Detriment. But the two Saturns are square by sign. This is a very loaded 1st house. But the 7th is loaded as well. The Sun is in the 7th and ruling the 7th, and it's conjunct the South Node. But here, the Moon is in an evil aspect to Saturn (Gadbury aphorism 10).

One may further note that SR-Neptune was conjunct the 7th house cusp of the radix. That's a little too close to the symbolism of drowning for comfort.

Dorothy Hamill's Marriage Merry-Go-Round

One likes to think that one's choices get better as one gets older, but of course, that's just a myth. We may learn many things, but some people don't seem to do a good job of learning how to pick better relationships. We have already seen in Mary Shelley's life that her father's first marriage to Mary Wollstonecraft was the special one. This is not to say that his marriage to Mary Clairmont was unhappy or unsuccessful. But if there are soul mates, then William G. and Mary W. were.

One gets the same sense with Dorothy Hamill. In her autobiography, it is the relationship to Dean Paul Martin that sends up sparks, where her marriage to Kenneth Forsythe reads like a bounce-back relationship gone bad that lasted too long. As for her third marriage, Dorothy is keeping things private, so all we can do is wish her the very best.

In examining her nativity with regard to marriage we are immediately struck by Pluto very tightly conjunct her 7th house cusp. Ouch! The ruler of the 7th is the Sun. *Her* inclination is to keep the marriage going, quite possibly for longer than it should. With Jupiter in Virgo in Detriment at the Bendings, I am reminded of colleague Dennis Harness' comment about marriage being for the purpose of burning karma at an accelerated rate! One is immediately struck by the astrology that argues that this area of life will be problematic for Dorothy, much more so than the other examples we have examined so far.

So we begin with Dean Paul Martin, whom Dorothy adored. But her chart for the year of their marriage looks a bit odd! Since the Jupiter-Saturn conjunction in her solar return that year was in Libra, a sign where both planets have dignity, but especially Saturn, we would dispense with the usual interpretation of Saturn associated with the 7th house as a bad thing. Remember that a malefic in dignity does not act as a malefic, according to Bonatti. The problem was that at the actual time of her solar return, SR-

Dorothy Hamill
Chicago, Illinois
Time Zone: 6 hours West

July 26, 1956
41 N 51 87 W 39
Tropical Regiomontanus
NATAL CHART

9:18 PM
Daylight Saving Time

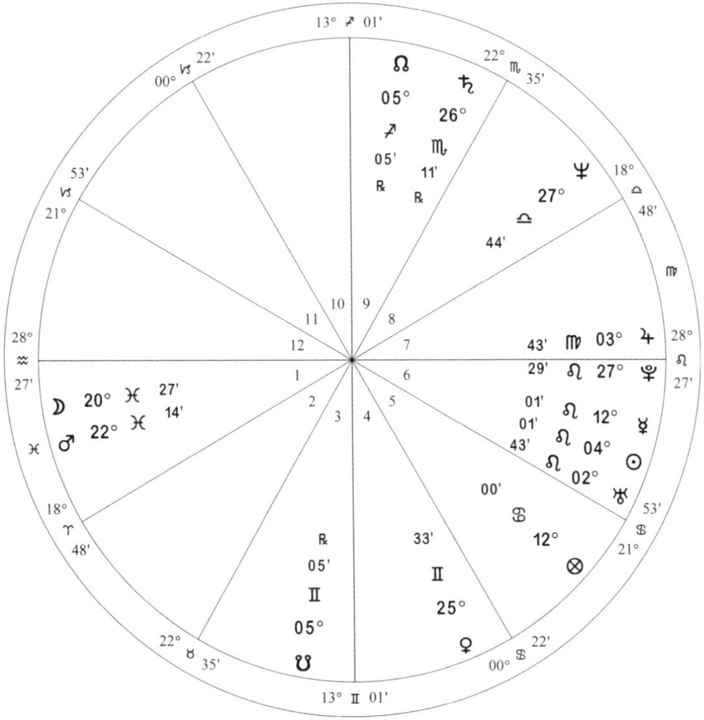

Dorothean Ess. Dig. (No Mut Rec. Points)

Pl	Ruler	Exalt	Tripl	Term	Face	Detri	Fall	Score
☉	☉ +	--	♃	♄	♄	♄	--	+5
☽	♃	♀	♂	♂	♂	☿	☿	- 5 P
☿	☉	--	♃	☿ +	♃	♄	--	+2
♀	☿	☊	☿	♂	☉	♃	--	- 5 P
♂	♃	♀	♂ +	♂ +	♂ +	☿	☿	+6
♃	☿	☿	☽	☿	☉	♃ -	♀	- 10 P
♄	♂	--	♂	☿	♀	♀	☽	- 5 P
☊	♃	☋	♃	♃	☿	☿	--	--
⊗	☽	♃	♂	♃	☿	♄	♂	--
As	♄	--	☿	♂	☽	☉	--	--
Mc	♃	☋	♃	♀	☽	☿	--	--
☋	☿	☊	☿	☿	♃	♃	--	--

Hs	Alm. (Pto)
1	♄
2	☉♂
3	☽
4	☿
5	☽
6	☽
7	☉
8	♀♄
9	♂
10	♃
11	♄
12	♂

Example 3-4. Dorothy Hamill nativity

Dorothy Hamill
Chicago, Illinois
Time Zone: 6 hours West

July 26, 1981
41 N 51 87 W 39
Tropical Regiomontanus
Solar Return for July 26, 1981 in Chicago, Illinois

10:35:38 PM
Daylight Saving Time

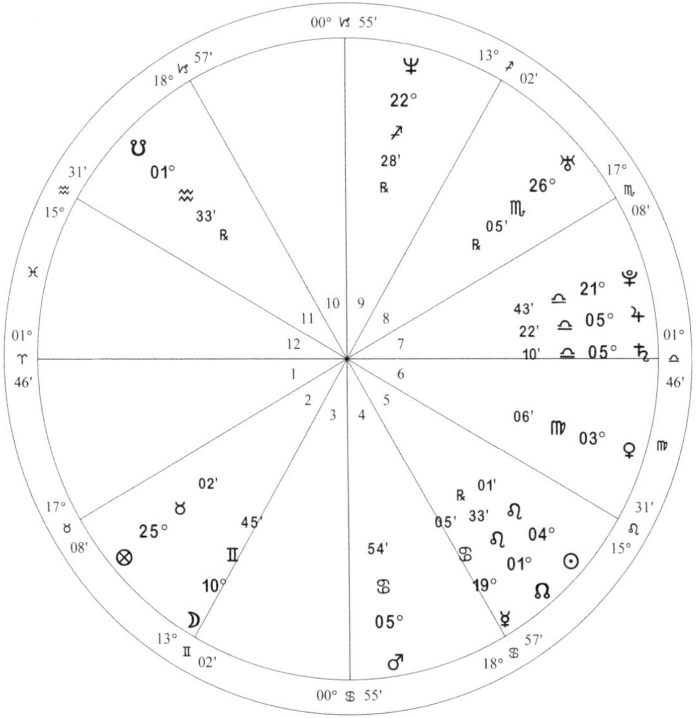

Dorothean Ess. Dig. (No Mut Rec. Points)

Pl	Ruler	Exalt	Tripl	Term	Face	Detri	Fall	Score
☉	☉ +	--	♃	♄	♄	♄	--	+5
☽	☿ m	☊	☿	♃	♂	♃	--	- 5 P
☿	☽ m	♃	♂	☿ +	☿ +	♄	♂	+3
♀	☿	☿	☽	☿	☉	♃	♀ -	- 9 P
♂	☽	♃	♂ +	♂ +	♀	♄	♂ -	+1
♃	♀	♄	☿	♄	☽	♂	☉	- 5 P
♄	♀	♄ +	☿	♄ +	☽	♂	☉	+6
☊	☉	--	♃	♄	♄	♄	--	--
⊗	♀	☽	☽	♄	♄	♂	--	--
As	♂	☉	♃	♃	♂	♀	♄	--
Mc	♄	♂	☽	♀	♃	☽	♃	--
☋	♄	--	☿	♄	♀	☉	--	--

Hs	Alm. (Pto)
1	♂
2	☽
3	☿
4	☽
5	☽
6	☉
7	♄
8	♂
9	♃
10	♄
11	♂♄
12	♄

Example 3-4a. Dorothy Hamill relationship solar return for 1981

Dorothy Hamill
Chicago, Illinois
Time Zone: 6 hours West

July 27, 1983
41 N 51 87 W 39
Tropical Regiomontanus
Solar Return for July 27, 1983 in Chicago, Illinois

10:02:54 AM
Daylight Saving Time

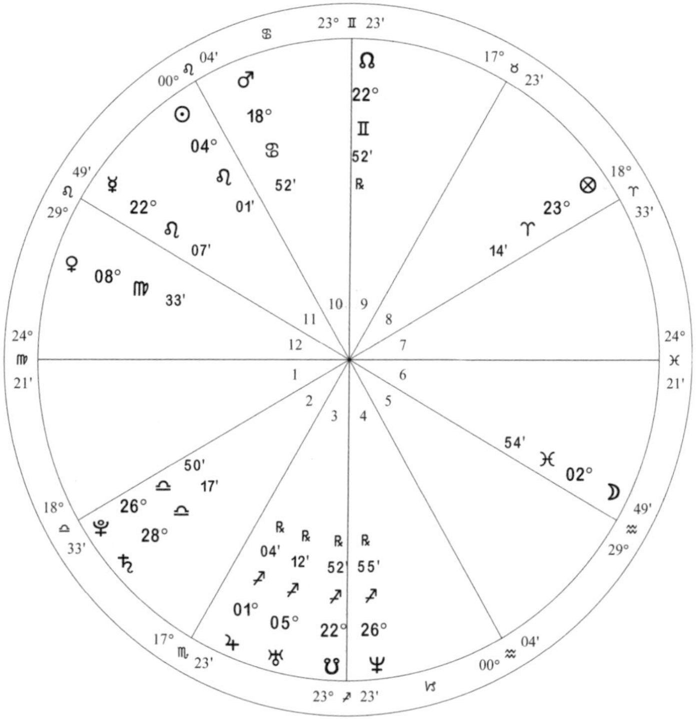

Dorothean Ess. Dig. (No Mut Rec. Points)								
Pl	Ruler	Exalt	Tripl	Term	Face	Detri	Fall	Score
☉	☉ +	--	☉ +	♄	♄	♄	--	+8
☽	♃	♀	♀	♀	♄	☿	☿	- 5 P
☿	☉	--	☉	♃	♂ m	♄	--	- 5 P
♀	☿	☿	♀ +	♀ +	☉	♃	♀ -	+1
♂	☽	♃	♀	☿	☿ m	♄	♂ -	- 9 P
♃	♃ +	☋	☉	♃ +	☿	☿	--	+7
♄	♀	♄ +	♄ +	☊	♃	♂	☉	+7
☊	☿	☊ +	♄	♄	☉	♃	--	--
⊗	♂	☉	☉	♂	♀	♀	♄	--
As	☿	☿	♀	♂	☿	♃	♀	--
Mc	☿	☊	♄	♄	☉	♃	--	--
☋	♃	☋	☉	♄	♄	☿	--	--

Hs	Alm. (Pto)
1	☿
2	♄
3	♂
4	♃
5	♄
6	♄
7	♂
8	☉
9	♀
10	☿♄
11	☉
12	☉

Example 3-4b. Dorothy Hamill relationship solar return for 1983

Dorothy Hamill
Chicago, Illinois
Time Zone: 6 hours West

July 27, 1986
41 N 51 87 W 39
Tropical Regiomontanus
Solar Return for July 27, 1986 in Chicago, Illinois

3:22:34 AM
Daylight Saving Time

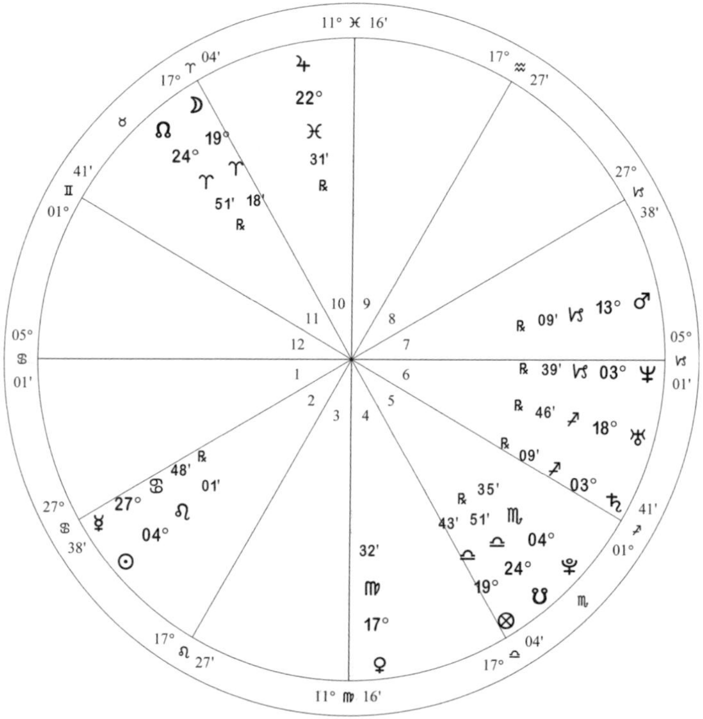

Dorothean Ess. Dig. (No Mut Rec. Points)								
Pl	Ruler	Exalt	Tripl	Term	Face	Detri	Fall	Score
☉	☉ +	--	♃	♄	♄	♄	--	+5
☽	♂	☉	♃	☿	☉	♀	♄	- 5 P
☿	☽	♃	♂	♄	☽	♄	♂	- 5 P
♀	☿	☿	☽	♃	♀ +	♃	♀ -	- 3
♂	♄	♂ +	☽	♃ m	♂ +	☽	♃	+5
♃	♃ +	♀	♂	♂ m	♂	☿	☿	+5
♄	♃	☋	♃	♃	☿	☿	--	- 5 P
☊	♂	☉	♃	♂	♀	♀	♄	--
⊗	♀	♄	☿	☿	♄	♂	☉	--
As	☽	♃	♂	♂	♀	♄	♂	--
Mc	♃	♀	♂	♃	♃	☿	☿	--
☋	♀	♄	☿	☊	♃	♂	☉	--

Hs	Alm. (Pto)
1	☽
2	☽
3	☉
4	☿
5	♀♄
6	♃
7	♄
8	♄
9	♄
10	♃
11	☉♂
12	☿

Example 3-4c. Dorothy Hamill relationship solar return for 1986

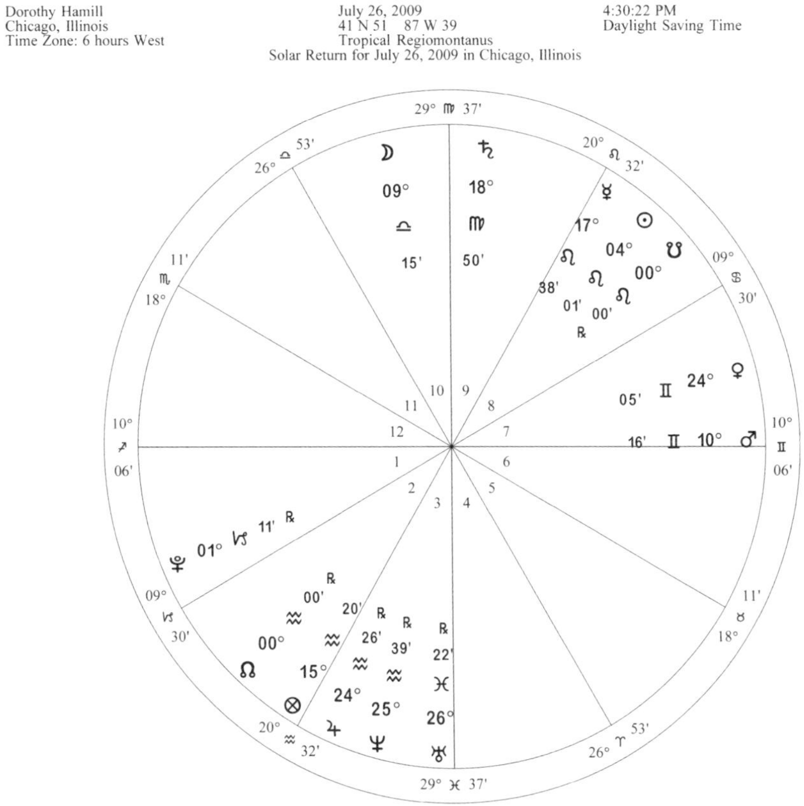
Dorothy Hamill
Chicago, Illinois
Time Zone: 6 hours West
July 26, 2009
41 N 51 87 W 39
Tropical Regiomontanus
Solar Return for July 26, 2009 in Chicago, Illinois
4:30:22 PM
Daylight Saving Time

Dorothean Ess. Dig. (No Mut Rec. Points)								
Pl	Ruler	Exalt	Tripl	Term	Face	Detri	Fall	Score
☉	☉ +	--	☉ +	♄	♄	♄	--	+8
☽	♀	♄	♄	♀	☽ +	♂	☉	+1
☿	☉	--	☉	♀	♃	♄	--	- 5 P
♀	☿	☊	♄ m	♄	☉	♃	--	- 5 P
♂	☿	☊	♄	♃	♂ +	♃	--	+1
♃	♄	--	♄	♃ +	☽	☉	--	+2
♄	☿	☿	♀ m	♄ +	♀	♃	♀	+2
☊	♄	--	♄	♄	♀	☉	--	--
⊗	♄	--	♄	♀	☿	☉	--	--
As	♃	☋	☉	♀	☽	☿	--	--
Mc	☿	☿	♀	♂	☿	♃	♀	--
☋	☉	--	☉	♄	♄	♄	--	--

Hs	Alm. (Pto)
1	♃
2	♄
3	♄
4	♃
5	☉
6	♀
7	☿
8	♃
9	☉
10	☿
11	♄
12	♂

Example 3-4d. Dorothy Hamill relationship solar return for 2009

Mars was in a partile square. This activates Gadbury's aphorism 10, which judges this an evil year for the marriage partner. Pluto in the 7th as well does not give me the warm fuzzies. The Moon was in a sign square the radix Moon, and none of the ptolemaic planets were in their radix signs, except the Sun of course, and Mars was in the same element. This absence of resonance with the nativity suggests that year as being of a "stranger in a strange land" ambiance. No matter how appealing the dream may be, it doesn't quite fit. Is this simply a harbinger of what happened when she did get married at this time?

Within two years, they were divorced, not because Dorothy wanted it that way, but because Dean wanted and felt he needed his freedom. They were divorced under her 1983 solar return. The solar return 7th house is pretty close to the radix Mars position, which tracks. Jupiter, ruling the 7th, and thus Dean, is strong in Sagittarius, but also applying to Uranus. SR-Venus was square her natal Venus by sign. The SR-Moon was opposite SR-Venus. All of these are arguments of difficulty in the marriage or with the marriage partner. Whether they add up to divorce or simply difficulty is open to interpretation.

They remained friends, and stayed in frequent contact. But shortly thereafter, Dorothy met Kenneth Forsythe, and in her autobiography, she described the attraction as being that he looked like Dean! This fact puts the next relationship clearly in the bounce-back category. She married him under her 1986 solar return. She did not tell Dean in advance. Less than three weeks later, the plane Dean was piloting crashed into a mountain and he was killed. Guilt, anyone?

So given the circumstances, it seems we have two different 7th house men to sort out in Dorothy's solar return. The question is: how? The answer is given to us by the phrase: *and they remained friends*. Often this cliché tells us what we need to know at this point. Under the 1986 solar return, *Kenneth was her 7th house man, while Dean was her 11th house friend.*[4]

But we can still read the marriage from the 7th house cusp. There, Saturn rules. While Saturn has mixed Triplicity in the fire signs, Saturn is cadent here – and Neptune is sitting on the 7th house cusp. This is not a configuration for a good marriage. Add to this the partile square of the Sun-Pluto, and the fact that Pluto has a marriage theme for Dorothy because it is natally on her 7th house cusp, and the combination denotes a miserable year with respect to marriage themes.

Meanwhile, in the friend department, we see the Moon and North Node in the 11th, disposed by Mars in the 7th, which also rules the cusp of the 11th. The particular friend, namely Dean, is completely tied in to the 7th house through the rulership patterns, showing what just seems obvious: while he may have thought that he didn't want to be Dorothy's partner, when confronted with the formal and legal reality that she had moved on, he became at the very least accident prone. If we carry this argument still further, then the 6th house is the 8th from the 11th – and there is Saturn, sitting right on the cusp.

The marriage ended under Dorothy's 1995 solar return, at which point, she also filed for bankruptcy. We can really see Dorothy exhausted, and at a low ebb at this time, with the Sun-Moon-Mercury conjunction in the 12th house, at the Bendings. The SR-Moon was exactly at Dorothy's radix Uranus. But with Mercury back in its natal sign, and the angles reversed by sign from her nativity, Dorothy was ready to move on.

Interestingly, this is a New Moon solar return – almost. We discussed the concept of New Moon solar returns in Chapter 2. Our examples of Theodore Roosevelt had the New Moon configuration just after the conjunction. Here, it is just before. This is the more difficult configuration, because the new times are looming, but there is this no man's land which needs to be traversed to get there.

One hopes that her third marriage has occurred after enough time so that the ghosts of numbers 1 and 2 are purged. We will hence be optimistic and only interpret the 7th house as it stands. Having the

malefic SR-Mars in a sign square its radix position, partile conjunct the 7th house cusp would not be my choice as ideal, but it may be mitigated somewhat by the trine from the Moon. Mercury rules the marriage partner, and Mercury had returned to its natal sign. Also Venus had returned to its radix sign, and was in the 7th house. Thus, there was more of a feeling of familiarity between the solar return chart and the natal chart, which should make the marriage much more pleasant for Dorothy.

The Choices of Madame Roosevelt

At this point in our history and western culture, most of us don't marry our cousins, no matter how distant. But we also don't marry future presidents, as a rule. In our current cultural context, we would most likely judge Eleanor's chart as indicating multiple marriage partners, with a mutable sign on the cusp, Saturn in Gemini in the 7th house, and Mercury ruling it. Both the 1st house ruler and the 7th house ruler were dignified by Triplicity. They were also sextile by sign, if not by orb. The equality by dignity implies that Eleanor would work best in a relationship where there was some equality or colleagiality among partners; unfortunately, she came from an era where this was still uncommon. And Saturn in the 7th does imply the potential for problems, although it too had dignity by Triplicity.

Our first chart is for the year of her marriage. Here, we see the 7th house cusp under Venus rulership, which is good, until we see Venus, which was debilitated in Scorpio. But Eleanor's natal Venus was in Virgo, hence Fall (and Triplicity) – here in her marriage solar return, Venus was in Detriment as well as Triplicity. We are reminded again that it is the match to the radix conditions that is important, so here we do have a match of mixed debility and dignity.

So if the Venus which is Franklin is in the 1st house, representing Eleanor, this should be a good thing. It is, however, partile square Saturn. But again SR-Saturn, like Venus, parallels the natal dignity. Eleanor's radix Saturn had Triplicity; here SR-Saturn had rulership

Eleanor Roosevelt
New York, New York
Time Zone: 5 hours West

October 11, 1884
40N42'51" 74W00'23"
Tropical Regiomontanus
NATAL CHART

11:00 AM
Standard Time

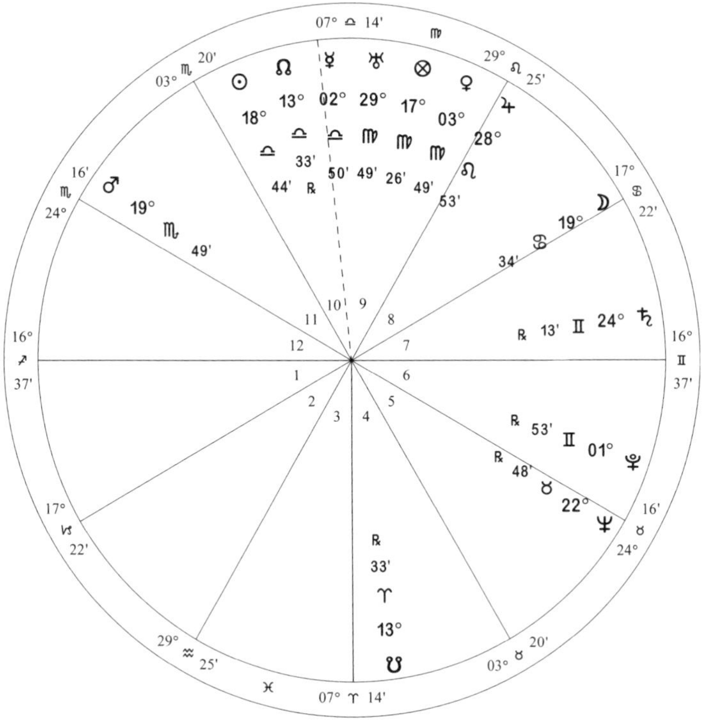

Dorothean Ess. Dig. (No Mut Rec. Points)

Pl	Ruler	Exalt	Tripl	Term	Face	Detri	Fall	Score
☉	♀	♄	♄	♃	♄ m	♂	☉ -	- 9 P
☽	☽ +	♃	♀	☿	☿ m	♄	♂	+5
☿	♀ m	♄	♄	♄	☽ m	♂	☉	- 5 P
♀	☿ m	☿	♀ +	☿	☉	♃	♀ -	- 1
♂	♂ +	--	♀	♀	☉	♀	☽	+5
♃	☉	--	☉	♂	♂	♄	--	- 5 P
♄	☿	☊	♄ +	♄ +	☉ m	♃	--	+5
☊	♀	♄	♄	♃	♄	♂	☉	--
⊗	☿	☿	♀	♃	♀	♃	♀	--
As	♃	☋	☉	☿	☽	☿	--	--
Mc	♀	♄	♄	♀	☽	♂	☉	--
☋	♂	☉	☉	♀	☉	♀	♄	--

Hs	Alm. (Pto)
1	♃
2	♂♄
3	♄
4	☉
5	♀
6	♀
7	☿
8	☽
9	☉
10	♀♄
11	♂
12	♂

Example 3-5. Eleanor Roosevelt nativity

and Triplicity. There is also an interesting interchange of Venus and Mars: Eleanor's radix had Venus in Virgo and Mars in Scorpio; the solar return had Venus in Scorpio and Mars in Virgo. The water and earth signs share Triplicity rulerships, so there is again some familiarity all around. However, in Eleanor's birth chart, the Moon was trine Mars; here the Moon was square Mars. There would definitely be some adjustments to be made.

In the early years of their marriage, Eleanor was the conventional wife: she bore children and stayed in the background while Franklin pursued his political career. This would change when Eleanor discovered that Franklin was having an affair with her secretary, Lucy Mercer. While suspicion had been growing, Eleanor made that discovery in September 1918, just a month before her next birthday. Divorce would destroy Franklin's career. Eleanor only agreed to stay married if sexual relations ceased – which they immediately did. I really don't think we need to go much further than that partile conjunction of Pluto and the South Node in the 7th house! It was probably the applying trine between Jupiter ruling Eleanor and Mercury ruling Franklin which allowed them to stay married. Eleanor's significator at the 7th house certainly would argue that she loved him a great deal, no matter how painful the revelation.

We also may note that there is a *trine* between the Sun and Uranus. Even in this time period, when divorce really was frowned upon, the smoking gun of Franklin's correspondence with Lucy that Eleanor inadvertently discovered would have been considered ample justification on her part to get the divorce. And with Mars opposite that Uranus, I have no doubt that Eleanor's anger was strong enough to have broken the marriage if she had not kept control over it.

And then things changed again when Franklin developed polio. This brought Eleanor more into the public eye, as they found that she could act as the spokesperson and the "eyes and ears" for her husband. She and Franklin maintained a close, if platonic,

Eleanor Roosevelt
New York, New York
Time Zone: 5 hours West

October 12, 1904
40N42'51" 74W00'23"
Tropical Regiomontanus

7:20:04 AM
Standard Time

Solar Return for October 12, 1904 in New York, New York

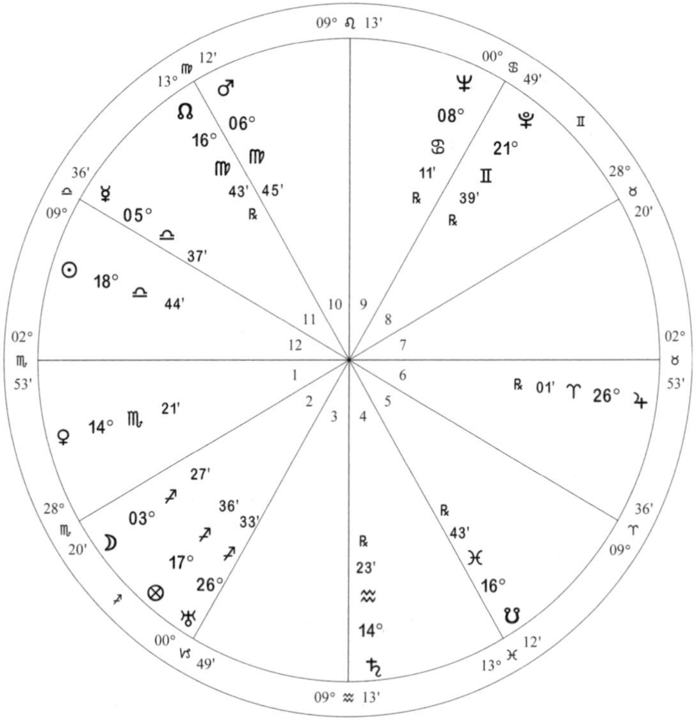

Dorothean Ess. Dig. (No Mut Rec. Points)								
Pl	Ruler	Exalt	Tripl	Term	Face	Detri	Fall	Score
☉	♀	♄	♄	♃	♄	♂	☉ -	- 9 P
☽	♃	☋	☉	♃	☿ m	☿	--	- 5 P
☿	♀	♄	♄	♄	☽ m	♂	☉	- 5 P
♀	♂	--	♀ +	♀ +	☉	♀ -	☽	+0
♂	☿	☿	♀	☿	☉	♃	♀	- 5 P
♃	♂	☉	☉	♄	♀	♀	♄	- 5 P
♄	♄ +	--	♄ +	♀	☿	☉	--	+8
☊	☿	☿	♀	♃	♀	♃	♀	--
⊗	♃	☋ +	☉	☿	☽	☿	--	--
As	♂	--	♀	♂	♂	♀	☽	--
Mc	☉	--	☉	☿	♄	♄	--	--
☋	♃	♀	♀	☿	♃	☿	☿	--

Hs	Alm. (Pto)
1	♂
2	♂
3	♀♄
4	♄
5	♃
6	☉
7	♀
8	♀
9	☽
10	☉
11	☿
12	♀♄

Example 3-5a. Eleanor Roosevelt relationship solar return for 1904

Eleanor Roosevelt
New York, New York
Time Zone: 5 hours West

October 12, 1917
40N42'51" 74W00'23"
Tropical Regiomontanus

10:48:24 AM
Standard Time

Solar Return for October 12, 1917 in New York, New York

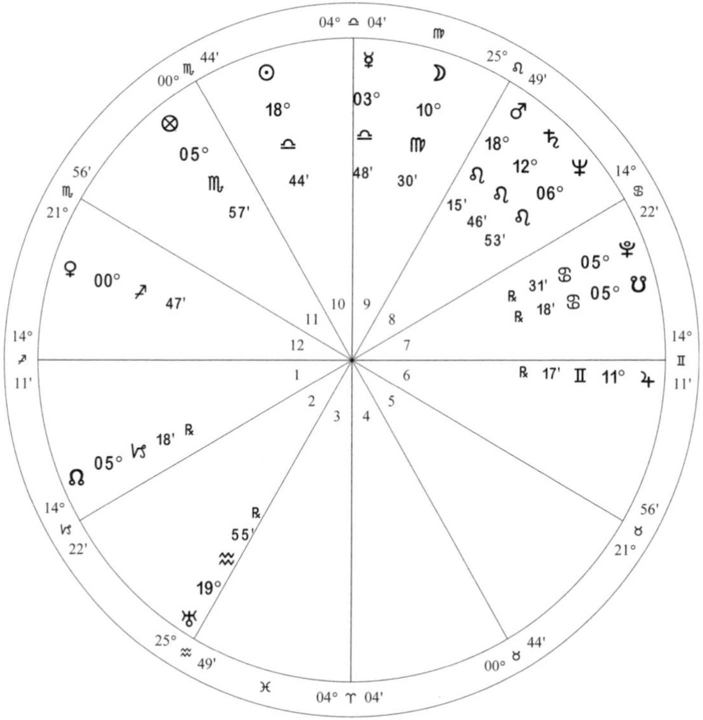

Dorothean Ess. Dig. (No Mut Rec. Points)								
Pl	Ruler	Exalt	Tripl	Term	Face	Detri	Fall	Score
☉	♀	♄	♄ m	♃	♄	♂	☉ -	- 9 P
☽	☿	☿	♀	♀	♀	♃	♀	- 5 P
☿	♀	♄	♄	♄ m	☽	♂	☉	- 5 P
♀	♃	☋	☉	♃	☿	☿	--	- 5 P
♂	☉	--	☉	♀	♃ m	♄	--	- 5 P
♃	☿	☊	♄	♃ +	♂ m	♃ -	--	- 3
♄	☉	--	☉ m	☿ m	♃	♄ -	--	- 10 P
☊	♄	♂	♀	♀	♃	☽	♃	--
⊗	♂	--	♀	♂	♂	♀	☽	--
As	♃	☋	☉	☿	☽	☿	--	--
Mc	♀	♄	♄	♄	☽	♂	☉	--
☋	☽	♃	♀	♂	♀	♄	♂	--

Hs	Alm. (Pto)
1	♃
2	♂♄
3	♄
4	☉
5	♀
6	♀
7	☿
8	☽
9	☉
10	♄
11	♂
12	♂

Example 3-5b. Eleanor Roosevelt relationship solar return for 1917

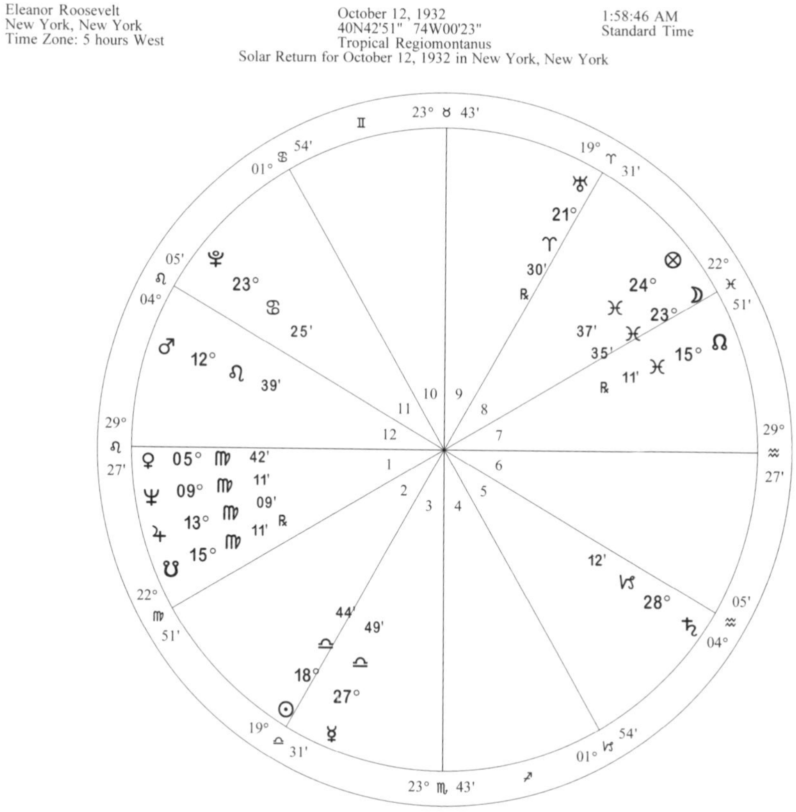

Eleanor Roosevelt
New York, New York
Time Zone: 5 hours West
October 12, 1932
40N42'51" 74W00'23"
Tropical Regiomontanus
Solar Return for October 12, 1932 in New York, New York
1:58:46 AM
Standard Time

Dorothean Ess. Dig. (No Mut Rec. Points)								
Pl	Ruler	Exalt	Tripl	Term	Face	Detri	Fall	Score
☉	♀	♄	☿	♃	♄ m	♂	☉ -	- 9 P
☽	♃	♀	♂	♂	♂	☿	☿	- 5 P
☿	♀ m	♄	☿ +	☊	♃	♂	☉	+3
♀	☿ m	☿	☽	☿	☉	♃	♀ -	- 9 P
♂	☉	--	♃	☿	♃	♄	--	- 5 P
♃	☿	☿	☽	♃ +	♀	♃ -	♀	- 3
♄	♄ +	♂	☽	♄ +	☉ m	☽	♃	+7
☊	♃	♀	♂	☿	♃	☿	☿	--
⊗	♃	♀	♂	♂	♂	☿	☿	--
As	☉	--	♃	♂	♂	♄	--	--
Mc	♀	☽	☽	♄	♄	♂	--	--
☋	☿	☿	☽	♃	♀	♃	♀	--

Hs	Alm. (Pto)
1	☉
2	☿
3	☿♀♄
4	♂
5	♄
6	♄
7	♄
8	♃
9	☉♂
10	☽
11	☽
12	☉

Example 3-5c. Eleanor Roosevelt relationship solar return for 1932

relationship for the rest of Franklin's life. But change was not done for Eleanor – then there was Lorena Hickock.

The discussion of her relationship with Lorena was coy, then cloaked, and only more recently discussed more freely when correspondence between them was published. What is now apparent was that Lorena was part of the lesbian underground of the time, and that Eleanor ended up quite integrated into that community. But this was a time when this was very closeted to the outside world.

Lorena was a reporter, and well-established in her field. She met Eleanor about five years before they apparently became lovers. The latter appears to have occurred in 1932, just after Eleanor's birthday. Like the Mary Shelley chart when she started her affair with Percy, it's a 29 degree Ascendant! And it's one active chart, with the modern configuration known as the cardinal cross. As we would note: the Sun, which rules the Ascendant, was opposite Uranus, and square Pluto, and also square Saturn, which ruled both the 7th house and the 5th house. Because that is the question: what house do we use for Lorena, because Eleanor's marriage to Franklin was still in present tense?

Hence, we have truly achieved the "it's complicated!" state, just as we did when Percy and Mary were sleeping together, while Percy was still married to Harriet. And to keep the complication going, Franklin *liked* Lorena! What does seem likely is that the sexual aspect of the relationship did not last as long as the friendship, and they did stay friends until Lorena's death. But this was surely the kind of year that would have jolted Eleanor out of any complacency she had at the time!

Theodore Roosevelt's Two Wives

Ted Roosevelt was a family man: he loved his two wives, and he loved his children and grandchildren. There seems to be no evidence of any affair lurking somewhere in the background. The

Theodore Roosevelt
New York, New York
Time Zone: 0 hours West

October 27, 1877
40N42'51" 74W00'23"
Tropical Regiomontanus

10:20:24 AM
Local Mean Time

Solar Return for October 27, 1877 in New York, New York

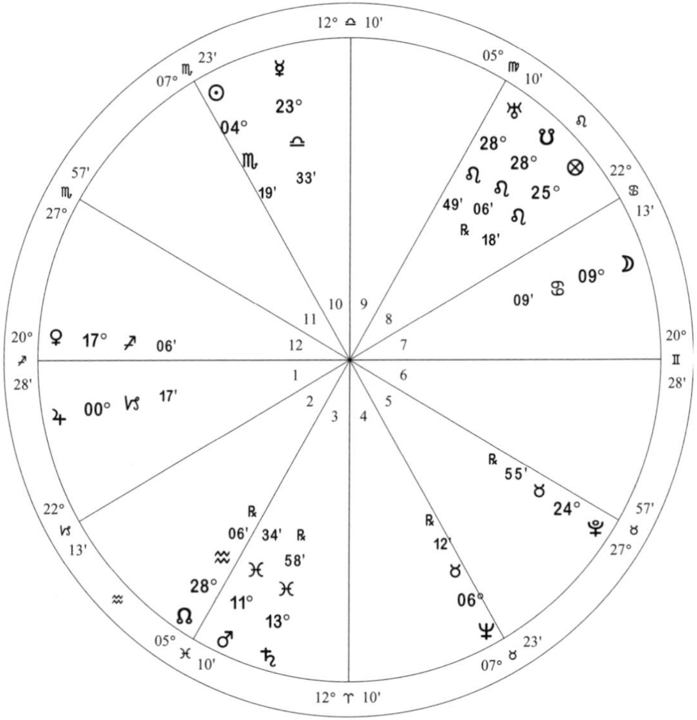

Dorothean Ess. Dig. (No Mut Rec. Points)								
Pl	Ruler	Exalt	Tripl	Term	Face	Detri	Fall	Score
☉	♂	--	♀ m	♂	♂	♀	☽	- 5 P
☽	☽ +	♃	♀	♃	♀ m	♄	♂	+5
☿	♀	♄	♄	☿ +	♃	♂	☉	+2
♀	♃	☋	☉ m	☿	☽ m	☿	--	- 5 P
♂	♃	♀	♀	♃	♃	☿	☿	- 5 P
♃	♄ m	♂	♀	♀	♃ +	☽	♃ -	- 3
♄	♃ m	♀	♀	♃	♃	☿	☿	- 5 P
☊	♄	--	♄	♂	☽	☉	--	--
⊗	☉	--	☉	♂	♂	♄	--	--
As	♃	☋	☉	♄	♄	☿	--	--
Mc	♀	♄	♄	♃	♄	♂	☉	--
☋	☉	--	☉	♂	♂	♄	--	--

Hs	Alm. (Pto)
1	♃
2	♂
3	♀
4	☉
5	♀
6	♀
7	☿
8	☽
9	☿
10	♄
11	♂
12	♂

Example 3-6a. Theodore Roosevelt relationship solar return for 1877

Theodore Roosevelt
New York, New York
Time Zone: 5 hours West

October 27, 1886
40N42'51" 74W00'23"
Tropical Regiomontanus

2:31:41 PM
Standard Time

Solar Return for October 27, 1886 in New York, New York

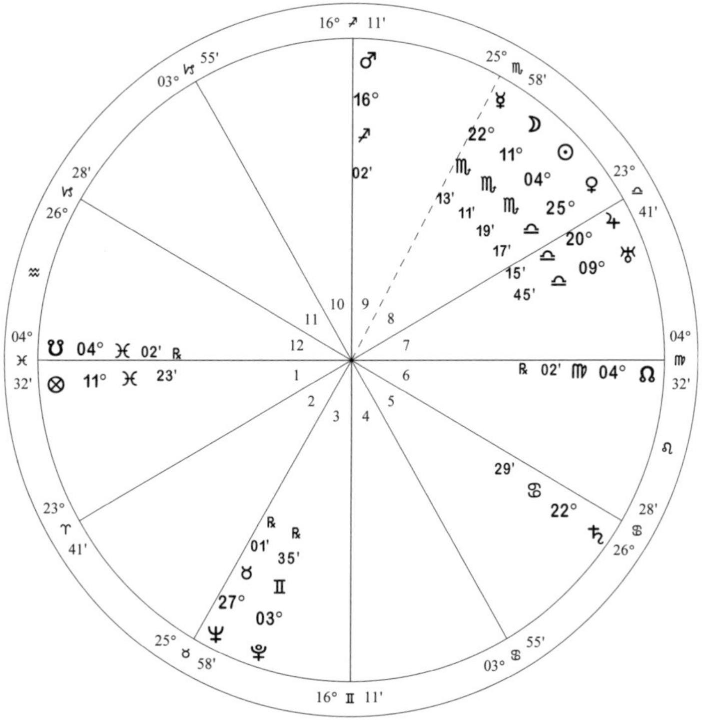

Dorothean Ess. Dig. (No Mut Rec. Points)								
Pl	Ruler	Exalt	Tripl	Term	Face	Detri	Fall	Score
☉	♂	--	♀	♂	♂	♀	☽	- 5 P
☽	♂	--	♀	♃	☉	♀	☽ -	- 9 P
☿	♂	--	♀	☿ +	♀	♀	☽	+2
♀	♀ +	♄	♄ m	☊	♃	♂	☉	+5
♂	♃	☋	☉	☿	☽	☿	--	- 5 P
♃	♀	♄ m	♄	☿	♃ +	♂	☉	+1
♄	☽	♃ m	♀ m	♀	☽	♄ -	♂	- 10 P
☊	☿	☿	♀	☿	☉	♃	♀	--
⊗	♃	♀	♀	♃	♃	☿	☿	--
As	♃	♀	♀	♀	♄	☿	☿	--
Mc	♃	☋	☉	☿	☽	☿	--	--
☋	♃	♀	♀	♀	♄	☿	☿	--

Hs	Alm. (Pto)
1	♀
2	☉♂
3	♀
4	☿
5	☽
6	☽
7	☿
8	♄
9	♂
10	♃
11	♀♄
12	♄

Example 3-6b. Theodore Roosevelt relationship solar return for 1886

closest TR came to "it's complicated" is that he met his first wife just after he broke off a burgeoning relationship with the girl/woman who would become his second wife. In other words, like any typical adolescent with hormones, he had already turned his attention to relationships.

The year that he met Alice Lee, who became his first wife, he was nineteen, and that means that his solar return would generally have the Moon in the same sign as the radix. As TR had the Moon in Cancer natally [SEE EXAMPLE 2-4 ON PAGE 43], this was one powerful Moon. Furthermore, the SR-Moon was in the 7th house, and trine Saturn. Ted was definitely getting serious about marriage! Mercury ruled the cusp of the 7th, and was in Triplicity, although not in the radix sign. SR-Mercury was in the 10th. Ted was a Harvard student, and the convention for his class was not to marry during college.

But courtship was just fine! It was this year that set up their relationship. They became engaged in January 1880, and they married on Ted's birthday in 1880. His life seemed set. That was until February 14, 1884, when both his mother *and* his wife died on the very same day in the same house. It was shortly after Alice delivered their daughter Alice, a solar return we shall examine in Chapter 11. TR was absolutely crushed. It wasn't for another three years before he married again – and after declaring strongly up to that point that second marriages were immoral!

On December 2, 1886, he married Edith Carrow, who thus became his partner for the rest of his life. It is to this 1886 chart that we shall turn. The north node is right on the 7th house! But obviously, that puts the South Node right on the Ascendant. The Descendant is ruled by Mercury, which is in its radix sign. This sets Mercury up to act as an accidentally dignified planet. As we have already seen, this chart was a New Moon solar return. This really did set up his life for the next phase. While the Moon was in mixed debility and dignity, it was trine its radix position.

One really does get some sense that this was TR's second choice marriage. And this would make sense. He knew Edith when he got involved with Alice. Alice was very dear to him, and with her death, he could barely speak her name for the rest of his life. Edith was perhaps more comfortable than the love of his life.

Percy Shelley's Version of, "It's Complicated"

We have examined Mary Godwin Shelley's relationship with Percy, and so it seems fitting to end with Percy's relationship with his two wives. But what a different story than for Theodore Roosevelt! Percy met and married Harriet before he met Mary.

For the year of his marriage to Harriet, the Ascendant-Descendant angles were almost precisely reversed. We have already seen that any such sign oppositions between radix and solar return are not a positive configuration. This marriage took place just a few months after he was expelled from Oxford, an event we will discuss in chapter 7.

Besides the flipped angles, Uranus in the 1st house is also not a good sign. Is is an argument of volatility, which is not a good condition for a marriage. Harriet, as Venus in Cancer, was willing and able, and the SR-Moon was trine Venus by sign, which starts to make this a good idea. But the Moon is afflicted by Neptune and also square Saturn by sign, and the Moon is further conjunct Pluto. Almost immediately upon their elopement, Percy first proposed a menage-a-trois living arrangement with his buddy Hogg, and then, when Harriet refused, he left her on her own to go politicking in Ireland. The presence of the Sun partile conjunct the 10th house cusp suggests that Percy was far more concerned about his reputation and place in the world than he was about his marriage, which looks almost an afterthought.

Then, just a couple of years later, he met Mary. For the year he began his affair with Mary while still married, he once again had Venus in Cancer in the solar return, like he did the year of his marriage to Harriet. What is prominent here is the Moon in the 9th: and this was the year of the whirlwind trip to the Continent

Percy Bysshe Shelley
Horsham, England
Time Zone: 0 hours West

August 4, 1792
51 N 04 0 W 21
Tropical Regiomontanus
NATAL CHART

10:00 PM
Local Mean Time

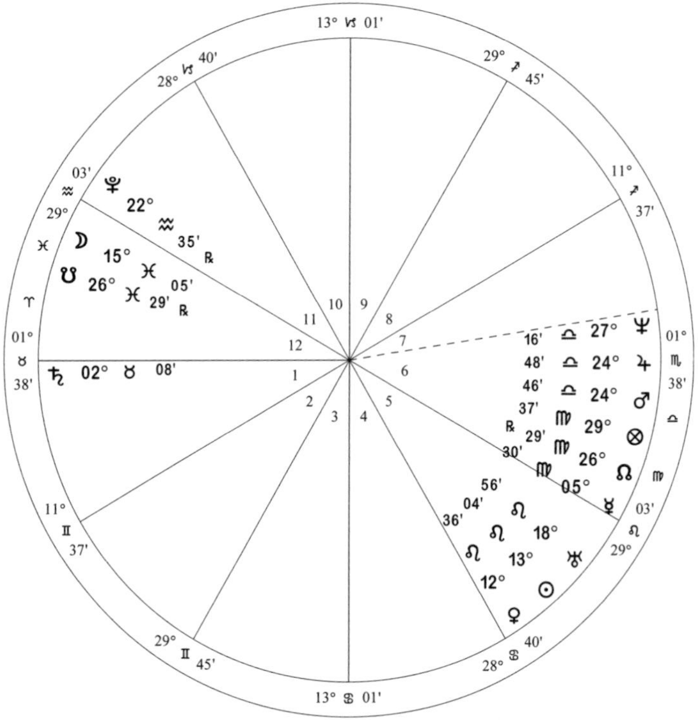

Dorothean Ess. Dig. (No Mut Rec. Points)								
Pl	Ruler	Exalt	Tripl	Term	Face	Detri	Fall	Score
☉	☉ +	--	♃	♀	♃	♄	--	+5
☽	♃	♀	♂	☿	♃	☿	☿	- 5 P
☿	☿ +	☿ +	☽	☿ +	☉	♃	♀	+11
♀	☉	--	♃	☿	♃	♄	--	- 5 P
♂	♀	♄	☿	☊	♃	♂ -	☉	- 10 P
♃	♀	♄	☿	☊	♃ +	♂	☉	+1
♄	♀	☽	☽	♀	☿	♂	--	- 5 P
☊	☿	☿	☽	♂	☿	♃	♀	--
⊗	☿	☿	☽	♂	☿	♃	♀	--
As	♀	☽	☽	♀	☿	♂	--	--
Mc	♄	♂	☽	♃	♂	☽	♃	--
☋	♃	♀	♂	♄	♂	☿	☿	--

Hs	Alm. (Pto)
1	☽♀
2	☿
3	☿
4	☽
5	☽
6	☉
7	♂
8	♃
9	♃
10	♂♄
11	♄
12	♄

Example 3-7. Percy Shelley nativity

Percy Bysshe Shelley
Horsham, England
Time Zone: 0 hours West

August 6, 1811
51 N 04 0 W 21
Tropical Regiomontanus
Solar Return for August 6, 1811 in Horsham, England

12:06:59 PM
Local Mean Time

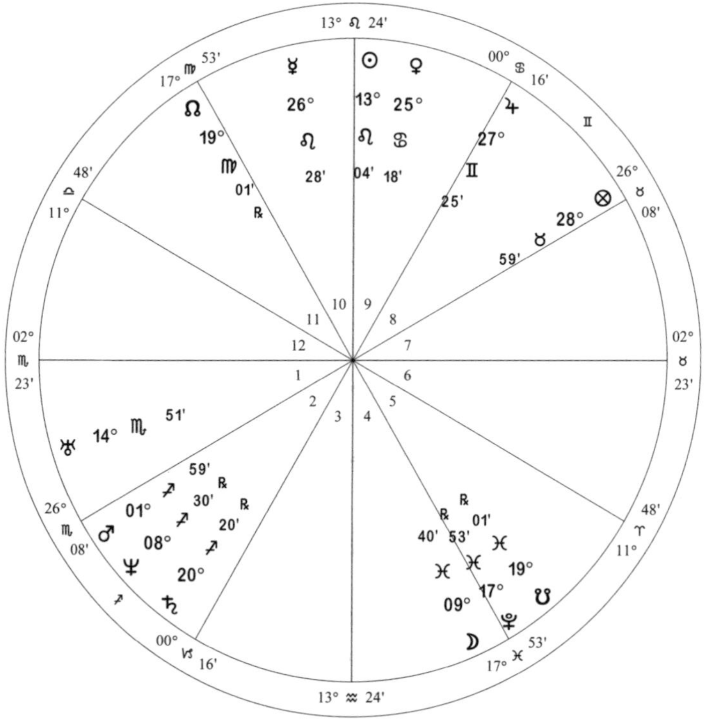

Dorothean Ess. Dig. (No Mut Rec. Points)								
Pl	Ruler	Exalt	Tripl	Term	Face	Detri	Fall	Score
☉	☉ +	--	☉ +	♀	♃ m	♄	--	+8
☽	♃	♀	♀	♃	♄	☿	☿	- 5 P
☿	☉	--	☉	♂	♂ m	♄	--	- 5 P
♀	☽	♃	♀ +	♀ +	☽	♄	♂	+5
♂	♃	☋	☉	♃ m	☿ m	☿	--	- 5 P
♃	☿	☊	♄	♂ m	☉ m	♃ -	--	- 10 P
♄	♃	☋	☉	♄ +	♄ +	☿	--	+3
☊	☿	☿	♀	♄	♀	♃	♀	--
⊗	♀	☽	♀	♂	♄	♂	--	--
As	♂	--	♀	♂	♂	♀	☽	--
Mc	☉	--	☉	♀	♃	♄	--	--
☋	♃	♀	♀	☿	♃	☿	☿	--

Hs	Alm. (Pto)
1	♂
2	♂
3	♀♄
4	♄
5	♃
6	☉
7	♀
8	♀
9	☽
10	☉
11	☿
12	♄

Example 3-7a. Percy Shelley relationship solar return for 1811

Percy Bysshe Shelley
Horsham, England
Time Zone: 0 hours West

August 6, 1814
51 N 04 0 W 21
Tropical Regiomontanus
Solar Return for August 6, 1814 in Horsham, England

5:40:47 AM
Local Mean Time

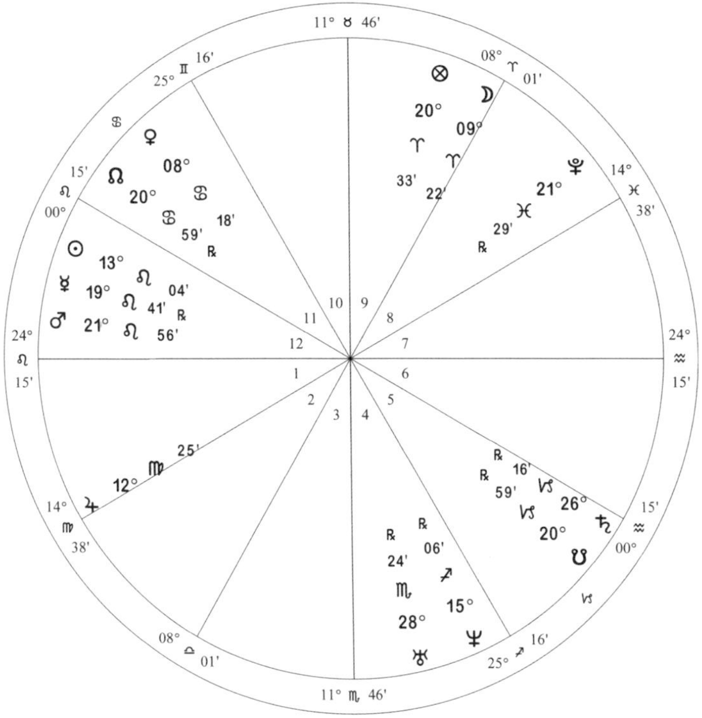

Dorothean Ess. Dig. (No Mut Rec. Points)								
Pl	Ruler	Exalt	Tripl	Term	Face	Detri	Fall	Score
☉	☉ +	--	☉ +	♀	♃	♄	--	+8
☽	♂	☉	☉	♀	♂	♀	♄	- 5 P
☿	☉	--	☉	♃	♃	♄	--	- 5 P
♀	☽	♃	♀ +	♃ m	♀ +	♄	♂	+4
♂	☉	--	☉	♃	♂ +	♄	--	+1
♃	☿	☿	♀	♀ m	♀	♃ -	♀	- 10 P
♄	♄ +	♂	♀	♄ +	☉	☽	♃	+7
☊	☽	♃	♀	♀	☽	♄	♂	--
⊗	♂	☉	☉	☿	♀	♀	♄	--
As	☉	--	☉	♃	♂	♄	--	--
Mc	♀	☽	♀	☿	☽	♂	--	--
☋	♄	♂	♀	♂	☉	☽	♃	--

Hs	Alm. (Pto)
1	☉
2	☿
3	♀♄
4	♂
5	♃
6	♄
7	♄
8	♃
9	☉
10	♀
11	☿
12	☉

Example 3-7b. Percy Shelley relationship solar return for 1814

Percy Bysshe Shelley
Horsham, England
Time Zone: 0 hours West

August 5, 1816
51 N 04 0 W 21
Tropical Regiomontanus
Solar Return for August 5, 1816 in Horsham, England

5:14:39 PM
Local Mean Time

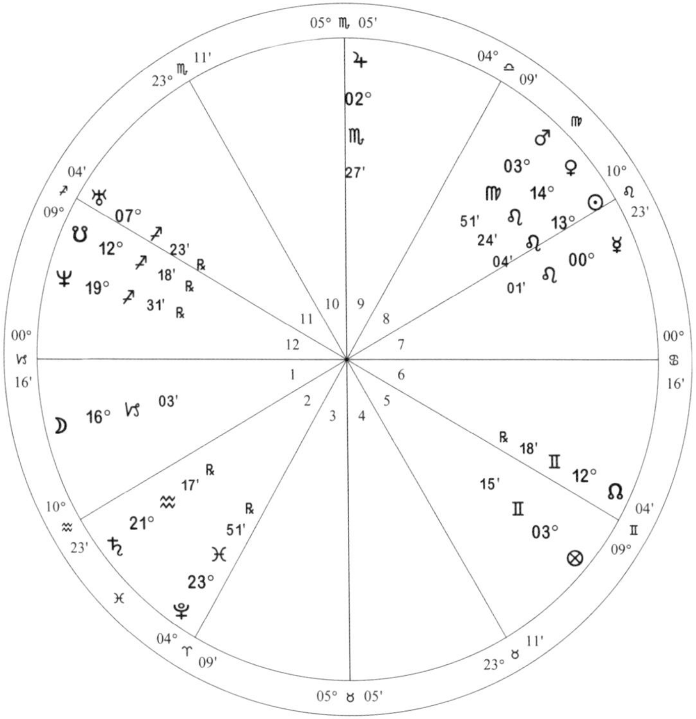

Dorothean Ess. Dig. (No Mut Rec. Points)								
Pl	Ruler	Exalt	Tripl	Term	Face	Detri	Fall	Score
☉	☉ +	--	☉ +	♀	♃	♄	--	+8
☽	♄	♂	♀	♃	♂	☽ -	♃	- 10 P
☿	☉	--	☉	♄	♄	♄	--	- 5 P
♀	☉	--	☉	♀ +	♃	♄	--	+2
♂	☿	☿	♀	☿	☉	♃	♀	- 5 P
♃	♂	--	♀	♂	♂	♀	☽	- 5 P
♄	♄ +	--	♄ +	♃	☽	☉	--	+8
☊	☿	☊ +	♄	♃	♂	♃	--	--
⊗	☿	☊	♄	☿	♃	♃	--	--
As	♄	♂	♀	♀	♃	☽	♃	--
Mc	♂	--	♀	♂	♂	♀	☽	--
☋	♃	☋	☉	♀	☽	☿	--	--

Hs	Alm. (Pto)
1	♀♄
2	♄
3	☉
4	♀
5	♀
6	☿
7	☽
8	☉
9	♄
10	♂
11	♂
12	♃

Example 3-7c. Percy Shelley relationship solar return for 1816

with Mary and Claire Clairmont, during which Mary got pregnant, but during which they had adventures as well, until called back by temporary destitution. Here we see Jupiter in Detriment in Virgo at his 2nd house cusp, which showed his profligate spending, further argued by the Part of Fortune at the Bendings. Meanwhile Harriet was shown by a very strong Saturn, but near the South Node. She was being publicly humiliated by Percy: thoughtlessly, most likely, with no aspect between the 1st and the 7th house rulers.

In 1816, Harriet committed suicide, and then Mary and Percy wed before the year was out. The Descendant is zero Cancer: and so now: who is Harriet and who is Mary in this chart? Unlike our example with Dorothy Hamill, at the beginning of this solar return, Harriet and Mary were both present: he was married to Harriet and living with Mary. Here, I have to surmise that Harriet, as his legal spouse at the beginning of the solar year, was the Moon in Capricorn in the 1st. She still wanted Percy, and was completely tied to him emotionally. But he was the imbecilic (retrograde) Saturn dignified – and in no aspect to the Moon. He was in the 2nd: her 8th. And he did benefit from her death, not so much materially, but because he was free to marry Mary. I would take Mary here as Venus, the ruler of the 5th: and in Leo, the sign of Venus in his radix. Venus is combust, but in her own Terms: Mary gets Percy. But it's in the 8th house, so it happens as a result of death. What a way to do it!

We have seen several ideas in this chapter for applying Gadbury's rules, but also ways to consider the complexities of relationships that people somehow manage to bring into their lives. In the next chapter, we'll consider another major area of most people's experience of life: jobs and business situations.

Chapter 3 Endnotes

1. Lilly, CA, p 737.

2. Good houses would be, first, the angular houses, and then the succedent houses. The cadent houses were the bad houses, although 6th and 12th were worse than 3rd and 9th.

3. Gadbury, John. Genethlialogia, or, the Doctrine of Nativities Containing the Whole Art of Directions and Annual Revolutions, Whereby Any Man (Even of an Ordinary Capacity) May Be Enabled to Discover the Most Remarkable and Occult Accidents of His Life ... : Also Tables for Calculating the Planets Places for Any Time, Either Past, Present, or to Come : Together with the Doctrine of Horarie Questions, Which (in the Absence of a Nativity) Is Sufficient to Inform Any One of All Manner of Contingencies Necessary to Be Known. Printed for William Miller ... London, 1661, pp 226-227.

4. This is not how they would be defined in her nativity, but the nativity covers the entire life, not just one year. In the nativity, the Medieval practice was to use the sequential Triplicity rulers for different people or things related to a house. I discussed this method at length in MAHA, Chapter 13. Under this method, Dean would be Jupiter, the In-sect Triplicity ruler for the 7th house (Dorothy was born at night, so this would be the nighttime Triplicity ruler.) Kenneth would be the Sun (the out-of-sect Triplicity ruler of Leo), while her third husband would be Saturn, the mixed Triplicity ruler of Leo.

4

Solar Returns for Jobs and Money

THE ANCIENTS WERE PRETTY CLEAR ABOUT THIS ISSUE: THEY SIMPLY CALLED IT RICHES. While we may list all sorts of reasons to work that involve fulfillment and service, how many of us would really choose to work very hard if we didn't have to? And yet, there are workaholics as well. In that case, the passion is first for the work (whatever it is), and then for the money that it generates.

The intertwining of these issues was not a topic discussed in the traditional astrology era. In the much simpler societal hierarchies of the day, the vast majority of the populace had the choice: work or starve. Work was physical, long, and hard. The establishment of the Medieval guild system in part served the purpose of providing an economic means for masters to retire, and for their widows to be cared for, should the master pre-decease them.

Even for the nobility, work was often long and hard, even if the conditions were vastly superior to those of their servants, serfs, or slaves. There were decisions about crops, hunting, soldiers, bridge repairs, animal breeding, taxes, enforcement – all sorts of matters that seldom make it into the movies that present the Medieval nobility as living a life of luxury. Castle life may have been better than hovel life, but it was still often dirty, cold, cramped, and certainly not private.

The only class that had what we might call idle time was the clergy. And even there, the times of prayer competed with the farming, cooking, cleaning, and other daily necessities of running a monastery or a parish. It was a small subset of clergy that didn't have those fixed duties so necessary for existence, who were really free to enjoy unfettered contemplation. And then there were the university dons, who either received payment for services, or the harvest of a particular property, who had the time to engage in intellectual pursuits.

Under these social conditions, the discussion of one's "job" would seem odd indeed. Your "job" was either what your father did, or a series of fixed options, like the army. There was a certain amount of social mobility, but it was often easiest to train "in house," or in the house of a neighbor, relative, or family friend.

What had developed through the traditional astrological method was several questions related to wealth, and its corollary, work, which we shall examine here:

1. Can the Native be wealthy at all, where wealth here is mostly defined relative to one's social class?
2. Will the Native fare better or worse than his father, or about the same?
3. Which periods in life will be best financially for the Native?
4. Will the Native prosper through foreign trade, or shipping, or the sale of large animals, or some other specific type of business?
5. Will the Native prosper through benefices?
6. Will the Native receive titles or properties from higher nobility?

Before we consider the specifics, let me make a few cultural comments. If you read biographies of people such as Jane Austen or William Godwin, whose families were in the clergy business, or you read Jane Austen's novels, you will understand that many of the ways that family economics worked were quite different than how we do things today.

Our modern approach is to see almost everything through money. However, during much of the Medieval period, land was the basis of wealth, not cash. Even as the trading cities of Italy and such groups as the Hanseatic League extended the importance of trade and money, the use of money continued to be secondary to wealth. The major reason was that much economic activity was never translated into cash at all. If you had land, you could farm it, or you could lease it to someone to farm it for you. Either way, the result was produce, because if you were the owner, you were paid in crops for the use of the land, just as you would "pay" your serfs in crops to keep them alive to work your land. You probably paid your taxes in crops. You could trade your crops for goods. Barter was the major form of economic exchange.

When Lilly discussed whether a priest would get a parsonage, he was discussing the very same question that Jane Austin had Edward Ferrars contemplating in *Sense and Sensibility*, and that Jane Austen's father himself grappled with in reality. A parsonage was not merely the building that was used by the vicar's family: it was a source of income through the lands associated with it. Different parsonages were more or less advantageous, because the land associated with them would produce greater or less wealth. Thus, it became common for the landed gentry to *buy* a parsonage for a religiously inclined son, because the purchase of it would provide an annual income. Of course, the local nobleman like Colonel Brandon might offer the clergyman a parish within his estate, but whether this would be sufficient to support a family, or even the clergyman himself, depended on the amount of land.

This same idea of benefices supported the clergy in Catholic countries as well, even when they were celibate, and thus not having to consider whether a parish was sufficient to feed a family. Within the university system, considered in the Middle Ages as falling under Church law, a particular professorship might be financed by a benefice.

The logic of owning rental property still hearkens to this system, where the annual rents form a basis of income. Tenants may now typically pay rents monthly, and in cash, but the principle is the same. Over the years, many a family and individual has created wealth through land ownership, and the use of rents. This type of wealth is shown through the 4th house astrologically, with the acquisition of rents being considered an ideal form of retirement income. Land has always been seen as a 4th house matter. But we may make a distinction between the *owning* or *holding* of the land in the 4th, and the income *from* the land.

There was also the concept of wages, where workmen were often paid a daily wage. Craftsmen were generally paid by the piece produced. These wages could be cash, food, or cloth – or potentially any other commodity.

Income *from* land or *from* labor, or *from* any other means is *substance*. Substance, as Bonatti tells us, based on earlier Arabic sources, is a matter of the second house.[1] Bonatti gives the method of determining the nature of one's wealth based on the house placement of the ruler of substance. He defined the ruler of substance by judging the three Triplicity Lords of the 2nd house, picking the strongest, and then using its house position to determine the best path for wealth.

In this method of delineation, he nowhere mentions rents. He refers to such substance from the 4th as being from fathers and grandfathers, not from land itself. The value of land was not in *reselling* it – it was in the income derived *from* its productivity. Thus, when Bonatti said the ruler of substance in the 4th gave income from the fathers, that could be through direct cash allowances, or through the inheritance of land, and thus the income derived from it.

When the United States was founded, its land that was not individually owned already was said to be owned by the federal government, since there was no crown. Born during the era of mercantilism, when all economic value was being converted to cash, property itself was seen as having cash value, not merely the value of rents. Without the system of landed nobility, and without the crown as owner, this newer understanding of land saw profit as coming from the sale of the land itself, as much as from income derived from the land.

Thus, we can see a different view of 4th house wealth than Lilly would have, because the means of profiting from land have changed because of these economic changes. Thus, we can see 4th house profit as follows:

1. The inheritance of land from one's family, what we might call the traditional method
2. Profit from the sale of properties as an owner
3. Profit from land owned, as the traditional idea of rents
4. Profit from the development of land, as with mining, finding treasure, or otherwise developing the resources of the land
5. Profit through buying land or buildings, improving them, and reselling
6. Profit through helping others to buy and sell land: a real estate agent, in other words

Modern astrology would tend to see the profit from all of these as the 2nd from the 4th, or the 5th house. The only case where I would definitely agree is case 6, the real estate agent. But I agree there because I would classify all income derived from *commissions* as 5th house. With this 5th house income, the agent is acting as an ambassador for the property – and ambassador is an old 5th house concept. As an ambassador, one is not selling something that one owns personally, but helping the owner to sell it, and then receiving a gift (commission) in return.

The idea of options 1-5 staying strictly in the 4th house, and not the 5th, is only comprehensible when you understand the history of European land use as we have outlined above. Then one understands that traditionally, the value of property was from the rents derived from the land, and not just from the land value itself.

This makes us thoroughly re-examine the idea of taking the second from a house to tell us something about making money from that area of life. In fact, the strong implication of the Medieval astrologers is that it is the house *itself* that shows the profit, *not* its 2nd house derivative.

Which brings us back to jobs. What is a job? It is generally a contract of time for money. We have tended to see that as a 6th house matter, because traditionally, the 6th house was slaves, and then servants, and so we can see hourly wage work as being like the work of servants. And yet Bonatti, in using the most dignified Triplicity ruler of the 2nd house as the ruler of substance, says that the ruler of substance in the 1st means that one acquires substance through the labor of one's hands.[2] This actually makes a great deal of sense, because the 1st house represents the body, and when one is primarily working through the body, which is manual labor, then there is a definite 1st house quality to that labor.

However, a lot of work in our culture is not exactly manual, and not exactly mental. This work may require computers, but for filling out forms, not programming. Or talking to customers. Or filling orders. These are probably the best description of servant jobs in our time.

When I wrote *Martial Art of Horary Astrology*, I discussed how title inflation had led to many jobs appearing to have a 10th house flavor when they are in fact 6th in nature. The watchword was given by Bonatti: when the ruler of substance is in the 10th, the substance comes from the kingdom or the profession.[3] The kingdom part is pretty straightforward. Within the feudal system, the king made grants to his vassals, who served him and protected the lands they were granted, while enjoying their substance. They in turn gave lesser vassals grants, and those lesser vassals in turn enjoyed the substance of the grants, while protecting the lands, and giving service to their lord. In our modern world, such a 10th house grant is a management promotion: but it has to be real management, not middle management. A business owner is essentially like a feudal lord, as would be a Chief Executive Officer (CEO), Chief Operating Officer (COO), or Chief Financial Officer (CFO). In a family business, the entire family may function as the Board, and hence they may all be in the 10th.

As for the question of profession, it's well to recall that Bonatti himself was a university professor. In the Italian universities of his day, there were only two "professional" degrees: law and medicine. In a number of Medieval cities, being a Doctor of Medicine gave the physician the social rank of Count. This is the sense of profession here: not biologist, computer programmer, librarian, or nurse. It has to be a high status profession to count as 10th house – and presumably, this is in line with considering a partner in a law firm as a 10th house figure, but not an attorney just out of law school.

Regarding substance, Gadbury in the *Genethlialogia* gives several general aphorisms before proceeding to specific matters of the houses:

4. When the Part of Fortune shall be in a good place of the Figure, viz., where the Fortunate Stars of the Radix were placed, or in good Aspect of them, chiefly if either of them be Lord or Governour of the second House of the Revolution, it declares unto the Native in that year an Augmentation of his Estate, and much gaine.

5. The Lord of the second of the Revolution in the Ascendant, portends much increase of gaine and substance unto the Native; and this to come unto him without much labour, or without his own seeking.

6. If a Planet were Peregrine in the second house of the Radix, and he happen to be in the Ascendant of the Revolution, it portends unto the Native gaine by some person or thing as he never imagined or hoped for: the nature of the planet may in some measure discover the matter, if compared with the nature of the Houses he is Lord of.

7. When the Lord of the Ascendant of the Revolution shall apply to the Lord of the second, the Native shall gain much that year by his labour. But if the Lord of the second shall separate from the Lord of the Ascendant, it denotes the contrary. But if the Lord of the Ascendant shall separate from the Lord of the second, the Native shall then be sollicitous and desirous of gaine; but he will very rarely attain much.

8. If a Fortune shall be in the Ascendant of a Revolution, or the Ascendant happen to be the place of a Fortune in the Radix, the Native shall in that year acquire riches and great honours; and (if in a condition suitable) he shall have a Child. But if the Ascendant be hindered, neither of them can come to pass but with much difficulty; and if the Infortunes behold the Ascendant, all the hopes of good are utterly destroyed

9. An infortune in the second of a Revolution, denotes unto the Native much damage and loss according to the nature of the infortune, (i.e.) if Saturn happen to him, the Native loses by

Saturnine Men and things; if Mars, he denotes much expence of Treasure, and loss and prejudice by Theeves and Robbers, by Fire, and by Men Martially inclined."[4]

What may perhaps be the most surprising about these aphorisms is Gadbury's reliance on the Ascendant with respect to financial gain or loss. Clearly, it's not enough to have things working in the 2nd if the Ascendant is afflicted. And this in turn reflects on the likelihood of uncommon financial gain in any particular year: it's difficult when two houses must be fortified.

Gadbury's specific method for substance includes the Part of Fortune as well as the second house. The method follows the typical patterns, so that fortunes associated with the 2nd house bring gain, while malefics bring loss. With respect to the Part of Fortune, the planet disposing it shows the nature of possible gain, so that, for instance, if Mercury disposes the Part of Fortune, gain will be through industry, commerce, or public employment; Venus, though women generally or a dowry.[5]

The Sun in the 2nd house of a revolution is unfortunate, as there is often much expense for egotistical reasons. Saturn brings problems if it's not dignified, so for example, Saturn retrograde in the 4th brings problems with lands or inheritance of lands.[6]

If the Lord of the 2nd and Fortuna are well dignified, then their interpretation is for gain according to the house(s) posited by them, thus, for example in the 6th, through servants, small animals, uncles or aunts, or the practice of medicine.[7]

As we examine these matters, we shall defer most discussion of 10th house situations until chapter 8. For now, we will examine the following examples:

- Buzz Aldrin's beginning of military service, landing on the Moon, and the year his wife's family business collapsed
- Marie Curie's faculty appointments to the École normale and the Sorbonne
- Dorothy Hamill's purchase and sale of the Ice Capades, and the year she filed bankruptcy
- René Lacoste's founding of his clothing company
- Louis Pasteur's chart in the year of the opening of the Institut Pasteur
- Theodore Roosevelt's early jobs he received through political appointment
- Percy Shelley's financial collapse as he pursued his romantic passion with Mary Godwin in Europe

Buzz Aldrin Taking Care of Business

Buzz Aldrin began his career looking like a successful military officer and pilot. Yet a brief view of his natal chart *[SEE EXAMPLE 3-1 ON PAGE 65]* suggests that the financial end of the matter just might not be the shortest distance between two points. One is immediately confronted by Pluto conjunct the 2nd house cusp. So: big losses, or big gains, or simply a few renditions of phoenix from the ashes? At first, we don't know.

So, inspired by Gadbury's analysis of the 1st and 2nd houses as an insertion point, we note Mercury in Aquarius retrograde and combust ruling his 1st. Mercury has dignity there, but Mercury is doubly imbecilic, being both Combust and retrograde. Jupiter might have been able to bail Mercury out, but Jupiter is likewise retrograde, and in Detriment as well. So, we have a sound (dignified) rational mind, a little quirky (the retrograde), but capable of some really *dumb* moves. Buzz himself, in his autobiography, would concur. He graduated third in his class at West Point, which definitely assures us he's not really dumb. He also ended up with a PhD from M.I.T., which isn't sloppy either. But every so often, he just has to make it a lot harder on himself!

So with the imbecilic 1st house ruler and the Pluto on the 2nd cusp: I'm voting big swings, some dumb moves, and some phoenix maneuvers as well. The thing is: this isn't *exactly* the flight path of your normal West Point guy.

We begin in 1952. Buzz has just taken up his job of flying planes. He's a junior officer at this time, gainfully employed flying combat missions during the Korean War. So, Venus ruled the 1st, in a conjunction with the Part of Fortune, disposed by Jupiter in Aries, where it has in-sect Triplicity. So far, not bad. Now there is this matter of Saturn and Neptune in his 1st house. But it's Saturn dignified, so there is no particular danger here. The Neptune? A number of people in the flying business have noted how many pilots seem to end up with strong religious beliefs. Perhaps it's the effect of being up in the air; perhaps they see things they cannot otherwise explain. By the time of his Apollo flight to the Moon, Buzz was sufficiently religiously inclined to decide to arrange to do communion on the Moon: something that NASA did not condone, and specifically asked him not to publicize. Is this the effect we are seeing in 1952? Perhaps.

The 1969 solar return is for the year that Buzz did what he is most known for – he walked on the Moon. So in a sense, this should look like his position in life fulfilled. And in a sense, it does. Buzz has the exalted Mars in Capricorn: how perfect for a career military officer. Here, the Mars was dignified in Scorpio at the Ascendant – Buzz was *doing it*. Here he was with a PhD in orbital rendezvous, on the ultimate mission. SR-Mercury had returned to its natal sign, and Venus was also dignified, albeit in a different type of dignity than his radix position.

Buzz had two very angular planets in that solar return: Mars at the Ascendant, and Mercury at the 4th. The Moon was in the same element as his radix Moon. It makes sense that the two angles activated were the Ascendant and the 4th, because Buzz was the *second* man on the Moon, an artifact of the design of the Lunar Excursion Module (LEM), from which one man could maneuver more easily to the door.

The question of course, afterwards, is: you're thirty-nine years old: what do you do now? Buzz's finances for the year look average to slightly better, with Jupiter in mixed Triplicity ruling the 2nd. It's

Edward "Buzz" Aldrin
Montclair, New Jersey
Time Zone: 5 hours West

January 20, 1952
40N49'33" 74W12'34"
Tropical Regiomontanus
Solar Return for January 20, 1952 in Montclair, New Jersey

10:22:23 PM
Standard Time

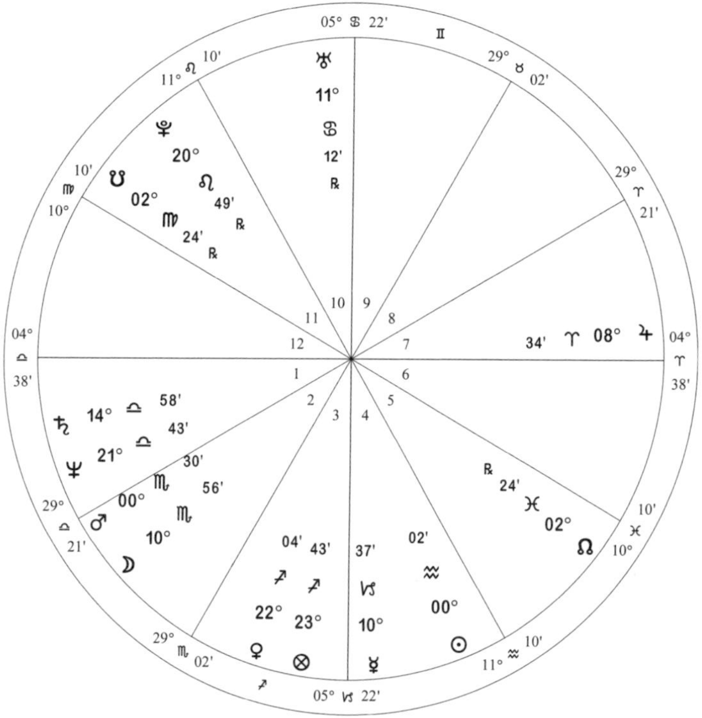

Dorothean Ess. Dig. (No Mut Rec. Points)								
Pl	**Ruler**	**Exalt**	**Tripl**	**Term**	**Face**	**Detri**	**Fall**	**Score**
☉	♄	--	☿	♄	♀	☉ -	--	- 10 P
☽	♂	--	♂	♃	☉	♀	☽ -	- 9 P
☿	♄	♂	☽	☿ +	♂	☽	♃	+2
♀	♃	☋	♃	♄	♄	☿	--	- 5 P
♂	♂ +	--	♂ +	♂ +	♂ +	♀	☽	+11
♃	♂	☉	♃ +	♀	♂	♀	♄	+3
♄	♀	♄ +	☿	♃	♄ +	♂	☉	+5
☊	♃	♀	♂	♀	♄	☿	☿	--
⊗	♃	☋ +	♃	♄	♄	☿	--	--
As	♀	♄	☿	♄	☽	♂	☉	--
Mc	☽	♃	♂	♂	♀	♄	♂	--
☋	☿	☿	☽	☿	☉	♃	♀	--

Hs	Alm. (Pto)
1	♄
2	♀
3	♂
4	♄
5	☿
6	♃
7	♂
8	♂
9	☽
10	☽
11	☉
12	☿

Example 4.1a. Buzz Aldrin money/job solar return for 1952

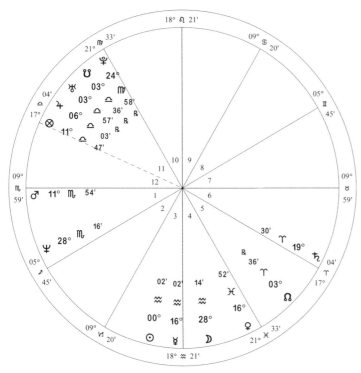

Example 4.1b. Buzz Aldrin money/job solar return for 1969

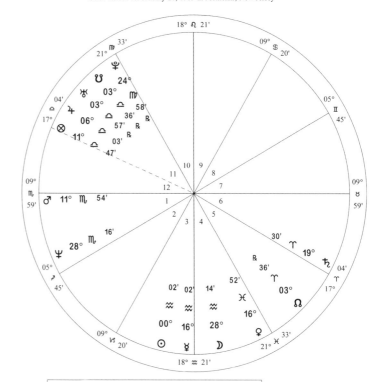

Example 4.1c. Buzz Aldrin money/job solar return for 1989

not like he got big bonuses for going to the Moon: this was his job, after all. And he remained in the military, where pay scales are pretty standard, and don't have special bonuses for unusual activities.

The Saturn in Aries in the 6th house, in contrast to his natal dignified Saturn, probably did make him uncomfortable and impatient with his working conditions. Before the launch, this probably simply registered as perfectionism. Afterwards, he was probably not that easy to be around.

This was, perhaps, a hint of the problems that he would develop later, leading to his separation both from his wife and the military. By his own description, the re-entry to Earth was tough. He would battle alcoholism and come out the other side.

But our last example for him was yet another tough assignment: the year his wife's family business collapsed. During this time period, almost one-quarter of the savings and loan banking institutions in the U.S. failed. Buzz's wife's family business was one of them. For our purposes, we are only examining this issue from the standpoint of how this affected Buzz's immediate family.

From Buzz's standpoint, this loss is 8th house, the wife's portion. Here, we see the Part of Fortune at the 8th house cusp, disposed by Mars in Taurus, in Detriment and in the 8th house. This is an afflicted Fortuna, which makes this the Part of Misfortune, and associated with his wife. His second house ruler, however, is Venus, which is dignified in Capricorn, where it has Triplicity. It is, however, conjunct Neptune and Saturn. Buzz was at his second Saturn return this year, and with Neptune – things were going to have to work in a different way, a not obvious way.

Likewise, the Moon is actually in very good condition: far better than it is natally. So what is the message of this solar return? The message is that Buzz's wife's finances are trashed this year, but Buzz himself shows good earning potential, but only if he does something that (for him) is a different approach.

All Buzz's life, his "work" life had been defined by the military and space. Now, we could make a good case for a Neptune component in space, given the number of unknowns there. But what happened was that his wife Lois and her daughter decided that this would be a good time to market Buzz as a motivational speaker, something that Buzz himself had never attempted. Neptune *does* resonate very well to marketing, because successful marketing touches your clients' aspirations: and not necessarily in a negative way. Buzz went out on the speaking circuit: and after some trial and error and a bit of a learning curve, did very well.

Marie Curie's Professorial Appointments

While by Marie Curie's time, women were not unusual as students of universities, there still were universities that banned them, and it was still unusual to have women faculty members. And especially so in science, where, for a long time, women encountered extra barriers, since the rationality of science was supposed to be difficult for women's brains. However, even in the 19th century, many women participated in the sciences: but often as daughters or wives.

Marie's 9th house natally was ruled by Venus in Scorpio [SEE EXAMPLE 3-2 ON PAGE 69]. We shall see in chapter 7 how this affected her time as a student. Teaching, however, is also a 9th house profession. Her Venus is disposed by a very dignified Mars – so this is an argument that she can benefit financially from teaching. Having the ruler of the 9th in the 10th is a great indicator of making a living at a 9th house job, of which teaching is one (law would be another, as would be religion). The Venus disposed by Mars is a beautiful signature for the fact that she was a fighter – she persisted, usually until she got what she wanted. This combination was crucial for the level of discrimination she experienced: it made it easier not to become a victim.

While the South Node in the 2nd house is not considered a great placement for money, Marie may have managed to mitigate some of the effects that might otherwise have occurred by keeping meticulous household financial records from the time of her marriage forward – which not only provides a magnificent historical document, but also kept their spending frugal and conscious, not spur of the moment. At least Jupiter in Aquarius ruled the 2nd – a benefic with Triplicity, although Jupiter can be a spendthrift if unchecked.

Marie Curie's grades at the Sorbonne exceeded her fellows, and when she began working in Pierre Curie's laboratory, there was no dismissing her as a mere helper. Her work on radioactivity which Pierre then joined ended up with a Nobel Prize. In 1900, she was named the first female faculty member of École normale supérieure at Sèvres.

Here we see a good example of Gadbury's emphasis on the 1st house in these matters, because what is outstanding is the Sun-Jupiter conjunction in the 1st house of the solar return for the year of her appointment. It's hard to see how Moon in Capricorn ruling the 9th helped her get the job, the job required a commute, and took time from her schedule. Marie was completely absorbed in her scientific studies, so this represented a considerable conflict.

The year of this appointment had an extremely active 2nd house. This, in an era where few women worked for a salary. The ruler of the 2nd was in the 2nd. That none of the planets there had any dignity except Saturn by mixed Triplicity does reflect that the salary was not fantastic: Venus, her radix 9th house ruler, shows the employment; that it was in her natal sign makes the whole configuration that much more propitious, even though Venus in Scorpio under other circumstances might not read so positively.

By all accounts, she was a good teacher, an excellent role model for women students, and she enjoyed teaching.

Our second example for Marie follows the tragic death of Pierre the previous April. The two of them had won the Nobel Prize together, and it was because of Pierre's laboratory facilities at the Sorbonne that both of them could work. It was under these rather unusual conditions that Marie was offered his faculty position to replace him. We have already examined this solar

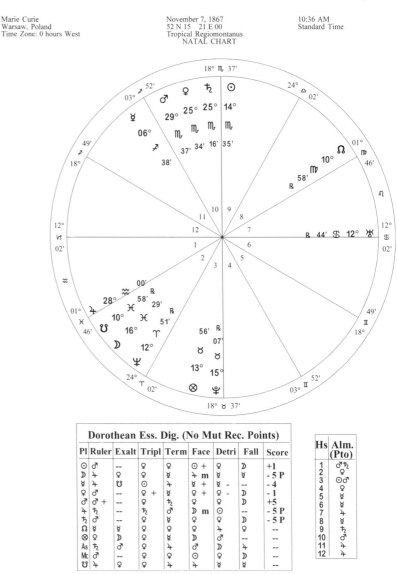

Marie Curie
Warsaw, Poland
Time Zone: 0 hours West

November 7, 1867
52 N 15 21 E 00
Tropical Regiomontanus
NATAL CHART

10:36 AM
Standard Time

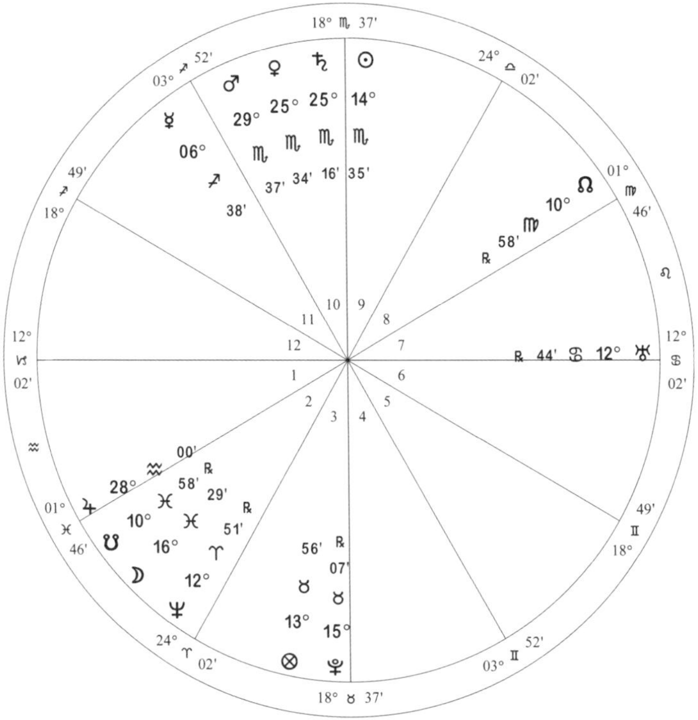

Dorothean Ess. Dig. (No Mut Rec. Points)								
Pl	Ruler	Exalt	Tripl	Term	Face	Detri	Fall	Score
☉	♂	--	♀	♀	☉ +	♀	☽	+1
☽	♃	♀	♀	☿	♃ m	☿	☿	- 5 P
☿	♃	☋	☉	♃	☿ +	☿ -	--	- 4
♀	♂	--	♀ +	☿	♀ +	♀ -	☽	- 1
♂	♂ +	--	♀	♄	♀	♀	☽	+5
♃	♄	--	♄	♂	☽ m	☉	--	- 5 P
♄	♂	--	♀	☿	♀	♀	☽	- 5 P
☊	☿	☿	♀	♀	♀	♃	♀	--
⊗	♀	☽	♀	☿	☽	♂	--	--
As	♄	♂	♀	♃	♂	☽	♃	--
Mc	♂	--	♀	♀	☉	♀	☽	--
☋	♃	♀	♀	♃	♃	☿	☿	--

Hs	Alm. (Pto)
1	♂♄
2	♀
3	☉♂
4	♀
5	☿
6	☿
7	♃
8	☿
9	♄
10	♂
11	♃
12	♃

Example 4-2a. Marie Curie money/job solar return 1899

Marie Curie
Warsaw, Poland
Time Zone: 1 hr 24 min East

November 7, 1905
52 N 15 21 E 00
Tropical Regiomontanus
Solar Return for November 7, 1905 in Warsaw, Poland

5:05:25 PM
Standard Time

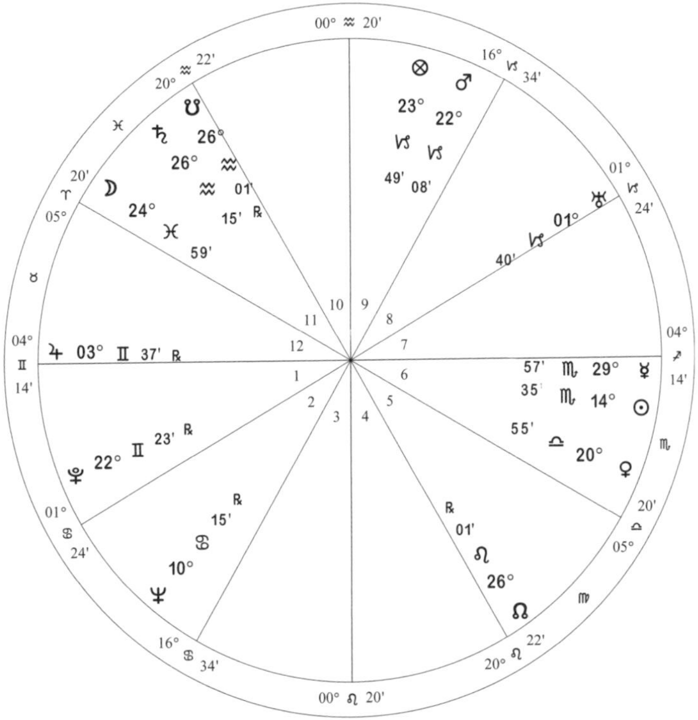

Dorothean Ess. Dig. (No Mut Rec. Points)								
Pl	Ruler	Exalt	Tripl	Term	Face	Detri	Fall	Score
☉	♂	--	♂	♀	☉ +	♀	☽	+1
☽	♃	♀	♂ m	♂	♂	☿	☿	- 5 P
☿	♂	--	♂	♄	♀	♀	☽	- 5 P
♀	♀ +	♄	☿	☿	♃	♂	☉	+5
♂	♄	♂ +	☽ m	♂ +	☉	☽	♃	+6
♃	☿	☊	☿	☿	♃ +	♃ -	--	- 4
♄	♄ +	--	☿	♂	☽	☉	--	+5
☊	☉	--	♃	♂	♂	♄	--	--
⊗	♄	♂	☽	♂	☉	☽	♃	--
As	☿	☊	☿	☿	♃	♃	--	--
Mc	♄	--	☿	♄	♀	☉	--	--
☋	♄	--	☿	♂	☽	☉	--	--

Hs	Alm. (Pto)
1	☿
2	☽
3	☽
4	☉
5	☉♃
6	♄
7	♃
8	♄
9	♂♄
10	♄
11	♄
12	♂

Example 4-2b. Marie Curie money/job solar return 1905

return in the last chapter to see it from the standpoint of their relationship. Here we re-examine the same solar return from the standpoint of the job.

In the 1899 solar return, the dispositor of the 9th house ruler was in the 2nd. In 1905, it was the co-ruler of the 9th exalted in its own house, conjunct the Part of Fortune. The Moon in Pisces ruling the 2nd likewise has mixed Triplicity, so she made out financially fairly well.

Obviously, the vocational side was a smaller piece of the interpretation of the 1905 solar return, but it is interesting that we can see this angle, as well as the far more major theme of her husband's death.

Dorothy Hamill's Roller-Coaster Financial Adventures

Peggy Fleming had created the script that Dorothy Hamill was able to walk in to: win a Ladies Gold Medal at the Olympics, take the Worlds, turn pro, and have a career not only with the Ice Capades, but as a celebrity. Largely, Dorothy followed the pattern. Scott Hamilton discussed in his autobiography how professional skating tended to prefer female skaters – he in fact considered himself somewhat of a ground-breaker as a professional headliner for that reason.

Neither Peggy nor Dorothy came from wealth, and so the greater financial rewards as a pro must have seemed wonderful. But as we saw in the last chapter, Dorothy went into two marriages that provided a lot of emotional turmoil. Her second husband, Kenneth Forsythe, left a successful practice as a physician to use Dorothy's star salary to support his financial plans, which mostly were unsuccessful. He also attempted to act as manager for her, for which he had no training. It was in the midst of this financial scheming that they actually bought the Ice Capades. But this wasn't the same Ice Capades of only a few years prior. For a number of reasons, the market had fragmented, and there was much stiffer business competition.

How do we see a financial investment? When you buy the Ice Capades, what do you get? Oftentimes when you buy a business, you get a property and other fixed assets, as well as the business itself. Here, while there were some fixed assets, what Dorothy and Kenneth basically got was a name and a set of contracts: with skaters, and with arenas that wanted to hire them. Fixed assets would be 4th house, contracts would be 7th house. Saturn ruling the SR-4th and dignified by sign is not a bad place to start for fixed assets. But the 4th house doesn't represent the profit in this business: it's the contracts. These look pretty lackluster: Venus in Leo looks flashy, but doesn't have any dignity. Now obviously, this was meant to be a showcase for Dorothy as well: but her stature in the skating community hardly required her purchase of the Ice Capades! She may be the Sun in Leo ruling the 10th – but she's cadent. This confirms my conclusion that she hardly needed to own it to skate in it. While SR-Jupiter has returned to its natal sign of Virgo, as a 2nd house ruler, it leaves a bit to be desired! With the North Node in the 2nd and Jupiter ruling it, there is going to be too much spending, and not enough earning. As a financial move, too much was spent chasing too little profit.

It should be noted that normally, Dorothy had pretty good earning power, with Mars in Triplicity ruling her 2nd and in the 1st, but being a manager is not her greatest gift.

The 1994 solar return is for when she and Kenneth sold the Ice Capades to a television network. With a sale, the big question is what impact does this show on the 2nd house? The SR-2nd house looks good, but not great. The Moon rules the 2nd, and not only has it returned to its radix sign, but it is in Triplicity.

While this year looked good financially, it wasn't enough for her. She had to declare bankruptcy the following year in the wake of her separation from Kenneth, shown in the solar return for 1995. This chart is *almost* a new moon; hence, the Part of Fortune just off the Ascendant. And that New Moon was square the Nodes. Dorothy truly was closing a cycle. With malefic Mars in the 2nd house in Detriment,

Dorothy Hamill
Chicago, Illinois
Time Zone: 6 hours West

July 26, 1992
41 N 51 87 W 39
Tropical Regiomontanus
Solar Return for July 26, 1992 in Chicago, Illinois

2:04:18 PM
Daylight Saving Time

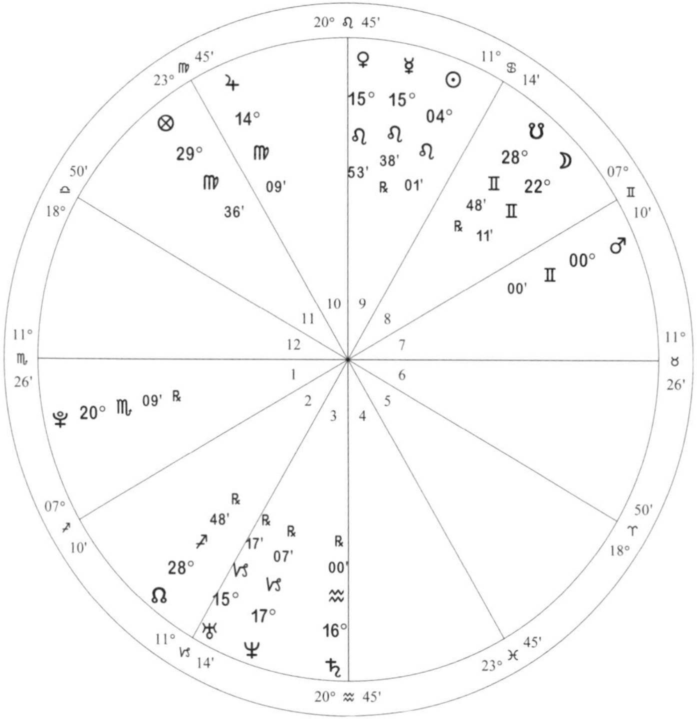

Dorothean Ess. Dig. (No Mut Rec. Points)								
Pl	Ruler	Exalt	Tripl	Term	Face	Detri	Fall	Score
☉	☉ +	--	☉ +	♄	♄	♄	--	+8
☽	☿	☊	♄	♄	☉	♃	--	- 5 P
☿	☉	--	☉	♀	♃	♄	--	- 5 P
♀	☉	--	☉	♀ +	♃ m	♄	--	+2
♂	☿	☊	♄	☿	♃	♃	--	- 5 P
♃	☿	☿	♀	♃ +	♀ m	♃ -	♀	- 3
♄	♄ +	--	♄ +	♀	☿	☉	--	+8
☊	♃	☋	☉	♂	♄	☿	--	--
⊗	☿	☿	♀	♂	☿	♃	♀	--
As	♂	--	♀	♃	☉	♀	☽	--
Mc	☉	--	☉	♃	♂	♄	--	--
☋	☿	☊	♄	♂	☉	♃	--	--

Hs	Alm. (Pto)
1	♂
2	♃
3	♂♄
4	♄
5	♃
6	☉
7	♀
8	☿
9	♃
10	☉
11	☿
12	♄

Example 4-3a. Dorothy Hamill money/job solar return 1992

Dorothy Hamill
Chicago, Illinois
Time Zone: 6 hours West

July 27, 1994
41 N 51 87 W 39
Tropical Regiomontanus
Solar Return for July 27, 1994 in Chicago, Illinois

1:39:36 AM
Daylight Saving Time

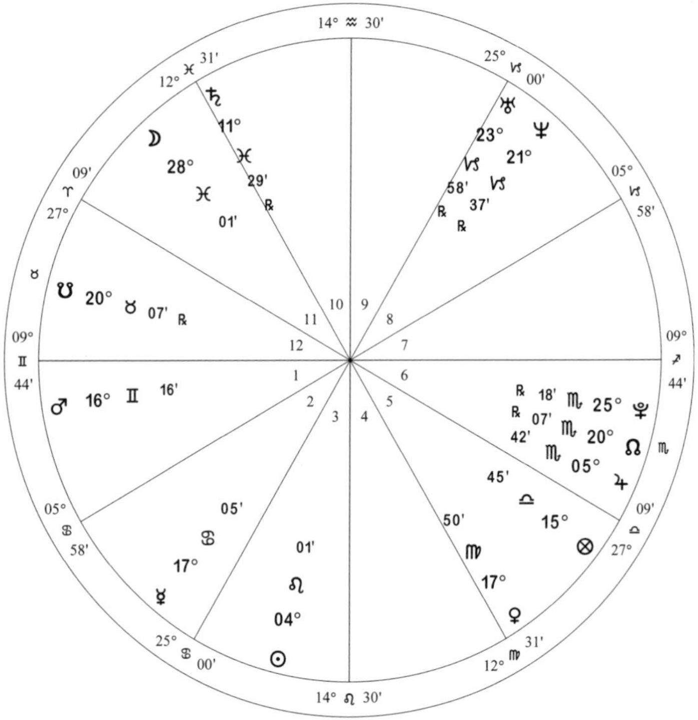

Dorothean Ess. Dig. (No Mut Rec. Points)

Pl	Ruler	Exalt	Tripl	Term	Face	Detri	Fall	Score
☉	☉ +	--	♃	♄	♄	♄	--	+5
☽	♃	♀	♂	♄	♂	☿	☿	- 5 P
☿	☽	♃	♂ m	☿ +	☿ +	♄	♂	+3
♀	☿	☿	☽	♃	♀ +	♃	♀ -	- 3
♂	☿	☊	☿ m	♀	♂ +	♃	--	+1
♃	♂	--	♂	♂	♂	♀	☽	- 5 P
♄	♃	♀	♂	♃	♃	☿	☿	- 5 P
☊	♂	--	♂	♀	♀	♀	☽	--
⊗	♀	♄	☿	♃	♄	♂	☉	--
As	☿	☊	☿	♃	♃	♃	--	--
Mc	♄	--	☿	♀	☿	☉	--	--
☋	♀	☽	☽	♃	♄	♂	--	--

Hs	Alm. (Pto)
1	☿
2	☽
3	☽
4	☉
5	☿
6	♀
7	♃
8	♄
9	♄
10	♄
11	♃
12	♂

Example 4-3b. Dorothy Hamill money/job solar return 1994

Dorothy Hamill
Chicago, Illinois
Time Zone: 6 hours West

July 27, 1995
41 N 51 87 W 39
Tropical Regiomontanus
Solar Return for July 27, 1995 in Chicago, Illinois

7:24:33 AM
Daylight Saving Time

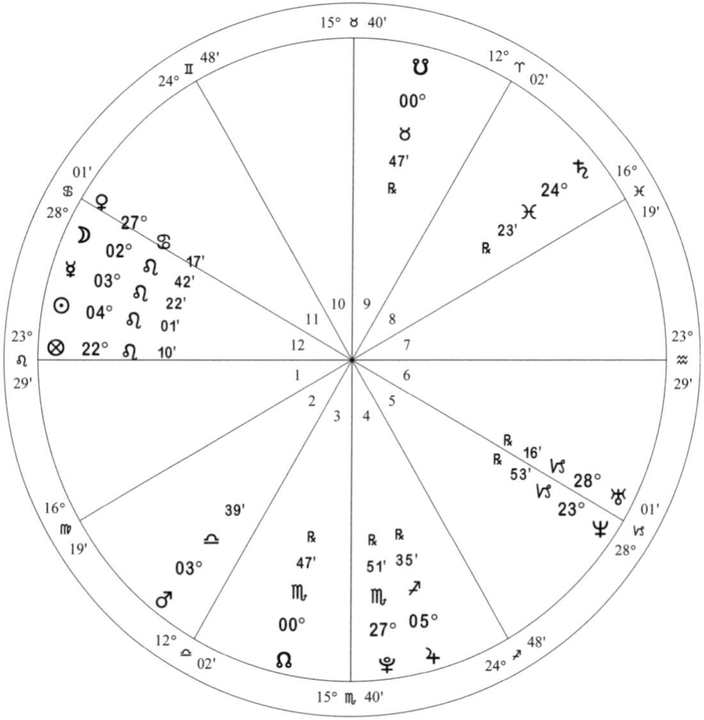

Dorothean Ess. Dig. (No Mut Rec. Points)

Pl	Ruler	Exalt	Tripl	Term	Face	Detri	Fall	Score
☉	☉ +	--	☉ +	♄	♄	♄	--	+8
☽	☉	--	☉	♄	♄	♄	--	- 5 P
☿	☉	--	☉	♄	♄	♄	--	- 5 P
♀	☽	♃	♀ +	♄	☽	♄	♂	+3
♂	♀	♄	♄	♄ m	☽	♂ -	☉	- 10 P
♃	♃ +	☋	☉	♃ +	☿	☿	--	+7
♄	♃	♀	♀	♂ m	♂	☿	☿	- 5 P
☊	♂	--	♀	♂	♂	♀	☽	--
⊗	☉	--	☉	♃	♂	♄	--	--
As	☉	--	☉	♃	♂	♄	--	--
Mc	♀	☽	♀	♃	☽	♂	--	--
☋	♀	☽	♀	♀	☿	♂	--	--

Hs	Alm. (Pto)
1	☉
2	☿
3	♄
4	♂
5	♃
6	♄
7	♄
8	♃
9	☉
10	♀
11	☿♄
12	☽

Example 4-3c. Dorothy Hamill money/job solar return 1995

her financial earning for the year is reduced, and the greater malefic Saturn is in the 8th house, of either debt, or the partner's portion, which probably didn't make much difference in interpretation.

We can thus see that this really was a financial nadir. Fortunately, she has since bounced back, but that is not part of our story line in this chapter.

René Lacoste Creates a Company

Unlike most of our example athletes in this book, René Lacoste did come from money. Even so, his father didn't just hand him an allowance: he found ways to encourage René's competitiveness and drive.

As a player, Lacoste was a pioneer, using fitness training earlier than was fashionable to give himself a competitive edge. It was during his playing days that he discovered the comfort of a polo shirt, which was not the standard issue for tennis of that era. After his playing days were over, he co-founded La Société Chemise Lacoste, which manufactured the shirts. This was a success, and the crocodile/alligator icon was born, although his son believed that it was the introduction of colored models some years later that really sent the brand into the fashion stratosphere.

Lacoste's natal chart has the ruler of the 2nd in the 12th, which isn't at first so encouraging. But to follow Bonatti's logic, we can examine the three Triplicity rulers of the 2nd house, and pick the most dignified to represent financial affairs. Here, we would have a choice of Saturn, with both sign rulership and Triplicity (but retrograde), or Jupiter, with out-of-sect Triplicity. Actually, here Jupiter ***renders*** Saturn, meaning that, because Jupiter sextiles Saturn, disposes the Air Signs by participating Triplicity, and has dignity itself, Jupiter renders the imbecility of Saturn's retrogradation. So this effectively gives us a fully functional Saturn, with a little help from Jupiter.

This Saturn is in the 8th of other people's money, and in a partile trine to Pluto. So there is the possibility here of some gigantic success, but also danger.

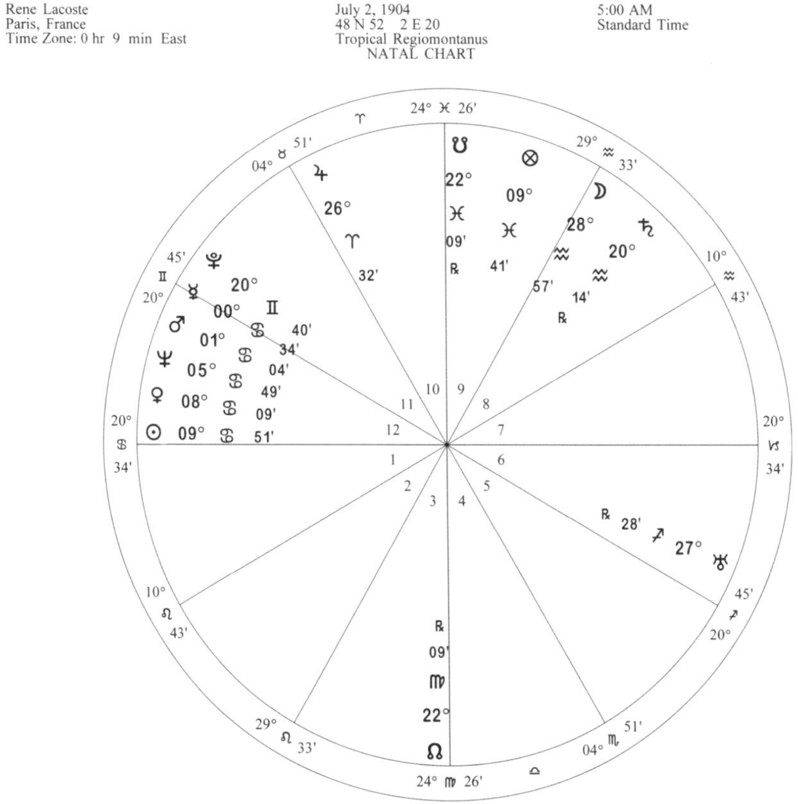

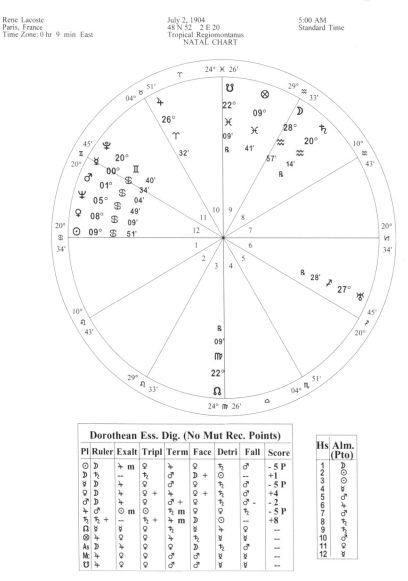

Rene Lacoste
Paris, France
Time Zone: 0 hr 9 min East
July 2, 1904
48 N 52 2 E 20
Tropical Regiomontanus
NATAL CHART
5:00 AM
Standard Time

Dorothean Ess. Dig. (No Mut Rec. Points)

Pl	Ruler	Exalt	Tripl	Term	Face	Detri	Fall	Score
☉	☽	♃ m	♀	♃	♀	♄	♂	- 5 P
☽	♄	--	♄	♂	☽ +	☉	--	+1
☿	☽	♃	♀	♂	♀	♄	♂	- 5 P
♀	☽	♃	♀ +	♃	♀ +	♄	♂	+4
♂	☽	♃	♀	♂ +	♀	♄	♂ -	- 2
♃	♂	☉ m	☉	♄ m	♀	♀	♄	- 5 P
♄	♄ +	--	♄ +	♃ m	☽	☉	--	+8
☊	☿	☿	♀	♄	☿	♃	♀	--
⊗	♃	♀	♀	♃	♄	☿	☿	--
As	☽	♃	♀	♀	☽	♄	♂	--
Mc	♃	♀	♀	♂	♂	☿	☿	--
☋	♃	♀	♀	♂	♂	☿	☿	--

Hs	Alm. (Pto)
1	☽
2	☉
3	☉
4	☿
5	♂
6	♃
7	♂
8	♄
9	♄
10	♂
11	♀
12	☿

Example 4-4. René Lacoste nativity

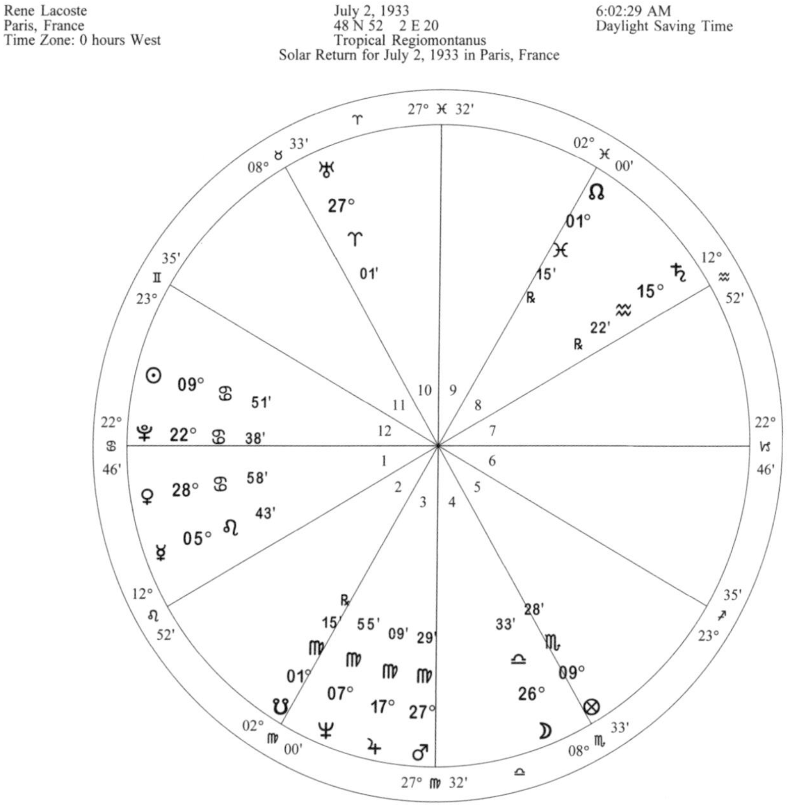
Rene Lacoste
Paris, France
Time Zone: 0 hours West
July 2, 1933
48 N 52 2 E 20
Tropical Regiomontanus
Solar Return for July 2, 1933 in Paris, France
6:02:29 AM
Daylight Saving Time

Dorothean Ess. Dig. (No Mut Rec. Points)								
Pl	Ruler	Exalt	Tripl	Term	Face	Detri	Fall	Score
☉	☽	♃	♀	♃	♀	♄	♂	- 5 P
☽	♀ m	♄	♄	☊	♃	♂	☉	- 5 P
☿	☉	--	☉	♄	♄ m	♄	--	- 5 P
♀	☽ m	♃	♀ +	♄ m	☽	♄	♂	+3
♂	☿	☿	♀	♂ +	☿	♃	♀	+2
♃	☿	☿	♀	♃ +	♀	♃ -	♀	- 3
♄	♄ +	--	♄ +	♀ m	☿ m	☉	--	+8
☊	♃	♀	♀	♀	♄	☿	☿	--
⊗	♂	--	♀	♃	♂	♀	☽	--
As	☽	♃	♀	♀	☽	♄	♂	--
Mc	♃	♀	♀	♄	♂	☿	☿	--
☋	☿	☿	♀	☿	☉	♃	♀	--

Hs	Alm. (Pto)
1	☽
2	☉
3	☿
4	☿
5	♂
6	♃
7	♂
8	♄
9	♀
10	♃
11	♀
12	☿♄

Example 4-4a. René Lacoste money/job solar return for 1933

In the year that the apparel company began production, we see that Pluto possibility coming into focus with SR-Pluto on the Ascendant. This company, unlike our Ice Capades example above, involved some serious 4th house assets, because manufacture had to happen. And here is Mars, the great planet of *doing*, in the 4th and in a sextile to 1st house Venus – so appropriate since this is clothing, which would fall under Venus's rulership, with Venus in its radix sign. The Part of Fortune is in the 5th, and that likewise makes sense for a *sports* apparel company – an activity done for pleasure, thus, ruled by the 5th house. But especially with the Part of Fortune ruled by Mars, since this was *sporting* apparel.

This was the year of Lacoste's Saturn return, which is also appropriate with Saturn so dignified, with the angles lining up so close to the radix position, and with that dignified Saturn ruling partnerships, the form of business structure he used.

Everything about this chart looks like the company he created. And it was amazingly successful!

The Institute that Bears Pasteur's Name

Unlike Marie Curie, I have not listed Pasteur's various professorships here, because we will examine them in a different context. In his case, accepting the positions meant moving, and so we shall examine his in chapter 6. Curie's jobs did not require relocation, so the delineation was a bit more straightforward.

However, Pasteur was honored in his lifetime to have a research institute built and named after him: his legacy for future medical, biological, and chemical research. This occurred in his sixties, and sadly, he did not have so many years left to enjoy the facilities created.

In Pasteur's time, a professorship gave a good solid income. I remember as a child finding some old copies of the *Ladies Home Journal* from the Theodore Roosevelt era, and seeing an article that gave the amount of yearly income for a number of professions, and professorships were near the top – long ago, in a galaxy far away!

Pasteur had Mars in Capricorn ruling his 2nd house. That's already an argument of a comfortable income. His father, shown by Saturn retrograde ruling the 4th, had been a tanner: reasonably successful in his own way, but very much a country job, and not the most pleasant to live around, given the chemicals and the smells.

Venus, ruling the 1st, and Mars, ruling the 2nd, are in the same sign, conveying the connection between the two which is so helpful to having stable financial resources.

But let us turn to the Pasteur Institute. The money for it came after Pasteur had spent a lifetime finding methods to improve French industrial and agricultural production, whether through his work on fermentation or his development of treatment for anthrax. Then, the development of the rabies vaccine proved a major medical miracle at the time. These developments meant that Pasteur had won a fair number of prizes over the years, and he received money from the sale of the vaccines. But while he donated a substantial sum of money to the Institute, he also was involved with fund-raising to increase contributions to the Institute as well. Let us be clear: this was an expansion of his research facilities, and certainly an opportunity for even more research, but *this was not necessary for him personally as a funding mechanism*. It is this latter fact which probably explains the nature of the solar return for the year that construction was begun. First, we see an emphasis on the 4th, which is perfect for *construction*. Second, we see Leo rising, which seems perfect for an institution that will bear his name – and that was known already under that name.

This is quite an angular chart, with a dignified Moon in Taurus at the MC. We can see that the ruler of the 2nd is in Detriment in the 4th, and this is not the sign of Pasteur's radix Mercury. The symbolism makes sense. Pasteur was donating money to the Institute, not the other way around. This also explains the ruler of the 4th in Fall in the 2nd: again, the flow of money was out, not in. Things would not stay that way of course, but this illustrates the period of the building of the Institute where it was too nascent to flourish yet, but where it required money to even come into existence. At this point, it looks

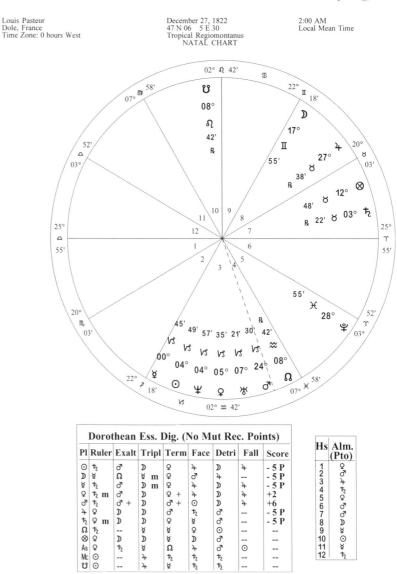

Louis Pasteur
Dole, France
Time Zone: 0 hours West

December 27, 1822
47 N 06 5 E 30
Tropical Regiomontanus
NATAL CHART

2:00 AM
Local Mean Time

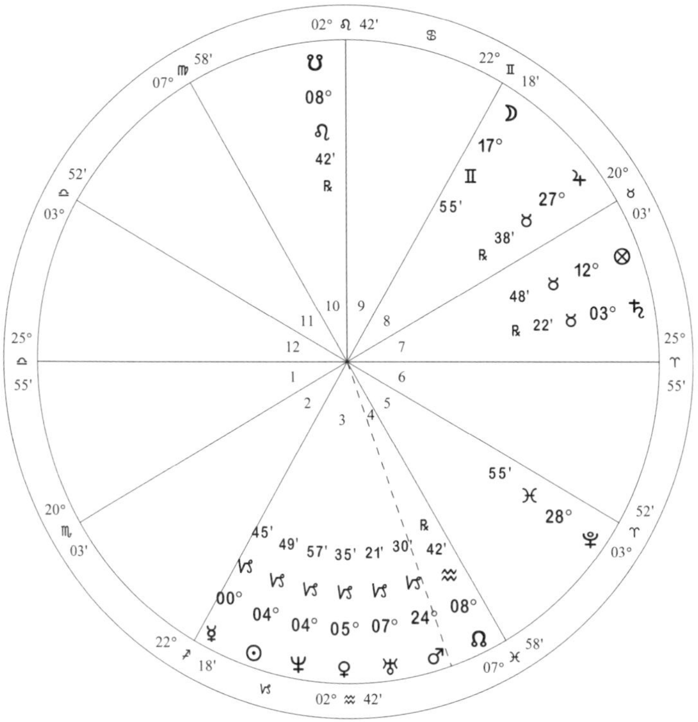

Dorothean Ess. Dig. (No Mut Rec. Points)								
Pl	Ruler	Exalt	Tripl	Term	Face	Detri	Fall	Score
☉	♄	♂	☽	♀	♃	☽	♃	- 5 P
☽	☿	☊	☿ m	♀	♂	♃	--	- 5 P
☿	♄	♂	☽ m	♀	♃	☽	♃	- 5 P
♀	♄ m	♂	☽	♀ +	♃	☽	♃	+2
♂	♄	♂ +	☽	♂ +	☉	☽	♃	+6
♃	♀	☽	☽	♂	♄	♂	--	- 5 P
♄	♀ m	☽	☽	♀	☿	♂	--	- 5 P
☊	♄	--	☿	☿	♀	☉	--	--
⊗	♀	☽	☽	☿	☽	♂	--	--
As	♀	♄	☿	☊	♃	♂	☉	--
Mc	☉	--	♃	♄	♄	♄	--	--
☋	☉	--	♃	☿	♄	♄	--	--

Hs	Alm. (Pto)
1	♀
2	♂
3	♃
4	♄
5	♀
6	♂
7	♂
8	☽
9	☿
10	☉
11	☿
12	♄

Example 4-5. Louis Pasteur nativity

Louis Pasteur December 26, 1887 8:46:27 PM
Dole, France 47 N 06 5 E 30 Local Mean Time
Time Zone: 0 hours West Tropical Regiomontanus
Solar Return for December 26, 1887 in Dole, France

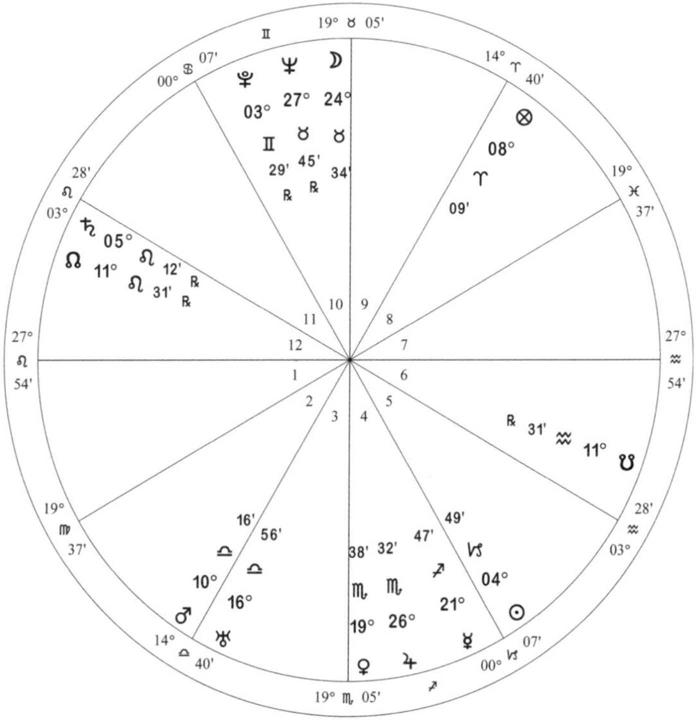

Dorothean Ess. Dig. (No Mut Rec. Points)								
Pl	Ruler	Exalt	Tripl	Term	Face	Detri	Fall	Score
☉	♄ m	♂	☽	♀	♃	☽	♃	- 5 P
☽	♀	☽ +	☽ +	♄	♄	♂	--	+7
☿	♃	☋	♃	♄	♄	☿ -	--	- 10 P
♀	♂ m	--	♂	♀ +	☉	♀ -	☽	- 3
♂	♀ m	♄	☿	♀	♄	♂ -	☉	- 10 P
♃	♂	--	♂	☿	♀	♀	☽	- 5 P
♄	☉ m	--	♃	♄ +	♄ +	♄ -	--	- 2
☊	☉	--	♃	☿	♃	♄	--	--
⊗	♂	☉	♃	♀	♂	♀	♄	--
As	☉	--	♃	♂	♂	♄	--	--
Mc	♀	☽	☽	♃	☽	♂	--	--
☋	♄	--	☿	☿	☿	☉	--	--

Hs	Alm. (Pto)
1	☉
2	☿
3	♀♄
4	♂
5	♄
6	♄
7	♄
8	♃
9	☉♂
10	☽
11	☽
12	☉

Example 4-5a. Louis Pasteur money/job solar return for 1887

like a liability. In fact, it turned into a flourishing institution that is still alive today.

Theodore Roosevelt's Appointments

What is especially good about this example is that Theodore Roosevelt's three appointments were exactly like the traditional idea of receiving honors from the king. The political spoils system – where the winning party to an election gets to hand out jobs – operates exactly in this fashion.

Roosevelt came from the upper class, but that doesn't mean he didn't need to work. He was actually far better at spending money than making it, so a job helped to pay for the staff that he and Edith needed to live their lifestyle. His first such honor came after campaigning for William Henry Harrison in 1888. He was appointed a Civil Service Commissioner, a thankless job that annoyed a lot of people and didn't pay very well. Nonetheless, it brought him to national attention, and gave him a chance to exercise his zeal for doing whatever was necessary for good, clean government.

Here, Mercury rules both 10th and 1st: Ted sees eye to eye with the king, or president in this case. Mercury is in its natal sign *[SEE EXAMPLE 2-4 ON PAGE 43]*. Not only that, the Moon was in its natal sign, and partile conjunct the North Node. TR managed to turn this job into a platform which commanded national attention, something which had not been done this way before. This was also the national position he occupied during the subsequent election when campaigning around the country. He burnished his reputation as a reformer at the same time that he claimed status as a good party man.

His second appointment was in New York City following the 1894 elections, where he was appointed a Police Commissioner (one of three), and then his fellows elected him Commission President. He used the post to launch an anti-corruption campaign. TR is shown by Saturn in Libra exalted; the mayor of New York, his

Theodore Roosevelt
New York, New York
Time Zone: 5 hours West

October 27, 1888
40N42'51" 74W00'23"
Tropical Regiomontanus
Solar Return for October 27, 1888 in New York, New York

2:25:38 AM
Standard Time

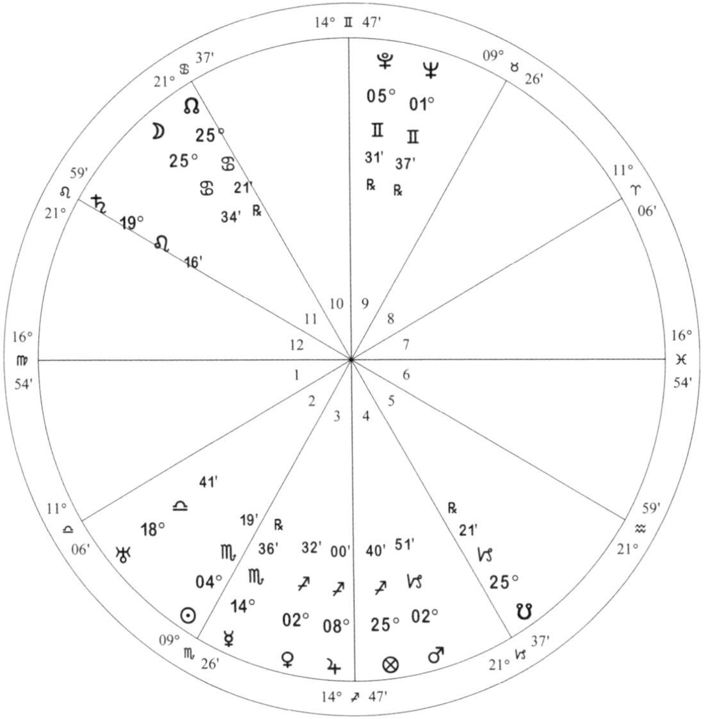

Dorothean Ess. Dig. (No Mut Rec. Points)								
Pl	Ruler	Exalt	Tripl	Term	Face	Detri	Fall	Score
☉	♂	--	♂	♂	♂	♀	☽	- 5 P
☽	☽ +	♃	♂ m	♀	☽ +	♄	♂	+6
☿	♂	--	♂	♀	☉	♀	☽	- 5 P
♀	♃	☋	♃	♃ m	☿	☿	--	- 5 P
♂	♄	♂ +	☽ m	♀	♃	☽	♃	+4
♃	♃ +	☋	♃ +	♀ m	☿	☿	--	+8
♄	☉	--	♃	♃	♃	♄ -	--	- 10 P
☊	☽	♃	♂	♀	☽	♄	♂	--
⊗	♃	☋ +	♃	♂	♄	☿	--	--
As	☿	☿	☽	♃	♀	♃	♀	--
Mc	☿	☊	☿	♀	♂	♃	--	--
☋	♄	♂	☽	♄	☉	☽	♃	--

Hs	Alm. (Pto)
1	☿
2	♀♄
3	♂
4	♃
5	♂
6	♄
7	♃
8	☉♂
9	☽
10	☿
11	☽
12	☉♃

Example 4-6a. Theodore Roosevelt job appointments solar return for 1888

Theodore Roosevelt
New York, New York
Time Zone: 5 hours West

October 27, 1894
40N42'51" 74W00'23"
Tropical Regiomontanus
Solar Return for October 27, 1894 in New York, New York

1:03:31 PM
Standard Time

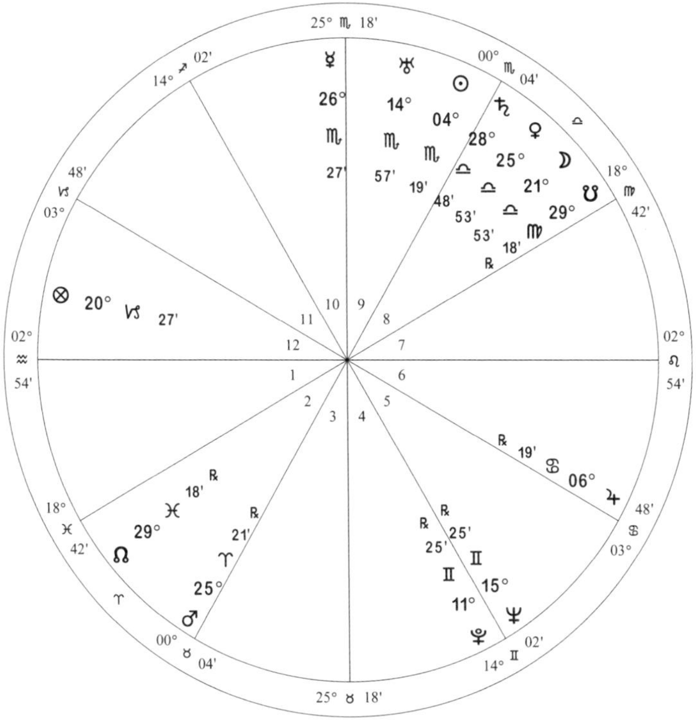

Dorothean Ess. Dig. (No Mut Rec. Points)								
Pl	Ruler	Exalt	Tripl	Term	Face	Detri	Fall	Score
☉	♂	--	♀	♂	♂	♀	☽	- 5 P
☽	♀	♄	♄	☿	♃	♂	☉	- 5 P
☿	♂	--	♀	☿ +	♀	♀	☽	+2
♀	♀ +	♄	♄	☊	♃ m	♂	☉	+5
♂	♂ +	☉	☉	♂ +	♀	♀	♄	+7
♃	☽	♃ +	♀	♃ +	♀ m	♄	♂	+6
♄	♀	♄ +	♄ +	☊	♃	♂	☉	+7
☊	♃	♀	♀	♄	♂	☿	☿	--
⊗	♄	♂	♀	♂	☉	☽	♃	--
As	♄	--	♄	♄	♀	☉	--	--
Mc	♂	--	♀	☿	♀	♀	☽	--
☋	☿	☿	♀	♂	☿	♃	♀	--

Hs	Alm. (Pto)
1	♄
2	♃
3	♀
4	♀
5	☿
6	☽
7	☉
8	☿
9	♂
10	♂
11	♃
12	♀♄

Example 4-6b. Theodore Roosevelt job appointments solar return for 1894

Theodore Roosevelt
New York, New York
Time Zone: 5 hours West

October 27, 1896
40N42'51" 74W00'23"
Tropical Regiomontanus
Solar Return for October 27, 1896 in New York, New York

12:41:07 AM
Standard Time

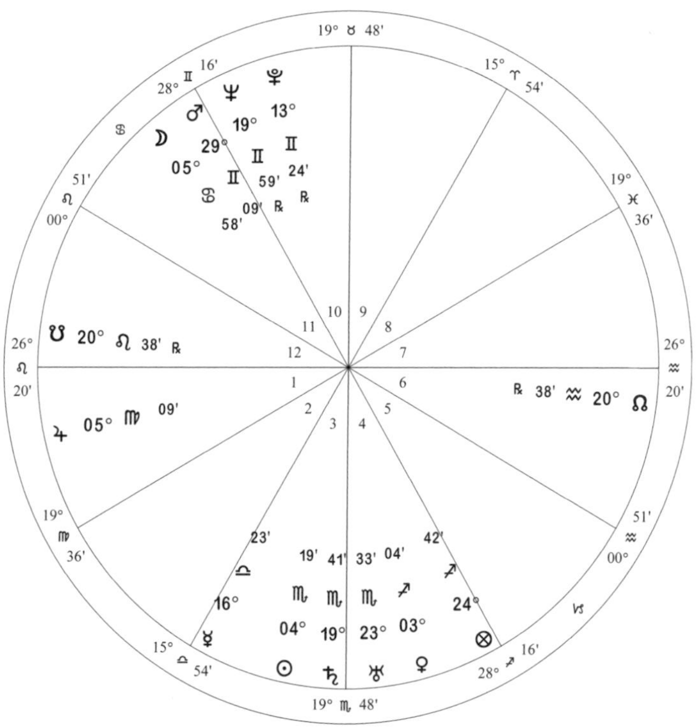

Dorothean Ess. Dig. (No Mut Rec. Points)

Pl	Ruler	Exalt	Tripl	Term	Face	Detri	Fall	Score
☉	♂	--	♂	♂	♂ m	♀	☽	- 5 P
☽	☽ +	♃	♂	♂	♀	♄	♂	+5
☿	♀	♄	☿ +	♃ m	♄	♂	☉	+3
♀	♃	☋	♃	♃	☿	☿	--	- 5 P
♂	☿	☊	☿	♂ +	☉ m	♃	--	+2
♃	☿	☿	☽	☿ m	☉	♃ -	♀	- 10 P
♄	♂	--	♂	♀	☉	♀	☽	- 5 P
☊	♄	--	☿	♃	☽	☉	--	--
⊗	♃	☋ +	♃	♄	♄	☿	--	--
As	☉	--	♃	♂	♂	♄	--	--
Mc	♀	☽	☽	♃	☽	♂	--	--
☋	☉	--	♃	♃	♂	♄	--	--

Hs	Alm. (Pto)
1	☉
2	☿
3	♀♄
4	♂
5	♃
6	♄
7	♄
8	♃
9	☉♂
10	☽
11	☿
12	☉

Example 4-6c. Theodore Roosevelt job appointments solar return for 1896

titular boss, is shown by Mars in sign, but retrograde. The mayor was more from the conservative wing of the party; TR from the reform wing. But they managed to create a working relationship, which is probably the double separation from opposition. The triple conjunction of Moon-Venus-Saturn, with two of them dignified, shows that Roosevelt was able to use this job effectively as a platform. He was becoming very popular with the voters (Moon) if not the party bosses.

The final member of this trio was his appointment following the 1896 presidential election to Assistant Secretary of the Navy. At first, this choice of jobs may seem very odd, but Roosevelt had written an extremely influential book on naval history and strategy, and he kept current with naval matters as a result. In these days, cabinet posts were often given to the president's largest financial backers, so it was often the people, like TR, who were at the level of assistants who did most of the administrative work of their respective departments. This perhaps explains the cadent position of the Sun: he wasn't head of the Navy Department, after all. Yet the Moon trined the Sun from its radix sign, so this would be a very useful plum for Roosevelt.

Roosevelt set about to increase naval preparedness and to insert the U.S. into the Spanish-American War. When this finally happened, it was TR's preparedness that partially allowed the war to be as short as it was. But this was behind-the-scenes stuff – a perfect application for a cadent Sun.

Notice also Mars, ruler of war, just about to change signs into Cancer, its Fall and Triplicity. This position is one of the very strong fighting signs, as we shall see shortly.

Percy Does Europe; Impoverishes Self

I thought it would be interesting to return to another example from chapter 3: Percy Shelley's sojourn with Mary Godwin and Claire Clairmont on the European Continent, where they had great adventures, but they returned completely destitute. Actually, the demolition of substance is a well-established story throughout history. Mary and Claire were raised by a man, William Godwin, who was always near or in debt. On the other hand, Percy's grandfather was quite wealthy, and Percy was almost always able to borrow substantially on his "prospects" as a result of being the eldest son. The irony turned out to be that both his grandfather and his father outlived him.

Percy's natal 2nd house *[SEE EXAMPLE 3-7 ON PAGE 84]* was ruled by Mercury in Virgo. This fact seemed to allow him to go through life, not worrying as much about money as his circumstances would sometimes suggest that he should. But his choice to be a romantic poet had an air of downward mobility about it.

In the year of the Great European Adventure, the conflict between theory and reality was expressed by Mercury again ruling the 2nd, but in Leo in the 12th, combust. Percy was going to do what Percy wanted to do, and the financial consequences be damned. Remember that in 1814, Percy is still married to Harriet, so Mary *must* be 5th house. The symbolism is so perfect your could weep: The ruler of the 5th house (Mars/Mary) is Jupiter in Virgo, i.e., in Detriment. Mary's maidenly reputation is trashed, she becomes pregnant (Jupiter), while the whole affair destroys Percy's finances (Jupiter in Detriment at the 2nd house cusp). But let's not forget that when he ran off with Mary, Harriet was pregnant: and she would give birth to Charles Shelley (1814-1826), who outlived his father, but not by much. Mary's baby was born prematurely, and soon died. Thus, the other meanings of the 5th house also play out during this year.

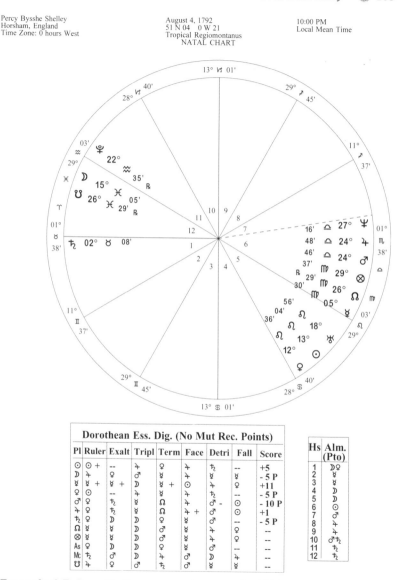

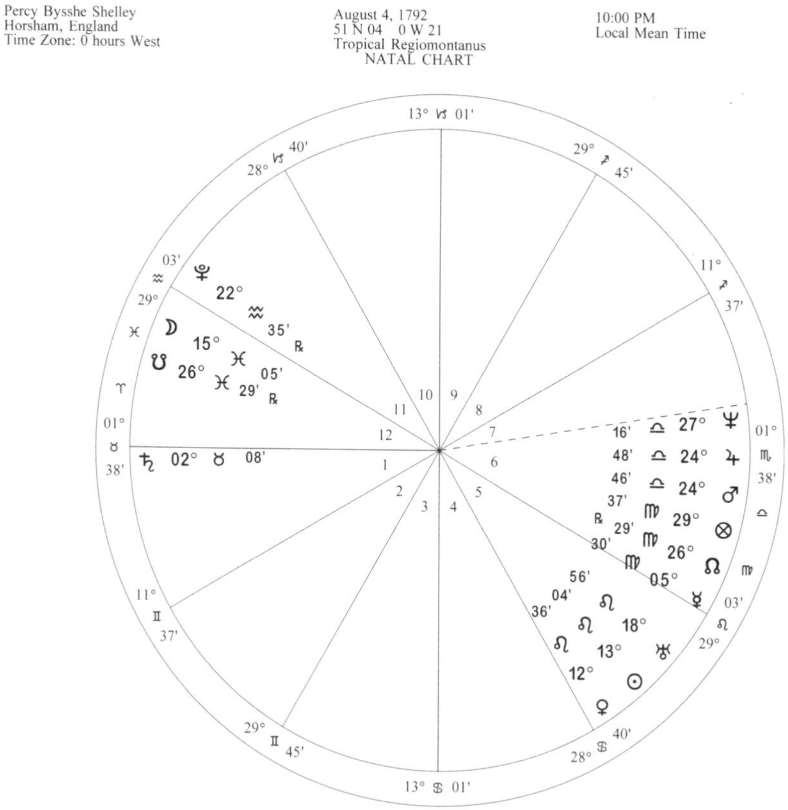
Percy Bysshe Shelley
Horsham, England
Time Zone: 0 hours West
August 4, 1792
51 N 04 0 W 21
Tropical Regiomontanus
NATAL CHART
10:00 PM
Local Mean Time

Dorothean Ess. Dig. (No Mut Rec. Points)

Pl	Ruler	Exalt	Tripl	Term	Face	Detri	Fall	Score
☉	☉ +	--	♃	♀	♃	♄	--	+5
☽	♃	♀	♂	☿	♃	☿	☿	- 5 P
☿	☿ +	☿ +	☽	☿ +	☉	♃	♀	+11
♀	☉	--	♃	☿	♃	♄	--	- 5 P
♂	♀	♄	☿	☊	♃	♂ -	☉	- 10 P
♃	♀	♄	☿	☊	♃ +	♂	☉	+1
♄	♀	☽	☽	♀	☿	♂	--	- 5 P
☊	☿	☿	☽	♂	☿	♃	♀	--
⊗	☿	☿	☽	♂	☿	♃	♀	--
As	♀	☽	☽	♀	☿	♂	--	--
Mc	♄	♂	☽	♃	♂	☽	♃	--
☋	♃	♀	♂	♄	♂	☿	☿	--

Hs	Alm. (Pto)
1	☽♀
2	☿
3	☿
4	☽
5	☽
6	☉
7	♂
8	♃
9	♃
10	♂♄
11	♄
12	♄

Example 4-7. Percy Shelley money solar return for 1814

We have seen how Bonatti's ideas combine well with Gadbury's to produce a clear read of the 2nd house. We have also seen that the modern tendency to take the 2nd from a house as the profit from it may not be compatible with traditional analysis.

In the next chapter, we shall examine solar returns for having children, so Percy's big 1814 year seems an appropriate transition.

Chapter 4 Endnotes

1. Bonatti (Dykes), pp 97-99.
2. Bonatti (Dykes), p 97.
3. Lehman, *MAHA*, Chapter 10.
4. Gadbury (*Genethlialogia*), pp 212-213.
5. Gadbury (*Genethlialogia*), p 218.
6. Gadbury (*Genethlialogia*), p 219.
7. Gadbury (*Genethlialogia*), p 219.

5

Solar Returns for Having Children

T HE TOPIC OF THIS CHAPTER REPRESENTS A GOOD EXAMPLE OF THE ADAPTATION OF ASTROLOGICAL METHOD TO CHANGED CULTURAL TIMES. In Lilly's day, and for the next couple of centuries, the poor and the rich generally did what they wanted, and the results were often lots of children. In between, the ideal was for the man to establish himself as economically able to have a wife and children, and then children were frequent.

Juxtaposed against this general picture is the fact that contraception, abortion, and infanticide have been practiced by many, and not just in modern times. In many times and places, methods were known – perhaps not as effective or easy as modern technologies, but sufficient to make a difference. Thus, we can read of Mary Shelley's half-sister Claire Clairmont, who seduced the poet Byron, but was then rebuffed by him when she became pregnant. Byron was a great believer in birth control, and not in the children that could result from its absence. St. Clair notes that it was a time when upper class women routinely used contraceptive sponges, and he speculates that Mary and Percy Shelley were using contraception within their marriage during certain periods.[1]

Perhaps of much more major concern was not the frequency or timing of children, but their longevity. In our current developed culture, the expectation is that *every* child born will live to maturity, and anything which prevents this from happening is considered extremely tragic. Contrast this with Mary and Percy Shelley, who had five children, of whom only one lived to maturity. At the turn of the 20th century, Eleanor Roosevelt, from one of America's wealthiest families, would lose one of her six children to illness during infancy. Ask in your own family tree about ancestors born before 1920 and their families, and you will see these same stories. My mother (b. 1916) lost two siblings to childhood diseases, and she herself almost died of scarlet fever. The advent of antibiotics massively changed childhood survival rates, and the present generation of superbugs may threaten childhood survival once again.

Whatever the expectations for childhood survival, what is obvious in developed countries is that the birth *rate* per woman has dropped enormously since 1900. My parents' generation as a group expected to plan how many children they had. My generation experienced the shift to where many couples *chose* not to have children at all.

These changes present astrological challenges to interpretation. With women having fewer children, the older astrological configurations which predicted them cannot be applied in the same fashion as before, or at least, with the same expectations. The further decoupling of marriage and children also changes what would have been the expectation of earlier astrologers in the sequencing of the life.

The classical system for evaluating fertility was through the examination of the Moon, 1st house, and 5th house. Specifically, the evaluation required that one compare the presence of fertile against infertile signs, looking for the bodies in or ruling these houses. The fertile signs are the water signs. The barren signs are Gemini, Leo and Virgo. In addition to the ancient model, I would include Taurus as a mostly fertile sign. The more fertile signs and the fewer barren signs, the greater the number of expected children. This system does not, however, predict whether the children will live to any great age. That would come from an evaluation of the condition of the 5th house apart from fertility concerns, and for the nativities of the children themselves.

We can see the classical interpretation for solar returns in Gadbury's discussion of the 5th house in a revolution:

1. *When the Signe Ascending in a Revolution shall devolve to the place of Jupiter or Venus in the Radix, and Jupiter or Venus in or neer the Ascendant, the Native in that yeer shall have Children. If the Sun in a Revolution shall be in the fifth House, and the Part of Children fall neer unto the Lord of the fifth, or Venus, the Native shall in that yeer have Children.*

2. *Venus, Jupiter, the Moon, North Node, or either of them, in the fifth of a Revolution, chiefly in fecund or fruitful Signes, as be Cancer, Scorpio, Pisces, demonstrate oftentimes Children unto the Native in that yeer. If they be with the Lord of the fifth, it denotes the same. It denoteth a pleasant yeer otherwise also.*

3. *When Venus, Jupiter, or Moon, shall be posited in the tenth, eleventh, fourth or fifth Houses of a Revolution, and no wayes impeded of the Malefiques, the Native in the yeer shall have a Child or Children.*

[4.] *If Jupiter in a Revolution shall come to the Part of Children, or behold the same with (good) Aspect, it denotes a Child or Children to the Native in that year.*

5. *The Lord of the fifth of the Revolution, in Conjunction, Sextile or Trine of Jupiter or Venus, and no wayes afflicted of the benevolent Planets, denotes an apt and propitious time to the Native for issue.*

6. *Saturn, Mars or Cauda Draconis, in the fifth House of a Revolution, oftentimes denotes the death of a Child or Children of the Natives in that yeer. If Saturn or Mars afflict the fifth House, or his Lord, by conjunction, square, or opposition, it portends the same; and also the loss and damage to the Native by voluptuous and unhandsome courses.*

7. *The Lord of the fifth in the Ascendant, is also very propitious unto the Native for Issue. But the Lord of the Fifth in the Twelfth House, it is being the eighth from the fifth, threatens much evil (many times death) unto the Natives Children.*

8. *The Lord of the Ascendant, the Moon, and Lord of the fifth, shall be in good Houses of the Revolution, having dignities there, always portends issue unto the Native in that yeer.*

9. *When the Lord of the Ascendant, the Moon, and the Lord of the fifth shall be in good Houses of the Revolution, beholding each other friendly, the Native in that yeer shall enjoy much*

pleasure and delight, and may have a child also; and if he have any Children living, they prove dutiful and obedient unto him.

10. If Mercury be afflicted in a Revolution (he being the general significator of Children) the Children of the Native will be in that yeer much grieved and perplexed; and this so much the more, if he be Lord of the fifth in the Nativity.

11. When Venus in a Revolution shall be afflicted by Saturn, Mars, or the Dragon's Tayl, the Native in that yeer cannot have issue. Saturn by diseases of cold and the like, destroyes the conception. Mars by Abortion, the Dragons Tayl by Poyson, or some other fright, &c. The Natives Delights are eclipsed also.

12. When all the significators of Children are in fruitful Signes, the Native may have more children than one in that yeer. If some happen in fruitful Signes, and others of them in sterile, the Native may have a Child, other arguments concurring; but if they all fortune to be in barren Signes, the Native cannot have issue in that yeer, unless a benevolent Direction be operating; rarely then.

14. Venus Lady of the fifth in Quartile or Opposition of Mars in the Revolution, declares the Native to be lascivious, and given to a voluptuous kind of life, haunting the Company of evil Women, thereby contracting hurtful Disease, such as be the Gonorrhea, Morbus Gallicus, &c., chiefly if Mars be in the Ascendant, or is found to have dignities there.[2]

Notice that aphorism 3 above is the real deal-maker here: when you allow *any* of three planets to be in *one-third* of the houses, and the *only* restriction is impedition of the classical malefics, which itself happens less than a quarter of the time, the odds are easily in favor of pregnancy in any year – even without consulting any additional aphorisms.

Also, the Part of Children that he referred to is probably the Bonatti part, which is Ascendant + Saturn – Jupiter, reversed at night.[3]

Maya Angelou's Son Guy Johnson

Maya Angelou wanted to dispense with all notions of virginity, and she did – and her one-night stand at the age of seventeen also produced her one child, Guy Johnson. We can begin by examining Maya's natal chart – where we see Leo Rising, a barren sign, with the Sun in Aries conjunct Jupiter, ruler of the 5th. Having the Ruler of the 5th combust would reduce fertility, because fertility is seen as "wet" and a combust planet is "burned up." So while the planet Jupiter would tend naturally toward fertility, its combustion may mitigate this effect. But obviously not completely!

Notice that this argument concerning fertility does not address whether she *wanted* to have children, or what she *thinks* about children in general: as usual, classical astrology tends to address the behavior and not the intention or motivation.

In her solar return for this year, Maya had three planets in their natal houses, and none but the Sun in their own signs: Mercury, Venus and Neptune were all in their radix houses. Venus is a critical planet here as a natural ruler of fertility: in this solar return retrograde, in the sign of Taurus, a sign I have found represents fertility, although it was not on the ancient lists. Her natal Venus is in Pisces, a fruitful sign, and one of the minority strong arguments of fertility in her nativity. Thus, in the year of Guy's birth, Venus was in a fertile sign. Although Saturn is not usually associated with fertility, here it rules the 5th from fertile Cancer.

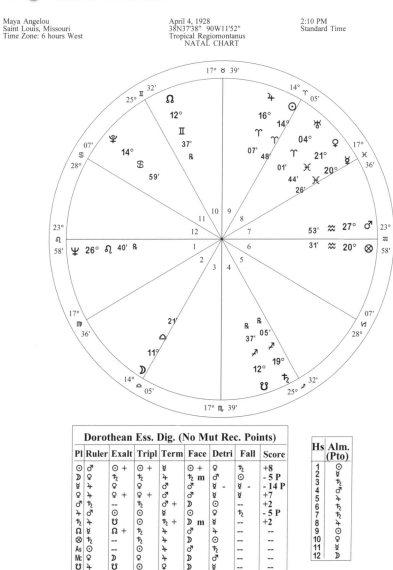

Maya Angelou
Saint Louis, Missouri
Time Zone: 6 hours West

April 4, 1928
38N37'38" 90W11'52"
Tropical Regiomontanus
NATAL CHART

2:10 PM
Standard Time

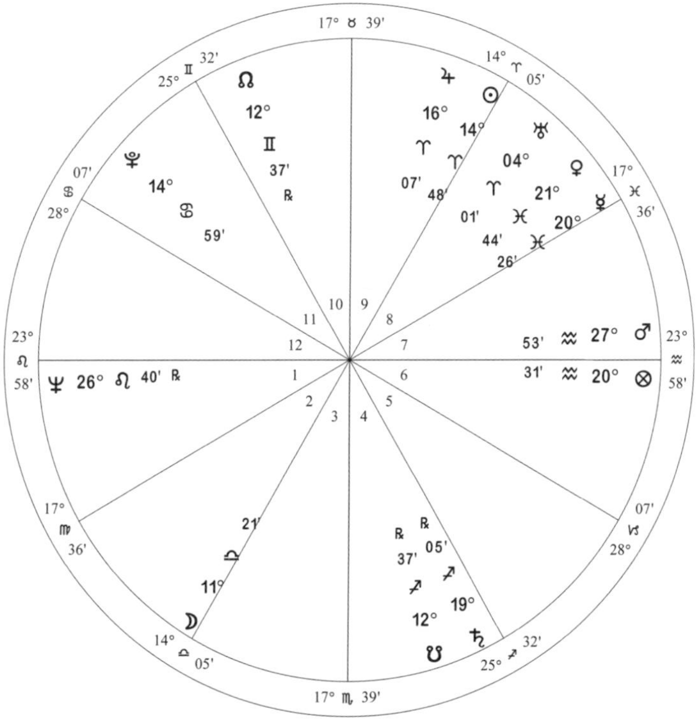

Pl	Ruler	Exalt	Tripl	Term	Face	Detri	Fall	Score
Dorothean Ess. Dig. (No Mut Rec. Points)								
☉	♂	☉ +	☉ +	☿	☉ +	♀	♄	+8
☽	♀	♄	♄	♃	♄ m	♂	☉	- 5 P
☿	♃	♀	♀	♂	♂	☿ -	☿ -	- 14 P
♀	♃	♀ +	♀ +	♂	♂	☿	☿	+7
♂	♄	--	♄	♂ +	☽	☉	--	+2
♃	♂	☉	☉	☿	☉	♀	♄	- 5 P
♄	♃	☋	☉	♄ +	☽ m	☿	--	+2
☊	☿	☊ +	♄	♃	♂	♃	--	--
⊗	♄	--	♄	♃	☽	☉	--	--
As	☉	--	☉	♃	♂	♄	--	--
Mc	♀	☽	♀	♃	☽	♂	--	--
☋	♃	☋	☉	♀	☽	☿	--	--

Hs	Alm. (Pto)
1	☉
2	☿
3	♄
4	♂
5	♃
6	♄
7	♄
8	♃
9	☉
10	♀
11	☿
12	☽

Example 5-1. Maya Angelou nativity

Maya Angelou
Saint Louis, Missouri
Time Zone: 6 hours West

April 4, 1945
38N37'38" 90W11'52"
Tropical Regiomontanus
Solar Return for April 4, 1945 in Saint Louis, Missouri

6:07:22 PM
War Time

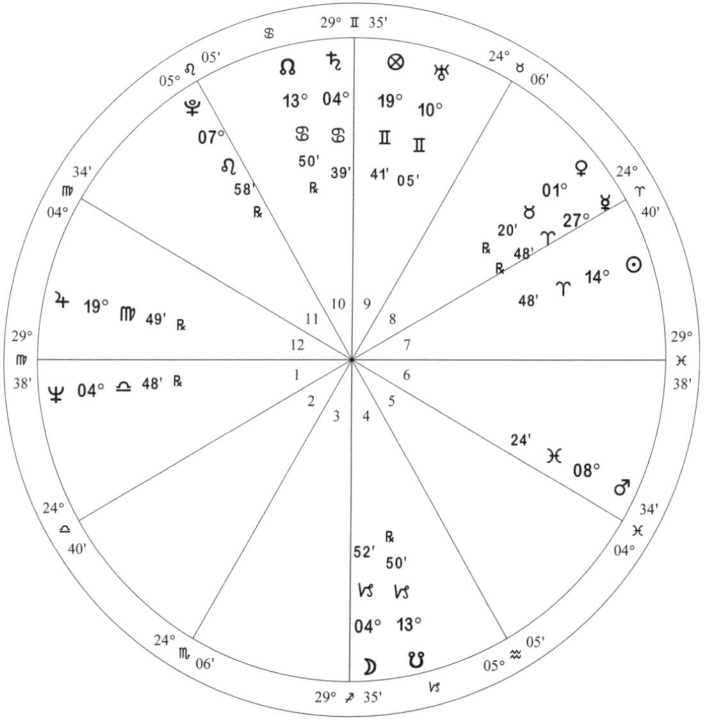

Pl	Ruler	Exalt	Tripl	Term	Face	Detri	Fall	Score
Dorothean Ess. Dig. (No Mut Rec. Points)								
☉	♂	☉ +	☉ +	☿	☉ +	♀	♄	+8
☽	♄ m	♂	♀	♀	♃	☽ -	♃	- 10 P
☿	♂	☉	☉	♄	♀ m	♀	♄	- 5 P
♀	♀ +	☽	♀ +	♀ +	☿ m	♂	--	+10
♂	♃	♀	♀	♃	♄	☿	☿	- 5 P
♃	☿	☿	♀	♄	♀	♃ -	♀	- 10 P
♄	☽ m	♃	♀	♂	♀	♄ -	♂	- 10 P
☊	☽	♃	♀	☿	☿	♄	♂	--
⊗	☿	☊	♄	♀	♂	♃	--	--
As	☿	☿	♀	♂	☿	♃	♀	--
Mc	☿	☊	♄	♂	☉	♃	--	--
☋	♄	♂	♀	♃	♂	☽	♃	--

Hs	Alm. (Pto)
1	☿
2	♄
3	♂
4	♃
5	♄
6	♀
7	♃
8	☉♂
9	♀
10	☿
11	☉
12	☿

Example 5-1a. Maya Angelou pregnancy solar return for 1945

Peggy Fleming's Son Andy

As we examine Peggy Fleming's solar return for the birth of her older son, let's recall a few facts. The probability of pregnancy from a single act of sexual intercourse without contraception is estimated at 3-5%. This is both a low and a high number, depending on one's desires at the time. The point is: very few adults of fertile years have sex only once, and the sociological experience that we know from eras past is that married women who proved fertile at all could expect to spend many if not most of their fertile years pregnant. As it is, there are estimates that the odds of a conception for a healthy couple in their twenties is around 85% for a year of unprotected sex. Babies definitely happen.

So when we examine the chart for Peggy, or any other married woman in her fertile years who is trying to get pregnant, what should we look for when we learn that the odds are 85% that she will become pregnant within a given year if she is not using birth control? Is pregnancy then an unusual enough event to remark upon? This begins to give us a hint that the biological side of our existence may not be seen extremely well from the chart, *if it is operating within the norms of our existence as a species.*

It is our choices that have made pregnancy a more unusual event; not our fate. It is our fate to be part of a biological matrix in which more reproductive potential can be manifested in a generation than our ecosystems can often support. As such, we can only expect the solar return to show issues of pregnancy when the curtain of fate is in an unusual position for us *personally.* What does this mean? It means that pregnancy only shows in the solar return chart (at the birth location) when the tendency toward fertility is either especially strong or especially weak. The default setting is: let nature take its course.

What I have said about nativities does not apply to horaries or electionals. There is a long history of asking about when one would have a child – and that is as much a legitimate question now as it ever was. Similarly, there was a traditional electional system for the begetting of children, especially for picking the gender. I have used the latter system in part for picking times for clinic fertility treatment procedures. These questions do not relate so much to our biology as to the path of choices followed by the fate we are currently traversing.

So as we address Peggy's situation leading to her first successful pregnancy, are we looking at the need for fate to take a left turn, or are we looking at things working out according to the laws of biology? As a world-class athlete, even a retired Olympian, Peggy kept herself in excellent physical condition. We know that in women, such conditioning can have an impact on the female hormones, disrupting the "normal" cycle of estrogen and progesterone. So it would be conceivable that Peggy would need an extra nudge to the finger of fate to get pregnant.

Peggy's natal chart shows average fertility. With Moon in the 5th house, it is not surprising she wanted children: Aries is not an especially fertile sign, but it's not barren either – and it does actually describe the outcome in her case, which was two boys. Venus rules her 5th, and her Venus is in Gemini, a double but barren sign. On the other hand, her Ascendant is late Scorpio, a fertile sign, and her Mars ruling that is weak in Libra, an average sign. She does have Jupiter in the first house, which is a fertile planet, but in an average sign and retrograde, so Jupiter doesn't add much to the delineation. And her Sun is in the barren sign of Leo.

Her natal chart thus shows a lower than average fertility, it does not deny fertility. The presence of barren planets suggests that there may well be periods where she is infertile, or there may be miscarriages along the way. This matches her personal history as she has given it.

Because the human gestation period is nine months, it is frequent that a woman becomes pregnant under one solar return, and gives birth in the next. This was the case with Peggy. Peggy became pregnant under her 1975 solar return, and then gave birth to Andy on 30 January 1977. She was 28 at the time. Her age tells

Peggy Fleming
San Jose, California
Time Zone: 8 hours West

July 27, 1948
37N20'07" 121W53'38"
Tropical Regiomontanus
NATAL CHART

3:39 PM
Daylight Saving Time

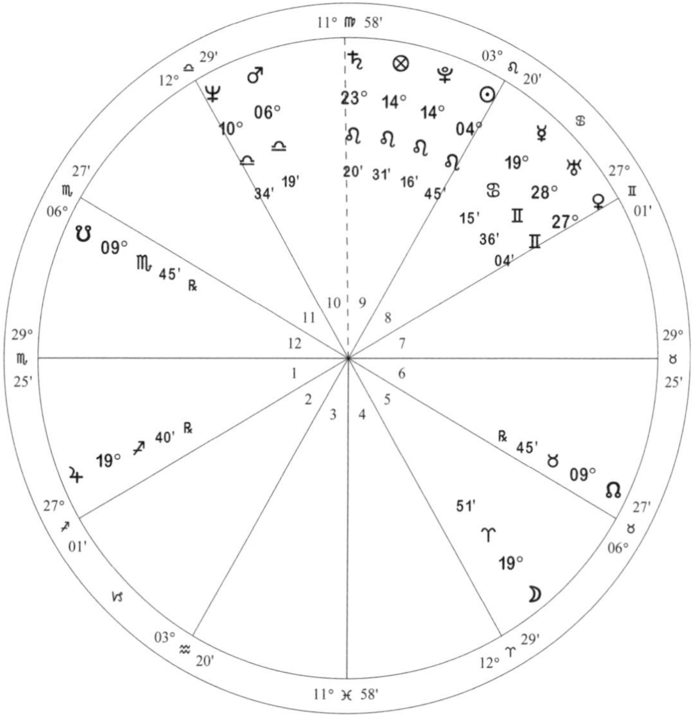

Peggy Fleming
San Jose, California
Time Zone: 8 hours West

July 28, 1975
37N20'07" 121W53'38"
Tropical Regiomontanus
Solar Return for July 28, 1975 in San Jose, California

3:54:15 AM
Daylight Saving Time

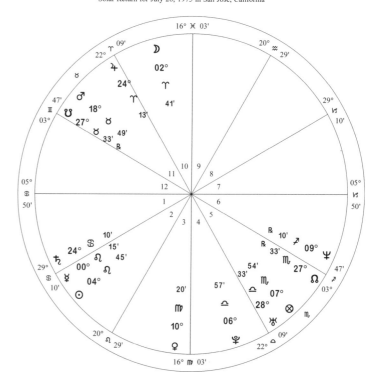

Example 5-2. Peggy Fleming nativity

Example 5-2a. Peggy Fleming pregnancy solar return for 1975

Dorothean Ess. Dig. (No Mut Rec. Points) — Nativity

Pl	Ruler	Exalt	Tripl	Term	Face	Detri	Fall	Score
☉	☉ +	--	☉ +	☉ +	♄	♄	♄	--	+8
☽	♂	☉	☉	☿	♀	♀	♄	- 5 P
☿	☿ +	☿ +	♃	♀ +	♀ +	♃	♂	+3
♀	☿	☊	♄	♂ m	♂ m	♃	☉	- 5 P
♂	♃ +	☌	♄	♀ m	♄ m	☿	☉	- 10 P
♃	♃ +	--	☉	♄	♂ m	☿	--	+5
♄	☿	--	♄	♀ m	☿	♃	--	- 10 P
☊	♃	☽	♃	♀	♀	☿	☿	--
⊗	♂	☉	☉	♀	♄	♀	♄	--
As	♂	--	♀	♄	♀	♀	☽	--
Mc	☿	--	♄	♀	♀	♃	☿	--
☋	☿	--	♀	♀	♃	♃	☉	--

Hs	Alm. (Pto)
1	
2	
3	
4	
5	
6	
7	
8	
9	
10	
11	
12	

Dorothean Ess. Dig. (No Mut Rec. Points) — Solar Return 1975

Pl	Ruler	Exalt	Tripl	Term	Face	Detri	Fall	Score
☉	☉ +	--	♃	♄	♄	♄	--	+5
☽	♂	☉	♃	♃	♂ m		♄	- 5 P
☿	☿ +	☿ +	♃	♃	♃	♀		- 5 P
♀	☿	☿	☽	♀ +	♀ +	♃	♀ -	- 1
♂	♂ +	☉	☽	♃ m	☽ m	♂ -		- 10 P
♃	☿	☊	♃ +	♀	♀	☿		+3
♄	☽	♃	♂	♂	♃	♄ -	--	- 10 P
☊	♃	♃	♃	♀	♀	☿	☿	--
⊗	♂	☉	♃	☿	♀	♀	♄	--
As	☽	♃	♂	♀	♀	♄	♂	--
Mc	♃	☊	♃	☿	☿	☿	--	--
☋	☿	--	♀	♀	♀	♃	☉	--

Hs	Alm. (Pto)
1	☽
2	♃ ☿
3	☉ ♃
4	
5	♃
6	☿ ♃
7	☽ ♃
8	♄ ♃
9	☿
10	♃
11	♄
12	☿

Peggy Fleming
San Jose, California
Time Zone: 8 hours West

July 27, 1976
37N20'07" 121W53'38"
Tropical Regiomontanus
Solar Return for July 27, 1976 in San Jose, California

9:45:56 AM
Daylight Saving Time

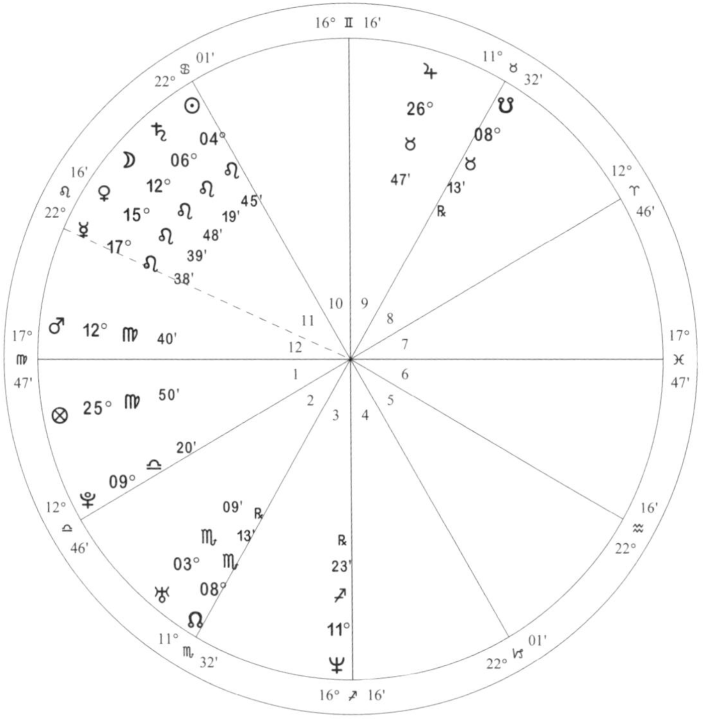

Dorothean Ess. Dig. (No Mut Rec. Points)								
Pl	Ruler	Exalt	Tripl	Term	Face	Detri	Fall	Score
☉	☉ +	--	☉ +	♄	♄	♄	--	+8
☽	☉	--	☉	☿	♃	♄	--	- 5 P
☿	☉	--	☉	♀	♃	♄	--	- 5 P
♀	☉	--	☉	♀ +	♃	♄	--	+2
♂	☿	☿	♀	♀	♀	♃	♀	- 5 P
♃	♀	☽	♀	♂	♄	♂	--	- 5 P
♄	☉	--	☉	☿	♄ +	♄ -	--	- 4
☊	♂	--	♀	♃	♂	♀	☽	--
⊗	☿	☿	♀	♂	☿	♃	♀	--
As	☿	☿	♀	♃	♀	♃	♀	--
Mc	☿	☊	♄	♀	♂	♃	--	--
☋	♀	☽	♀	☿	☿	♂	--	--

Hs	Alm. (Pto)
1	☿
2	♄
3	♂
4	♃
5	♂
6	♄
7	♃
8	☉
9	♀
10	☿
11	☽
12	☉

Example 5-2b. Peggy Fleming pregnancy solar return for 1976

you what a quick check of the chart confirms: that transiting Saturn had gotten back to the sign of her natal Saturn at the time she gave birth. But it had not done so when she became pregnant.

The year of her pregnancy, the SR-Moon was in the same sign as her radix Moon. SR-Venus was in the other Mercury-ruled sign: Virgo instead of her natal Gemini. Peggy's natal Mars is in Detriment; this solar return, Mars was again in Detriment, but in Venus's other sign, Taurus. These two situations are both variations on the idea of ***planets on the same journey***: the Hellenistic concept that planets in signs ruled by the same dispositor become linked, because the same planet rules their fate.

Peggy's 1975 solar return had three placements in the 5th house: Uranus, the Part of Fortune, and the North Node. The Ascendant was the fertile sign of Cancer, and Saturn was in Cancer in the 1st. The nodal axis was in the opposite signs from their natal positions.

All of this leads to the conclusion that Peggy was more fertile than usual in that year, and Venus, ruling the developing fetus, was trine the malefics, which argues that there was no intrinsic danger to it. But as the following year rules the second part of the pregnancy and the birth itself, we now turn to the 1976 solar return to see if any later issues appear.

In the 1976 solar return, the pregnancy and birth is ruled by Saturn in Detriment – but in this case, in the sign of Peggy's natal Saturn. This fortifies the position of Saturn, not weakens it. Saturn is combust, which isn't so good. The death of the foetis would be shown from the 8th from the 5th, which is the 12th. Here, Saturn ruled as well. Mars was in the 12th, but conjunct the angle: and not afflicting Saturn in any case. The Moon was separating from Saturn. There is no argument of death. I suspect that the combustion of Saturn may show the challenge that faces the child of a famous parent: that of not being lost in the glow. But it was not an argument of life-threatening danger.

Peggy Fleming's Second Son Todd

Here is the solar return chart for Peggy's second son. By the time she had Todd, she was forty. She and her husband Greg really wanted a second child, and had been trying for some time to conceive. The process had become frustrating enough that they were beginning to consider adoption as an alternative. As a result, I am showing three solar returns. Peggy delivered Todd in 1988 a bit over a month after her birthday: so the majority of her pregnancy took place under her 1987 solar return. But I have included the 1986 one to also show the process that was leading up to the successful pregnancy – and why it did not take place earlier under the 1986 solar return period.

There was a time during the 20th century when pregnancy at the age of forty was considered dangerous, but this particular prejudice was gone by the time that Peggy reached that age. In fact, her continued athleticism both contributed to her overall vigor, but possibly provided a check to her fertility. And so we see in her solar return for 1986, the unsuccessful outcome is shown almost exclusively from the condition of SR-Mercury:

- SR-Mercury retrograde in Cancer rules the 5th (Peggy's natal Mercury is in Cancer, but direct)
- SR-Mercury square Uranus
- SR-Mercury at the Bendings
- SR-Mercury at the 7th house cusp which *could* give a danger of miscarriage
- The SR-Ascendant 29 degrees, which does give rather a tinge of desperation
- The SR-Moon void of course

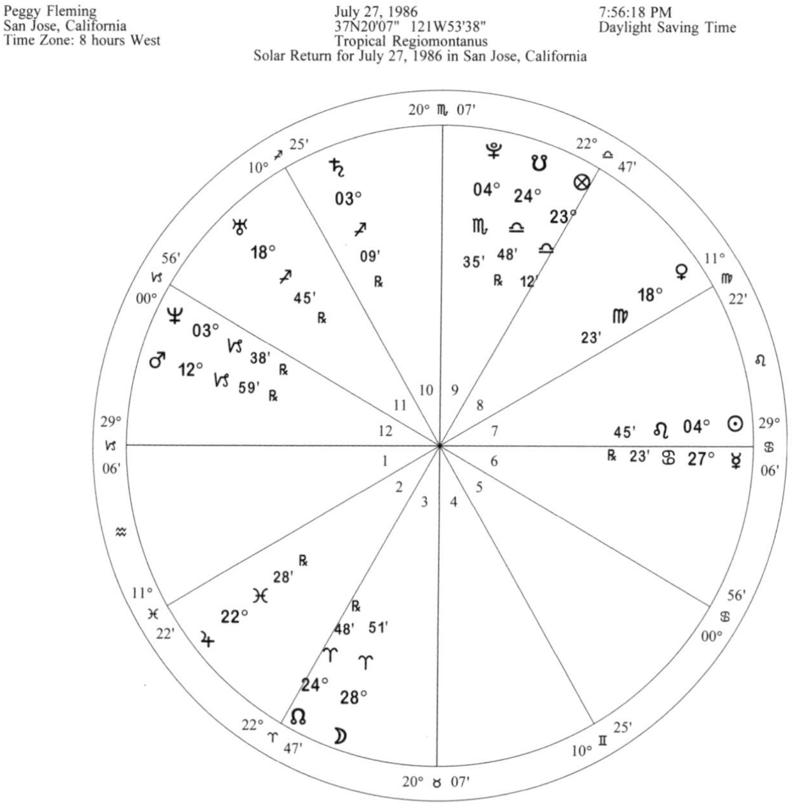
Peggy Fleming
San Jose, California
Time Zone: 8 hours West
July 27, 1986
37N20'07" 121W53'38"
Tropical Regiomontanus
7:56:18 PM
Daylight Saving Time
Solar Return for July 27, 1986 in San Jose, California

Dorothean Ess. Dig. (No Mut Rec. Points)								
Pl	Ruler	Exalt	Tripl	Term	Face	Detri	Fall	Score
☉	☉ +	--	☉ +	♄	♄	♄	--	+8
☽	♂	☉	☉	♄	♀	♀	♄	- 5 P
☿	☽	♃	♀	♄	☽	♄	♂	- 5 P
♀	☿	☿	♀ +	♄	♀ +	♃	♀ -	+0
♂	♄	♂ +	♀	♃ m	♂ +	☽	♃	+5
♃	♃ +	♀	♀	♂ m	♂	☿	☿	+5
♄	♃	☋	☉	♃	☿	☿	--	- 5 P
☊	♂	☉	☉	♂	♀	♀	♄	--
⊗	♀	♄	♄	☿	♃	♂	☉	--
As	♄	♂	♀	♄	☉	☽	♃	--
Mc	♂	--	♀	♀	♀	♀	☽	--
☋	♀	♄	♄	☊	♃	♂	☉	--

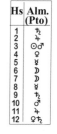

Hs	Alm. (Pto)
1	♄
2	♃
3	☉♂
4	♀
5	☿
6	☽
7	☽
8	☿
9	♄
10	♂
11	♃
12	♀♄

Example 5-3a. Peggy Fleming pregnancy solar return for 1986

Peggy Fleming
San Jose, California
Time Zone: 8 hours West

July 28, 1987
37N20'07" 121W53'38"
Tropical Regiomontanus
Solar Return for July 28, 1987 in San Jose, California

1:34:06 AM
Daylight Saving Time

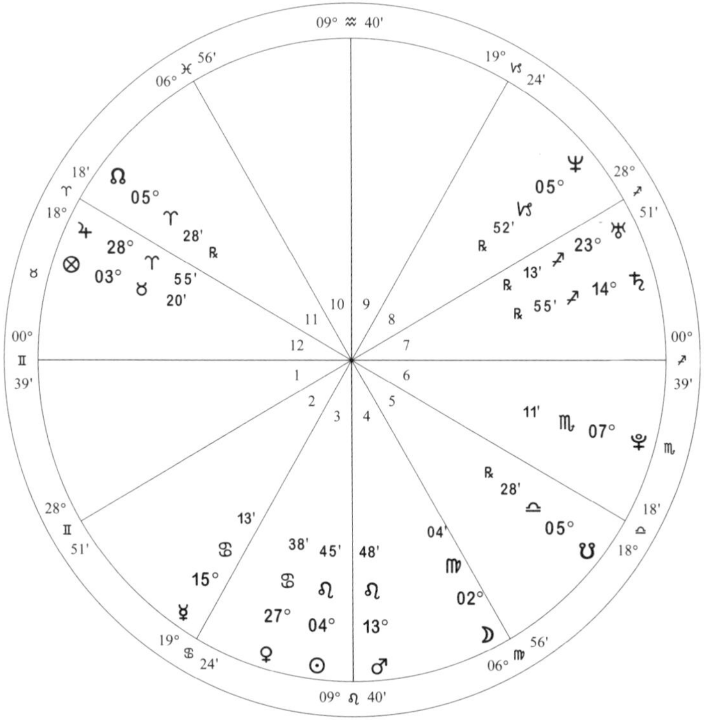

Dorothean Ess. Dig. (No Mut Rec. Points)								
Pl	Ruler	Exalt	Tripl	Term	Face	Detri	Fall	Score
☉	☉ +	--	♃	♄	♄	♄	--	+5
☽	☿ m	☿	☽ +	☿	☉	♃	♀	+3
☿	☽ m	♃	♂	☿ +	☿ +	♄	♂	+3
♀	☽	♃	♂	♄	☽	♄	♂	- 5 P
♂	☉	--	♃	♀	♃	♄	--	- 5 P
♃	♂	☉	♃ +	♄	♀	♀	♄	+3
♄	♃	☋	♃	☿	☽	☿	--	- 5 P
☊	♂	☉	♃	♃	♂	♀	♄	--
⊗	♀	☽	☽	♀	☿	♂	--	--
As	☿	☊	☿	☿	♃	♃	--	--
Mc	♄	--	☿	☿	♀	☉	--	--
☋	♀	♄	☿	♄	☽	♂	☉	--

Hs	Alm. (Pto)
1	☿
2	☿
3	☽
4	☉
5	☿
6	♀♄
7	♃
8	♃
9	♂
10	☿♄
11	♀
12	☉♂

Example 5-3b. Peggy Fleming pregnancy solar return for 1987

Peggy Fleming
San Jose, California
Time Zone: 8 hours West

July 28, 1987
37N20'07" 121W53'38"
Tropical Regiomontanus
Solar Return for July 28, 1987 in San Jose, California

1:34:06 AM
Daylight Saving Time

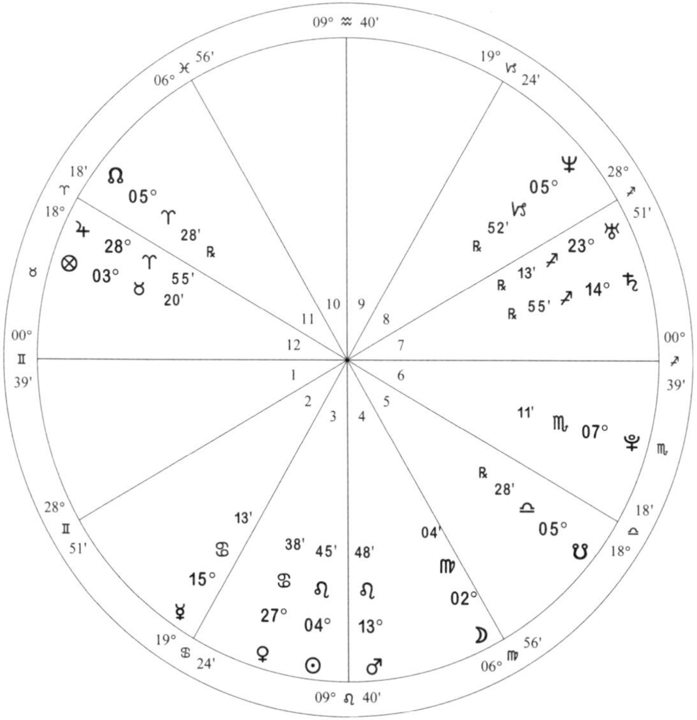

Dorothean Ess. Dig. (No Mut Rec. Points)								
Pl	Ruler	Exalt	Tripl	Term	Face	Detri	Fall	Score
☉	☉ +	--	♃	♄	♄	♄	--	+5
☽	☿ m	☿	☽ +	☿	☉	♃	♀	+3
☿	☽ m	♃	♂	☿ +	☿ +	♄	♂	+3
♀	☽	♃	♂	♄	☽	♄	♂	- 5 P
♂	☉	--	♃	♀	♃	♄	--	- 5 P
♃	♂	☉	♃ +	♄	♀	♀	♄	+3
♄	♃	☋	♃	☿	☽	☿	--	- 5 P
☊	♂	☉	♃	♃	♂	♀	♄	--
⊗	♀	☽	☽	♀	☿	♂	--	--
As	☿	☊	☿	☿	♃	♃	--	--
Mc	♄	--	☿	☿	♀	☉	--	--
☋	♀	♄	☿	♄	☽	♂	☉	--

Hs	Alm. (Pto)
1	☿
2	☿
3	☽
4	☉
5	☿
6	♀♄
7	♃
8	♃
9	♂
10	☿♄
11	♀
12	☉♂

Example 5-3c. Peggy Fleming pregnancy solar return for 1988

Contrast this with 1987, where again, Mercury rules the 5th house cusp:

- SR-Mercury in Cancer is now direct, matching Peggy's natal Mercury
- The Moon is Virgo in a barren sign, but at the 5th house cusp, in an early degree
- The SR-Ascendant is 0 Gemini.
- SR-Mars in Cancer: Mars rules Peggy's 5th natally.

There are still quite a few barren signs represented, but the late degrees from the previous solar return have disappeared, and early degrees suggest that something new is happening, not the end of an old story. The actual birth fell in the following year. Here, the presence of three Outer Planets in the 5th does suggest a little help from modern medicine at the birth. Does SR-Pluto at the IC act as a signature for Todd being her last child? I don't know.

Mary Godwin Shelley's First Successful Pregnancy

Mary Shelley marks an interesting transition, because according to her biographer, there is some evidence that she and Percy began using contraception: but not at first. They were in the circle of Byron – and he was notorious for it, and we know there was a personal connection here, because Mary's half-sister Claire Clairmont seduced Byron and got pregnant by him – and he was evidently quite furious that she didn't use contraception.[4]

In 1815, Mary was young, in love, and soon pregnant, and then soon miscarrying, and then soon pregnant again. In 1815, Mary's solar return had Saturn ruling the 5th – SR-Saturn retrograde in Aquarius. Jupiter and Venus were in the 1st house in Libra, with the SR-Moon in Leo opposite that Saturn. Despite the barrenness of Leo, this wasn't enough to prevent pregnancy, although it may have contributed to the miscarriage. In the following year, SR-Uranus was conjunct the

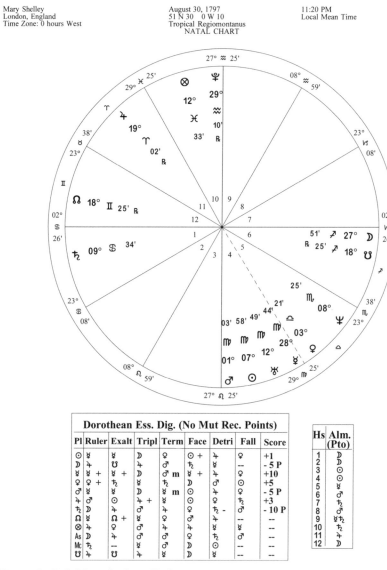

Mary Shelley
London, England
Time Zone: 0 hours West

August 30, 1797
51 N 30   0 W 10
Tropical Regiomontanus
NATAL CHART

11:20 PM
Local Mean Time

Example 5-4. Mary Godwin Shelley nativity

Mary Shelley
London, England
Time Zone: 0 hours West

September 1, 1815
51 N 30 0 W 10
Tropical Regiomontanus
Solar Return for September 1, 1815 in London, England

7:47:33 AM
Local Mean Time

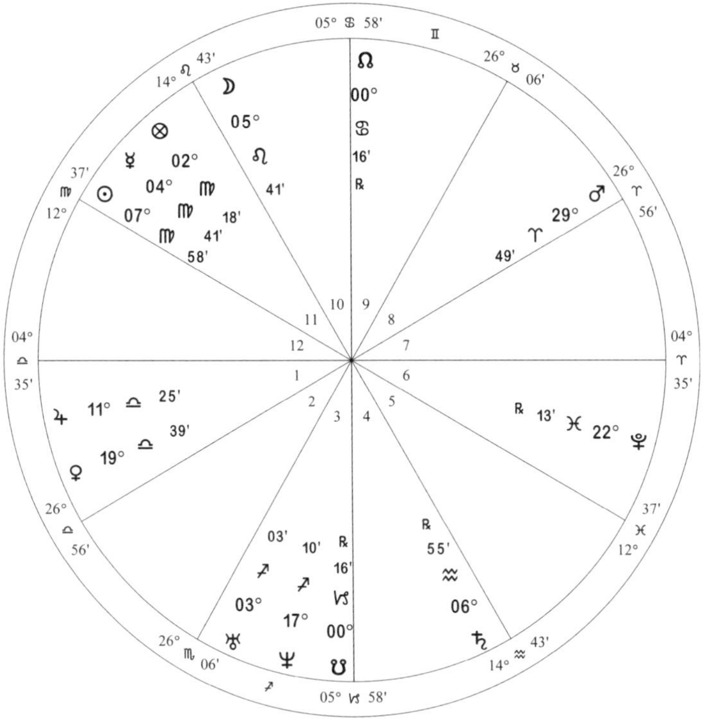

Dorothean Ess. Dig. (No Mut Rec. Points)

Pl	Ruler	Exalt	Tripl	Term	Face	Detri	Fall	Score
☉	☿	☿	♀	♀	☉ +	♃	♀	+1
☽	☉	--	☉	♄	♄	♄	--	- 5 P
☿	☿ +	☿ +	♀	☿ +	☉	♃	♀	+11
♀	♀ +	♄	♄	☿	♄ m	♂	☉	+5
♂	♂ +	☉	☉	♄	♀	♀	♄	+5
♃	♀	♄	♄	♃ +	♄	♂	☉	+2
♄	♄ +	--	♄ +	☿	♀ m	☉	--	+8
☊	☽	♃	♀	♂	♀	♄	♂	--
⊗	☿	☿	♀	☿	☉	♃	♀	--
As	♀	♄	♄	♄	☽	♂	☉	--
Mc	☽	♃	♀	♂	♀	♄	♂	--
☋	♄	♂	♀	♀	♃	☽	♃	--

Hs	Alm. (Pto)
1	♄
2	♄
3	♂
4	♀♄
5	♄
6	♃
7	☉
8	☉
9	♀
10	☽
11	☉
12	☿

Example 5-4a. Mary Godwin Shelley pregnancy solar return for 1815

Mary Shelley
London, England
Time Zone: 0 hours West

August 31, 1816
51 N 30 0 W 10
Tropical Regiomontanus
Solar Return for August 31, 1816 in London, England

1:36:16 PM
Local Mean Time

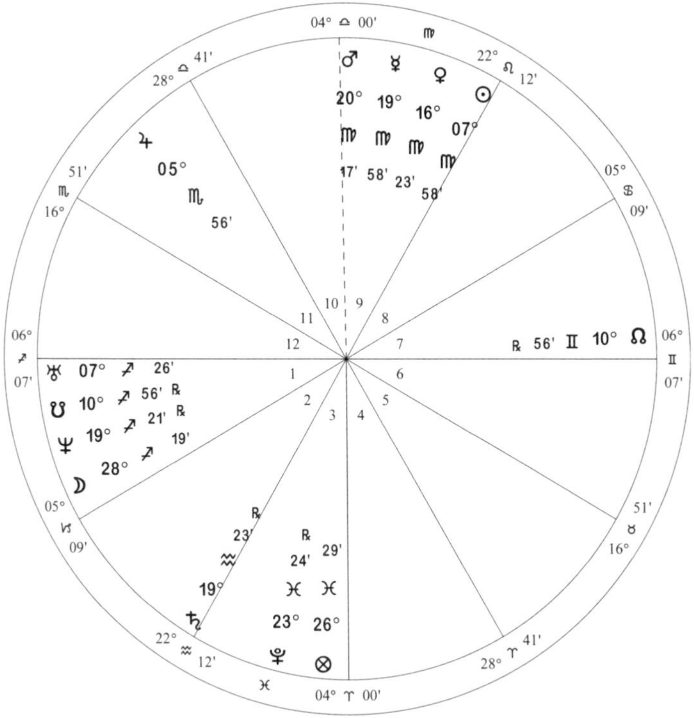

Dorothean Ess. Dig. (No Mut Rec. Points)

Pl	Ruler	Exalt	Tripl	Term	Face	Detri	Fall	Score
☉	☿	☿	♀	♀	☉ +	♃	♀	+1
☽	♃	☋	☉	♂	♄	☿	--	- 5 P
☿	☿ +	☿ +	♀	♄	♀	♃	♀	+9
♀	☿	☿	♀ +	♃	♀ +	♃	♀ -	+0
♂	☿	☿	♀	♄	☿	♃	♀	- 5 P
♃	♂	--	♀	♂	♂	♀	☽	- 5 P
♄	♄ +	--	♄ +	♀	☿	☉	--	+8
☊	☿	☊ +	♄	♃	♂	♃	--	--
⊗	♃	♀	♀	♄	♂	☿	☿	--
As	♃	☋	☉	♃	☿	☿	--	--
Mc	♀	♄	♄	♄	☽	♂	☉	--
☋	♃	☋	☉	♀	☽	☿	--	--

Hs	Alm. (Pto)
1	♃
2	♀♄
3	♄
4	☉
5	☉
6	♀
7	☿
8	☽
9	☉
10	♄
11	♄
12	♂

Example 5-4b. Mary Godwin Shelley pregnancy solar return for 1816

solar return Ascendant, and SR-Mars ruled the 5th. Mars was in Virgo, the sign of Mary's natal Mars [SEE PAGE 116], and SR-Mercury was likewise in Mary's natal sign. Again, having some barren signs was not enough to prevent the pregnancy, or, in this case, the birth either. SR-Moon at 28 Sagittarius was partile trine the 5th house cusp.

I cannot honestly say that this has developed an argument for me that her son William, born January 24, 1816, would die at the age of three. Here, I think we would have to look at *his* nativity, and possibly hers and Percy's for the death year.

We are again seeing the situation given that the default argument is that, if Percy and Mary were having a sexual relationship, then Mary would get pregnant. In this biological mode, pregnancy is likely, and miscarriage is not uncommon.

Mary Godwin Shelley's Final Miscarriage

Life can be so strange. In the summer of 1822, Mary Godwin Shelley had a miscarriage and hemorrhaging from it that was so severe that she almost died. It was quick thinking by Percy to have her sit in cold water to stop the bleeding that saved her life. A month later, he was dead from drowning. We shall discuss this chart in Chapter 11 as it related to Percy's death, but I want to use this to raise the question, as we will with Eleanor Roosevelt's child who died: is it possible to see the *unsuccessful* pregnancies in a solar return? We have already established that pregnancy itself is such an extremely normal outcome for couples of average health in their early adult years, but the same argument should apply to miscarriages which, without some of the more aggressive methods of modern medicine, ought to also be fairly common.

In choosing this case, we are choosing an extreme. At the time of Mary's miscarriage, there couldn't have been a thought about this being her last pregnancy – once she survived the miscarriage, anyway! Both she and Percy were still in their twenties, and no doubt expected a much longer life together than they had.

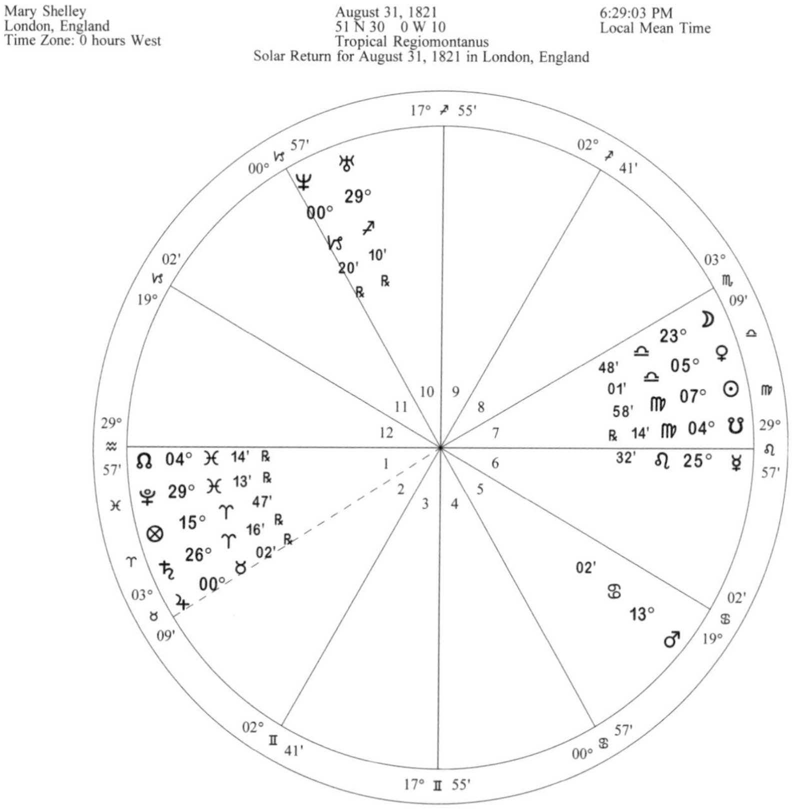
Mary Shelley
London, England
Time Zone: 0 hours West
August 31, 1821
51 N 30 0 W 10
Tropical Regiomontanus
Solar Return for August 31, 1821 in London, England
6:29:03 PM
Local Mean Time

Dorothean Ess. Dig. (No Mut Rec. Points)

Pl	Ruler	Exalt	Tripl	Term	Face	Detri	Fall	Score
☉	☿ m	☿	♀	♀	☉ +	♃	♀	+1
☽	♀	♄	♄	☿	♃	♂	☉	- 5 P
☿	☉ m	--	☉	♂ m	♂ m	♄	--	- 5 P
♀	♀ +	♄	♄	♄	☽	♂	☉	+5
♂	☽	♃	♀	☿ m	☿ m	♄	♂ -	- 9 P
♃	♀	☽	♀	♀	☿	♂	--	- 5 P
♄	♂	☉	☉	♄ +	♀	♀	♄ -	- 2
☊	♃	♀	♀	♀	♄	☿	☿	--
⊗	♂	☉	☉	☿	☉	♀	♄	--
As	♄	--	♄	♂	☽	☉	--	--
Mc	♃	☋	☉	☿	☽	☿	--	--
☋	☿	☿	♀	☿	☉	♃	♀	--

Hs	Alm. (Pto)
1	♄
2	♀
3	☿
4	☿
5	☽
6	☽
7	☉
8	♂
9	♃
10	♃
11	♀♄
12	♂

Example 5-5. Mary Godwin Shelley miscarriage solar return for 1821

Mary had become pregnant under this solar return. We see Cancer on the 5th house cusp, a fertile sign. We also see the Moon applying to the opposition to Saturn, which actually makes sense as an argument for miscarriage, in an era where that was quite common. That 5th house cusp was quite close to Mary's natal Ascendant. The 29 Aquarius rising of the solar return was just a shade before fertile Pisces, again hinting at fertility shortly after the solar return. Venus was in Libra, the sign of her natal Venus: but squared by Mars, thereby negating the positive outcome of Gadbury's Aphorism #1 and providing the negative report of Aphorism #11. Mars in the 5th activates Gadbury's Aphorism #6 about the death of a child [SEE PAGES 108-109].

Is the Uranus square Pluto at 29 degrees the signature for this as Mary's last pregnancy? That square touches her natal Moon, Mercury, *and* Pluto, as well as her 5th house cusp. That 29 degree Aquarius Ascendant is partile conjunct her radix Pluto. So perhaps we do have some suggestive ideas for what happened. Her fertility was coming to an end, wrenched from her by a massive tragedy that divided her life into before and after.

Dorothy Hamill's Daughter Alexandra

Bouncing back to the era of more widespread contraception, we can begin by simply asking: does Dorothy have a chart which supports the argument of having children? Yes, she does [SEE EXAMPLE 3-4 ON PAGE 75]. While her Ascendant is ruled by Saturn, she has the Moon and Mars in the 1st house in Pisces, a fruitful sign. She has the fruitful sign Cancer on the 5th house cusp, and the Part of Fortune in the 5th. From her standpoint, everything else is choice and circumstance, unless her husband of the time is infertile.

When she married Kenneth Forsythe, she did want to settle down, and to many people, having a child is part of that process. Dorothy became pregnant under her 1987 solar return, and delivered under her 1988 one. In the 1987 return, Saturn was ruler

Dorothy Hamill
Chicago, Illinois
Time Zone: 6 hours West

July 27, 1987
41 N 51   87 W 39
Tropical Regiomontanus
Solar Return for July 27, 1987 in Chicago, Illinois

9:00:44 AM
Daylight Saving Time

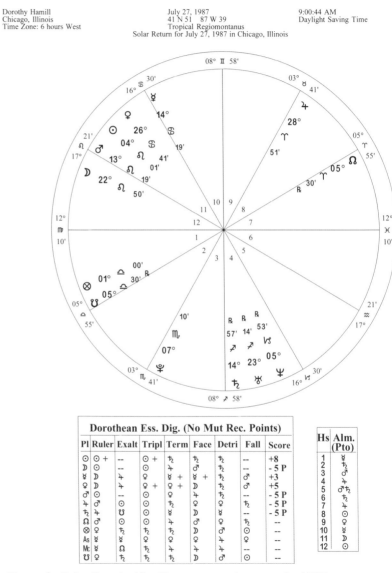

Example 5-6a. Dorothy Hamill pregnancy solar return for 1987

Dorothy Hamill
Chicago, Illinois
Time Zone: 6 hours West

July 26, 1988
41 N 51 87 W 39
Tropical Regiomontanus
Solar Return for July 26, 1988 in Chicago, Illinois

2:48:59 PM
Daylight Saving Time

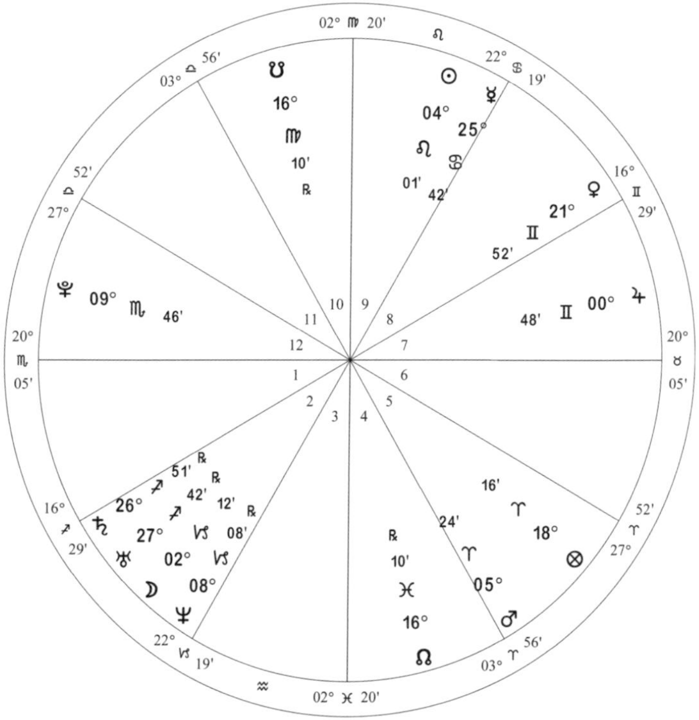

Dorothean Ess. Dig. (No Mut Rec. Points)								
Pl	Ruler	Exalt	Tripl	Term	Face	Detri	Fall	Score
☉	☉ +	--	☉ +	♄	♄	♄	--	+8
☽	♄	♂	♀	♀	♃	☽ -	♃	- 10 P
☿	☽	♃	♀	♀	☽	♄	♂	- 5 P
♀	☿	☊	♄	♄	☉	♃	--	- 5 P
♂	♂ +	☉	☉	♃	♂ +	♀	♄	+6
♃	☿	☊	♄	☿	♃ +	♃ -	--	- 4
♄	♃	☋	☉	♂	♄ +	☿	--	+1
☊	♃	♀	♀	☿	♃	☿	☿	--
⊗	♂	☉	☉	☿	☉	♀	♄	--
As	♂	--	♀	♀	♀	♀	☽	--
Mc	☿	☿	♀	☿	☉	♃	♀	--
☋	☿	☿	♀	♃	♀	♃	♀	--

Hs	Alm. (Pto)
1	♂
2	♃
3	♂
4	♀
5	☉
6	☉
7	♀
8	☿
9	☽
10	☿
11	♄
12	♄

Example 5-6b. Dorothy Hamill pregnancy solar return for 1988

of the 5th, in Sagittarius retrograde. Saturn has Triplicity in the Fire signs, so Saturn is essentially dignified. When she delivered, a very dignified Mars ruled the 5th from the 5th itself, so no problems there. Again, her chart for 1987 doesn't scream pregnancy – but it doesn't have to. After all, she was the right age, they were trying, and so pregnancy happened.

Scott Hamilton's First Son Aidan

So far, we have seen only women's solar returns, and of course, men are involved in the process as well! Scott did not end up getting married until his professional skating career was winding down – but he is hardly retired, since he also has a career in broadcasting! The age of 45 is not impossibly late for a first-time father, but still, it's later than average.

So first: what does his natal chart say about children? We may note that the classic works on astrology indicate that the expectation was that the client was male, so when the astrologer refers to the 5th house for children, we know that they meant the same thing for men as for women. Scott's Moon is in the 5th house, an argument of children. Saturn rules his 5th house cusp, perhaps an argument of children delayed.

In 2003 when his first son was born, Saturn again was ruling the 5th house in the solar return, although the 5th house cusp was in the other sign of Saturn. Saturn was in Sagittarius, its sign of mixed Triplicity. The Moon was in the barren sign Virgo, conjunct the Part of Fortune. Scott had already suffered testicular cancer, and so he was in the process of transitioning to medically-directed hormones. Evidently, the Mars-Uranus conjunction in fertile Pisces gave him a productive opportunity. He took it!

Scott Hamilton
Toledo, Ohio
Time Zone: 5 hours West

August 28, 1958
41N39'50" 83W39'50"
Tropical Regiomontanus
NATAL CHART

9:00 AM
Standard Time

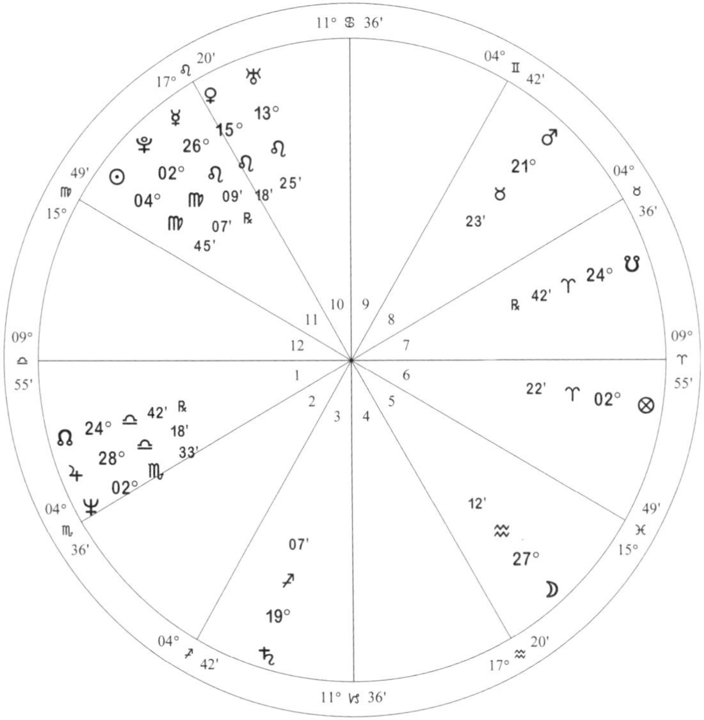

Dorothean Ess. Dig. (No Mut Rec. Points)								
Pl	Ruler	Exalt	Tripl	Term	Face	Detri	Fall	Score
☉	☿ m	☿	♀ m	☿	☉ +	♃	♀	+1
☽	♄	--	♄	♂	☽ +	☉	--	+1
☿	☉ m	--	☉	♂	♂	♄	--	- 5 P
♀	☉	--	☉ m	♀ +	♃	♄	--	+2
♂	♀	☽	♀	♃	♄	♂ -	--	- 10 P
♃	♀	♄	♄	☊	♃ +	♂	☉	+1
♄	♃	☋	☉	♄ +	☽	☿	--	+2
☊	♀	♄	♄	☊ +	♃	♂	☉	--
⊗	♂	☉	☉	♃	♂	♀	♄	--
As	♀	♄	♄	♀	☽	♂	☉	--
Mc	☽	♃	♀	♃	☿	♄	♂	--
☋	♂	☉	☉	♂	♀	♀	♄	--

Hs	Alm. (Pto)
1	♀♄
2	♂
3	♃
4	♂♄
5	♄
6	♃
7	☉
8	♀
9	☿
10	♃
11	☉
12	☿

Example 5-7. Scott Hamilton nativity

Scott Hamilton
Toledo, Ohio
Time Zone: 5 hours West

August 28, 2003
41N39'50" 83W33'19"
Tropical Regiomontanus
Solar Return for August 28, 2003 in Toledo, Ohio

7:19:57 AM
Daylight Saving Time

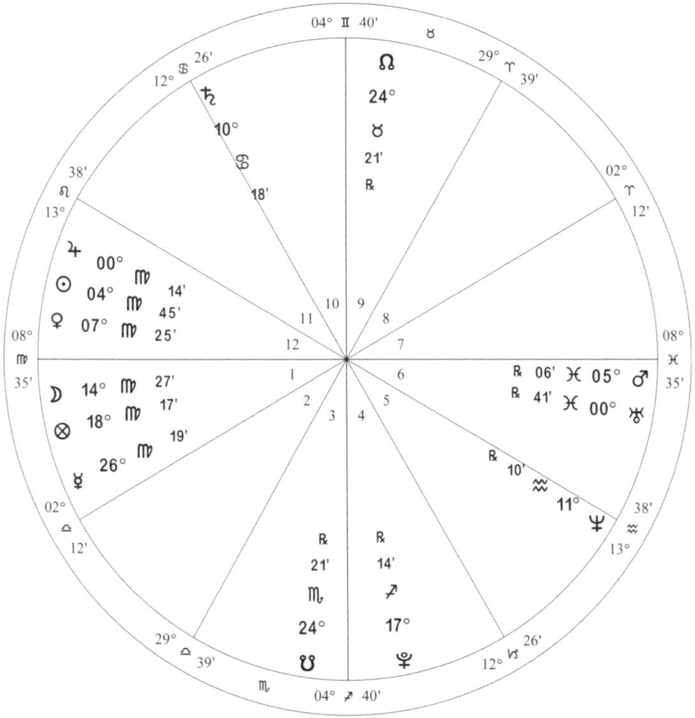

Dorothean Ess. Dig. (No Mut Rec. Points)								
Pl	Ruler	Exalt	Tripl	Term	Face	Detri	Fall	Score
☉	☿	☿	♀	☿	☉ +	♃	♀	+1
☽	☿	☿	♀	♃	♀	♃	♀	- 5 P
☿	☿ +	☿ +	♀	♂	☿ +	♃	♀	+10
♀	☿	☿	♀ +	♀ +	☉	♃	♀ -	+1
♂	♃	♀	♀	♀	♄	☿	☿	- 5 P
♃	☿	☿	♀	☿	☉	♃ -	♀	- 10 P
♄	☽	♃	♀	♃	☿	♄ -	♂	- 10 P
☊	♀	☽	♀	♄	♄	♂	--	--
⊗	☿	☿	♀	♄	♀	♃	♀	--
As	☿	☿	♀	♀	☉	♃	♀	--
Mc	☿	☊	♄	☿	♃	♃	--	--
☋	♂	--	♀	☿	♀	♀	☽	--

Hs	Alm. (Pto)
1	☿
2	♄
3	♄
4	♃
5	♂♄
6	♄
7	♃
8	☉
9	☉
10	☿
11	♃
12	☉

Example 5-7a. Scott Hamilton fatherhood solar return for 2003

Eleanor Roosevelt's Children

Eleanor and Franklin's history of having children shows every evidence of the biological pattern of fertility. There is no evidence that any contraception was considered, under the probable situation of, "we can afford any children we have." What stopped the process in the end was Eleanor's discovery of Franklin's affair, at which point, she stopped sleeping with him. But for the sake of argument, I have taken her solar returns for the first five years of her marriage. She was pregnant in four of them.

To begin: Eleanor had Taurus on the 5th house cusp natally *[see example 3-5 on page 79]*, with Venus in barren Virgo in a partile trine to the 5th house cusp. She also had the Moon in Cancer – the opposite argument from barren Virgo. It's fascinating here that Eleanor had the Sun-Moon square: here's the signature of the difficulty between the marriage partners when Eleanor discovered her husband's affair, and the signature marker for the end of her reproductive phase.

In these examples, I will also rather rigorously apply and discuss Gadbury's aphorisms, to give you an idea of how this can work in practice.

1905: daughter Anna is conceived. Jupiter was retrograde in the sign of its barren Detriment in the 5th house when Anna was conceived. The Capricorn Ascendant was ruled by Saturn in Aquarius retrograde. This isn't wildly fertile. It's clear from Gadbury's aphorisms that the condition of Venus and Jupiter are important. Venus is in its natal sign placement, which I would interpret as meaning that this was personally a good time for Eleanor to get pregnant, as long as her natal chart did not preclude child-bearing, which it did not. Jupiter is in the 5th according to Gadbury's aphorism 2, but in a barren sign, not a fertile one.

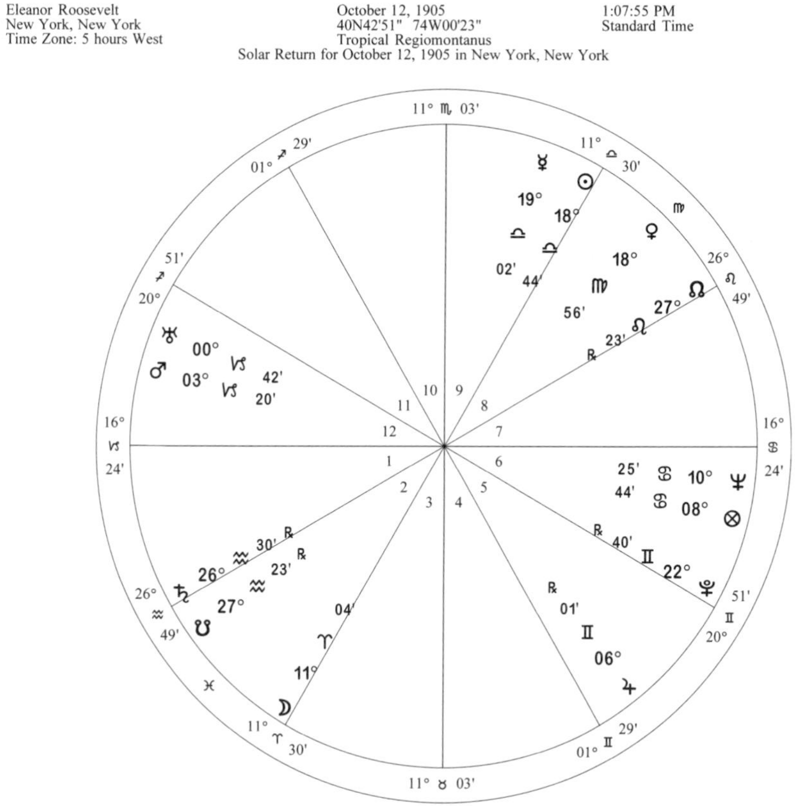
Eleanor Roosevelt
New York, New York
Time Zone: 5 hours West
October 12, 1905
40N42'51" 74W00'23"
Tropical Regiomontanus
1:07:55 PM
Standard Time
Solar Return for October 12, 1905 in New York, New York

Dorothean Ess. Dig. (No Mut Rec. Points)								
Pl	Ruler	Exalt	Tripl	Term	Face	Detri	Fall	Score
☉	♀	♄	♄	♃	♄	♂	☉ -	- 9 P
☽	♂	☉	☉	♀	☉	♀	♄	- 5 P
☿	♀ m	♄	♄	☿ +	♄	♂	☉	+2
♀	☿ m	☿	♀ +	♄	♀ +	♃	♀ -	+0
♂	♄	♂ +	♀	♀	♃	☽	♃	+4
♃	☿	☊	♄	☿	♃ +	♃ -	--	- 4
♄	♄ +	--	♄ +	♂	☽	☉	--	+8
☊	☉	--	☉	♂	♂	♄	--	--
⊗	☽	♃	♀	♃	♀	♄	♂	--
As	♄	♂	♀	♃	♂	☽	♃	--
Mc	♂	--	♀	♃	☉	♀	☽	--
☋	♄	--	♄	♂	☽	☉	--	--

Hs	Alm. (Pto)
1	♂♄
2	♄
3	☉
4	♀
5	☿
6	☿
7	☽
8	☉
9	♄
10	♂
11	♃
12	♃

Example 5-8a. Eleanor Roosevelt pregnancy solar return for 1905

1906: son James is conceived. The Sun was the ruler of the 5th, with Mars in barren Virgo in the 5th. Here we have Eleanor's natal 5th house sign Taurus as the Ascendant sign, with Venus in Sagittarius, a sign of average fertility. Eleanor's chart matched Gadbury's aphorism #6, concerning Mars in the 5th, which could preclude pregnancy. But we may note that Mars was in a barren sign (a negative of a negative, perhaps?) but possibly more importantly, in strong dignity by Triplicity, which could well negate the negative effect. Venus here is square Saturn, which puts it in conflict with Gadbury's Aphorism 11, which should preclude children.

1907: no conception, but son James is born. SR-Moon conjunct Uranus in the 5th house, with Jupiter in Leo conjunct the SR-Ascendant ruling it. Jupiter in Leo was Eleanor's radix Jupiter sign, thereby activating Gadbury's Aphorism #1. The Moon was in the 5th and not impedited by the traditional malefics, although it did apply to Uranus. So, this matches Gadbury Aphorism #3. The Lord of the 5th *is* Jupiter, which I believe corresponds to Gadbury's Aphorism #5. The South Node is technically moved back to the 6th, so just missing the negative argument of Gadbury's Aphorism #6. Jupiter conjunct the Ascendant activates Gadbury's positive Aphorism #7. Venus is technically afflicted by Mars, being square, and thus activating Gadbury's Aphorism #11, but since Mars is in Capricorn and thus exalted, I do not believe that Mars was acting as a malefic in this particular chart, so I would ignore Aphorism #11.

1908: son Franklin, their only child to die in infancy, is born. Empty 5th house in SR, but fertile Pisces on the cusp, with Jupiter in Virgo conjunct Venus in Virgo, with the Venus ruling the Ascendant. Venus in Virgo was Eleanor's natal placement, but not near the Ascendant, as in Gadbury Aphorism #1. Venus and Jupiter were conjunct in Virgo in the 11th and not impedited by the traditional malefics, thereby matching Gadbury's Aphorism #3. Jupiter ruled the 5th unimpedited, thus matching Aphorism #5. Perhaps the Moon in the 8th is a possible argument of death here?

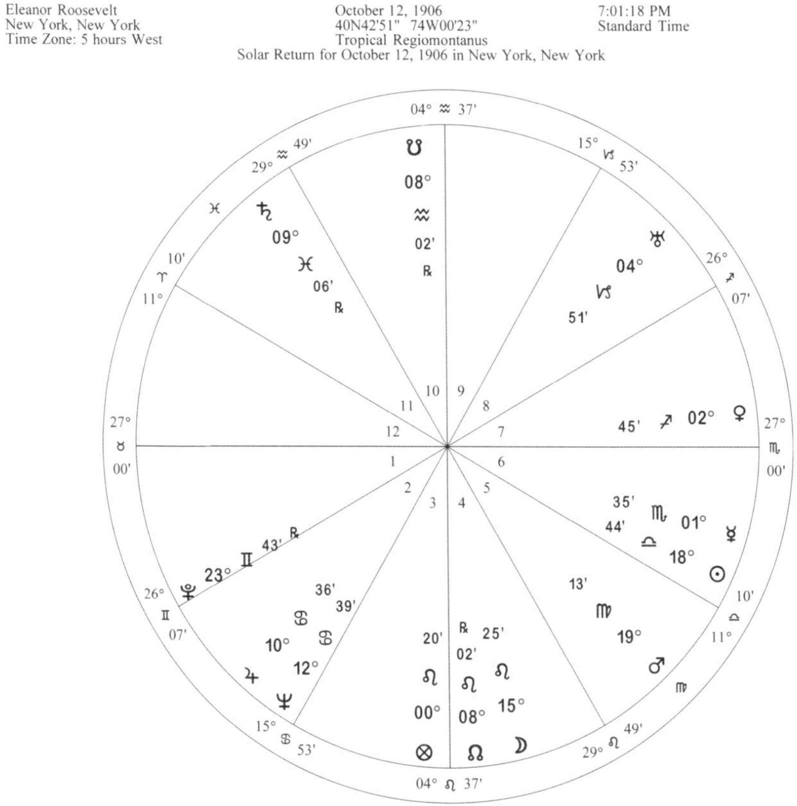
Eleanor Roosevelt
New York, New York
Time Zone: 5 hours West
October 12, 1906
40N42'51" 74W00'23"
Tropical Regiomontanus
7:01:18 PM
Standard Time
Solar Return for October 12, 1906 in New York, New York

Dorothean Ess. Dig. (No Mut Rec. Points)

Pl	Ruler	Exalt	Tripl	Term	Face	Detri	Fall	Score
☉	♀	♄	☿	♃	♄	♂	☉ -	- 9 P
☽	☉	--	♃	♀	♃	♄	--	- 5 P
☿	♂ m	--	♂	♂	♂	♀	☽	- 5 P
♀	♃	☋	♃	♃	☿	☿	--	- 5 P
♂	☿ m	☿	☽	♄	♀	♃	♀	- 5 P
♃	☽	♃ +	♂	♃ +	☿	♄	♂	+6
♄	♃	♀	♂	♃	♄ +	☿	☿	+1
☊	☉	--	♃	☿	♄	♄	--	--
⊗	☉	--	♃	♄	♄	♄	--	--
As	♀	☽	☽	♂	♄	♂	--	--
Mc	♄	--	☿	♄	♀	☉	--	--
☋	♄	--	☿	☿	♀	☉	--	--

Hs	Alm. (Pto)
1	☽
2	☿
3	☽
4	☉
5	☉
6	♀♄
7	♂
8	♃
9	♂♄
10	♄
11	♄
12	☉♂

Example 5-8b. Eleanor Roosevelt pregnancy solar return for 1906

Eleanor Roosevelt
New York, New York
Time Zone: 5 hours West

October 13, 1907
40N42'51" 74W00'23"
Tropical Regiomontanus
Solar Return for October 13, 1907 in New York, New York

12:48:20 AM
Standard Time

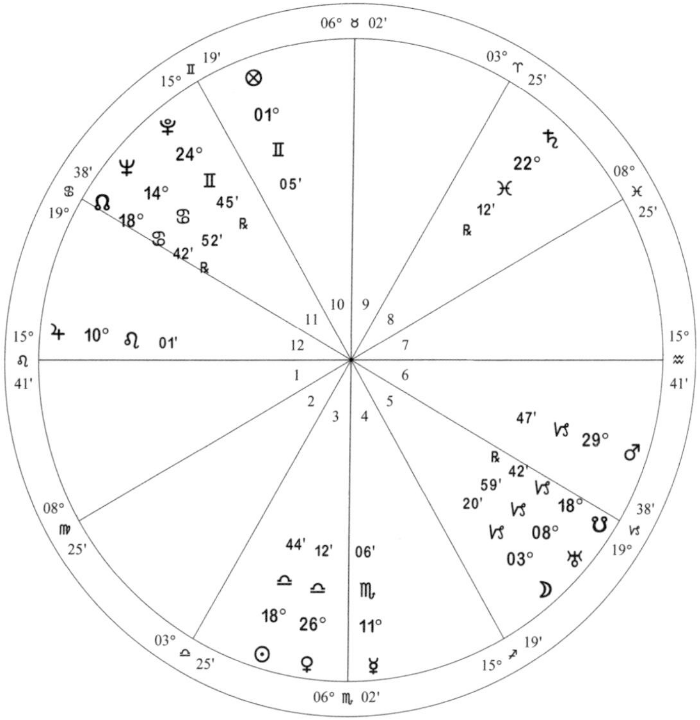

Dorothean Ess. Dig. (No Mut Rec. Points)								
Pl	Ruler	Exalt	Tripl	Term	Face	Detri	Fall	Score
☉	♀	♄	☿	♃	♄	♂	☉ -	- 9 P
☽	♄	♂	☽ +	♀	♃	☽ -	♃	- 2
☿	♂	--	♂	♃ m	☉	♀	☽	- 5 P
♀	♀ +	♄ m	☿	☊	♃	♂	☉	+5
♂	♄	♂ +	☽	♄ m	☉	☽	♃	+4
♃	☉	--	♃ +	☿ m	♃ +	♄	--	+4
♄	♃	♀ m	♂	♂ m	♂	☿	☿	- 5 P
☊	☽	♃	♂	☿	☿	♄	♂	--
⊗	☿	☊	☿	☿	♃	♃	--	--
As	☉	--	♃	♀	♃	♄	--	--
Mc	♀	☽	☽	♀	☿	♂	--	--
☋	♄	♂	☽	♃	♂	☽	♃	--

Hs	Alm. (Pto)
1	☉
2	☿
3	♄
4	♂
5	♃
6	♂
7	♄
8	♃
9	♂
10	☽♀
11	☿
12	☽

Example 5-8c. Eleanor Roosevelt pregnancy solar return for 1907

Eleanor Roosevelt
New York, New York
Time Zone: 5 hours West

October 12, 1908
40N42'51" 74W00'23"
Tropical Regiomontanus
Solar Return for October 12, 1908 in New York, New York

6:39:42 AM
Standard Time

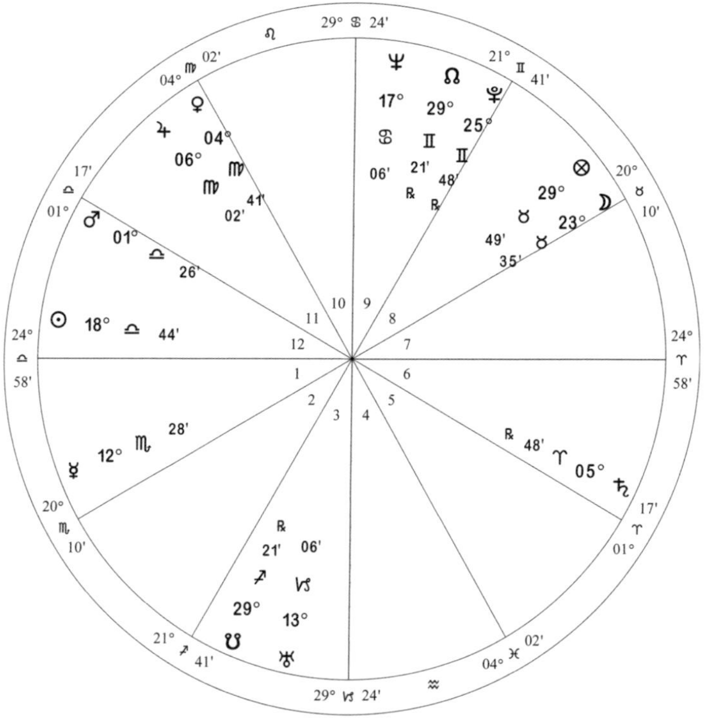

Dorothean Ess. Dig. (No Mut Rec. Points)								
Pl	Ruler	Exalt	Tripl	Term	Face	Detri	Fall	Score
☉	♀	♄ m	♄ m	♃	♄	♂	☉ -	- 9 P
☽	♀	☽ +	♀	♄	♄	♂	--	+4
☿	♂	--	♀	♃ m	☉	♀	☽	- 5 P
♀	☿	☿	♀ +	☿	☉	♃	♀ -	- 1
♂	♀	♄	♄	♄	☽	♂ -	☉	- 10 P
♃	☿	☿	♀	☿ m	☉	♃ -	♀	- 10 P
♄	♂	☉ m	☉ m	♃	♂	♀	♄ -	- 9 P
☊	☿	☊ +	♄	♂	☉	♃	--	--
⊗	♀	☽	♀	♂	♄	♂	--	--
As	♀	♄	♄	☊	♃	♂	☉	--
Mc	☽	♃	♀	♄	☽	♄	♂	--
☋	♃	☋	☉	♂	♄	☿	--	--

Hs	Alm. (Pto)
1	♄
2	♂
3	♃
4	♄
5	♀
6	☉
7	☉♂
8	♀
9	☿♄
10	☽
11	☿
12	♄

Example 5-8d. Eleanor Roosevelt pregnancy solar return for 1908

Eleanor Roosevelt
New York, New York
Time Zone: 5 hours West

October 12, 1909
40N42'51" 74W00'23"
Tropical Regiomontanus
Solar Return for October 12, 1909 in New York, New York

12:28:14 PM
Standard Time

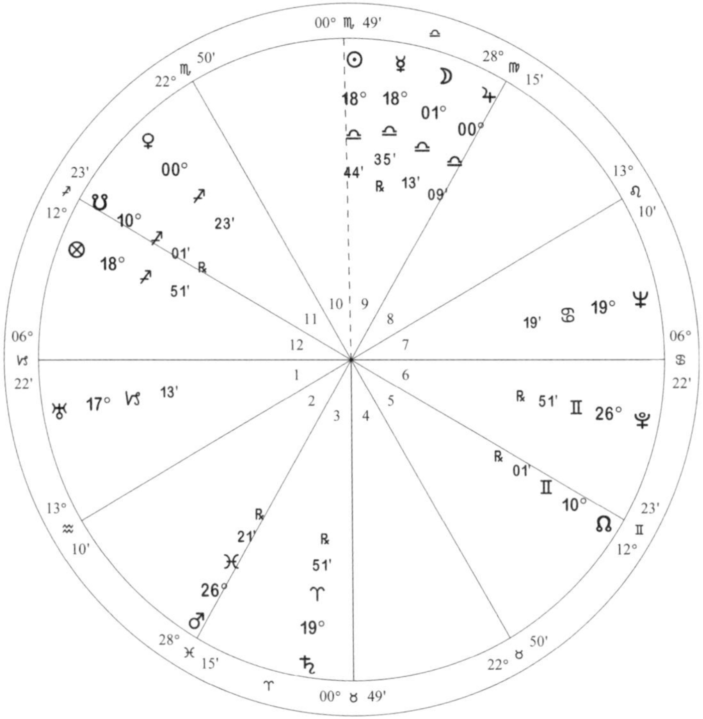

Dorothean Ess. Dig. (No Mut Rec. Points)								
Pl	Ruler	Exalt	Tripl	Term	Face	Detri	Fall	Score
☉	♀	♄ m	♄ m	♃	♄ m	♂	☉ -	- 9 P
☽	♀	♄	♄	♄	☽ +	♂	☉	+1
☿	♀	♄	♄	♃	♄	♂	☉	- 5 P
♀	♃ m	☋	☉	♃	☿	☿	--	- 5 P
♂	♃	♀	♀	♄	♂ +	☿	☿	+1
♃	♀ m	♄	♄	♄	☽	♂	☉	- 5 P
♄	♂	☉ m	☉ m	☿	☉ m	♀	♄ -	- 9 P
☊	☿	☊ +	♄	♃	♂	♃	--	--
⊗	♃	☋ +	☉	☿	☽	☿	--	--
As	♄	♂	♀	☿	♃	☽	♃	--
Mc	♂	--	♀	♂	♂	♀	☽	--
☋	♃	☋	☉	♀	☽	☿	--	--

Hs	Alm. (Pto)
1	♄
2	♄
3	♃
4	♀
5	♀
6	☿
7	♃
8	☉
9	☿
10	♂
11	♂
12	♃

Example 5-8e. Eleanor Roosevelt pregnancy solar return for 1909

1909: son Franklin died of flu. SR-South Node at the 12th house cusp, the 8th from the 5th. The 5th ruled by Venus in Sagittarius, and the Ascendant ruled by Saturn in Aries retrograde. Only Venus was in one of the approved houses for fertility (i.e., not Jupiter or the Moon), and it is widely impedited by the South Node, thereby grading toward a negative reading of Aphorism #3. Aphorism #5 applies, if we agree that the orb between Venus and the South Node is too wide. Mercury is very definitely afflicted in this chart, which makes a direct hit to the negative consequences of aphorism #10. We would probably argue for the problem being the Lord of the Ascendant in Detriment and retrograde square Uranus in the 1st. However, that would tend to suggest that it was Eleanor herself in trouble, not her son.

For examining this series of years, Gadbury's aphorisms leave a lot to be desired, thereby supporting the thesis that this aspect of biology may simply not show astrologically unless the process is in some way unusual. Eleanor's situation was not unusual for the time, except that the Roosevelts experienced fewer than average deaths of their young children. It also raises the question of whether Gadbury's aphorisms will produce too many false positives in our modern climate of contraception.

Contraception perhaps may be understood here as one of the ways that we consciously change fate. And while contraceptive methods may have improved in the 20th century, and knowledge of them became more accessible, contraception has a long history, as well as the more extreme forms of birth control. Thus, humans have been tampering with fertility for a long time, and thus, changing fate.

We may therefore learn from this that the prediction of children astrologically has its limitations. However, Peggy Fleming's example in particular may give food for thought about the way that we can understand family planning. For those who do *not* want children, but are in heterosexual relationships, contraception is probably a universally good idea! And what we *see* is that fate from this direction *can* be changed, at least the fate of ignorance, if not necessity.

But Peggy and her husband Greg *wanted* children, and there, the solar returns did seem to provide guidance about the possibilities for greater than average (for Peggy!) fertility over a period of time. Whether through fertility treatment, or just plain trying harder, some years will be more fertile than others, and this can be used as a planning tool.

Chapter 5 Endnotes

1. St. Clair, William. *The Godwins and the Shelleys : The Biography of a Family.* New York: Norton, 1989, p 464.

2. Gadbury, 1661, pp 223-224.

3. Bonatti (Dykes), p 1060.

4. St. Clair, p. 464.

6

Solar Returns for Relocation

RELOCATION CAN HAPPEN FOR MANY REASONS, AND SOME OF THEM WILL OVERLAP WITH OTHER CHAPTERS IN THIS BOOK. One thing is certain: relocation is more common now than it was when traditional astrology was being devised. That said, many people throughout history have moved great distances, either individually or collectively.

What is a move, and how much of a move does it need to be for one to expect to see it in a solar return? The answer may well be like the question of what distinguishes a 3rd house from a 9th house trip, where the answer seems to be: it depends. Someone who has lived in the same house for fifty years, with that house having been occupied by ancestors for umpteen generations, who is forced to move because the land has been condemned by the state to build a new airport, is going to find moving unbelievably more traumatizing than a college student who moves every six months. A move three blocks away for someone who hasn't moved in twenty years is likely to be far harder than a move across the country for someone who just moved two years ago. And this isn't even accounting for the general astrological lore that fixed signs would have the toughest time moving, while cardinal signs would have the easiest time!

Moving rates as one of the more difficult things for many people because it mixes multiple challenges:

- If it is a move of any distance, it disrupts friendships.
- The familiar environment (read: the unconscious environment) is overturned, with the need to find new schools, shopping, recreation, and services.
- It involves a new work environment and new schools for the children.
- One even loses the ability to navigate one's living environment in the dark!
- The actual process of moving, with packing, throwing away, giving away, selling, supervising, renting, or hiring the truck or moving company, is difficult, time-consuming, and expensive.
- Physically relocating pets, children, aging parents, not to mention oneself and partner can be trying.

As I have iterated some of the obvious effects of moving, it doesn't take long to realize that many houses of the chart could reflect a move, and not just a single one, such as the 4th house. There are yet further complications. Moving from or to a rental, which is 6th, is different than if one owns the properties. Splitting up the move into the buy/sell vs. the actual relocation provides different complications. Moving where one person goes ahead while the rest of the family stays behind could also show differently, as could a retirement move compared to moving because of a job relocation. "Moving up" may well look different than downsizing. And for the person who moves regularly, moving may not look terribly different than traveling. As we go through our scenarios, we shall attempt to sort out which of these stories applies.

We shall study:

- Maya Angelou's move to St. Louis when she was seven, after which she was raped
- Maya Angelou's move to Ghana in 1962
- Jane Austen's family's "downsizing" to Bath in 1801
- Jane Austen, sister Cassandra and her mother's move to Chawton July 1809 after Jane and Cassandra's father had died
- Martin Luther King's move back to Atlanta in 1960
- Louis Pasteur's move to Strasbourg in 1849, where he took a job, met his future wife, and married her
- Louis Pasteur's move to Paris in 1857, which was a step up for his career
- Eleanor Roosevelt's move to Albany in 1911, accompanying her husband when he was elected to the State Senate
- Mary Godwin Shelley's move back to England in 1823 following the death of Percy

Two of Maya Angelou's Moves

Maya Angelou has lived many places, but this pair is representative of what we might call the negative and the positive. In the first case, not only was she raped but, when she revealed the identity of her attacker and her relatives punished him, she chose

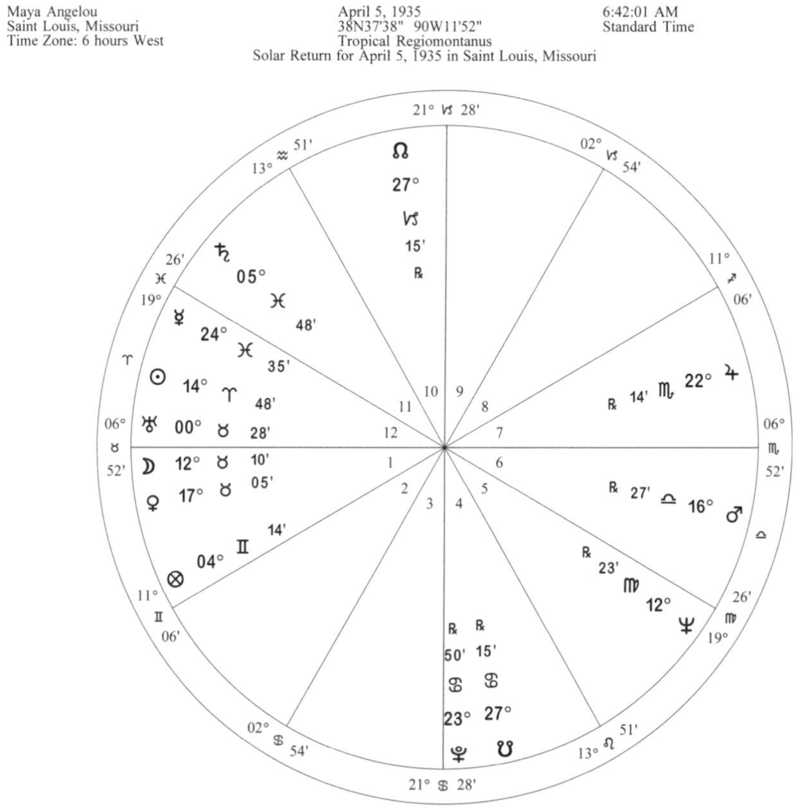
Maya Angelou
Saint Louis, Missouri
Time Zone: 6 hours West
April 5, 1935
38N37'38" 90W11'52"
Tropical Regiomontanus
6:42:01 AM
Standard Time
Solar Return for April 5, 1935 in Saint Louis, Missouri

Dorothean Ess. Dig. (No Mut Rec. Points)								
Pl	Ruler	Exalt	Tripl	Term	Face	Detri	Fall	Score
☉	♂	☉ +	☉ +	☿	☉ +	♀	♄	+8
☽	♀	☽ +	♀	☿	☽ +	♂	--	+5
☿	♃	♀	♀	♂	♂	☿ -	☿ -	- 14 P
♀	♀ +	☽	♀ +	♃	☽	♂	--	+8
♂	♀	♄	♄	♃	♄	♂ -	☉	- 10 P
♃	♂	--	♀	☿	♀	♀	☽	- 5 P
♄	♃	♀	♀	♀	♄ +	☿	☿	+1
☊	♄	♂	♀	♄	☉	☽	♃	--
⊗	☿	☊	♄	☿	♃	♃	--	--
As	♀	☽	♀	♀	☿	♂	--	--
Mc	♄	♂	♀	♂	☉	☽	♃	--
☋	☽	♃	♀	♄	☽	♄	♂	--

Hs	Alm. (Pto)
1	♀
2	☿
3	☽
4	☽
5	☉
6	☿
7	♂
8	♃
9	♀♄
10	♂
11	♄
12	♃

Example 6-1a. Maya Angelou relocation solar return for 1935

Maya Angelou
Saint Louis, Missouri
Time Zone: 6 hours West

April 4, 1962
38N37'38" 90W11'52"
Tropical Regiomontanus
Solar Return for April 4, 1962 in Saint Louis, Missouri

7:49:58 PM
Standard Time

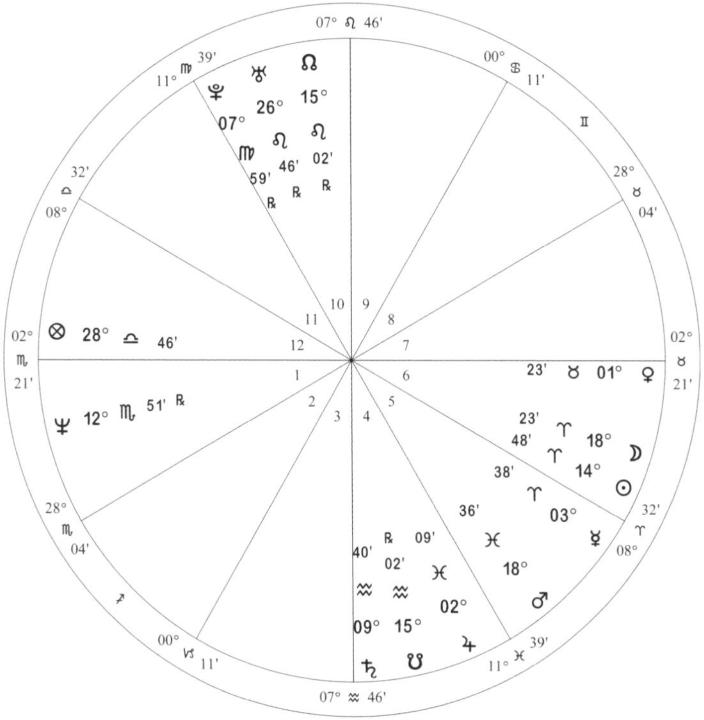

Dorothean Ess. Dig. (No Mut Rec. Points)								
Pl	Ruler	Exalt	Tripl	Term	Face	Detri	Fall	Score
☉	♂	☉ +	♃	☿	☉ +	♀	♄	+5
☽	♂	☉	♃	☿	☉	♀	♄	- 5 P
☿	♂	☉	♃	♃	♂	♀	♄	- 5 P
♀	♀ +	☽	☽	♀ +	☿	♂	--	+7
♂	♃	♀	♂ +	☿	♃	☿	☿	+3
♃	♃ +	♀	♂	♀	♄	☿	☿	+5
♄	♄ +	--	☿	☿	♀	☉	--	+5
☊	☉	--	♃	♀	♃	♄	--	--
⊗	♀	♄	☿	☊	♃	♂	☉	--
As	♂	--	♂	♂	♂	♀	☽	--
Mc	☉	--	♃	☿	♄	♄	--	--
☋	♄	--	☿	♀	☿	☉	--	--

Hs	Alm. (Pto)
1	♂
2	♂
3	♄
4	☿♄
5	♃
6	♂
7	☽♀
8	☽
9	☽
10	☉
11	☿
12	♀

Example 6-1b. Maya Angelou relocation solar return for 1962

to remain silent for years afterwards because she was at least as traumatized by the revenge against him as the act itself.

Modern astrology would unequivocally use the 4th house to represent moves, and here is Pluto in Cancer, right at the IC. Not only does this describe the rape, but it describes the silence afterwards: the water signs are also known as the mute signs. Not far from Pluto is the South Node, also in the 4th, and thus another indicator that moving at this time would not be a good plan.

Or is it? If the 4th house is the home, then two malefics in the home mean problems in the home. Would moving mitigate that, since a move by itself is disruptive? The obvious answer is: it would depend on whether the move "solves" anything. In other words, the move *could* be a solution if the home itself has become unstable. In Maya's case, it wasn't. She had a very happy life with her grandmother which was disrupted when her mother decided that she wanted her children with her. Here, the move was indicative *of* the disruption, rather than a move away *from* existing disruption. The presence of a cardinal sign on the 4th makes moving easier – but that also doesn't argue that a move *will* take place.

There is a horary method in Lilly for removal (moving house) in which he compares the condition of the 1st house and the 7th house. If the 1st house is stronger, then it's better to stay. In this case, Venus in Taurus in the 1st and ruling the 1st would make a strong case for staying in Stamps, Arkansas, where she was living at the time of her solar return. The 7th was ruled by Mars in Detriment in a cadent house, another strong argument for staying in Stamps.

So far, both these methods argue that it would be better not to move. But *will* she move? For now, I want to defer that question until we can examine some more charts, and follow the arguments.

Our second case with Maya is for when she moved to Ghana from Egypt in 1962. Ghana was a revelation for both her and her son. She taught, wrote, and met Malcolm X when she was there, returning to the USA in 1964 to help to build the Organization of

African American Unity. Furthermore, this move represented moving on from a relationship that had failed.

In this case, the angles are reversed from the abortive 1935 move. Now staying is represented by a succedent Mars in Pisces, where it has Triplicity. But moving has Venus in Taurus again, conjunct the 7th house of the move. The classical horary method thus gives a strong "thumbs up" to the move.

These two charts of moving share the South Node in the 4th house. The home situation has become untenable. Saturn at the IC in Aquarius is actually a pretty strong and generally positive influence. But we might note that Maya has the South Node in the 4th natally [SEE EXAMPLE 5-1 ON PAGE 110]. She has moved a lot in her life! Despite her natal fixed angles, she has been a wandering stone.

Jane Austen's Moves

In *Sense and Sensibility*, Jane Austen wrote movingly about how, in her time, women could be displaced from "their" homes because oftentimes the inheritance of the residence was entailed, and more often passed father to son. In real life, as a spinster, she and her sister moved when their parents moved. And when their father died, they and their mother moved again, as their brothers arranged for their maintenance.

Neither move was an especially happy one, although the second one was a better move, because it was going to a comfortable situation. The other factor which weighed against the first move was that they were moving from Jane and Cassandra's childhood home, in an arrangement that favored one of their brothers, who happened to have an obnoxious wife, making visits "back home" uncomfortable and brief.

Jane shared with Maya the Neptune rising natally, but not the house placement of the South Node. While Jane and her sister both visited with other households frequently, often for weeks or months, she did have home as a strong base. And Cassandra seemed to do more visiting than Jane. Jane's natal Sun was in the 4th house, and home was where her writing happened. Jane was very much a private person, at least from the portrait of her devised by her sister, when she selectively burned Jane's correspondence after her death. The 4th house was ruled by Jupiter in Gemini: not the strongest placement, being in Detriment and Triplicity. Jane's father was by no means rich. He had a parsonage and too many children: eight brothers and two sisters. The children did seem to make the best of it, which may well be shown by the exalted Mars, ruling Jane's third. One of her brothers was adopted out of the family by a fourth cousin, which resulted in an extensive estate, and the eventually better situation for the Austen women with the move to Chawton when the brothers took over support of the ladies. Two of her other brothers took military careers where they flourished as officers, both eventually becoming admirals.

In the 1800 solar return which covered the move to Bath in 1801, this time we see the South Node in the 1st house. This does describe Jane's position regarding the move: it was a loss. Financial circumstances required that they sell most of their furniture rather than pay to move it. The process took months and a lot of work, as a move does. Jane had already completed and extensively revised the manuscript for *Sense and Sensibility*, *Pride and Prejudice*, and *Northanger Abbey*. Her productivity dropped completely upon the move, and didn't resume until after Bath.

While we might at first be tempted to see the South Node in the 1st as an argument against staying in Steventon, when we do the 1st house – 7th house comparison, we see an entirely different picture. Venus in Capricorn in Triplicity ruled Steventon; Mars in Taurus mixed with Detriment and Triplicity ruled Bath. No contest. Steventon wins. If we use the co-Almutens of the 1st and 7th, then we see the same pattern as the Nodes: Saturn ruling the 1st is in Detriment, and the Sun ruling the 7th is in Triplicity in Sagittarius.

Comparing this solar return to her natal chart, the Moon is square radix Moon, already setting up an uncomfortable pattern. Jane's natal Saturn was exalted; we have already seen that the solar return Saturn was in Detriment. Jane's solar return Mercury was in the same sign, Sagittarius, as its radix position. This is actually illuminating, because a successful adaptation of Mercury in Sagittarius seems to best operate when the Native can establish a regular pattern or structure within which to operate. Jane had that pattern established in Steventon: she lost it at Bath. Venus and Mars flipped like Saturn, being in reverse dignity from the natal placements, where radix Venus was debilitated and Mars exalted; to Venus in Triplicity and Mars in Detriment. That's a lot of stress in the solar return when compared to the natal. Did posterity lose a novel or two over this move? It's entirely possible.

One can argue that the move to Chawton largely restored balance. It was after this move that Jane became published, and wrote several more works. In this solar return, It's the 3rd house with the greatest prominence, showing the efforts of her brothers which achieved this more stable situation for them. The Sun is in the 4th, Jane's radix Sun house position.

Just running the rulership of the 1st and 7th houses shows the situation as well: the 1st house is ruled by Mercury in Detriment, while the 7th is ruled by Jupiter in rulership. Notice that, for this assessment, the fact that Mercury is in its radix sign is not part of the assessment. The presence of Mercury in Detriment works literally in the argument about stay or go, but it works symbolically in the understanding of the year, where its presence in the radix sign means that the experience of the year will be more comfortable for her relating to the affairs of Mercury.

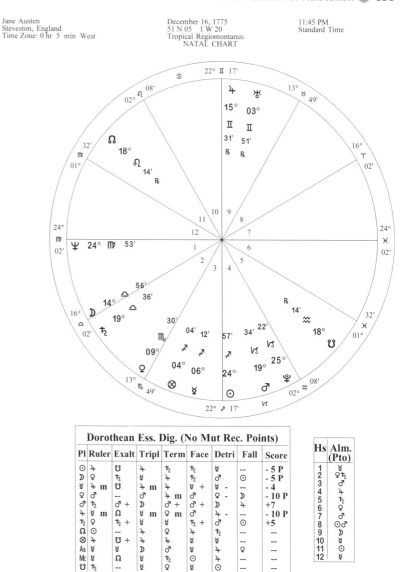

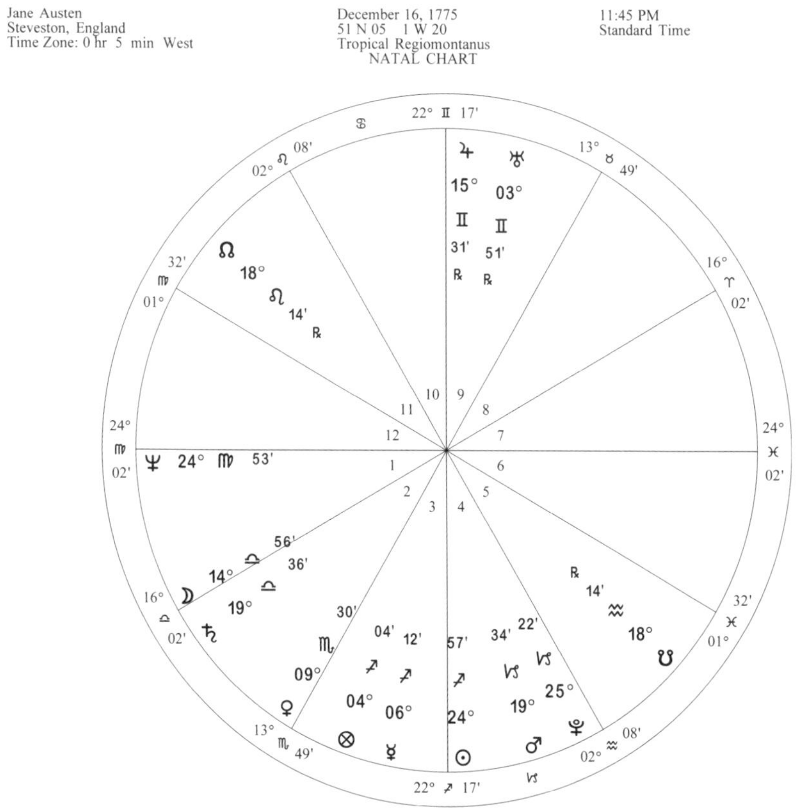
Jane Austen
Steveston, England
Time Zone: 0 hr 5 min West
December 16, 1775
51 N 05 1 W 20
Tropical Regiomontanus
NATAL CHART
11:45 PM
Standard Time

Dorothean Ess. Dig. (No Mut Rec. Points)

Pl	Ruler	Exalt	Tripl	Term	Face	Detri	Fall	Score
☉	♃	☋	♃	♄	♄	☿	--	- 5 P
☽	♀	♄	☿	♃	♄	♂	☉	- 5 P
☿	♃ m	☋	♃ m	♃	☿ +	☿ -	--	- 4
♀	♂	--	♂	♃ m	♂	♀ -	☽	- 10 P
♂	♄	♂ +	☽	♂ +	♂ +	☽	♃	+7
♃	☿ m	☊	☿ m	♀ m	♂	♃ -	--	- 10 P
♄	♀	♄ +	☿	☿	♄ +	♂	☉	+5
☊	☉	--	♃	♀	♃	♄	--	--
⊗	♃	☋ +	♃	♃	☿	☿	--	--
As	☿	☿	☽	♂	☿	♃	♀	--
Mc	☿	☊	☿	♄	☉	♃	--	--
☋	♄	--	☿	♀	☿	☉	--	--

Hs	Alm. (Pto)
1	☿
2	♀♄
3	♂
4	♃
5	♄
6	♀
7	♂
8	☉♂
9	☽
10	☿
11	☉
12	☿

Example 6-2. Jane Austen nativity

Jane Austen
Steveston, England
Time Zone: 0 hours West

December 17, 1800
51 N 05 1 W 20
Tropical Regiomontanus
Solar Return for December 17, 1800 in Steveston, England

1:26:20 AM
Standard Time

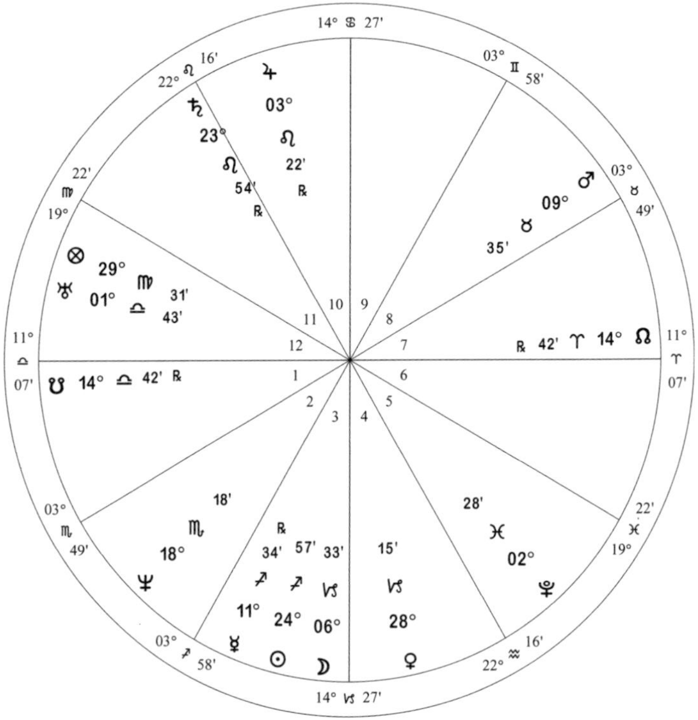

Dorothean Ess. Dig. (No Mut Rec. Points)								
Pl	Ruler	Exalt	Tripl	Term	Face	Detri	Fall	Score
☉	♃ m	☋	♃	♄	♄	☿	--	- 5 P
☽	♄	♂ m	☽ +	☿	♃	☽ -	♃	- 2
☿	♃	☋	♃	♀	☽	☿ -	--	- 10 P
♀	♄	♂	☽	♄	☉	☽	♃	- 5 P
♂	♀	☽ m	☽	☿	☿	♂ -	--	- 10 P
♃	☉ m	--	♃ +	♄ m	♄	♄	--	+3
♄	☉	--	♃	♃ m	♂	♄ -	--	- 10 P
☊	♂	☉	♃	☿	☉	♀	♄	--
⊗	☿	☿	☽	♂	☿	♃	♀	--
As	♀	♄	☿	♃	♄	♂	☉	--
Mc	☽	♃	♂	☿	☿	♄	♂	--
☋	♀	♄	☿	♃	♄	♂	☉	--

Hs	Alm. (Pto)
1	♀♄
2	♂
3	♃
4	♂♄
5	♄
6	♃
7	☉♂
8	☽♀
9	☿
10	☽
11	☉♃
12	☿

Example 6-2a. Jane Austen relocation solar return for 1800

Jane Austen
Steveston, England
Time Zone: 0 hours West

December 17, 1808
51 N 05 1 W 20
Tropical Regiomontanus
Solar Return for December 17, 1808 in Steveston, England

12:00:09 AM
Standard Time

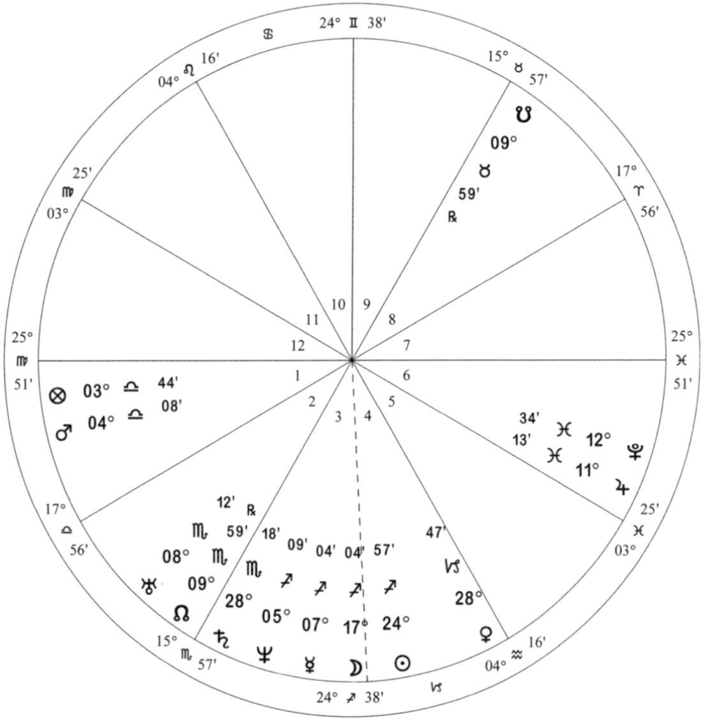

Dorothean Ess. Dig. (No Mut Rec. Points)								
Pl	Ruler	Exalt	Tripl	Term	Face	Detri	Fall	Score
☉	♃	☋	♃	♄	♄	☿	--	- 5 P
☽	♃	☋	♃	☿	☽ +	☿	--	+1
☿	♃	☋	♃	♃	☿ +	☿ -	--	- 4
♀	♄	♂	☽	♄	☉	☽	♃	- 5 P
♂	♀	♄	☿	♄	☽	♂ -	☉	- 10 P
♃	♃ +	♀	♂	♃ +	♃ +	☿	☿	+8
♄	♂	--	♂	♄ +	♀	♀	☽	+2
☊	♂	--	♂	♃	♂	♀	☽	--
⊗	♀	♄	☿	♄	☽	♂	☉	--
As	☿	☿	☽	♂	☿	♃	♀	--
Mc	☿	☊	☿	♄	☉	♃	--	--
☋	♀	☽	☽	☿	☿	♂	--	--

Hs	Alm. (Pto)
1	☿
2	♀♄
3	♂
4	♃
5	♄
6	♀
7	♂
8	☉♂
9	☽
10	☿
11	☉
12	☿

Example 6-2b. Jane Austen relocation solar return for 1808

Martin Luther King's Move Back to Atlanta, and Mohandas Gandhi's Move Back to India

Every decision that Martin Luther King made about his life, he seemed to make very deliberately and carefully, and often, with much prayer.

King had come to national prominence because of his activities in the Montgomery, Alabama, bus boycott. As one of the local pastors, his influence had been considerable. We shall examine these matters in the next chapter, in the overlap between the Church and higher education. We will not examine his actual move to Montgomery, because, frankly, the move overlaps too much with the start of a new job and with the completion of his PhD.

Doing a quick evaluation of the solar return for his return to Atlanta, we see that Mars, ruling the 1ˢᵗ house, was exalted, and Venus, ruling the 7ᵗʰ house, was peregrine, as was the Moon, co-Almuten of the 7ᵗʰ house. By this argument, it would have been better to have stayed in Montgomery. And perhaps it would have been. He had a thriving church where he was pastor.

So why did he decide to move? Two reasons. First, at this point in time, Atlanta was seen as the capital of the Civil Rights movement, which meant that this move put him even more into the middle of this political process. And secondly, it was to his father's church, the church he remembered.

There is one very interesting natal argument for the move: his natal Jupiter partile conjunct the 7ᵗʰ house cusp. I actually have a very similar configuration in one case in my private files. A woman who did move across country to join a lover had the Moon in Taurus ruling the 1ˢᵗ of her solar return, and Saturn in Scorpio ruling her 7ᵗʰ. By this method, this was an easy call for staying, just as with King's example here. However, her natal Moon was right on the 7ᵗʰ house cusp. As she described it, she had moved several times before, but *never had she moved her pots and pans.* This move turned out to be a move into a long-term relationship, and home was where the

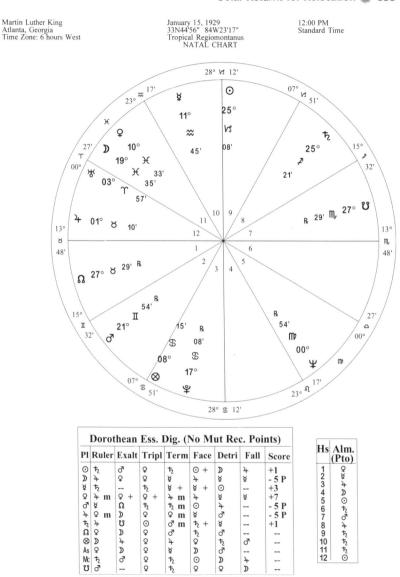

Martin Luther King
Atlanta, Georgia
Time Zone: 6 hours West

January 15, 1929
33N44'56" 84W23'17"
Tropical Regiomontanus
NATAL CHART

12:00 PM
Standard Time

Example 6-3. Martin Luther King nativity

Martin Luther King
Atlanta, Georgia
Time Zone: 5 hours West

January 16, 1960
33N44'56" 84W23'17"
Tropical Regiomontanus
Solar Return for January 16, 1960 in Atlanta, Georgia

1:27:11 AM
Standard Time

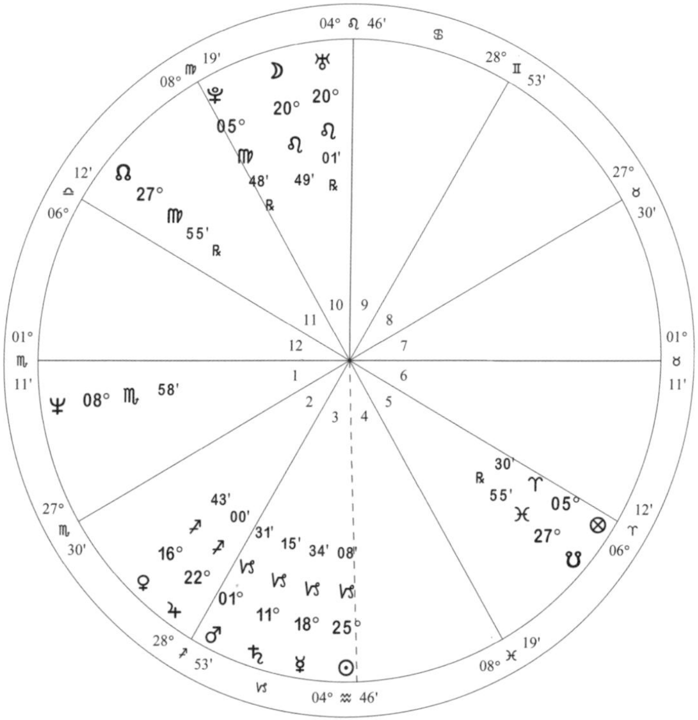

Dorothean Ess. Dig. (No Mut Rec. Points)								
Pl	Ruler	Exalt	Tripl	Term	Face	Detri	Fall	Score
☉	♄	♂	☽	♄	☉ +	☽	♃	+1
☽	☉	--	♃	♃	♂	♄	--	- 5 P
☿	♄	♂	☽	♃	♂	☽	♃	- 5 P
♀	♃	☋	♃	☿	☽	☿	--	- 5 P
♂	♄	♂ +	☽	♀	♃	☽	♃	+4
♃	♃ +	☋	♃ +	♄	♄	☿	--	+8
♄	♄ +	♂	☽	☿	♂	☽	♃	+5
☊	☿	☿	☽	♂	☿	♃	♀	--
⊗	♂	☉	♃	♃	♂	♀	♄	--
As	♂	--	♂	♂	♂	♀	☽	--
Mc	☉	--	♃	♄	♄	♄	--	--
☋	♃	♀	♂	♄	♂	☿	☿	--

Hs	Alm. (Pto)
1	♂
2	♂
3	♃
4	♄
5	♃
6	♂
7	☽♀
8	☽
9	☿
10	☉
11	☿
12	♀

Example 6-3a. Martin Luther King relocation solar return for 1960

pots were. In fact, her solar return was so powerful that year, that one would have been tempted to say that any major decision that she would make would be for the good.

It appears that a natal planet right on the 1st or the 7th house cusp of the solar return may make that removing situation that much more "fated," regardless of whether the rest of the model judges "stay" or "go." In my private case, the meaning is double, because the move also involved a relationship, another 7th house matter. In King's case, Jupiter is a natural ruler of organized religion, so a move which involved taking over a church position was especially appropriate.

But let's explore further. For King's 1960 solar return, the Moon was in a partile conjunction with Uranus. This conjunction occurred near the radix Northern Bending. A Moon-Uranus conjunction in the solar return will tend to make the Native feel restless – ready to move on to the next adventure. Here, it was in the 10th house of profession, thereby making that area of life the focus for change. But it was fixed change, being in a fixed sign. This means that the Native is rarely starting something new so much as perhaps going into new circumstances to apply a system already established.

We can see the logic of fixed change in an entirely appropriate example, that of Mohandas Gandhi, one of the men who was a great inspiration for Martin Luther King. Gandhi developed his system of nonviolent political confrontation in South Africa; in July 1914, Gandhi returned to his native India, to apply the same system there to help to achieve independence from the British. His solar return Moon in Scorpio activated his natal Venus-Mars opposite Jupiter-Pluto, all in fixed signs. Here, the argument about moving was clearly in favor of doing so, with Moon in Scorpio ruling the Ascendant, while Saturn, the 7th house ruler, had Triplicity. One has to wonder with Pluto so close to the solar return Ascendant whether he wasn't close to being killed in South Africa. I suspect one could make a good case for it.

Mohandas Gandhi
Porbandar, India
Time Zone: 0 hours West

October 2, 1869
21 N 38 69 E 36
Tropical Regiomontanus
NATAL CHART

7:11 AM
Local Mean Time

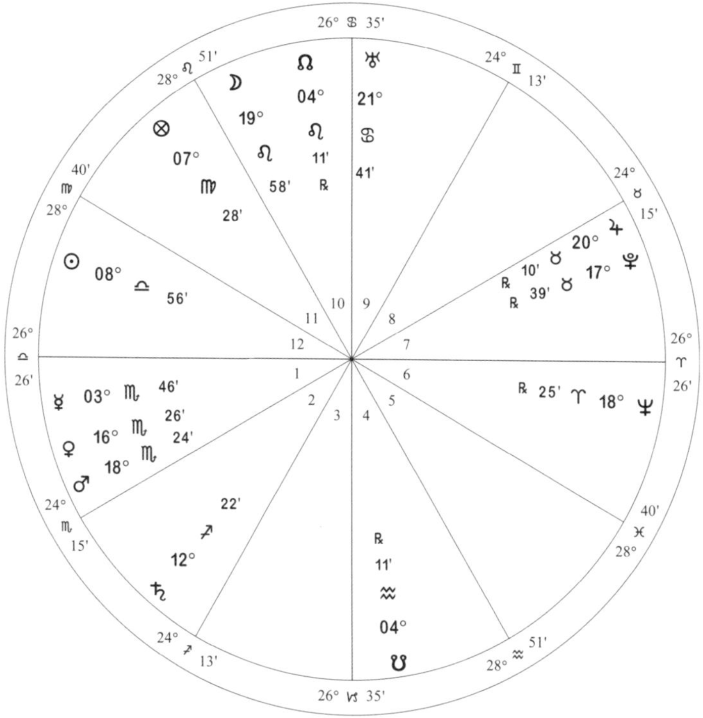

Dorothean Ess. Dig. (No Mut Rec. Points)								
Pl	Ruler	Exalt	Tripl	Term	Face	Detri	Fall	Score
☉	♀	♄	♄ m	♀	☽	♂	☉ -	- 9 P
☽	☉	--	☉	♃	♃	♄	--	- 5 P
☿	♂	--	♀	♂	♂	♀	☽	- 5 P
♀	♂	--	♀ +	♀ +	☉	♀ -	☽	+0
♂	♂ +	--	♀	♀	☉	♀	☽	+5
♃	♀	☽	♀	♃ +	♄	♂	--	+2
♄	♃	☋	☉ m	♀	☽	☿	--	- 5 P
☊	☉	--	☉	♄	♄	♄	--	--
⊗	☿	☿	♀	♀	☉	♃	♀	--
As	♀	♄	♄	☊	♃	♂	☉	--
Mc	☽	♃	♀	♀	☽	♄	♂	--
☋	♄	--	♄	♄	♀	☉	--	--

Hs	Alm. (Pto)
1	♄
2	♂
3	♃
4	♄
5	♄
6	♃
7	☉
8	♀
9	☿♄
10	☽
11	☉
12	☿

Example 6-3b. Mohandes Gandhi nativity

Mohandas Gandhi
Porbandar, India
Time Zone: 5 hr 30 min East

October 2, 1913
21 N 38 69 E 36
Tropical Regiomontanus
Solar Return for October 2, 1913 in Porbandar, India

11:28:40 PM
Standard Time

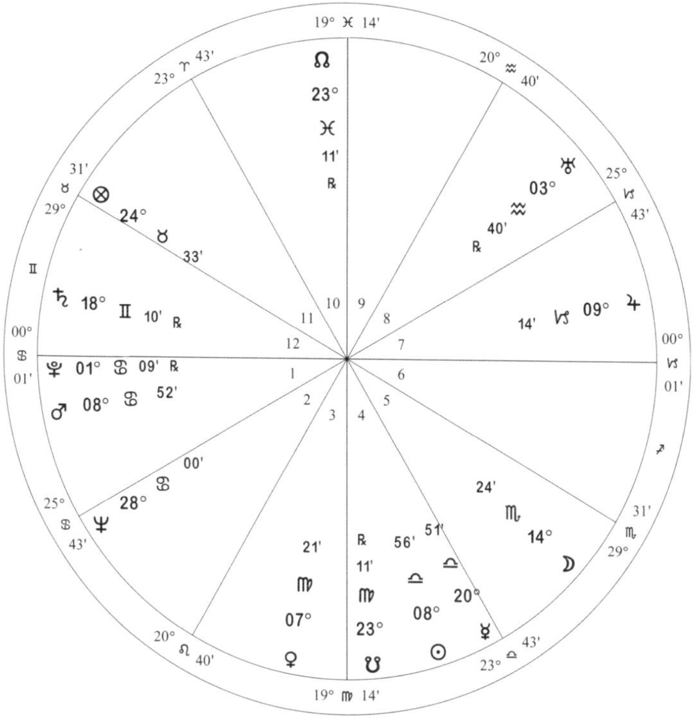

Dorothean Ess. Dig. (No Mut Rec. Points)								
Pl	Ruler	Exalt	Tripl	Term	Face	Detri	Fall	Score
☉	♀	♄	☿	♀	☽ m	♂	☉ -	- 9 P
☽	♂ m	--	♂	♀	☉ m	♀	☽ -	- 9 P
☿	♀ m	♄	☿ +	☿ +	♃	♂	☉	+5
♀	☿ m	☿	☽	♀ +	☉	♃	♀ -	- 2
♂	☽ m	♃ m	♂ +	♃	♀	♄	♂ -	- 1
♃	♄	♂ m	☽	☿	♃ +	☽	♃ -	- 3
♄	☿	☊	☿	♀	♂	♃	--	- 5 P
☊	♃	♀	♂	♂	♂	☿	☿	--
⊗	♀	☽	☽	♄	♄	♂	--	--
As	☽	♃	♂	♂	♀	♄	♂	--
Mc	♃	♀	♂	☿	♃	☿	☿	--
☋	☿	☿	☽	♄	☿	♃	♀	--

Hs	Alm. (Pto)
1	☽
2	☽
3	☉♃
4	☿
5	☿♀
6	♂
7	♄
8	♄
9	♄
10	♃
11	♂
12	☽

Example 6-3c. Mohandes Gandhi relocation solar return for 1913

In fact, this nonviolent confrontation that Gandhi so practiced has evidence of a lot of fixed energy, which is so characteristic of his nativity. While peaceful, these protests were unrelenting. Gandhi's natal Mars was strong in Scorpio, in an opposition to Jupiter. This 1913 solar return recapitulates the opposition between these planets, but with Mars and Jupiter in Fall.

But to return to King's 1960 solar return, the focus on the 3rd house does suggest that it was the return to the old neighborhood, so to speak, that was at least as important as his ambitions in the civil rights movement through the 10th house. The Moon-Uranus there was not trivial. King was being called home.

Pasteur's Vocational Moves

I suppose one would expect that, with someone as earthy as Pasteur, the moves would be for practical purposes. But really – he was desperate. When he received his PhD, he discovered there were practically no teaching jobs. (Hmm: was this 19th century, 20th, or 21st? Hard to say!) So he took the only one he could, which was at a secondary school in Dijon, where the class sizes were off the scale, the pay was bad, and the laboratory facilities primitive. (Déja vu, all over again!) When a temporary position at the University of Strasbourg opened up, he was ready to fly away! His solar year opened with the South Node in the 1st house, a signature we have seen before in the charts of people who moved, when the 1st-7th calculation was not in their favor. Here, there's no real call: Saturn ruling the 1st is just as peregrine as the Sun ruling the 7th. This is no argument either way. *[SEE EXAMPLE 4-5 ON PAGE 101 FOR PASTEUR'S NATAL CHART.]*

But one has to assume that the South Node near Saturn in the 1st shows his working conditions, at least at the beginning of the year. In fact, this chart in general is pretty weak. But there are two bright spots. Diurnally, the Sun is "escaping" the 12th house, meaning that things are just beginning to look better. And with Jupiter dignified in the 7th house, he won a wife – the daughter of the university rector,

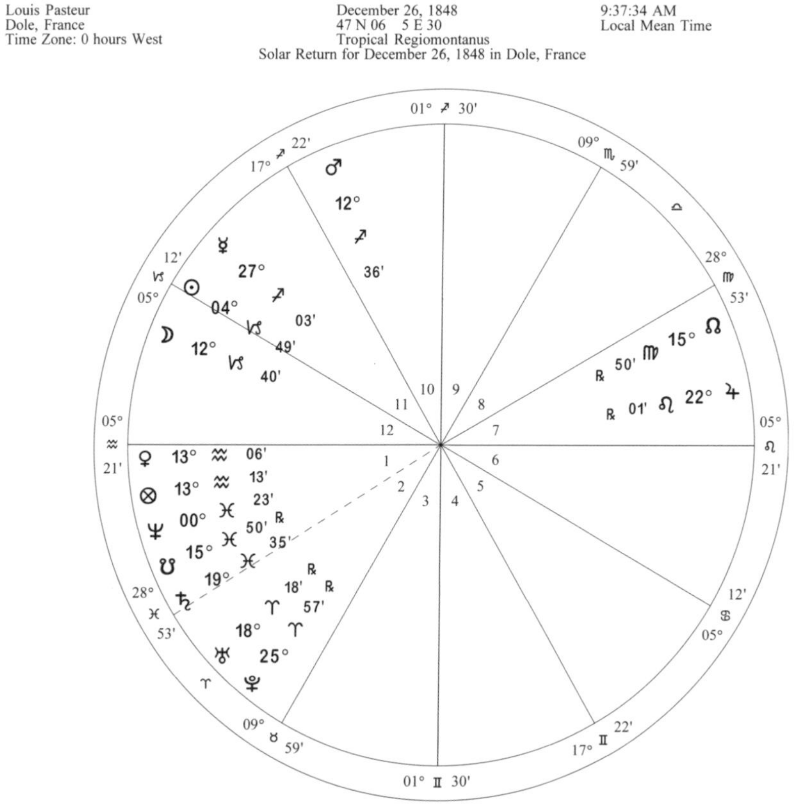
Louis Pasteur
Dole, France
Time Zone: 0 hours West
December 26, 1848
47 N 06 5 E 30
Tropical Regiomontanus
Solar Return for December 26, 1848 in Dole, France
9:37:34 AM
Local Mean Time

Dorothean Ess. Dig. (No Mut Rec. Points)								
Pl	Ruler	Exalt	Tripl	Term	Face	Detri	Fall	Score
☉	♄	♂	♀	♀	♃	☽	♃	- 5 P
☽	♄	♂	♀	♃	♂ m	☽ -	♃	- 10 P
☿	♃	☋	☉	♂	♄	☿ -	--	- 10 P
♀	♄	--	♄ m	♀ +	☿	☉	--	+2
♂	♃	☋	☉	♀	☽ m	☿	--	- 5 P
♃	☉	--	☉	♃ +	♂	♄	--	+2
♄	♃	♀	♀ m	☿	♃	☿	☿	- 5 P
☊	☿	☿	♀	♃	♀	♃	♀	--
⊗	♄	--	♄	♀	☿	☉	--	--
As	♄	--	♄	♄	♀	☉	--	--
Mc	♃	☋	☉	♃	☿	☿	--	--
☋	♃	♀	♀	☿	♃	☿	☿	--

Hs	Alm. (Pto)
1	♄
2	♃
3	♀
4	☿
5	☿
6	☽
7	☉
8	☿
9	♂
10	♃
11	♃
12	♀♄

Example 6-4a. Louis Pasteur relocation solar return 1848

Louis Pasteur
Dole, France
Time Zone: 0 hours West

December 26, 1856
47 N 06 5 E 30
Tropical Regiomontanus
Solar Return for December 26, 1856 in Dole, France

8:16:48 AM
Local Mean Time

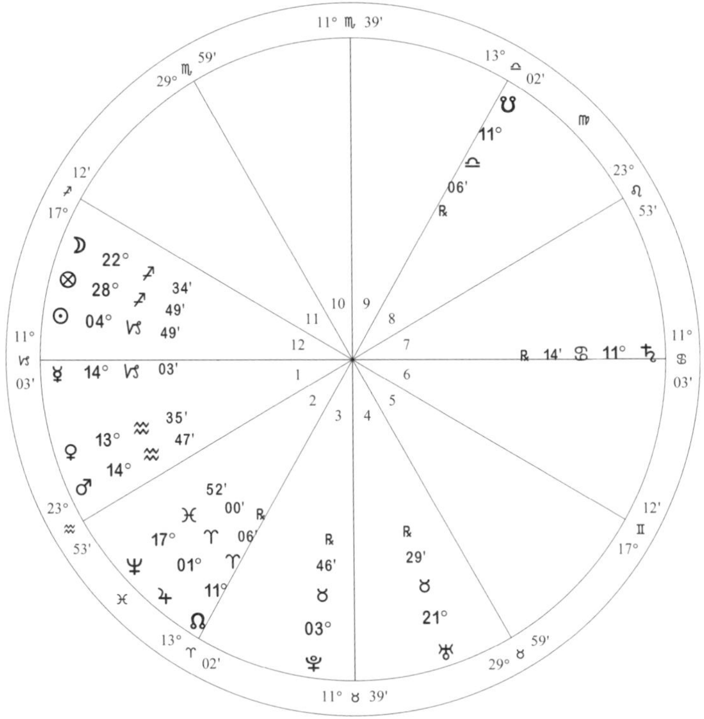

Dorothean Ess. Dig. (No Mut Rec. Points)								
Pl	Ruler	Exalt	Tripl	Term	Face	Detri	Fall	Score
☉	♄	♂	♀	♀	♃	☽	♃	- 5 P
☽	♃	☋	☉	♄	♄	☿	--	- 5 P
☿	♄	♂	♀	♃	♂ m	☽	♃	- 5 P
♀	♄	--	♄ m	♀ +	☿	☉	--	+2
♂	♄	--	♄	♀	☿ m	☉	--	- 5 P
♃	♂	☉	☉	♃ +	♂	♀	♄	+2
♄	☽	♃	♀ m	♃	☿	♄ -	♂	- 10 P
☊	♂	☉	☉	♀	☉	♀	♄	--
⊗	♃	☋ +	☉	♂	♄	☿	--	--
As	♄	♂	♀	☿	♂	☽	♃	--
Mc	♂	--	♀	♃	☉	♀	☽	--
☋	♀	♄	♄	♃	♄	♂	☉	--

Hs	Alm. (Pto)
1	♂♄
2	♄
3	☉
4	♀
5	♀
6	☿
7	♃
8	☉
9	♄
10	♂
11	♂
12	♃

Example 6-4b. Louis Pasteur relocation solar return 1856

no less. Jupiter that year also ruled the 11th – and Pasteur sent off to one of his best friends to join him, who then wooed and won the rector's younger daughter!

Madame Pasteur proved worthy to the challenge of being a fine academic wife: she not only ran his household, she helped him with his notes and publications. This was not yet the time of Marie Curie. In Pasteur's natal chart, his wife is shown by exalted Mars in Capricorn. Here, in the solar return where he met her, the Sun rules the 7th, showing his new focus on marriage.

Our second example from Pasteur's life was his move back to Paris from Lille, when he was promoted to administrator and director of scientific studies at École normale in Paris, October 1857. This was definitely a career move up. While he had distinguished himself in the provinces, all scientific roads in 19th century France ran to Paris.

With the Ruler of the 1st in Detriment partile conjunct the 7th house cusp, and the ruler of the 7th merely peregrine, the choice about moving was clear. From this point, Pasteur's career flourished, thanks initially to his mentors, and then later, to his brilliance. In this solar return year, Mercury had returned to its natal sign. What is perhaps most significant was the South Node conjunct the 9th house cusp. It was this appointment which began to reduce his teaching responsibilities, which in turn gave him more available time for his researches, which are what proved so brilliant. We don't actually have a good house placement for scientific research, but it may well not be the 9th house. Here, it seems to prefigure an end to his classroom teaching, even if he was still within academia.

I could make a good case for research being a 12th house enterprise: at least the scientific research prior to the huge teams of scientists that we saw develop in the latter half of the 20th century. Pasteur's own success actually began to drive that process, as he progressed from a couple of research assistants – not unusual in the days of gentlemen scientists – to the Pasteur Institute, one of the great early research facilities. But we are getting ahead of ourselves!

In this year in which he could suddenly do more research, there was quite a 12th house focus, with both the Sun and Moon there. The 12th house was ruled by Jupiter in Aries, in out-of-sect Triplicity.

So Pasteur's decision to return to Paris seemed to pick up several diverse threads in this solar return. The Venus-Mars in the 1st house were probably indicative of his intrinsic workaholism. The greater angular focus of this year may also be reflected in the recognition within the scientific community of his discovery of lactic acid yeast fermentation, published in this solar year. This was the second of many of his discoveries which, individually, would have been adequate to mark his as a highly distinguished career.

Eleanor and Franklin Move to Albany

By the time that Franklin Delano Roosevelt was elected a State Senator in New York, he and Eleanor had been married five years, and she had borne four children, three of them still surviving. This was in the great Before of Eleanor's life: before Franklin developed polio, before either of them had met Lucy Mercer (Franklin's paramour), and before Eleanor had met Lorena Hickock. At this time, Eleanor was just one of your normal political wives: someone to smile from the platform during a campaign stop.

According to our 1st-7th equation, this move was not so good: Venus in Libra ruled staying, while Mars in Libra ruled moving. A clear call, except for the question of what to say about Saturn conjunct the Ascendant. At this stage in her life, the hint for this is seen in the partile opposition of Uranus and Neptune at her MC/IC axis, where Saturn ruled the 10th. Eleanor was an orphan, raised by her maternal grandmother. So Franklin's mother was a real shock. Franklin was a serious mother's boy, and his mother Sara, whom Eleanor had known as a cousin before the marriage, continued to dominate the marriage for many years afterward. Thus, while overall, the move to Albany represented isolation for Eleanor, it did

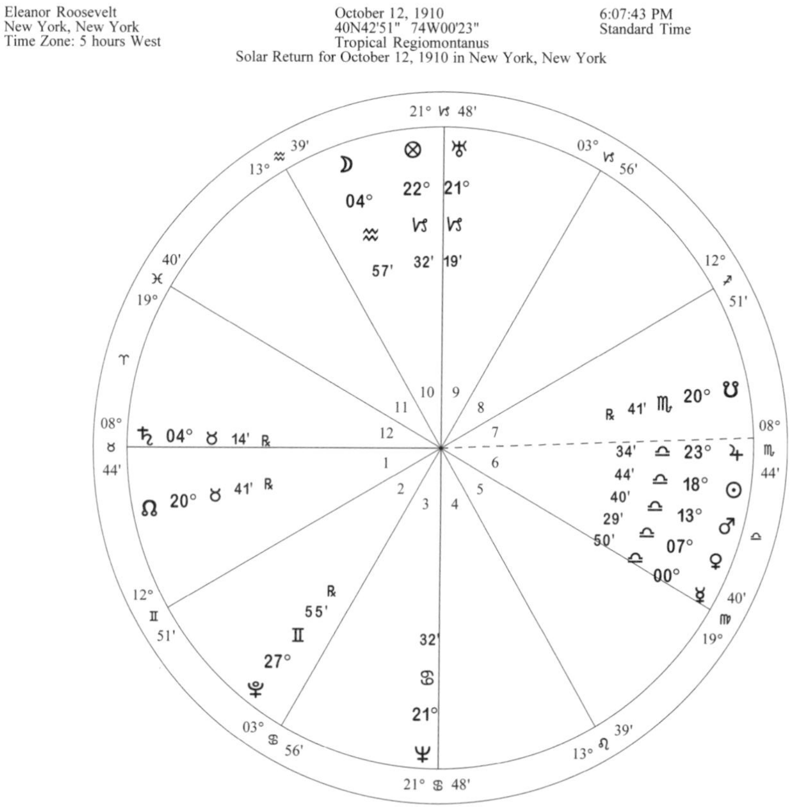
Eleanor Roosevelt
New York, New York
Time Zone: 5 hours West
October 12, 1910
40N42'51" 74W00'23"
Tropical Regiomontanus
Solar Return for October 12, 1910 in New York, New York
6:07:43 PM
Standard Time

Dorothean Ess. Dig. (No Mut Rec. Points)								
Pl	Ruler	Exalt	Tripl	Term	Face	Detri	Fall	Score
☉	♀	♄	☿	♃	♄	♂	☉ -	- 9 P
☽	♄	--	☿	♄	♀ m	☉	--	- 5 P
☿	♀	♄	☿ +	♄	☽	♂	☉	+3
♀	♀ +	♄	☿	♀ +	☽ m	♂	☉	+7
♂	♀	♄	☿	♃	♄	♂ -	☉	- 10 P
♃	♀	♄	☿	☿	♃ +	♂	☉	+1
♄	♀	☽	☽	♀	☿	♂	--	- 5 P
☊	♀	☽	☽	♃	♄	♂	--	--
⊗	♄	♂	☽	♂	☉	☽	♃	--
As	♀	☽	☽	☿	☿	♂	--	--
Mc	♄	♂	☽	♂	☉	☽	♃	--
☋	♂	--	♂	♀	♀	♀	☽	--

Hs	Alm. (Pto)
1	☽
2	☿
3	☽
4	☽
5	☉
6	☿
7	♂
8	♃
9	♄
10	♂
11	♄
12	♃

Example 6-5. Eleanor Roosevelt relocation solar return for 1910

have the value for her of isolating both Franklin and her from her mother-in-law.

It's worth mentioning that there was never any doubt about this move, once Franklin was elected to the State Senate. Eleanor had no say-so about moving. Normally today, when we examine solar return charts for clients, we assume that they can make or at least contribute to decisions about matters like moving. Even if married, one presumes that both of the partners have a say in major family matters like relocation. Not so for a married woman in 1910 – or even in 1965!

While that Uranus-Neptune opposition right on an angle is certainly a striking feature of the year, its long-term influence upon Eleanor is questionable. The opposition was tightest to Eleanor's natal Neptune *[SEE EXAMPLE 3-5 ON PAGE 79]*, although it was within orb of both her Sun, Moon, and Mars. Call this the first taste of freedom from parental control. Eleanor was a naturally shy girl, and so standing up for herself was a skill she would only learn slowly and gradually.

Mary Godwin Shelley's Return to England

Mary and Percy Shelley had lived quite a life on the European Continent. They had had four children, although only one survived. They had loved, created poetry and novels, and experienced the movements for political independence. And then all of a sudden, Percy drowned. Percy had a modest income of his own, but mainly, he was the sole heir to a large fortune. Mary, on the other hand, had a father who was perennially in debt, regularly bailed out by his friends, and even several times by Percy.

With Percy's sudden death, their surviving son was now the heir to the fortune. But Mary had no control, because Percy had no control: his very conventional father had no use for Percy's radical lifestyle, nor that of his wife and now widow. Mary's return

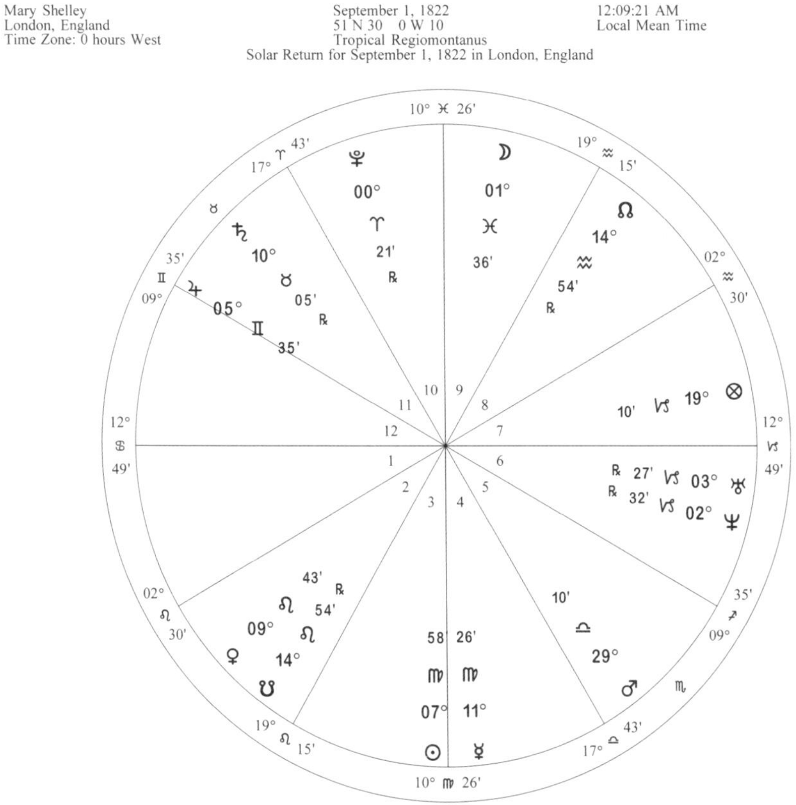
Mary Shelley
London, England
Time Zone: 0 hours West
September 1, 1822
51 N 30 0 W 10
Tropical Regiomontanus
12:09:21 AM
Local Mean Time
Solar Return for September 1, 1822 in London, England

Dorothean Ess. Dig. (No Mut Rec. Points)

Pl	Ruler	Exalt	Tripl	Term	Face	Detri	Fall	Score
☉	☿	☿	☽	♀	☉ +	♃	♀	+1
☽	♃	♀	♂	♀	♄ m	☿	☿	- 5 P
☿	☿ +	☿ +	☽	♀ m	♀	♃	♀	+9
♀	☉	--	♃	☿ m	♄	♄	--	- 5 P
♂	♀	♄	☿	☊	♃	♂ -	☉	- 10 P
♃	☿	☊	☿	☿	♃ +	♃ -	--	- 4
♄	♀	☽	☽	☿	☽ m	♂	--	- 5 P
☊	♄	--	☿	♀	☿	☉	--	--
⊗	♄	♂	☽	♂	♂	☽	♃	--
As	☽	♃	♂	♃	☿	♄	♂	--
Mc	♃	♀	♂	♃	♃	☿	☿	--
☋	☉	--	♃	♀	♃	♄	--	--

Hs	Alm. (Pto)
1	♃
2	☉
3	♃
4	☿
5	♀♄
6	♃
7	♂♄
8	♄
9	♄
10	♃
11	☉♂
12	☿

Example 6-6. Mary Shelley relocation solar return for 1822

to England was to put her financial house in order, and then get an allowance for her son, and to go back to work as a writer, as her father had done before her. Was the move a good idea? Did she have any choice?

There are several ways to read her circumstances in the solar return. While the Moon is the sign ruler of the 1st, Jupiter is the Almuten. Given her circumstances at the time, Jupiter in Detriment does seem to describe her better than a Moon with Triplicity! The 7th also had two options: Saturn or Mars.

The critical piece in understanding this is to see Mars in the 5th: her son, Percy Florence. He was the trump card. Saturn was in bad shape, as was Mars in Detriment: but Mars was just about to go into dignity, thus, about to improve.

This chart shows so many of her circumstances for the year. First, when she arrived in London, she lived with her father until she could establish her own place. The Sun was at the 4th house cusp: literally, the place of the father. It took her a while to manage to reach an *entente* with her father-in-law, but she did. In fact, she did something highly unusual and probably highly unpredictable: she raised Percy Florence to be absolutely conventional, far more like his grandfather than his father. The Mercury in Virgo, the same sign as in her natal [*SEE EXAMPLE 3-3 ON PAGE 71*], went to work, and she supported herself and her son with her writing until 1844, when her father-in-law died, then Percy Florence supported her until her death.

Thus, the Part of Fortune in the 7th in this case showed fortune both from the move, and from her late husband's family, even if grudgingly. But her father supplied great moral support, and father and daughter buried their differences.

Does this system of comparing 1st and 7th to test the question of whether staying or moving is the better argument *always* work out? Like any other idea in astrology, the answer is no. Consider this idea a little more carefully. Do people move *every other year*, or, alternately, *should* they? Because this is one case where one could expect that roughly half the time, the argument would point to the 1st, and half the time, the argument would point to the 7th. Like most arguments in astrology, this is suggestive only.

But I cannot emphasize enough: not all people will move given any particular set of astrological configurations. There are simply people who find moving to be a solution to an impasse, whereas others would never think to do so. Mary and Percy's escape to the European continent was fairly unusual in their day. Many people's economic circumstances have made moving difficult. Trying to balance the logic of a move when an entire family is involved is much more difficult than a single person. A change in property values can completely change the possibility of moving. Many circumstances, both individual and cultural, are involved.

So it is probably better to say in a given period that the solar return chart supports or doesn't support a move if there are other circumstances which would suggest it.

7

Solar Returns for Education
and other 9ᵗʰ House Matters

WHAT DOES EDUCATION LOOK LIKE IN THE CHART? Our general model for education revolves around the 3ʳᵈ/9ᵗʰ house axis. The 3ʳᵈ house in contemporary astrology is referred to as childhood education, which is a modern translation of the older idea of apprenticeship. A child in any society has to learn how to function as an adult. Whether this is in the form of learning a trade, learning what foods to gather which are ripe or edible, or learning the multiplication tables, the 3ʳᵈ house is said to rule two things: what everybody knows, and what everybody in one's trade knows. One is not assumed to have achieved mastery in the 3ʳᵈ house: only adequacy. Thus, al-Biruni is one of the few ancient authors to list a house rulership for schools, which he gave to the 3ʳᵈ.[1] Education was generally given to Mercury;[2] scholars (or those already educated) to Jupiter.[3] Yet, al-Biruni could also give education to the 1ˢᵗ, perhaps because Mercury joys there.[4]

But now we must address this question from a different direction, and that is through another great 3ʳᵈ house association: neighbors, siblings, and cousins. In many if not most societies, what a boy does is more or less what his father does, and what a girl does is more or less what her mother does. So the simple answer is: in such societies younger children learned a lot from their older siblings, and only the oldest boy or oldest girl learned exclusively from the parents – and that's if older cousins were not around. As each child learns how to do something, they are teaching the next oldest how to do what they already know, just as they are mastering the next lesson from the sibling or cousin before. Then, father or mother simply stands at the top of the chain, providing overall authority and supervision. While Mercury may rule the mental wiring that we possess which helps us learn, learning is learning, whether it involves sums, or setting type, or learning how to bend iron, or blow glass. In almost all societies and situations, it is agreed that the best way to learn is by doing, and hierarchies of peers provide the mechanism, as the older relatives assist the younger ones in how to do their future jobs. So it is actually this hands-on learning which is so characteristic of the 3ʳᵈ house.

There is a tendency in today's astrology to divide formal education, putting primary education in the 3ʳᵈ house, and university training in the 9ᵗʰ house, perhaps reflecting the family's expectations or history. While I would certainly agree with the attributions of these extreme points, I would question the intermediate steps, and the logic for how to place other models of learning between the two houses. It is here I will step out a little from my colleagues in part through the model that I observed in Asian martial arts. There is much that is traditional about martial arts, and it is to this tradition that we must turn.

When a student begins training in the martial arts of Japan or Korea (and I assume for many other types, although I have not directly experienced them), the starting place is the same, no matter the age. The white belt beginner is not presumed to be stupid, inept, or incompetent, but simply unlearned. As a white belt, there are certain goals that are established that have to be learned in order to advance. The white belt stays at that level until these goals are reached. Once the student has met the requirements, he or she is allowed to test – and then advance to the next level, where the process is repeated. So my question: how is this education different, for a child or an adult? The goal is the same. So could this really be 3rd house for one, and 9th house for the other? It's not the age that the person does the training: it's the nature of how it is done.

As one proceeds up the belt levels, a lot of how one learns is from one's peers, exactly as if this were the family business, and the peers were relatives or fellow apprentices. And the reasoning around why this is true is also the same: in martial arts, the goal is to acquire certain bodily skills – to learn through doing. The grading system of the belts may provide a certain ego satisfaction for the person going through the process, but the learning-by-doing mode is what actually characterizes the 3rd house, rather than the age at which it occurs.

Modern primary education in developed societies has somewhat confused these learning objectives, as the educational requirements shift increasingly toward intellectual achievements. However, it remains true that at these levels of learning, peer interaction often enhances learning. When children are forced to learn in isolation, the overall result is often stunted compared to those children who learn the same lessons in a classroom which allows peer interaction.

Systems such as Montessori don't work exclusively because they have more teachers. They also work because the students learn to help each other, not just pursue their own private goals. It is the very social nature of our humanity that makes learning together satisfying, fun, and productive.

But what happens when one achieves a black belt, or passes on to "higher" education? The answer is: the goals shift. One of the odd juxtapositions for many modern astrologers to understand is the combination of higher education and religion both sharing the 9th house. Considering history, this oddity makes sense. In the Middle Ages, the university was part of the Church. The curriculum included a large dose of philosophy, which gave the primary means of reasoning.

Consider again the almost mystical symbolism of the black belt in martial arts studies. Whoever made it a goal to get a brown belt? Or a yellow one? Except as an intermediate step along the way to the *real* goal, of course. More to our point, once you attain a black belt, your whole curriculum changes. You become a teacher in a different way. The black belt community is designed to encompass the *serious* students – the ones who made it through the preliminary steps and continue anyway. They are the ones who demonstrate perseverance. This is not terribly different from the psychology of attaining a university degree. Who has the goal of becoming a junior? Whether it's a piece of black cloth or a piece of sheepskin, the object is to complete a round of training that has a title attached to it.

In the Medieval guild system, every apprentice did not become a master if they simply stayed with the program long enough. Almost any apprentice *could* become a journeyman. Mastery required a demonstration of skill that established the journeyman as possessing a master's skills. In Medieval times, the *Master* of Arts was the terminal degree in the faculty of the Arts. Doctorates were only available in three fields: theology, medicine, and law. It is when learning occurs within an environment in which the students already have achieved a certain level of expertise, that 9th house learning can be said to occur. In this learning, masters are creating peers.

Now really: what is the difference with Lilly's day? It is revealing that in Lilly's section on nativities, his subtitle for the 9th house lists "Of Journeys and Religion."[5] *You didn't "go to the 9th" to learn a trade: you went to the 3rd*. Remember that university was not there to teach a vocation: it was the arts of free men, which didn't really include the trade class. It was where the sons of the wealthy or nobles went. The degree was a general one and one that was not applicable to a specific vocation. The two "vocational" degrees, namely law and medicine, were highly technical professions whose graduates were *part* of the upper classes. The one profession that relied most heavily on the university system was the Church, which always was somewhat open to the brighter sons of the lesser classes. Here we see again that our modern association of the 9th with higher education, church, and law really isn't a random aggregation.

And yet – in his horary section, Lilly lists the question, if one shall profit by his knowledge.[6] In that case, he looked for a dignified ruler of the 9th, ideally a benefic, in an easy aspect to the Ruler of the Ascendant for "good" knowledge. Aspect by square or opposition meant that the knowledge was there, but it would do no good. Here, perhaps we have the germ upon which to build our reasoning. Most people are not studying merely for personal enjoyment – although such a desire might show as well through Lilly's horary model. In Gadbury's section on the 9th house in solar returns, the aphorisms break out into thirteen related to journeying, mostly for business; one for trouble from the law; and one concerning religious matters. Again, nothing about education.[7]

It is also worth studying Lilly's section on obtaining benefices.[8] We may even see how this works in such fiction as Jane Austen's *Sense and Sensibility*. One often *bought* a parsonage, which meant that, having purchased it, the rents of the land were one's yearly income, but these were granted not as ownership, but as tenancy. One had to obtain a cleric licensure, which meant that one had to have some university education, but this wouldn't necessarily entail a degree. So now, this makes more sense as a model for the acquisition of a position based on education.

Here, we are going to examine six case studies relating to education:

- Buzz Aldrin graduated from West Point with a B.S. Degree, and then later went back for his doctorate.
- Marie Curie studied at a Polish gymnasium before enrolling at the Sorbonne, eventually taking a doctorate.
- Martin Luther King, Jr. was ordained as a minister before receiving any academic degree, but he was working on his B.A. He then received a Bachelor of Divinity, and finally, a doctorate. This will also allow us to examine these two different 9th house activities.
- Michelle Kwan received her B.A. degree after her amateur skating career was completed.
- Louis Pasteur studied near his home in Arbois before attending college in Paris, ultimately receiving his doctorate.
- Percy Bysshe Shelley matriculated at Oxford and was then expelled for his political views.

This may seem like a lot of doctorates! Here, my "sample" is skewed by being famous people. Pasteur and Curie worked in a field where the doctorate was necessary for success. Our list of biographies also includes a number of sports champions. In many sports, college is completely useless, because the person must already be mostly formed as an athlete before the age of college. So among our athletes, except in a field like U.S. football or basketball, where college play is effectively an apprenticeship for professional play, college is something for after the competitive career has ended. Thus, Michelle Kwan is very proud of her academic achievement as something which will help her in the rest of her life. In the earlier amateur period of figure skating, which in the U.S. is to say before Peggy Fleming trail-blazed a new professional trajectory, academic achievement was quite common. Both Dick Button, the 1948 and

1952 Men's Olympic gold medalist, and Hayes Jenkins, the 1956 Olympic gold medalist, went on to study law at Harvard, while Tenley Albright, 1956 Women's Olympic gold medalist, also went to Harvard, but for medicine.

However, in judging actual cases, the issue is far less which degree the person achieves, than whether one's education is dramatically more or less than one's parents. As early as Hellenistic astrology, the consideration of whether the Native's social status would be higher or lower than one's parents was already embedded as an astrological consideration. Pasteur's father was a tanner, so any academic achievement on his part broke a family mold. Curie's parents were both teachers, so while her doctorate trumped their degrees, it was of the same nature, and thus, less surprising. Shelley went to Oxford because his family was rich, and because that was where rich boys went. Martin Luther King, Sr., attended the same school, Morehead College, where Martin Jr. would later get his B.A. This was in a time when preaching in the South was not seen to require any degree at all. But King Sr. did not get the doctorate as his son later did.

So here we will focus on what the attainment of education looks like.

Buzz Aldrin and West Point

West Point, like all the military academies, mixes military training and discipline with academic rigor. The successful result is a commission *and* an academic degree. Thus, the experience is very different than a civilian university experience. Further, a graduate of a military academy is already on active service, so graduation brings an automatic job assignment.

Buzz's father was also in the military, so we can also view his time at West Point as following in the family tradition. How well adapted to this life was he? The **Almuten of his Profession** is Mercury. With Mercury ruling two of the angles, and Jupiter the other two,

one would expect one or the other to dominate. In Buzz's case, Mercury is in out-of-sect Triplicity, close to the 9th house cusp, but in the 8th, and trine Jupiter, ruler of his MC.

His two most dignified planets, however, are Mars and Saturn: Mars by Exaltation and Face, and also mixed Triplicity, and Saturn by sign. Both are in the 7th, although Mars is close enough to the 8th house cusp to be considered succedent. That very dignified Saturn rules his 9th house. This indicates that he will be successful in structured educational programs. A military academy is about as structured as it gets!

If a typical college experience lasts four years, it is about as impossible to have four (or five) consecutive solar returns that present the same pattern as it is to experience all four years of college as being of the same nature. One year is often easier or more difficult than the one before, or the one after.

Being born in January, Buzz always experienced each school year under two different influences. The Fall term would be under the solar return of the prior January; the Spring term of the following January. Just as most businesses run on the civil calendar, most academic endeavors run on the school year. But the time of the birthday may break this pattern up. In a sense, people born during Summer may have the easiest time with the academic year, because their personal solar change happens between the two school years.

Here, to graph Buzz's undergraduate experience, we actually need five solar returns, not four. His freshman year fell under his 1947 and 1948 solar returns. His sophomore year fell under his 1948 and 1949 solar returns. His junior year fell under his 1949 and 1950 solar returns. His senior year fell under his 1950 and 1951 solar returns.

Beginning with his 1947 solar return, there is a Saturn-Sun opposition straddling the Ascendant-Descendant axis. Immediately he is challenged – but that is exactly the kind of hazing process one expects at the beginning of the military experience. A freshman has a lowly status that only time will mitigate. Buzz's 1947 solar return was very saturnian, from the Saturn rising, to the Moon in Capricorn. But this was an environment that wasn't foreign to him. Solar return Mars was in the same sign as his natal Mars [SEE EXAMPLE 3-1 ON PAGE 65]. The 6th house focus of the chart was probably just as well, as this is a cadent house. One imagines in this circumstance that any freshman who rebelled against the seniority system undoubtedly had a tougher time: this tendency to stick out would be shown by a very angular chart for the year, which Buzz didn't have.

Buzz's 1948 solar return had Neptune rising. I cannot think of a better place for Neptune for a freshman at a military academy. One of the very obvious effects of a prominent Neptune is invisibility. This is one of the better times in one's life to be invisible!

Now that the solar return is moving into Buzz's second year in college, what exactly are we looking for? The average college student goes to college, disappears into the process, and emerges typically four to five years later with a degree. Honestly, all we can expect to see are the deviations from that path.

Buzz's natal 9th house is ruled by Saturn, which is both essentially dignified and angular. One would conclude that higher education should not be problematic for him, and that he should have little difficulty pursuing it, and in fact, he will probably excel at it. So in Buzz's case, we are really only looking for an argument of a temporary catastrophic failure of a magnitude to derail the natal chart argument of success. There isn't one.

Buzz's freshman-sophomore solar return, with its dignified Taurus Moon, shows he remains on track. However, this year represents a quadrature change in the solar return, where the rising sign shifts to cardinal. This shift sometimes denotes a change in one's perception of life. Going from fixed as it had been in 1946

and 1947, life opens out a bit. I have no doubt that the Uranus-Fortuna conjunction in his 9th for that year brought some interesting diversions or disruptions, but with Fortuna there, they didn't cause him any harm. Perhaps he had some great insights, or perhaps he wasn't caught in some rebellion!

The 1949 return had several recapitulations of the natal chart: the Moon, Venus, and Mercury were all in their natal signs. There's also a kind of recapitulation that isn't officially in the books, but may be worth noting. Buzz's natal Jupiter is debilitated by being in Detriment in Gemini. In that year, his Jupiter was debilitated by being in Fall. It's just enough of a similarity that it may be meaningful.

Generally, a year with a lot of natal recapitulation is a good year, because it's as if the natal chart were shining through more strongly. This is good, unless the natal chart is really challenging. As we have seen, Buzz's chart shows good natal 9th house strength, so this should be a good year for him academically.

His 1950 solar return, which bridged his junior and senior years, had Neptune angular, like his 1948 return. Mercury had returned to his natal sign of Capricorn, but it was retrograde. The Moon and Jupiter were in signs trine to their natal positions, but perhaps most importantly, the Descendant was the degree of his natal Moon. That Jupiter ruled his solar return 9th, and was dignified – again, nothing to interfere with the natal 9th house strength.

His final term in 1951 had his SR-Mercury again in his natal sign, but this time direct. Saturn rules his 9th natally; here, it was exalted, although retrograde, and doubly approaching the trine to the Sun. Jupiter ruled his solar return 9th, and Jupiter was right there dignified in Pisces, with the highly dignified Moon in Cancer trine to it. Buzz finished third in his graduating class, allowing him to begin his military career with an assignment to his liking.

Edward "Buzz" Aldrin
Montclair, New Jersey
Time Zone: 5 hours West

January 20, 1947
40N49'33" 74W12'34"
Tropical Regiomontanus
Solar Return for January 20, 1947 in Montclair, New Jersey

5:15:30 PM
Standard Time

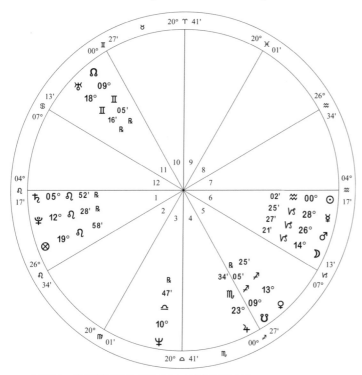

Edward "Buzz" Aldrin
Montclair, New Jersey
Time Zone: 5 hours West

January 20, 1948
40N49'33" 74W12'34"
Tropical Regiomontanus
Solar Return for January 20, 1948 in Montclair, New Jersey

11:02:24 PM
Standard Time

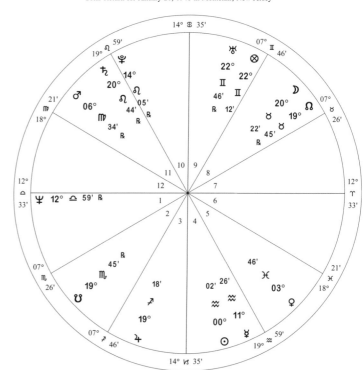

Example 7-1a. Buzz Aldrin education solar return for 1947

Example 7-1b. Buzz Aldrin education solar return for 1948

Edward "Buzz" Aldrin
Montclair, New Jersey
Time Zone: 5 hours West

January 20, 1949
40N49'33" 74W12'34"
Tropical Regiomontanus

4:52:34 AM
Standard Time

Solar Return for January 20, 1949 in Montclair, New Jersey

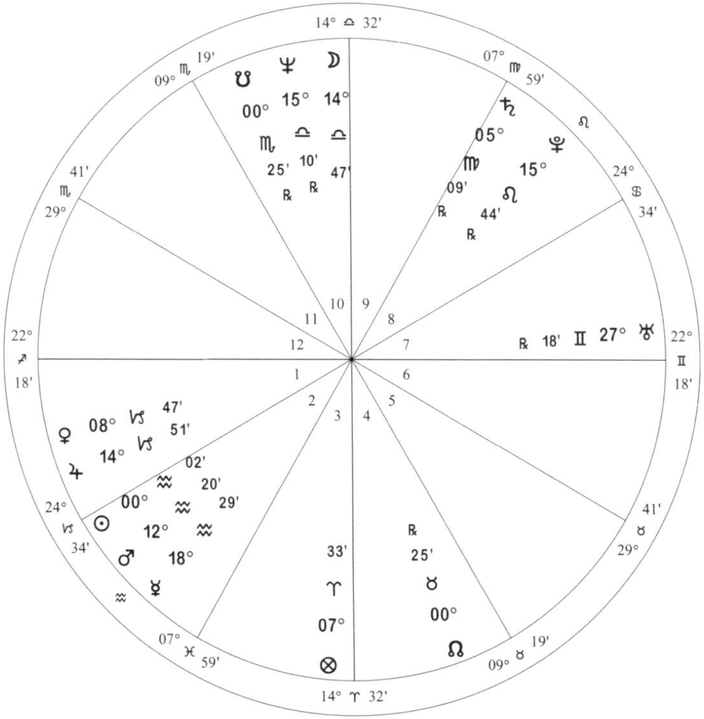

Pl	Ruler	Exalt	Tripl	Term	Face	Detri	Fall	Score
☉	♄	--	☿	♄	♀	☉ -	--	- 10 P
☽	♀	♄	☿	♃	♄	♂	☉	- 5 P
☿	♄ m	--	☿ +	♀ m	☿ +	☉	--	+4
♀	♄	♂	☽	☿ m	♃	☽	♃	- 5 P
♂	♄	--	☿	♀	☿	☉	--	- 5 P
♃	♄	♂	☽	♃ +	♂	☽	♃ -	- 2
♄	☿ m	☿	☽	☿	☉	♃	♀	- 5 P
☊	♀	☽	☽	♀	☿	♂	--	--
⊗	♂	☉	♃	♀	♂	♀	♄	--
As	♃	☋	♃	♄	♄	☿	--	--
Mc	♀	♄	☿	♃	♄	♂	☉	--
☋	♂	--	♂	♂	♂	♀	☽	--

Dorothean Ess. Dig. (No Mut Rec. Points)

Hs	Alm. (Pto)
1	♃
2	♂
3	♀
4	☉♂
5	☽
6	☽
7	☿
8	☽
9	☿
10	♀♄
11	♂
12	♂

Example 7-1c. Buzz Aldrin education solar return for 1949

Edward "Buzz" Aldrin
Montclair, New Jersey
Time Zone: 5 hours West

January 20, 1950
40N49'33" 74W12'34"
Tropical Regiomontanus

10:43:36 AM
Standard Time

Solar Return for January 20, 1950 in Montclair, New Jersey

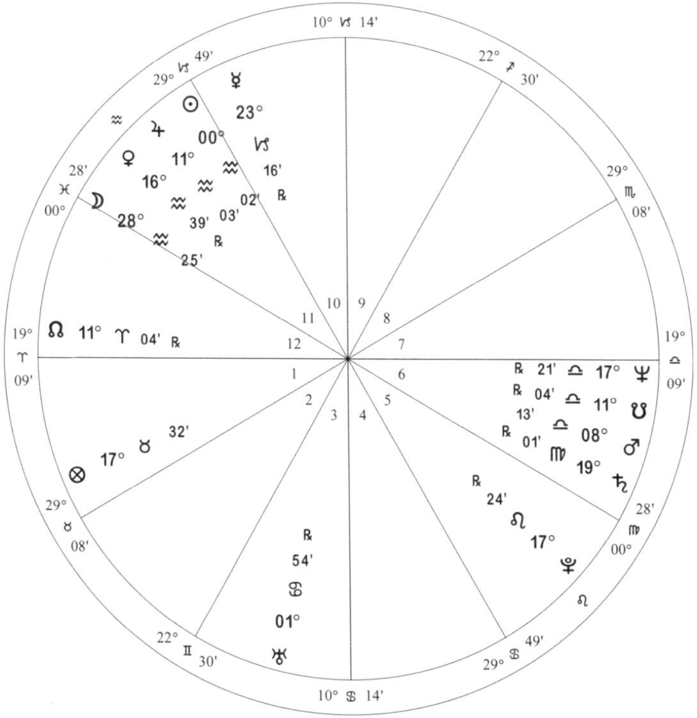

Pl	Ruler	Exalt	Tripl	Term	Face	Detri	Fall	Score
☉	♄	--	♄	♄	♀	☉ -	--	- 10 P
☽	♄	--	♄	♂	☽ +	☉	--	+1
☿	♄ m	♂	♀	♂	☉	☽	♃	- 5 P
♀	♄	--	♄ m	♀ +	☿	☉	--	+2
♂	♀	♄	♄	♀	☽	♂ -	☉	- 10 P
♃	♄	--	♄	☿	☿	☉	--	- 5 P
♄	☿ m	☿	♀ m	♄ +	♀	♃	♀	+2
☊	♂	☉	☉	♀	☉	♀	♄	--
⊗	♀	☽	♀	♃	☽	♂	--	--
As	♂	☉	☉	☿	☉	♀	♄	--
Mc	♄	♂	♀	☿	♂	☽	♃	--
☋	♀	♄	♄	♃	♄	♂	☉	--

Dorothean Ess. Dig. (No Mut Rec. Points)

Hs	Alm. (Pto)
1	☉
2	♀
3	☿♄
4	♃
5	☽
6	☿
7	♄
8	♂
9	♃
10	♂♄
11	♄
12	♀

Example 7-1d. Buzz Aldrin education solar return for 1950

Edward "Buzz" Aldrin
Montclair, New Jersey
Time Zone: 5 hours West

January 20, 1951
40N49'33" 74W12'34"
Tropical Regiomontanus
Solar Return for January 20, 1951 in Montclair, New Jersey

4:36:04 PM
Standard Time

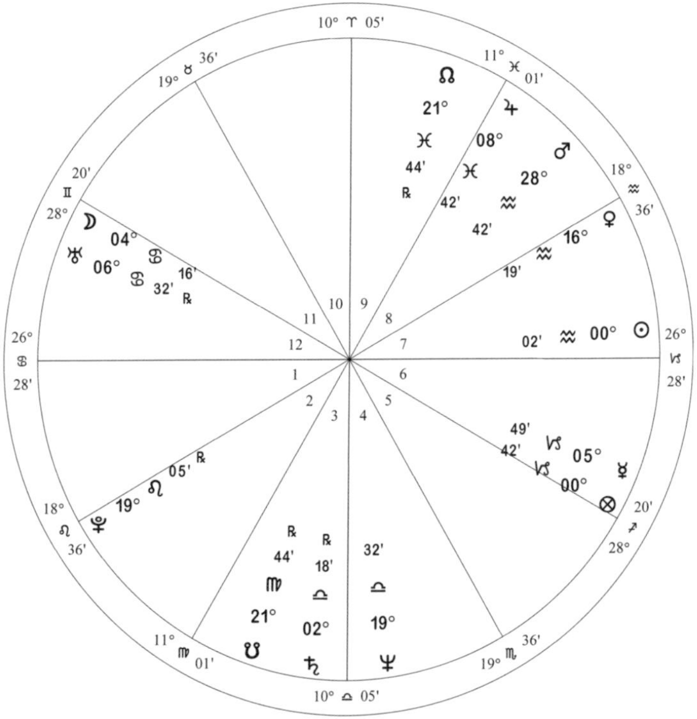

Dorothean Ess. Dig. (No Mut Rec. Points)								
Pl	Ruler	Exalt	Tripl	Term	Face	Detri	Fall	Score
☉	♄	--	♄	♄	♀	☉ -	--	- 10 P
☽	☽ +	♃	♀	♂	♀	♄	♂	+5
☿	♄	♂	♀	♀	♃	☽	♃	- 5 P
♀	♄ m	--	♄	♀ +	☿	☉	--	+2
♂	♄	--	♄	♂ +	☽	☉	--	+2
♃	♃ +	♀	♀	♃ +	♄	☿	☿	+7
♄	♀ m	♄ +	♄ +	♄ +	☽	♂	☉	+9
☊	♃	♀	♀	♂	♂	☿	☿	--
⊗	♄	♂	♀	♀	♃	☽	♃	--
As	☽	♃	♀	♀	☽	♄	♂	--
Mc	♂	☉	☉	♀	☉	♀	♄	--
☋	☿	☿	♀	♄	☿	♃	♀	--

Hs	Alm. (Pto)
1	☽
2	☉
3	☿
4	♄
5	♂
6	♃
7	♄
8	♄
9	♃
10	☉
11	♀
12	☿

Example 7-1e. Buzz Aldrin education solar return for 1951

Marie Curie: PhD after the Fact

As mentioned, both of Marie Curie's parents were teachers. However, because of the political issues related to Russian occupation of Poland, her family was poor. She had worked as a governess, in part to support her older sister's medical studies at the Sorbonne, under an agreement that first she would aid her sister, and then her sister in turn would help her.

Marie Curie is an excellent example to use when someone asks, but what do I do with my planets in detriment? Marie had Venus in Detriment ruling the 9th house. Her family background may have said yes to education, but her gender and her nationality said *no*. Having a planet in detriment means that you have to expend more effort to get something done – it doesn't mean you cannot do it. The quintessential image of Marie Curie is processing *tons* of pitchblende to obtain a large enough sample of radium to measure an atomic weight. And this latter point really adds to the difficulty factor: she didn't need to purify that much radium in order to prove that she had discovered a new element: she'd already done *that*. She did it to follow the standard procedures for a new element, which included establishing an atomic weight.

So we may say that Marie succeeded academically despite her Venus in Scorpio, which means that we have to go looking for another factor to back it up. The Sun-Pluto opposition is a good place to start, but even here, the Sun is fortified by its dispositor Mars in Scorpio: which also disposes that Venus. It would have been very easy for her to simply stay in Poland and be a governess, or to do just enough to get a teaching license, or simply to get married. She didn't. Every step of the way, she took the harder path, shown by the opposition.

So, she arrived in Paris to begin studying at the Sorbonne in October 1891, just a month before her birthday. So we begin with her solar return for 1890. And this was not an easy year for her. She didn't like leaving her father. (Note the South Node conjunct the 4th house cusp – the father.) The trip was a difficult one. (The Neptune-Pluto conjunction is in the 9th, square her radix Nodes.) She had recently come out of a failed love relationship. (7th house ruler Jupiter was conjunct a peregrine, and thus thoroughly malefic, Mars.) When she arrived in Paris, her sister wasn't there to meet her, and her new brother-in-law was loquacious, just when she wanted quiet to study. (Her brother-in-law would be the 9th, her sister's husband, ruled by Venus in Sagittarius.)

For most of the year 1890, Marie was waiting for a marriage proposal that never came. Jupiter, which ruled the marriage partner was in its natal sign [SEE EXAMPLE 3-2 ON PAGE 69]. Unfortunately, for the state of her emotions, the Moon was in the sign opposite her natal Moon sign. The Moon-Saturn in the 12th suggests the possibility of an emotional disappointment. This reading is further affirmed when we observe that the Moon was actually translating the light between Neptune and Pluto and Saturn – by square, no less! This is emphatically *not* a signature for a nice warm happy year, as one would have expected, given that the marriage she had in mind was for love.

It was as she reached the *apoklima* of her Sun position that she moved to France – and to higher education. And so we might wonder whether we shall see the changes in the 1890 or in the 1891 solar return. The Moon-Mercury in Virgo was no doubt hypersensitive to the environment. Marie's natal Mercury debilitated may be thought of as having the same qualities as well. As I have stated repeatedly, I do not consider the debilities to represent a lack of talent. But a debilitated Mercury can find that in order to thrive, the environment for learning needs careful control. In a year with the Moon-Saturn, that control must extend to solitude.

This need for the perfect learning conditions was only heightened in the 1891 solar return, where we see the partile Neptune-Pluto conjunction opposite her natal Mercury and square her Nodes. But after her birthday, she ruthlessly created her own environment in a tiny walk-up apartment, where there literally was nothing to distract her from her purpose at the time.

The Moon in Capricorn might not have been the most comfortable position, but it was sextile her Sun, and her solar return Venus was nearly exactly her natal Venus. Also observe the South Node in the 1st conjunct Venus in Detriment, her radix Venus sign. The South Node in the 1st represents a difficult year energetically, because one is tired all the time. Marie to a certain extent created those conditions anyway through overwork and stress, but this is obviously an easier road for a young person than somebody older.

It was under the following solar return, the 1892 one, that she received her license (degree) in physics, ranking first, in the Spring of 1893. Here, we see a more prominent 9th house than in the other two years. Mercury was in the house, in Sagittarius, its radix sign. Normally, we would wonder about the strength of Mercury there, but it acts as if it has accidental dignity, being in its natal sign.

But really: what did we expect to see? For Marie, this was just the first step. Her older sister, after all, had achieved the M.D., and her whole family was educated. This was the first step – very nice, with the first and all, but it's not like she was about to take a gap year or go off into academia immediately and accomplish great things. The physics degree was over, let the mathematics begin! She had proved herself, but now she had more work to do.

The 1893 solar return shows her license in mathematics. It was only *after* this degree that she began working as a physicist and later began teaching. In 1893, her Mercury is back to within a degree of its natal position, as she completed her entry-level credentials to her chosen profession, science. It was a mathematics degree, and Mercury is the ancient ruler of mathematics, whether what we call it is mathematics, or astrology.[9] Saturn rules the 9th and it was exalted, although complicated by being part of a rather significant planetary cluster.

Marie lived in the time when both the sciences and higher education were still undergoing rapid change. As such, circumstances were more fluid than today, when both fields are more established. In a time of rapid growth of a profession, credentials do seem to be less important. The concept of accreditation was barely emerging in academic circles, and science itself was emerging from being more of an avocation than a profession. Marie's credentials were perhaps more important for teaching than for lab work. But her same credentials today would doom her to nothing more than being a lab technician until such time as she finished her PhD.

As was not uncommon in that more open era, she did some of her most profound work before she "got around" to taking the PhD almost nine years later. No lab tech, she! She had already begun to work on Bequerel rays, discovered two chemical elements, and coined the term "radioactivity!" She had also been named the first female faculty member of École normale supérieure at Sèvres, thus beginning her formal teaching career.

Her 1902 solar return gives the year that she received her PhD, although, apart from that, it wasn't a great year, because she was sick most of it, possibly with anemia.

Here, the 9th house is again ruled by Mars, in Triplicity – not as dignified as radix Mars perhaps, but sextile by sign. Mars is in the 1st, tying together 1st and 9th very neatly. While there is a fair amount of angularity in this chart, the focus is the Sun at the 4th house cusp, which is the least public of the angular houses. This makes sense. Marie did not become known because of her PhD work – she was already establishing her reputation well before it. For her, it was simply the final credential, not the entry requirement.

Her health problems can be seen from Moon-Jupiter in the 6th, especially since Jupiter has some relationship to blood diseases. Her work had already been at a fever pitch and had extended beyond exhaustion. We have already seen her capacity to over-work in her natal chart.

Venus rules the 10th, which would be honors. Venus was back in her radix sign, and in a close sextile to her dispositor Mars. Fortuna also fell in the 10th. Mercury was conjunct the North Node, perhaps indicating the intellectual fruitfulness of her PhD topic.

Marie went on to win the Nobel Prize twice, but for that, we will turn to Chapter 8.

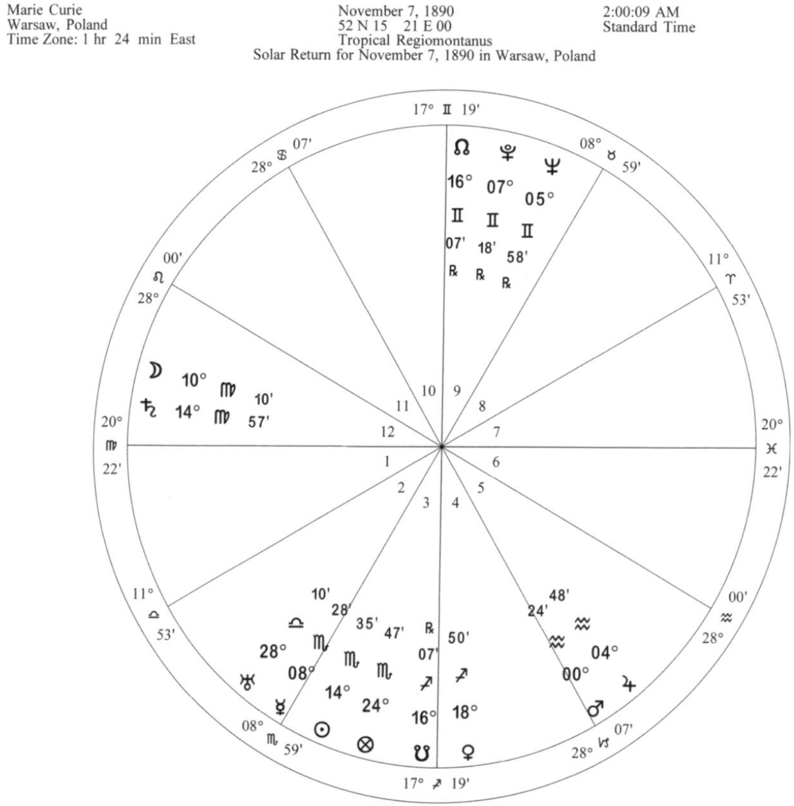
Marie Curie
Warsaw, Poland
Time Zone: 1 hr 24 min East
November 7, 1890
52 N 15 21 E 00
Tropical Regiomontanus
Solar Return for November 7, 1890 in Warsaw, Poland
2:00:09 AM
Standard Time

Dorothean Ess. Dig. (No Mut Rec. Points)								
Pl	Ruler	Exalt	Tripl	Term	Face	Detri	Fall	Score
☉	♂	--	♂	♀	☉ +	♀	☽	+1
☽	☿	☿	☽ +	♀	♀ m	♃	♀	+3
☿	♂	--	♂ m	♃	♂	♀	☽	- 5 P
♀	♃	☋	♃	☿	☽ m	☿	--	- 5 P
♂	♄	--	☿ m	♄	♀	☉	--	- 5 P
♃	♄	--	☿	♄ m	♀	☉	--	- 5 P
♄	☿	☿	☽	♃ m	♀	♃	♀	- 5 P
☊	☿	☊ +	☿	♀	♂	♃	--	--
⊗	♂	--	♂	☿	♀	♀	☽	--
As	☿	☿	☽	♄	☿	♃	♀	--
Mc	☿	☊	☿	♀	♂	♃	--	--
☋	♃	☋	♃	☿	☽	☿	--	--

Hs	Alm. (Pto)
1	☿
2	♀♄
3	♂
4	♃
5	♄
6	♄
7	♃
8	☉♂
9	☽
10	☿
11	☽
12	☉

Example 7-2a. Marie Curie education solar return for 1890

Marie Curie
Warsaw, Poland
Time Zone: 1 hr 24 min East

November 7, 1891
52 N 15 21 E 00
Tropical Regiomontanus
Solar Return for November 7, 1891 in Warsaw, Poland

7:44:44 AM
Standard Time

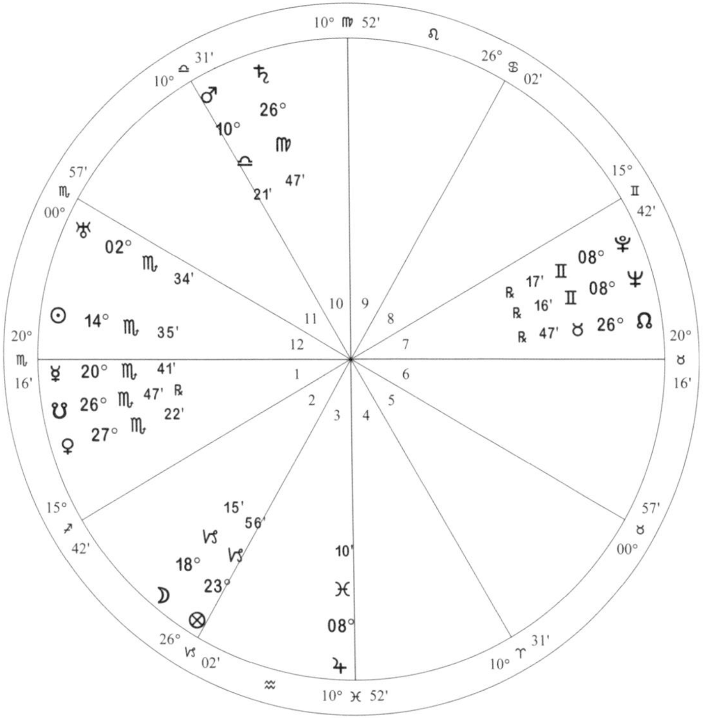

Dorothean Ess. Dig. (No Mut Rec. Points)								
Pl	**Ruler**	**Exalt**	**Tripl**	**Term**	**Face**	**Detri**	**Fall**	**Score**
☉	♂	--	♀	♀	☉ +	♀	☽	+1
☽	♄	♂	♀	♃	♂	☽ -	♃	- 10 P
☿	♂	--	♀	♀	♀	♀	☽	- 5 P
♀	♂ m	--	♀ +	♄	♀ +	♀ -	☽	- 1
♂	♀ m	♄	♄	♀	♄	♂ -	☉	- 10 P
♃	♃ +	♀	♀	♃ +	♄	☿	☿	+7
♄	☿	☿	♀	♂	☿	♃	♀	- 5 P
☊	♀	☽	♀	♂	♄	♂	--	--
⊗	♄	♂	♀	♂	☉	☽	♃	--
As	♂	--	♀	♀	♀	♀	☽	--
Mc	☿	☿	♀	♀	♀	♃	♀	--
☋	♂	--	♀	☿	♀	♀	☽	--

Hs	Alm. (Pto)
1	♂
2	♃
3	♄
4	♃
5	☉
6	♀
7	♀
8	☿
9	☽
10	☿
11	♄
12	♂

Example 7-2b. Marie Curie education solar return for 1891

Marie Curie
Warsaw, Poland
Time Zone: 1 hr 24 min East

November 6, 1892
52 N 15 21 E 00
Tropical Regiomontanus
Solar Return for November 6, 1892 in Warsaw, Poland

1:33:05 PM
Standard Time

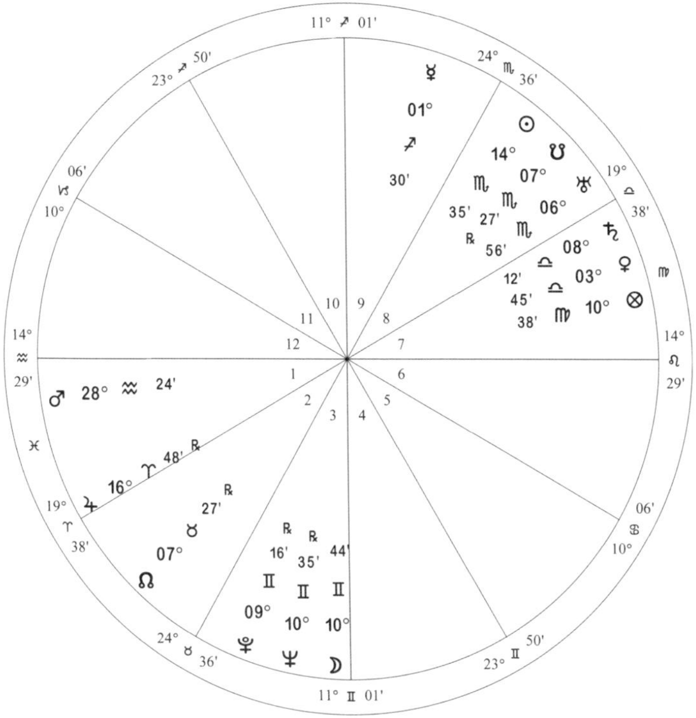

Dorothean Ess. Dig. (No Mut Rec. Points)								
Pl	**Ruler**	**Exalt**	**Tripl**	**Term**	**Face**	**Detri**	**Fall**	**Score**
☉	♂	--	♀	♀	☉ +	♀	☽	+1
☽	☿	☊	♄	♃	♂ m	♃	--	- 5 P
☿	♃	☋	☉	♃ m	☿ +	☿ -	--	- 4
♀	♀ +	♄	♄	♄ m	☽	♂	☉	+5
♂	♄	--	♄	♂ +	☽ m	☉	--	+2
♃	♂	☉	☉	☿ m	☉	♀	♄	- 5 P
♄	♀	♄ +	♄ +	♀ m	☽	♂	☉	+7
☊	♀	☽	♀	♀	☿	♂	--	--
⊗	☿	☿	♀	♀	♀	♃	♀	--
As	♄	--	♄	♀	☿	☉	--	--
Mc	♃	☋	☉	♀	☽	☿	--	--
☋	♂	--	♀	♃	♂	♀	☽	--

Hs	Alm. (Pto)
1	♄
2	☉
3	♀
4	☿
5	☿♄
6	♃
7	☉
8	♄
9	♂
10	♃
11	♃
12	♂♄

Example 7-2c. Marie Curie education solar return for 1892

Marie Curie
Warsaw, Poland
Time Zone: 1 hr 24 min East

November 6, 1893
52 N 15 21 E 00
Tropical Regiomontanus
Solar Return for November 6, 1893 in Warsaw, Poland

7:21:14 PM
Standard Time

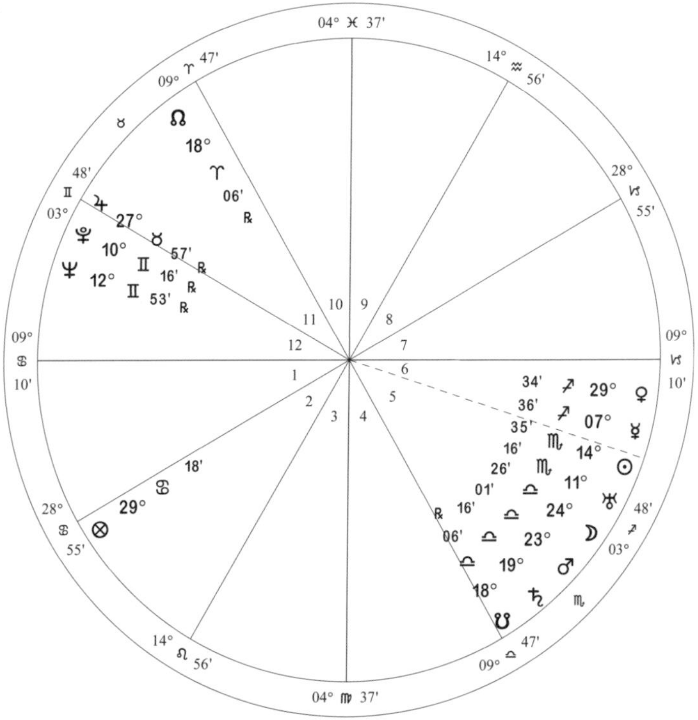

Dorothean Ess. Dig. (No Mut Rec. Points)								
Pl	**Ruler**	**Exalt**	**Tripl**	**Term**	**Face**	**Detri**	**Fall**	**Score**
☉	♂	--	♂	♀	☉ +	♀	☽	+1
☽	♀	♄	☿	☊	♃	♂	☉	- 5 P
☿	♃	☋	♃	♃	☿ +	☿ -	--	- 4
♀	♃ m	☋	♃	♂	♄	☿	--	- 5 P
♂	♀	♄	☿	☿	♃	♂ -	☉	- 10 P
♃	♀ m	☽	☽	♂	♄	♂	--	- 5 P
♄	♀	♄ +	☿	☿	♄ +	♂	☉	+5
☊	♂	☉	♃	☿	☉	♀	♄	--
⊗	☽	♃	♂	♄	☽	♄	♂	--
As	☽	♃	♂	♃	♀	♄	♂	--
Mc	♃	♀	♂	♀	♄	☿	☿	--
☋	♀	♄	☿	♃	♄	♂	☉	--

Hs	Alm. (Pto)
1	♃
2	☽
3	☉
4	☿
5	♀
6	♃
7	♄
8	♄
9	♄
10	♀
11	♂
12	☿

Example 7-2d. Marie Curie education solar return for 1893

Marie Curie
Warsaw, Poland
Time Zone: 1 hr 24 min East

November 7, 1902
52 N 15 21 E 00
Tropical Regiomontanus
Solar Return for November 7, 1902 in Warsaw, Poland

11:33:33 PM
Standard Time

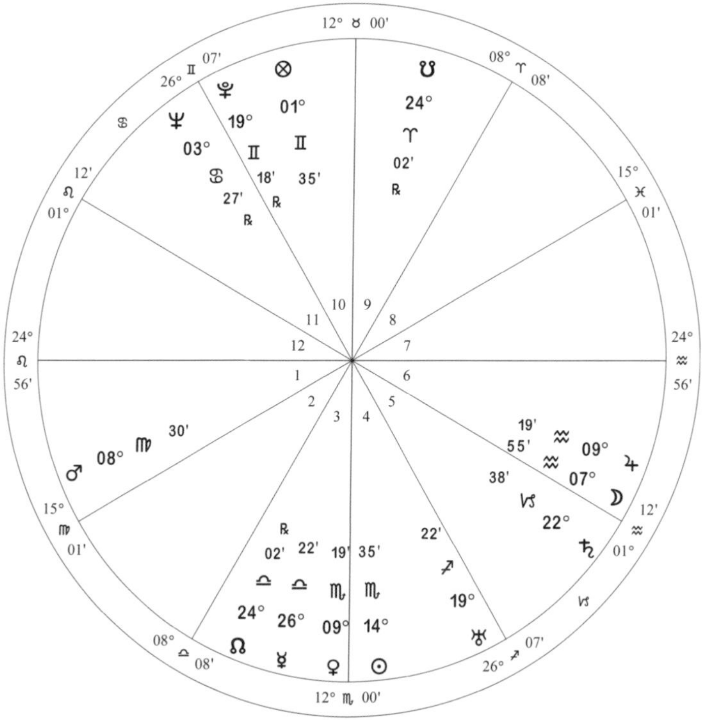

Dorothean Ess. Dig. (No Mut Rec. Points)								
Pl	**Ruler**	**Exalt**	**Tripl**	**Term**	**Face**	**Detri**	**Fall**	**Score**
☉	♂	--	♂	♀	☉ +	♀	☽	+1
☽	♄	--	☿	☿	♀	☉	--	- 5 P
☿	♀	♄	☿ +	☊	♃	♂	☉	+3
♀	♂	--	♂	♃	♂	♀ -	☽	- 10 P
♂	☿	☿	☽	♀	☉	♃	♀	- 5 P
♃	♄	--	☿	☿	♀	☉	--	- 5 P
♄	♄ +	♂	☽	♂	☉	☽	♃	+5
☊	♀	♄	☿	☊ +	♃	♂	☉	--
⊗	☿	☊	☿	☿	♃	♃	--	--
As	☉	--	♃	♃	♂	♄	--	--
Mc	♀	☽	☽	☿	☽	♂	--	--
☋	♂	☉	♃	♂	♀	♀	♄	--

Hs	Alm. (Pto)
1	☉♃
2	☿
3	♀
4	♂
5	♃
6	♄
7	♄
8	♃
9	♂
10	☽
11	☿
12	☉

Example 7-2e. Marie Curie education solar return for 1902

Martin Luther King: Preacher and Doctor of Philosophy

Martin Luther King is invaluable to our study, because we can see both 9th house issues of education and religion occurring. We begin with 1948, when the two themes are mixed: King was ordained in February 1948, and received his B.A. Later that year in May.

In King's natal chart [SEE EXAMPLE 6-3 ON PAGE 133], the 9th house is ruled by Saturn. One interpretation of this relates to Saturn being the classical ruler of the father. King followed his father in many ways: by going into his father's profession, by being ordained by his father, and by first serving in his father's church. If one accepts racial attributions (and I am doubtful about this, given the complete porosity of the human genome of any individual), then there are sources that give Saturn as the ruler of the "negro race." [10] King used the term "negro" extensively, as he was the last generation before the term "black" became dominant. But in King's day, these were much more real distinctions than they are now, and he was a major contributor to why the status of all minorities has improved. So perhaps that use of Saturn is appropriate in his case. King's Saturn was in the 8th, in Jupiter's sign, where it has dignity by mixed Triplicity. The Moon, also in Triplicity and Jupiter's sign, was in an approaching square to that Saturn. He would preach justice, and he would appeal to others for Christian values, and he would die for his efforts.

With a dignified ruler of the 9th, education was not a difficult thing for him, and with the same planet ruling both 9th and 10th, affairs of the 9th house easily become the area of one's profession. His Sun was at the 10th, the metaphorical placement for the birth of kings. He actually had quite a bit of dignity in his chart, with the Moon, Mercury, Venus, and Saturn all with strong dignity.

One further note we might make: in his writings, King rejected fundamentalism. One might expect otherwise, given the Saturn rulership. But we should note that his 3rd is as strong as his 9th. The 3rd house is also related to religion, and often of a heretical or at least recessive type of a culture. The Moon, which we have already noted, had Triplicity, ruled his 3rd, Fortuna was there, and Pluto was there. Thus, if anything, King's 3rd was stronger than the 9th. In the works compiled to create his autobiography, it is clear that he thought long and hard about these issues, and that his model of God as love conquered any idea of literal interpretation: and what a symbolism with the Moon square Saturn!

In 1948, we see this intermixing of 3rd and 9th, with the Sun at the 3rd house cusp by the five degree rule, Mercury and Venus in the 3rd, and Saturn and Pluto in the 9th. Mars was partile conjunct the 10th. Let's sort through these symbols.

The intermixing of 3rd and 9th probably has nothing to do with the educational part of the year: he was studying in a 9th house location. But it could have to do with his religious profession. We have already seen that King came to the conclusion that fundamentalism wasn't the right approach. He, like so many before him, had his own spiritual crisis to go through. But he was also being ordained in his childhood church, the church of his father. From this point, his path would change. This was much more of a direct effect than his college graduation.

In 1948, the Moon and Mercury had returned to their natal signs. The ruler of the 1st was partile conjunct the MC and dignified by mixed Triplicity: he was becoming his profession. 1949 and 1950 were years of study for him in Pennsylvania. We can see this especially in 1949, with the cadent placement in the 12th house of the Sun and Mars, ruler of the 9th. We begin to see more of an angular focus in 1950, but he was also working with his father on vacations, where he would have been more visible, thus angular.

In 1954 he interviewed for, and received, the pastorship of Dexter Avenue Baptist Church in Montgomery, Alabama. At the time, he was still working on his doctorate at Boston University School of Theology. He was, in academic-speak, ABD – All but Dissertation. He had completed his classwork, and was putting together his thesis.

Martin Luther King
Atlanta, Georgia
Time Zone: 5 hours West

January 16, 1948
33N44'56" 84W23'17"
Tropical Regiomontanus
Solar Return for January 16, 1948 in Atlanta, Georgia

3:36:58 AM
Standard Time

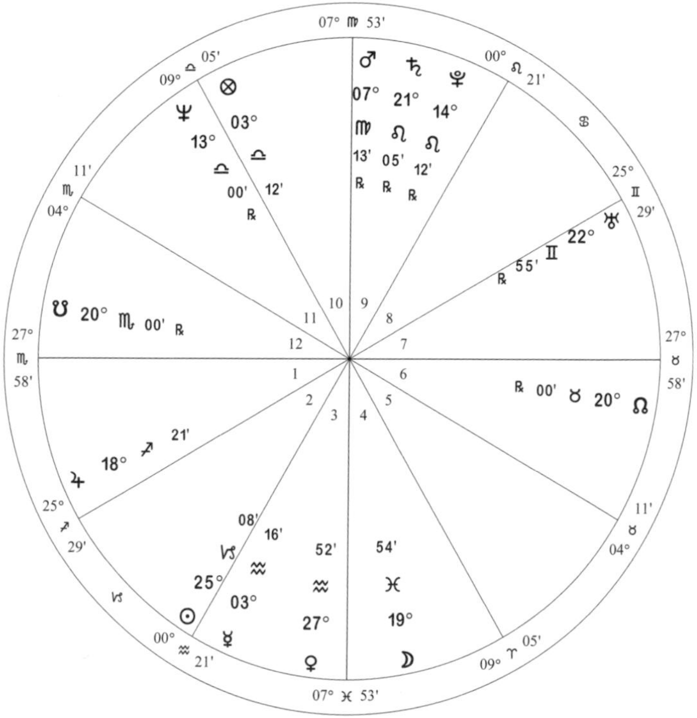

Dorothean Ess. Dig. (No Mut Rec. Points)								
Pl	Ruler	Exalt	Tripl	Term	Face	Detri	Fall	Score
☉	♄ m	♂	☽	♄	☉ +	☽	♃	+1
☽	♃	♀	♂ m	☿	♃ m	☿	☿	- 5 P
☿	♄	--	☿ +	♄	♀	☉	--	+3
♀	♄	--	☿	♂ m	☽	☉	--	- 5 P
♂	☿	☿	☽ m	♀ m	☉	♃	♀	- 5 P
♃	♃ +	☋	♃ +	☿	☽ m	☿	--	+8
♄	☉ m	--	♃	♃	♂	♄ -	--	- 10 P
☊	♀	☽	☽	♃	♄	♂	--	--
⊗	♀	♄	☿	♄	☽	♂	☉	--
As	♂	--	♂	♄	♀	♀	☽	--
Mc	☿	☿	☽	♀	☉	♃	♀	--
☋	♂	--	♂	♀	♀	♀	☽	--

Hs	Alm. (Pto)
1	♂
2	♃
3	♄
4	♀
5	♂
6	☽♀
7	☽
8	☿
9	☉
10	☿
11	♀
12	♂

Example 7-3a. Martin Luther King education solar return for 1948

Martin Luther King
Atlanta, Georgia
Time Zone: 5 hours West

January 15, 1949
33N44'56" 84W23'17"
Tropical Regiomontanus
Solar Return for January 15, 1949 in Atlanta, Georgia

9:25:01 AM
Standard Time

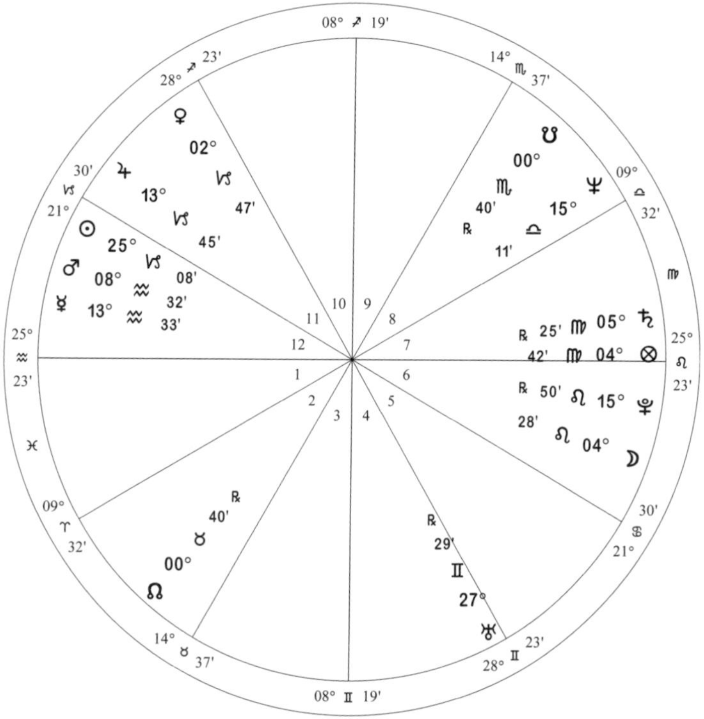

Dorothean Ess. Dig. (No Mut Rec. Points)								
Pl	Ruler	Exalt	Tripl	Term	Face	Detri	Fall	Score
☉	♄	♂	♀	♄	☉ +	☽	♃	+1
☽	☉	--	☉	♄	♄	♄	--	- 5 P
☿	♄ m	--	♄	♀	☿ +	☉	--	+1
♀	♄	♂	♀ +	♀ +	♃	☽	♃	+5
♂	♄	--	♄	☿	♀	☉	--	- 5 P
♃	♄	♂	♀	♃ +	♂	☽	♃ -	- 2
♄	☿ m	☿	♀	☿	☉	♃	♀	- 5 P
☊	♀	☽	♀	♀	☿	♂	--	--
⊗	☿	☿	♀	☿	☉	♃	♀	--
As	♄	--	♄	♂	☽	☉	--	--
Mc	♃	☋	☉	♀	☿	☿	--	--
☋	♂	--	♀	♂	♂	♀	☽	--

Hs	Alm. (Pto)
1	♄
2	☉
3	♀
4	☿
5	☿
6	☽
7	☉
8	♀♄
9	♂
10	♃
11	♃
12	♂

Example 7-3b. Martin Luther King education solar return for 1949

Martin Luther King
Atlanta, Georgia
Time Zone: 5 hours West

January 15, 1950
33N44'56" 84W23'17"
Tropical Regiomontanus
Solar Return for January 15, 1950 in Atlanta, Georgia

3:20:42 PM
Standard Time

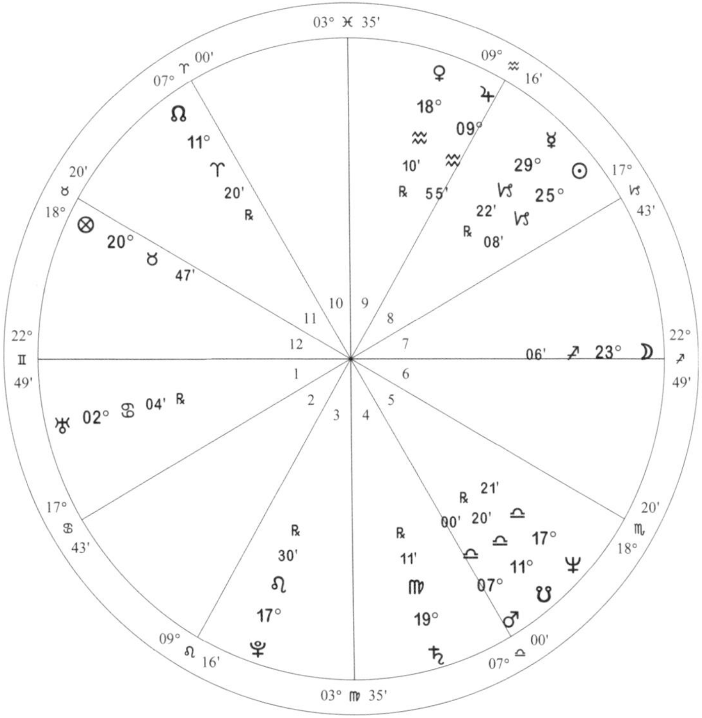

Dorothean Ess. Dig. (No Mut Rec. Points)

Pl	Ruler		Exalt	Tripl		Term		Face		Detri		Fall	Score
☉	♄		♂	♀		♄		☉	+	☽		♃	+1
☽	♃		☋	☉		♄		♄		☿		--	- 5 P
☿	♄	m	♂	♀		♄		☉		☽		♃	- 5 P
♀	♄		--	♄	m	♀	+	☿		☉		--	+2
♂	♀		♄	♄		♀		☽		♂	-	☉	- 10 P
♃	♄		--	♄		☿		♀		☉		--	- 5 P
♄	☿	m	☿	♀	m	♄	+	♀		♃		♀	+2
☊	♂		☉	☉		♀		☉		♀		♄	--
⊗	♀		☽	♀		♃		♄		♂		--	--
As	☿		☊	♄		♄		☉		♃		--	--
Mc	♃		♀	♀		♀		♄		☿		☿	--
☋	♀		♄	♄		♃		♄		♂		☉	--

Hs	Alm. (Pto)
1	☿♄
2	☽
3	☉
4	☿
5	♀♄
6	♂
7	♃
8	♂♄
9	♄
10	♀
11	☉
12	♀

Example 7-3c. Martin Luther King education solar return for 1950

Martin Luther King
Atlanta, Georgia
Time Zone: 5 hours West

January 15, 1954
33N44'56" 84W23'17"
Tropical Regiomontanus
Solar Return for January 15, 1954 in Atlanta, Georgia

2:26:39 PM
Standard Time

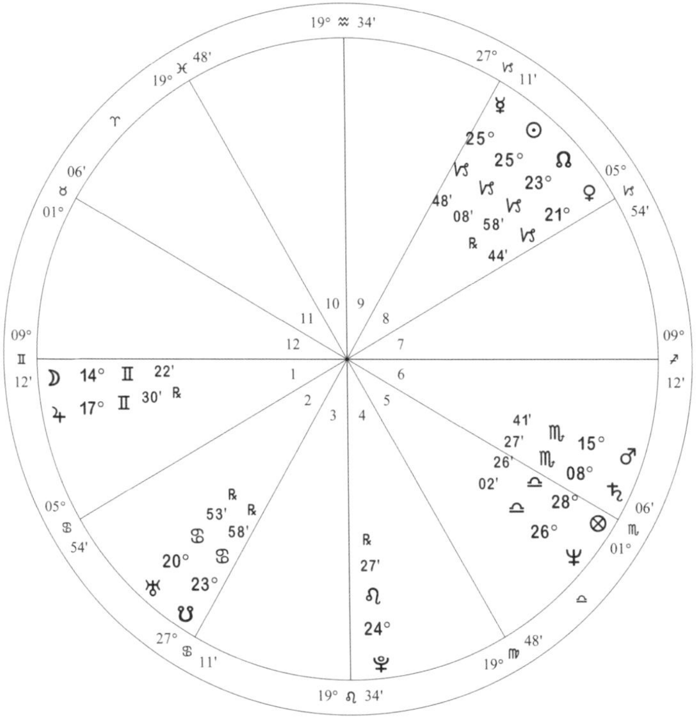

Dorothean Ess. Dig. (No Mut Rec. Points)

Pl	Ruler		Exalt	Tripl		Term		Face		Detri		Fall	Score
☉	♄		♂	♀		♄		☉	+	☽		♃	+1
☽	☿		☊	♄		♀		♂		♃		--	- 5 P
☿	♄		♂	♀		♄		☉		☽		♃	- 5 P
♀	♄		♂	♀	+	♂	m	☉		☽		♃	+3
♂	♂	+	--	♀		♀	m	☉		♀		☽	+5
♃	☿		☊	♄		♀		♂		♃	-	--	- 10 P
♄	♂		--	♀		♃		♂		♀		☽	- 5 P
☊	♄		♂	♀		♂		☉		☽		♃	--
⊗	♀		♄	♄		☊		♃		♂		☉	--
As	☿		☊	♄		♃		♃		♃		--	--
Mc	♄		--	♄		♀		☿		☉		--	--
☋	☽		♃	♀		♀		☽		♄		♂	--

Hs	Alm. (Pto)
1	☿
2	☽
3	☽
4	☉
5	☿
6	♂
7	♃
8	♀♄
9	♄
10	♄
11	♃
12	♀

Example 7-3d. Martin Luther King education solar return for 1954

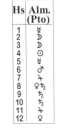

Martin Luther King
Atlanta, Georgia
Time Zone: 5 hours West

January 15, 1955
33N44'56" 84W23'17"
Tropical Regiomontanus
Solar Return for January 15, 1955 in Atlanta, Georgia

8:21:26 PM
Standard Time

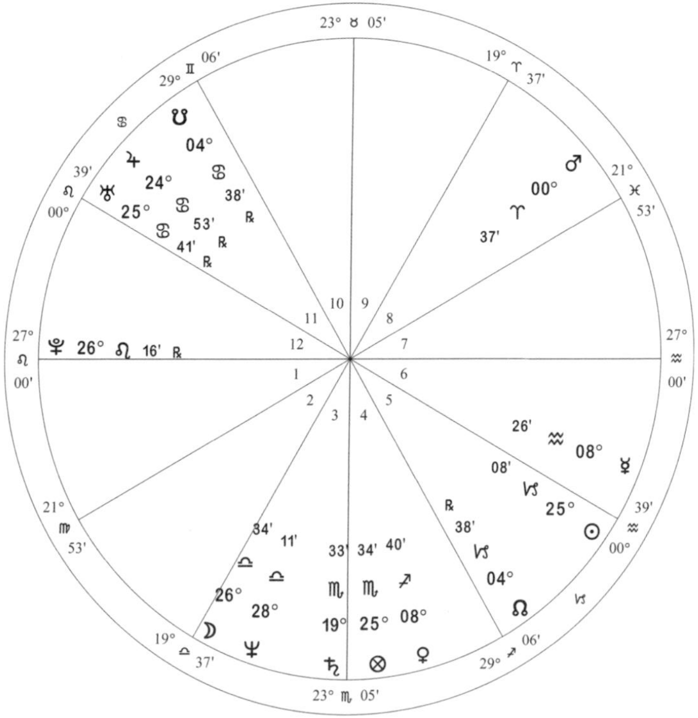

Dorothean Ess. Dig. (No Mut Rec. Points)								
Pl	Ruler	Exalt	Tripl	Term	Face	Detri	Fall	Score
☉	♄	♂ m	☽	♄	☉ +	☽	♃	+1
☽	♀	♄	☿	☊	♃ m	♂	☉	- 5 P
☿	♄	--	☿ +	☿ +	♀ m	☉	--	+5
♀	♃	☋	♃	♀ +	☿ m	☿	--	+2
♂	♂ +	☉ m	♃ m	♃	♂ +	♀	♄	+6
♃	☽	♃ +	♂ m	♀	☽ m	♄	♂	+4
♄	♂	--	♂	♀	☉	♀	☽	- 5 P
☊	♄	♂	☽	♀	♃	☽	♃	--
⊗	♂	--	♂	☿	♀	♀	☽	--
As	☉	--	♃	♂	♂	♄	--	--
Mc	♀	☽	☽	♄	♄	♂	--	--
☋	☽	♃	♂	♂	♀	♄	♂	--

Hs	Alm. (Pto)
1	☉
2	☿
3	☿♀♄
4	♂
5	♃
6	♄
7	♄
8	♃
9	☉♂
10	☽
11	☿
12	☉

Example 7-3e. Martin Luther King education solar return for 1955

This was his first independent appointment – and one that would launch him onto the national stage, although he didn't know that yet! What at first appears to be an 8th house emphasis is in fact a 9th house one, because three out of the four positions are conjunct the 9th house cusp, and the fourth gets dragged into it by conjunction with the others.

While Venus lacked its natal Exaltation, it did have Triplicity. The North Node was loosely trine its natal position, and Mercury added to this clustering of attendants to the Sun. The opposition of this cluster to Uranus must be seen as a prefiguring of the extent to which King would find himself a lightening rod in a very short time. A very tight cardinal pattern was completed with Neptune square all of the above.

What was strong in this solar return was Mars, a planet not strong in his nativity. It was strong in the 6th. King would find much of his greatest support from 6th house people: not his servants and employees, but those invisible soldiers of civil rights, often embedded in the houses of the white community, which was dependent upon black labor. The Mars was cadent. The fight did not start yet, but his presence in the community was the vital catalyst to begin to forge the community that would so shortly be tested.

Indian spiritual masters have pointed the way to liberation through many paths: often more clearly than has been done in the West. King was exposed to Gandhi's teaching in college, and its effect on him was very profound. This can be understood as part of the path of *karma yoga*: active work in the world, purified through selfless work on behalf of others. King's biography makes clear that he also practiced what we might call *raja yoga*: the path of contemplation.

The Moon-Jupiter conjunction in the 1st in this solar return suggests that he still had not completely found his spiritual path – but that he was seeking it. Jupiter is the planet of organized religion, and Mercury – disposing the Moon, Jupiter and Ascendant – is right at the 9th house cusp. His involvement with spiritual matters at this point was profound, even if it wasn't entirely public, or entirely formed.

In the 1955 solar return, King received his PhD, his oldest daughter was born, and the Montgomery bus boycott began through the actions of Rosa Parks. The next era of the civil rights movement was birthing just as King had completed his highest degree.

How can one not stop to gaze at that Pluto rising? It just so happened to be in a partile trine with the 3ʳᵈ house Moon, relating it to spiritual matters. Mars ruled the 9ᵗʰ – and it was the warrior Mars in Aries. For two years, King enjoyed a strong Mars. But in 1955, the Mars was no longer cadent. The zero Mars in Aries is also suggestive of both beginning something, and the modern idea of the World Axis, further suggested by that Mars being at the Bendings, and specifically, the Northern Bending.

It is impossible to emphasize how important the spiritual side was to the early Civil Rights movement. It probably would have failed without this influence. The black community met at the black churches. The various pastors came together to coordinate activities. They discouraged any kind of revenge, which could easily have led to all-out warfare. And perhaps most importantly, as King had understood from Gandhi's work, they provided a moral focus that the white community of the United States would find difficult to challenge.

That King was ready to step up to this spiritual challenge and perhaps sacrifice, is shown with the Sun in a partile opposition to Uranus, with exalted Jupiter coming to conjoin that Uranus. Further, the Moon is applying to the conjunction to Neptune. Pretty much all the spiritual factors are activated.

But what of his PhD? Where is the educational achievement in this chart? As we have seen, the 9ᵗʰ house was certainly dignified through its ruler. King's natal 9ᵗʰ house ruler Saturn was also disposed by Mars, ruling the 9ᵗʰ house.

But let's ask ourselves: what actually happened here? Buzz Aldrin went on to use his degree in the sense of becoming a military officer. Marie Curie went on to a career in science, although, as we saw, the degree in many respects was an afterthought in her time.

Undoubtedly, King's PhD was useful to him, but not necessary for his job. Where it *was* most useful was in the title it bestowed. Throughout the civil rights movement, he was known as "Dr. King." The Moon in this solar return was Almuten of the MC, trine the Ascendant and the Pluto rising, square the Sun – and not far from the highly positive fixed star Sirius. The marketing worked. The "Dr. King" label produced an element of respect even among persons who otherwise did try very hard to minimize his message and his person.

Michelle Kwan

Michelle Kwan's skating accomplishments were so stellar that she will require an effort of supreme magnitude to surpass them in any other field. Like so many sportspeople, the very years when she needed to develop her athletics were also the usual years where conventional education occurs. So Michelle deferred her education, but she has not chosen to forego it, even if technically she didn't need it.

That she would be successful at higher education can be seen from her natal Moon exalted in Taurus in the 9ᵗʰ house. That her schooling might be somewhat erratic is perhaps shown by the Moon opposite Uranus. It may also be shown by Venus in the common (*i.e.*, mutable) sign Gemini ruling the 9ᵗʰ house. Michelle's Mercury, the natural ruler of the rational side of the mind, is in Cancer retrograde, also not the easiest placement for the way conventional educational training occurs. People with placements that are not so encouraged by the straight educational establishment may well do better later in life, when they have more fully developed their personal Mercury functions, and are less likely to find the educational system and hierarchies intimidating.

In the year that Michelle received her Bachelor's degree, her solar year encompassed her entire senior year. Mercury is temporarily fortified by being in its ruling sign Gemini, and it also ruled her 1ˢᵗ house and was conjunct her Ascendant. Saturn, ruling the 9ᵗʰ,

Michelle Kwan
Los Angeles, California
Time Zone: 8 hours West

July 7, 1980
34N03'08" 118W14'34"
Tropical Regiomontanus
NATAL CHART

10:05 AM
Daylight Saving Time

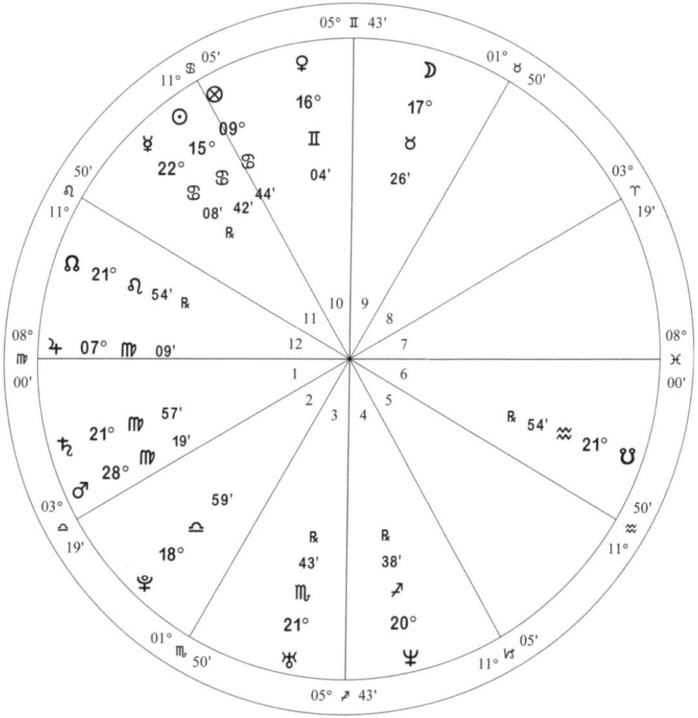

Pl	Ruler	Exalt	Tripl	Term	Face	Detri	Fall	Score
☉	☽	♃	♀	☿	☿	♄	♂	- 5 P
☽	♀	☽ +	♀	♃	☽ +	♂	--	+5
☿	☽	♃ m	♀	♀	☽	♄	♂	- 5 P
♀	☿	☊	♄ m	♀ +	♂	♃	--	+2
♂	☿	☿	♀	♂ +	☿	♃	♀	+2
♃	☿	☿ m	♀	♀	☉	♃ -	♀	- 10 P
♄	☿	☿	♀ m	♄ +	☿	♃	♀	+2
☊	☉	--	☉	♃	♂	♄	--	--
⊗	☽	♃	♀	♃	♀	♄	♂	--
As	☿	☿	♀	♀	☉	♃	♀	--
Mc	☿	☊	♄	☿	♃	♃	--	--
☋	♄	--	♄	♃	☽	☉	--	--

Dorothean Ess. Dig. (No Mut Rec. Points)

Hs	Alm. (Pto)
1	☿
2	♄
3	♂
4	♃
5	♂♄
6	♄
7	♃
8	☉
9	♀
10	☿
11	♃
12	☉

Example 7-4. Michelle Kwan nativity

Michelle Kwan
Los Angeles, California
Time Zone: 8 hours West

July 7, 2008
34N03'08" 118W14'34"
Tropical Regiomontanus
Solar Return for July 7, 2008 in Los Angeles, California

4:07:48 AM
Daylight Saving Time

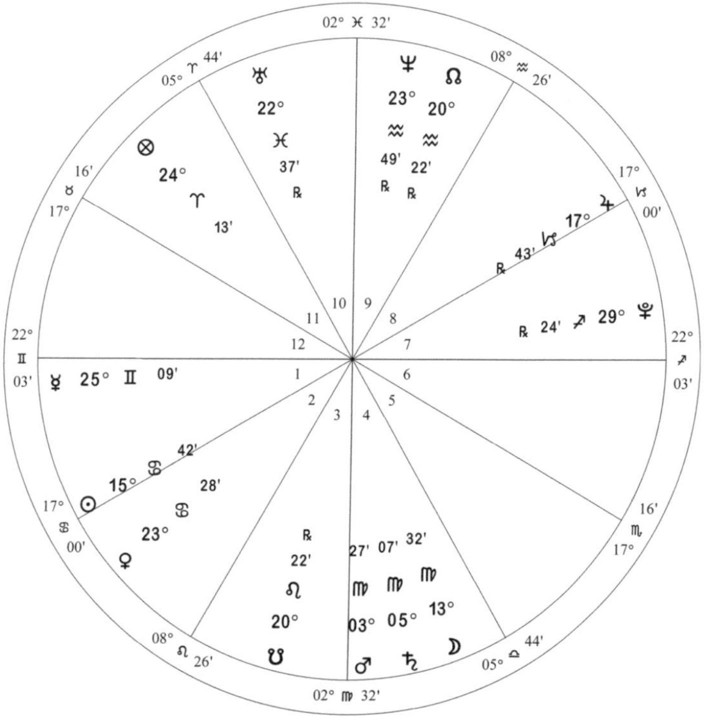

Dorothean Ess. Dig. (No Mut Rec. Points)

Pl	Ruler	Exalt	Tripl	Term	Face	Detri	Fall	Score
☉	☽	♃	♂	☿	☿ m	♄	♂	- 5 P
☽	☿	☿	☽ +	♃	♀ m	♃	♀	+3
☿	☿ +	☊	☿ +	♂ m	☉ m	♃	--	+8
♀	☽	♃	♂	♀ +	☽ m	♄	♂	+2
♂	☿	☿	☽	☿ m	☉	♃	♀	- 5 P
♃	♄	♂	☽	♃ +	♂	☽	♃ -	- 2
♄	☿	☿	☽	☿	☉	♃	♀	- 5 P
☊	♄	--	☿	♃	☽	☉	--	--
⊗	♂	☉	♃	♂	♀	♀	♄	--
As	☿	☊	☿	♄	☉	♃	--	--
Mc	♃	♀	♂	♀	♄	☿	☿	--
☋	☉	--	♃	♃	♂	♄	--	--

Hs	Alm. (Pto)
1	☿
2	☽
3	☉
4	☿
5	♄
6	♂
7	♃
8	♂♄
9	☿♄
10	♀
11	♂
12	☽

Example 7-4a. Michelle Kwan education solar return for 2008

was angular in the 4th and in its natal sign, and disposed by that very powerful Mercury. The Moon in Virgo was dignified, and in a sign trine her natal Moon. Mars was in its radix sign. Jupiter was in debility, a condition also found in her natal chart. Thus, there was a lot of resonance with her radix.

We might note that Michelle's radix Mercury in Cancer (retrograde, no less!) is in a mute sign, which is not normally associated with verbal forthrightness. However, Michelle's job as a competitive skater did not allow her any such verbal reticence. She was forced to learn what to do when a microphone was shoved in her face, whether her performance was good or bad, to address an audience of millions. Whatever Michelle's natural inclinations, she had to express herself. Whatever her *fate* as a mute Mercury, she had to *exercise free will and learn* to express herself verbally. Once she learned this new pattern, she then could make it her own.

Michelle has since moved on to graduate school.

Louis Pasteur

The world of Louis Pasteur spanned the period from just after Napoleon (his father had been a supporter) to the Third Republic, the form of government in France from 1870-1940. Napoleon I had changed French education considerably, creating technical education at the expense of the older Latin-dominated liberal arts. Thus, the system created and then developed over the intervening decades was favorable to Pasteur's scientific interests.

What makes a scientist? In the Gauquelin data, the answer is Saturn. But the criticism has been made that Gauquelin's successful scientists were dominated by those who were members of the French Academy of Sciences, a group which tended to be dominated by older men who probably never thought to set the world on fire. And it was very definitely *men* – Marie Curie was not allowed into that august body. Although Pasteur was, I think we have to examine his Mercury-Sun-Neptune-Venus-Uranus conjunction, all trine Saturn.

To say that Pasteur was practical is a bit of an understatement!

Within that stellium, it is Venus and Mars that have Triplicity, with those two planets ruling half his houses: the 12th, 1st, 2nd, 6th, 7th, and 8th. Venus and Saturn were in mutual reception. Following the Venus symbolism, Pasteur at one point distinguished himself well enough as an artist that this could have been a career path.

With Mercury peregrine ruling the 9th, education wasn't always easy for Pasteur. Certainly, it wasn't a straight-line proposition, as we shall see shortly. He had prodigious study skills, the ability to work as hard at a project as was necessary, and a remarkable ability to cut through the data to a brilliant hypothesis. The latter was the talent which I would attribute to the Sun-Neptune. He could think outside the box (the Sun-Uranus), but he was always willing to provide extensive repetition (Saturn), and he was very hands-on in the laboratory (all that earth).

The first solar return we are examining was one of his unsuccessful years. His greatest success would have to occur in the City, so at age fifteen, he was sent off to study in Paris, where he lasted barely three months before returning home. For his solar return of 1837, the abrupt move to the city is shown by Uranus in the 9th. Why didn't it work? Pasteur was ruled by the Moon in Sagittarius in the 6th, cadent. That's a Moon position opposite his natal sign position [SEE EXAMPLE 4-5 ON PAGE 101], with Saturn in the sign opposite his natal Saturn. These positions express a level of discomfort! Mercury and Mars were in their natal signs, but the Moon and Saturn put a damper on the other two planets.

In 1839, he received his *Baccalauréat* in Letters (Arts). For him, with his scientific interests, this would not be a terminal degree. But it was a start, and it was further than his father had gone. What we find in this year is focus on a house: the third house, the same house which is the most active in his natal chart. While Mars and Uranus are both there, the other focus is on the 1st: and that shows a struggle. A Mercury-Saturn conjunction, with Mercury retrograde in its Detriment, and conjunct Saturn—this wasn't easy for him. Since

Louis Pasteur
Dole, France
Time Zone: 0 hours West

December 26, 1837
47 N 06 5 E 30
Tropical Regiomontanus
Solar Return for December 26, 1837 in Dole, France

5:31:19 PM
Local Mean Time

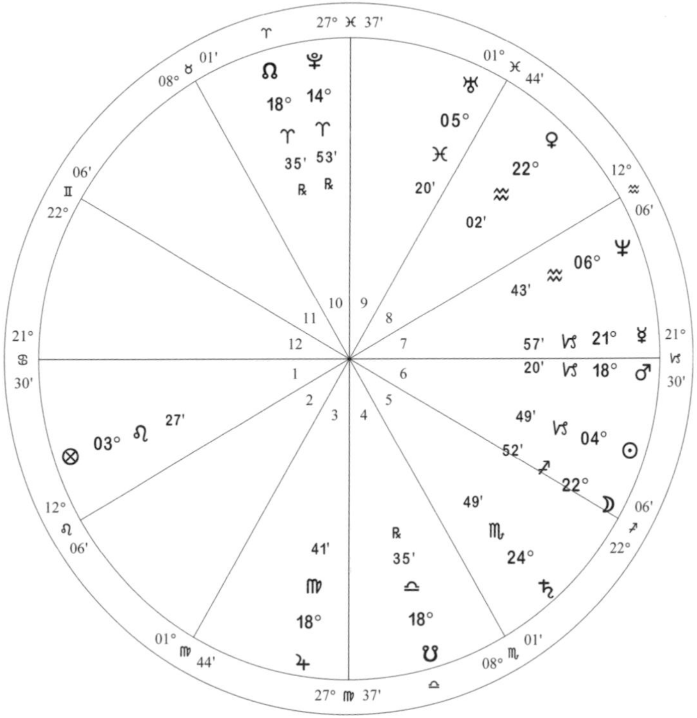

Dorothean Ess. Dig. (No Mut Rec. Points)								
Pl	Ruler	Exalt	Tripl	Term	Face	Detri	Fall	Score
☉	♄	♂	☽	♀	♃	☽	♃	- 5 P
☽	♃	☋	♃ m	♄	♄	☿	--	- 5 P
☿	♄	♂	☽	♂	☉	☽	♃	- 5 P
♀	♄	--	☿	♃	☽	☉	--	- 5 P
♂	♄ m	♂ +	☽	♃	♂ +	☽	♃	+5
♃	☿	☿	☽ m	♄	♀	♃ -	♀	- 10 P
♄	♂ m	--	♂	☿	♀	♀	☽	- 5 P
☊	♂	☉	♃	☿	☉	♀	♄	--
⊗	☉	--	♃	♄	♄	♄	--	--
As	☽	♃	♂	♀	☽	♄	♂	--
Mc	♃	♀	♂	♄	♂	☿	☿	--
☋	♀	♄	☿	♃	♄	♂	☉	--

Hs	Alm. (Pto)
1	☽
2	☉
3	☿
4	☿
5	♂
6	♃
7	♂
8	♄
9	♀
10	♃
11	☽
12	☿

Example 7-5a. Louis Pasteur education solar return for 1837

Louis Pasteur
Dole, France
Time Zone: 0 hours West

December 27, 1839
47 N 06 5 E 30
Tropical Regiomontanus
Solar Return for December 27, 1839 in Dole, France

5:03:20 AM
Local Mean Time

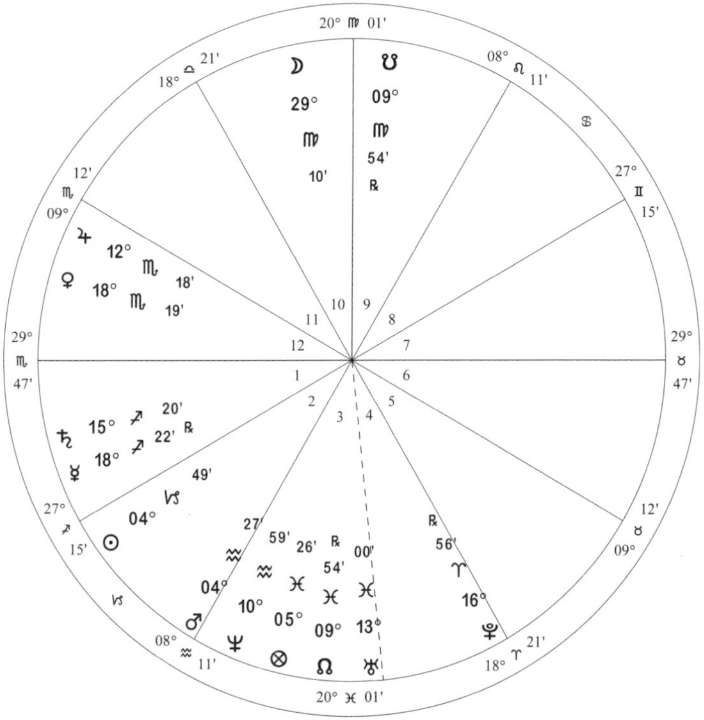

Dorothean Ess. Dig. (No Mut Rec. Points)								
Pl	Ruler	Exalt	Tripl	Term	Face	Detri	Fall	Score
☉	♄	♂	☽	♀	♃ m	☽	♃	- 5 P
☽	☿	☿	☽ +	♂	☿ m	♃	♀	+3
☿	♃	☋	♃	☿ +	☽ m	☿ -	--	- 3
♀	♂	--	♂	♀ +	☉	♀ -	☽	- 3
♂	♄	--	☿	♄	♀	☉	--	- 5 P
♃	♂	--	♂	♃ +	☉ m	♀	☽	+2
♄	♃	☋	♃	☿	☽	☿	--	- 5 P
☊	♃	♀	♂	♃	♄	☿	☿	--
⊗	♃	♀	♂	♀	♄	☿	☿	--
As	♂	--	♂	♄	♀	♀	☽	--
Mc	☿	☿	☽	♄	☿	♃	♀	--
☋	☿	☿	☽	♀	☉	♃	♀	--

Hs	Alm. (Pto)
1	♂
2	♃
3	☿♄
4	♃
5	☉♂
6	☽
7	☽
8	☿
9	☉
10	☿
11	♀♄
12	♂

Example 7-5b. Louis Pasteur education solar return for 1839

Louis Pasteur
Dole, France
Time Zone: 0 hours West

December 26, 1840
47 N 06 5 E 30
Tropical Regiomontanus
Solar Return for December 26, 1840 in Dole, France

10:49:30 AM
Local Mean Time

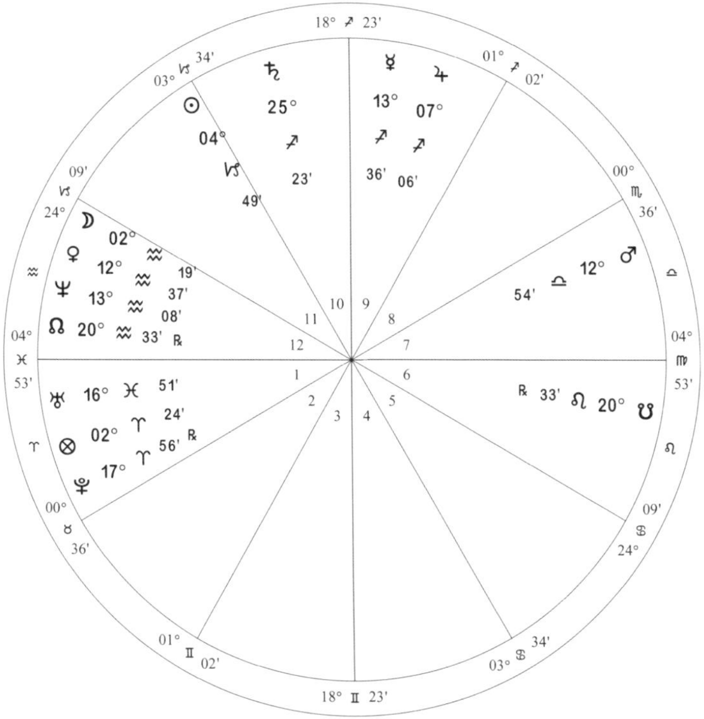

Dorothean Ess. Dig. (No Mut Rec. Points)

Pl	Ruler	Exalt	Tripl	Term	Face	Detri	Fall	Score
☉	♄	♂	♀	♀	♃	☽	♃	- 5 P
☽	♄	--	♄	♄	♀	☉	--	- 5 P
☿	♃	☋	☉	♀	☽	☿ -	--	- 10 P
♀	♄	--	♄	♀ +	☿	☉	--	+2
♂	♀	♄	♄	♃	♄	♂ -	☉	- 10 P
♃	♃ +	☋	☉	♃ +	☿	☿	--	+7
♄	♃	☋	☉	♂	♄ +	☿	--	+1
☊	♄	--	♄	♃	☽	☉	--	--
⊗	♂	☉	☉	♃	♂	♀	♄	--
As	♃	♀	♀	♀	♄	☿	☿	--
Mc	♃	☋	☉	☿	☽	☿	--	--
☋	☉	--	☉	♃	♂	♄	--	--

Hs	Alm. (Pto)
1	♀
2	♀
3	☿
4	☿
5	☽
6	☽
7	☿
8	♂
9	♃
10	♃
11	♀♄
12	♂

Example 7-5c. Louis Pasteur education solar return for 1840

Louis Pasteur
Dole, France
Time Zone: 0 hours West

December 26, 1841
47 N 06 5 E 30
Tropical Regiomontanus
Solar Return for December 26, 1841 in Dole, France

4:36:46 PM
Local Mean Time

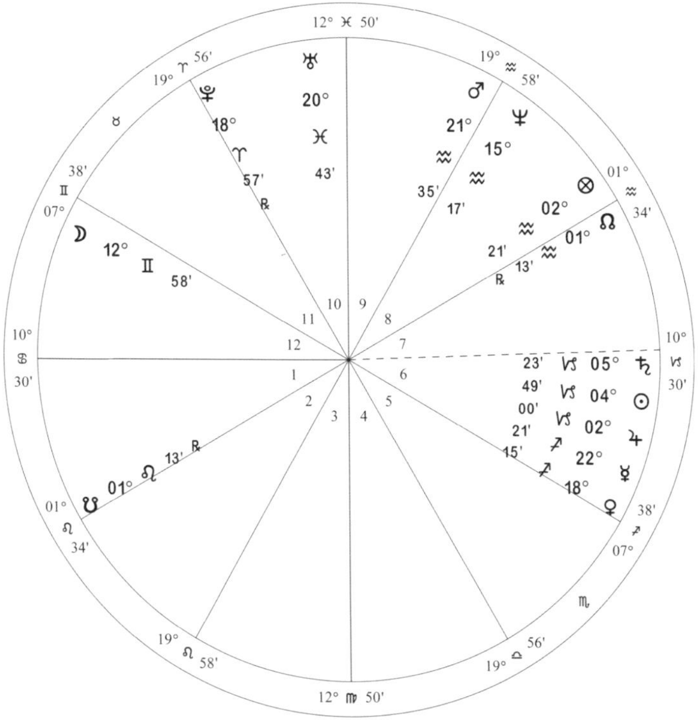

Dorothean Ess. Dig. (No Mut Rec. Points)

Pl	Ruler	Exalt	Tripl	Term	Face	Detri	Fall	Score
☉	♄	♂	☽	♀	♃	☽	♃	- 5 P
☽	☿	☊	☿	♃	♂ m	♃	--	- 5 P
☿	♃	☋	♃	♄	♄	☿ -	--	- 10 P
♀	♃	☋	♃	☿	☽	☿	--	- 5 P
♂	♄	--	☿	♃	☽ m	☉	--	- 5 P
♃	♄	♂	☽	♀	♃ +	☽	♃ -	- 3
♄	♄ +	♂	☽	♀	♃	☽	♃	+5
☊	♄	--	☿	♄	♀	☉	--	--
⊗	♄	--	☿	♄	♀	☉	--	--
As	☽	♃	♂	♃	☿	♄	♂	--
Mc	♃	♀	♂	♃	♃	☿	☿	--
☋	☉	--	♃	♄	♄	♄	--	--

Hs	Alm. (Pto)
1	♃
2	☉
3	♃
4	☿
5	☿♀♄
6	♃
7	♂♄
8	♄
9	♄
10	♃
11	☉♂
12	☿

Example 7-5d. Louis Pasteur education solar return for 1841

Louis Pasteur
Dole, France
Time Zone: 0 hours West

December 26, 1842
47 N 06 5 E 30
Tropical Regiomontanus
Solar Return for December 26, 1842 in Dole, France

10:35:26 PM
Local Mean Time

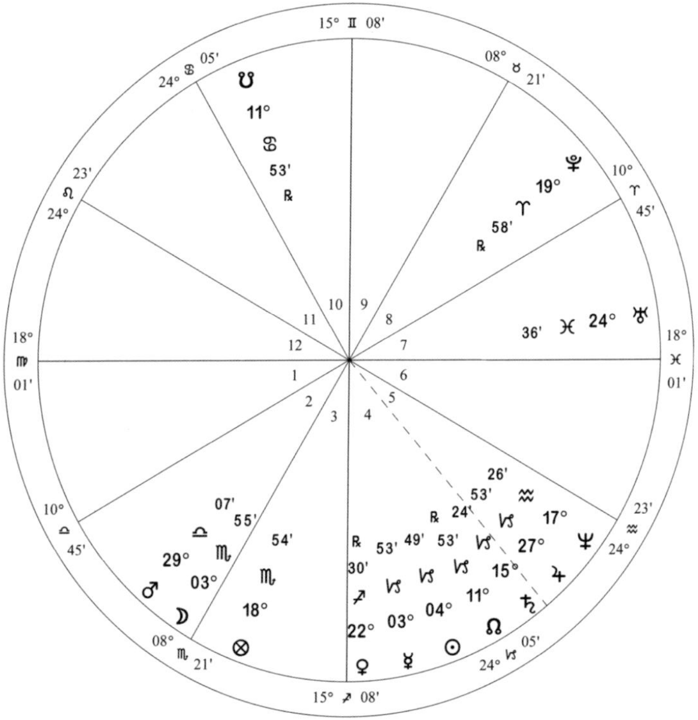

Pl	Ruler	Exalt	Tripl	Term	Face	Detri	Fall	Score
☉	♄	♂	☽	♀	♃ m	☽	♃	- 5 P
☽	♂	--	♂	♂	♂	♀	☽ -	- 9 P
☿	♄	♂	☽	♀	♃	☽	♃	- 5 P
♀	♃	☋	♃	♄	♄	☿	--	- 5 P
♂	♀	♄ m	☿	☊	♃	♂ -	☉	- 10 P
♃	♄	♂	☽	♄ m	☉ m	☽	♃ -	- 9 P
♄	♄ +	♂ m	☽	♃ m	♂	☽	♃	+5
☊	♄	♂	☽	☿	♂	☽	♃	--
⊗	♂	--	♂	♀	☉	♀	☽	--
As	☿	☿	☽	♄	♀	♃	♀	--
Mc	☿	☊	☿	♀	♂	♃	--	--
☋	☽	♃	♂	♃	☿	♄	♂	--

Dorothean Ess. Dig. (No Mut Rec. Points)

Hs	Alm. (Pto)
1	☿
2	♀
3	♂
4	♃
5	♂
6	♄
7	♃
8	☉♂
9	☽
10	☿
11	☽
12	☉♃

Example 7-5e. Louis Pasteur education solar return for 1842

Louis Pasteur
Dole, France
Time Zone: 0 hours West

December 26, 1845
47 N 06 5 E 30
Tropical Regiomontanus
Solar Return for December 26, 1845 in Dole, France

4:05:39 PM
Local Mean Time

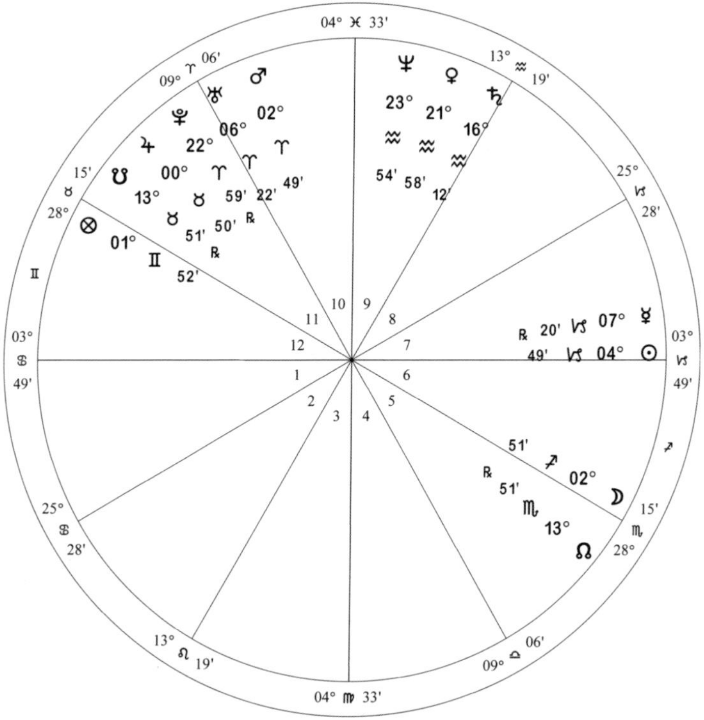

Pl	Ruler	Exalt	Tripl	Term	Face	Detri	Fall	Score
☉	♄	♂ m	♀	♀	♃	☽	♃	- 5 P
☽	♃	☋	☉	♃	☿	☿	--	- 5 P
☿	♄	♂	♀	☿ +	♃ m	☽	♃	+2
♀	♄	--	♄	♃ m	☽	☉	--	- 5 P
♂	♂ +	☉ m	☉	♃	♂ +	♀	♄	+6
♃	♀	☽	♀	♀ m	☿ m	♂	--	- 5 P
♄	♄ +	--	♄ +	♀	☿	☉	--	+8
☊	♂	--	♀	♃	☉	♀	☽	--
⊗	☿	☊	♄	☿	♃	♃	--	--
As	☽	♃	♀	♂	♀	♄	♂	--
Mc	♃	♀	♀	♀	♄	☿	☿	--
☋	♀	☽	♀	☿	☽	♂	--	--

Dorothean Ess. Dig. (No Mut Rec. Points)

Hs	Alm. (Pto)
1	☽
2	☽
3	☉
4	☿
5	♀♄
6	♂
7	♀♄
8	♄
9	♄
10	♀
11	☉
12	♀

Example 7-5f. Louis Pasteur education solar return for 1845

Louis Pasteur
Dole, France
Time Zone: 0 hours West

December 26, 1846
47 N 06 5 E 30
Tropical Regiomontanus
Solar Return for December 26, 1846 in Dole, France

9:52:09 PM
Local Mean Time

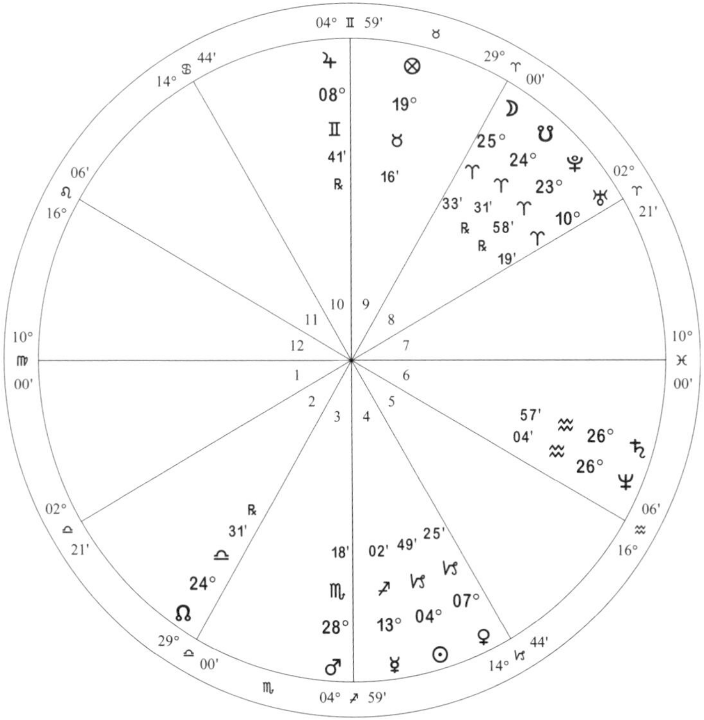

Dorothean Ess. Dig. (No Mut Rec. Points)								
Pl	Ruler	Exalt	Tripl	Term	Face	Detri	Fall	Score
☉	♄	♂	☽	♀	♃	☽	♃	- 5 P
☽	♂	☉	♃	♂	♀	♀	♄	- 5 P
☿	♃ m	☋	♃ m	♀ m	☽	☿ -	--	- 10 P
♀	♄	♂	☽	☿ m	♃	☽	♃	- 5 P
♂	♂ +	--	♂ +	♄ m	♀	♀	☽	+8
♃	☿ m	☊	☿ m	♃ +	♃ +	♃ -	--	- 2
♄	♄ +	--	☿	♂ m	☽	☉	--	+5
☊	♀	♄	☿	☊ +	♃	♂	☉	--
⊗	♀	☽	☽	♃	☽	♂	--	--
As	☿	☿	☽	♀	♀	♃	♀	--
Mc	☿	☊	☿	☿	♃	♃	--	--
☋	♂	☉	♃	♂	♀	♀	♄	--

Hs	Alm. (Pto)
1	☿
2	♄
3	♀
4	♃
5	♂♄
6	♄
7	♃
8	♂
9	♂
10	☿
11	☽
12	☉

Example 7-5g. Louis Pasteur education solar return for 1846

Saturn had some dignity, it helped the situation somewhat. However, he was still unsure of himself, and he had not really blossomed yet. When a person exceeds the family expectations as Pasteur had, it's hard for all but the most confident to feel comfortable about what they are doing.

He continued to study for the science *Baccalauréat*. In the following year, he took the exam and failed. Two years in a row, he had solar return Mercury in Sagittarius. Someone who has Mercury in Sagittarius natally learns how to make that Mercury position work. But the other Sun Scorpios and Capricorns who regularly encounter this Mercury position in their solar returns do not have the continuity to learn how to make this work readily for them.[11] Pasteur was still relatively young, so this wasn't easy for him. In any case, these end-of-degree exams were not easy. Uranus in the 1st house was evidently more disruptive to his thought processes than Jupiter in Sagittarius, ruling and in the 9th, was helpful.

Under his 1841 solar return, he received the *Baccalauréat* in Science. Here, Saturn in Capricorn took command of his 9th house. He was in his third consecutive year of Mercury in Sagittarius, so perhaps by this time, he had figured out how to structure his studying more successfully.

Perhaps because of his recent failure on the exam, or his earlier failure in Paris, he decided to spend an extra year preparing for the École normale. This extra year of study continued into his 1842 solar return. The Moon and Venus co-rule the 9th, but perhaps more importantly, Mercury moved to its natal sign of Capricorn, which must have seemed a considerable relief.

Observe the lower hemisphere emphasis of the 1842 chart. This was a quiet year for Pasteur, and in August, he passed the rest of his entrance exam, then started school in Paris in the Autumn of 1842.

We skip ahead to 1845. At this point, Pasteur had passed his physics exam, and was staying on at the École normale as a graduate student, doing the work which would allow him to take his doctorate in science the following year. He was already doing ground-breaking work in crystallography, his first area of expertise. Once again, Mercury was in Capricorn and Mars was dignified; this time in Aries. Not surprisingly with the 7th house Sun-Mercury, Pasteur's work was beginning to be noticed.

His 1846 solar return marked the culmination of his student years in the awarding of the D.Sc.[12] We saw earlier the configuration of several bodies lining up on the 8th house side of the 9th house cusp. Martin Luther King's 1954 solar return, when he received his appointment in Montgomery, Alabama, occurred when he was still working on his doctorate. Here, Louis Pasteur was finishing his. While the Moon didn't have dignity in Aries, its dispositor Mars was in Scorpio.

Honestly, this doesn't look as strong as his prior solar return. In the immediate sense, it wasn't. Pasteur struggled to get a teaching job after he finished the degree. He barely got one, and that reality probably overshadowed the immediate accomplishment.

Percy Bysshe Shelley

Not just anyone gets thrown out of Oxford for atheism. Accordingly, I couldn't resist looking at Percy Shelley. He had actually matriculated the prior year, but then he was expelled from Oxford March 25, 1811, because of his published pamphlet, *The Necessity of Atheism*.

His views had not changed between the two years, but what happened? Shelley is classified as a Romantic, and he both was enthusiastic and, with a wide square of Sun and Saturn, not averse to spitting in the face of authority. Shelley's 9th is ruled by Jupiter, which had mixed Triplicity. But of perhaps greater significance, it was partile conjunct Mars in Detriment. We have already observed that the Mars in debility is the more dangerous one. It rather looks like Percy couldn't resist being deliberately provocative. With both of them conjunct Neptune as well, if not as closely, it's entirely possible that Percy would do something provocative, and then be surprised by the result because he misjudged the probable effect.

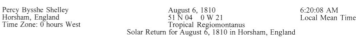

Percy Bysshe Shelley
Horsham, England
Time Zone: 0 hours West
August 6, 1810
6:20:08 AM
Local Mean Time
51 N 04 0 W 21
Tropical Regiomontanus
Solar Return for August 6, 1810 in Horsham, England

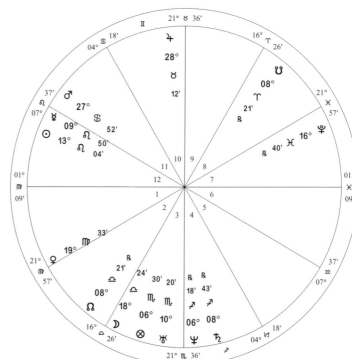

Example 7-6a. Percy Shelley education solar return for 1810

Percy Bysshe Shelley
Horsham, England
Time Zone: 0 hours West

August 6, 1811
51 N 04 0 W 21
Tropical Regiomontanus
Solar Return for August 6, 1811 in Horsham, England

12:06:59 PM
Local Mean Time

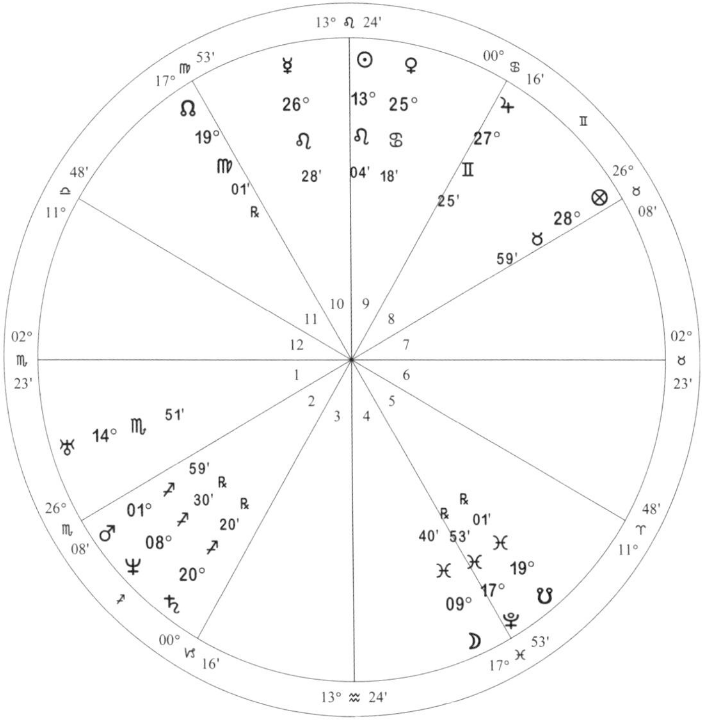

Dorothean Ess. Dig. (No Mut Rec. Points)								
Pl	Ruler	Exalt	Tripl	Term	Face	Detri	Fall	Score
☉	☉ +	--	☉ +	♀	♃ m	♄	--	+8
☽	♃	♀	♀	♃	♄	☿	☿	- 5 P
☿	☉	--	☉	♂	♂ m	♄	--	- 5 P
♀	☽	♃	♀ +	♀ +	☽	♄	♂	+5
♂	♃	☋	☉	♃ m	☿ m	☿	--	- 5 P
♃	☿	☊	♄	♂ m	☉ m	♃ -	--	- 10 P
♄	♃	☋	☉	♄ +	♄ +	☿	--	+3
☊	☿	☿	♀	♄	♀	♃	♀	--
⊗	♀	☽	♀	♂	♄	♂	--	--
As	♂	--	♀	♂	♂	♀	☽	--
Mc	☉	--	☉	♀	♃	♄	--	--
☋	♃	♀	♀	☿	♃	☿	☿	--

Hs	Alm. (Pto)
1	♂
2	♂
3	♀♄
4	♄
5	♃
6	☉
7	♀
8	♀
9	☽
10	☉
11	☿
12	♄

Example 7-6b. Percy Shelley education solar returns for 1811

One can see instances of this phenomenon throughout Percy's biography. For example, Percy had set out to meet William Godwin (his future father-in-law) because he absolutely worshiped his writings. But he couldn't help exclaiming to the elder Godwin that he had assumed he was already dead! Ironically, the elder Godwin ended up outliving him by decades. Later, when Percy, Mary, and Mary's half sister Claire were busily practicing the free love that Godwin had since rejected in his life after writing about it before they were born, the three of them continued to read William's writings aloud to each other, invoking a parental figure who no longer existed! This configuration of planets would have a bit of a foot-in-mouth quality.

Percy was very bright, very well read, and Oxford should have been a walk in the park for him. In solar year 1810, when he matriculated, Mars was ruling the 9th, in mixed dignity in Cancer (Fall and Triplicity), but sextile Jupiter. Jupiter, which barely ruled Percy's natal 9th *[SEE EXAMPLE 3-7 ON PAGE 84]*, has no strong dignity in Taurus, but it was in a Venus-ruled sign, like his radix Jupiter.

This matriculation did look like a big deal. It probably wasn't. Percy was from a social class where education was hardly necessary for his "profession," which was actually simply being of his class. While most young men of his standing may have attended university, graduation was strictly optional.

So the next year, Percy gets himself into trouble by being very publicly indiscreet. He was hardly the first British writer to profess atheism – that honor should probably go to David Hume. Even if Oxford and Cambridge had moved over to the Church of England with the Protestant revolution of the 16th century, they were still associated with the Church. Thus, a direct attack on belief by a member of one of their own community was not to be tolerated.

Seeing this within context, Percy's "stunt" can thus be seen as doubly affecting the 9th house: of both university and church. In 1811, we see Jupiter at the 9th house cusp. As we saw, Jupiter ruled

Percy's natal 9th house. In the solar return it was Jupiter in Gemini: Jupiter in Detriment. Like the year before, Mercury and Jupiter were sextile, resonating to his radix conjunction of these planets. The solar return Jupiter was in a partile trine to Percy's natal Neptune, and Jupiter was at the natal Bendings: the Southern Bending, which is the one that has more of a scapegoat quality.[13] In the solar return Saturn was at the SR-Southern Bending, with Saturn ruling the 3rd house of heresy. The nodal axis in the solar return was almost reverse the natal position.

Does this look like an intentional attack on Percy's part? One may justly ask: what is intention? If the question is, did Percy expect to be kicked out of Oxford for his publication, I would suspect that the answer is no. The solar return Moon, ruling the 9th house, is closer to the square of Neptune than of Mars. He may have sincerely believed that he was speaking the truth, and he may have sincerely believed that the truth was self evident. He, however, was ruled by that Mars in Sagittarius: his exuberance definitely had come into conflict with the Church. The Church won. But by how much? Percy didn't *need* the degree. And what he lost in extra education, he gained in notoriety: which he may have considered more valuable anyway.

Chapter 7 Endnotes

1. Al-Biruni, 1934, p 276.
2. For example, Lilly, p 279
3. For example, Ramesey, p 52.
4. al-Biruni, p 275.
5. Lilly, *CA*, p 606
6. Lilly, *CA*, p 429.
7. Gadbury, 1661, pp 228-229.
8. Lilly, *CA*, pp 432-434.
9. See Lehman, J. Lee. *The Book of Rulerships*. Atglen, PA: Schiffer Press, 1992, for a full list of citations.
10. For this we need to go to a modern source: see Bills, Rex, *The Rulership Book*, Richmond, VA: Macoy, p 94. As I am writing this, my spellchecker picked up "negro" as a misspelling, which itself perhaps is a victory.
11. It's worth considering that, given the geocentric limitation of Mercury's zodiacal distance from the Sun, it typically falls in the solar return in only three signs: the sign of the Sun, and the two signs around it. When the Sun is close to the beginning or ending of a sign, it will typically be in only two signs. What this means is that it is impossible for the solar return Mercury to be in both Sign or Exaltation *and* Detriment or Fall. From the standpoint of Mercury's dignity, the two best Sun signs are Virgo and Libra, for in both cases, Mercury would be in both of those signs perhaps two-thirds of the time. Since Mercury has sign and Exaltation in Virgo, and Triplicity in Libra, that's as good as it gets.
12. The D.Sc. Is the Doctor of Science. In many institutions, this degree is not given, but scientists receive a Ph.D. (Doctor of Philosophy) instead.
13. Lehman, *CAML*, pp 208-209, 213.

8

Solar Returns for Awards and Honors

THERE IS NO SHORTAGE OF HONORS AND AWARDS AMONG THE EMINENT PEOPLE SELECTED FOR THIS WORK. And yet I find myself wanting to take an award here or there from some of the sportspeople and award it to Jane Austen instead. Here was someone who wrote books that shortly would be called classics – but who never even saw them published with her own name on them, much less grasp that later generations would call them classics. Mary Shelley saw more of her name in print: but even she couldn't know how influential her work would remain.

When our classical writers wrote of honors and awards, they didn't distinguish types. But let me suggest that it is possible that there may be such, and we will explore that question here, because we have several good test types.

When an individual such as Martin Luther King or Marie Curie wins the Nobel Prize, while one might argue that there are some politics involved, there are few people who could get anywhere near that award without having already distinguished themselves greatly in their field. And yet, it is possible with lesser prizes like the Motion Picture Academy Awards (Oscars), given every year in multiple categories (24, at current count), there is much greater probability that in a given year, the field of nominees can be quite different, so that in one year, there may be two or three extremely worthy candidates, and in another year, none. Yet in both cases, one wins. Still, there is honor and prestige in the award.

Either of these cases represents a form of honor where others, whether a benefactor, committee, or group of peers, declares the work of the individual to be of extraordinary merit. This is probably quite close to the spirit of honor that we find in the traditional material.

However, we have noted that, in sports and a few other areas of life, there are competitions that an individual can enter and attempt to win. Here we present examples of this, mainly from figure skating. The difference in this case may be that there is no less honor, but the activity is much more directed toward the *goal* of the honor.

Also, because we are highlighting sports, there is a definite age and maturity issue. In most Olympic sports today, a person over the age of twenty-five is *old*. This may not be true of an equestrian competitor, for example. But in figure skating, if a skater has not reached a certain level of placement by their early twenties, they probably will never earn a top placement at a world competition.

Also because we are considering Olympic achievement here, the typical pattern has been to compete as an amateur, and then become a professional once achieving the highest competitive level that that person can expect to attain. Since this is entirely possible in one's late teens or early twenties, these competitive periods seem very short. When you take into account that most skaters have begun to skate by age nine or so, this commitment represents a decade or more – at an age where we rarely expect children to be so disciplined.

In electional astrology, Ramesey gave competition as a 1st-7th event, loosely based on Bonatti's rules of war.[1] So this raises the question: should we even consider the 10th house in these cases? A person who wins the Nobel Prize or the Oscar has been doing very high quality work: but not against a field of competitors. Marie Curie's extraction of pitchblende was not conducted as a public spectacle, with teams of scientists each attempting to find the new element first! Even if one could *hope* for an Academy Award, even possibly change a nuance here or there to perhaps improve one's chances, *the body of work must stand on its own*. In a competition, you must prove yourself better than the other people you are up against – in the moment.

And yet – an Olympic gold medal is the achievement of a lifetime, an honor that will always distinguish you for the rest of your life. So our sports scenario may well have both the 1st-7th and the 10th house markers.

In our examples, one of the most telling could well be Michelle Kwan. Michelle was U.S. Ladies Figure Skating champion *nine times* – compare this to Peggy Fleming's five and Dorothy Hamill's three. Michelle was World Champion four times, compared to Peggy's three and Dorothy's one. On this basis, Michelle should be counted one of the greats of U.S. ladies figure skating. But she never won an Olympic gold medal – and she competed twice. It was this fact that kept her competing longer than Peggy or Dorothy had to: because the professional transition is almost automatic in the year of winning

the Olympic gold medal. The year before Peggy won the Olympic gold, she was World Champion; in the year before Dorothy won she was Silver Medalist at Worlds. The year before Michelle won the Olympic Silver, she was also World Champion.

Because the Olympics take place only every four years, a particular athlete may not be entirely in sync with the Olympic schedule: not being at peak for the first time, possibly being past peak for the second. Or in Michelle's case, having that crucial injury or illness right at the time of the Olympics that dashes all hope for four years.

Before we go on to consider how these ideas work in practice, let's add a few aphorisms from Gadbury, who cites Schoener and Argolus.

2. Jupiter, Venus or the Dragon's Head in the tenth House, makes the Native famous in his Profession, gives him great gaine therein, gives him some eminent Office or Preferment in the place wherein he lives in that year; it mightily augments unto his Credit or Reputation in all things.

3. If Mars shall be in Quartile or Opposition of the Ascendant of the Radix, or of his Lord, it portends many labours and difficulties, and loss of Trade, &c. If Mars shall be in the tenth of a Revolution, it portends dangers from Magistrates, or Men in Power, loss of Preferment or Office, &c.

4. The Lord of the Mid-Heaven in a Revolution in the Ascendant, portends Honour and Preferment unto the Native in that year.

5. When the Sun, Moon, Lord of the Ascendant, &c. Shall be in good Aspect with the Lord of the tenth, or well dignified in the tenth House of a Revolution, the Native in that year shall attain unto a great degree of Preferment; and if he be a Mechanique, shall thrive well in his Trade or Profession.

6. Kingly fixed Stars in the Ascendant or Mid-heaven, (of a Revolution) denotes Honours and Preferment unto the Native in that year beyond his Condition or Expectation; chiefly when they shall be assisted with the friendly Rays of Jupiter or Venus.

7. ...When in a Revolution the beneficial Planets are in the tenth House, they always portend Honours unto the Native.

8. The Lord of the Tenth of a Revolution in the eighth House, presages fears and sorrows, &c. unto the Native from Princes and great Persons. Also danger unto his Mother.

9. Mars, Mercury and Venus (being the proper significators of Trade)[2] afflicted in a Revolution, denotes much labour, sorrow and difficulty unto the Native in his Profession or imployment in that year.

10. The Malevolent Planets beholding the Sun, Jove, the Lord of the Mid-heaven, or the Mid-heaven itself, by square or opposition, such Configurations are always found obnoxious to the Natives honour and Preferment. The like also to his Trade or Employment.

<...>

12. A Comet (or an Eclipse) happening in the Mid-heaven, as well as of the Radix as the Revolution, and Sol or Mars beholding the same, portends that the Native in that yeer shall come into great Dignity and Preferment.[3]

We should now be prepared to begin our examples.

Buzz Aldrin's Promotion to Commandant

Here we have a good example of the promotion scenario. Once he landed on the Moon, Buzz Aldrin's astronaut assignment was effectively finished, especially given that the U.S. space program was cut back massively after the goal of reaching the Moon was achieved. Buzz's promotion to Commandant of the U.S. Air Force Test Pilot School at Edwards Air Force Base should have been a good appointment, because Buzz had great respect both as a pilot and as an astronaut. However, after such a major life-altering event, Buzz was about to embark on a journey to the dark side of the soul: that portion that asks, "Is this all there is?" Landing on the Moon definitely qualified as a life-altering event!

Seeing this simply as a promotion, the SR-Ascendant is the same as Buzz's radix, which already is a positive. The Part of Fortune was almost precisely in the natal position [SEE EXAMPLE 3-1 ON PAGE 65]. But significantly, Jupiter, ruler of Buzz's natal MC, and SR-MC was in Sagittarius, almost exactly opposite its radix position. We recall that, when a planet is square or opposite its radix position, there will be problems, regardless of the fact that the opposing position itself might be dignified. In this case, we might interpret this as follows. Buzz gets a promotion to a reasonably high visibility job, but it doesn't work out for him. The dignity reversal doesn't preclude the promotion, but it made taking advantage of the new circumstances difficult.

Note also the focus on the 6th house. A cadent focus is likewise not an appropriate expression for a high-profile job, which should look angular in focus. With the Sun in the 9th, Buzz was still trying to break through his question about "what now:" the spiritual crisis where he found himself.

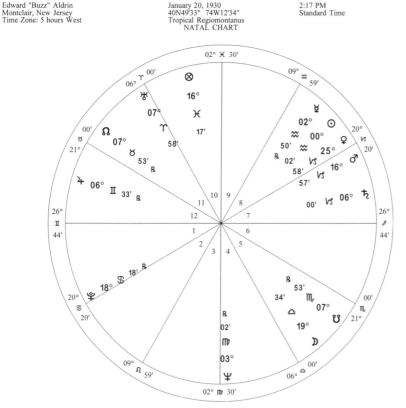

Edward "Buzz" Aldrin
Montclair, New Jersey
Time Zone: 5 hours West

January 20, 1930
40N49'33" 74W12'34"
Tropical Regiomontanus
NATAL CHART

2:17 PM
Standard Time

Maya Angelou's Presidential Medal of Freedom

Like the vast majority of such awards, Maya Angelou's did not come easy. She documented the pain of the black experience, but also its joys, strengths, and the commitment of its people. Angelou was given this award by President Obama in recognition of her inspirational qualities.

Angelou's radix 10th house has Venus exalted in Pisces ruling it. In the solar return chart, Jupiter is ruling the 10th – but again in Pisces where it is likewise dignified. The Part of Fortune is partile conjunct the 10th house cusp, again disposed by that prominent Jupiter. The radix Jupiter is dignified by Triplicity, so here the likewise dignified SR-Jupiter is a blessing, even extending the natal meaning. The SR-Sun in the 10th also argues that this is a year when she will receive recognition. [SEE EXAMPLE 5-1 ON PAGE 110 FOR ANGELOU'S NATIVITY]

Venus, the ruler of the radix 10th, is also more strongly dignified than in the radix, in Taurus. This continues the argument that this will be an exceptionally good year from the standpoint of honor.

Dorothean Ess. Dig. (No Mut Rec. Points)								
Pl	Ruler	Exalt	Tripl	Term	Face	Detri	Fall	Score
☉	♄	--	♄	♄	♀ m	☉ -	--	- 10 P
☽	♀	♄	♄	☿	♄	♂	☉	- 5 P
☿	♄	--	♄	♄ m	♀	☉	--	- 5 P
♀	♄	♂	♀ +	♄	☉ m	☽	♃	+3
♂	♄	♂ +	♀	♀	♂ +	☽	♃	+5
♃	☿	♏	♄	♄	♃ m	♃ -	♃	- 4
♄	♄ +	♂	♀	☿ m	♃	☽	♃	+5
☊	♀	♃	♀	♀	☿	♂	--	--
⊗	♃	♀	♀	☿	♃	☿	☿	--
As	☿	☊	♄	♂	☉	♃	--	--
Mc	♃	♀	♀	♀	♄	♀	--	--
☋	♂	--	♀	♃	♂	♀	☽	--

Hs	Alm. (Pto)
1	♀
2	☽
3	☉
4	☿
5	♀ ♄
6	♂
7	♀
8	♂
9	♄
10	☿
11	☉
12	♀

Example 8-1. Buzz Aldrin honors solar return for 1971

Maya Angelou
Saint Louis, Missouri
Time Zone: 6 hours West

April 4, 2010
38N37'38" 90W11'52"
Tropical Regiomontanus
Solar Return for April 4, 2010 in Saint Louis, Missouri

11:46:09 AM
Daylight Saving Time

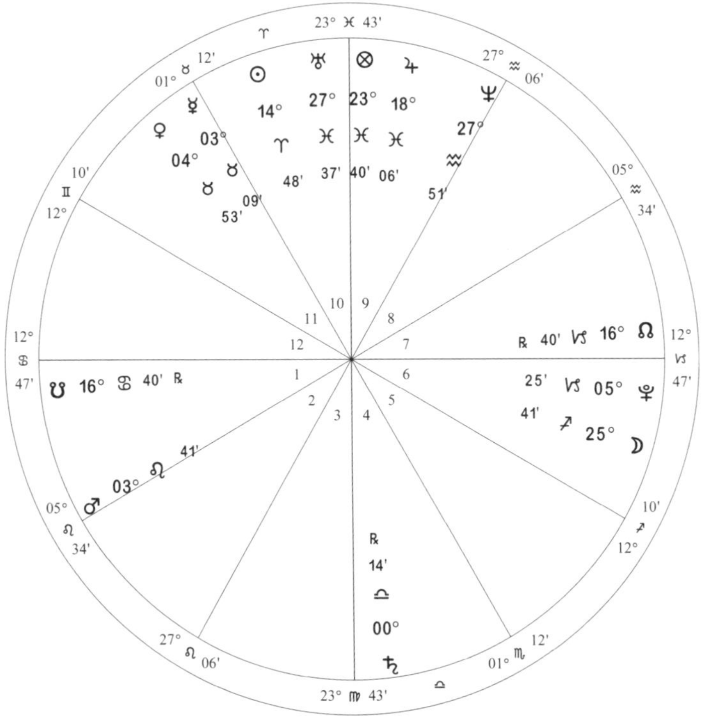

Dorothean Ess. Dig. (No Mut Rec. Points)								
Pl	Ruler	Exalt	Tripl	Term	Face	Detri	Fall	Score
☉	♂ m	☉ +	☉ +	☿	☉ +	♀	♄	+8
☽	♃	☋	☉	♂	♄ m	☿	--	- 5 P
☿	♀	☽	♀	♀	☿ +	♂	--	+1
♀	♀ +	☽	♀ +	♀ +	☿	♂	--	+10
♂	☉ m	--	☉	♄	♄	♄	--	- 5 P
♃	♃ +	♀	♀	☿	♃ +	☿	☿	+6
♄	♀	♄ +	♄ +	♄ +	☽ m	♂	☉	+9
☊	♄	♂	♀	♃	♂	☽	♃	--
⊗	♃	♀	♀	♂	♂	☿	☿	--
As	☽	♃	♀	♃	☿	♄	♂	--
Mc	♃	♀	♀	♂	♂	☿	☿	--
☋	☽	♃	♀	☿	☿	♄	♂	--

Hs	Alm. (Pto)
1	♃
2	☉
3	☉
4	☿
5	♂
6	♃
7	♂♄
8	♄
9	♄
10	♃
11	♀
12	☿

Example 8-2. Maya Angelou honors solar return for 2010

Marie Curie's Two Nobel Prizes

One Nobel Prize is impressive: two is amazing. It is no wonder that virtually every female child of a scientific bent becomes obsessed with Marie Curie's life! Examining her natal chart from the standpoint of the 10th house, here is exceptionally strong Mars ruling and in the 10th house *[SEE EXAMPLE 3-2 ON PAGE 69]*. The translation here is that Marie will not get points for who she *is*, but for what she *does*. Hard work produces reward – and she was nothing if not a hard worker.

Curie's first Nobel Prize was for the work she and Pierre did to discover and characterize new radioactive elements. Becquerel, who originally discovered radioactivity (originally called Becquerel rays), was also honored with them.

It's hard to say which was the more important factor for her about the award: the award itself, or the cash that it brought – mostly put into more research, but also funding a vacation for them. I'd say from the chart that the money was the more appealing aspect, with the Sun so close to the 2nd house cusp. The Sun itself ruled the 10th. As we shall continue to observe, the Sun in a solar return is treated as automatically dignified *when it refers to the Native*. Here, with the Sun ruling the 10th, she is coming into her own power, honor, and dignity. The three dignified planets are Mars, Jupiter and Saturn, where Jupiter and Mars were dignified in her radix chart. The Moon in Gemini in the solar return was square her radix Moon in Pisces. Given the frequency with which Pluto has been assigned to radioactivity, perhaps its conjunction to the Moon is also meaningful, given the subject of the Nobel Prize. In this year, her SR-Mars was dignified, analogous to her radix, and her SR-Venus was debilitated, also analogous to her radix. So this chart has some strong resonances with her birth chart. What is actually quite remarkable are the similarities between the 1903 and the 1911 solar return charts, the two years she won the prize. Venus is in the same degree – but of course, the second chart is eight years later, which follows the Venus cycle. The Moon is in Gemini in the 9th house in both charts. In 1911, Saturn was

Marie Curie
Warsaw, Poland
Time Zone: 1 hr 24 min East

November 8, 1903
52 N 15 21 E 00
Tropical Regiomontanus
Solar Return for November 8, 1903 in Warsaw, Poland

5:29:01 AM
Standard Time

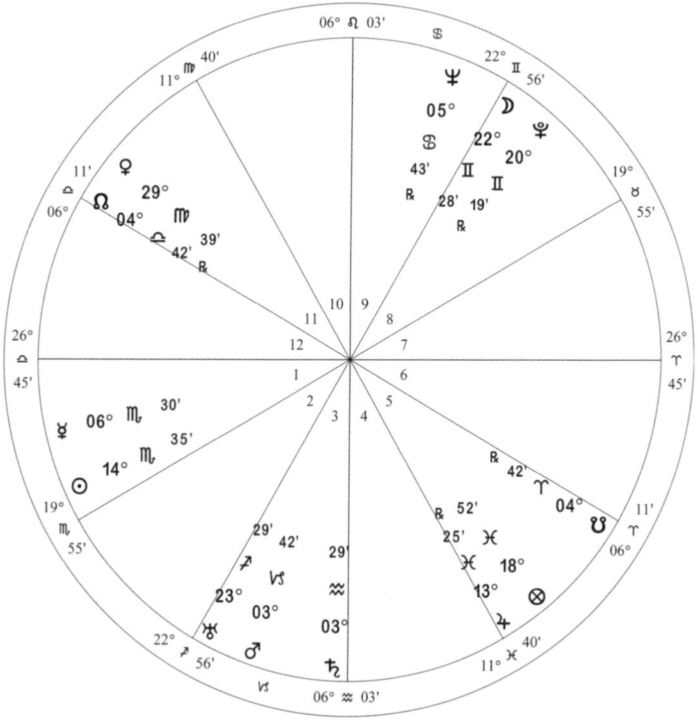

Pl	Ruler	Exalt	Tripl	Term	Face	Detri	Fall	Score
☉	♂	--	♂	♀	☉ +	♀	☽	+1
☽	☿	☊	☿	♄	☉	♃	--	- 5 P
☿	♂	--	♂	♃	♂	♀	☽	- 5 P
♀	☿	☿	☽	♂ m	☿	♃	♀ -	- 9 P
♂	♄	♂ +	☽	♀ m	♃	☽	♃	+4
♃	♃ +	♀	♂	♃ +	♃ +	☿	☿	+8
♄	♄ +	--	☿	♄ +	♀	☉	--	+7
☊	♀	♄	☿	♄	☽	♂	☉	--
⊗	♃	♀	♂	☿	♃	☿	☿	--
As	♀	♄	☿	☊	♃	♂	☉	--
Mc	☉	--	♃	☿	♄	♄	--	--
☋	♂	☉	♃	♃	♂	♀	♄	--

Dorothean Ess. Dig. (No Mut Rec. Points)

Hs	Alm. (Pto)
1	♀
2	♂
3	♃
4	☿♄
5	♃
6	♂
7	♂
8	☽
9	☿
10	☉
11	☿
12	♀

Example 8-3a. Marie Curie honors solar return for 1903

Marie Curie
Warsaw, Poland
Time Zone: 1 hr 24 min East

November 8, 1911
52 N 15 21 E 00
Tropical Regiomontanus
Solar Return for November 8, 1911 in Warsaw, Poland

4:02:34 AM
Standard Time

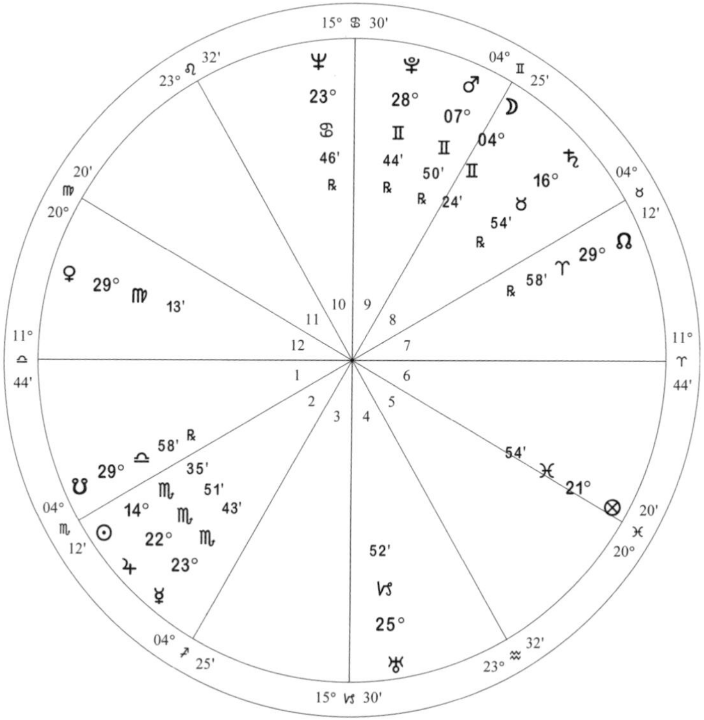

Pl	Ruler	Exalt	Tripl	Term	Face	Detri	Fall	Score
☉	♂	--	♂	♀	☉ +	♀	☽	+1
☽	☿	☊	☿	☿	♃	♃	--	- 5 P
☿	♂ m	--	♂ m	☿ +	♀ m	♀	☽	+2
♀	☿	☿	☽	♂	☿ m	♃	♀ -	- 9 P
♂	☿ m	☊	☿ m	♃	♃	♃	--	- 5 P
♃	♂	--	♂	☿	♀	♀	☽	- 5 P
♄	♀	☽	☽	♃	☽	♂	--	- 5 P
☊	♂	☉	♃	♄	♀	♀	♄	--
⊗	♃	♀	♂	♂	♂	☿	☿	--
As	♀	♄	☿	♃	♄	♂	☉	--
Mc	☽	♃	♂	☿	☿	♄	♂	--
☋	♀	♄	☿	☊	♃	♂	☉	--

Dorothean Ess. Dig. (No Mut Rec. Points)

Hs	Alm. (Pto)
1	♀♄
2	♂
3	♃
4	♂♄
5	♄
6	♃
7	☉♂
8	☽♀
9	☿
10	☽
11	☉♃
12	☿

Example 8-3b. Marie Curie honors solar return for 1911

opposite radix Saturn: this year the scandal over her affair with Paul Langevin broke. But SR-Pluto trine radix Jupiter is quite a signature in her case! The unprecedented qualities of these substances were clearly on everyone's minds.

Peggy Fleming's Skating Accomplishments

How do you tell the difference between a Gold Medal year and a good year? Ultimately, not every person born at roughly Peggy Fleming's time and date of birth had either her grace or athletic ability! Was she the only possible Gold Medalist of 1968? I would argue no – at the very least, there is the question of illness or injury. Michelle Kwan would later fail to skate at her maximum potential in Olympic years because of both of these. Winter sports competitions take place by definition during influenza season among global competitors who are constantly exposed to people who may be carriers. How many athletes lose because they get sick at just the wrong time? And one competitor may skate the performance of a lifetime, only to be followed by another one skating the performance of a lifetime. Really, an individual is only "responsible" for his or her own performance.

But be that as it may, let's examine Peggy's solar returns for the three years where she was at the top of her field. In 1965 she won her first World Championship. This may also show as a case of the highs and lows, because it was only a few weeks later that her father died.

Recall that her chart has the athletic signature of a Mars in Detriment: a stunningly frequent occurrence in top athletes that could well speak to extreme competitiveness [SEE EXAMPLE 5-2 ON PAGE 112]. And note: in this first year where she won the Worlds, Mars was right back in Libra. Possibly best for her was that the MC was the benefic fixed star Spica, which would certainly be advantageous for her on the world stage. The focus on the 8th house is most probably her father's death.

We have already seen repeatedly that a recapitulation of the radix condition sets up an advantageous resonance for the year. (But not necessarily wonderful: see Chapter 11 for a discussion of her father's death in this same year.) We have also seen that there are several ways to see that resonance. In Peggy's solar return for 1965, we have several such variations:

- Mars in its radix sign
- Venus and Uranus are in a Mercury-ruled sign
- Jupiter is in the sign opposite the natal Jupiter
- The Part of Fortune is in a sign trine the radix Part of Fortune

We have seen that having the Moon in the sign square its radix position should provide some imbalance or stress: her father's death fulfilled this. But I cannot help but think that having the solar return Moon so dignified must also be helpful at the same time, provided that the natal Moon is not debilitated by dignity and not merely peregrine, as is her Aries Moon. This return Moon, while strong by dignity, is not quite so strong by aspect as Peggy's natal Moon, with its partile sextile to Venus and partile trine to Jupiter.

Figure skating is one of those sports with a conservative component which is introduced because the judging is, by necessity, subjective. What this means in practice is that the judges know the competitors, and the competitors know the judges, and the coaches know everybody. To a degree, it is possible to adapt one's program to the judging of a time period in order to achieve a better score. It also means that skaters who have been seen by the judges and are collectively believed to be top competitors will often be judged less harshly for errors than newcomers. After all, the judges have seen these same competitors perform these moves time after time. By winning the Worlds in 1966 (the 1965 solar return), Peggy increased her chances in the next few competitive years. Thus, unlike some sports, which give the champion a more difficult schedule in the year after the championship, Peggy's success made her the favorite for the following year, especially as her age indicated that she could well not have peaked yet.

In her 1966 solar return (1966-1967 competitive season), Peggy had:

- A dignified Jupiter
- The SR-Moon conjunct radix Jupiter
- The nodal axis in the radix signs
- Mars debilitated
- Another gold medal at Worlds

The only thing about this solar return which was worrisome was Saturn at the fixed star Alcyone, ruling the MC. However, Mars was co-Almuten of the 10th house cusp, which, given the debilitated strength of Peggy's natal Mars, was a good thing for her.

The 1967 solar return was the key, because that was the solar return which covered her Olympic year. Here, the presence of Mars so dignified isn't automatically a good omen, because Peggy's Mars is strong – but debilitated. Further, it's in a partile square to the Sun. In *Traditional Medical Astrology*, I quoted from Peggy's autobiography about how she would use anger to focus her skating: in fact, she told how her mother would deliberately infuriate her in order to release her competitive fervor. That would look a lot like Sun square Mars, especially with the Sun in the 1st and Mars in the 4th, a parental house.[4]

In 1967, Peggy's solar return had:

- The Moon in its radix sign
- Mercury in its radix sign
- Venus in the other sign ruled by Mercury
- Mars in reverse dignity
- Saturn debilitated (radix in Detriment; here in Fall)
- Jupiter not as dignified, but still dignified by Triplicity

Peggy Fleming
San Jose, California
Time Zone: 8 hours West

July 27, 1965
37N20'07" 121W53'38"
Tropical Regiomontanus
Solar Return for July 27, 1965 in San Jose, California

6:15:11 PM
Daylight Saving Time

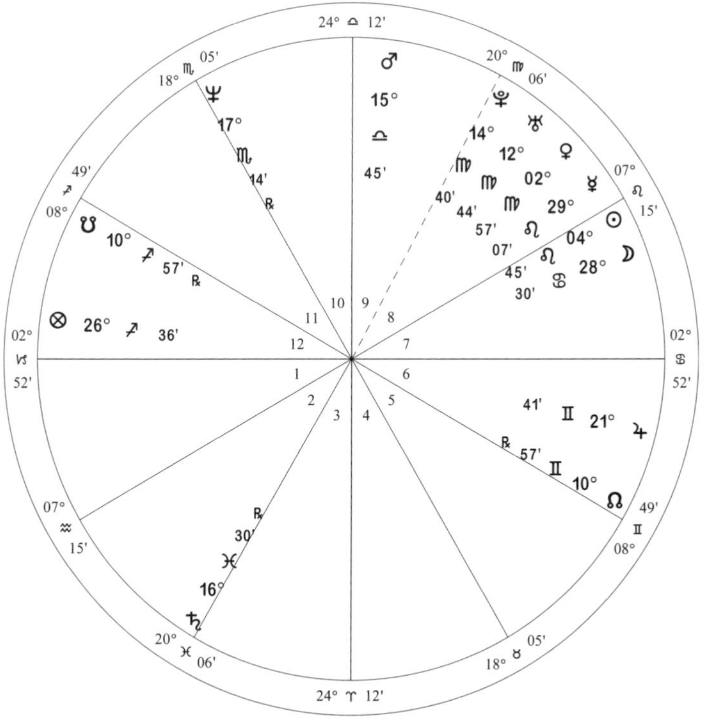

Dorothean Ess. Dig. (No Mut Rec. Points)								
Pl	Ruler	Exalt	Tripl	Term	Face	Detri	Fall	Score
☉	☉ +	--	☉ +	♄	♄	♄	--	+8
☽	☽ +	♃	♀	♄	☽ +	♄	♂	+6
☿	☉	--	☉	♂	♂	♄	--	- 5 P
♀	☿	☿	♀ +	☿	☉	♃	♀ -	- 1
♂	♀	♄	♄	♃	♄	♂ -	☉	- 10 P
♃	☿	☊	♄	♄	☉	♃ -	--	- 10 P
♄	♃	♀	♀	☿	♃	☿	☿	- 5 P
☊	☿	☊ +	♄	♃	♂	♃	--	--
⊗	♃	☋ +	☉	♂	♄	☿	--	--
As	♄	♂	♀	♀	♃	☽	♃	--
Mc	♀	♄	♄	☊	♃	♂	☉	--
☋	♃	☋	☉	♀	☽	☿	--	--

Hs	Alm. (Pto)
1	♀♄
2	♄
3	♃
4	☉♂
5	♀
6	☿
7	☽
8	☉
9	☿
10	♄
11	♂
12	♃

Example 8-4a. Peggy Fleming honors solar return for 1965

Peggy Fleming
San Jose, California
Time Zone: 8 hours West

July 27, 1966
37N20'07" 121W53'38"
Tropical Regiomontanus
Solar Return for July 27, 1966 in San Jose, California

11:52:53 PM
Daylight Saving Time

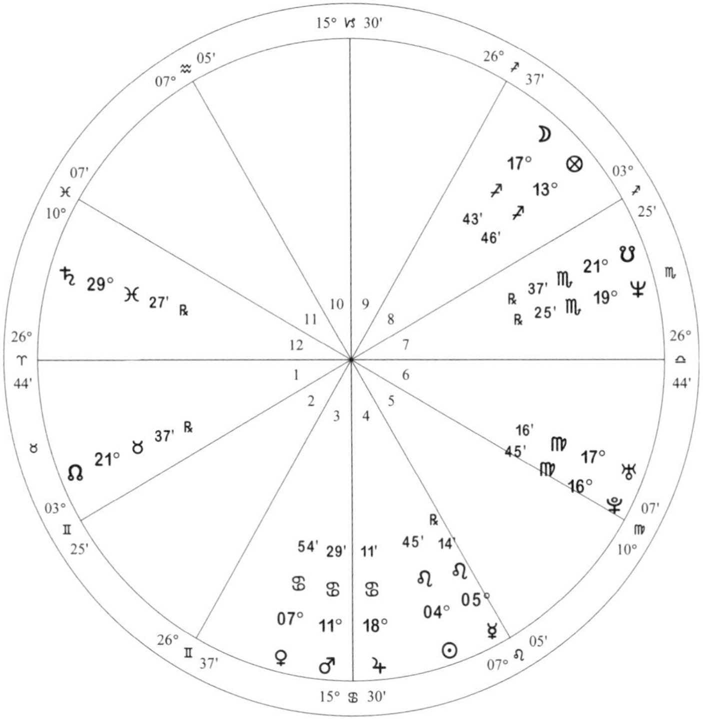

Dorothean Ess. Dig. (No Mut Rec. Points)								
Pl	Ruler	Exalt	Tripl	Term	Face	Detri	Fall	Score
☉	☉ +	--	♃	♄	♄	♄	--	+5
☽	♃ m	☋	♃	☿	☽ +	☿	--	+1
☿	☉	--	♃	♄	♄	♄	--	- 5 P
♀	☽	♃	♂	♃	♀ +	♄	♂	+1
♂	☽	♃	♂ +	♃	☿	♄	♂ -	- 1
♃	☽ m	♃ +	♂	☿	☿	♄	♂	+4
♄	♃	♀	♂	♄ +	♂	☿	☿	+2
☊	♀	☽	☽	♃	♄	♂	--	--
⊗	♃	☋ +	♃	♀	☽	☿	--	--
As	♂	☉	♃	♄	♀	♀	♄	--
Mc	♄	♂	☽	♃	♂	☽	♃	--
☋	♂	--	♂	☿	♀	♀	☽	--

Hs	Alm. (Pto)
1	♂
2	☿
3	☿
4	☽
5	☉
6	☿
7	♀
8	♃
9	♃
10	♂♄
11	☿♄
12	♃

Example 8-4b. Peggy Fleming honors solar return for 1966

Peggy Fleming
San Jose, California
Time Zone: 8 hours West

July 28, 1967
37N20'07" 121W53'38"
Tropical Regiomontanus
Solar Return for July 28, 1967 in San Jose, California

5:47:10 AM
Daylight Saving Time

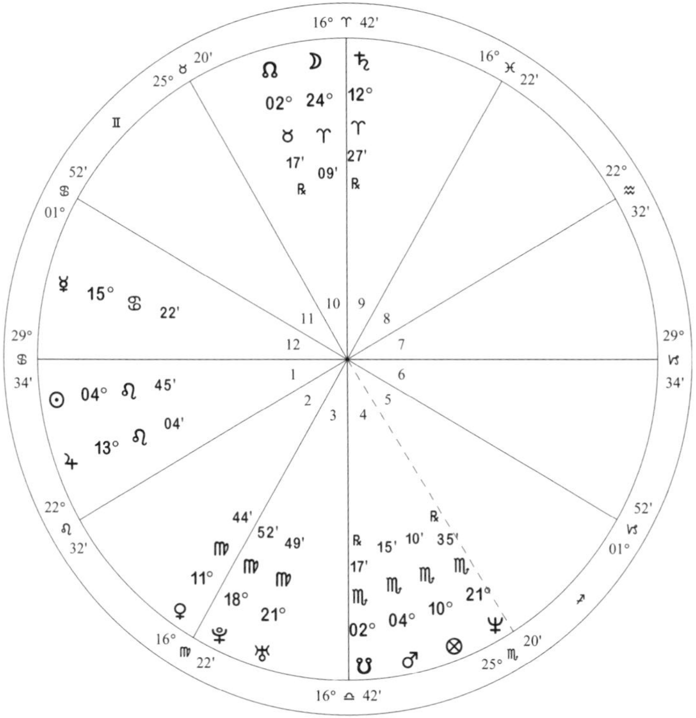

Dorothean Ess. Dig. (No Mut Rec. Points)								
Pl	Ruler	Exalt	Tripl	Term	Face	Detri	Fall	Score
☉	☉ +	--	♃	♄	♄ m	♄	--	+5
☽	♂	☉	♃	♂	♀	♀	♄	- 5 P
☿	☽	♃	♂	☿ +	☿ +	♄	♂	+3
♀	☿	☿	☽	♀ +	♀ +	♃	♀ -	- 1
♂	♂ +	--	♂ +	♂ +	♂ +	♀	☽	+11
♃	☉	--	♃ +	♀	♃ +	♄	--	+4
♄	♂	☉	♃	♀	☉ m	♀	♄ -	- 9 P
☊	♀	☽	☽	♀	☿	♂	--	--
⊗	♂	--	♂	♃	☉	♀	☽	--
As	☽	♃	♂	♄	☽	♄	♂	--
Mc	♂	☉	♃	☿	☉	♀	♄	--
☋	♂	--	♂	♂	♂	♀	☽	--

Hs	Alm. (Pto)
1	☽
2	☉♃
3	☿
4	♀♄
5	♂
6	♄
7	♄
8	♄
9	♃
10	☉♂
11	☽
12	☽

Example 8-4c. Peggy Fleming honors solar return for 1967

- The Ascendant partile trine the radix Ascendant
- SR-Venus conjunct radix MC

Thus, we can see that there is powerful resonance between the 1967 solar return and Peggy's radix chart, not to mention the hit to the MC with Venus. There should be. This would be the year that set up Peggy's life patterns through her victory in the Olympics. The amount of angularity would be one sign that a lot could change.

Dorothy Hamill's Ride to the Top

From everything that we can see on the outside, both Peggy Fleming and Dorothy Hamill are very classy ladies – now. Peggy talks in her biography about how much the skating community changed after the Sabena Airlines crash that killed the U.S. world skating team of 1961, creating a gulf between her and Carol Heiss Jenkins, the previous U.S. gold medalist. By the end of the 1960s, Peggy's options were very different, and Dorothy also benefited from these changes, as well as direct help from Peggy and her mother as supporters, and as problem solvers.

Both Peggy and Dorothy had established themselves in the global skating community by standing on the platform of the World Championships for the two years prior to the Olympics. The only difference was that Peggy stood in the #1 spot, while Dorothy stood in the #2 position. But in the end, both were lucky to be able to peak in an Olympic year, and stand on the podium at both the Olympics and the Worlds as the gold medalist.

Dorothy's natal setup for success is the hard way *[SEE EXAMPLE 3-4 ON PAGE 75]*. Jupiter ruling the 10th house natally is a good starting place, except that Dorothy's natal Jupiter in Virgo means that she needs a little extra time to get established. That Jupiter also rules her Moon, and most importantly for competition, Mars.

In her 1973 solar return, when she won the U.S. championships, and then came in second in the Worlds, Dorothy's Mars was in Aries in a Gauquelin sector: a strong placement even stronger than her natal Mars in Triplicity.[5] The Moon-Saturn conjunction in her solar return was fairly close to her natal Venus. That Mars was square the MC and opposite Uranus, giving some dynamism, which could represent a change in status, although up or down might be harder to project.

SR-Saturn ruled her 10th – a participating Triplicity which is not wildly strong, but a bit stronger than her radix position. But this chart hasn't quite synced yet. *Her radix positions don't resonate in this solar return*: she didn't have a personal comfort zone yet.

The following year, in 1974, she has the same results at both the U.S. and the Worlds. The Sun is in the 1st house and ruling the 1st: there she is, ready to do her job. The Part of Fortune is at the 10th house, showing the plan. But again, nothing is synced. None of her solar return personal planets show resonance with her natal chart, so things just aren't quite operating easily. I have to suspect with the Moon in Scorpio, which was at least trine her natal position, but in Fall, and Mars in late Leo, that perhaps she was trying a bit too hard at this point. Also, the dignified Jupiter isn't helping, because it's opposite the natal position. She's holding her own, but she's not able to advance.

Then next is her 1975 solar return, which covers the Olympic gold medal competition. Now she has:

- The Moon in the same sign as the radix, and ruling the 10th
- Venus in a Mercury-ruled sign, like the radix and ruling the 1st
- Mars in debility, but with Triplicity and sextile the radix. While the Mars in debility doesn't match Dorothy's, it's the hyper-competitive Mars.
- The Moon is trine Saturn in Detriment. Dorothy's radix Saturn is so-so, but remember the undignified malefics are the really competitive ones.

Dorothy Hamill
Chicago, Illinois
Time Zone: 6 hours West

July 26, 1973
41 N 51 87 W 39
Tropical Regiomontanus
Solar Return for July 26, 1973 in Chicago, Illinois

11:50:35 PM
Daylight Saving Time

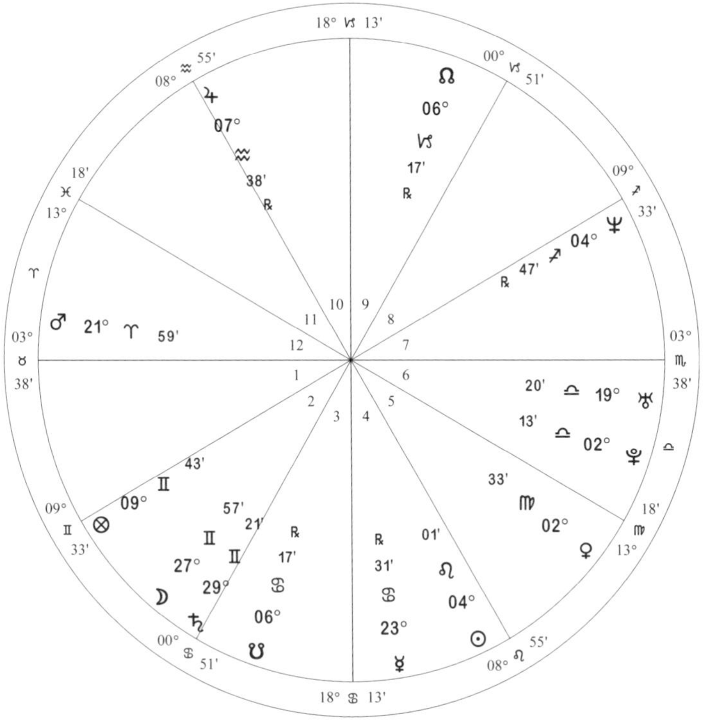

Dorothean Ess. Dig. (No Mut Rec. Points)								
Pl	Ruler	Exalt	Tripl	Term	Face	Detri	Fall	Score
☉	☉ +	--	♃	♄	♄ m	♄	--	+5
☽	☿ m	☊	☿	♂	☉	♃	--	- 5 P
☿	☽ m	♃	♂	♀ m	☽	♄	♂	- 5 P
♀	☿	☿	☽	☿ m	☉	♃	♀ -	- 9 P
♂	♂ +	☉	♃	♂ +	♀	♀	♄	+7
♃	♄	--	☿	☿	♀	☉	--	- 5 P
♄	☿	☊	☿	♂	☉ m	♃	--	- 5 P
☊	♄	♂	☽	☿	♃	☽	♃	--
⊗	☿	☊	☿	♃	♃	♃	--	--
As	♀	☽	☽	♀	☿	♂	--	--
Mc	♄	♂	☽	♃	♂	☽	♃	--
☋	☽	♃	♂	♃	♀	♄	♂	--

Hs	Alm. (Pto)
1	☽♀
2	☿
3	☽
4	☽
5	☉
6	☿
7	♂
8	♃
9	♄
10	♂♄
11	☿♄
12	♃

Example 8-5a. Dorothy Hamill honors solar return for 1973

Dorothy Hamill
Chicago, Illinois
Time Zone: 6 hours West

July 27, 1974
41 N 51 87 W 39
Tropical Regiomontanus
Solar Return for July 27, 1974 in Chicago, Illinois

5:26 AM
Daylight Saving Time

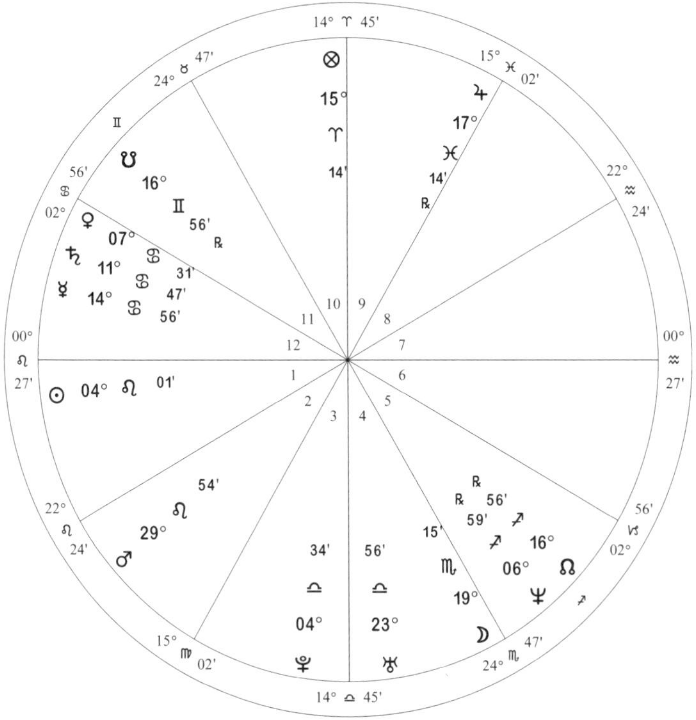

Dorothean Ess. Dig. (No Mut Rec. Points)								
Pl	Ruler	Exalt	Tripl	Term	Face	Detri	Fall	Score
☉	☉ +	--	♃	♄	♄	♄	--	+5
☽	♂	--	♂	♀	☉	♀	☽ -	- 9 P
☿	☽	♃	♂	☿ +	☿ +	♄	♂	+3
♀	☽	♃ m	♂	♃	♀ +	♄	♂	+1
♂	☉	--	♃ m	♂ +	♂ +	♄	--	+3
♃	♃ +	♀ m	♂ m	☿	♃ +	☿	☿	+6
♄	☽	♃	♂	♃	☿	♄ -	♂	- 10 P
☊	♃	☋	♃	☿	☽	☿	--	--
⊗	♂	☉	♃	☿	☉	♀	♄	--
As	☉	--	♃	♄	♄	♄	--	--
Mc	♂	☉	♃	☿	☉	♀	♄	--
☋	☿	☊	☿	♀	♂	♃	--	--

Hs	Alm. (Pto)
1	☉
2	☉♃
3	☿
4	♀♄
5	♂
6	♄
7	♄
8	♄
9	♃
10	☉♂
11	☽
12	☽

Example 8-5b. Dorothy Hamill honors solar return for 1974

Dorothy Hamill
Chicago, Illinois
Time Zone: 6 hours West

July 27, 1975
41 N 51 87 W 39
Tropical Regiomontanus
Solar Return for July 27, 1975 in Chicago, Illinois

11:20:22 AM
Daylight Saving Time

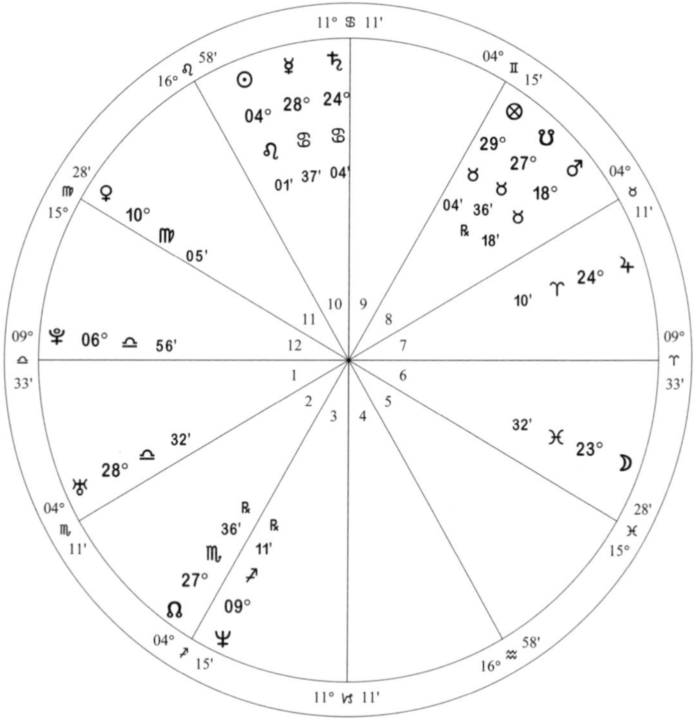

Dorothean Ess. Dig. (No Mut Rec. Points)								
Pl	**Ruler**	**Exalt**	**Tripl**	**Term**	**Face**	**Detri**	**Fall**	**Score**
☉	☉ +	--	☉ +	♄	♄	♄	--	+8
☽	♃	♀	♀	♂	♂ m	☿	☿	- 5 P
☿	☽	♃	♀	♄	☽	♄	♂	- 5 P
♀	☿	☿	♀ +	♀ +	♀ +	♃	♀ -	+2
♂	♀	☽	♀	♃ m	☽ m	♂ -	--	- 10 P
♃	♂	☉	☉	♂ m	♀	♀	♄	- 5 P
♄	☽	♃	♀	♀	☽	♄ -	♂	- 10 P
☊	♂	--	♀	♄	♀	♀	☽	--
⊗	♀	☽	♀	♂	♄	♂	--	--
As	♀	♄	♄	♀	☽	♂	☉	--
Mc	☽	♃	♀	♃	☿	♄	♂	--
☋	♀	☽	♀	♂	♄	♂	--	--

Hs	Alm. (Pto)
1	♀♄
2	♂
3	♃
4	♂♄
5	♄
6	♃
7	☉
8	♀
9	☿
10	♃
11	☉
12	☿

Example 8-5c. Dorothy Hamill honors solar return for 1975

What about the Pluto rising? For as good a competitor as Dorothy, I'm tempted to say that it couldn't possibly hurt! She wasn't just going for a local competition, she was potentially engaging in a life-altering process. Peggy may not have entirely understood what winning would mean for her – but Dorothy did. Peggy's victory was at the dawn of U.S. television coverage of the Olympics: by Dorothy's time, it had expanded even more.

We thus see an interesting contrast between Peggy and Dorothy: Peggy's Olympic year synched a little more than Dorothy's did – but Dorothy had both the malefics in highly competitive signs *generally*, not specific to her radix. Peggy succeeded by getting into a groove; Dorothy succeeded by stepping up her competitive nature.

Scott Hamilton Overcomes

The bulk of U.S. sports coverage is team sports, a fact and an obsession which, as astrologers, we might recall led to an awkward moment for us, when Michel Gauquelin was called upon to repeat his results with data from U.S. sports champions. In France, the sports that were greatly prized were tennis and cycling, two sports characterized by individual effort and achievement. It is not at all apparent that athletes who compete in team sports would have the same configuration. Likewise, though figure skating is either individual or paired, one isn't on the ice racing against direct competitors or the clock, as with short track or speed skating. As we arrive at our next example, Scott Hamilton, a brief examination of three top figure skaters from the 1960s, 1970s, and 1980s shows that none of these three had their Mars position in a Gauquelin sector – and yet all three have talked about competition and their competitive spirit – the essence of Mars for each of them.

As we have mentioned, the usual career trajectory for a skater who wins is to turn pro just after the Olympics and the Worlds afterward in the same year. The logic is simple: an Olympic gold is the highest accolade one can collect, and performing at the Worlds in the same year is a service to one's country, because a high finish at the Worlds in one year guarantees more slots for that country in the following year.

So it is extremely common to see someone suddenly "appear" at the top of the rankings either the year after the Olympics, or the following year. Scott jumped to the top the year after the Olympics, which was a little harder than Peggy and Dorothy, because he had to stay at the top one extra year to get the gold.

Scott is not somebody you would pick as a natural athlete, perhaps because of his small stature.[6] But he is a very persistent guy who is not afraid of hard work, and who will push himself to the limit – a Sun-Pluto [SEE EXAMPLE 5-7 ON PAGE 121]. His Mars is also one of the hyper-competitive ones, the signs in detriment. Easy-going and humorous as Scott can be, he takes his competitiveness seriously. He has Mars, Jupiter and Saturn in Triplicity – all of them participating, which is the weakest Triplicity of the three. Scott is going to have to really work his way through the ranks to get what he wants, but he also has a little help from the fixed star Sirius, which is in the ecliptic projected degree of his North Node.

In 1980, the solar return for the first year he won the U.S., and then the Worlds, showed Mars ruling his SR-10th: and in the other sign of Venus from his natal. With both the Moon and Mars at 29 degrees, one worries that this could be a year when Scott pushed too hard and too fast and skated beyond his limits: or could it be the harbinger of simply getting to a new level?

Notice: while there are some good indicators here, this situation doesn't sync with his natal chart. The twenty-nine degree situation provides a challenge: one he clearly mastered. But could he continue?

The 1981 solar return continued the twenty-nine degree symbolism, this time with the Nodes. The SR-Moon was opposite his natal Moon by sign, but conjunct his radix Venus-Uranus conjunction. SR-Mercury was in Virgo, where it had been the year before. There was a Venus-Jupiter-Saturn conjunction in Libra, the one sign where they all have dignity. 1981 finds Jupiter back in its natal sign, and a conjunction of the benefics is a good thing. Saturn in Triplicity was ruling the MC. Solar return Mars was debilitated, this time in Fall, which we have seen is beneficial for Scott. Except for the Moon, these are good indicators for him.

In 1982, we see Venus rising in Leo, the sign of his radix Venus, and in a sextile to Saturn, which was still dignified. That Venus rules the MC, which I have to take as a good sign, since this is close to his radix Venus position. There is an interesting Moon-Neptune trine Fortuna in the 5th and 9th: perhaps this shows Scott's more playful side coming out a bit more clearly. Mars is in Scorpio, its own sign, but square Venus, not so fortunate for Scott. Whether this would have been the best solar return for *starting* Scott's run at the top, I am uncertain; but the fixed rising, *and* angular fixed Venus ruling the fixed MC, shows him *maintaining* his position.

In the solar return for his Olympic year, 1983, Scott had Pluto rising trine his natal Moon, as had Dorothy Hamill: a configuration for digging deep and just getting on with it. Here, we have the return of the twenty-nine degree theme, with Venus and Mercury there. Mercury was back in Virgo, where it was for three out of four of these championship years. Not his radix position, but when posited in Virgo, Mercury is as strong as it gets. Venus was in its radix sign, while Jupiter was strong in Sagittarius. The Moon was in Taurus, a strong Moon, even if square its radix position by sign. That SR-Moon was in a partile Moon-Saturn opposition, and square Mars, the most elevated planet. By dignity, the Moon wins in this configuration.

As for the MC, it's ruled by the Sun, whose own dispositor is very strong, and it's in a fixed sign, again arguing for maintaining his position. Scott was the front-runner, and so he won.

Scott Hamilton
Toledo, Ohio
Time Zone: 5 hours West

August 27, 1980
41N39'50" 83W33'19"
Tropical Regiomontanus
Solar Return for August 27, 1980 in Toledo, Ohio

5:56:10 PM
Daylight Saving Time

Scott Hamilton
Toledo, Ohio
Time Zone: 5 hours West

August 27, 1981
41N39'50" 83W33'19"
Tropical Regiomontanus
Solar Return for August 27, 1981 in Toledo, Ohio

11:49:05 PM
Daylight Saving Time

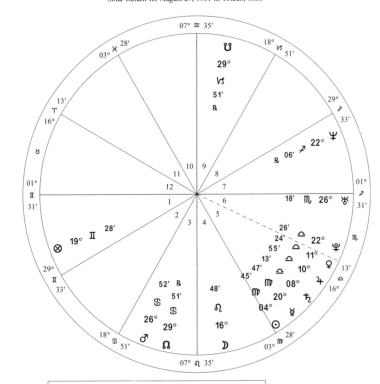

Example 8-6a. Scott Hamilton honors solar return for 1980

Example 8-6b. Scott Hamilton honors solar return for 1981

Scott Hamilton
Toledo, Ohio
Time Zone: 5 hours West

August 28, 1982
41N39'50" 83W33'19"
Tropical Regiomontanus
Solar Return for August 28, 1982 in Toledo, Ohio

5:28:10 AM
Daylight Saving Time

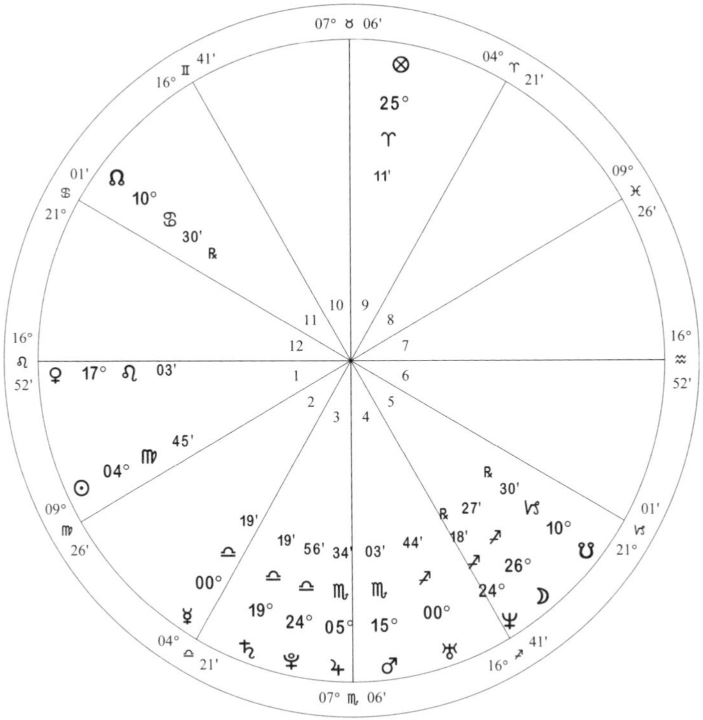

Pl	Ruler	Exalt	Tripl	Term	Face	Detri	Fall	Score
☉	☿	☿	☽	☿	☉ +	♃	♀	+1
☽	♃	☋	♃	♂	♄	☿	--	- 5 P
☿	♀	♄	☿ +	♄ m	☽	♂	☉	+3
♀	☉	--	♃	♀ +	♃	♄	--	+2
♂	♂ +	--	♂ +	♀	☉	♀	☽	+8
♃	♂	--	♂	♂	♂	♀	☽	- 5 P
♄	♀	♄ +	☿	☿ m	♄ +	♂	☉	+5
☊	☽	♃	♂	♃	☿	♄	♂	--
⊗	♂	☉	♃	♂	♀	♀	♄	--
As	☉	--	♃	♀	♃	♄	--	--
Mc	♀	☽	☽	♀	☿	♂	--	--
☋	♄	♂	☽	☿	♂	☽	♃	--

Dorothean Ess. Dig. (No Mut Rec. Points)

Hs	Alm. (Pto)
1	☉
2	☿
3	♄
4	♂
5	♃
6	♂
7	♄
8	♃
9	♂
10	☽♀
11	☿
12	☽

Example 8-6c. Scott Hamilton honors solar return for 1982

Scott Hamilton
Toledo, Ohio
Time Zone: 5 hours West

August 28, 1983
41N39'50" 83W33'19"
Tropical Regiomontanus
Solar Return for August 28, 1983 in Toledo, Ohio

11:23:35 AM
Daylight Saving Time

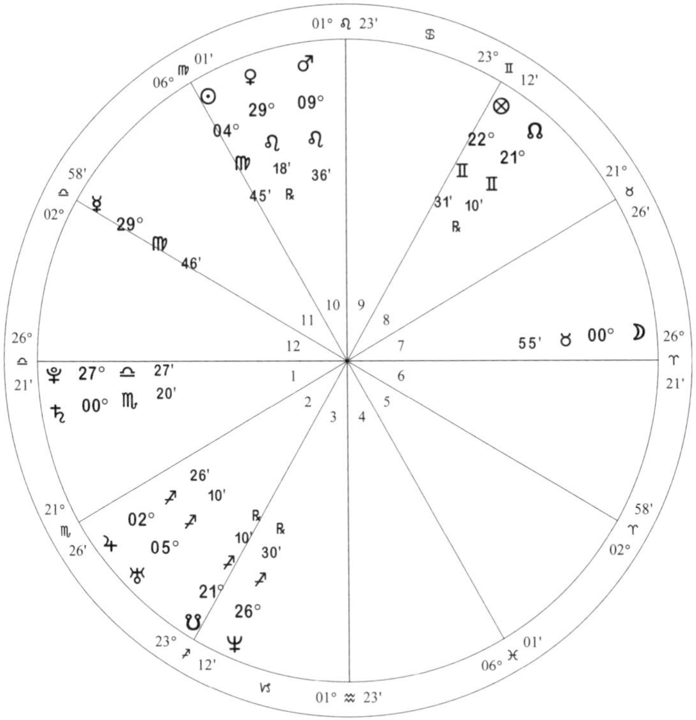

Dorothean Ess. Dig. (No Mut Rec. Points)

Pl	Ruler	Exalt	Tripl	Term	Face	Detri	Fall	Score
☉	☿	☿	♀ m	☿	☉ +	♃	♀	+1
☽	♀	☽ +	♀	♀	☿	♂	--	+4
☿	☿ +	☿ +	♀	♂ m	☿ +	♃	♀	+10
♀	☉	--	☉ m	♂	♂	♄	--	- 5 P
♂	☉	--	☉	☿ m	♄ m	♄	--	- 5 P
♃	♃ +	☋	☉	♃ +	☿	☿	--	+7
♄	♂	--	♀	♂	♂ m	♀	☽	- 5 P
☊	☿	☊ +	♄	♄	☉	♃	--	--
⊗	☿	☊	♄	♄	☉	♃	--	--
As	♀	♄	♄	☊	♃	♂	☉	--
Mc	☉	--	☉	♄	♄	♄	--	--
☋	♃	☋	☉	♄	♄	☿	--	--

Hs	Alm. (Pto)
1	♄
2	♂
3	♃
4	♄
5	♀
6	☉
7	☉
8	♀
9	☿♄
10	☉
11	☿
12	♄

Example 8-6d. Scott Hamilton honors solar return for 1983

Martin Luther King's Nobel Prize

Martin Luther King was born at noon, already highlighting his 10th house. The MC and his Sun are disposed by Saturn, which has participating Triplicity. Continuing to examine his nativity, we actually see better than the average amount of strong dignity (rulership, Exaltation or Triplicity):

- The Moon has mixed Triplicity
- Mercury has out-of-sect Triplicity
- Venus has both Exaltation and in-sect Triplicity
- Saturn has mixed Triplicity

So, does one need a great deal of dignity to win a Nobel Prize? The person with angular placements, especially dignified, should be noticed more than average in a given situation, according to our model. We can actually use this example in another way to test this idea by comparing Martin Luther King with Ralph Abernathy. Abernathy's nativity is shown here as Figure 8-7b.

The story is quite fascinating from an astrological perspective. King and Ralph Abernathy met and became friends as students, and they stayed friends for life. Abernathy was Pastor of the largest Black church in Montgomery at the time of the Montgomery Bus Boycott: thus, he and King were together throughout King's time in the Civil Rights Movement, and Abernathy frankly had as much claim to the leadership as King did. And yet, it was *King* who was the most public face, it was *King* who won the Nobel Prize (by himself), it was *King* whose speeches electrified the nation. It was also King who publicly called Abernathy his best friend, and it was Abernathy who picked up the pieces once King was assassinated.

Thus, we have a perfect what-if: two men, both Pastors of churches, at a critical moment in time. When we examine Ralph Abernathy's chart, we see that the one angular ptolemaic planet he had was Mars, and it's exalted. There is no question that Abernathy was a fighter, even if his methodology was nonviolent. He had organized his first protest while still a student. His home and church were bombed during the Montgomery action, just as King's were. Both men had to confront the danger this presented to their wives and children, who were all fortunately unharmed.

However, when confronted with an angular Sun at the MC with a dignified dispositor by participating Triplicity, and an angular dignified Mars in the 1st, it's the Sun that is seen as the leader. This is exactly what our astrology would predict.

The year that Dr. King won the Nobel Prize his solar return showed a *partile* reversal of the MC/IC axis. That placed his Sun squarely on the 4th house cusp – angular again, but perhaps not the angle we would expect. It is, however, a remarkable solar return. A very large proportion of planets are ruled by a very dignified Saturn in Aquarius. *All* of the ptolemaic planets are either strongly dignified, or their dispositors are.

We have seen how each year, the Sun "moves" around the wheel approximately one quadrant in the solar return, going in a diurnal direction. Thus, we could expect (and we would be right) that in 1966 – two years later – the solar return Sun would be approximately conjunct the MC. So why wasn't this year (1966) the year of the Nobel Prize? In 1966, we see the resonance with his birth angle signs, and the placement of the Sun at the MC. But in this chart, the Saturn-ruled placements are ruled by a Saturn in *Pisces*, not Aquarius, and the Moon is in debilitated Scorpio, approaching Neptune. While the IC angle may not be the ideal one for the recognition of the Nobel Prize, the chart itself is *very* strong for 1964.

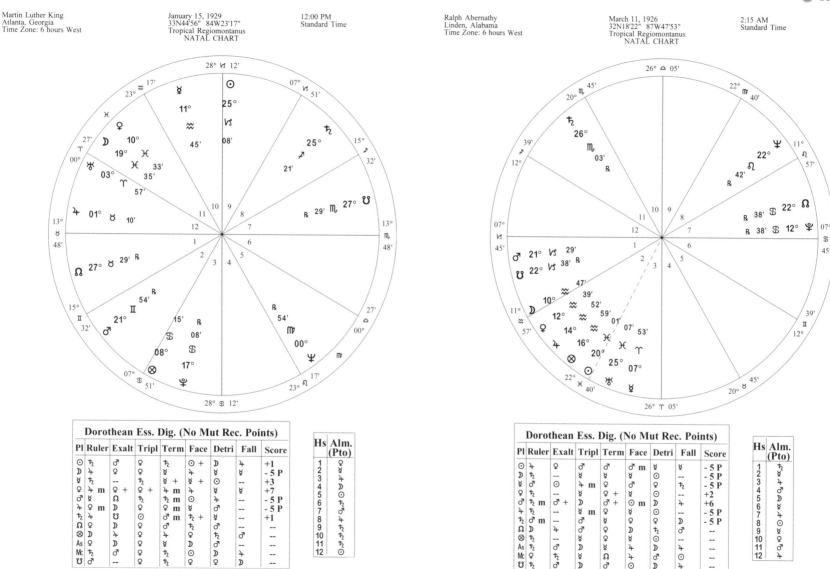

Example 8-7a. Martin Luther King nativity

Example 8-7b. Ralph Abernathy nativity

Martin Luther King
Atlanta, Georgia
Time Zone: 5 hours West

January 16, 1964
33N44'56" 84W23'17"
Tropical Regiomontanus
Solar Return for January 16, 1964 in Atlanta, Georgia

1:00:56 AM
Standard Time

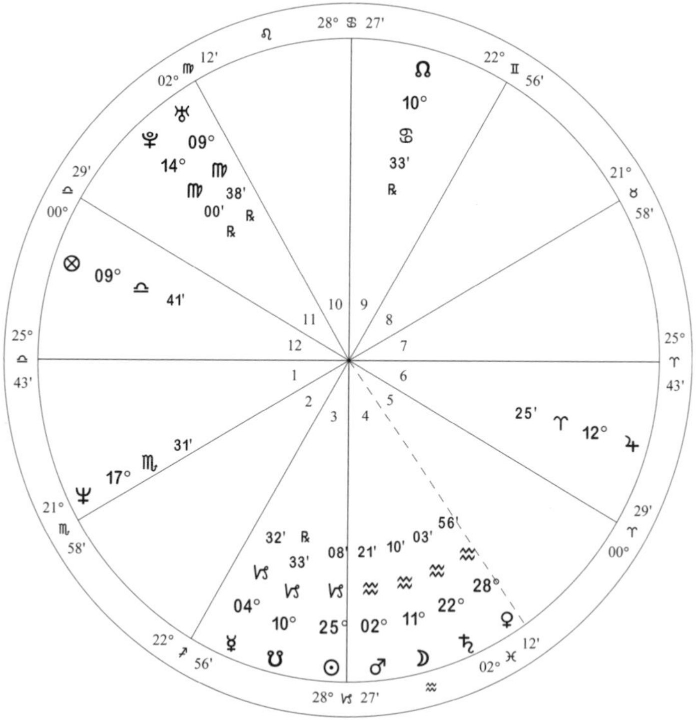

Dorothean Ess. Dig. (No Mut Rec. Points)								
Pl	Ruler	Exalt	Tripl	Term	Face	Detri	Fall	Score
☉	♄	♂	☽	♄	☉ +	☽	♃	+1
☽	♄	--	☿ m	☿	☿	☉	--	- 5 P
☿	♄	♂	☽ m	♀	♃	☽	♃	- 5 P
♀	♄	--	☿	♂	☽	☉	--	- 5 P
♂	♄	--	☿	♄	♀	☉	--	- 5 P
♃	♂	☉	♃ +	♀	☉	♀	♄	+3
♄	♄ +	--	☿	♃	☽	☉	--	+5
☊	☽	♃	♂	♃	☿	♄	♂	--
⊗	♀	♄	☿	♀	☽	♂	☉	--
As	♀	♄	☿	☊	♃	♂	☉	--
Mc	☽	♃	♂	♄	☽	♄	♂	--
☋	♄	♂	☽	☿	♂	☽	♃	--

Hs	Alm. (Pto)
1	♀
2	♂
3	♃
4	♄
5	♀
6	♂
7	♂
8	☽
9	☿
10	☽
11	☿
12	♄

Example 8-7c. Martin Luther King honors solar return for 1964

Martin Luther King
Atlanta, Georgia
Time Zone: 5 hours West

January 15, 1966
33N44'56" 84W23'17"
Tropical Regiomontanus
Solar Return for January 15, 1966 in Atlanta, Georgia

12:39:44 PM
Standard Time

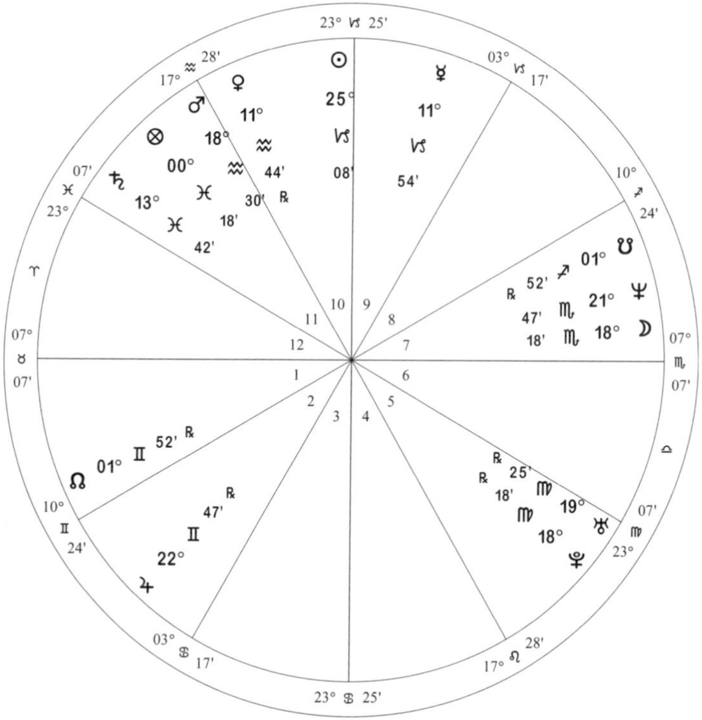

Dorothean Ess. Dig. (No Mut Rec. Points)								
Pl	Ruler	Exalt	Tripl	Term	Face	Detri	Fall	Score
☉	♄	♂	♀	♄	☉ +	☽	♃	+1
☽	♂	--	♀	♀	☉	♀	☽ -	- 9 P
☿	♄	♂	♀	☿ +	♂ m	☽	♃	+2
♀	♄	--	♄ m	☿	☿	☉	--	- 5 P
♂	♄	--	♄	♀	☿ m	☉	--	- 5 P
♃	☿	☊	♄	♄ m	☉	♃ -	--	- 10 P
♄	♃	♀	♀ m	♃ m	♃	☿	☿	- 5 P
☊	☿	☊ +	♄	☿	♃	♃	--	--
⊗	♃	♀	♀	♀	♄	☿	☿	--
As	♀	☽	♀	♀	☿	♂	--	--
Mc	♄	♂	♀	♂	☉	☽	♃	--
☋	♃	☋	☉	♃	☿	☿	--	--

Hs	Alm. (Pto)
1	♀
2	☿
3	☽
4	☽
5	☉
6	☿
7	♂
8	♃
9	♀♄
10	♂
11	♄
12	♃

Example 8-7d. Martin Luther King honors solar return for 1966

Michelle Kwan's Skating Excellence

Even as a Junior competitor, Michelle Kwan stood out. Michelle would end up skating her own path: one we know must not have been her preferred choice entirely. The legendary Sonja Henie stands out with *ten* consecutive world championships: the record. Michelle tied Carol Heiss for the most World Championships by a U.S. woman, five. Peggy Fleming had three, Dorothy Hamill only one. The difference between Carol and Michelle is that Carol won them five years in a row, whereas Michelle won them over eight years – an eternity in the fast pace of skating culture. During that same time period, Michelle would stand on the podium at the Olympics – but with two different American women on the winner's tier: Tara Lipinski in 1998, and Sarah Hughes in 2002. Tara won Worlds in 1997, and Sarah never did. And in a totally amazing run, Michelle was U.S. champion from 1998-2005, beating both Tara *and* Sarah, as well as Sasha Cohen, who would be the next U.S. ladies medalist at the Olympics in 2006, just one year later.

So what we have with Michelle is an immensely talented, persistent, popular young woman whose timing, luck, or competitive edge evaporated only at the Olympics – the pinnacle moment. Sarah Hughes could retire as an Olympics gold medalist without a U.S. win, without a world win – and nobody cares. Tara Lipinsky could retire as an Olympics gold medalist with a single U.S. win, a single Worlds win, and nobody cares. Michelle worked herself to the maximum for those eight years, and the absence of that one win amidst all of the other ones gives still at least a slightly bad taste.

She was a *very* successful skater. When there are thousands of competitors who started the process when she did, the fact that she didn't end up #1 in *every* competition in the world may not be something that we can see in the chart. Or maybe it is, if we consider it from a different perspective. We have examined three Olympic Gold Medalists here – Peggy Fleming, Dorothy Hamill, and Scott Hamilton. In all three cases, we have said a lot about Mars.

In *Traditional Medical Astrology*, I also delineated Dick Button, the two-time Olympics and five times World Gold Medalist for the men. He has Scorpio Rising with Mars in Virgo at the MC. Mars again.

When we examine Michelle's chart, we are confronted with Mercury ruling both Ascendant and MC [SEE EXAMPLE 7-4 ON PAGE 158]: and her Mercury is not strong, by anyone's read.[7] We don't often discuss this, but with classical rulerships, there are only a few planetary rulership pairs possible for any Ascending sign: Mars-Venus (with Aries, Taurus, Libra, or Scorpio Rising); Mercury-Jupiter (Gemini, Virgo, Sagittarius or Pisces Rising); and the Saturn pairs, Saturn-Sun (Aquarius or Leo Rising) and Saturn-Moon (Cancer or Capricorn Rising). The Mercury-Jupiter pairing simply does not seem to be dominated by competition or combativeness as the primary motivating principle. The passions of Venus and Mars, or the ego/dominance structures of Saturn and the Lights produce much more consistently competitive types. With Mercury and Jupiter, the result is more likely moments of pure virtuosity and style, but not unrelenting *drive*.

In Michelle's chart, four of the seven ptolemaic bodies are ruled by Mercury: Venus, Mars, Jupiter and Saturn. That's a lot of Mercury, especially in somebody who doesn't at first seem to be so Mercurial, being a Cancer Sun and Taurus Moon. So let's follow the logic. Michelle's Moon is by far the strongest planet in her chart. Loosely trine the Ascendant and Jupiter, trine Saturn, and sextile the Sun and Mercury, the Moon is the body that renders Michelle's Mercury from being imbecilic as a result of its retrograde condition. It's a great Moon for many things, but there is something just a little stubborn and indolent about it! Being lunar in nature, with the Moon so strong and the Moon disposing the Sun, Michelle will need continual motivation. Now: sometimes she really can do it: she's got Sun square Pluto, after all. But other times, one suspects she really needs that extra caffeine to get going. Being as talented as she is, she can try to get by sometimes, just letting her talent shine without pushing herself. That's a more lunar approach to life. If she had the talent (and she clearly did), this approach can work – to a point.

So in the absence of continual motivation, we have to examine just what does drive Michelle to her point of personal excellence – and when she is only going through the motions.

We should begin by noting that Michelle did not win the U.S. Figure Skating Championships in her first attempt. She came in second three times. The first time she came in second was extraordinary, being the year that Tonya Harding won after Nancy Kerrigan was assaulted at the U.S. Championships. When Harding's ex-husband was later implicated in the attack, Harding's first place finish was withdrawn, but the USFSA chose not to move the other competitors up in the standings. Nancy was selected for the Olympic team along with Tonya, with Michelle as alternate.

We would expect Michelle's 1993 solar return, which covered the 1993-1994 skating season, to look pretty good, because she was in the years of progressing from junior talent to established senior. A second in the nationals the year after qualifying as a Senior, and taking the 1994 World Junior Championships is hardly a bad year, especially when followed by finishing eighth in her first Worlds. But already, Michelle had begun to show her own initiatives, as she deliberately qualified for seniors a year before her coach, Frank Carroll, wanted her to do so.

In fact, the 1993 solar return is remarkable. Here is the Sun conjunct the MC in a year where Michelle really made it to the world stage – both through winning the world Juniors, placing at the U.S. seniors, and placing 8th at the Worlds. Venus, ruling the Ascendant, is in her natal sign, as was Mars. But: MC and Ascendant ruler are in square, and then there is the Uranus-Neptune conjunction right at the IC, definitely showing the weirdness in the rankings, the competitions, not to mention Michelle's very personal overlap between Juniors and Seniors.

In the 1994-1995 competitions, Michelle would again place second. So we will return to her 1995 solar return, which covers the 1995-1996 season, when she first won the U.S. Championships, and captured her first World title. We see here the same shuffle that we previously

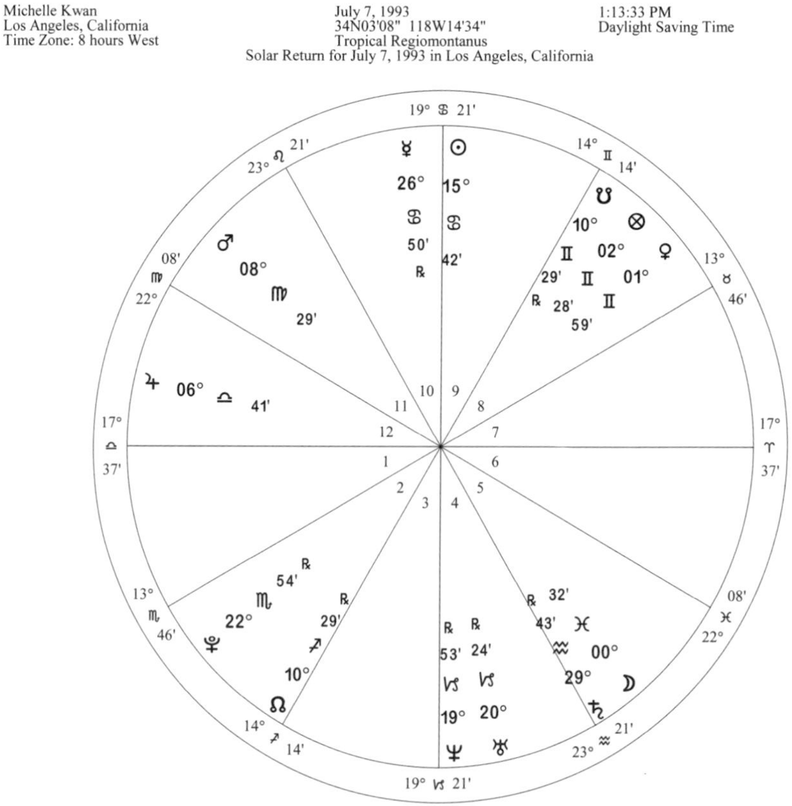
Michelle Kwan
Los Angeles, California
Time Zone: 8 hours West
July 7, 1993
34N03'08" 118W14'34"
Tropical Regiomontanus
Solar Return for July 7, 1993 in Los Angeles, California
1:13:33 PM
Daylight Saving Time

Dorothean Ess. Dig. (No Mut Rec. Points)								
Pl	Ruler	Exalt	Tripl	Term	Face	Detri	Fall	Score
☉	☽	♃	♀	☿	☿	♄	♂	- 5 P
☽	♃	♀	♀	♀	♄ m	☿	☿	- 5 P
☿	☽	♃	♀	♀ m	☽	♄	♂	- 5 P
♀	☿	☊	♄	☿ m	♃	♃	--	- 5 P
♂	☿	☿	♀	♀	☉	♃	♀	- 5 P
♃	♀	♄	♄	♀	☽	♂	☉	- 5 P
♄	♄ +	--	♄ +	♂	☽ m	☉	--	+8
☊	♃	☋	☉	♀	☽	☿	--	--
⊗	☿	☊	♄	☿	♃	♃	--	--
As	♀	♄	♄	♃	♄	♂	☉	--
Mc	☽	♃	♀	☿	☿	♄	♂	--
☋	☿	☊	♄	♃	♂	♃	--	--

Hs	Alm. (Pto)
1	♄
2	♂
3	♃
4	♂
5	♄
6	♃
7	☉
8	♀
9	☿
10	☽
11	☉
12	☿

Example 8-8a. Michelle Kwan honors solar return for 1993

observed with Martin Luther King, the two year shift from MC Sun to IC Sun or *vice versa*. In 1995, there was a trine between the Sun and the Moon, although the Moon was in the sign opposite its radix position, which is not so good. But look at Mercury: it's dignified in Gemini. We have a very functional Mercury for somebody who has a strong Mercury nature that normally needs some help. And the angles? Michelle's Ascendant is ruled by Mars, which is in its radix sign. And Mars is Almuten of the 10th, giving it dignity there as well. Mercury is on board, Mars is on board; Michelle breaks through and wins.

Her 1996-1997 season was covered by her 1996 solar return. In 1997, Michelle would lose her U.S. and World crowns and place second to Tara Lipinski in both. She was in the middle of a growth spurt, and had equipment problems.

In the 1996 solar return, we see the quadrant shift of the Sun bringing it into the 12th house, and not conjunct the Ascendant either. The Moon was in Aries at the MC, which could well have indicated a really fiery competitiveness, except that the Moon was conjunct the South Node: that energy was just going into the toilet, metaphorically. The Moon was also square her Sun, which could not have been comfortable either. Notice that Mercury is back in Cancer, its radix position, but it is combust, and thus imbecilic again. But this time, the Moon doesn't have the dignity to render it. Mars is not in an especially strong placement either, but Fortuna is in Aries in the 10th: fortune from sports. She didn't collapse totally, but this was not her best year.

In the 1997-1998 season, governed by her 1997 solar return, she would re-take the U.S. and Worlds, but lose out to Tara Lipinski at the Olympics. She struggled with two injuries. Again, we see the two year return to the MC/IC axis for the Sun. Obviously, not everyone has such a configuration every two years! But that was the sequence that Michelle was encountering. Michelle's SR-Mercury was back in its radix sign, but this year, it was only barely Under Beams, so not imbecilic. So the Moon wasn't necessary to render it, which was a good thing, because the Moon had no dignity itself, and was square the radix Moon.

Michelle Kwan
Los Angeles, California
Time Zone: 8 hours West

July 8, 1995
34N03'08" 118W14'34"
Tropical Regiomontanus
Solar Return for July 8, 1995 in Los Angeles, California

12:42:28 AM
Daylight Saving Time

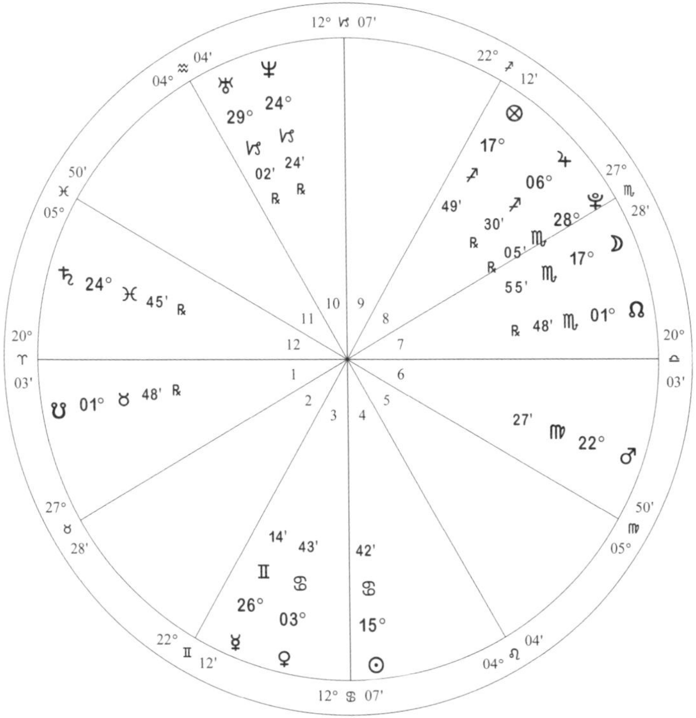

Dorothean Ess. Dig. (No Mut Rec. Points)								
Pl	Ruler	Exalt	Tripl	Term	Face	Detri	Fall	Score
☉	☽	♃	♂	☿	☿ m	♄	♂	- 5 P
☽	♂	--	♂ m	♀	☉	♀	☽ -	- 9 P
☿	☿ +	☊	☿ +	♂	☉ m	♃	--	+8
♀	☽	♃	♂	♂	♀ +	♄	♂	+1
♂	☿	☿	☽ m	♄ m	☿	♃	♀	- 5 P
♃	♃ +	☋	♃ +	♃ +	☿	☿	--	+10
♄	♃	♀	♂	♂ m	♂	☿	☿	- 5 P
☊	♂	--	♂	♂	♂	♀	☽	--
⊗	♃	☋ +	♃	☿	☽	☿	--	--
As	♂	☉	♃	☿	♀	♀	♄	--
Mc	♄	♂	☽	♃	♂	☽	♃	--
☋	♀	☽	☽	♀	☿	♂	--	--

Hs	Alm. (Pto)
1	♂
2	☽
3	☿
4	♃
5	☉
6	☿
7	☿♀
8	♂
9	♃
10	♂♄
11	♄
12	♀

Example 8-8b. Michelle Kwan honors solar return for 1995

Michelle Kwan
Los Angeles, California
Time Zone: 8 hours West

July 7, 1996
34N03'08" 118W14'34"
Tropical Regiomontanus
Solar Return for July 7, 1996 in Los Angeles, California

6:41:20 AM
Daylight Saving Time

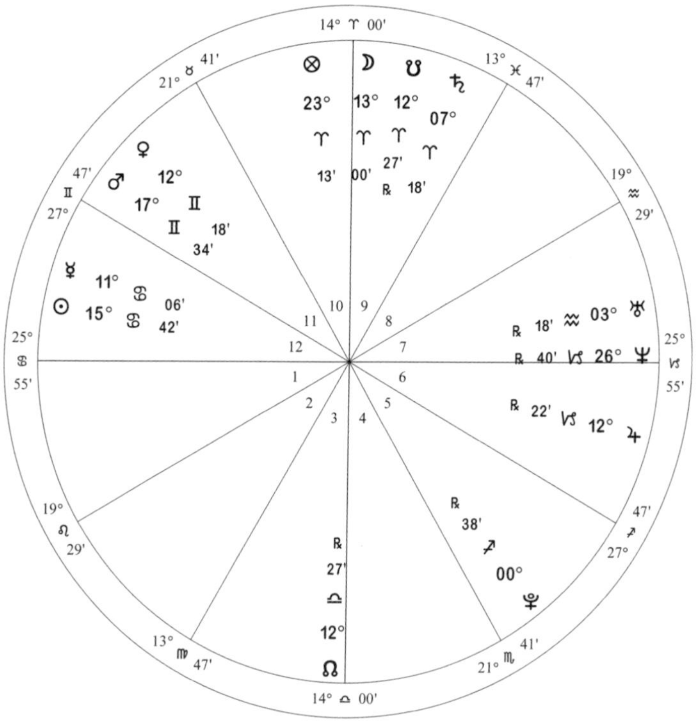

Dorothean Ess. Dig. (No Mut Rec. Points)								
Pl	Ruler	Exalt	Tripl	Term	Face	Detri	Fall	Score
☉	☽	♃	♀	☿	☿	♄	♂	- 5 P
☽	♂	☉	☉	♀	☉	♀	♄	- 5 P
☿	☽	♃	♀	♃	☿ +	♄	♂	+1
♀	☿	☊	♄	♃	♂	♃	--	- 5 P
♂	☿	☊	♄	♀	♂ +	♃	--	+1
♃	♄	♂	♀	♃ +	♂	☽	♃ -	- 2
♄	♂	☉	☉	♀	♂	♀	♄ -	- 9 P
☊	♀	♄	♄	♃	♄	♂	☉	--
⊗	♂	☉	☉	♂	♀	♀	♄	--
As	☽	♃	♀	♀	☽	♄	♂	--
Mc	♂	☉	☉	☿	☉	♀	♄	--
☋	♂	☉	☉	♀	☉	♀	♄	--

Hs	Alm. (Pto)
1	☽
2	☉
3	☿
4	♄
5	♂
6	♃
7	♄
8	♄
9	♃
10	☉
11	♀
12	☿

Example 8-8c. Michelle Kwan honors solar return for 1996

Michelle's competitive edge was maintained that year by Mars in Libra, the combative Mars, conjunct the Ascendant. The problem was injuries. Any malefic associated with the 6th house can bring illness: this is a basic tenet I discuss in *Traditional Medical Astrology*. So here, the South Node in the 6th gives her problems, and she does not have the perfect year that her wonderful program that year presaged. And then she made the difficult decision: she would stay in amateurs so that she could compete at yet another Olympics.

In the 1998-1999 season, here shown through her 1998 solar return, she maintained her U.S. Championship (as she would for the next eight seasons) but she took second at Worlds. The Sun was technically in the 7th house in the solar return, but read in the 8th. Venus is in its radix position, which stabilizes the MC somewhat, although having the ruler of the MC at the Descendant does suggest the competition winning. But Jupiter is ruling the Ascendant in dignity, though opposite her radix position. Mars is in one of its difficult signs, which is generally a good thing for an athlete. But its 7th house position tends to suggest that one's competitors are the ones with the focus.

The Moon was in the 1st house square to and disposed by that Jupiter: Michelle's attention was really not on competing. This even showed in how she changed her routine for the year, skipping many of the early competitive events.

The 1999-2000 season brought Michelle back to the World title – and here we are in her 1999 solar return, with the Sun in the 4th house and the Moon in the 1st in Taurus, her radix Moon sign. While Saturn in Taurus isn't especially strong, as Co-Almuten of the 10th, Saturn is at least in a sign trine her radix Saturn. This time the Mars in the 7th doesn't favor the competitors, because this is the "good" Mars, which is less optimal for competing.

The 2000-2001 season, Michelle accomplished something she had never done before: she successfully defended her World title. Heretofore, she needed the Sun in the 4th or the 10th, but this time, it was conjunct the Ascendant instead of buried in the 12th. With

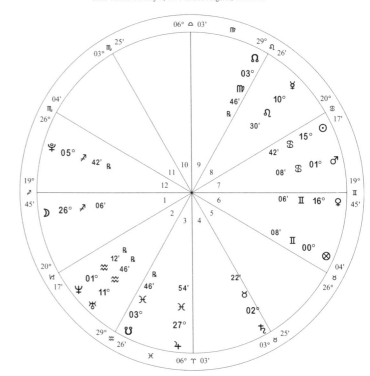

Example 8-8d. Michelle Kwan honors solar return for 1997

Example 8-8e. Michelle Kwan honors solar return for 1998

Michelle Kwan
Los Angeles, California
Time Zone: 8 hours West

July 8, 1999
34N03'08" 118W14'34"
Tropical Regiomontanus

12:06:03 AM
Daylight Saving Time

Solar Return for July 8, 1999 in Los Angeles, California

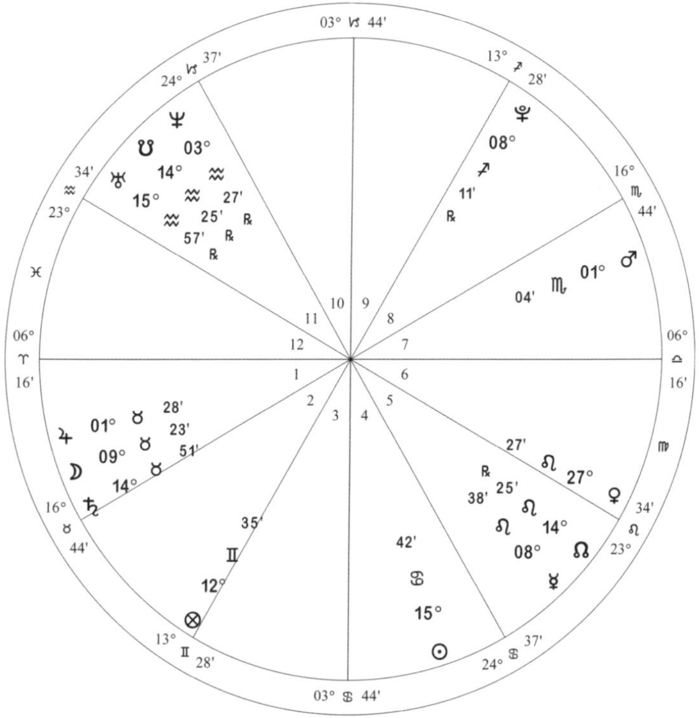

Dorothean Ess. Dig. (No Mut Rec. Points)								
Pl	Ruler	Exalt	Tripl	Term	Face	Detri	Fall	Score
☉	☽	♃	♂	☿	☿	♄	♂	- 5 P
☽	♀	☽ +	☽ +	☿	☿	♂	--	+7
☿	☉	--	♃	☿ +	♄	♄	--	+2
♀	☉	--	♃	♂	♂	♄	--	- 5 P
♂	♂ +	--	♂ +	♂ +	♂ +	♀	☽	+11
♃	♀	☽	☽	♀	☿	♂	--	- 5 P
♄	♀	☽	☽	☿	☽	♂	--	- 5 P
☊	☉	--	♃	♀	♃	♄	--	--
⊗	☿	☊	☿	♃	♂	♃	--	--
As	♂	☉	♃	♀	♂	♀	♄	--
Mc	♄	♂	☽	♀	♃	☽	♃	--
☋	♄	--	☿	♀	☿	☉	--	--

Hs	Alm. (Pto)
1	♂
2	☽
3	☿
4	☽
5	☽
6	☉♃
7	♀
8	♂
9	♃
10	♄
11	♂
12	♄

Example 8-8f. Michelle Kwan honors solar return for 1999

an angry Mars ruling the 10th, and the Sun its Almuten, she was able to defend.

Then, in 2001-2002, Michelle again did something she had not done before: she lost the Worlds in a solar return year (2001) in which she had Sun in the 10th. And to make matters worse, this was an Olympics year, and she finished third. Why did her winning pattern break down? There are a couple of answers we can give. First, notice that in her entire run to this point, the dreaded Mercury-Jupiter pairing that I had discussed with her nativity had not been ruling the MC/IC axis. Here, in the very year that her solar return angles matched her radix ones by sign, her competitive grip slipped just a bit. And what should have been equally obvious by now is that, at the Worlds anyway, Michelle was encountering competition that was of a quality nature. She was not the only elite athlete competing, and thus only losing if she actively *lost* the competition through mistakes. For the past few years, the Russian skater Irena Slutskaya was breathing down her neck: and Slutskaya beat her at the Worlds that year, and finished ahead of her at the Olympics. Sarah Hughes, who had been finishing second or third behind Michelle at the nationals suddenly rushed in and grabbed gold at the Olympics. And it certainly had not helped that she had ended her coaching relationship with Frank Carroll.

In that 2002 Olympics, the Moon was again square her radix Moon and conjunct Neptune – certainly not an argument of good judgment or outwardly-directed desire. The twenty-nine degrees on the angles is suggestive that she was at a critical phase: a moment of transition. There would be no more Olympics.

But that hardly means that she was washed out. Michelle made the even more difficult decision to try to remain competitive for a third Olympics, an extremely difficult endeavor. In so doing, she tried to skate smart. She again limited her engagements and hired a new coach. In the 2002-2003 season, she grabbed her last Worlds, while still retaining her streak of U.S. Championships.

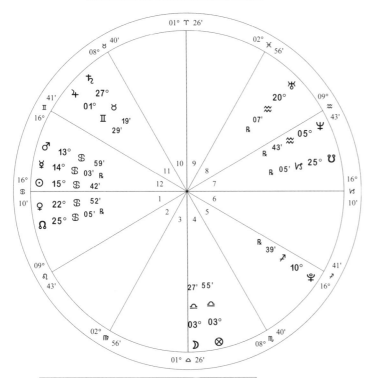

Example 8-8g. Michelle Kwan honors solar return for 2000

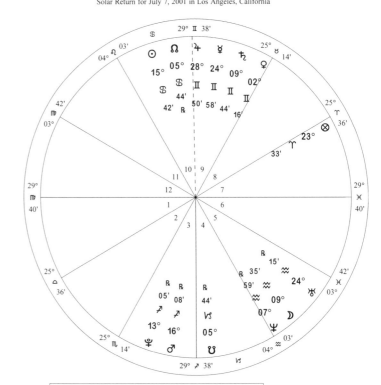

Example 8-8h. Michelle Kwan honors solar return for 2001

What has happened in her solar returns is that there has been a drift away from the MC/IC axis for the Sun position. To win, she must find another method: which she did very effectively in this particular year. The partile Pluto-Moon opposition across the Ascendant-Descendant is striking to say the least. Now from a competitive standpoint, if there had to be one answer it would be: Pluto. On a positive note, we also see the return of the Jupiter-Mars conjunction by sign that is in her radix: but here it is much tighter, and in a sign where both Mars and Jupiter have dignity, while Mars also has the debility that makes it a mean competitor.

The bad side of this solar return was that the Pluto was conjunct the South Node. This was metaphorically the danger of blowing everything in one attempt.

The following year, 2003-2004, continued the pattern of the Sun moving into the succedent houses, not the angular ones. Mercury is back to being imbecilic, and Mars is buried in the 12th, in the sign opposite the radix. Jupiter ruling the solar return Ascendant is in a cadent house, which is the weakest placement. And obviously, the radix angular rulership patterns were reversed between Jupiter and Mercury, which is also not a good omen.

And what was angular? A Venus-Saturn partile conjunction in the 4th house. Venus was Almuten of the Ascendant, which wouldn't be too bad, except for being the dignified Venus, which is less competitive. But Saturn is in one of its problem signs. Now, this could have boded well, except for one thing. The International Skating Union had decided to change the scoring and judging system. The last major change had been the elimination of the school figures, but now a more reproducible system of scoring was supposed to eliminate some of the uncertainty from judge to judge. The problem for skaters who were already established was that they had to learn a new system. This was extremely late in Michelle's career to go through this level of retrofit. Thus, the Saturn in debility makes perfect sense for the circumstances of the season.

Michelle hired a different coach with the intention of working on improving the technical nature of her program, but instead, she had technical problems at the Worlds. She would finish in third, her last medal in nine consecutive medal-winning World Championships.

But Michelle continued. In the 2004-2005 season, she hired Christopher Dean to choreograph her "Bolero" as her long program. While she won the U.S., at the Worlds, the new judging system resulted in her being edged out of third place by points, even though she came in third in both the short and the long program.

In her 2004 solar return, There's a Sun-Saturn conjunction in the 1st house. In water, this literally is a wet blanket. The MC/IC axis has reversed rulerships from her nativity. The Moon has dignity, and elevation, and a square to Pluto. All in mutable signs, she was capable of flashes of brilliance, but that's part of the problem with mutable signs – sustaining and creating a consistency. Michelle achieved her ninth U.S. title, which tied the record of Maribel Vinson-Owen from 1928-1937. This did not carry over to the Worlds.

But even if the 2004-2005 season was disappointing, it didn't have the appeal to Michelle, because it could not give her the elusive Olympic gold. That could only come in the following season. Unfortunately for Michelle, this was to be a season plagued with injuries. She could not defend her U.S. title because of an injury. While she succeeded in petitioning her way into the Olympics, in the end, yet another injury kept her from competing. She retired from amateur skating.

The 2005 solar return has Uranus in the 6th, and a malefic Saturn in Cancer ruling the 6th. These are both arguments of injury, and even more so when Saturn is conjunct the Moon.

It is often sad to look at an athlete's chart at the end of their career, because it is so incredibly rare for an athlete to retire at precisely their prime, with no decline in capabilities. In fact, we have seen an amazing run of solar returns for Michelle, even if there was a bit of an alternation in consecutive years. But the frequency

Michelle Kwan
Los Angeles, California
Time Zone: 8 hours West

July 7, 2002
34N03'08" 118W14'34"
Tropical Regiomontanus

5:36:55 PM
Daylight Saving Time

Solar Return for July 7, 2002 in Los Angeles, California

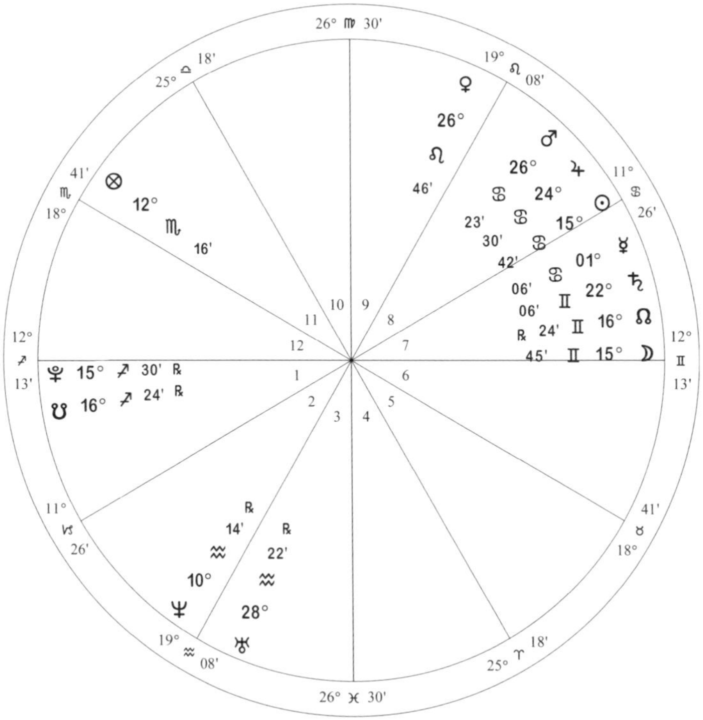

Dorothean Ess. Dig. (No Mut Rec. Points)								
Pl	Ruler	Exalt	Tripl	Term	Face	Detri	Fall	Score
☉	☽	♃	♀ m	☿	☿	♄	♂	- 5 P
☽	☿ m	☊	♄	♀	♂ m	♃	--	- 5 P
☿	☽ m	♃	♀	♂	♀	♄	♂	- 5 P
♀	☉	--	☉ m	♂ m	♂	♄	--	- 5 P
♂	☽	♃	♀	♀ m	☽ m	♄	♂ -	- 9 P
♃	☽	♃ +	♀	♀	☽	♄	♂	+4
♄	☿	☊	♄ +	♄ +	☉	♃	--	+5
☊	☿	☊ +	♄	♀	♂	♃	--	--
⊗	♂	--	♀	♃	☉	♀	☽	--
As	♃	☋	☉	♀	☽	☿	--	--
Mc	☿	☿	♀	♂	☿	♃	♀	--
☋	♃	☋	☉	☿	☽	☿	--	--

Hs	Alm. (Pto)
1	♃
2	♂♄
3	♄
4	♃
5	☉♂
6	♀
7	☿
8	♃
9	☉
10	☿
11	♄
12	♂

Example 8-8i. Michelle Kwan honors solar return for 2002

Michelle Kwan
Los Angeles, California
Time Zone: 8 hours West

July 7, 2003
34N03'08" 118W14'34"
Tropical Regiomontanus

11:16:58 PM
Daylight Saving Time

Solar Return for July 7, 2003 in Los Angeles, California

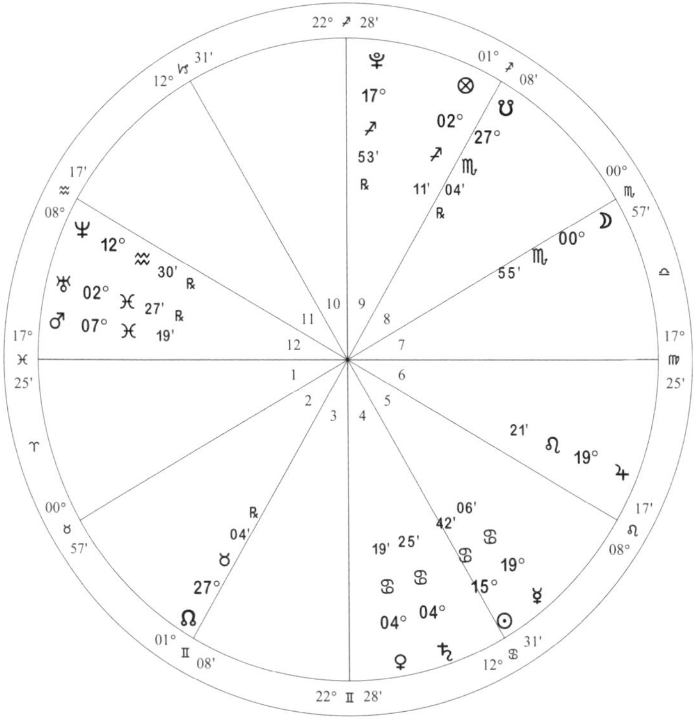

Dorothean Ess. Dig. (No Mut Rec. Points)								
Pl	Ruler	Exalt	Tripl	Term	Face	Detri	Fall	Score
☉	☽	♃	♂	☿	☿	♄	♂	- 5 P
☽	♂	--	♂	♂	♂	♀	☽ -	- 9 P
☿	☽	♃	♂	☿ +	☿ +	♄	♂	+3
♀	☽	♃	♂	♂ m	♀ +	♄	♂	+1
♂	♃	♀	♂ +	♀ m	♄	☿	☿	+3
♃	☉	--	♃ +	♃ +	♃ +	♄	--	+6
♄	☽	♃	♂	♂	♀	♄ -	♂	- 10 P
☊	♀	☽	☽	♂	♄	♂	--	--
⊗	♃	☋ +	♃	♃	☿	☿	--	--
As	♃	♀	♂	☿	♃	☿	☿	--
Mc	♃	☋	♃	♄	♄	☿	--	--
☋	♂	--	♂	♄	♀	♀	☽	--

Hs	Alm. (Pto)
1	♃
2	☽♀
3	☿
4	☿
5	♃
6	☉
7	☿
8	♂
9	♃
10	♃
11	♂♄
12	☿♄

Example 8-8j. Michelle Kwan honors solar return for 2003

Michelle Kwan
Los Angeles, California
Time Zone: 8 hours West

July 7, 2004
34N03'08" 118W14'34"
Tropical Regiomontanus

5:12:43 AM
Daylight Saving Time

Solar Return for July 7, 2004 in Los Angeles, California

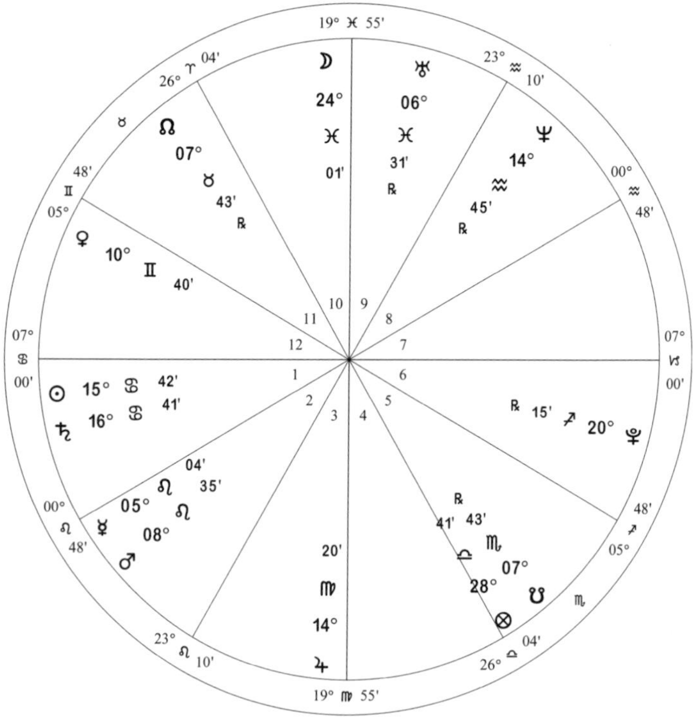

Pl	Ruler	Exalt	Tripl	Term	Face	Detri	Fall	Score
☉	☽	♃	♂	☿	☿	♄	♂	- 5 P
☽	♃	♀	♂	♂	♂	☿	☿	- 5 P
☿	☉	--	♃	♄ m	♄ m	♄	--	- 5 P
♀	☿	☊	☿	♃	♂	♃	--	- 5 P
♂	☉	--	♃	☿	♄	♄	--	- 5 P
♃	☿	☿	☽	♃ +	♀	♃ -	♀	- 3
♄	☽	♃	♂	☿ m	☿ m	♄ -	♂	- 10 P
☊	♀	☽	☽	♀	☿	♂	--	--
⊗	♀	♄	☿	☊	♃	♂	☉	--
As	☽	♃	♂	♃	♀	♄	♂	--
Mc	♃	♀	♂	☿	♃	☿	☿	--
☋	♂	--	♂	♃	♂	♀	☽	--

Dorothean Ess. Dig. (No Mut Rec. Points)

Hs	Alm. (Pto)
1	♃
2	☉
3	☉♃
4	☿
5	♀
6	♃
7	♄
8	♄
9	♄
10	♃
11	♂
12	☿

Example 8-8k. Michelle Kwan honors solar return for 2004

Michelle Kwan
Los Angeles, California
Time Zone: 8 hours West

July 7, 2005
34N03'08" 118W14'34"
Tropical Regiomontanus

10:57:22 AM
Daylight Saving Time

Solar Return for July 7, 2005 in Los Angeles, California

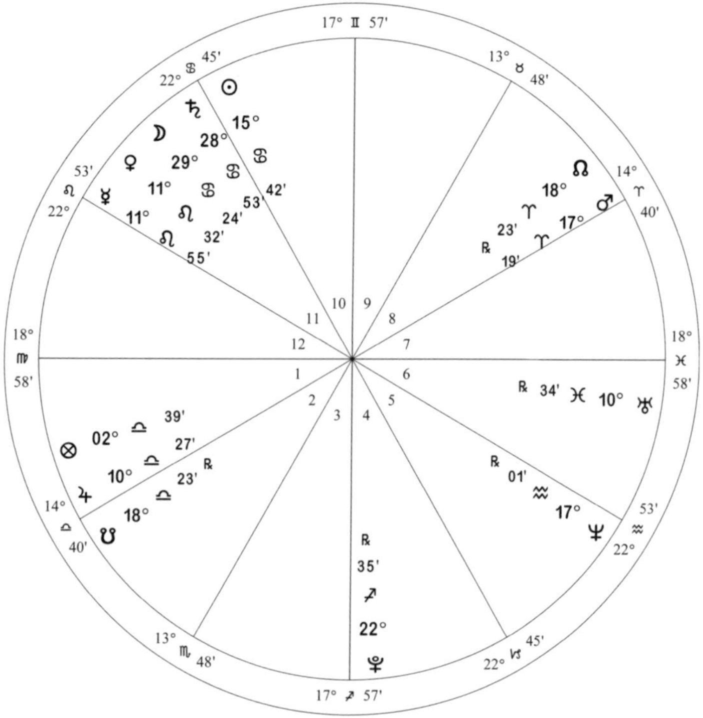

Pl	Ruler	Exalt	Tripl	Term	Face	Detri	Fall	Score
☉	☽	♃	♀ m	☿	☿	♄	♂	- 5 P
☽	☽ +	♃	♀	♄	☽ +	♄	♂	+6
☿	☉	--	☉	☿ +	♃	♄	--	+2
♀	☉	--	☉ m	☿	♃	♄	--	- 5 P
♂	♂ +	☉	☉	☿	☉	♀	♄	+5
♃	♀	♄ m	♄	♀	♄	♂	☉	- 5 P
♄	☽	♃ m	♀	♄ +	☽	♄ -	♂	- 3
☊	♂	☉	☉	☿	☉	♀	♄	--
⊗	♀	♄	♄	♄	☽	♂	☉	--
As	☿	☿	♀	♄	♀	♃	♀	--
Mc	☿	☊	♄	♀	♂	♃	--	--
☋	♀	♄	♄	♃	♄	♂	☉	--

Dorothean Ess. Dig. (No Mut Rec. Points)

Hs	Alm. (Pto)
1	☿
2	♄
3	♂
4	♃
5	♂
6	♄
7	♃
8	☉
9	♀
10	☿
11	☽
12	☉

Example 8-8l. Michelle Kwan honors solar return for 2005

of angular placements over that period of time should remind us of how very difficult it is to stay at the top of one's game over long periods. That the run ends is a statement of the human condition. In the end, Michelle's spirit was willing (Sun in the 10th) even if her flesh was weak (strong 6th house).

Louis Pasteur: Scientific Brilliance in the 19th Century

Louis Pasteur was a beacon to everyone regarding the scientific life. While it is almost impossible to overstate his achievements in chemistry, physics, biology, and medicine, one also is confronted with the fact that Pasteur was benefited by the same system that would later be so infuriating for Marie Curie: the French scientific establishment and its organizations. One cannot compare the two brilliant scientists and easily say that one was more brilliant than the other. But Pasteur had three things going for him that Curie did not: he was French, he was male, and he had mentors who eased his path.

It is in reading his biography that we are struck by his very down-to-earth Capricornian attitude: he simply assumed that hard work, perseverance, and results would bring rewards. It's hardly surprising that Pasteur would have this attitude, given his earthy stellium.

Pasteur's natal 10th house is not especially dignified [SEE EXAMPLE 4-5 ON PAGE 101]. The Sun rules it, and the Sun is peregrine, disposed by Saturn, which itself is both peregrine and retrograde. The South Node is in it. Saturn, which disposes his Capricorn stellium, is thus imbecilic, and it's even at the Bendings. So does this mean that Pasteur spends his entire life toiling, without ever getting his just desserts?

No. It simply means that honors are not going to be out of proportion to his actual accomplishments. Take, for example, U.S. President Barack Obama [SEE EXAMPLE 12-21 ON PAGE 291]. As a Sun in Leo, many astrologers were somewhat bemused when, as President-elect, he already created a public persona for what is an interim situation, one normally mostly in the background during the transition. But the real surprise was him receiving the Nobel Peace Prize in the first year of his term of office, before he had accomplished anything at all. In Obama's case, Mars in Virgo, which has Triplicity, rules his 10th house, and is unafflicted otherwise. This would be an example of someone receiving honors out-of-proportion to his actual accomplishments.

So Pasteur's position of work hard for one's rewards seems modest enough. We are going to examine his chart for five different events:

- His 1852 solar return, when he won a 1,500 franc cash prize from Society of Pharmacy of Paris for preparing racemic acid from tartaric acid
- His 1856 solar return, when he was rejected for membership in the Academy of Sciences
- His 1858 solar return, when he was awarded the prize for experimental physiology by the Academy of Sciences
- His 1861 solar return, when he was elected to the Academy of Sciences
- His 1880 solar return, when he was elected to the Académie française

We could further state that it was only by 1861 with his election to the Academy of Sciences that he began to stand on his own apart from his mentors, curious as that idea sounds to us now, because Pasteur so eclipsed his mentors within the history of science. But like so many of his fellows in the French academies, he was elected to succeed one of those mentors who died, creating the vacancy that he then filled. These positions were thus the ultimate Old Boys Network.

Whatever we might think of the reactionary tendencies of such a system, the fact was that Pasteur was very proud of his memberships and accomplishments. So we may be sure that these honors meant a great deal to him.

The first award with the 1852 solar return brought him money as well as honor. It was also for work done, not to win the prize, but his first major scientific breakthrough. Pasteur began as a physicist and then branched into chemistry. He later branched into biology because he was asked to examine chemical problems of biological systems.

Pasteur's natal 2nd house is ruled by Mars, which is in Exaltation and mixed Triplicity: one of his two most dignified planets. For most of his life, he had few money problems. His father supported him through school, and then he was gainfully employed in academia, often with supplements, based on his willingness (and success) in taking on industrial problems and solving them.

In this year of the cash prize, dignified Jupiter ruled his SR-2nd house, while Mars in his radix sign of Capricorn ruled his 10th house. Symbolically, it is interesting that this solar return is close to a full Moon: he was being recognized for work he had done, not for work that he had just done in order to compete for a prize. Thus, the prize was for the culmination of a body of work.

This chart for 1852 is a more dignified chart than his natal, but without a lot of resonance to the radix other than Mars.

In 1856, he had campaigned for, then failed to be elected to a vacant seat in the Academy of Sciences. We have already seen that he would eventually be elected; so this should be understood as only a temporary setback.

In 1856, Mars again ruled his MC: but this time it was conjunct Venus in a sign that is strong for neither of them. Furthermore, Saturn, in Detriment and retrograde, ruled the Ascendant and conjunct the 7th: he was at the mercy of his enemies, literally. Quite simply, there is nothing about this year that suggests any recognition at all, quite the contrary.

In 1858, we see Pluto in a partile conjunction to the MC. We have seen with the skaters that Pluto is a good thing for competition, and so we have to interpret it the same way here. In fact, without the argument of Pluto, I don't see him winning the prize, because the other indicators are simply not strong. Venus, the 10th house

Louis Pasteur
Dole, France
Time Zone: 0 hours West

December 26, 1852
47 N 06 5 E 30
Tropical Regiomontanus
Solar Return for December 26, 1852 in Dole, France

8:54:12 AM
Local Mean Time

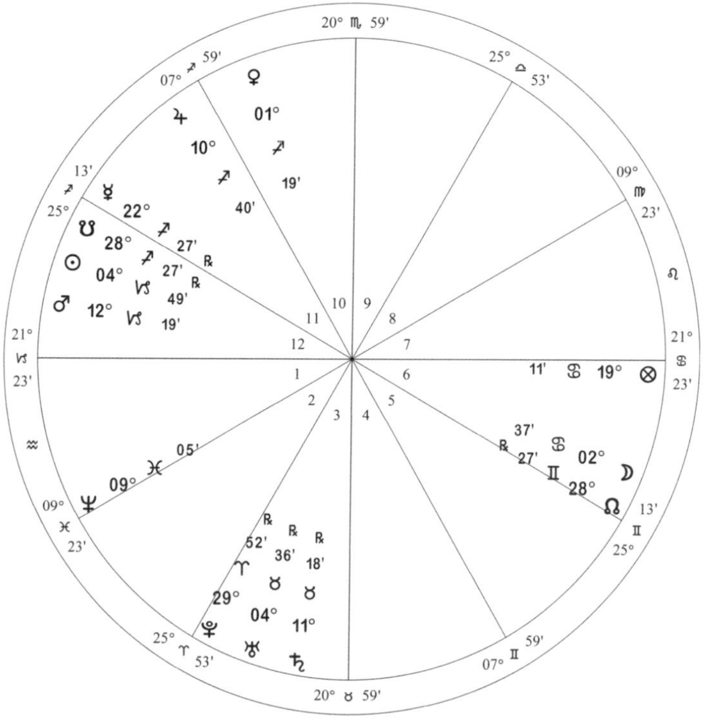

Dorothean Ess. Dig. (No Mut Rec. Points)

Pl	Ruler	Exalt	Tripl	Term	Face	Detri	Fall	Score
☉	♄	♂	♀ m	♀	♃	☽	♃	- 5 P
☽	☽ +	♃	♀	♂	♀	♄	♂	+5
☿	♃	☋	☉	♄ m	♄	☿ -	--	- 10 P
♀	♃	☋	☉ m	♃ m	☿	☿	--	- 5 P
♂	♄	♂ +	♀	♃	♂ +	☽	♃	+5
♃	♃ +	☋	☉	♀ m	☽	☿	--	+5
♄	♀	☽	♀	☿ m	☽	♂	--	- 5 P
☊	☿	☊ +	♄	♂	☉	♃	--	--
⊗	☽	♃	♀	☿	☿	♄	♂	--
As	♄	♂	♀	♂	☉	☽	♃	--
Mc	♂	--	♀	♀	♀	♀	☽	--
☋	♃	☋	☉	♂	♄	☿	--	--

Hs	Alm. (Pto)
1	♂
2	♃
3	☉♂
4	♀
5	☿
6	☿
7	☽
8	☿
9	♄
10	♂
11	♃
12	♃

Example 8-9a. Louis Pasteur honors solar return for 1852

Louis Pasteur
Dole, France
Time Zone: 0 hours West

December 26, 1856
47 N 06 5 E 30
Tropical Regiomontanus
Solar Return for December 26, 1856 in Dole, France

8:16:48 AM
Local Mean Time

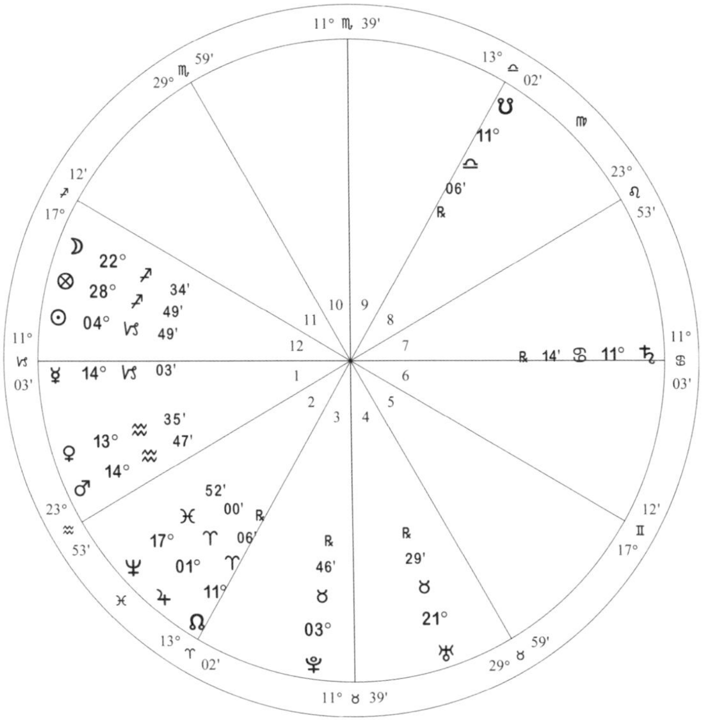

Dorothean Ess. Dig. (No Mut Rec. Points)								
Pl	Ruler	Exalt	Tripl	Term	Face	Detri	Fall	Score
☉	♄	♂	♀	♀	♃	☽	♃	- 5 P
☽	♃	☋	☉	♄	♄	☿	--	- 5 P
☿	♄	♂	♀	♃	♂ m	☽	♃	- 5 P
♀	♄	--	♄ m	♀ +	☿	☉	--	+2
♂	♄	--	♄	♀	☿ m	☉	--	- 5 P
♃	♂	☉	☉	♃ +	♂	♀	♄	+2
♄	☽	♃	♀ m	♃	☿	♄ -	♂	- 10 P
☊	♂	☉	☉	♀	☉	♀	♄	--
⊗	♃	☋ +	☉	♂	♄	☿	--	--
As	♄	♂	♀	☿	♂	☽	♃	--
Mc	♂	--	♀	♃	☉	♀	☽	--
☋	♀	♄	♄	♃	♄	♂	☉	--

Hs	Alm. (Pto)
1	♂♄
2	♄
3	☉
4	♀
5	♀
6	☿
7	♃
8	☉
9	♄
10	♂
11	♂
12	♃

Example 8-9b. Louis Pasteur honors solar return for 1856

Louis Pasteur
Dole, France
Time Zone: 0 hours West

December 26, 1858
47 N 06 5 E 30
Tropical Regiomontanus
Solar Return for December 26, 1858 in Dole, France

7:51:47 PM
Local Mean Time

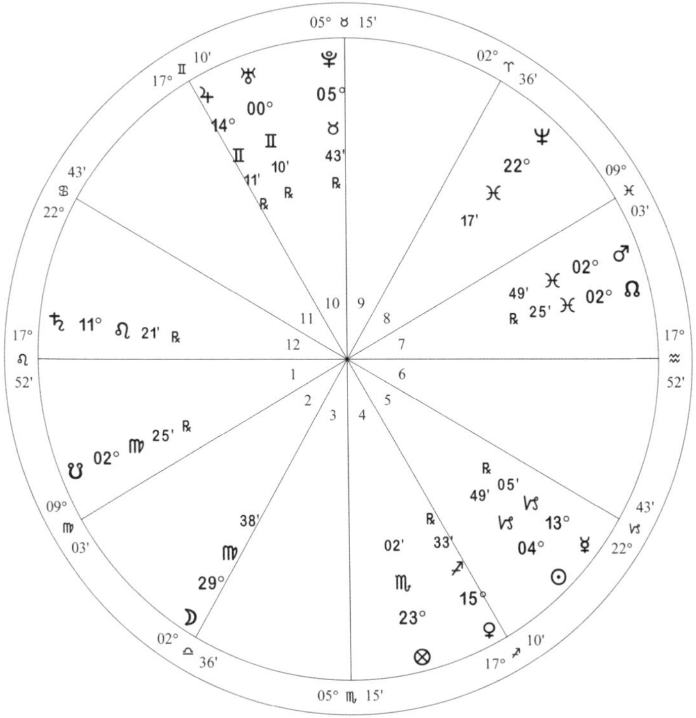

Dorothean Ess. Dig. (No Mut Rec. Points)								
Pl	Ruler	Exalt	Tripl	Term	Face	Detri	Fall	Score
☉	♄ m	♂	☽	♀	♃	☽	♃	- 5 P
☽	☿	☿	☽ +	♂	☿	♃	♀	+3
☿	♄	♂	☽	♃	♂	☽	♃	- 5 P
♀	♃	☋	♃	☿	☽	☿	--	- 5 P
♂	♃	♀	♂ +	♀	♄	☿	☿	+3
♃	☿	☊	☿	♀	♂	♃ -	--	- 10 P
♄	☉ m	--	♃	☿	♃	♄ -	--	- 10 P
☊	♃	♀	♂	♀	♄	☿	☿	--
⊗	♂	--	♂	☿	♀	♀	☽	--
As	☉	--	♃	♀	♃	♄	--	--
Mc	♀	☽	☽	♀	☿	♂	--	--
☋	☿	☿	☽	☿	☉	♃	♀	--

Hs	Alm. (Pto)
1	☉
2	☿
3	♄
4	♂
5	♃
6	♂
7	♄
8	♃
9	♂
10	☽♀
11	☿
12	☽

Example 8-9c. Louis Pasteur honors solar return for 1858

Louis Pasteur
Dole, France
Time Zone: 0 hours West

December 26, 1861
47 N 06 5 E 30
Tropical Regiomontanus
Solar Return for December 26, 1861 in Dole, France

1:14:35 PM
Local Mean Time

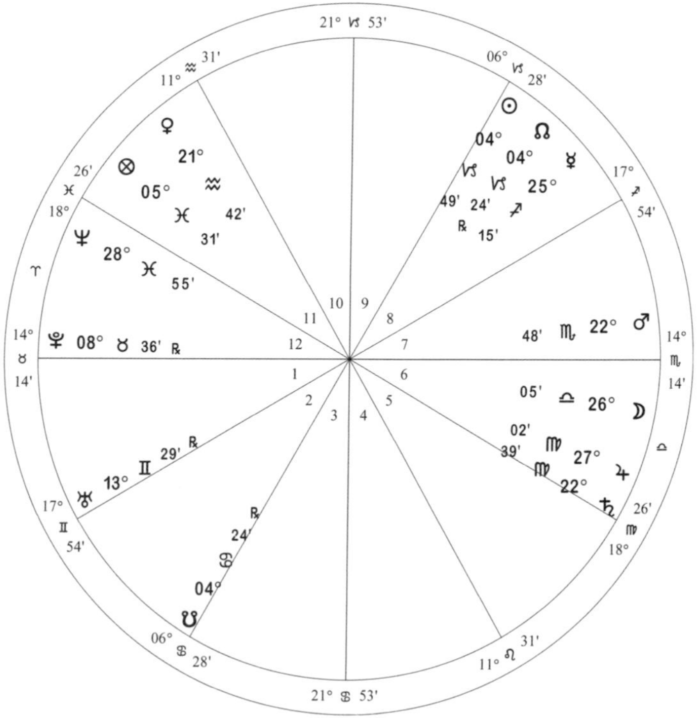

Pl	Ruler	Exalt	Tripl	Term	Face	Detri	Fall	Score
☉	♄	♂	♀	♀	♃	☽	♃	- 5 P
☽	♀	♄	♄	☊	♃	♂	☉	- 5 P
☿	♃ m	☋	☉	♂ m	♄ m	☿ -	--	- 10 P
♀	♄	--	♄ m	♃	☽	☉	--	- 5 P
♂	♂ +	--	♀	☿ m	♀	♀	☽	+5
♃	☿ m	☿	♀	♂	☿	♃ -	♀	- 10 P
♄	☿	☿	♀ m	♄ +	☿ m	♃	♀	+2
☊	♄	♂	♀	♀	♃	☽	♃	--
⊗	♃	♀	♀	♀	♄	☿	☿	--
As	♀	☽	♀	☿	☽	♂	--	--
Mc	♄	♂	♀	♂	☉	☽	♃	--
☋	☽	♃	♀	♂	♀	♄	♂	--

Dorothean Ess. Dig. (No Mut Rec. Points)

Hs	Alm. (Pto)
1	♀
2	☿
3	♃
4	☽
5	☉
6	☿
7	♂
8	♃
9	♄
10	♂
11	♄
12	♃

Example 8-9d. Louis Pasteur honors solar return for 1861

Louis Pasteur
Dole, France
Time Zone: 0 hours West

December 26, 1880
47 N 06 5 E 30
Tropical Regiomontanus
Solar Return for December 26, 1880 in Dole, France

3:59:36 AM
Local Mean Time

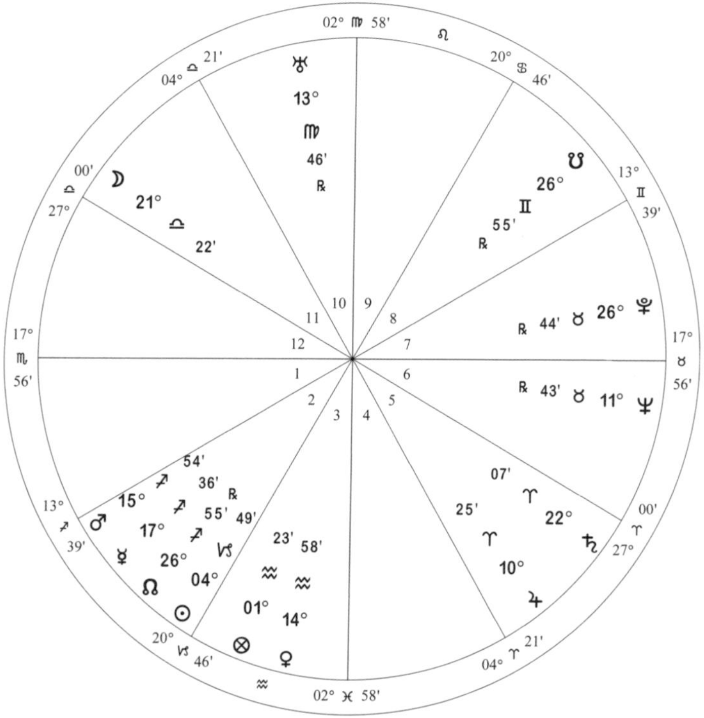

Dorothean Ess. Dig. (No Mut Rec. Points)

Pl	Ruler	Exalt	Tripl	Term	Face	Detri	Fall	Score
☉	♄	♂	☽	♀	♃ m	☽	♃	- 5 P
☽	♀	♄	☿	☿	♃	♂	☉	- 5 P
☿	♃	☋	♃	☿ +	☽	☿ -	--	- 3
♀	♄	--	☿	♀ +	☿	☉	--	+2
♂	♃ m	☋	♃	☿	☽	☿	--	- 5 P
♃	♂ m	☉	♃ +	♀	☉ m	♀	♄	+3
♄	♂	☉	♃	♂	♀	♀	♄ -	- 9 P
☊	♃	☋	♃	♂	♄	☿	--	--
⊗	♄	--	☿	♄	♀	☉	--	--
As	♂	--	♂	♀	☉	♀	☽	--
Mc	☿	☿	☽	☿	☉	♃	♀	--
☋	☿	☊	☿	♂	☉	♃	--	--

Hs	Alm. (Pto)
1	♂
2	♃
3	♂
4	♀
5	♂
6	♂
7	☽
8	☿
9	☽
10	☿
11	♄
12	♀

Example 8-9e. Louis Pasteur honors solar return for 1880

ruler, is not in a good sign, and retrograde besides; Moon, the 10th house Almuten has Triplicity, but is at twenty-nine degrees. Apart from that questionable Moon, Mars has dignity – not as much as natally, but then, Mars doesn't rule the relevant houses.

In 1861 for his election to the Academy of Sciences, we again see Pluto, this time associated with the Ascendant. But this is a stronger chart than the 1858 solar return, quite apart from the Pluto. Mars is Almuten of the MC, and here Mars is very strong in Scorpio. Jupiter and Saturn are conjunct; in the radix they are in the same sign, but further apart. Their solar return sign is trine the radix sign, so that is harmonious as well. The Sun is conjunct the North Node.

Finally, in 1880 for his election to the Académie française, we have another example where Jupiter and Saturn were in the same sign, and the Moon was trine its radix position. With Mercury in Sagittarius ruling the MC, I frankly don't see this as a very strong solar return.

What perhaps begins to make sense is to put this year into context. At the time, the major project that Pasteur was working on was the anthrax vaccine, which was an extremely important discovery for veterinary science. It was also extremely controversial, and he had been engaged in rather extreme polemics about it for several years running. In this context, the Mercury-Mars conjunction square Uranus in the 10th house becomes much clearer – he was, at this point, the most famous French scientist alive, and the arguments about the effectiveness of the vaccine were fast becoming ridiculous. His election to the Académie at that time had the effect of quelling the sniping which was continuing to the detriment of French farming. Thus, we are presented with a situation which was much more complex than a simple honor – although honor it was.

We entered this chapter with the question of whether the 10th house would even be relevant to persons who receive prizes in open competition, compared to other more diffuse honors, such as for a body of work. We have seen that the 10th house seems to apply in either case.

Chapter 8 Endnotes

1. Ramesey, 1654, pp 179-181. Those rules are in: Bonatti (Dykes), pp 760-768.
2. Gadbury's reference to these planets as the proper significators of trade comes from Ptolemy, *IV*.4
3. Gadbury, *Genethlialogia*, pp 229-230.
4. While you will not find this in any of the classical sources, a personal note: I have repeatedly observed that, when one parent dies (as was the case for Peggy during this time period), the surviving parent often takes over qualities of both parents astrologically as well as in other dimensions. Thus, before Peggy's father died, I would not have interpreted a 4th house position as applying to her mother, but to her father.
5. The Gauqulein sectors were the sections of the birth chart most occupied by the planet in question: they tended to be on the cadent side of the angles, with about a five degree overlap onto the angular side of the cusp. Gauquelin, Michel, and Françoise Gauquelin. *Birth and Planetary Data Gathered since 1949 – Coordonnées Natales Et Planétaires Rassemblées Depuis 1949. Series C, Volume 1, Profession – Heredity, Results of Series A & B, Profession – Hérédité, Résultats Des Séries A & B*. Paris: Laboratoire d'étude des relations entre rythmes cosmiques et psychophysiologiques, 1972.
6. Part of his short stature was because of an endocrine problem as a child when he simply stopped growing for several years. I treat those solar returns in: *Traditional Medical Astrology*, Chapter 7.
7. This is something that I probably would not have even noticed were it not for results obtained in Brady, Bernadette and J. Lee Lehman. "Twelfth century castle besiegement in sport," *The Astrological Journal* 39(3): 27-44, 1998.

9

Solar Returns for Medical Problems

In *Traditional Medical Astrology* Chapter 7, I considered how solar returns could be used in the prediction of medically significant periods of life – but without presenting the full theory of solar returns. Now, in a sense, I do the opposite: present medical examples without being able to present the whole medical model. As I have indicated in that work, the traditional view of medical astrology was not so much to predict the *type* of diseases that one would have, as the periods in which one was subject to illness. Malefics associated with the 6th house bring illness. We shall see this model quite clearly when we examine Gadbury's rules for the 6th house. In the *Genethlialogia*, he gives the following delineation of the sixth house in a revolution:

1. Evil Planets posited in the sixth House of a Revolution, declares a dangerous year for infirmities unto the Native. If the Lord of the sixth be afflicted of them, either by Conjunction, Quartile or Opposition, the same.

2. The Lord of the Ascendant of the Revolution in Quartile or Opposition to the Lord of the sixth in the Radix, denotes

an unfortunate year to the Native in respect of his health. The Luminaries in the sixth, in Opposition to the Lord of the sixth in the twelfth House, denotes the same.

3. The Lord of the Ascendant of the Radix with the South Node in the sixth, in Opposition to the Moon, Mars or Saturn, denotes many tedious and grievous infirmities in that year unto the Native; it will indeed be a year of evil to him.

4. If Saturn in a Revolution shall be in the Ascendant or sixth House, it portends diseases to invade the Native, of the nature of Saturn.

5. The Sun Lord of the sixth House, and posited in the Ascendant in conjunction of Saturn, denotes a very sickly year unto the Native. If Saturn shall be in opposition to the Sun from the seventh House, it denotes great danger unto the Natives life in that year; chiefly if an evil Direction concurs in Signification.

6. The Luminaries in Opposition from Angles in a Revolution, bids the Native beware of hurts in his Eyes; chiefly, if Mars or the Dragons Tayl shall afflict either of them. If Mercury and Saturn be in conjunction in the eighth, in Quartile to the Lord of the Ascendant or the Moon in the twelfth, the Native shall in that year receive impediment in his hearing.

7. But when the Lord of the Ascendant, Luminaries, and Lord of the sixth House of the Revolution shall be strong, and in good Aspect to each other, it denotes a healthful year unto the Native, and sickness will not much hurt him.

10. The Lord of the sixth House of a Revolution afflicted by an evil Planet, and he be Lord of the fifth, it portends many infirmities to happen to the Native by reason of drinking and haunting Taverns or Ale-houses; as Surfeits, Fevers, or the like. If the Lord of the seventh be the evil Planet afflicting, he contracts Diseases of a Venerous quality, by consorting with ill Women. If he be Lord of the Twelfth, the private Enemies of the Native conspire against him, and so subject him to infirmities, or imprisonments, banishment, &c. Which may occasion much grief. If the Lord of the second be the ill Planet afflicting, the want of money makes him despair.

11. The Figures of the Revolution and Radix differing, or Antipathetical each unto other, denotes an evil year to the Native.

12. Observe the Planet or Planets occasioning the sickness or infirmity, and so may you find what distempers they are the Native is most subject unto that year.[1]

On the later point of distempers, what Gadbury and the other ancients meant was twofold: an identification of an organ or sense organ, or which kind of derangement in terms of imbalance of the four humors of the body. Thus, one might be able to see that an excess of choler (hot and dry) could affect the head (Sun or Aries). Such definitions might or might not translate into a form which we could easily identify as a disease within our own parlance. Fever translates easily, but a bacterial infection?

While medical astrology involves much more than the interpretation of solar returns, our model for use here is to examine the condition of the 6th house in the return chart, both with respect to the return and the radix, to see if sickness is a likely theme for the year.

Buzz Aldrin's Alcoholism

Examining Buzz's natal chart, we see Mars in Capricorn ruling the 6th house [SEE EXAMPLE 3-1 ON PAGE 65]. Knowing that he trained at West Point, we would be tempted to see his lifetime illnesses as being those associated with his trade: namely battle injuries, or other accidents. Buzz's Mars is in Capricorn and thus dignified by Exaltation: but it is close to the 8th house cusp, suggesting the possibility of chronic disease.[2]

When we come to the condition of alcoholism, we are up against a disease that was not recognized as such in the ancient world. I discuss alcoholism briefly in *Traditional Medical Astrology*, Chapter 5 (pages 180-182) in the case of Marlene Dietrich. The modern convention is to see it as Neptune. Personally, I have no problem with assigning "new" diseases to the outer planets. However, I would nominate the obsessive-compulsiveness of Pluto as being at least as good a candidate for addiction as the cluelessness, dissatisfaction, and unconsciousness of Neptune. In Buzz's case, he's got a Mars-Pluto opposition square his Moon: every time that he gets uncomfortable on his Moon, the Mars-Pluto will kick in. Emotional discomfort gives anger and obsessive-compulsive behavior. Buzz's alcoholism only manifested after he had traveled to the Moon, after which he found himself in an existential crisis, asking what to do with his life *now*.

Edward "Buzz" Aldrin
Montclair, New Jersey
Time Zone: 5 hours West

January 20, 1975
40N49'33" 74W12'34"
Tropical Regiomontanus
Solar Return for January 20, 1975 in Montclair, New Jersey

12:20:14 PM
Standard Time

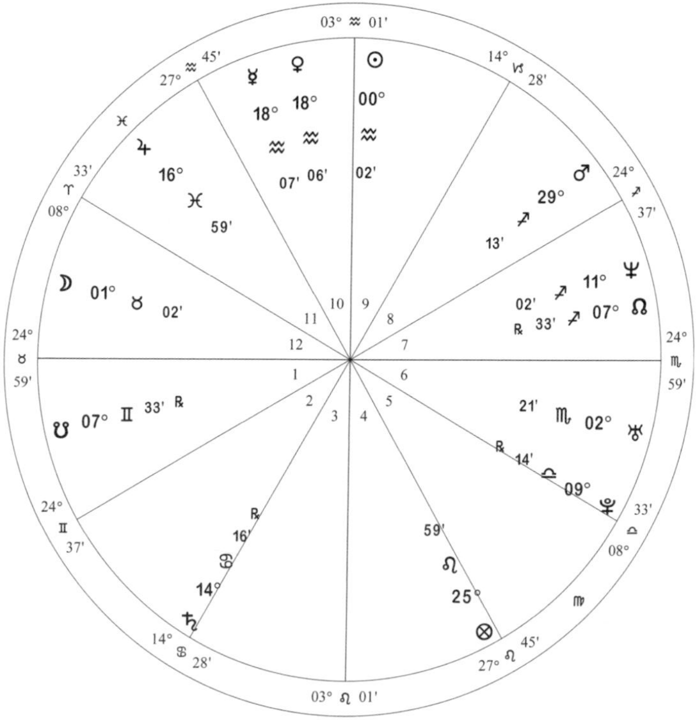

Dorothean Ess. Dig. (No Mut Rec. Points)								
Pl	Ruler	Exalt	Tripl	Term	Face	Detri	Fall	Score
☉	♄	--	♄	♄	♀	☉ -	--	- 10 P
☽	♀	☽ +	♀	♀	☿	♂	--	+4
☿	♄	--	♄	♀	☿ +	☉	--	+1
♀	♄	--	♄ m	♀ +	☿	☉	--	+2
♂	♃	☋	☉	♂ +	♄	☿	--	+2
♃	♃ +	♀	♀	☿	♃ +	☿	☿	+6
♄	☽	♃	♀ m	☿	☿	♄ -	♂	- 10 P
☊	♃	☋	☉	♃	☿	☿	--	--
⊗	☉	--	☉	♂	♂	♄	--	--
As	♀	☽	♀	♄	♄	♂	--	--
Mc	♄	--	♄	♄	♀	☉	--	--
☋	☿	☊	♄	♃	♃	♃	--	--

Hs	Alm. (Pto)
1	♀
2	☿♄
3	☽
4	☉
5	☉
6	♀♄
7	♂
8	♃
9	♂♄
10	♄
11	♄
12	☉

Example 9-1a. Buzz Aldrin medical solar return for 1975

Edward "Buzz" Aldrin
Montclair, New Jersey
Time Zone: 5 hours West

January 20, 1978
40N49'33" 74W12'34"
Tropical Regiomontanus
Solar Return for January 20, 1978 in Montclair, New Jersey

5:48 AM
Standard Time

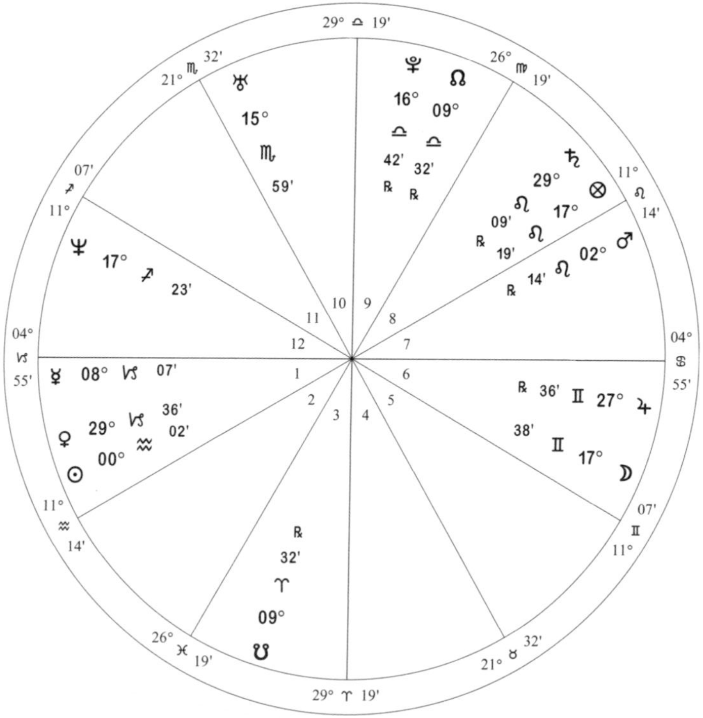

Dorothean Ess. Dig. (No Mut Rec. Points)								
Pl	Ruler	Exalt	Tripl	Term	Face	Detri	Fall	Score
☉	♄ m	--	☿	♄	♀ m	☉ -	--	- 10 P
☽	☿	☊	☿ m	♀	♂	♃	--	- 5 P
☿	♄	♂	☽ m	☿ +	♃	☽	♃	+2
♀	♄	♂	☽	♄	☉ m	☽	♃	- 5 P
♂	☉	--	♃	♄ m	♄ m	♄	--	- 5 P
♃	☿	☊	☿	♂	☉	♃ -	--	- 10 P
♄	☉ m	--	♃	♂ m	♂ m	♄ -	--	- 10 P
☊	♀	♄	☿	♀	☽	♂	☉	--
⊗	☉	--	♃	♀	♃	♄	--	--
As	♄	♂	☽	♀	♃	☽	♃	--
Mc	♀	♄	☿	☊	♃	♂	☉	--
☋	♂	☉	♃	♀	♂	♀	♄	--

Hs	Alm. (Pto)
1	♄
2	☿
3	♃
4	♂
5	☽
6	☿
7	☽
8	☉
9	☿
10	♀
11	♂
12	♃

Example 9-1b. Buzz Aldrin medical solar return for 1978

It's tough to come up with an exact time that his alcoholism started; thus, we can only look at when he first began treatment, during his 1975 solar return. In this chart, we see Pluto sitting right on the 6th house cusp, with Uranus in the 6th. This was not going to be an easy year for him. Only Mercury of the ptolemaic planets was in its own sign. Jupiter and Saturn were in reverse dignity to the natal. The Ascendant was the fixed star Algol. The Moon was strong, but in the 12th house and square the Sun. This fact alone, given that it is not in his radix, suggests that he had not really come to grips fully with his condition. The South Node in the 1st generally produces a difficult year physically. While I can completely understand why this solar return produced a circumstance where Buzz was able to seek treatment, it's not an argument of solving the problem. Because there is so little resonance with the radix, this year would not feel comfortable enough to produce lasting change: it would simply be too strange.

Buzz didn't stop drinking until his 1978 solar return. As several former smokers have said to me, the thing about doing something for the last time is that you don't know that you've really succeeded until you die! In Buzz's case, we can at least say that he has been successful for over a Saturn cycle! This solar return doesn't look like a complete resonance with the nativity, but there are more elements than the 1975 solar return possessed.

Both solar returns have a more significant 6th house focus than his radix chart has: not surprising, given the importance of these years from a medical perspective. However, the resonances with the radix for 1978 are:

- Moon in the same element as the radix
- Venus in the same sign as the radix
- Jupiter in the same sign and direction (i.e., retrograde) as the radix

It is not everything, but it's something to build upon. In contrast to 1975, in 1978 there were no malefics associated with the 6th house. One theme I discuss in *Traditional Medical Astrology* which emerges from the natal studies is that illness is associated with the 6th house when malefics are associated with that house. In 1978, there is at least a greater focus on the 1st house of health, as well as the absence of malefics associated with the 6th house. Collectively, these two arguments add up to a much more positive outcome.

It is also in the 1978 chart that Neptune makes its appearance, opposed by the solar return Moon. With the SR-Moon aspecting both Neptune and Pluto, there is a better chance to be able to confront *both* sets of issues presented by these difficult planets. And the trine between natal Moon and solar return Moon doesn't hurt either.

Dorothy Hamill's Professional Skating Injuries

Injuries come with athletics. There are few exceptions, whether occasional, amateur, or professional. However, as the body ages, injuries tend to take more of a toll than they do on a young body.

Dorothy's nativity has a large 6th house focus to begin with, with the Sun, Mercury and Uranus in the 6th, and the 1st house Moon ruling it [SEE EXAMPLE 3-4 ON PAGE 75]. The Sun-Uranus conjunction makes it difficult for Dorothy to hold concentration without being distracted, although obviously, being in the fixed signs, she's better than most other Sun-Uranus combinations. Having the ruler of the 6th in the 1st is already an argument of the Native being the cause of her or his own disease: this works out in practice to diseases either being caused by stress, or the Native voluntarily going into dangerous places. An ice rink is a dangerous place! We should also mention that the Moon conjunct Mars could easily be a signature for anger, or at least being quick to anger. One presumes that a person in a martial pursuit channels this energy into a better performance, but if anger is allowed to build up, this may not be so easy.

In her solar return year for 1993, Dorothy broke a rib. The twenty-nine degrees on the 6th house cusp is suggestive: Mercury ruling the cusp is in the 6th, peregrine and in the sign of her radix 6th.

Dorothy Hamill
Chicago, Illinois
Time Zone: 6 hours West

July 26, 1993
41 N 51 87 W 39
Tropical Regiomontanus
Solar Return for July 26, 1993 in Chicago, Illinois

7:46:29 PM
Daylight Saving Time

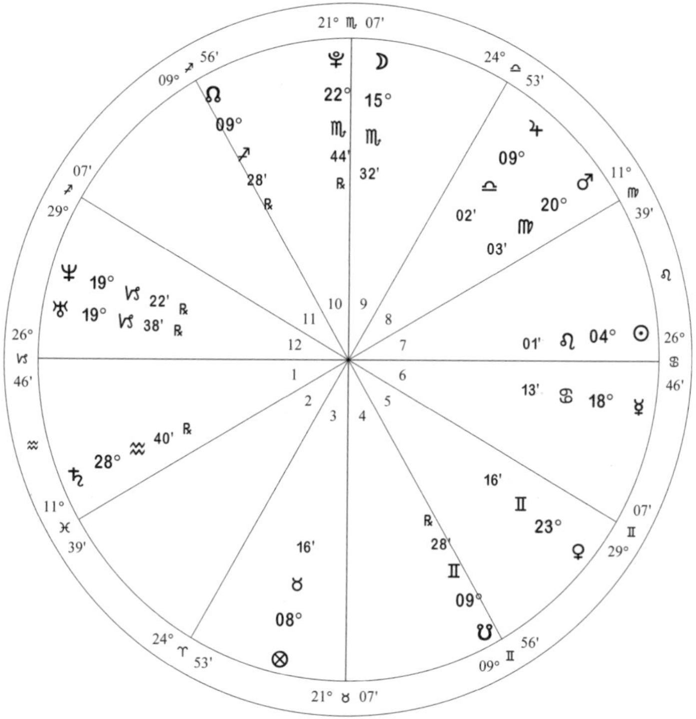

Pl	Ruler	Exalt	Tripl	Term	Face	Detri	Fall	Score
☉	☉ +	--	☉ +	♄	♄	♄	--	+8
☽	♂	--	♀	♀	☉	♀	☽ -	- 9 P
☿	☽	♃	♀	☿ +	☿ +	♄	♂	+3
♀	☿	☊	♄	♄	☉	♃	--	- 5 P
♂	☿	☿	♀	♄ m	☿	♃	♀	- 5 P
♃	♀	♄	♄	♀	☽	♂	☉	- 5 P
♄	♄ +	--	♄ +	♂ m	☽	☉	--	+8
☊	♃	☋	☉	♀	☿	☿	--	--
⊗	♀	☽	♀	☿	☿	♂	--	--
As	♄	♂	♀	♄	☉	☽	♃	--
Mc	♂	--	♀	☿	♀	♀	☽	--
☋	☿	☊	♄	♃	♃	♃	--	--

Dorothean Ess. Dig. (No Mut Rec. Points)

Hs	Alm. (Pto)
1	♄
2	♃
3	☉♂
4	♀
5	☿
6	☿
7	☽
8	☿
9	♄
10	♂
11	♃
12	♃

Example 9-2a. Dorothy Hamill medical solar return for 1993

Dorothy Hamill
Chicago, Illinois
Time Zone: 6 hours West

July 27, 1998
41 N 51 87 W 39
Tropical Regiomontanus
Solar Return for July 27, 1998 in Chicago, Illinois

12:49:57 AM
Daylight Saving Time

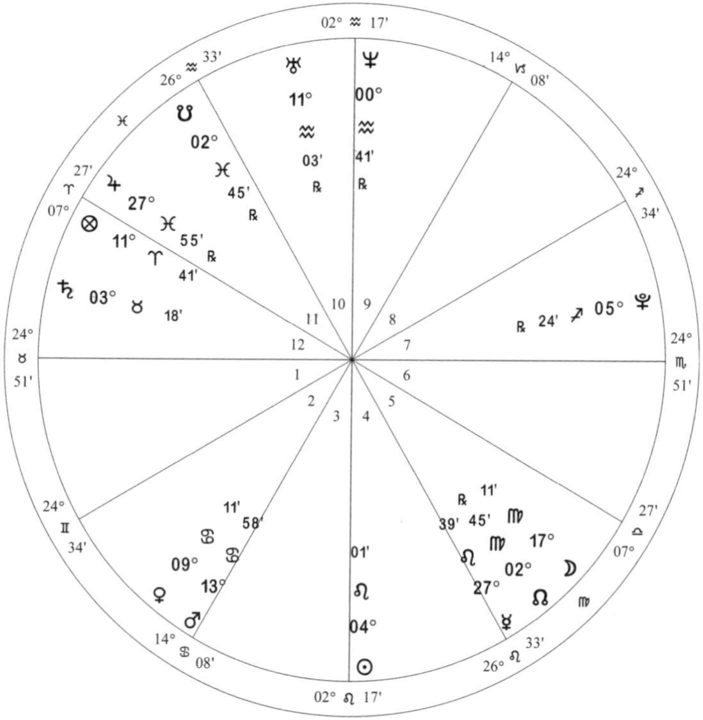

Pl	Ruler	Exalt	Tripl	Term	Face	Detri	Fall	Score
☉	☉ +	--	♃	♄	♄	♄	--	+5
☽	☿	☿	☽ +	♃	♀	♃	♀	+3
☿	☉	--	♃	♂ m	♂ m	♄	--	- 5 P
♀	☽	♃ m	♂	♃	♀ +	♄	♂	+1
♂	☽	♃	♂ +	☿ m	☿ m	♄	♂ -	- 1
♃	♃ +	♀ m	♂	♄	♂	☿	☿	+5
♄	♀	☽	☽	♀	☿	♂	--	- 5 P
☊	☿	☿	☽	☿	☉	♃	♀	--
⊗	♂	☉	♃	♀	☉	♀	♄	--
As	♀	☽	☽	♄	♄	♂	--	--
Mc	♄	--	☿	♄	♀	☉	--	--
☋	♃	♀	♂	♀	♄	☿	☿	--

Dorothean Ess. Dig. (No Mut Rec. Points)

Hs	Alm. (Pto)
1	☽
2	☿
3	☽
4	☉
5	☉
6	♀
7	♂
8	♃
9	♂♄
10	♄
11	♄
12	♂

Example 9-2b. Dorothy Hamill medical solar return for 1998

The Moon, which rules the rest of the house, is in Fall in Scorpio. What is interesting to me about the cusp being in Gemini is that it gives the anatomical location: the region of the *lungs*. Mercury in that solar return is opposite Uranus-Neptune, which is as good an indicator of an accident – or bone break – as you are likely to see. On the other hand, Saturn ruled Dorothy's SR-Ascendant, like her radix Ascendant. And in the solar return, Saturn was quite dignified. It was, however, transiting the natal Ascendant and square her natal Saturn. So at least, she could heal and get back on her feet.

The collarbone, the site of Dorothy's later injury in solar return 1998, is in the zone ruled by Taurus: the neck. So what do we see but SR-Taurus rising, at Algol, no less! Continuing the theme, we have Saturn in Taurus, in the sign opposite Dorothy's natal Saturn. Venus rules 1st and 6th, tying these two houses together completely. The Saturn was square Dorothy's Sun, and osteoarthritis is an especially painful, often degenerative condition, that is unquestionably ruled by Saturn. Neptune also was in the picture, with the Sun opposite Neptune, and Saturn square Neptune in the return chart. A true competitor to the core, Dorothy did not use this as a reason to retire, and continued to skate professionally.

Venus in Dorothy's radix is peregrine; here, in the 1998 solar return, it has out-of-sect Triplicity. But it is conjunct an unfortunate Mars in Fall. Dorothy has those two planets in square natally: here, the conjunction literally brought a crisis to a head. In addition, the nodes were in the signs square the radix nodes.

In 1998, Dorothy had both the Moon and Jupiter in signs opposite the radix. All these factors together make 1998 a worse year for her than 1993. But with the Sun trine Pluto, she endured it, and moved on.

Scott Hamilton's Brain Tumor and its Complications

Throughout his skating career, the human interest story on Scott focused on how, as a child, he stopped growing for several years, took up skating, and the rest, as we say, is history. I discussed his solar returns during that childhood period in *Traditional Medical Astrology* on pages 246-249. Physiologically, when one mentions growth, the pituitary gland in the brain comes to mind, since it is pituitary hormones that control much of the growth process.

So it is perhaps not so surprising at all that, as an adult, Scott developed a benign brain tumor. This was first diagnosed and treated in his 2004 solar return. It was then operated upon in his 2009 return. Surgery also happened a year later to repair an artery that was nicked during the solar 2009 procedure.

In Scott's natal chart, we see Jupiter ruling the 6th house *[SEE EXAMPLE 5-7 ON PAGE 121]*. How many astrologers have repeated the mantra about Jupiter meaning growth and expansion? In medicine, that may well mean a tumor, which is something that grows and expands too much. In Scott's chart, Jupiter has participating Triplicity – and perhaps his example should serve as one of the warnings that the participating Triplicity is in fact not as strong as in-sect or out-of-sect. The Moon is trine his Jupiter, with Venus and Saturn strongly disposing it, having sign and exaltation disposition respectively.

Venus is in Leo, not a strong sign for Venus, but in Term. Saturn has participating Triplicity. None of these three planets is seriously afflicted, except for the separating conjunction of Venus with Uranus. Now, that probably isn't a terribly bad description for suddenly stopping growing, and then starting again several years later. But as for the pituitary? This is a gland that was not recognized in antiquity. So applying our rulership logic to this problem, we either go with Sun and Aries for the head (its anatomical location), or Jupiter for growth (its functional purpose).

In the year 2004, when the problem was diagnosed, what do we get on the 6th house cusp but Aries? Mars rules both 1st and 6th, and it is combust – although at least in a sign in the same element as the radix position. But Jupiter, not to be outdone, is in Detriment in Virgo, and square Pluto. This configuration does relate to Scott's health because Jupiter rules his 6th natally. So we have two strong arguments of the brain problem in this year. Notice that Mercury, ruling the 8th in the solar return, is not providing additional danger by becoming enmeshed in this configuration we have already discussed. Mercury is almost at its radix position, the Moon is in the same sign as his radix Moon, so both are providing anchors into the strength of his nativity.

In Scott's nativity, the Venus-Uranus may have had something to do with his growth problem, but in 2004, it was the Sun partile opposed to Uranus in angular houses. This certainly argues for the problem manifesting: but it's no argument of the problem being permanently solved. The North Node in the 6th house would normally be considered a benefic, but not for a condition that involves *growth*. The Moon was in Aquarius, Scott's radix sign, but at the Southern Bending. This shows a crisis point, not a release. So that is an argument that whatever happens in this year is not the end of the problem.

It wasn't. But before we move on to the next phase, let's consider the details of what happened to him medically in November 2004 and immediately after, so we can understand the dimensions of the problem. In 2004, Scott was given radiation to destroy the tumor – but the radiation also destroyed the pituitary itself. Now, for the first time since his childhood, Scott was back in "no growth" mode. In the interim, many additional medical procedures had been developed – and most importantly, Scott was an adult, not a child, and not expected to physically enlarge. But like other victims of pituitary tumors, he needs to take a whole regimen of injections, pills, and gels to attempt to replicate the normal functioning of a gland critical to metabolic functioning.

Benign tumors generally don't happen overnight, and we may note that Scott's diagnosis occurred barely two months after his birthday. To see the development, we need to go back to 2003. And here we see a year focused on the 6th-12th, with some Ascendant action as well. Scott's son Aiden was born in this year, a miracle of modern science, since Scott earlier had testicular cancer, had lost one testicle, and was about to have the other stop functioning. We have reviewed this year already with respect to that matter. But in 2003, Neptune was lurking at the 6th house cusp, a good argument for a health problem that would either be difficult to diagnose, or develop in secret. With the five planets involved in opposition in the 6th-12th, and Mars and Uranus as part of them, we could figure the other testicle, or Mars, as it relates to metabolism, would also stop working. Here, with a partile Uranus opposite Jupiter, it's not hard to pick out the pituitary, given Scott's personal history.

What was hidden in 2003 becomes fully manifest in 2004, with the heavy 10th-4th axis. Scott is a celebrity, and so anything he goes through not only tends to end up public, it tends to end up in one of his autobiographies! This was no exception. And so before we proceed to 2009, let's consider one more impact of this crisis in his life.

When Scott was experiencing testicular cancer, he had been an active professional skater with an outstanding network of friends, but a girlfriend with whom he would shortly break up. In the meantime, he had met and married the girl of his dreams. This new health crisis was the first one she would face. In the 2004 solar return, we see the 7th house cusp being ruled by a dignified Venus in Triplicity, right at the cusp of his 9th, and applying to Saturn in the 9th. When Scott told her, instead of caving in to the news as he had feared, she dropped down on her knees in prayer. Scott was so overwhelmed that he joined her, and what ensued was a religious conversion for him.

In Chapter 7, when we considered the 9th house, we looked primarily at education because, frankly, in our secular society, education is the more likely read when it comes to the 9th house.

Scott Hamilton
Toledo, Ohio
Time Zone: 5 hours West

August 28, 2003 7:19:57 AM
41N39'50" 83W33'19" Daylight Saving Time
Tropical Regiomontanus
Solar Return for August 28, 2003 in Toledo, Ohio

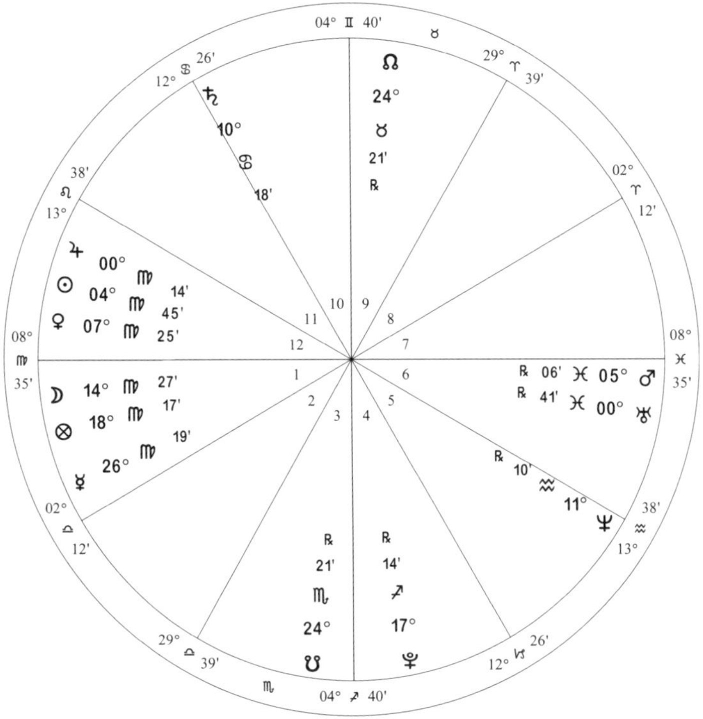

Dorothean Ess. Dig. (No Mut Rec. Points)								
Pl	Ruler	Exalt	Tripl	Term	Face	Detri	Fall	Score
☉	☿	☿	♀	☿	☉ +	♃	♀	+1
☽	☿	☿	♀	♃	♀	♃	♀	- 5 P
☿	☿ +	☿ +	♀	♂	☿ +	♃	♀	+10
♀	☿	☿	♀ +	♀ +	☉	♃	♀ -	+1
♂	♃	♀	♀	♀	♄	☿	☿	- 5 P
♃	☿	☿	♀	☿	☉	♃ -	♀	- 10 P
♄	☽	♃	♀	♃	☿	♄ -	♂	- 10 P
☊	♀	☽	♀	♄	♄	♂	--	--
⊗	☿	☿	♀	♄	♀	♃	♀	--
As	☿	☿	♀	♀	☉	♃	♀	--
Mc	☿	☊	♄	☿	♃	♃	--	--
☋	♂	--	♀	☿	♀	♀	☽	--

Hs	Alm. (Pto)
1	☿
2	♄
3	♄
4	♃
5	♂♄
6	♄
7	♃
8	☉
9	☉
10	☿
11	♃
12	☉

Example 9-3a. Scott Hamilton medical solar return for 2003

Scott Hamilton
Toledo, Ohio
Time Zone: 5 hours West

August 27, 2004 1:08:13 PM
41N39'50" 83W33'19" Daylight Saving Time
Tropical Regiomontanus
Solar Return for August 27, 2004 in Toledo, Ohio

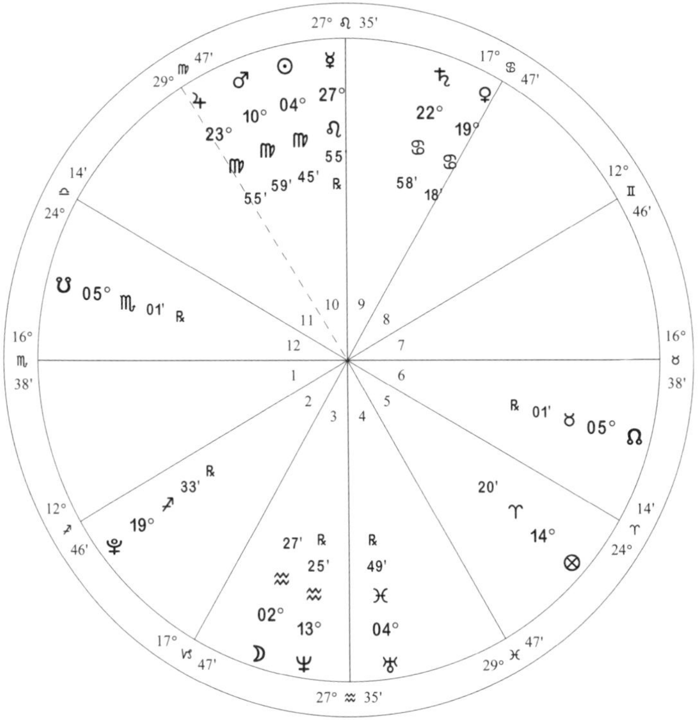

Dorothean Ess. Dig. (No Mut Rec. Points)								
Pl	Ruler	Exalt	Tripl	Term	Face	Detri	Fall	Score
☉	☿ m	☿	♀	☿	☉ +	♃	♀	+1
☽	♄ m	--	♄	♄	♀	☉	--	- 5 P
☿	☉ m	--	☉	♂	♂	♄	--	- 5 P
♀	☽	♃	♀ +	☿	☿	♄	♂	+3
♂	☿	☿	♀	♀	♀	♃	♀	- 5 P
♃	☿	☿	♀	♄	☿	♃ -	♀	- 10 P
♄	☽ m	♃	♀	♀	☽	♄ -	♂	- 10 P
☊	♀	☽	♀	♀	☿	♂	--	--
⊗	♂	☉	☉	☿	☉	♀	♄	--
As	♂	--	♀	♀	☉	♀	☽	--
Mc	☉	--	☉	♂	♂	♄	--	--
☋	♂	--	♀	♂	♂	♀	☽	--

Hs	Alm. (Pto)
1	♂
2	♃
3	♂♄
4	♄
5	♃
6	☉♂
7	♀
8	☿
9	☽
10	☉
11	☿
12	♄

Example 9-3b. Scott Hamilton medical solar return for 2004

In Lilly's day, the religious profession (which is to say, intensity of belief) was a much more dramatic concern than it tends to be today. Briefly, the Native's religious profession is given by the planets in and ruling the 3rd and the 9th houses, plus Jupiter.[3] Elsewhere, I have discussed the observation that the 3rd house may relate to less common religions within one's culture, whereas the 9th could relate to the dominant religious culture.

From a natal perspective, Scott's profession looks adequate, but not overwhelming. He has Jupiter in Triplicity ruling the 3rd and disposing Saturn, the only planet in 3rd or 9th. A malefic associated with the 3rd or 9th can destroy belief, but since Saturn in Sagittarius has dignity, the reverse would be the argument. What intrigues me is that in Scott's nativity, the emphasis is placed on the 3rd. Christianity is the dominant religion of the U.S., but there may still be a twist here. Scott grew up in the North. His wife is from the South. There is a definite difference in fervor that tends to be fairly obvious when you compare the behavior of Northerners and Southerners with regard to religion – Northerners tend to be "colder" about it.

Scott's description of his wife's behavior in his autobiography sounds exactly normal for a Southerner – but it sounds pretty unusual for a Northerner. Thus, the cultural difference shown here may actually be a regional approach to the same religion! At any rate, in the year 2004, the religious focus in the return was pretty strong, with four planets in the 3rd and 9th.

But back to Scott's medical condition. In 2004, the benign tumor was discovered and irradiated, and his pituitary gland was destroyed in the process of shrinking the tumor. But the tumor came back. Under the 2009 return, Scott had to undergo surgery on the tumor. For 2009, we see Mars in the 6th house in Fall, opposite Pluto in the 12th. With this configuration, there is no doubt in my mind that surgery was absolutely necessary. Saturn, ruling Scott's vitality, was in the 8th. Mercury, ruling the SR-6th was also in the 8th. These are both serious indicators: not of death, but of *unto death*: it's

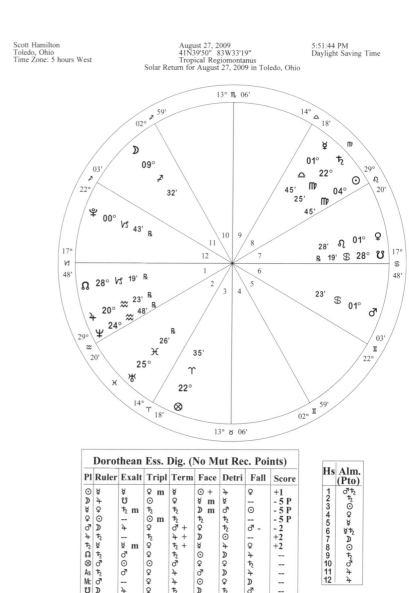

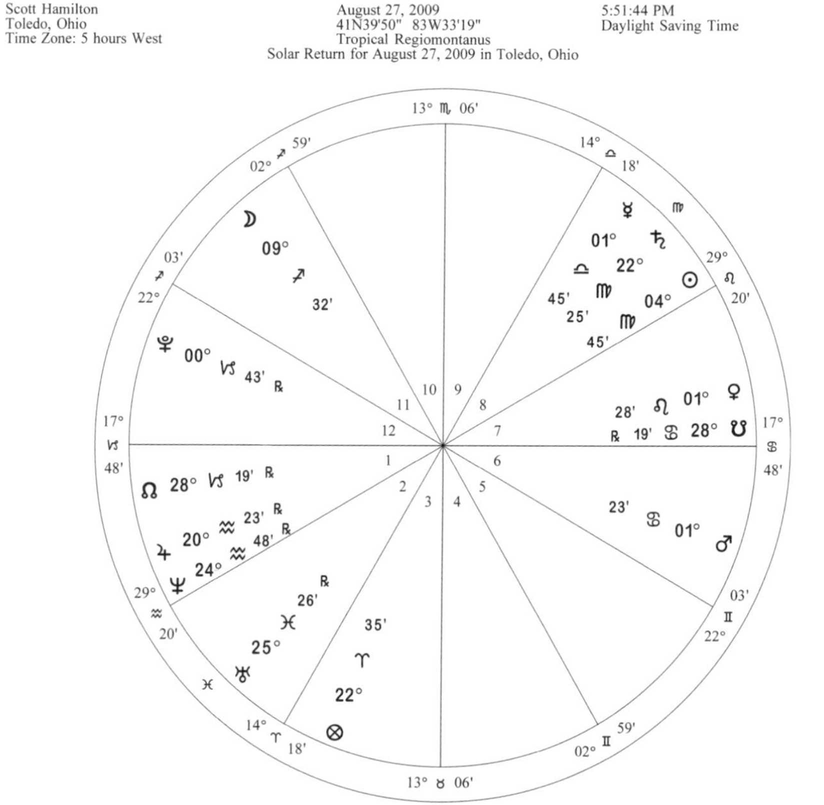
Scott Hamilton
Toledo, Ohio
Time Zone: 5 hours West
August 27, 2009
41N39'50" 83W33'19"
Tropical Regiomontanus
Solar Return for August 27, 2009 in Toledo, Ohio
5:51:44 PM
Daylight Saving Time

Dorothean Ess. Dig. (No Mut Rec. Points)								
Pl	**Ruler**	**Exalt**	**Tripl**	**Term**	**Face**	**Detri**	**Fall**	**Score**
☉	☿	☿	♀ m	☿	☉ +	♃	♀	+1
☽	♃	☋	☉	♀	☿ m	☿	--	- 5 P
☿	♀	♄ m	♄	♄	☽ m	♂	☉	- 5 P
♀	☉	--	☉ m	♄	♄	♄	--	- 5 P
♂	☽	♃	♀	♂ +	♀	♄	♂ -	- 2
♃	♄	--	♄	♃ +	☽	☉	--	+2
♄	☿	☿ m	♀	♄ +	☿	♃	♀	+2
☊	♄	♂	♀	♄	☉	☽	♃	--
⊗	♂	☉	☉	♂	♀	♀	♄	--
As	♄	♂	♀	♃	♂	☽	♃	--
Mc	♂	--	♀	♃	☉	♀	☽	--
☋	☽	♃	♀	♄	☽	♄	♂	--

Hs	Alm. (Pto)
1	♂♄
2	♄
3	☉
4	♀
5	☿
6	☿♄
7	☽
8	☉
9	♄
10	♂
11	♃
12	♃

Example 9-3c. Scott Hamilton medical solar return for 2009

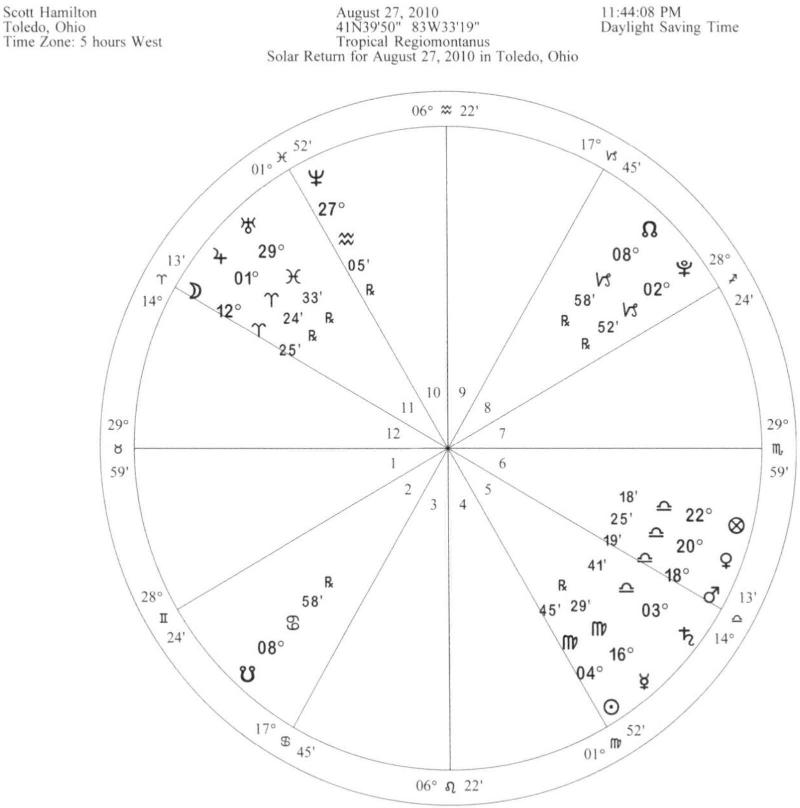
Scott Hamilton
Toledo, Ohio
Time Zone: 5 hours West
August 27, 2010
41N39'50" 83W33'19"
Tropical Regiomontanus
Solar Return for August 27, 2010 in Toledo, Ohio
11:44:08 PM
Daylight Saving Time

Pl	Ruler	Exalt	Tripl	Term	Face	Detri	Fall	Score
☉	☿	☿	☽	☿	☉ +	♃	♀	+1
☽	♂	☉	♃	♀	☉	♀	♄	- 5 P
☿	☿ +	☿ +	☽	♃	♀	♃	♀	+9
♀	♀ +	♄	☿	☿	♃	♂	☉	+5
♂	♀	♄	☿	♃	♄	♂ -	☉	- 10 P
♃	♂	☉	♃ +	♃ +	♂	♀	♄	+5
♄	♀	♄ +	☿	♄ +	☽	♂	☉	+6
☊	♄	♂	☽	☿	♃	☽	♃	--
⊗	♀	♄	☿	☿	♃	♂	☉	--
As	♀	☽	☽	♂	♄	♂	--	--
Mc	♄	--	☿	☿	♀	☉	--	--
☋	☽	♃	♂	♃	♀	♄	♂	--

Dorothean Ess. Dig. (No Mut Rec. Points)

Hs	Alm. (Pto)
1	☽
2	☿
3	☽
4	☉
5	☿
6	♀♄
7	♂
8	♃
9	♂♄
10	☿♄
11	♀
12	☉♂

Example 9-3d. Scott Hamilton medical solar return for 2010

the configuration for sickness patterns that last until death without necessarily causing it.

This is all true enough, because, as we have seen, Scott will not be able to go very long for the rest of his life without having to take supplements to stay alive. Mars is the classic planet of surgery, and here it's highlighted. Its debility may be a key to its success, because Scott's own natal Mars is debilitated. Scott's problem for the year was that his vitality was given by Saturn ruling the SR-Ascendant, with Jupiter and Neptune in the 1st. Of the three, Saturn was the strongest, having dignity by Term. While Jupiter had participating Triplicity, it was also retrograde. But Saturn was in the 8th.

Neptune associated with the 1st could be a low immune system, mysterious illnesses, or general confusion or cluelessness. Under the circumstances, I would nominate Neptune for showing the problem with the operation, namely, that a moment of unconsciousness or distraction could well have caused the nick to his artery that required the follow-up surgery the next year.

So in 2010, Scott again had Mars associated with the 6th house, this time in Libra, the other sign of Detriment. Also there was Venus, ruling Scott's SR-Ascendant – barely! But this year, Venus was in good condition, and Scott was actually in much better shape to face the surgery than he had been the year before.

Still, the ruler of the 1st in the 6th for a solar return is a year of confronting illness, so no matter how much stronger he felt, the emphasis on disease was still present.

Michelle Kwan's Hip and Abdominal Injuries

We have already reviewed Michelle Kwan's 2005 solar return to see the end of her amazing string of U.S. Figure Skating Championships. Michelle was stopped from competing at her third Olympics by injury. In the following year, she had arthroscopic surgery to repair the labrum. It is to this pair of years, 2005 and 2006, that we now return.

In her 2005 solar return, we see Uranus in Pisces in the 6th. Uranus is a good argument for an injury, a break, or a tear. Neptune hovering near the 6th house cusp doesn't add clarity to the whole question of injuries. Saturn ruling the 6th and in Detriment points to the bones. And we can see clearly this is Michelle's natal configuration, except that her radix Saturn is not debilitated, but in Term [*SEE EXAMPLE 7-4 ON PAGE 158*]. However, the South Node in the 6th in Aquarius was a natal warning: her bones and their limitations could not be denied indefinitely.

In *The Martial Art of Horary Astrology*, I gave a table from Saunders that related disease rulerships by sign and planet that I admitted some caution about, because I felt it was not possible to study the table in any quantitatively meaningful way at that time.[4] But I do return to it periodically to try to understand its application more clearly. Michelle's radix 6th house ruler is Saturn, in Virgo. In Saunders' table, that combination gives thighs, the genitals, and the feet. The reference to the thighs does seem interesting as a specific localization that wasn't the knees – and the knees were not the focus of Michelle's problems. So perhaps this is suggestive, but I still haven't been able to get the table to work with the consistency that produces "ooh's" and "aah's" from the audience (me).

The major thing that strikes me about the 2005 chart is that very late separating Moon-Saturn conjunction, not just the Saturn itself. Michelle was pushing with every fiber of her being – and her body was leaving her -- just a little short. Mars was also square her Sun: Mars in one of the dignified signs, which are not always so great for athletes. A Sun-Mars can be a bit physically dangerous as well, and so Michelle no doubt was willing to push harder than the physical resources she had left could tolerate.

When I had stopped doing Tae Kwon Do, and then decided to practice some of the forms, I was stunned at how crisply I could do them – until the next day, when I was practically prostrate in pain. Even at my lowly level, the body develops a memory of how it should move. You can hold on to that for a little, but you

Michelle Kwan
Los Angeles, California
Time Zone: 8 hours West

July 7, 2005
34N03'08" 118W14'34"
Tropical Regiomontanus
Solar Return for July 7, 2005 in Los Angeles, California

10:57:22 AM
Daylight Saving Time

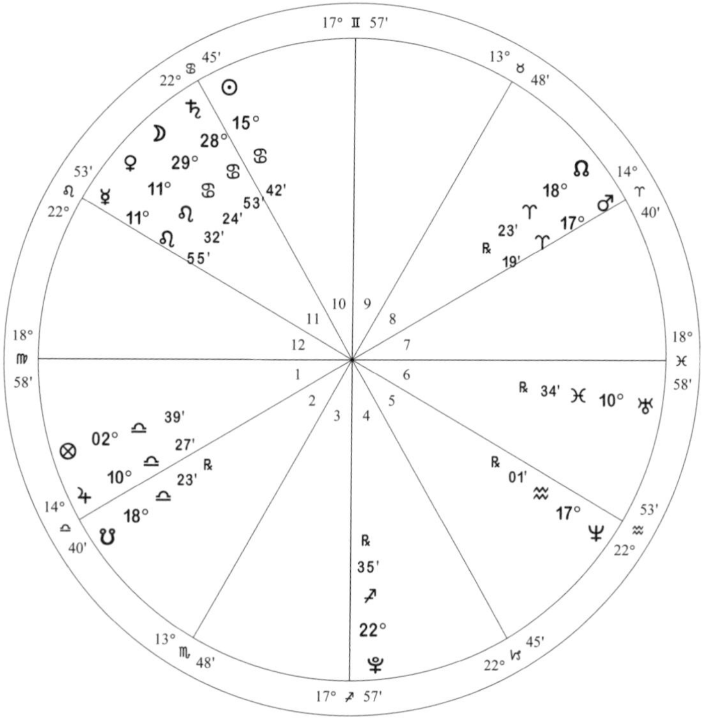

Dorothean Ess. Dig. (No Mut Rec. Points)

Pl	Ruler	Exalt	Tripl	Term	Face	Detri	Fall	Score
☉	☽	♃	♀ m	☿	☿	♄	♂	- 5 P
☽	☽ +	♃	♀	♄	☽ +	♄	♂	+6
☿	☉	--	☉	☿ +	♃	♄	--	+2
♀	☉	--	☉ m	☿	♃	♄	--	- 5 P
♂	♂ +	☉	☉	☿	☉	♀	♄	+5
♃	♀	♄ m	♄	♀	♄	♂	☉	- 5 P
♄	☽	♃ m	♀	♄ +	☽	♄ -	♂	- 3
☊	♂	☉	☉	☿	☉	♀	♄	--
⊗	♀	♄	♄	♄	☽	♂	☉	--
As	☿	☿	♀	♄	♀	♃	♀	--
Mc	☿	☊	♄	♀	♂	♃	--	--
☋	♀	♄	♄	♃	♄	♂	☉	--

Hs	Alm. (Pto)
1	☿
2	♄
3	♂
4	♃
5	♂
6	♄
7	♃
8	☉
9	♀
10	☿
11	☽
12	☉

Example 9-4a. Michelle Kwan medical solar return for 2005

Michelle Kwan
Los Angeles, California
Time Zone: 8 hours West

July 7, 2006
34N03'08" 118W14'34"
Tropical Regiomontanus
Solar Return for July 7, 2006 in Los Angeles, California

4:32:56 PM
Daylight Saving Time

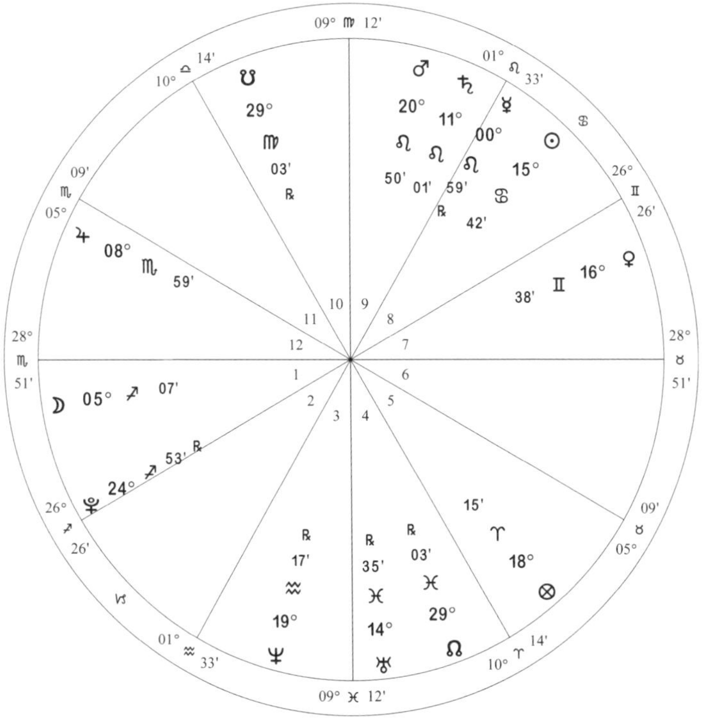

Dorothean Ess. Dig. (No Mut Rec. Points)

Pl	Ruler	Exalt	Tripl	Term	Face	Detri	Fall	Score
☉	☽	♃	♀	☿	☿	♄	♂	- 5 P
☽	♃	☋	☉	♃	☿	☿	--	- 5 P
☿	☉	--	☉	♄ m	♄	♄	--	- 5 P
♀	☿	☊	♄	♀ +	♂	♃	--	+2
♂	☉	--	☉	♃	♂ +	♄	--	+1
♃	♂	--	♀	♃ +	♂	♀	☽	+2
♄	☉	--	☉	☿ m	♃	♄ -	--	- 10 P
☊	♃	♀	♀	♄	♂	☿	☿	--
⊗	♂	☉	☉	☿	☉	♀	♄	--
As	♂	--	♀	♄	♀	♀	☽	--
Mc	☿	☿	♀	♀	☉	♃	♀	--
☋	☿	☿	♀	♂	☿	♃	♀	--

Hs	Alm. (Pto)
1	♂
2	♃
3	♄
4	♃
5	☉
6	♀
7	♀
8	☿
9	☉
10	☿
11	♄
12	♂

Example 9-4b. Michelle Kwan medical solar return for 2006

better have the strength to back it up! Michelle no doubt knew exactly what she was asking her body to do, and exactly how it would work. But at twenty-nine degrees, it was slipping out of her grasp.

The following year, with the Solar Return South Node transiting her natal Mars, Michelle had surgery to repair the damage. But what is striking about this year is that it doesn't look like a medical year. And largely – it wasn't. Michelle was transitioning her life – something that would result in a B.A. degree a couple of years later. The ruler of the 1st is in the 9th, along with Saturn, and with Mercury on the 9th house cusp.

And yet... Venus was ruling her solar return 6th house, with dignity by Term. Peregrine Mars was ruling her vitality, along with the Moon in the 1st house. The Venus position was partile Michelle's natal position. Benefics do not normally create health problems, so here is the chance to improve her health, not make it worse.

Louis Pasteur's Strokes

The symptoms of stroke were described by Hippocrates, and known to the ancient world under the name apoplexy. It wasn't until the 17th century that any evidence accumulated that these were related to the brain.

In Pasteur's biography, his first incident was called hemiplagia, which is a reference to paralysis on one side of the body. The medicine of his time called for bleeding, which he reported improved his condition at the time of his first stroke. Now, this is interesting for several reasons. First, many people might be surprised that bleeding was still practiced as late as 1867 – but it was. No better medical protocol had been proposed at this stage, and so the traditional methods tended to continue.

Second, according to Pasteur's own biographer, he reported improvement after the bleeding. Now, Louis Pasteur was not some "superstitious" type, but a trained observer. How could he possibly report an improvement from venesection? Lost in the later propaganda against obsolete medical procedures is the acknowledgement that bleeding was not prescribed for just anything. Doctors had an extensive pharmacopia, and many of these traditional medicines have been found to have active properties that worked on the conditions for which they were used. Venesection was also known under the name refrigeration, and that was the point: it was used for hot conditions. In the modern era, there's been discussion of the use of cold baths to reduce stroke damage. Venesection might not be our first choice of treatment, but we are just plain biased if we refuse to admit the possibility that there might have been some perception of improvement.

In Pasteur's natal chart, the 6th house cusp is Aries *[SEE EXAMPLE 4-5 ON PAGE 101]*. That immediately introduces the head as a possible site for issues. Mars in his chart was exalted, but square the Ascendant. Mars was also trine Jupiter, and sextile Pluto. The Sun-Uranus conjunction (which was part of a broader conjunctional pattern) would automatically suggest the possibility of some sort of acute condition as having importance in his health make-up.

In the year of his first stroke, Mars was conjunct the Sun at the IC, opposite Uranus, and square Neptune. It's interesting that Venus and Mars in the solar return had virtually swapped positions from the radix. Jupiter, ruling the SR-6th, was in a loose conjunction with the South Node.

This was a serious stroke: Pasteur didn't walk for three months, although he never lost consciousness when the stroke occurred. For his solar return in 1867, the Ascendant-Descendant were in the same signs as for the radix. This put Sun, Mercury and Mars in the 3rd, his natal configuration. However, this put Jupiter as ruler of the 6th, not Mars. Jupiter was highly dignified, but it was conjunct the South Node *and* it was square Saturn.

But is this chart "bad" enough to look like a stroke? Normally, the argument for serious illness is a malefic associated with the 6th house.

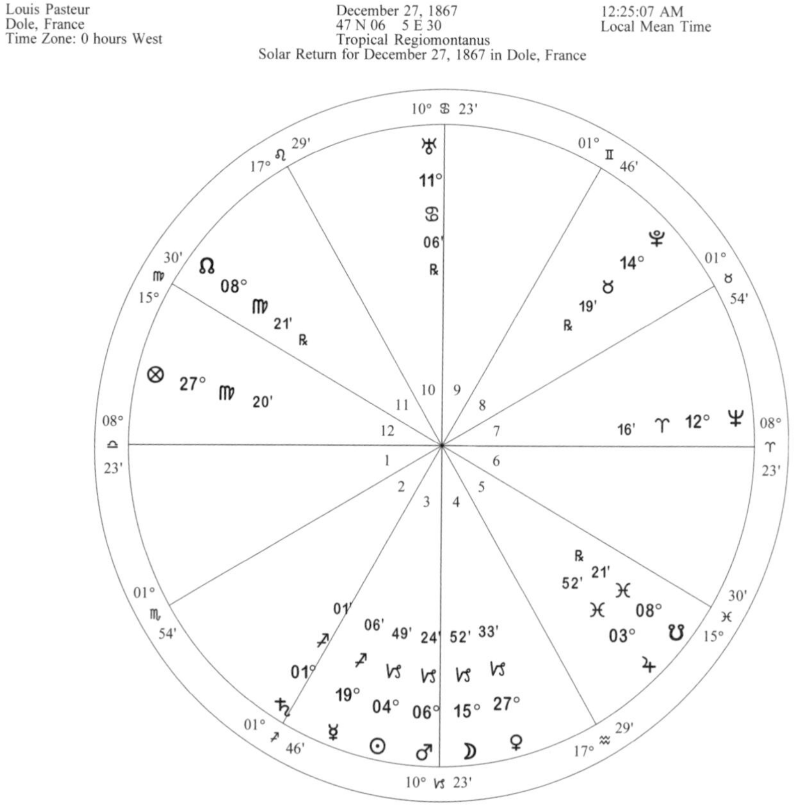
Louis Pasteur
Dole, France
Time Zone: 0 hours West
December 27, 1867
47 N 06 5 E 30
Tropical Regiomontanus
Solar Return for December 27, 1867 in Dole, France
12:25:07 AM
Local Mean Time

Dorothean Ess. Dig. (No Mut Rec. Points)								
Pl	Ruler	Exalt	Tripl	Term	Face	Detri	Fall	Score
☉	♄	♂	☽	♀	♃	☽	♃	- 5 P
☽	♄	♂	☽ +	♃	♂	☽ -	♃	- 2
☿	♃	☋	♃	♄	☽	☿ -	--	- 10 P
♀	♄	♂	☽	♄	☉	☽	♃	- 5 P
♂	♄	♂ +	☽	☿	♃	☽	♃	+4
♃	♃ +	♀	♂	♀	♄	☿	☿	+5
♄	♃	☋	♃	♃	☿	☿	--	- 5 P
☊	☿	☿	☽	♀	☉	♃	♀	--
⊗	☿	☿	☽	♂	☿	♃	♀	--
As	♀	♄	☿	♀	☽	♂	☉	--
Mc	☽	♃	♂	♃	☿	♄	♂	--
☋	♃	♀	♂	♃	♄	☿	☿	--

Hs	Alm. (Pto)
1	♀
2	♂
3	♃
4	♂♄
5	♄
6	♃
7	♂
8	☽♀
9	☿
10	♃
11	☉
12	☿

Example 9-5a. Louis Pasteur medical solar return for 1867

Louis Pasteur
Dole, France
Time Zone: 0 hr 9 min East

December 26, 1893
47 N 06 5 E 30
Tropical Regiomontanus
Solar Return for December 26, 1893 in Dole, France

7:37:42 AM
Standard Time

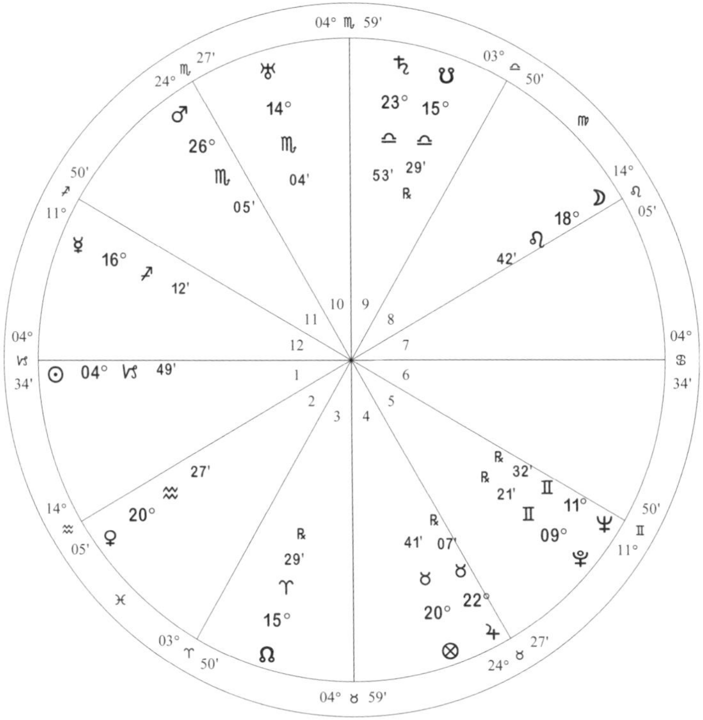

Dorothean Ess. Dig. (No Mut Rec. Points)								
Pl	Ruler	Exalt	Tripl	Term	Face	Detri	Fall	Score
☉	♄	♂	☽	♀	♃	☽	♃	- 5 P
☽	☉	--	♃ m	♀	♃	♄	--	- 5 P
☿	♃	☋	♃	☿ +	☽	☿ -	--	- 3
♀	♄ m	--	☿	♃	☽	☉	--	- 5 P
♂	♂ +	--	♂ +	☿	♀	♀	☽	+8
♃	♀	☽	☽ m	♄	♄ m	♂	--	- 5 P
♄	♀ m	♄ +	☿	☿	♃ m	♂	☉	+4
☊	♂	☉	♃	☿	☉	♀	♄	--
⊗	♀	☽	☽	♃	♄	♂	--	--
As	♄	♂	☽	♀	♃	☽	♃	--
Mc	♂	--	♂	♂	♂	♀	☽	--
☋	♀	♄	☿	♃	♄	♂	☉	--

Hs	Alm. (Pto)
1	♄
2	♄
3	♂
4	☽♀
5	☽
6	☿
7	☽
8	☉
9	♄
10	♂
11	♂
12	♃

Example 9-5b. Louis Pasteur medical solar return for 1893

Jupiter in Pisces is certainly *not* a malefic. However, one can argue that strokes are in part Jupiterian, being a vascular problem. So Pasteur's illness precisely matched the characteristics of the 6th house ruler, malefic or not. The other two hints come from the fixed stars. Here, we see two significant fixed star conjunctions. Mars was conjunct Facies, a difficult star. But more importantly, the Ascendant was conjunct Vindemiatrix, the widow's star.

There is no classical equivalent of the planetary patterns developed by M.E. Jones and later astrologers, so we have no classical interpretation for the fact that all the traditional bodies fall between the Saturn-Jupiter square, or even Saturn-South Node one. Perhaps this acts as a kind of besiegement.

Our second stroke example for Pasteur came the year before his death. And this is a notable chart, with the Sun just on the Ascendant. Now we do have to be careful, because that is not an argument of danger or death, but more of a rebirth: the dawning of a new day. His later years were filled with all sorts of honors and awards, not to mention the opening of the Institut Pasteur.

Saturn ruled the solar return Ascendant from the sign of Libra, the other Venus sign besides his radix placement. This was not the problem. But Neptune conjunct the 6th house cusp, with Pluto so close as well, makes a much more dangerous 6th house situation. The ruler of the 6th was in the 12th, which is a place of confinement. And the Moon is in the 8th, disposed by the Sun at the 1st, tying these two critical houses together. In addition, Saturn was trine Venus, radix ruler of the 8th, recapitulating the natal Venus-Saturn trine, and further highlighting the danger through their mutual reception. None of this argues for a physically strong year, given the strong emphasis on the 8th house.

Eleanor and Franklin: Polio

I have included this example to address a very simple methodological question. Often, we are delineating a solar return, or even natal chart, and the major symbolism involves another person. How much can you see in one person's chart about a second person?

This question will be addressed in detail relating to death in Chapter 11. But more generally, if you see the focus of a solar return being in the 7th house, how much can you actually say about the partner? Or can you simply say that partnership issues will be on the agenda for that year?

To consider this question, I have picked the solar return for Eleanor Roosevelt during which Franklin manifested the symptoms of polio. We will examine this in his solar returns in Chapter 12. The diagnosis was not as neat as it would be today; nor was the treatment. Within the medical milieu of the time, he easily could have died, and it was certainly more than expected that his political career was over. Instead, Franklin and Eleanor found a way through their marriage to keep his career not merely alive, but flourishing. As she became more of his "eyes and ears," she also found a much more satisfying role for herself than passive political wife. *[See Example 3-5 on page 79 for Eleanor's nativity.]*

As far as we know, Eleanor herself had no serious medical problems in this year. Her 1st house ruler Mercury was peregrine, but "besieged" between benefic North Node and benefic Venus, although Venus in Scorpio is not a happy placement. There's a big emphasis on the 2nd house, which would normally lead one to believe that money issues would be a big item this year. The expenditures for health care that year were large.

But Franklin himself? He was Jupiter in Virgo, in Detriment, in the 12th house. Eleanor's 12th, of course, was Franklin's 6th. Viewing the chart from Franklin's standpoint, his ruler was debilitated, in his 6th house, with the Sun right at his 8th house cusp, the Moon in

Eleanor Roosevelt
New York, New York
Time Zone: 5 hours West

October 12, 1920
40N42'51" 74W00'23"
Tropical Regiomontanus
Solar Return for October 12, 1920 in New York, New York

5:14:37 AM
Daylight Saving Time

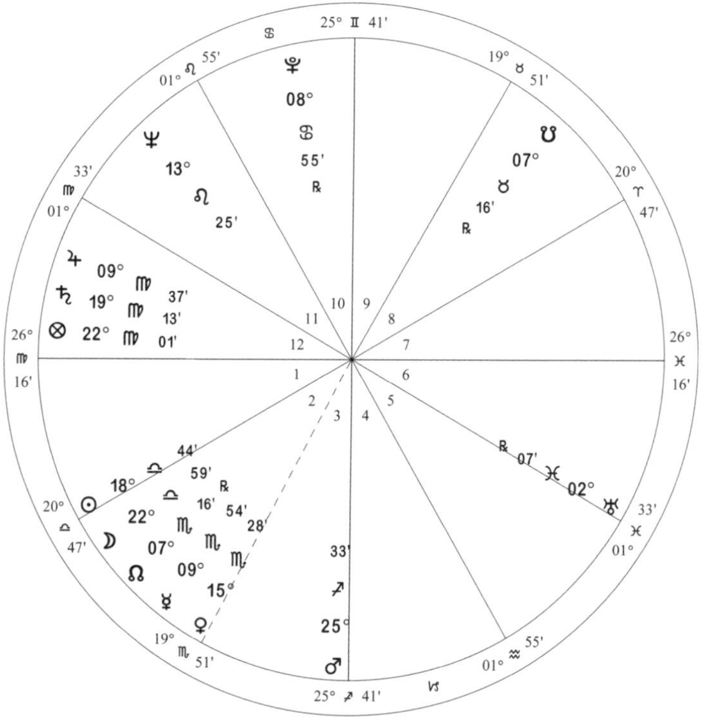

Dorothean Ess. Dig. (No Mut Rec. Points)								
Pl	Ruler	Exalt	Tripl	Term	Face	Detri	Fall	Score
☉	♀	♄	☿	♃	♄	♂	☉ -	- 9 P
☽	♀	♄	☿	☿	♃	♂	☉	- 5 P
☿	♂	--	♂	♃	♂	♀	☽	- 5 P
♀	♂	--	♂	♀ +	☉	♀ -	☽	- 3
♂	♃	☋	♃	♂ +	♄	☿	--	+2
♃	☿	☿	☽	♀	☉	♃ -	♀	- 10 P
♄	☿	☿	☽	♄ +	♀	♃	♀	+2
☊	♂	--	♂	♃	♂	♀	☽	--
⊗	☿	☿	☽	♄	☿	♃	♀	--
As	☿	☿	☽	♂	☿	♃	♀	--
Mc	☿	☊	☿	♂	☉	♃	--	--
☋	♀	☽	☽	♀	☿	♂	--	--

Hs	Alm. (Pto)
1	☿
2	☿♀
3	♂
4	♃
5	♄
6	♀
7	♃
8	♂
9	☽
10	☿
11	☉
12	☿

Example 9-6a. Eleanor Roosevelt medical solar returns for 1920

the 8ᵗʰ, and the ruler of his 6ᵗʰ in his 8ᵗʰ. This entire configuration shows a very grave disease that would become chronic, and with the potential to last for the rest of his life.

We can thus see that, at least in a case such as this, where Eleanor was called upon as Nurse Extraordinaire, and where Franklin's illness changed *her* life as well, we are completely confident reading his health crisis in her chart.

In Chapter 11, we shall see this idea expanded as we contemplate a more extreme case: death.

Chapter 9 Endnotes

1. Gadbury, John. *Genethlialogia*, pp 224-225.
2. We are skipping over a lot of medical procedure here that is addressed more fully in *Traditional Medical Astrology*, but in an interrogatory about a medical condition the connection between 6ᵗʰ and 8ᵗʰ means a chronic disease, i.e., one will have *it until* death, but not necessarily *causing* death.
3. For example, Lilly, *Christian Astrology*, pp 611-613.
4. Lehman, *MAHA* p 167. The original citation was: Saunders, Richard. *The Astrological Judgment and Practice of Physick, Deduced from the Position of the Heavens at the Decumbiture of the Sick Person, &C.* London: Thomas Sawbridge, 1677, pp 37-38.

10

Solar Returns for Life-Changing Years

SOME EXPERIENCES THAT PEOPLE HAVE JUST DON'T FIT INTO THE CATEGORIES COMPRISING THESE CHAPTERS. For this chapter, I have selected some events that fit between the lines. In Chapter 12, when we examine Franklin Roosevelt's life, we will see a number of other examples, because our goal then is to see solar returns develop chronologically, not to fit them into different and distinct categories.

Dorothy Hamill's Jewelry Loss

One doesn't need the glamor of ice skating to appreciate fine jewelry. For Dorothy Hamill, jewelry was something that she could enjoy collecting and wearing, and something that reminded her of her success. The money she made as a professional skater allowed her to indulge her tastes pretty freely. And she traveled with her jewelry, always taking care to lock it in safes along the way – except once, which was once too much. During a stopover in San Francisco, her entire collection of jewelry was stolen, right down to her wedding ring.

A theft is not merely a loss of property, it's a form of violation. All of a sudden, this piece of your personal history is gone. People who have, collect, and appreciate jewelry seldom have random collections: each piece has a story, and each piece is meaningful. In Dorothy's case, she tells in her autobiography how at that point in her life, "it was the only thing that I had that was mine. And it brought me great joy and made me feel good about myself."[1]

Can we see this personal loss in her solar return? Jewelry has a long natural rulership association with the planet Venus, so we shall start there. Her natal Venus is peregrine, in Gemini, in the 4ᵗʰ house [SEE EXAMPLE 3-4 ON PAGE 75]. This does not look like an especially strong placement of Venus, which is further confirmed by its squares to Mars and from the Moon, and its trine to Neptune.

However, we should mention one other factor. Dorothy is a Leo, and the metal associated with the sign Leo is gold. So much of fine jewelry contains gold, even if the stone is considered to be the principal interest in the particular piece. When we are reminded of Dorothy's four planets in Leo, we see clearly how it developed that jewelry became so precious to her. In her own account of the theft, and her subsequent feelings, she described how she was ultimately able to take this as a lesson to not become too wrapped up in material objects. Not that it was an easy lesson! But in light

Dorothy Hamill
Chicago, Illinois
Time Zone: 6 hours West

July 27, 1982
41 N 51 87 W 39
Tropical Regiomontanus
Solar Return for July 27, 1982 in Chicago, Illinois

4:10:40 AM
Daylight Saving Time

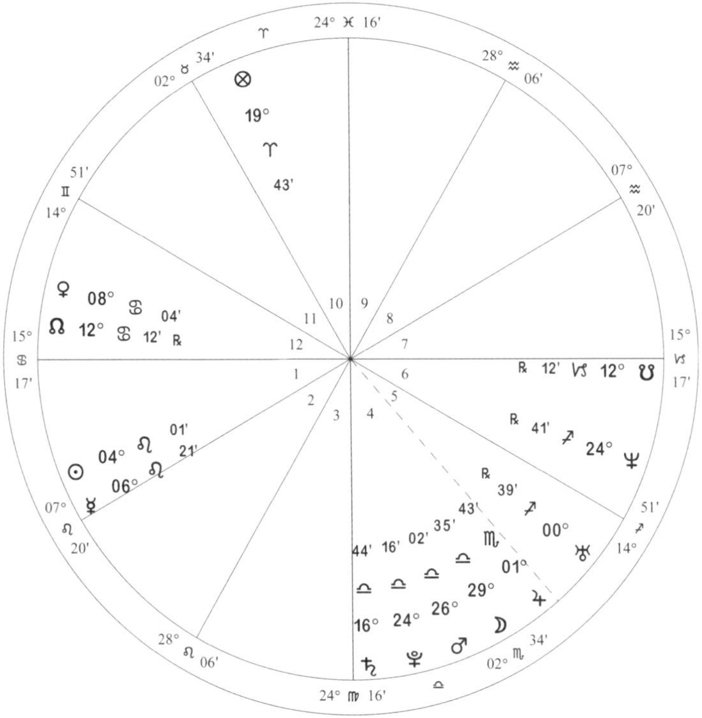

Dorothean Ess. Dig. (No Mut Rec. Points)

Pl	Ruler	Exalt	Tripl	Term	Face	Detri	Fall	Score
☉	☉ +	--	♃	♄	♄	♄	--	+5
☽	♀ m	♄	☿	☊	♃	♂	☉	- 5 P
☿	☉	--	♃	☿ +	♄	♄	--	+2
♀	☽ m	♃	♂	♃	♀ +	♄	♂	+1
♂	♀	♄	☿	☊	♃ m	♂ -	☉	- 10 P
♃	♂	--	♂	♂	♂ m	♀	☽	- 5 P
♄	♀	♄ +	☿	♃	♄ +	♂	☉	+5
☊	☽	♃	♂	♃	☿	♄	♂	--
⊗	♂	☉	♃	☿	☉	♀	♄	--
As	☽	♃	♂	☿	☿	♄	♂	--
Mc	♃	♀	♂	♂	♂	☿	☿	--
☋	♄	♂	☽	♃	♂	☽	♃	--

Hs	Alm. (Pto)
1	☽
2	☉
3	☉
4	☿
5	♂
6	♃
7	♂♄
8	☿♄
9	♄
10	♂
11	☽♀
12	☿

Example 10-1. Dorothy Hamill's Jewelry Loss

of this insight, we may observe that her one natal planet in earth was Jupiter, in detriment in Virgo. Truly, the material world would not easily serve her in this life.

In the solar return for her loss, we have the Sun at the 2nd house cusp along with Mercury in its radix sign. Venus is in the 12th. The Moon is at 29 degrees Libra, just short of going into Scorpio, applying to peregrine Jupiter in Scorpio. The Venus in Triplicity probably shows the quality of her collection rather than anything about the loss, although the 12th house location is suggestive.

But what's missing from this chart? Earth!! This return turns out to mimic Dorothy's natal earth deficit, and even more so. It was SR-Neptune squaring the radix Venus and opposite 1st house Moon-Mars that probably best illustrates the mental slip which left her jewelry unguarded. And shall we call the South Node on the Descendant a harbinger of thieves? Were this a horary delineation, we would be focusing in on the Moon and Mars, the two angular peregrine planets, as possible thieves. The hotel maid testified that she let a man into Dorothy's room when she was gone, knowing full well that it was Dorothy's room and not his. The proximity of the SR-Sun to the 2nd house shows the financial lesson. But while insurance money may prevent this from officially being a loss, Dorothy had a hard lesson in values indeed.

Scott Hamilton's Back Flip

From this title, you might think that this is really very trivial, but guess again. It's easy enough to learn to do a gymnastics back flip, although in my younger days, I certainly never attempted it! But a back flip on ice? Scott discussed the development of the back flip in his autobiography – and it wasn't easy.[2] First, he had to learn how to do the back flip on a gymnastics mat: he learned this from fellow skater Michael Weiss's father, a gymnastics coach (which is perhaps why it's no surprise that Michael is one of the few other skaters who does this move). Then, he needed the help of comedic professional skaters to teach him how to land it on ice, which has the further complications of a very powerful take-off, and a horrendous fall if anything is missed. It took him over a year to learn this. He used the jump in a Pro-Am competition in November 1992, where he placed third. Even placing third, however, he grabbed the headline in the *New York Times* for November 25, 1992, with a byline by Filip Bondy called "Scott Hamilton Takes the Dare, Back Flip and All." Not bad for a third place finish!

The reason that I have chosen to include this as an example is because this back flip became Scott's signature move. The back flip is illegal at an amateur competition, most probably because the take-off can really injure the ice surface, not to mention the possibility of injury to the skater. However, Scott's description of it really makes the point that it is far more appropriate for a professional, meaning, an adult. It requires patience to master, and time – neither of which the average youth is likely to find appealing. It is, however, very flashy, and I would not dispute Scott's contention that he was a much more successful professional skater for having it. Thus, we can see this as an example of achievement following hard work.

Because we are looking at professional achievement, we should probably go right to the 10th house, which is ruled by Venus, with Saturn as Almuten. Venus is in Virgo, in Fall, but with Triplicity. Saturn, however, is dignified by sign and Triplicity. With Saturn in Scott's 2nd house and dignified, this achievement will positively impact his 2nd house financial bottom line. Perfect!

Mars was in a partile square to Jupiter, but also ruling Pluto in a non-**beholding** quincunx.[3] Scott has a natal Sun-Pluto conjunction, so these two configurations surely demonstrate that his competitive juices were flowing just fine.

That was very close to being a New Moon chart for him, which, as we saw in Chapter 2, is a chart that not everybody gets so closely, but if it happens, it happens roughly every nineteen years. Thus, this shows that he was just stepping into a new era of his life. He literally was, one back flip at a time.

Scott Hamilton
Toledo, Ohio
Time Zone: 5 hours West

August 27, 1992
41N39'50" 83W33'19"
Tropical Regiomontanus
Solar Return for August 27, 1992 in Toledo, Ohio

3:21:18 PM
Daylight Saving Time

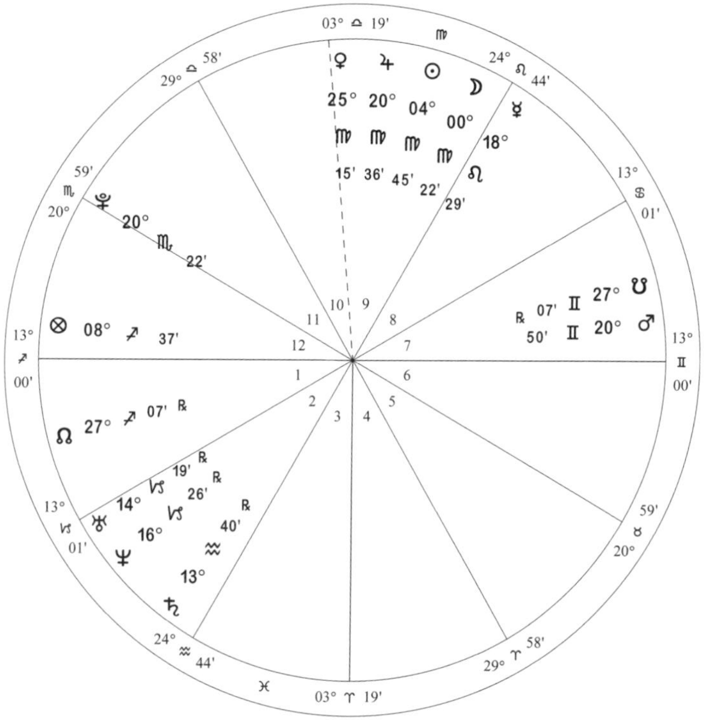

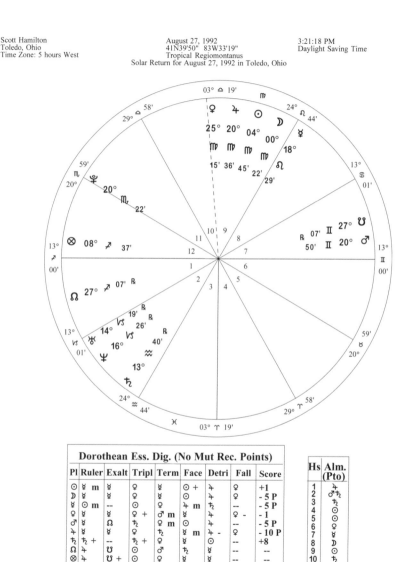

Dorothean Ess. Dig. (No Mut Rec. Points)								
Pl	Ruler	Exalt	Tripl	Term	Face	Detri	Fall	Score
☉	☿ m	☿	♀	☿	☉ +	♃	♀	+1
☽	☿	☿	♀	☿	☉	♃	♀	- 5 P
☿	☉ m	--	☉	♀	♃ m	♄	--	- 5 P
♀	☿	☿	♀ +	♂ m	☿	♃	♀ -	- 1
♂	☿	☊	♄	♀ m	☉	♃	--	- 5 P
♃	☿	☿	♀	♄	☿ m	♃ -	♀	- 10 P
♄	♄ +	--	♄ +	♀	☿	☉	--	+8
☊	♃	☋	☉	♂	♄	☿	--	--
⊗	♃	☋ +	☉	♀	☿	☿	--	--
As	♃	☋	☉	♀	☽	☿	--	--
Mc	♀	♄	♄	♄	☽	♂	☉	--
☋	☿	☊	♄	♂	☉	♃	--	--

Hs	Alm. (Pto)
1	♃
2	♂♄
3	♄
4	☉
5	☉
6	♀
7	☿
8	☽
9	☉
10	♄
11	♄
12	♂

Example 10-2. Scott Hamilton's Back Flip

Martin Luther King's Dream

If we could only still have one speech by Martin Luther King, this would be it. King was an amazing orator, and incredibly moving to hear. But this was the pinnacle. How do you capture the aspirations of a people, and communicate them beyond that group, to others who might either be neutral or even antagonistic toward those hopes? Much less try to find a way, through the expression of these desires, to move forward toward their accomplishment?

It was with this speech alone that King acquired immortality. But this speech was not for himself. It was for an entire community. And it really *was* a dream. So what was Saturn doing on the Descendant in this solar return?

Saturn rules King's natal 9th house: the house of prophetic dreams *[SEE EXAMPLE 6-3 ON PAGE 133]*. While modern astrology would go immediately to Neptune for dreams, ancient astrology distinguished kinds of dreams. Actually, it was considered a completely legitimate horary question to ask if a dream would come true, a usage seldom experienced anymore by modern persons. A prophetic dream was a dream which would come true. Hopes and wishes, long associated with the 11th house, may indicate the desire for an outcome, but desire does not guarantee result.

Thus, King's natal ruling planet of prophetic dreams conjunct the 7th house cusp in his solar return reflects his ability to convey those dreams to the masses, yes, even to his *enemies*. And more poignantly, it was a Mercury dignified by Triplicity conjunct Saturn, with Mercury in its radix sign, the ability to *speak* those dreams. And Mercury is trine the Moon, allowing the fortification of the telling with the emotion behind the story.

The Sun rules the Ascendant – *he* is the subject of this life, and this year. *He* is in the house of slavery, the 6th house. *He* is speaking dreams that he hopes will come true, *must* come true. Mars rules the 9th, even as the Sun has dignity there; Mars is in the 1st; the dream is with him; the dream *is* him. And Mars has dignity only by Face,

Martin Luther King
Atlanta, Georgia
Time Zone: 5 hours West

January 15, 1963
33N44'56" 84W23'17"
Tropical Regiomontanus
Solar Return for January 15, 1963 in Atlanta, Georgia

7:12:31 PM
Standard Time

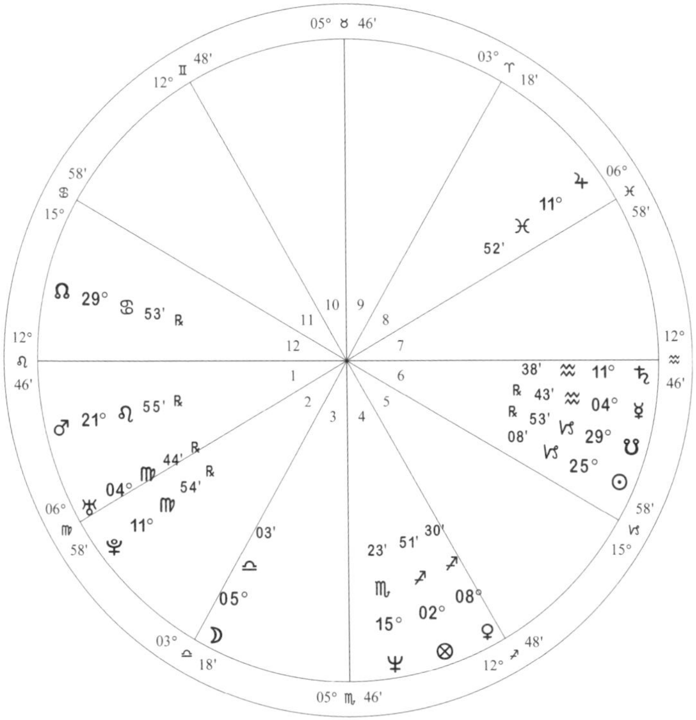

Dorothean Ess. Dig. (No Mut Rec. Points)

Pl	Ruler	Exalt	Tripl	Term	Face	Detri	Fall	Score
☉	♄	♂	☽	♄	☉ +	☽	♃	+1
☽	♀	♄	☿	♄	☽ +	♂	☉	+1
☿	♄	--	☿ +	♄ m	♀ m	☉	--	+3
♀	♃	☋	♃	♀ +	☿ m	☿	--	+2
♂	☉	--	♃ m	♃	♂ +	♄	--	+1
♃	♃ +	♀	♂ m	♃ +	♃ +	☿	☿	+8
♄	♄ +	--	☿	☿ m	☿	☉	--	+5
☊	☽	♃	♂	♄	☽	♄	♂	--
⊗	♃	☋ +	♃	♃	☿	☿	--	--
As	☉	--	♃	☿	♃	♄	--	--
Mc	♀	☽	☽	♀	☿	♂	--	--
☋	♄	♂	☽	♄	☉	☽	♃	--

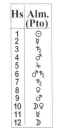

Hs	Alm. (Pto)
1	☉
2	☿
3	♄
4	♂
5	♃
6	♂♄
7	♄
8	♀
9	♂
10	☽♀
11	☿
12	☽

Example 10-3. Martin Luther King's Dream

so he is anxious about this. The angular Mars must be shared as surely as the angular Saturn.

And can we even speculate on the human cost of this dream, as we see the Sun approaching the South Node? Are we seeing the danger of self annihilation in the telling of the dream? This too is possible.

René Lacoste's Racquet

In this chapter, we are seeing life-changing years, whether positively, through initiative and imagination, or negatively, through victimization. The conventional wisdom when it comes to new ideas is that new ideas are the province of the young: that the early work, before the age of forty, captures innovation. Like most conventional ideas, while it may contain a kernel of wisdom, it is not the whole enchilada.

We know that in 1963, René Lacoste produced the first commercially viable metal tennis racquet. This new technology was picked up by Wilson in the USA, where tennis competitors like Jimmy Connors and Billie Jean King exploited its power potential to move the game to new heights of speed and athleticism. Since its introduction, the idea of anyone going back to a wood racquet and winning is simply unthinkable. This invention created a clear Before and After.

Because we know the year of its introduction, and because Lacoste was born in July, we don't actually know which solar return year refers to its public roll-out [SEE EXAMPLE 4-4 ON PAGE 99]. But I have chosen to use his 1962 solar return under the logic that there was an amount of time which went into its production before its public unveiling.

When we do this, what are we confronted with but a New Moon solar return? Here is this man in his late fifties, known for his athletic exploits from his teens and twenties, revolutionizing the sport for which he was known thirty years earlier! And as he lived to the age of 92, it can hardly be said that the experience of a New Moon in his fifties by any means was too late!

The lunation took place in the 12th house. Of course, in theory, it could have taken place in any house, but the definition of the calculation of the Part of Fortune means that it will be conjunct the Ascendant at the time of the New Moon, just as it will be conjunct the Descendant at the time of the Full Moon.

The success of the idea is shown by Jupiter, ruling the 10th in Pisces, one of the signs of its rulership. The Moon in Cancer rules the Ascendant, so this is definitely a good year. The North Node near the 2nd house cusp bodes well for financial outcome.

The New Moon in the 12th I suspect shows the work that occurred behind the scenes, which then allowed the commercial production of the racquet. Lacoste was not the first man to propose a steel racquet: he was the first to create one that could be mass-produced commercially. That meant that he had to work out the dynamics of the racquet, both from a player standpoint, and a manufacturer one. That was actually quite a challenge.

Lacoste's own nativity had an extremely strong 12th house flavor. When he decided to become a serious tennis player, the drive and determination, not to mention the sheer ability to work behind the scenes, allowed him to achieve the results he achieved. Hard work was not something foreign to him when a goal was involved.

The amount of work this invention took is further shown by the partile Saturn-South Node conjunction, especially when in a partile square with Neptune. Since Barbara Watters, there has been a tendency to see partile conjunctions with the Nodes as fated, if not fatal degrees.[4] This is not always the case. This is a dignified Saturn in the same sign as Lacoste's radix Saturn. But if it's not as dangerous as fatal, that doesn't mean one doesn't have to be concerned about the South Node! At the very least, this suggests a *lot* of work to get things right. The square with Neptune suggests to me that there was some real perfectionism going on, because Neptune can so easily represent dissatisfaction and criticality.

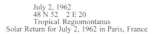

Rene Lacoste
Paris, France
Time Zone: 1 hours East

July 2, 1962
48 N 52 2 E 20
Tropical Regiomontanus
Solar Return for July 2, 1962 in Paris, France

6:14:20 AM
Standard Time

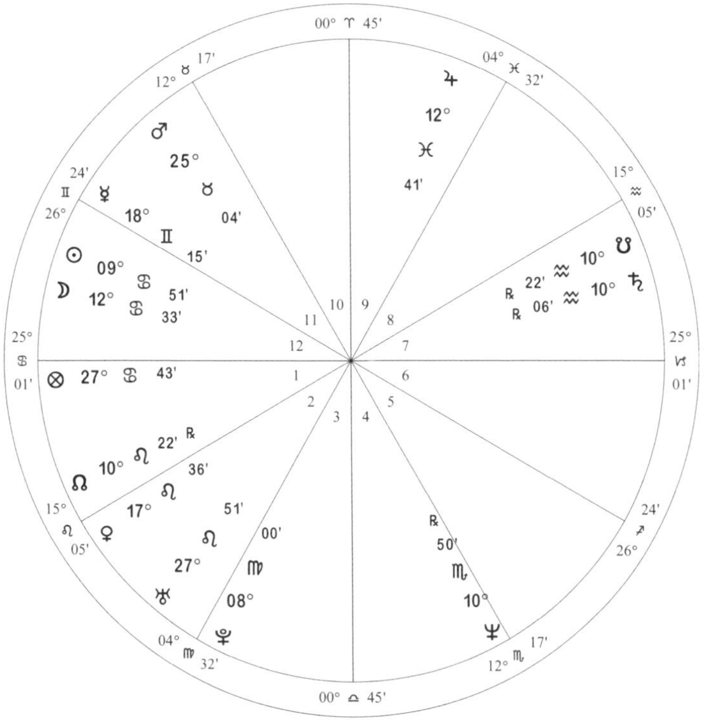

Dorothean Ess. Dig. (No Mut Rec. Points)								
Pl	Ruler	Exalt	Tripl	Term	Face	Detri	Fall	Score
☉	☽	♃	♀ m	♃	♀	♄	♂	- 5 P
☽	☽ +	♃	♀	♃	☿	♄	♂	+5
☿	☿ +	☊	♄	♀	♂	♃	--	+5
♀	☉	--	☉ m	♀ +	♃	♄	--	+2
♂	♀	☽	♀	♄	♄	♂ -	--	- 10 P
♃	♃ +	♀	♀	♃ +	♃ +	☿	☿	+8
♄	♄ +	--	♄ +	☿	☿	☉	--	+8
☊	☉	--	☉	☿	♃	♄	--	--
⊗	☽	♃	♀	♄	☽	♄	♂	--
As	☽	♃	♀	♀	☽	♄	♂	--
Mc	♂	☉	☉	♃	♂	♀	♄	--
☋	♄	--	♄	☿	☿	☉	--	--

Hs	Alm. (Pto)
1	☽
2	☉
3	☿
4	♄
5	♂
6	♃
7	♄
8	♄
9	♀
10	☉
11	♀
12	☿

Example 10-4. René Lacoste's Racquet

Louis Pasteur Discovers Microbiology

It's not everyday that a person gets to create a new field of knowledge. But Louis Pasteur had the kind of brilliant mind where such an outcome was possible. But he didn't set out to do it. Pasteur's biographer notes that in 1856, E. Bigo asked Pasteur to study the production of beet root alcohol, and some of the industrial problems that this production engendered. To this point, Pasteur's work had been in crystallography. However, throughout his life, Pasteur believed that scientists had a civic responsibility to study matters of economic import to their region and their country. He took up the challenge. His background as a physicist and chemist may not at first have been ideal, but his experimental method was impeccable. Along the way, he discovered that fermentation, the process of producing alcohol, was being carried out by tiny single-celled organisms: that it was a process occurring in living organisms, which was not the accepted theory of his day. In the process of publishing three papers on the subject in 1857, he laid down the rules and procedures for studying these microorganisms, thus creating microbiology in the process. We have already studied this solar return in chapters 6 and 8, so now we return to it with the question: can we see something that looks like the discovery of a discipline?

Given that the discipline in question was science, I was immediately drawn to the Mercury-Saturn opposition across the Ascendant-Descendant angles. Why? In the Gauquelin studies of successful professionals, the planet Saturn was associated with scientists: and here it was in a Gauquelin sector! These three papers would all be seen as ground-breaking: hence, Mercury rising also seems appropriate for the *way* that the development of the discipline occurred. [SEE EXAMPLE 4-5 ON PAGE 101 FOR PASTEUR'S NATIVITY]

Louis Pasteur
Dole, France
Time Zone: 0 hours West

December 26, 1856
47 N 06 5 E 30
Tropical Regiomontanus
Solar Return for December 26, 1856 in Dole, France

8:16:48 AM
Local Mean Time

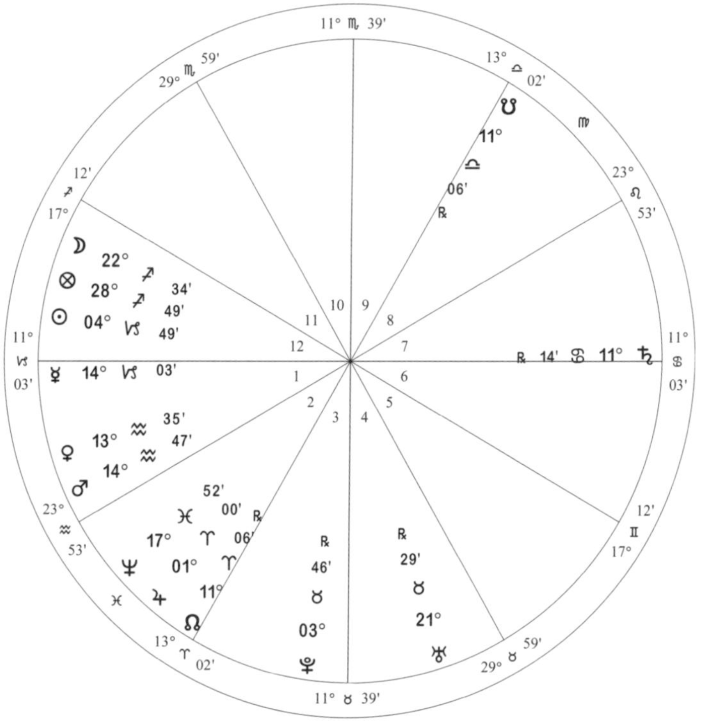

Dorothean Ess. Dig. (No Mut Rec. Points)								
Pl	Ruler	Exalt	Tripl	Term	Face	Detri	Fall	Score
☉	♄	♂	♀	♀	♃	☽	♃	- 5 P
☽	♃	☋	☉	♄	♄	☿	--	- 5 P
☿	♄	♂	♀	♃	♂ m	☽	♃	- 5 P
♀	♄	--	♄ m	♀ +	☿	☉	--	+2
♂	♄	--	♄	♀	☿ m	☉	--	- 5 P
♃	♂	☉	☉	♃ +	♂	♀	♄	+2
♄	☽	♃	♀ m	♃	☿	♄ -	♂	- 10 P
☊	♂	☉	☉	♀	☉	♀	♄	--
⊗	♃	☋ +	☉	♂	♄	☿	--	--
As	♄	♂	♀	☿	♂	☽	♃	--
Mc	♂	--	♀	♃	☉	♀	☽	--
☋	♀	♄	♄	♃	♄	♂	☉	--

Hs	Alm. (Pto)
1	♂♄
2	♄
3	☉
4	♀
5	♀
6	☿
7	♃
8	☉
9	♄
10	♂
11	♂
12	♃

Example 10-5. Louis Pasteur discovers microbiology

Eleanor Roosevelt Arrested

If it could be said that Franklin was following in the family tradition of Progressivism, but giving it a more liberal tint than Uncle Ted had, then Eleanor could be downright radical at times. She was raised to the idea that the privilege of wealth made it her social duty to reach out to those less fortunate, and she took this duty extremely seriously. Especially as she created her own life in the wake of Franklin's affair and his polio, she spoke out forcefully for civil rights, whether women's rights, or those of people of color, to use an expression more in keeping with her time. In 1926, this included being arrested for participating in a women's labor action, which cost her little in reality, but gained great publicity for the cause.

So what is the astrological marker for civil disobedience? This isn't a topic I can recall in any of the old texts! There is a model, though, in some of Lilly's horaries relating to imprisonment.[5] Here, we have the same ruler of the 1st and the 12th. Imprisonment is definitely a 12th house matter, and any connection between 1st and 12th is a bad thing when the topic of imprisonment is possible. I find it fascinating that the planet ruling is Mars, whom Lilly calls a felon.[6] Mars is in Libra: and that pretty much shows the circumstances: not only was Eleanor concerned about justice, but in a sense, she had become like the athletes who thrive on Mars in debility: the kind of fighter with the super-Mars that takes additional risks and fights especially hard. Furthermore, her solar return Sun and Mercury, returned to their radix signs, were in the house of political organizations, the 11th house. She saw herself as a *soldier* (Mars) for a *cause* (11th), further specified by Venus, ruling the 6th house of labor unions, conjunct the Ascendant. *[See Example 3-5 on page 79 for Eleanor's nativity.]*

Furthermore, in her solar return, the Moon was in Leo (public showmanship), in a partile semi-sextile to her own radix Moon, but also in a partile square to her radix Mars. This is as if she truly felt the need to witness for others this year, using her ability to generate headlines to help the cause.

Eleanor Roosevelt
New York, New York
Time Zone: 5 hours West

October 12, 1925
40N42'51" 74W00'23"
Tropical Regiomontanus
Solar Return for October 12, 1925 in New York, New York

9:34:43 AM
Standard Time

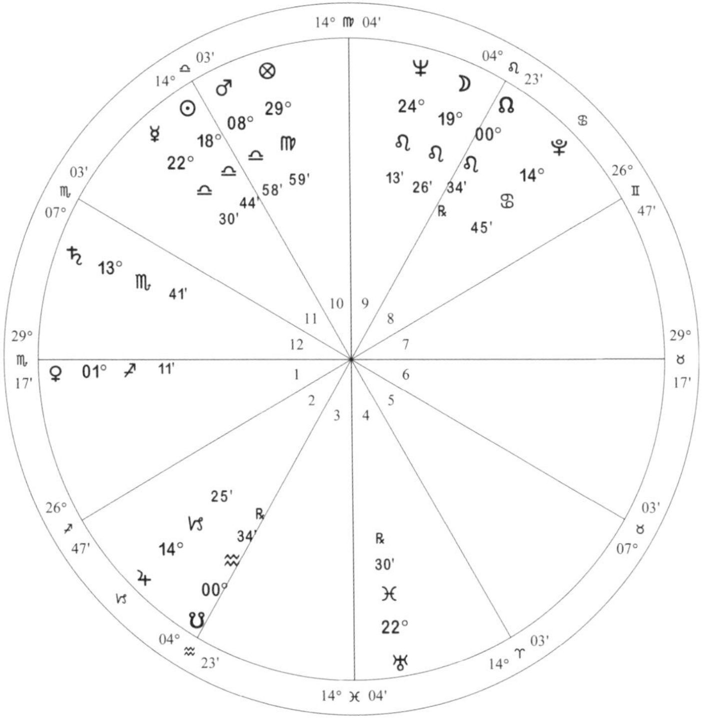

Dorothean Ess. Dig. (No Mut Rec. Points)								
Pl	Ruler	Exalt	Tripl	Term	Face	Detri	Fall	Score
☉	♀	♄	♄	♃	♄ m	♂	☉ -	- 9 P
☽	☉	--	☉	♃	♃	♄	--	- 5 P
☿	♀	♄	♄	☿ +	♃	♂	☉	+2
♀	♃	☋	☉	♃	☿	☿	--	- 5 P
♂	♀	♄	♄	♀	☽	♂ -	☉	- 10 P
♃	♄	♂	♀	♃ +	♂	☽	♃ -	- 2
♄	♂	--	♀	♃	☉ m	♀	☽	- 5 P
☊	☉	--	☉	♄	♄	♄	--	--
⊗	☿	☿	♀	♂	☿	♃	♀	--
As	♂	--	♀	♄	♀	♀	☽	--
Mc	☿	☿	♀	♃	♀	♃	♀	--
☋	♄	--	♄	♄	♀	☉	--	--

Hs	Alm. (Pto)
1	♂
2	♃
3	♄
4	♃
5	☉
6	♀
7	♀
8	☿
9	☉
10	☿
11	♄
12	♂

Example 10-6. Eleanor Roosevelt Arrested

Eleanor Roosevelt resigns from the DAR

Eleanor was quite capable of seeing morality simply, and when she had concluded something was immoral she acted upon it. The Daughters of the American Revolution (DAR) was (and is) a non-profit organization only open to women whose families were settled in the United States prior to the Revolutionary War. Go to their website today, and the organization appears to be about genealogy. This benign purpose today masks a very real fact of discrimination of 19th century America. Today, we call ourselves a nation of immigrants, but earlier, the people eligible for membership in the DAR were horrified at what they saw as wave after wave after wave of immigrants who were "not like them." These immigrants were not from England, Scotland, or the Netherlands, the three usual countries of origin for the families of DAR members. Of course, the DAR had never been open to Native Americans, thereby proving that this really could be relabeled *white* women whose families were settled in the United States prior to the Revolutionary War. And they were not open to blacks. In the society of the 1930s when our tableaux is taking place, white women did not mix socially with black women.

Roosevelt proved herself allergic to discrimination, because she apparently saw people as people first. She was also raised with a profound sense of social justice. This meant that ultimately, she would clash with an organization like the DAR. But she would clash from the inside, because the Roosevelts were one of those old families eligible for membership.

She rapidly discovered that one of the advantages to being First Lady was that she could highlight causes of interest to her. One of those causes that held her attention was the plight of black women. When she was unable to convince her fellow DAR members of her point of view, she resigned in protest, a resignation that received full media attention. Thus, we can see this primarily as a political action.

Eleanor Roosevelt
New York, New York
Time Zone: 5 hours West

October 12, 1938
40N42'51" 74W00'23"
Tropical Regiomontanus
Solar Return for October 12, 1938 in New York, New York

12:51:56 PM
Standard Time

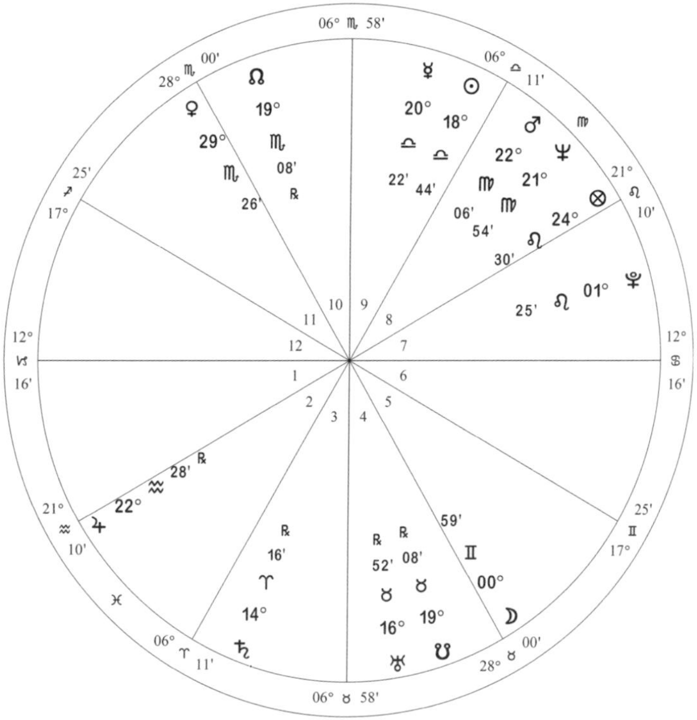

Dorothean Ess. Dig. (No Mut Rec. Points)								
Pl	Ruler	Exalt	Tripl	Term	Face	Detri	Fall	Score
☉	♀	♄ m	♄ m	♃	♄ m	♂	☉ -	- 9 P
☽	☿	☊	♄	☿	♃ m	♃	--	- 5 P
☿	♀	♄	♄	☿ +	♃	♂	☉	+2
♀	♂	--	♀ +	♄	♀ +	♀ -	☽	- 1
♂	☿	☿	♀	♄	☿	♃	♀	- 5 P
♃	♄	--	♄	♃ +	☽ m	☉	--	+2
♄	♂	☉ m	☉ m	☿	☉ m	♀	♄ -	- 9 P
☊	♂	--	♀	♀	☉	♀	☽	--
⊗	☉	--	☉	♃	♂	♄	--	--
As	♄	♂	♀	♃	♂	☽	♃	--
Mc	♂	--	♀	♃	♂	♀	☽	--
☋	♀	☽	♀	♃	☽	♂	--	--

Hs	Alm. (Pto)
1	♂♄
2	♄
3	☉
4	♀
5	♀
6	☿
7	♃
8	☉
9	♀♄
10	♂
11	♂
12	♃

Example 10-7. Eleanor Roosevelt resigns from the DAR

So that raises the question: what rules political action? Unlike our civil disobedience example that we just covered, there's no threat of the law in this case, no threat of incarceration. The answer is: we don't have a classical model for this, so we will have to use logic to construct a new one. Since Eleanor's action was to resign from an organization, that *must* bring in the 11th house. In fact, we could choose to see this as the relationship between 1st and 11th: Eleanor and the organization.

And how appropriate. The 11th house cusp is Scorpio, so the organization is Mars in Virgo, where it has mixed Triplicity, but the conjunction to Neptune. Also, right in the 11th house is Venus in Scorpio, mixed between Detriment and Triplicity. Eleanor is Saturn in Aries: she's on the warpath, and a Saturn in Aries is fundamentally an angry person. That Saturn is opposite her Sun, whereas in her radix, these two planets are trine. With Mars ruling both the 10th and 11th, any such dispute was bound to be very public, which of course it was.

Percy Shelley's Break-In

How would we look at the propensity for violence in a nativity? Or for the likelihood of being the victim of theft, or any other crime?

The difficulty with this question is to consider whether isolated events set up a pattern for the life. And this is not to say that an event cannot have so profound an impact that there literally is Before and After. So perhaps other ways we could ask this question of the nativity would be:

- Are there natal factors so strong that they preclude ever having the possibility of a break-in or violence?
- Are there natal factors so strong that they scream that violence or crime is a major theme of the chart, whether as a perpetrator, victim, or profession (as in, the police)?

If neither of the strong scenarios is present, there is still the possibility of a temporary configuration that would argue for these effects. In this case, the condition may last for a year or two but, while it may cause ripples within the life, the result would probably not be a major theme.

It's difficult to know what to do with this in the case of Percy, because ten years after this year, he would be dead. Percy had already lived two-thirds of his life: but it could not possibly have felt like this was true.

The basic model we should begin with would be afflictions from Mars. Mars was the planet of mayhem and murder. In his nativity, Percy had the triple conjunction of Mars, Jupiter, and Neptune in a sign where Mars was in Detriment and Jupiter had Triplicity *[SEE EXAMPLE 3-7 ON PAGE 84]*. In the older parlance, the greater dignity of Jupiter would make it the dominant partner in the conjunction, although I might question that the absolute value of the debility probably makes Mars dominant in a negative way. One could make the point that Percy's erotic desires did not seem tempered at all by any concerns for his sexual partners: either their reputations, or their ease.

However, conjunctions to malefics are not generally classified as being of equally baleful character as squares and oppositions. Percy's Sun is conjunct Venus, which made him generally more likable, surely. The Mars conjunctions are in the 6th, which again isn't very strong. So I'd say that Percy's natal does not have a strong argument of crime or violence.

However, on the other hand, there is the Sun-Uranus! It's always worth remembering that what to us non-possessors may seem strange or extreme always feels normal to the possessor. There are two common manifestations of a Sun-Uranus: a short attention span, and what we might call unself-consciously outrageous speech. The short attention span in a slower era might simply be characterized as restlessness: which Percy had. The second may be classified as saying whatever comes to mind, regardless of the consequences. A

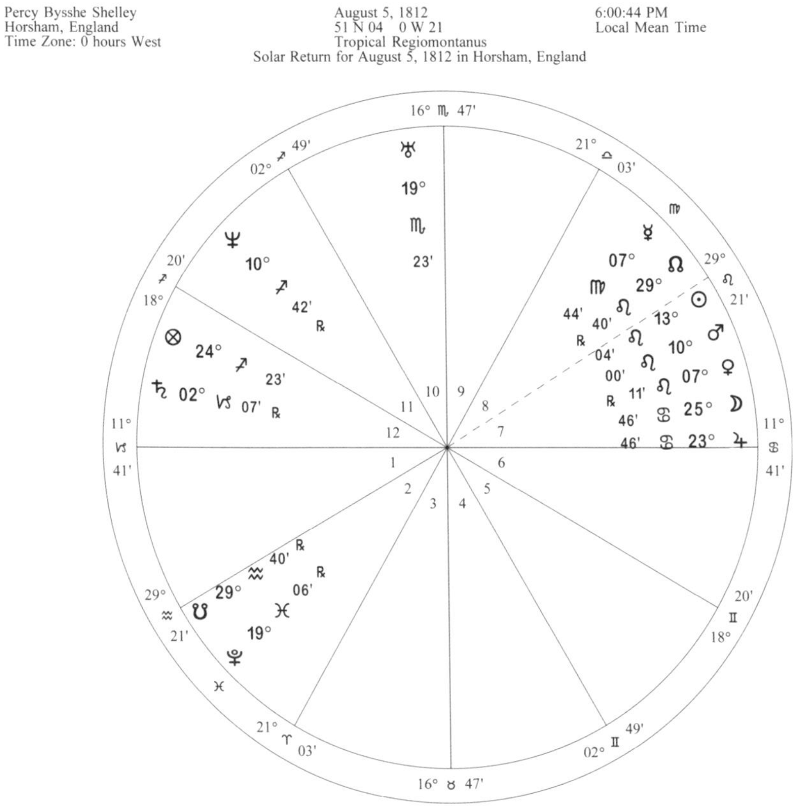
Percy Bysshe Shelley
Horsham, England
Time Zone: 0 hours West
August 5, 1812
51 N 04 0 W 21
Tropical Regiomontanus
Solar Return for August 5, 1812 in Horsham, England
6:00:44 PM
Local Mean Time

Dorothean Ess. Dig. (No Mut Rec. Points)

Pl	Ruler	Exalt	Tripl	Term	Face	Detri	Fall	Score
☉	☉ +	--	☉ +	♀	♃	♄	--	+8
☽	☽ +	♃	♀	♀	☽ +	♄	♂	+6
☿	☿ +	☿ +	♀	♀ m	☉	♃	♀	+9
♀	☉	--	☉	☿ m	♄	♄	--	- 5 P
♂	☉	--	☉	☿	♃	♄	--	- 5 P
♃	☽	♃ +	♀	♀	☽	♄	♂	+4
♄	♄ +	♂	♀	♀	♃	☽	♃	+5
☊	☉	--	☉	♂	♂	♄	--	--
⊗	♃	☋ +	☉	♄	♄	☿	--	--
As	♄	♂	♀	☿	♂	☽	♃	--
Mc	♂	--	♀	♀	☉	♀	☽	--
☋	♄	--	♄	♂	☽	☉	--	--

Hs	Alm. (Pto)
1	♂♄
2	♄
3	☉♂
4	♀
5	☿
6	☿
7	♃
8	☉
9	♄
10	♂
11	♃
12	♃

Example 10-8. Percy Shelley's Break-In

Sun-Uranus would find it difficult to impossible to filter speech to moderate the impact of what is said. The Native is virtually naive about the effect of such speech.

In Percy's case, when he discovered atheism, his Sun-Uranus would tell everybody within a two-mile radius his new revelation. It would absolutely never occur to him that anybody might actually take offense at whatever he said. This constitutional cluelessness would make it absolutely impossible for him to understand the effect of his words on others. *This* tendency could have major negative impact on his reputation whenever he would express a strong opinion.

Zoom in on solar year 1812. In horary analysis, personal danger is shown through the 7th house.[7] The 7th house is also the default ruler of a thief, if no more appropriate planet can be found.[8] Theft is the only form of crime typically mentioned in the ancient texts, except for Mars ruling murderers.[9] These ideas suggest that, in a particular year, afflictions by Mars, or to the 7th house, may be interpreted as possible indicators of the threat of crime. Notice, however, that these are not the only interpretations. Afflictions to the 7th house, as we have already seen, can also indicate problems with one's significant other.

In 1812, Percy was married to Harriet, and there *were* problems: Harriet was not thrilled with Percy's infidelities, and not thrilled when Percy tried to set up alternate partners for her either. Percy's 7th house was certainly full, including a combust peregrine Mars. The preferred planet over the 7th house ruler for a thief was a peregrine planet in an angle; here Mars fits the bill, plus being Mars adds the dimension of violence as a possibility, simply because violence is in the nature of Mars.

If we begin a conventional analysis of this year, the Moon in the 7th, ruling the 7th from the sign of Cancer was a good thing. In the old parlance, it meant his wife was virtuous in this year. By such conventional standards, Harriet appears to have been a virtuous wife; it's just not clear that Percy *wanted* a virtuous wife. In this year when the Moon was also conjunct Jupiter in Cancer, its exaltation sign, she gave birth to a daughter.

But then there's a second theme in the 7th house, the Venus-Mars conjunction also combust and peregrine. It may be great for the Sun to have companions, but that means the companions are combust, and that is not an indicator of fine, upstanding companions, especially when they are peregrine. Add to this configuration a second one: a very strong Mercury square Neptune. Percy seemed never at a loss for words, and this was his natal Mercury sign. But the square to Neptune meant that he was even more disconnected than usual from the emotional impact of his words. It is a sad commentary on human nature that persons for whom the word is their primary method of expression (like writers) are so naive in understanding that the human body seems wired to a direct connection between the ear and the fist. Wordsmiths often believe that words either do not hurt, or can only be responded to by a verbal riposte. Their listeners may find more direct methods to respond.

Thus, for a person like Percy who clearly enjoyed saying whatever he wanted, the idea that his words could literally enrage somebody to the point of violence or worse, is a difficult lesson. This combination in his solar return gives the set-up for that lesson to occur. His biographer states that the armed break-in he experienced that year could well have been an assassination attempt. Based on this solar return, I believe it.

But also based on this solar return, he survived, and I am afraid he didn't learn the lesson either. The danger is further shown by the North Node conjunct the 8th house cusp. Mercury in the 8th in this configuration does hint that his mouth was working against his interests, given the square to Neptune: that his words were dangerous, literally. But the survival? The Sun is in the 7th, but not conjunct either 7th or 8th cusp. The Sun is not conjunct death on the 8th house side, or the Portals of Death for the 7th house cusp. Saturn, ruling the Ascendant, joys in the 12th, and is dignified in Capricorn, although the retrogradation again implies some imbecility for the year.

My conclusion is thus that Percy's tendency to speak unchecked could well have set up the break-in, which may not have been a formal assassination attempt, but perhaps "that will teach him a lesson." But really, neither Saturn nor Sun seem so afflicted that this was probably much other than a temporary inconvenience for him.

In our next chapter, we shall consider the topic most difficult for us to discuss: death.

Chapter 10 Endnotes

1. Hamill, p 157.
2. Scott explained what was involved in Chapter 7 of: Hamilton, Scott. *The Great Eight : How to Be Happy (Even When You Have Every Reason to Be Miserable)*. Nashville, Tenn.: Thomas Nelson, Inc., 2008.
3. See *CAML*, Chapter 9, for a refresher on the beholding and non-beholding aspects.
4. See Watters, Barbara H. *Horary Astrology and the Judgment of Events*. [Washington]: Valhalla, 1973.
5. See Lilly, *Christian Astrology*, pp 461-465, 470-471.
6. Lilly, *Christian Astrology*, p 464.
7. Lilly, *Christian Astrology*, pp 366-368.
8. al-Biruni, p 276; Lilly, *Christian Astrology*, p 331.
9. Ptolemy, *Tetrabiblos* (Loeb), p 185; Lilly, *Christian Astrology*, p 66.

11

Solar Returns for Death

THIS CHAPTER ENCOMPASSES TWO TOPICS: THE ACTUAL DEATH OF THE NATIVE, AND THE DEATH OF PEOPLE CLOSE TO THE NATIVE. But before we proceed with these topics, I need to clarify our definitions. Death was a common topic in a classical astrological reading – there were none of the restrictions that modern astrology has placed on the discussion of this topic. In saying this, I am neither justifying the ancient program, nor criticizing the modern attempt to place ethical constraints upon this subject.

As I noted in *Traditional Medical Astrology*, any discussion of death is best done within the context of remembering that "death" means that the person would have died in the 17th century, given the same medical circumstances. Death is in part a matter of demographics. When we compare our society to that earlier European one, they had much higher infant and childhood mortality than we do now. Death from childbirth was relatively common. However, if one lived to be forty, one had a good chance of living into one's sixties – or beyond.

The significance of this is that everyone who lives past infancy experiences a series of blockages in the life: and a certain number of these can be understood to be what I like to call "exit visas" –

times when the individual is challenged to transform or to die.[1] We come up against the fact that part of our adaptation mechanism is no longer working. While we could be making adjustments to our behavior throughout our lives, inertia means that we will tend to stay within the patterns we have already adopted. Sometimes, that isn't enough to cope with our environment. An illness can result, and if one is sufficiently out-of-sync with what is happening, we can become ill, or even die. On the other hand, we can recuperate from the illness: but if the mechanisms are still in place which allowed the illness to manifest in the first place, then the inevitable result may simply be postponed. We are stressed in our lives, we eat a bad diet, we expose ourselves to toxic substances, and get no exercise – and then we get sick. Do we ignore the warning and just pop pills, or do we change anything? If we don't change anything, the chances are, we will get another wake up call, with this one being bigger than the last one. This is what I mean by an exit visa.

In my opinion, it is possible to astrologically predict the exit visa times, but it's not possible to predict what one will do about it. So it would be true to say that on an absolute level, we cannot predict death, but we can predict deathly *weather*, so to speak. And if we can find a way to talk about this process with our clients, and not run from perceived ethical considerations, then we may be helping our clients enormously.

Please notice that I am not trivializing the ethical issues. If there is one thing that we should have learned from psychology, it is the brain's almost infinite capacity to create its own reality. As such, it is completely possible to talk oneself into the idea that this is The Big One, and so create the psychological conditions that turn the possibility of death into the probability of death, and then into the certainty of death. It is not unusual to have exit visas *every decade* of the life, and sometimes more so. While modern astrology might highlight the times of Outer Planet hard aspects, the classical system had more specific ideas.

Here we will examine the solar returns for people who have died – but also for people who have faced the kind of danger which *could* result in death. In *Traditional Medical Astrology*, I give the example of actress Mary Martin's experience of a taxi accident, in which one of her fellow passengers was killed and she personally experienced serious injury. This is an exit visa moment. One cannot entirely say *why* Mary Martin didn't die. And from the outside, we never can.

From a practical standpoint, if we don't always die when we encounter an exit visa moment, then what can we legitimately say to our clients about this? At the very least, we can say that the chart indicates that the stress level for the period is high enough that illness or accident is strongly indicated if they cannot identify and reduce the cause(s) of the stress. We can indicate that this represents a time when it is important to work to resolve impasses – outmoded processes or behaviors that are a drag on the life.

Working historically, we have seen that the exit visa not taken was also a possibility in the past. One of the examples we shall consider in this Chapter was from our old friend Morinus – a solar return year of his that he gave in the *Astrologia Gallica*

as likely to have fatal consequences for him – but which he outlived. And having said this, we should not view Morin as a lesser astrologer for having outlived a chance to die! There is a story related by Derek Walters that we should take to heart. He was discussing how Jerome Cardan's reputation as an astrologer was enhanced by the belief that he had predicted the time of his death. And yet, there was a Chinese astrologer in the 20th century who perceived a personal exit visa. In studying the matter, he determined that only by adhering to a very unusual living circumstance could he fulfill the conditions of the period of time and still live. So he did. This required sacrificing his position and life in the city, and moving to a remote location. After the period of danger, he re-emerged. But the knowledge of the changes that he had made and their consequences enhanced his reputation, and he became even more eminent in his field. Derek's point was obviously to make us consider that a correct death prediction is a pyrrhic victory at best. Personally, I would hope to have the serenity and conviction of the Chinese sage, when next this challenge comes my way.

Arguments of an Exit Visa in a Solar Return	Morin	Gadbury[2]
The Lights conjoined in the 4th or 7th give the death of a parent		✓
Ruler of the revolutionary Ascendant retrograde in the 8th can bring sickness unto death[3]		✓
An eclipse near the degree of the Sun, Moon or Ascendant portends death		✓
Saturn and Mars conjunct in the revolutional 10th brings the death of the mother, and loss of honor	✓	
Aries on the revolutionary Ascendant brings fear of a violent death	✓	
Revolutionary Ruler of the 8th in square or opposition to the Ascendant Ruler is danger of death		✓

Arguments of an Exit Visa in a Solar Return	Morin	Gadbury
Revolutionary Ruler of the 8th in the 1st is a danger of death		✓
Revolutionary Ruler of the Ascendant in the 8th afflicted by malefics is danger of death	✓	✓
Ruler of the radix 4th or 8th square or opposite the Revolutionary Ruler of the Ascendant is danger of death	✓	✓
Revolutionary Sun and Saturn in opposition to each other across the the 2nd and 8th is grave danger of death		✓
Radix 8th house Ruler as Ruler of the Ascendant means danger of death	✓	
Revolutionary Ruler of the 12th at the 8th house cusp is an argument of death	✓	

In addition to the general aphorisms given above, Gadbury gave a specific series for the 8th house.

1. The Lord of the eighth House in Quartile or Opposition to the Lord of the Ascendant or Moon from evil places of the Figure, denotes great danger of death unto the Native in that year.

<...>

3. When the Lord of the Nativity happens to be an Infortune, and posited in the Ascendant of a Revolution, it presages great danger of death unto the Native in that year.

4. An Eclipse of the Sun in the place of the South Node in the Radix, happening in the very same degree, declares that the Native shall die that year: but if it happen to be near the same degree, he will onely be in danger of death.

5. An Eclipse in any of the Angles of the Radix, chiefly in the Ascendant, in the very degree thereof, threatens great danger of death unto the Native.

6. When Saturn in a Nativity shall be in a fiery Signe, and the Significator of life in a Watry or Earthy, and both these in Opposition in a Revolution, it denotes in that year danger of death unto the Native.

7. The Lord of the Ascendant afflicted of evil Planets in the eighth House of a Revolution, denotes danger unto the Native in that year. If the Luminaries are in Opposition at the same time, or in Opposition to the Lord of the Ascendant, it portends the death of the Native.

8. Good planets in Conjunction with the Moon or Lord of the Ascendant in the eighth, denotes gain unto the Native by Inheritances, or by Wills and Legacies of persons deceased; sometimes a rich dowry with a Wife. If they be in sextile or trine (from good parts of the Figure) with good Planets, chiefly if it happen that the Lord of the eighth be a good Planet, it then portends the same to the Native.

9. The Lord of the eighth and fourth in the Radix in Opposition or Quartile of the Lord of the Ascendant in the Revolution, portends unto the Native danger of death in that year; if they afflict the Lord of the second after the same manner, it denotes much loss of Substance to the Native in that year, by Wills, Legacies, &c.

10. When the Ascendant of the Revolution shall be the eighth in the Radix, it denotes great peril of death in that year: If the sixth of the Radix shall ascend in the Revolution, it will be a sickly year.

11. The Sun and Saturn in Opposition from the second and eighth Houses of a Revolution, denote unto the Native death in that year....

12. When the Significator of Life shall be corporally afflicted of the Malefiques in an Angle, chiefly in the seventh House, they denote great danger of death unto the Native in that year. If the Sun and Saturn shall be in Quartile from the fourth and first Houses, they portend the same..."[4]

Solar Returns with Exit Visas

Mary Shelley's solar return for 1822: miscarriage with hemorrhaging.

On June 16, 1822, Mary Shelley had a miscarriage with so much loss of blood that she nearly died. It was Percy's insistence in getting her into a bath of very cold water that saved her life. This was not her only miscarriage, but it was the only one that was extremely dangerous for her. [SEE EXAMPLE 3-3 ON PAGE 71 FOR MARY'S NATIVITY.]

Taking place in June 1822, it fell within her 1821 solar return. The chart for her solar return is dramatically dangerous: Mars in Fall is in the 5th (hemorrhaging from childbirth), ruling the 8th house of death. The South Node is only a few degrees from the 7th house cusp, the Portals of Death.

In this solar return year:

- Venus is in her natal sign (age 24, divisible by 8)
- The Moon is conjunct natal Fortuna
- Jupiter is trine natal Mars (*lots* of blood), ruler of radix 6th, trine Neptune, trine natal Mars, and sextile natal Pluto
- Saturn is trine natal Moon
- Pluto is opposite natal Mercury and square natal Moon
- Uranus is conjunct natal Moon and square natal Mercury
- The natal ruler of the 8th house is the solar return Ascendant ruler

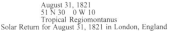

Mary Shelley
London, England
Time Zone: 0 hours West

August 31, 1821
51 N 30 0 W 10
Tropical Regiomontanus
Solar Return for August 31, 1821 in London, England

6:29:03 PM
Local Mean Time

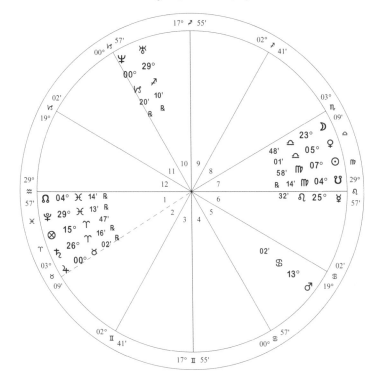

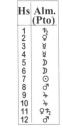

Dorothean Ess. Dig. (No Mut Rec. Points)								
Pl	Ruler	Exalt	Tripl	Term	Face	Detri	Fall	Score
☉	☿ m	☿	♀	♀	☉ +	♃	♀	+1
☽	♀	♄	♄	☿	♃	♂	☉	- 5 P
☿	☉ m	--	☉	♂ m	♂ m	♄	--	- 5 P
♀	♀ +	♄	♄	♄	☽	♂	☉	+5
♂	☽	♃	♀	☿ m	☿ m	♄	♂ -	- 9 P
♃	♀	☽	♀	♀	☿	♂	--	- 5 P
♄	♂	☉	☉	♄ +	♀	♀	♄ -	- 2
☊	♃	♀	♀	♀	♄	☿	☿	--
⊗	♂	☉	☉	☿	☉	♀	♄	--
As	♄	--	♄	♂	☽	☉	--	--
Mc	♃	☋	☉	☿	☽	☿	--	--
☋	☿	☿	♀	☿	☉	♃	♀	--

Hs	Alm. (Pto)
1	♄
2	♀
3	☿
4	☿
5	☽
6	☽
7	☉
8	♂
9	♃
10	♃
11	♀♄
12	♂

Example 11-1. Mary Shelley's solar return for 1821: miscarriage with hemorrhaging.

This is definitely a dangerous chart. As for what changed in her life, sadly we know. Less than a month later, her husband Percy was drowned in a boating accident. Now the affliction to the 7th house becomes clear. What also is clear is that Mary herself genuinely was in danger this year. What we see is a very strong 1st – 7th emphasis. Percy's death had an immediate impact on Mary's finances, quite apart from the usual expectations of the time. Percy's grandfather completely disapproved of their marriage, and while convention had required him to give Percy an allowance, Mary would have to fight for continued support for their son. This is also when her writing had to transition to supporting herself financially.

Mary Shelley's Death

For the solar return year of Mary Shelley's death, 1850, the SR-Moon was within a degree of the position of the Solar return IC. Saturn, radix ruler of her 8th house is in the SR-1st house, opposed by Venus, ruler of her natal 12th. What is interesting is that the 1821 exit visa and her actual death year both show a strong 1st – 7th axis: an emphasis not otherwise found in her natal chart.

We have seen the death aphorisms that the Sun opposed by Saturn is a dangerous configuration: here we have Sun-Neptune, which surely cannot be any better. This year has the following features:

- The SR-Sun is in the SR-6th house of illness.
- Sickness in the solar return is ruled by the Moon, at the SR-IC.
- The greater benefic Jupiter is in Detriment, partile square her natal Moon, and ruler of the SR-Ascendant.
- The SR-Mercury-Mars conjunction was square her natal Ascendant.
- SR-Venus had returned to its natal sign, but unfortunately was opposite Saturn.

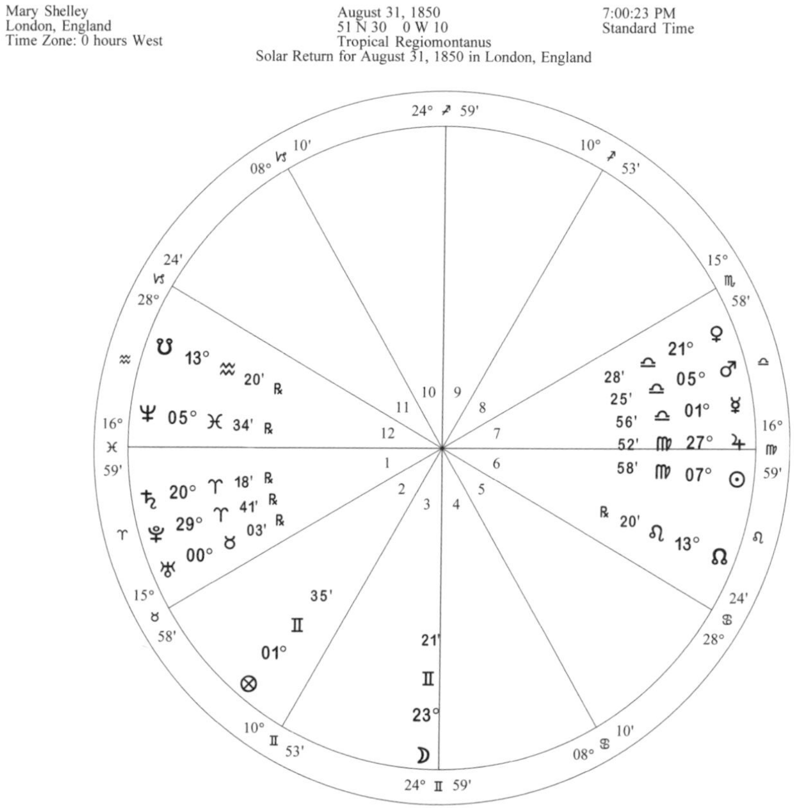

Mary Shelley
London, England
Time Zone: 0 hours West
August 31, 1850
51 N 30 0 W 10
Tropical Regiomontanus
Solar Return for August 31, 1850 in London, England
7:00:23 PM
Standard Time

Dorothean Ess. Dig. (No Mut Rec. Points)								
Pl	Ruler	Exalt	Tripl	Term	Face	Detri	Fall	Score
☉	☿	☿	☽	♀	☉ +	♃	♀	+1
☽	☿	☊	☿	♄	☉	♃	--	- 5 P
☿	♀	♄	☿ +	♄ m	☽	♂	☉	+3
♀	♀ +	♄	☿	☿	♃	♂	☉	+5
♂	♀	♄	☿	♄	☽	♂ -	☉	- 10 P
♃	☿	☿	☽	♂	☿	♃ -	♀	- 10 P
♄	♂	☉	♃	☿ m	♀	♀	♄ -	- 9 P
☊	☉	--	♃	♀	♃	♄	--	--
⊗	☿	☊	☿	☿	♃	♃	--	--
As	♃	♀	♂	☿	♃	☿	☿	--
Mc	♃	☋	♃	♄	♄	☿	--	--
☋	♄	--	☿	♀	☿	☉	--	--

Hs	Alm. (Pto)
1	♃
2	☽
3	☿
4	☿
5	♃
6	☽
7	☿
8	♂
9	♃
10	♃
11	♄
12	♄

Example 11-2. Mary Shelley's Death, 1850

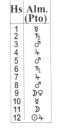

This year had a very difficult configuration, but honestly not worse than the prior exit visa year, 1821.

Jane Austen's Death

It's not always possible to identify which events are the exit visas. From what we know of Jane Austen – and this is problematic because her family chose to destroy a lot of documentation in their quest for the perfect Aunt Jane – Jane spent far more time as nurse than being nursed. Her nativity shows Jupiter ruling the 6th house, in Detriment and imbecilic, but rendered by Saturn [*see Example 6-2 on page 131*]. Having a benefic ruling the 6th house natally is very advantageous, because the worst diseases tend to be caused by the malefics. In *Traditional Medical Astrology*, I noted that malefics associated with the 6th house is a classic signature for lifelong health problems. The fact that her 8th house ruler is well-dignified shows that death will not be very quick – and it wasn't, as her condition deteriorated for months.

The year of her death, a very dignified Saturn was sitting right on the 6th house cusp. She was ill for that year. Although Saturn was dignified, it was conjunct her natal South Node.

In this solar return year:

- Solar return Mars, her radix 8th house ruler, was conjunct the South Node
- Mercury was in its natal sign
- The SR-Sun was in its radix house, but *not* conjunct the IC
- SR-Mercury, the SR-Ascendant ruler, was conjunct Neptune and combust – and partile square Pluto
- SR-Saturn was partile trine its natal position
- The SR- South Node was transiting her natal Mercury
- SR-South Node was conjunct the SR-IC

There was a strong interaction here with the natal chart, but not so much because of absolute similarity. The solar return

Jane Austen
Steventon, England
Time Zone: 0 hours West

December 16, 1816
51 N 13 1 W 13
Tropical Regiomontanus
Solar Return for December 16, 1816 in Steventon, England

10:50:56 PM
Standard Time

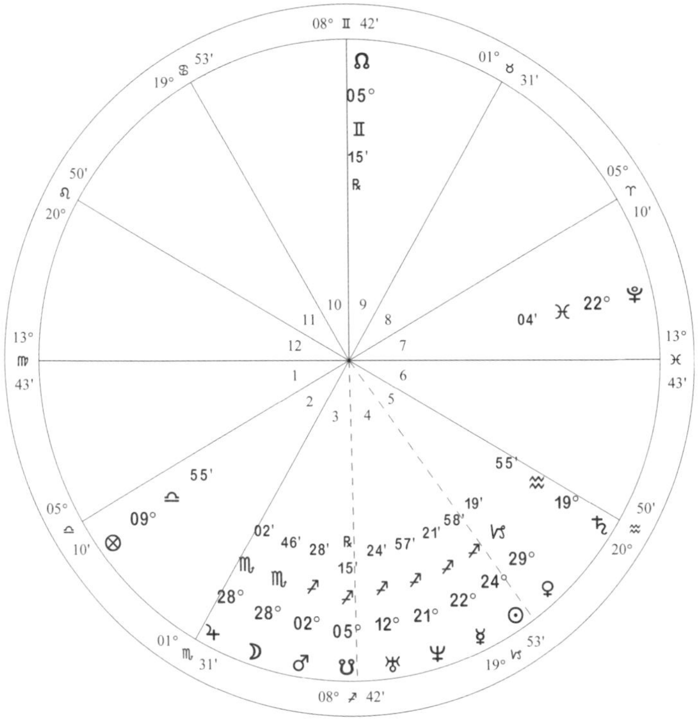

Dorothean Ess. Dig. (No Mut Rec. Points)								
Pl	Ruler	Exalt	Tripl	Term	Face	Detri	Fall	Score
☉	♃	☋	♃	♄	♄	☿	--	- 5 P
☽	♂	--	♂	♄	♀	♀	☽ -	- 9 P
☿	♃	☋	♃	♄	♄ m	☿ -	--	- 10 P
♀	♄	♂	☽	♄ m	☉	☽	♃	- 5 P
♂	♃ m	☋	♃ m	♃	☿	☿	--	- 5 P
♃	♂ m	--	♂ m	♄	♀	♀	☽	- 5 P
♄	♄ +	--	☿	♀ m	☿ m	☉	--	+5
☊	☿	☊ +	☿	☿	♃	♃	--	--
⊗	♀	♄	☿	♀	☽	♂	☉	--
As	☿	☿	☽	♃	♀	♃	♀	--
Mc	☿	☊	☿	♃	♃	♃	--	--
☋	♃	☋	♃	♃	☿	☿	--	--

Hs	Alm. (Pto)
1	☿
2	♄
3	♂
4	♃
5	♂
6	♄
7	♃
8	♂
9	☽♀
10	☿
11	☽
12	☉♃

Example 11-3. Jane Austen's Death, 1816

Rene Lacoste
Paris, France
Time Zone: 1 hours East

July 1, 1996
48 N 52 2 E 20
Tropical Regiomontanus
Solar Return for July 1, 1996 in Paris, France

12:18:11 PM
Daylight Saving Time

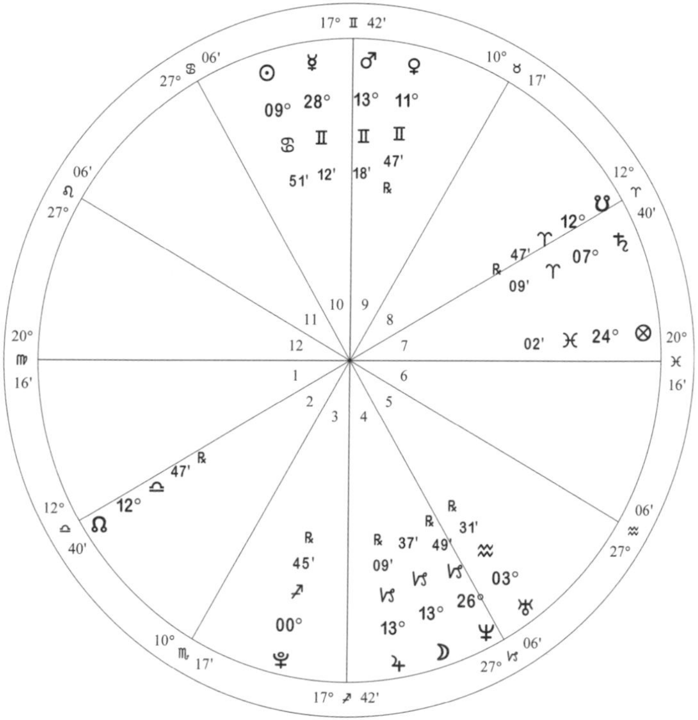

Dorothean Ess. Dig. (No Mut Rec. Points)								
Pl	Ruler	Exalt	Tripl	Term	Face	Detri	Fall	Score
☉	☽	♃	♀	♃	♀	♄	♂	- 5 P
☽	♄	♂	♀	♃	♂	☽ -	♃	- 10 P
☿	☿ +	☊	♄	♂	☉	♃	--	+5
♀	☿	☊	♄	♃	♂	♃	--	- 5 P
♂	☿	☊	♄	♃	♂ +	♃	--	+1
♃	♄	♂	♀	♃ +	♂	☽	♃ -	- 2
♄	♂	☉	☉	♀	♂	♀	♄ -	- 9 P
☊	♀	♄	♄	♃	♄	♂	☉	--
⊗	♃	♀	♀	♂	♂	☿	☿	--
As	☿	☿	♀	♄	☿	♃	♀	--
Mc	☿	☊	♄	♀	♂	♃	--	--
☋	♂	☉	☉	♀	☉	♀	♄	--

Hs	Alm. (Pto)
1	☿
2	♄
3	♂
4	♃
5	♄
6	♄
7	♃
8	☉
9	♀
10	☿
11	☽
12	☉

Example 11-4. René Lacoste's Death, 1996

does show Jane's debilities for the year, through the Saturn placement.

René Lacoste's Death

Lacoste lived what we would all agree was a long life. His natal chart would not at first suggest this *[SEE EXAMPLE 4-4 ON PAGE 99]*. He had a strong 12th house. In his own life experience, Lacoste was a supreme self-starter: he himself admitted that he was not a natural athlete, but he taught himself how to perform at the top by supreme conditioning, which was unusual at the time.

Saturn ruled his natal 8th, and it was dignified in the 8th. At its best, Saturn ruling the 8th does suggest death via the diseases of old age. This, however, was no guarantee. In his twenties he developed a lung condition which ended his playing days, and appeared to be akin to tuberculosis.

In the year of his death, none of the planets, with the exception of the Sun, was in their natal signs in the solar return. Only Saturn, ruler of the 8th natally, was in the SR-8th, by the 5 degree rule. The solar return chart has a partile conjunction of the Moon and Jupiter, both in debility, and posited in the 4th house. The South Node conjunct the 8th house cusp and the Moon-Jupiter at the bendings is a pretty strong statement, as is Saturn square Venus and the Sun of his radix chart.

Eleanor Roosevelt: An Exit Visa and her Death

At the age of two, Eleanor Roosevelt and her parents were in the shipwreck of the *Britannic* – all of them survived. Examining Eleanor's natal chart reveals that she could have drowned, given the Moon in Cancer so close to the 8th house cusp – a definite suggestion of water related to death *[SEE EXAMPLE 3-5 ON PAGE 79]*. This example is of particular interest to us with the theory of exit visas, because at age 2, we could hardly attribute great powers of choice to Eleanor, but rather loving attention on the part of her parents. But here, we demonstrate that exit visas can occur at any age, and it is not at all clear that the default is to go through the door.

At age 2, Eleanor's SR-Ascendant was almost exactly her natal 8th house cusp: a very dangerous signal. Furthermore, Saturn in Detriment in Cancer was very close to the SR-Ascendant: and that Saturn ruled the SR-8th house. This is one more argument of danger that year. The SR-Moon was in Aries opposite SR-Uranus in the 4th, which is not a bad descriptor for a shipwreck.

That year, Eleanor had:

- SR-Mercury in its natal sign
- Ruler of the 8th in the 1st
- SR-Sun Square Saturn
- SR-Moon opposite Uranus

Her father, the parent Eleanor felt closer to, is shown as prominent in this chart, with the SR-4th house ruler Venus in the 4th and dignified by sign.

The chart for 1962, the actual year of her death, does not look worse than the year of the shipwreck. But exit visa it was, with SR-Saturn in a partile conjunction with the South Node. In this year, the configuration included:

- SR-Saturn was partile conjunct the SR-South Node, SR-Mars opposed SR-Saturn. SR-Mars was the ruler of the SR-Ascendant.
- Mercury ruled the SR-8th, and was being opposed by SR-Moon, which was in partile sextile to the SR-Saturn-South Node conjunction. Additionally, the SR-Mercury was in its natal sign – but retrograde. The Moon was the ruler of the 8th in the radix, and here in the solar return, natal 8th house ruler Moon comes to opposition with SR-8th house ruler Mercury.

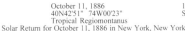

Eleanor Roosevelt
New York, New York
Time Zone: 5 hours West
October 11, 1886
40N42'51" 74W00'23"
Tropical Regiomontanus
10:36:45 PM
Standard Time
Solar Return for October 11, 1886 in New York, New York

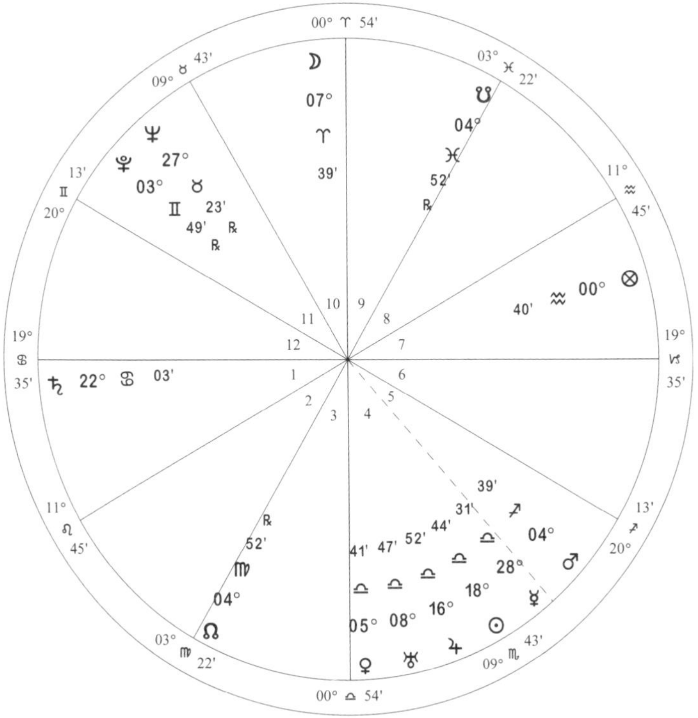

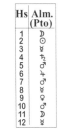

Dorothean Ess. Dig. (No Mut Rec. Points)								
Pl	Ruler	Exalt	Tripl	Term	Face	Detri	Fall	Score
☉	♀	♄	☿	♃	♄	♂	☉ -	- 9 P
☽	♂	☉	♃	♀	♂	♀	♄	- 5 P
☿	♀	♄	☿ +	☊	♃	♂	☉	+3
♀	♀ +	♄	☿	♄ m	☽	♂	☉	+5
♂	♃	☋	♃	♃	☿	☿	--	- 5 P
♃	♀	♄ m	☿	♃ +	♄	♂	☉	+2
♄	☽	♃ m	♂	♀ m	☽	♄ -	♂	- 10 P
☊	☿	☿	☽	☿	☉	♃	♀	--
⊗	♄	--	☿	♄	♀	☉	--	--
As	☽	♃	♂	☿	☿	♄	♂	--
Mc	♂	☉	♃	♃	♂	♀	♄	--
☋	♃	♀	♂	♀	♄	☿	☿	--

Hs	Alm. (Pto)
1	☽
2	☉
3	☿
4	♄
5	♂
6	♃
7	♂
8	☿
9	♀
10	♂
11	☽
12	☿

Example 11-5a. Eleanor Roosevelt: an Exit Visa and her Death, 1886

Eleanor Roosevelt
New York, New York
Time Zone: 5 hours West

October 12, 1962
40N42'51" 74W00'23"
Tropical Regiomontanus
Solar Return for October 12, 1962 in New York, New York

9:29:32 AM
Daylight Saving Time

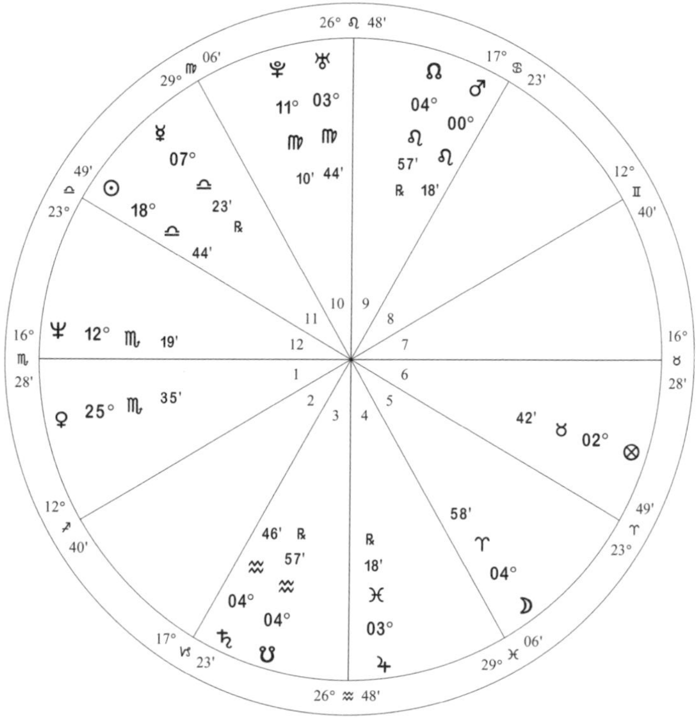

Dorothean Ess. Dig. (No Mut Rec. Points)								
Pl	Ruler	Exalt	Tripl	Term	Face	Detri	Fall	Score
☉	♀	♄	♄	♃	♄	♂	☉ -	- 9 P
☽	♂	☉	☉	♃	♂	♀	♄	- 5 P
☿	♀	♄	♄	♀ m	☽	♂	☉	- 5 P
♀	♂	--	♀ +	☿ m	♀ +	♀ -	☽	- 1
♂	☉	--	☉	♄	♄	♄	--	- 5 P
♃	♃ +	♀	♀	♀	♄	☿	☿	+5
♄	♄ +	--	♄ +	♄ +	♀	☉	--	+10
☊	☉	--	☉	♄	♄	♄	--	--
⊗	♀	☽	♀	♀	☿	♂	--	--
As	♂	--	♀	♀	☉	♀	☽	--
Mc	☉	--	☉	♂	♂	♄	--	--
☋	♄	--	♄	♄	♀	☉	--	--

Hs	Alm. (Pto)
1	♂
2	♃
3	♂♄
4	♄
5	♃
6	☉♂
7	♀
8	☿
9	☽
10	☉
11	☿
12	♄

Example 11-5b. Eleanor Roosevelt: an Exit Visa and her Death, 1962

There are a couple of notes to be said about this that don't fit into the routine format. I mentioned that the cause of death was tuberculosis, but that was only determined upon autopsy: the original cause of death was listed as something else. Perhaps here we have some of the confusion suggested by the Neptune rising. At the time, it was not known that tuberculosis could be harbored within the body for so many years, as Eleanor had contracted the disease in her late teens. When the symptoms disappeared shortly thereafter, it was *assumed* she was permanently cured.

But is there any way to see the danger from the tuberculosis long-term? I believe there is. The usual rulership of the lungs is Jupiter, given by many sources going back as far as Ptolemy. Presumably, part of the justification was the large size of the lungs. However, Lilly also listed the sign Cancer,[5] as did Saunders.[6] A couple of other sources like Partridge also gave Mercury for lung *disease*.[7] If the use of Mercury as a ruler seems strange, remember that traditional medicine operated using the contraries as well as the similars; so within this system, a Mercury-ruled herb could potentially treat a Jupiter-ruled condition, because Mercury's sign rulerships (Gemini and Virgo) and Jupiter's (Sagittarius and Pisces) are opposite. Actually, there is something to say about this whole cluster in Eleanor's chart. Her natal 6th house ruler was Venus in Virgo which, given the debility, was likely to manifest as a problem. Pluto in Gemini was in the 6th natally. Jupiter has emphasis in her natal chart through her Sagittarius Ascendant.

In her last solar return, a number of these symbols reassembled. Jupiter was in her 4th, dignified but retrograde. Mercury has returned to its natal sign, while the Moon comes to oppose Mercury. SR-Uranus was partile conjunct her natal Venus, ruler of the 6th.

Percy Shelley's Less than Excellent Adventure

We return to just after Mary Shelley had her miscarriage where she almost died. It was Percy's quick action that saved her. Percy must

Percy Bysshe Shelley
Horsham, England
Time Zone: 0 hours West

August 5, 1821
51 N 04 0 W 21
Tropical Regiomontanus
Solar Return for August 5, 1821 in Horsham, England

10:05:02 PM
Local Mean Time

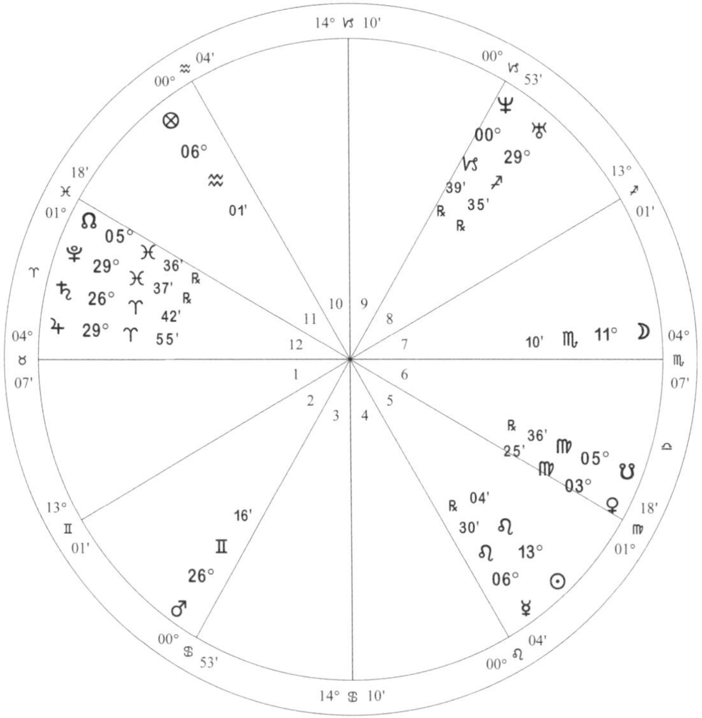

Dorothean Ess. Dig. (No Mut Rec. Points)								
Pl	Ruler	Exalt	Tripl	Term	Face	Detri	Fall	Score
☉	☉ +	--	♃	♀	♃	♄	--	+5
☽	♂	--	♂	♃	☉	♀	☽ -	- 9 P
☿	☉	--	♃	☿ +	♄	♄	--	+2
♀	☿	☿	☽	☿	☉	♃	♀ -	- 9 P
♂	☿	☊	☿	♂ +	☉	♃	--	+2
♃	♂	☉	♃ +	♄	♀	♀	♄	+3
♄	♂	☉	♃	♄ +	♀	♀	♄ -	- 2
☊	♃	♀	♂	♀	♄	☿	☿	--
⊗	♄	--	☿	☿	♀	☉	--	--
As	♀	☽	☽	♀	☿	♂	--	--
Mc	♄	♂	☽	♃	♂	☽	♃	--
☋	☿	☿	☽	☿	☉	♃	♀	--

Hs	Alm. (Pto)
1	☽♀
2	☿
3	☽
4	☽
5	☉
6	☿
7	♂
8	♃
9	♄
10	♂♄
11	♄
12	♀

Example 11-6. Percy Shelley's Less than Excellent Adventure, 1821

have felt enormous relief when she recovered, since it is doubtful that they could ever completely forget that Mary's mother had died giving birth to her.

Shortly afterwards, Percy embarked on a sailing trip, which proved fatal to him. Percy's natal 8th house cusp was ruled by Jupiter, which was in a partile conjunction with Mars *[SEE EXAMPLE 3-7 ON PAGE 84]*. He did not appear to have a lot of vitality, judging from the calculation of these matters.[8] A Mars-Jupiter conjunction in the 6th, may suggest a degree of recklessness that could be dangerous.

The solar return for the year shows both his wife's danger and his death. The danger to his wife is shown by the SR-Moon so close to his Descendant, and in Scorpio. This was not going to be an easy year for Mary with that configuration. But what about Percy? His year shows as this:

- Percy's SR-Ascendant is within only a few degrees of his natal Ascendant.
- SR-Venus, ruling SR-Ascendant, applies to a conjunction with the South Node.
- The SR-South Node is partile conjunct the natal Mercury.
- The partile Uranus-Pluto square in the solar return is also square/opposite his natal Fortuna.
- The solar return has a Mars-Uranus opposition in the 2nd-8th.
- That SR-Mars is partile Percy's natal Bendings

The preponderance of planets in the 6th, 8th, and 12th of the solar return at the very least suggests that Percy's judgment about what is and isn't dangerous is impaired in this year.

Morinus Had Lots of Exit Visas

Poor Jean-Baptiste Morin. He quite simply led a colorful life. In putting a couple of examples of my own life in this book, I am a paragon of boredom compared to our esteemed earlier colleague, who escaped certain death on quite a few occasions. However, I have chosen only two years from his later life to examine here: 1649, the year that he published in *Astrologia gallica* as likely his last (but he outlived it); and 1656, the year he actually died. The latter year was previously examined by Anthony Louis using slightly different reasoning, and so perhaps this may also be an interesting exercise for students of classical astrology to examine differences in methods.

Morinus picked 1649 as his fatal year, but we shall refer to it as an exit visa. Because this year was in his future when he wrote his *magnum opus*, we don't know what actually happened, apart from the fact that he survived it.

In 1649, we have a nasty Mars-Saturn square from the 6th to the 2nd, with Saturn conjunct the North Node. We also see Pluto there, which Morin of course would not have known. The South Node is quite close to the 8th house cusp, and we see Uranus and Neptune there as well. Those factors by themselves would qualify as an exit visa. Notice that Jupiter rules the 8th in both natal and solar return *[SEE EXAMPLE 2-3 ON PAGE 41]*. Jupiter in the 6th is retrograde, and disposed by an angry Venus in Detriment in the 12th, ruling the Ascendant. There isn't much to like about this chart except the trine between the Sun and the Moon, and the fact that he actually survived it.

Morin gave the following arguments for his probable death in 1646:

- There would be an eclipse that year square his radix Sun and Jupiter, which rule his natal 6th and 8th houses, respectively
- In primary directions, the Sun directed to square Saturn, Jupiter is directed to the Moon
- The Moon would be in the place of radix Mars[9]

The actual year of his death, 1656, honestly doesn't look as bad as 1649. Anthony begins his discussion of 1656 by attempting to reconstruct the delineation of fever as the cause of death as given in a

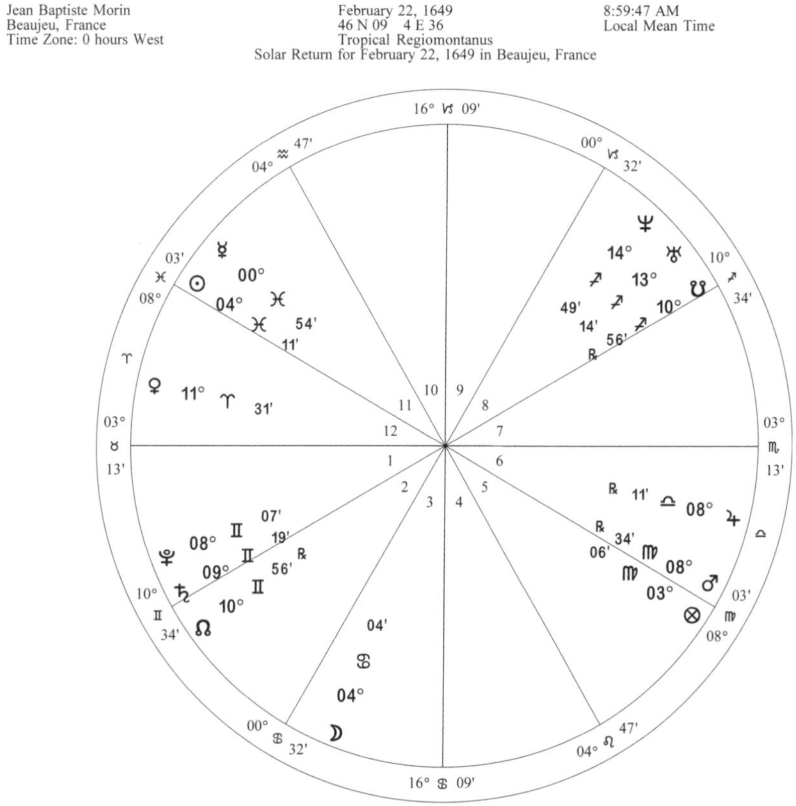
Jean Baptiste Morin
Beaujeu, France
Time Zone: 0 hours West
February 22, 1649
46 N 09 4 E 36
Tropical Regiomontanus
8:59:47 AM
Local Mean Time
Solar Return for February 22, 1649 in Beaujeu, France

Dorothean Ess. Dig. (No Mut Rec. Points)								
Pl	Ruler	Exalt	Tripl	Term	Face	Detri	Fall	Score
☉	♃	♀ m	♀ m	♀	♄	☿	☿	- 5 P
☽	☽ +	♃	♀	♂	♀	♄	♂	+5
☿	♃	♀	♀	♀	♄	☿ -	☿ -	- 14 P
♀	♂	☉ m	☉ m	♀ +	☉	♀ -	♄	- 3
♂	☿	☿	♀	♀	☉	♃	♀	- 5 P
♃	♀	♄	♄	♀	☽	♂	☉	- 5 P
♄	☿	☊	♄ +	♃	♃	♃	--	+3
☊	☿	☊ +	♄	♃	♂	♃	--	--
⊗	☿	☿	♀	☿	☉	♃	♀	--
As	♀	☽	♀	♀	☿	♂	--	--
Mc	♄	♂	♀	♃	♂	☽	♃	--
☋	♃	☋	☉	♀	☽	☿	--	--

Hs	Alm. (Pto)
1	♀
2	☿
3	☽
4	☽
5	☉
6	☿
7	♂
8	♃
9	♀♄
10	♂♄
11	♄
12	♃

Example 11-7a. Morinus had lots of Exit Visas: 1649

Jean Baptiste Morin
Beaujeu, France
Time Zone: 0 hours West

February 23, 1656
46 N 09 4 E 36
Tropical Regiomontanus
Solar Return for February 23, 1656 in Beaujeu, France

1:39:03 AM
Local Mean Time

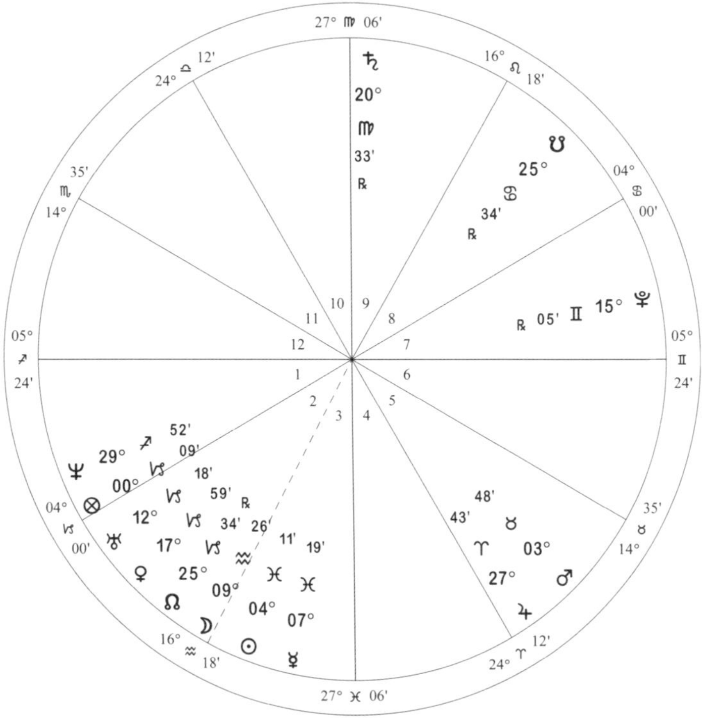

Dorothean Ess. Dig. (No Mut Rec. Points)								
Pl	Ruler	Exalt	Tripl	Term	Face	Detri	Fall	Score
☉	♃	♀	♂	♀	♄	☿	☿	- 5 P
☽	♄	--	☿	☿	♀	☉	--	- 5 P
☿	♃	♀	♂	♀	♄ m	☿ -	☿ -	- 14 P
♀	♄	♂	☽	♃	♂	☽	♃	- 5 P
♂	♀	☽	☽	♀	☿	♂ -	--	- 10 P
♃	♂	☉	♃ +	♄	♀	♀	♄	+3
♄	☿	☿	☽	♄ +	☿ m	♃	♀	+2
☊	♄	♂	☽	♄	☉	☽	♃	--
⊗	♄	♂	☽	♀	♃	☽	♃	--
As	♃	☋	♃	♃	☿	☿	--	--
Mc	☿	☿	☽	♂	☿	♃	♀	--
☋	☽	♃	♂	♀	☽	♄	♂	--

Hs	Alm. (Pto)
1	♃
2	♄
3	♄
4	♃
5	♂
6	☽
7	☿
8	☽
9	☉
10	☿
11	♀
12	♂

Example 11-7b. Morinus had lots of Exit Visas: 1656

brief description by Thomas Callanan, which sadly is unreferenced.[10] Anthony concludes the natal chart could show this because Jupiter, ruler of the 8th, and Venus, intercepted ruler of the 1st, are combust – and because the Sun itself is conjunct the 12th house.

I would suggest a different historical approach. First, it is not at all clear to me that the ancients put that much faith into determining the cause of death in the way that it tends to obsess us, in great part because we operate under the premise that there are things we can do to reduce our chances of dying of a particular condition, such as ingesting lots of anti-oxidants to help prevent cancer.[11] But quite apart from whether they were that concerned about it, the pathway to fever is much more direct. Jupiter ruled Morin's 8th house. Jupiter was listed as a ruler of fever almost as much as Mars.[12] The presence of Jupiter in Pisces would tend to increase the likelihood of sweating with the fever, thereby giving it a higher moisture, like the qualities of Jupiter itself. So fever as a cause of death is definitely within reason here.

Morin's natal chart has a very loaded 12th house, so perhaps that explains at least some of his "adventures." As Anthony notes, Morin's own calculations showed an Ascendant of 27 Aries (we get 21 Aries for the same time), so SR-Jupiter, ruler of his radix 8th was conjunct the natal Ascendant. That's a pretty profound hit. The Sun was square the SR-Ascendant, and SR-Jupiter is at the SR-Bendings – with the SR-South Node in the 8th house.

Theodore Roosevelt: The Rough Rider Had It Rough

Theodore Roosevelt, being the epitome of the late 19th century ideal of the manly man, practically worked to put himself in danger. His adventures as a Rough Rider that made him famous and set up his presidency may have been brash and bold, but he was hardly in combat for an extended period. But where his luck really failed was with his 1913 expedition to South America. After his failed presidential attempt, and after the assassination attempt, he embarked on an expedition to South America, where he expected to write a chronicle, for which he would be paid. What actually happened was that he injured his leg, developed an infection, and then developed malaria on top of it. He worried that keeping him alive was endangering the rest of the expedition. It was only the determination of his son Kermit which got him out alive, although TR afterwards said that the trip took ten years off his life.

As an exit visa year, this had a lot going for it:

- SR-Moon was partile square natal Moon
- SR-Pluto was square SR-Ascendant
- SR-Moon square Mars
- SR-Mars opposite radix Mars, with Mars ruling the SR-8th house
- Sun square SR-Uranus (perhaps the leg injury accident?)

What probably saved him was the 1st house Moon trine Saturn in Triplicity, where Saturn ruled Kermit. *[See Example 2-4 for T. Roosevelt's nativity on page 43.]*

We may compare 1913 to the exit visa that TR actually took, given by his solar return of 1918. In this fatal solar return, he had:

- 29 degrees rising
- Mercury ruling the 8th trine Jupiter, a planet in the 8th
- Moon conjunct Saturn in Detriment
- Sun at the 12th house cusp
- SR-Mars, co-almuten of the natal 8th in the SR-1st, and ruling the SR-Ascendant

None of these factors alone makes it an exit visa, but like 1913, there was an accumulation of arguments. He was diagnosed with inflammatory rheumatism in November, and died of a heart attack the following January.

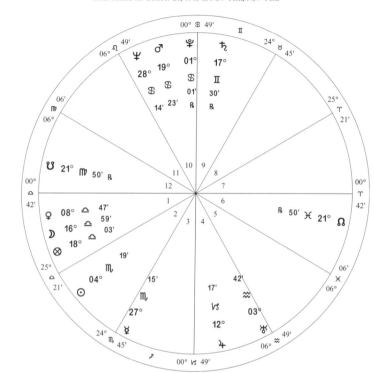

Theodore Roosevelt
New York, New York
Time Zone: 5 hours West

October 28, 1913
40N42'51" 74W00'23"
Tropical Regiomontanus
Solar Return for October 28, 1913 in New York, New York

3:35:15 AM
Standard Time

Dorothean Ess. Dig. (No Mut Rec. Points)								
Pl	Ruler	Exalt	Tripl	Term	Face	Detri	Fall	Score
☉	♂	--	♂	♂	♂	♀	☽	- 5 P
☽	♀	♄	☿	♃	♄	♂	☉	- 5 P
☿	♂	--	♂	♄	♀	♀	☽	- 5 P
♀	♀ +	♄	☿	♀ +	☽	♂	☉	+7
♂	☽	♃ m	♂ +	☿	☿	♄	♂ -	- 1
♃	♄	♂ m	☽	♃ +	♂	☽	♃ -	- 2
♄	☿	☊	☿	♀	♂	♃	--	- 5 P
☊	♃	♀	♂	♂	♂	☿	☿	--
⊗	♀	♄	☿	♃	♄	♂	☉	--
As	♀	♄	☿	♄	☽	♂	☉	--
Mc	☽	♃	♂	♂	♀	♄	♂	--
☋	☿	☿	☽	♄	☿	♃	♀	--

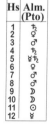

Hs	Alm. (Pto)
1	♄
2	♀
3	♂
4	♄
5	☿♄
6	♀
7	♂
8	♂
9	☽
10	☽
11	☉
12	☿

Example 11-8a. Theodore Roosevelt: The Rough Rider Had It Rough, 1913

Theodore Roosevelt
New York, New York
Time Zone: 5 hours West

October 28, 1918
40N42'51" 74W00'23"
Tropical Regiomontanus
Solar Return for October 28, 1918 in New York, New York

8:35:44 AM
Standard Time

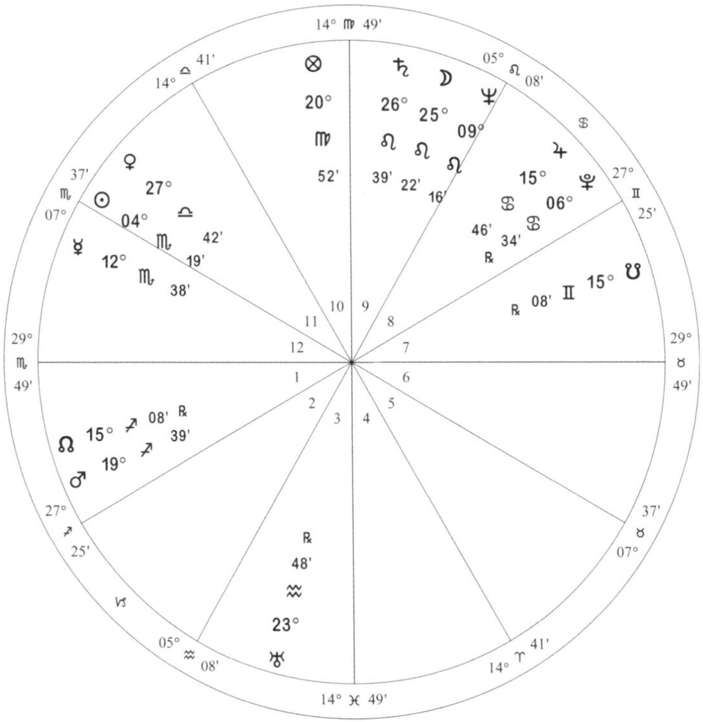

Dorothean Ess. Dig. (No Mut Rec. Points)								
Pl	Ruler	Exalt	Tripl	Term	Face	Detri	Fall	Score
☉	♂	--	♀	♂	♂	♀	☽	- 5 P
☽	☉	--	☉	♂	♂ m	♄	--	- 5 P
☿	♂	--	♀	♃ m	☉	♀	☽	- 5 P
♀	♀ +	♄	♄	☊	♃	♂	☉	+5
♂	♃	☋	☉	♄ m	☽ m	☿	--	- 5 P
♃	☽	♃ +	♀	☿ m	☿	♄	♂	+4
♄	☉	--	☉	♂ m	♂	♄ -	--	- 10 P
☊	♃	☋	☉	☿	☽	☿	--	--
⊗	☿	☿	♀	♄	☿	♃	♀	--
As	♂	--	♀	♄	♀	♀	☽	--
Mc	☿	☿	♀	♃	♀	♃	♀	--
☋	☿	☊	♄	♀	♂	♃	--	--

Hs	Alm. (Pto)
1	♂
2	♃
3	♄
4	♃
5	☉
6	♀
7	♀
8	☿
9	☉
10	☿
11	♄
12	♂

Example 11-8b. Theodore Roosevelt: The Rough Rider Had It Rough, 1918

Solar Returns for the Deaths of Others

We may only die once in a lifetime, but if we live for any length of time, we will have years where we are distressed by the deaths of others close to us. So it is to this second theme of death that we now turn.

Let us begin by asking whether this idea of exit visas has any relevance to the astrology of second-hand death. The answer seems to be that it could. If you live through your loved one's exit visa consciously, you may face almost as much unpleasantness and emotional angst as they do. Obviously, in that case, there is no mourning at the end, more likely relief, but the lead-up can be devastating. However, here we will concentrate on actual deaths.

Buzz Aldrin's Mother's Suicide

About a year before Buzz Aldrin went to the Moon, his mother evidently committed suicide through an overdose. Buzz's father, who was also in the military, survived her. It is extremely likely that the depression that Buzz talks about himself in *Magnificent Desolation* also affected her.

When we look for the death of a loved one in the chart of a survivor, the patterns are somewhat different than for the person's own death. The typical allocation of parents by rulership in the traditional period was that the mother was ruled by the 10th house, and the father by the 4th. While that may, at first, seem opposite to one's expectations, one of the primary arguments for the father's associations with the 4th house is the land, or to use the somewhat archaic term, the patrimony.

At first, Buzz's life followed the pattern of military father producing military son. In his biography, Buzz does not sound like he felt especially close to his father, but there certainly was some commonality of experience. In his natal chart, Buzz's mother is read through Jupiter, ruler of the 10th, while his father is Mercury, ruler of the 4th house *[SEE EXAMPLE 3-1]*. His mother is shown as being a secret enemy to him (remember that in reading others from the Native's chart, we are not seeing them, but how they interact with the Native). She is Jupiter in Gemini retrograde in his 12th house: a weak, imbecilic influence. This is not to say he didn't love her: Jupiter (her) is trine Mercury (him, as the Ascendant ruler). This configuration would suggest that, despite their mutual feelings for each other, she had difficulty reaching him, and what she would try often backfired (the 12th house placement at the same time that their significators were trine). That's the base or natal configuration.

Enter 1968. Buzz had:

- A Mercury-ruled Ascendant, like his natal chart
- Neptune conjunct the IC, as in his natal
- Mercury in the same sign as the natal
- Jupiter in Detriment and retrograde, as in the natal (but in Mercury's other sign)
- The Moon in the same sign as the natal
- SR-Saturn partile conjunct natal Uranus and square natal Saturn

These relationships are enough to declare this year more significant than most. But what of his mother? Venus rules his SR-10th – the mother – and the death of the mother is given from the SR-5th house, meaning, the 8th from the 10th. Here, SR-Saturn in Detriment rules his mother's death and is in the unturned SR-8th, bringing the issue of the possibility of the mother's death into focus. To confirm its import, the SR-Moon is just approaching the opposition to that Saturn. Both these bodies are square his natal Saturn, ruler of the radix 8th. And as we saw, SR-Saturn is partile conjunct natal Uranus: a sudden event that could be the death of the mother.

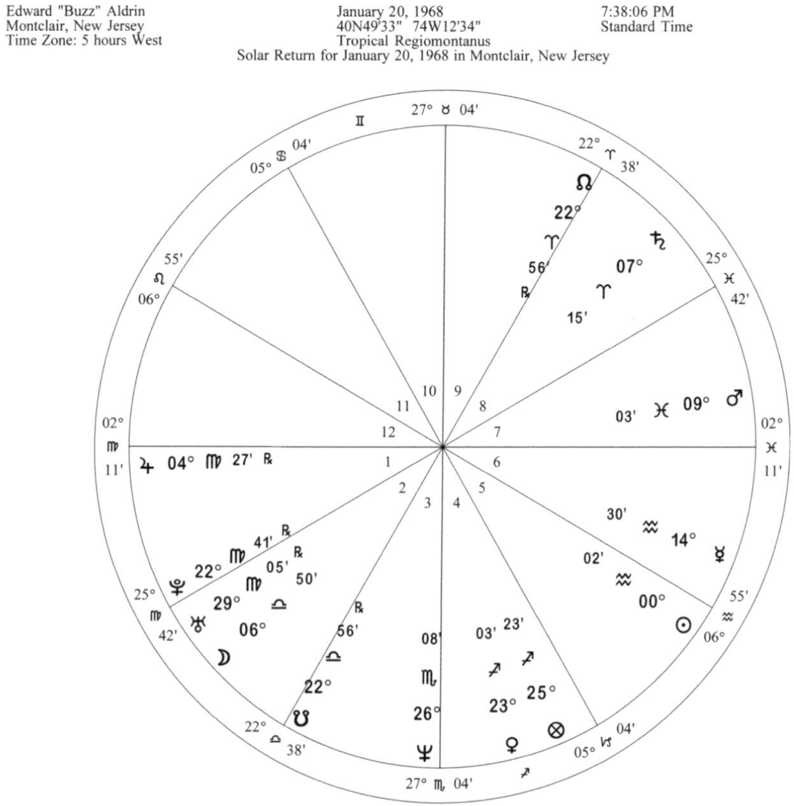
Edward "Buzz" Aldrin
Montclair, New Jersey
Time Zone: 5 hours West
January 20, 1968
40N49'33" 74W12'34"
Tropical Regiomontanus
7:38:06 PM
Standard Time
Solar Return for January 20, 1968 in Montclair, New Jersey

Dorothean Ess. Dig. (No Mut Rec. Points)

Pl	Ruler	Exalt	Tripl	Term	Face	Detri	Fall	Score
☉	♄	--	☿	♄	♀	☉ -	--	- 10 P
☽	♀	♄	☿	♀	☽ +	♂	☉	+1
☿	♄	--	☿ +	♀	☿ +	☉	--	+4
♀	♃	☋	♃	♄ m	♄	☿	--	- 5 P
♂	♃	♀	♂ +	♃	♄ m	☿	☿	+3
♃	☿	☿	☽	☿	☉	♃ -	♀	- 10 P
♄	♂	☉	♃	♀ m	♂ m	♀	♄ -	- 9 P
☊	♂	☉	♃	♂	♀	♀	♄	--
⊗	♃	☋ +	♃	♂	♄	☿	--	--
As	☿	☿	☽	☿	☉	♃	♀	--
Mc	♀	☽	☽	♂	♄	♂	--	--
☋	♀	♄	☿	☿	♃	♂	☉	--

Hs	Alm. (Pto)
1	☿
2	☿
3	☿♀
4	♂
5	♄
6	☿♄
7	♀
8	♂
9	♂
10	☽
11	☽
12	☉

Example 11-9. Buzz Aldrin's Mother's Suicide 1968

Jane Austen's Father's Death

Jane Austen's radix Sun was partile conjunct the IC, a sure sign that her father was an important influence, although whether by presence or absence remains to be seen. Jane lost her father in the year of her Saturn return.

Jane's father was an Anglican minister who was anything but rich, and who frankly would have done much better with fewer children. However, he had a good library, and encouraged both his daughters to use it and to learn from it. The sons, with the exception of one who was feeble-minded and sent off to the country, mostly did well in finding their way into the world. The year her father died, Jane had the following configuration:

- Venus and Saturn were in their natal signs
- The SR-Sun and SR-Moon were opposite
- SR-Mars, ruler of the SR-8th was in the 11th – one meaning of which is the death of the father. In other words, the house of death is specifically linked to the house of the father's death.
- The same sign was the SR-cusp and radix cusp for the following houses: 2nd, 3rd, 5th, 6th, 8th, 9th, 11th, and 12th.

In Austen's day, the death of a father could be a major problem for his widow and any unwed daughters – as the plots of her novels amply demonstrated. Indeed, the parsonage in which they grew up had already been occupied by one of her brothers, and relations with the brother's wife were not the easiest. But in Jane's nativity, her sibling brothers are collectively shown by Mars, which is dignified in Capricorn: Jane did well by her brothers [SEE EXAMPLE 6-2 ON PAGE 131]. In the year of her father's death, the 3rd house of siblings was ruled by Mars, posited in the 11th, which is the 8th from the 4th. The brothers would have to take on the financial dependency of their sisters and mother – which they did. But the transition was not completely ideal – as can be seen from Venus ruling the 2nd,

Jane Austen
Steveston, England
Time Zone: 0 hours West

December 17, 1804
51 N 05 1 W 20
Tropical Regiomontanus

12:30:14 AM
Standard Time

Solar Return for December 17, 1804 in Steveston, England

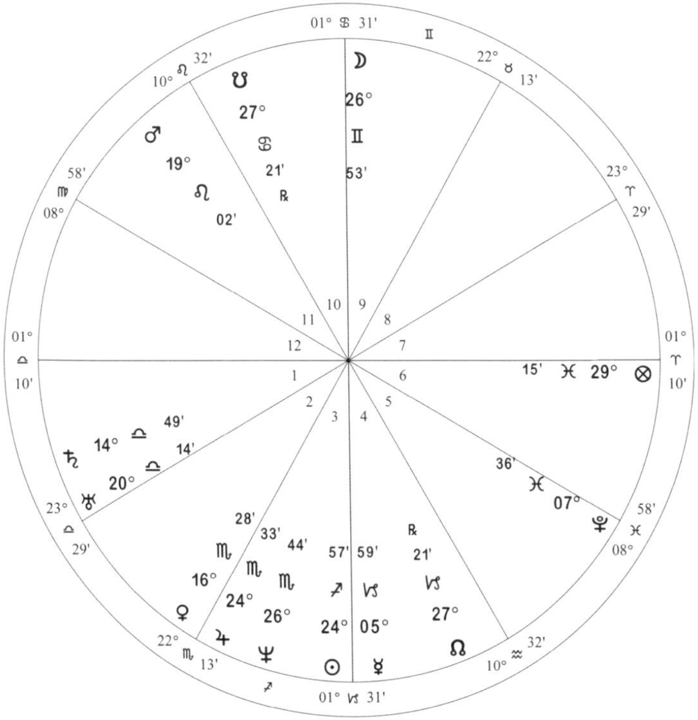

Dorothean Ess. Dig. (No Mut Rec. Points)								
Pl	**Ruler**	**Exalt**	**Tripl**	**Term**	**Face**	**Detri**	**Fall**	**Score**
☉	♃	☋	♃	♄	♄	☿	--	- 5 P
☽	☿	☊	☿ m	♂	☉	♃	--	- 5 P
☿	♄	♂	☽ m	♀	♃	☽	♃	- 5 P
♀	♂	--	♂	♀ +	☉	♀ -	☽	- 3
♂	☉	--	♃ m	♃	♃	♄	--	- 5 P
♃	♂	--	♂ m	☿	♀	♀	☽	- 5 P
♄	♀	♄ +	☿	♃	♄ +	♂	☉	+5
☊	♄	♂	☽	♄	☉	☽	♃	--
⊗	♃	♀	♂	♄	♂	☿	☿	--
As	♀	♄	☿	♄	☽	♂	☉	--
Mc	☽	♃	♂	♂	♀	♄	♂	--
☋	☽	♃	♂	♄	☽	♄	♂	--

Hs	Alm. (Pto)
1	♄
2	☿♀
3	♂
4	♄
5	☿
6	♃
7	♂
8	♂
9	☽
10	☽
11	☉
12	☿

Example 11-10. Jane Austen's Father's Death 1804

in Detriment. The brothers got together and prepared to take on the burden: but the timing for them wasn't ideal, and it would be a couple of years before the women were fully settled.

If the financial matters seem a shade more prominent here than sensibility, it is sad – but also sadly true that the change in circumstances brought on by such a death could be the dominant factor.

Peggy Fleming's Father's Death

How frequent is it, that a daughter or son reaches a major milestone right around the time a parent dies? Peggy Fleming was a driven young lady once she discovered skating, and while her mother was the parent who worked with Peggy day-to-day during the development of her skating skills, it was her father's athletic enthusiasm that helped her to find her path in the first place.

With her father's death under her 1965 solar return, Peggy had experienced two major deaths, as one of her coaches had died in the Sabina Airlines crash that had killed the US Olympic team in 1961. Peggy's SR-8th house is loaded in this year, beginning with SR-Sun conjunct the 8th house cusp, with Mercury, Venus, Uranus, and Pluto all in the SR-8th.

Mars ruled both the 4th and the 11th: the father, and the father's death. The term in classical astrology for when a single planet rules two houses is planets going on the same journey, or in the Hellenistic Period, planets within the [same] belt.[13] Whatever the name, the concept is that the multiple houses ruled by a single planet are combined to show a single pathway. Here, in this particular year, the father and his own death are strongly linked. This alone does not guarantee death: we could say that this sets up an exit visa for him. Other arguments would be necessary to make death more certain. Here, Neptune conjunct the house cusp of his death makes his death more likely. *[See Example 5-2 on page 112 for Peggy's nativity.]*

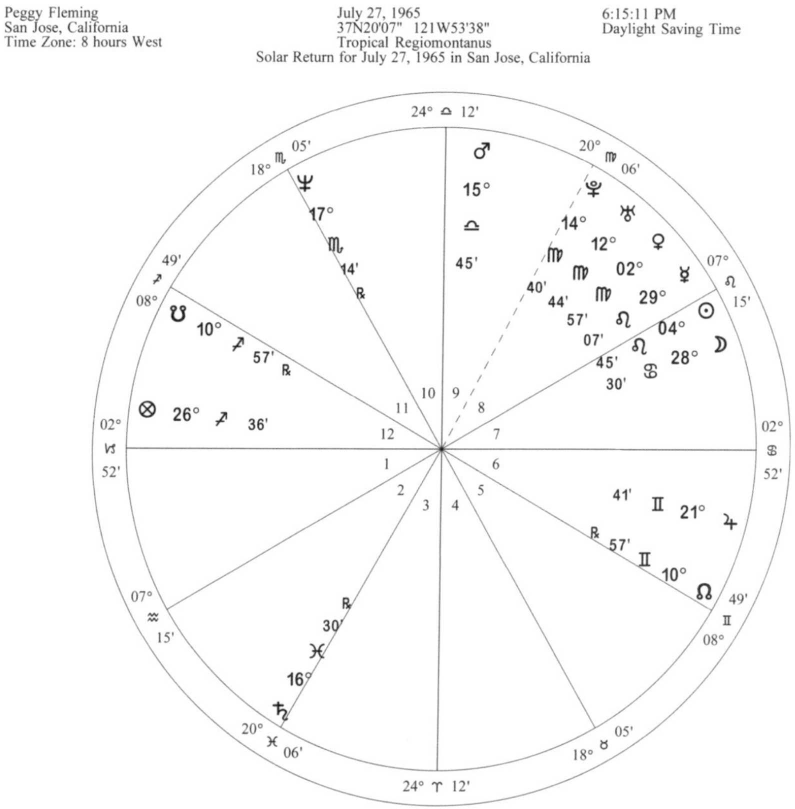
Peggy Fleming
San Jose, California
Time Zone: 8 hours West
July 27, 1965
37N20'07" 121W53'38"
Tropical Regiomontanus
Solar Return for July 27, 1965 in San Jose, California
6:15:11 PM
Daylight Saving Time

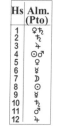

Dorothean Ess. Dig. (No Mut Rec. Points)								
Pl	Ruler	Exalt	Tripl	Term	Face	Detri	Fall	Score
☉	☉ +	--	☉ +	♄	♄	♄	--	+8
☽	☽ +	♃	♀	♄	☽ +	♄	♂	+6
☿	☉	--	☉	♂	♂	♄	--	- 5 P
♀	☿	☿	♀ +	☿	☉	♃	♀ -	- 1
♂	♀	♄	♄	♃	♄	♂ -	☉	- 10 P
♃	☿	☊	♄	♄	☉	♃ -	--	- 10 P
♄	♃	♀	♀	☿	♃	☿	☿	- 5 P
☊	☿	☊ +	♄	♃	♂	♃	--	--
⊗	♃	☋ +	☉	♂	♄	☿	--	--
As	♄	♂	♀	♀	♃	☽	♃	--
Mc	♀	♄	♄	☊	♃	♂	☉	--
☋	♃	☋	☉	♀	☽	☿	--	--

Hs	Alm. (Pto)
1	♀♄
2	♄
3	♃
4	☉♂
5	♀
6	☿
7	☽
8	☉
9	☿
10	♄
11	♂
12	♃

Example 11-11. Peggy Fleming's Father's Death 1965

Mars is in Detriment, the same sign as her natal Mars. In her natal chart, Jupiter ruled the 4th. In this return, Jupiter is in Gemini: in Detriment again. That Jupiter is in the radical 6th of illness, only a couple of degrees away from opposite her natal Jupiter. Morin especially emphasized the danger of return planets opposite the positions in the nativity, and this is an example.

Mary Shelley's Father's Death

Mary's mother, Mary Wollstonecraft, died a few days after Mary's birth of complications from childbirth. We can see this, first, through Pluto conjunct the 10th house of the mother in Mary's nativity [SEE EXAMPLE 3-3 ON PAGE 71]. Saturn, ruling the mother, was in Detriment, in the 1st house.

When her father William Godwin died, it was three years after Mary's half-brother died of cholera, and nine years after her beloved Percy drowned. In her natal chart, her father is shown through Saturn, a natural ruler of fathers, and through her 4th house. Saturn rules the 10th – her mother – and is in the 1st. I take this to be the grieving William, shorn of the love of his life, the one woman who had been his undisputed intellectual equal. The 4th house ruler is the Sun, disposed by a very dignified Mercury. With the Sun in the 4th conjunct Mars, here was her father as writer.

In the year of William's death, the solar return 4th house was ruled by Mars, now in Detriment, instead of dignified by Triplicity, as Mars was at her birth. Mercury in Virgo rules his 8th, the SR-11th. The two planets showing her father's possible death – the SR-11th house ruler and Jupiter in the 11th house – are both dignified, while William's own ruler Mars is in Detriment. The SR-South Node is in the 4th house, with the Sun-Mercury conjunction at the Bendings. SR-Jupiter in the 11th also rules her SR-8th, so here, the themes of death tie together.

Mary Shelley
London, England
Time Zone: 0 hours West

September 1, 1835
51 N 30 0 W 10
Tropical Regiomontanus
Solar Return for September 1, 1835 in London, England

3:45:38 AM
Local Mean Time

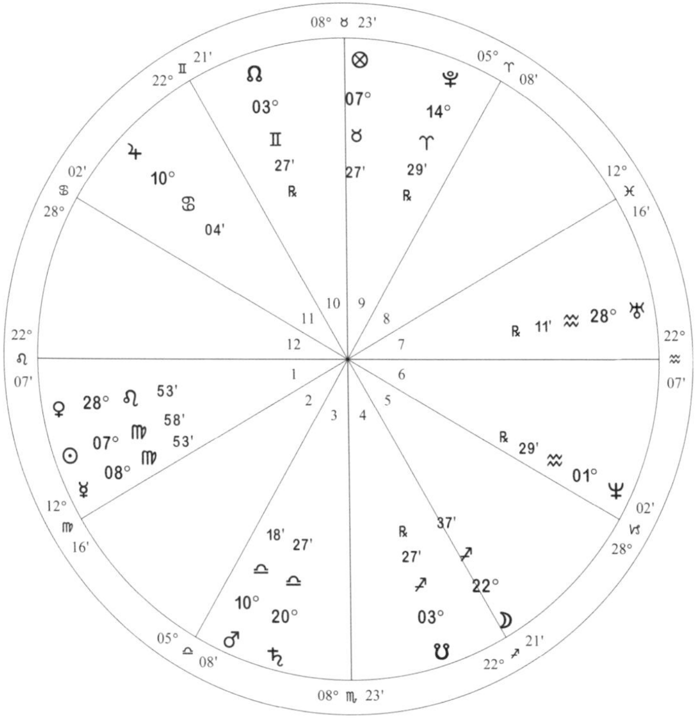

Dorothean Ess. Dig. (No Mut Rec. Points)								
Pl	Ruler	Exalt	Tripl	Term	Face	Detri	Fall	Score
☉	☿	☿	☽	♀	☉ +	♃	♀	+1
☽	♃ m	☋	♃	♄	♄	☿	--	- 5 P
☿	☿ +	☿ +	☽	♀	☉	♃	♀	+9
♀	☉	--	♃	♂ m	♂	♄	--	- 5 P
♂	♀	♄	☿	♀ m	♄	♂ -	☉	- 10 P
♃	☽ m	♃ +	♂	♃ +	☿	♄	♂	+6
♄	♀	♄ +	☿	☿	♃	♂	☉	+4
☊	☿	☊ +	☿	☿	♃	♃	--	--
⊗	♀	☽	☽	♀	☿	♂	--	--
As	☉	--	♃	♃	♂	♄	--	--
Mc	♀	☽	☽	☿	☿	♂	--	--
☋	♃	☋	♃	♃	☿	☿	--	--

Hs	Alm. (Pto)
1	☉♃
2	☿
3	♄
4	♂
5	♃
6	♄
7	♄
8	♃
9	♂
10	☽
11	☿
12	☽

Example 11-12. Mary Shelley's Father's Death 1835

The Death of Dorothy Hamill's Prince

If we could only have one major event in a year, it would make prediction so much easier! In solar return year 1986, Dorothy married for a second time. And then, scarcely two weeks later, Dean Paul Martin, her first husband, was killed in a plane crash in which he was the pilot. Let's try to sort this out!

To say in a solar return year when Neptune is conjunct the 7th house cusp that one is either confused or delusional about marriage partner(s) is perhaps an understatement. In Dorothy's nativity, the Sun rules the 7th, and the Sun is in Leo: partnerships are more than normally important for her sense of well being [SEE EXAMPLE 3-4 ON PAGE 75]. The natal Pluto at the 7th house seems tragically fulfilled by Martin's death.

The death of a spouse is the 2nd, which is the 8th from the 7th. But she and Martin were divorced, and this raises questions about how to look at an ex. Here, in the solar return we see the Sun in the 2nd, which would tend to suggest her attention in the very house that would be highlighted if Martin is treated as a 7th house person. From her description that she had been drawn to her second husband because he looked like her first, we conclude that she had not given up on Dean in her mind. I think he was still 7th house.

On the other hand, if we use the 11th – the official status of Martin at that point – the Moon in Aries is at the cusp, and the death of a friend would be given by the 6th: the 8th from the 11th. Saturn is on the cusp of the 6th, with Uranus there as well! Thus, in this case, it's not possible to decide.

But this does illustrate the complications that we have in our culture of divorce. The older concept of "til death do us part" did have the advantage of not having confusion about multiple options for the 7th house who are living simultaneously, and thus, who could be the subject of the delineation.

However you look at it, this was a difficult year for Dorothy.

Dorothy Hamill
Chicago, Illinois
Time Zone: 6 hours West

July 27, 1986
41 N 51 87 W 39
Tropical Regiomontanus
Solar Return for July 27, 1986 in Chicago, Illinois

3:22:34 AM
Daylight Saving Time

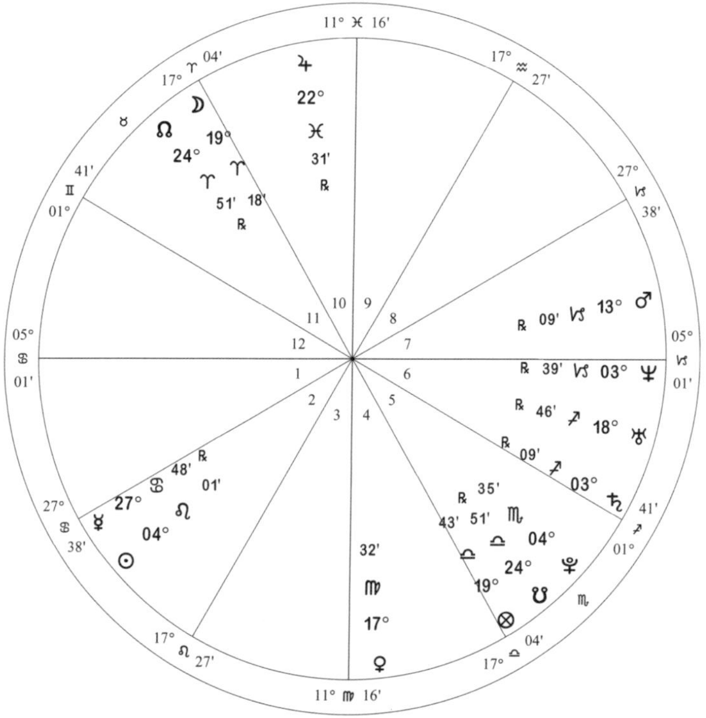

Dorothean Ess. Dig. (No Mut Rec. Points)								
Pl	Ruler	Exalt	Tripl	Term	Face	Detri	Fall	Score
☉	☉ +	--	♃	♄	♄	♄	--	+5
☽	♂	☉	♃	☿	☉	♀	♄	- 5 P
☿	☽	♃	♂	♄	☽	♄	♂	- 5 P
♀	☿	☿	☽	♃	♀ +	♃	♀ -	- 3
♂	♄	♂ +	☽	♃ m	♂ +	☽	♃	+5
♃	♃ +	♀	♂	♂ m	♂	☿	☿	+5
♄	♃	☋	♃	♃	☿	☿	--	- 5 P
☊	♂	☉	♃	♂	♀	♀	♄	--
⊗	♀	♄	☿	☿	♄	♂	☉	--
As	☽	♃	♂	♂	♀	♄	♂	--
Mc	♃	♀	♂	♃	♃	☿	☿	--
☋	♀	♄	☿	☊	♃	♂	☉	--

Hs	Alm. (Pto)
1	☽
2	☽
3	☉
4	☿
5	♀♄
6	♃
7	♄
8	♄
9	♄
10	♃
11	☉♂
12	☿

Example 11-13. The Death of Dorothy Hamill's Prince 1986

- None of her planets, except the Sun, of course, were in their natal signs.
- Only Venus was in its birth house.
- SR-Saturn was near her natal Saturn.
- SR-Mercury, in the 8th from the 7th; or simply the 2nd, was retrograde and at the SR-Bendings.
- The Sun in the 2nd shows the focus on money – or the death of the partner. The partile square with Pluto definitely does not help.
- SR-Neptune on the Descendant with Mars in the SR-7th house shows a disturbing cluelessness combined with conflict, which is no recipe for a good start to a marriage.

The absence of much overlap with the natal makes the situation during the solar return year seem foreign: it is hard for Dorothy to understand what is happening to her, and to make good decisions.

Scott Hamilton's Father

It may seem strange that there can be a touch of humor, or at least irony, about the time someone dies, but it happens. After my father died, my brother commented that our parents proved themselves teachers to the end, with Mom dying at Spring Break, and Dad during Christmas holidays. Scott Hamilton got to experience that strange calendar timing when his own father died during the Olympics – but nine years after Scott's own Gold Medal.

In his natal chart, Scott's father is shown as Saturn: doubly, because Saturn is both the natural ruler of fathers, and because Saturn rules his 4th house [SEE EXAMPLE 5-7 ON PAGE 121]. His Saturn has Triplicity in Sagittarius, and Venus, Scott's Ascendant ruler, forms a trine to it.

One would normally think that, with dignified Mercury in Virgo ruling the 4th house of the solar return, that Scott's father would be

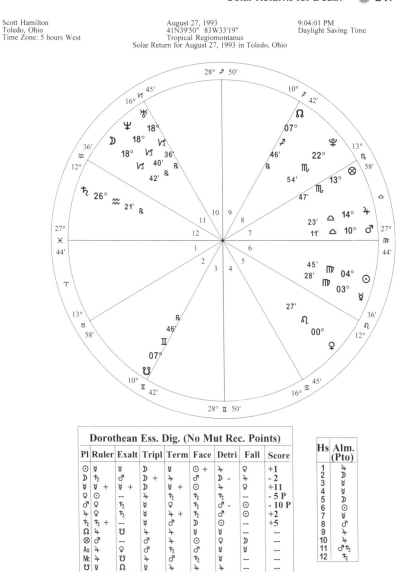

Scott Hamilton   August 27, 1993   9:04:01 PM
Toledo, Ohio   41N39'50" 83W33'19"   Daylight Saving Time
Time Zone: 5 hours West   Tropical Regiomontanus
Solar Return for August 27, 1993 in Toledo, Ohio

Example 11-14. Scott Hamilton's Father 1993

just fine. But SR-Mercury is combust and conjunct natal Pluto, and the bigger argument comes from an unusual configuration a triple partile conjunction of Moon, Neptune, and Uranus in Scott's 11th house – the house of the death of the father (8th from the 4th). Scott's father was in his retirement years, and he did outlive his wife. Here, we also see Pluto in the SR-8th, and the Part of Fortune at the 8th house cusp. When it is the death of the second parent, one often sees an indication of inheritance in the solar returns of the children. In Scott's case, his father did not have the earning power that he did, and this we can see by Fortuna at the 8th showing death and legacy – but Fortuna disposed by Mars in Detriment.

The Death of my Father

Like Scott's case, my father outlived my mother. Dad was a very vital and healthy individual, until the last few years of his life. Then, he broke his ankle, and followed his Christian Science beliefs by not treating it medically, with the result that he never walked properly again, and so his physical stamina declined.

Like Scott's case, Dad was shown in the chart by SR-Mercury in Virgo, which in my case, is further strengthened by being the sign of my natal Mercury. It is Under Beams, so the debility is not as strong as the combustion, although the combustion would be my natal state. But here, Mercury is in a partile opposition to Uranus. When Dad became ill it was quick: less than two weeks from the onset of serious symptoms to his death. The MC/IC axis is really highlighted in this year, not only because Pluto was sitting so close to the MC, but the IC position is my natal Jupiter. The Moon in Scorpio in the 8th house and in Fall is a strong signal that I will be unhappy about something related to death – and I surely was. This is definitely marked as an extreme year. With the Sun conjunct the Portals of Death, the seriousness of the issue of death is further argued.

Before leaving this example, let me mention one observation that I might not have noticed in my clients had it not been for my

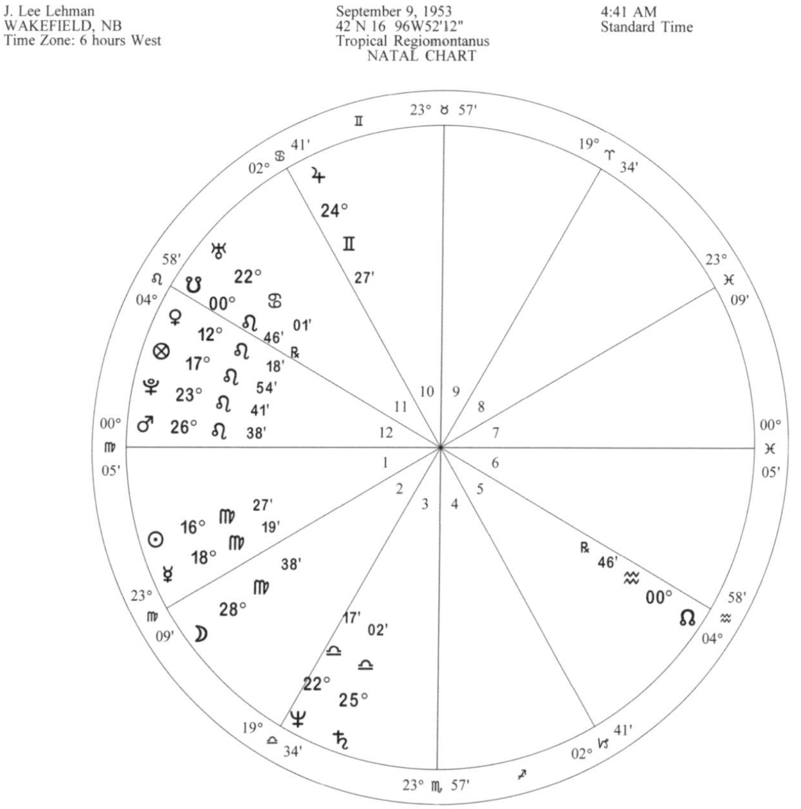
J. Lee Lehman
WAKEFIELD, NB
Time Zone: 6 hours West
September 9, 1953
42 N 16 96W52'12"
Tropical Regiomontanus
NATAL CHART
4:41 AM
Standard Time

Dorothean Ess. Dig. (No Mut Rec. Points)								
Pl	Ruler	Exalt	Tripl	Term	Face	Detri	Fall	Score
☉	☿	☿	☽	♃	♀	♃	♀	- 5 P
☽	☿	☿	☽ +	♂	☿	♃	♀	+3
☿	☿ +	☿ +	☽	♄	♀	♃	♀	+9
♀	☉	--	♃	☿	♃	♄	--	- 5 P
♂	☉	--	♃	♂ +	♂ +	♄	--	+3
♃	☿	☊	☿	♄	☉	♃ -	--	- 10 P
♄	♀	♄ +	☿	☊	♃	♂	☉	+4
☊	♄	--	☿	♄	♀	☉	--	--
⊗	☉	--	♃	♀	♃	♄	--	--
As	☿	☿	☽	☿	☉	♃	♀	--
Mc	♀	☽	☽	♄	♄	♂	--	--
☋	☉	--	♃	♄	♄	♄	--	--

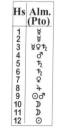

Hs	Alm. (Pto)
1	☿
2	☿
3	☿♀♄
4	♂
5	♄
6	♄
7	♀
8	♃
9	☉♂
10	☽
11	☽
12	☉

Example 11-15. Lee Lehman's nativity

J. Lee Lehman
WAKEFIELD, NB
Time Zone: 0 hours West

September 9, 2005
42 N 16 96W52'12"
Tropical Regiomontanus

12:46:01 AM
Standard Time

Solar Return for September 9, 2005 in WAKEFIELD, NB

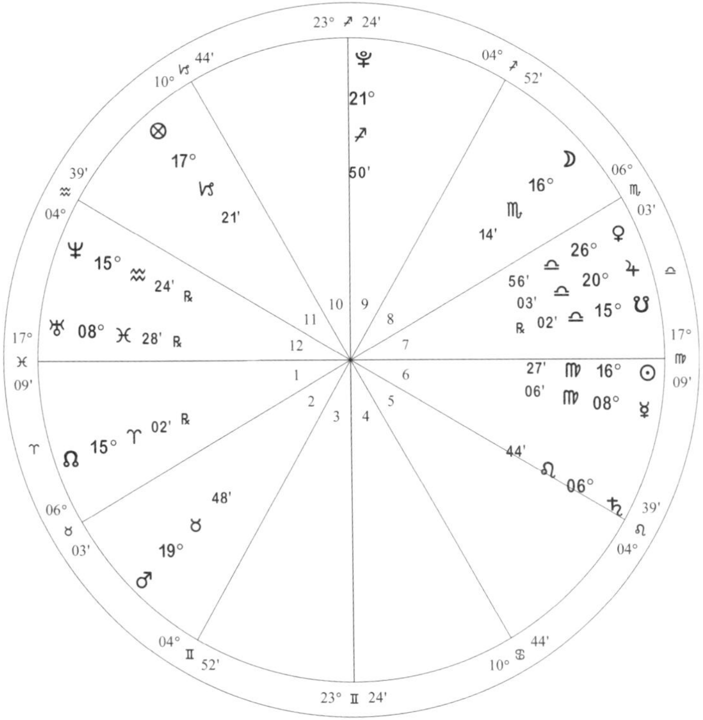

Dorothean Ess. Dig. (No Mut Rec. Points)								
Pl	Ruler	Exalt	Tripl	Term	Face	Detri	Fall	Score
☉	☿	☿	☽	♃	♀	♃	♀	- 5 P
☽	♂	--	♂ m	♀	☉	♀	☽ -	- 9 P
☿	☿ +	☿ +	☽	♀	☉	♃	♀	+9
♀	♀ +	♄	☿	☊	♃	♂	☉	+5
♂	♀	☽	☽ m	♃	☽	♂ -	--	- 10 P
♃	♀	♄	☿	☿	♃ +	♂	☉	+1
♄	☉	--	♃	☿	♄ +	♄ -	--	- 4
☊	♂	☉	♃	☿	☉	♀	♄	--
⊗	♄	♂	☽	♃	♂	☽	♃	--
As	♃	♀	♂	☿	♃	☿	☿	--
Mc	♃	☋	♃	♄	♄	☿	--	--
☋	♀	♄	☿	♃	♄	♂	☉	--

Hs	Alm. (Pto)
1	♃
2	☽♀
3	☿
4	☿
5	♃
6	☉
7	☿
8	♂
9	♃
10	♃
11	♂♄
12	♄

Example 11-15a. The Death of Her Father 2005

own experience. When one parent dies, the other parent often seems to take on some of the parenting duties from the other, whether consciously or unconsciously. Just as one can see this expansion of role in life, one can often see the surviving parent "taking over" the whole MC/IC axis. I have used this idea to good effect in both my horary and natal work.

I should also mention that the usual allocation of in-laws as the partner's parents isn't always that clear either. My partner lost her father at a very early age from cancer. Her father and my father shared almost the same birthday (different years). She bonded very strongly with my father. In her charts, my father would more likely show up as 4th than as 10th.

Louis Pasteur's Mother's Death

Louis Pasteur was the only son of a couple who hoped and planned for him to come home after he bettered his social position through education. At first, Paris life most emphatically didn't agree with the country boy, but he needed to go to Paris for his doctorate, and he was in Paris when his mother died unexpectedly of a stroke.

This solar year, which encompassed the Paris Riots of 1848, was a major one for Pasteur's career, as he made a major discovery in organic chemistry. The SR-Moon in the 10th thus tells two stories, not one. The Moon's dispositor is the same as for his nativity [*see Example 4-5 on page 101*]. The solar return feature of a partile opposition of the Moon and Saturn is one of the most diagnostic aspects for the death of a parent, whether it's found in the solar return, or it's the transit of Saturn over the natal Moon. Here, it's even enhanced by being in the MC/IC axis. The mother's death is further argued with the SR-South Node in the 8th from the 10th (the 5th). And further, SR-Uranus also in the 5th of the mother's death shows the circumstances – an unexpected acute attack. The 29 degrees on the MC/IC axis may well be implicated as well, and if more confirmation were needed, there's the Sun at the Bendings.

Louis Pasteur
Dole, France
Time Zone: 0 hours West

December 27, 1847
47 N 06 5 E 30
Tropical Regiomontanus
Solar Return for December 27, 1847 in Dole, France

3:47:01 AM
Local Mean Time

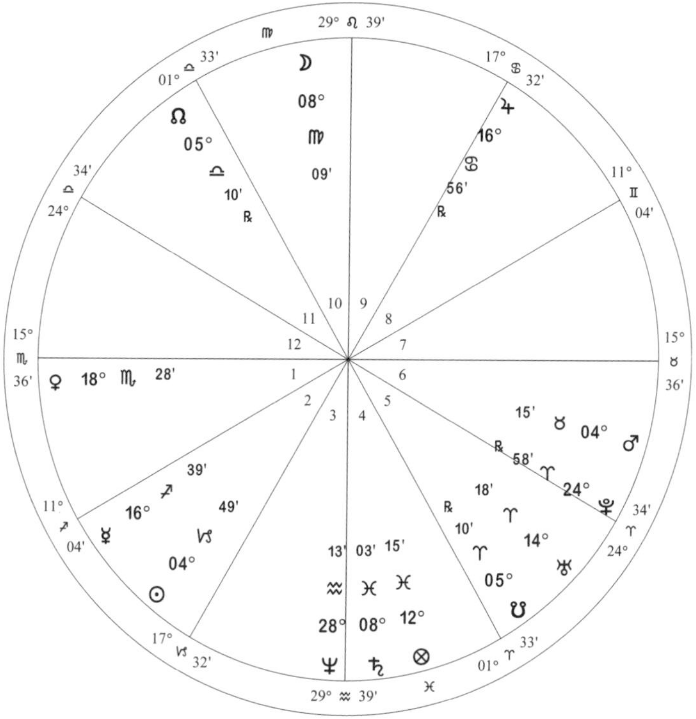

Dorothean Ess. Dig. (No Mut Rec. Points)

Pl	Ruler	Exalt	Tripl	Term	Face	Detri	Fall	Score
☉	♄	♂	☽	♀	♃	☽	♃	- 5 P
☽	☿	☿	☽ +	♀	☉	♃	♀	+3
☿	♃	☋	♃	☿ +	☽	☿ -	--	- 3
♀	♂ m	--	♂	♀ +	☉	♀ -	☽	- 3
♂	♀ m	☽	☽	♀	☿	♂ -	--	- 10 P
♃	☽	♃ +	♂	☿	☿	♄	♂	+4
♄	♃	♀	♂	♃	♄ +	☿	☿	+1
☊	♀	♄	☿	♄	☽	♂	☉	--
⊗	♃	♀	♂	♃	♃	☿	☿	--
As	♂	--	♂	♀	☉	♀	☽	--
Mc	☉	--	♃	♂	♂	♄	--	--
☋	♂	☉	♃	♃	♂	♀	♄	--

Hs	Alm. (Pto)
1	♂
2	♃
3	♂♄
4	♄
5	♂
6	♂
7	☽
8	☿
9	☽
10	☉
11	♄
12	♀

Example 11-16. Louis Pasteur's Mother's Death 1847

Like Dorothy Hamill's experience of the year of her first husband's death and her second marriage, the absence of planets in their natal signs gives the "stranger in a strange land" effect. How odd it must have been, going back home after getting ensconced in his intellectual life in Paris! And yet – for the rest of the year, the Moon in Triplicity in the 10th, and trine so many natal planets may have been key to the beginning of his public recognition as a promising young scientist.

Theodore Roosevelt's Horrible Day

In the summer of 1883, things had to be looking up for Theodore. His beloved wife Alice was pregnant with their first child. He was making a splash in his first term in the New York State Assembly. He was building his cattle ranch in North Dakota, and it looked like a promising enterprise. Life was good.

It all fell apart for him on Valentine's Day 1884. His mother, who was ailing, died. And if that were not bad enough, his wife not only died on the same day after giving birth to their daughter Alice, she died in the same house as her mother-in-law. TR was absolutely devastated. He was so devastated that he couldn't bring himself to mention his wife's name again for the rest of his life.

As we might expect, the solar return for the year looks pretty bad:

- While the SR-MC (ruling the mother) is in the same sign as the radix, Jupiter, ruling the MC, was at the Bendings, square the Sun, and square natal Pluto. *[SEE EXAMPLE 2-4 ON PAGE 43]*
- The SR-8th house is ruled by Saturn, dignified by Triplicity, but conjunct the 12th house cusp.
- The SR-7th house (ruling the wife) is that very same Saturn.
- The SR-5th (the 8th from the 10th, and thus, in part, the death of the mother) was ruled by Mars, which was in a partile square to radix Pluto.

- The SR-2nd (the 8th from the 7th, and thus, in part, his wife's death, or the possibility thereof) was ruled by the Sun, which was square Mars and Jupiter, and, by definition, opposite his natal Pluto.
- The SR-Ascendant was the natal Moon. I don't think this relates so much to the death theme, as what TR chose to do afterwards, which was to "retire" to his North Dakota ranch.
- SR-Mars was partile square natal Pluto, in the 2nd house.

The decision to move to North Dakota and give up his New York base was motivated by both his grief over his wife's death, but also by his love of the West, adventure, and manly things. TR had rather painted himself into a corner at this stage, since he had acquired the conviction that remarrying was a moral weakness. He certainly did not expect to be tested on this belief at the age of 25!

But what is so interesting about this particular configuration was that the SR-Moon was in Libra in the 4th. TR did have an abiding love of the land and nature, and the house placement of the Moon in this year shows how this general ideal came to the fore. Uranus at the 4th house cusp also suggests the move, but, being Uranus, we wonder whether it would be permanent. The Moon being peregrine suggests the probable short-term duration of this situation as well. As we saw in Chapter 3, it was in the year of TR's second marriage that his North Dakota holdings were destroyed as an investment.

The difficulty with the natal Sun-Pluto opposition meant that anytime the Sun ruled something in a solar return, it would, by necessity be afflicted by natal Pluto. While TR himself was adapted to this, other people or things were not. The Sun ruling something in his solar return should be treated as a malefic as a result.

Theodore Roosevelt
New York, New York
Time Zone: 0 hours West

October 27, 1883
40N42'51" 74W00'23"
Tropical Regiomontanus
Solar Return for October 27, 1883 in New York, New York

9:08:03 PM
Local Mean Time

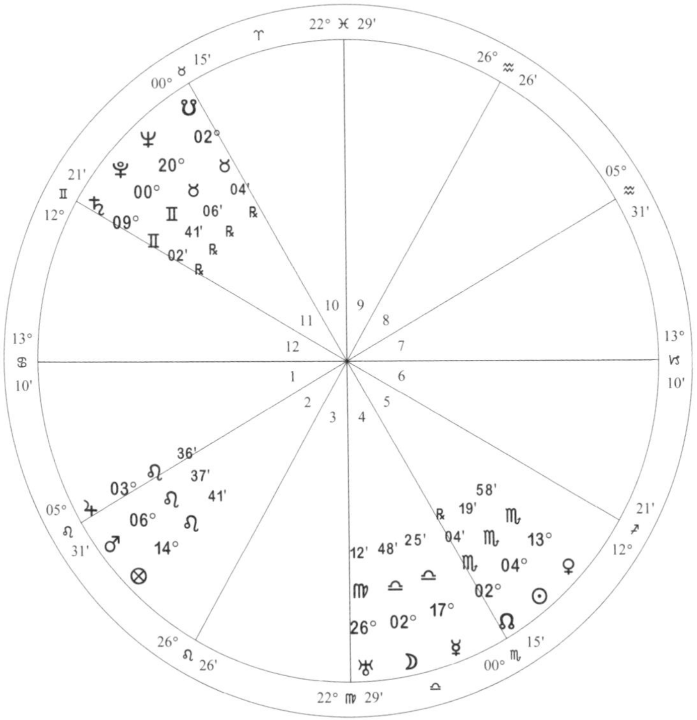

Dorothean Ess. Dig. (No Mut Rec. Points)

Pl	Ruler	Exalt	Tripl	Term	Face	Detri	Fall	Score
☉	♂ m	--	♂	♂	♂	♀	☽	- 5 P
☽	♀	♄	☿	♄	☽ +	♂	☉	+1
☿	♀	♄	☿ +	♃	♄	♂	☉	+3
♀	♂	--	♂	♃	☉	♀ -	☽	- 10 P
♂	☉ m	--	♃	☿	♄	♄	--	- 5 P
♃	☉	--	♃ +	♄ m	♄ m	♄	--	+3
♄	☿	☊	☿	♃ m	♃ m	♃	--	- 5 P
☊	♂	--	♂	♂	♂	♀	☽	--
⊗	☉	--	♃	♀	♃	♄	--	--
As	☽	♃	♂	☿	☿	♄	♂	--
Mc	♃	♀	♂	♂	♂	☿	☿	--
☋	♀	☽	☽	♀	☿	♂	--	--

Hs	Alm. (Pto)
1	☽
2	☉
3	☉
4	☿
5	♂
6	♃
7	♂♄
8	♄
9	♄
10	♃
11	☽♀
12	☿

Example 11-17. Theodore Roosevelt's Horrible Day 1883

Eleanor Roosevelt's One-Two Punch

Eleanor Roosevelt lost her parents in two consecutive years, when she was 8-9. Now: this did not set up an immediate change in social and financial status, as it might have been, had Eleanor not come from a rich family. It certainly resulted in severe emotional consequences, and it resulted in her being raised in a more conservative social environment than might have happened otherwise. But she was still the niece of the President of the United States for part of her childhood and adolescence. She became a shy, uncertain girl, but a bright one, and one with good language skills, especially French.

Her mother died of diphtheria in a solar return year in which young Eleanor had the Moon in the 8th house. The fact that it was dignified didn't make it any easier! The Neptune-Pluto conjunction that was the signature mundane event of this period fell in her 7th house. Her SR-Mars was square her natal Mars. That Mars ruled her 5th: her mother's death, among other possible meanings of the 5th house. Her SR-Mercury was in the same sign as her natal Mercury, and Venus was almost conjunct its natal placement, as one would expect for age 8. Diphtheria has now become quite rare in developed countries, and is easily treated by antibiotics and antitoxin. Neither of these methods had been invented in Eleanor's time. The symptoms of diphtheria don't become obvious until the sufferer is past the contagion stage, so perhaps we should ask another question: why did Eleanor survive, when it is almost a foregone conclusion that she was unwittingly exposed to the virus by her mother?

Eleanor's SR-Ascendant was zero Sagittarius, an earlier degree, but in the same sign as her natal Ascendant. Jupiter, while retrograde, had dignity. And perhaps most importantly, Eleanor had two benefics associated with the 6th of disease: the North Node partile conjunct the cusp, and Venus ruling the 6th. While Venus in Virgo has the mixture of Fall plus Triplicity, I note how a benefic ruling the 6th house would be at most an unusual indicator of disease in

Eleanor Roosevelt
New York, New York
Time Zone: 5 hours West

October 11, 1892
40N42'51" 74W00'23"
Tropical Regiomontanus
Solar Return for October 11, 1892 in New York, New York

9:40 AM
Standard Time

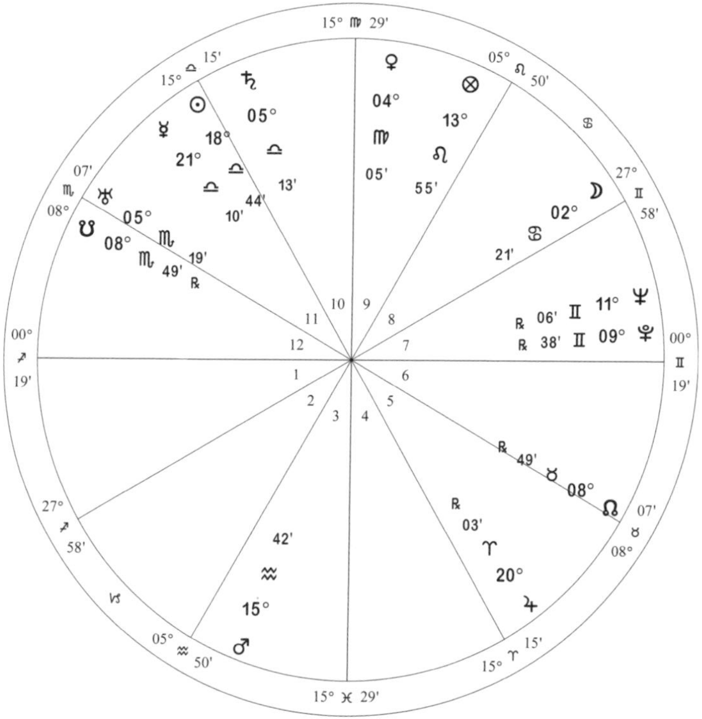

Dorothean Ess. Dig. (No Mut Rec. Points)								
Pl	Ruler	Exalt	Tripl	Term	Face	Detri	Fall	Score
☉	♀	♄	♄	♃	♄	♂	☉ -	- 9 P
☽	☽ +	♃	♀	♂	♀	♄	♂	+5
☿	♀ m	♄	♄	☿ +	♃	♂	☉	+2
♀	☿ m	☿	♀ +	☿	☉	♃	♀ -	- 1
♂	♄	--	♄	♀	☿	☉	--	- 5 P
♃	♂	☉	☉	☿	♀	♀	♄	- 5 P
♄	♀	♄ +	♄ +	♄ +	☽	♂	☉	+9
☊	♀	☽	♀	☿	☿	♂	--	--
⊗	☉	--	☉	♀	♃	♄	--	--
As	♃	☋	☉	♃	☿	☿	--	--
Mc	☿	☿	♀	♃	♀	♃	♀	--
☋	♂	--	♀	♃	♂	♀	☽	--

Hs	Alm. (Pto)
1	♃
2	♃
3	♄
4	♃
5	☉
6	♀
7	☿
8	☿
9	☉
10	☿
11	♄
12	♂

Example 11-18a. Eleanor Roosevelt's One-Two Punch 1892

Eleanor Roosevelt
New York, New York
Time Zone: 5 hours West

October 11, 1893
40N42'51" 74W00'23"
Tropical Regiomontanus
Solar Return for October 11, 1893 in New York, New York

3:24:41 PM
Standard Time

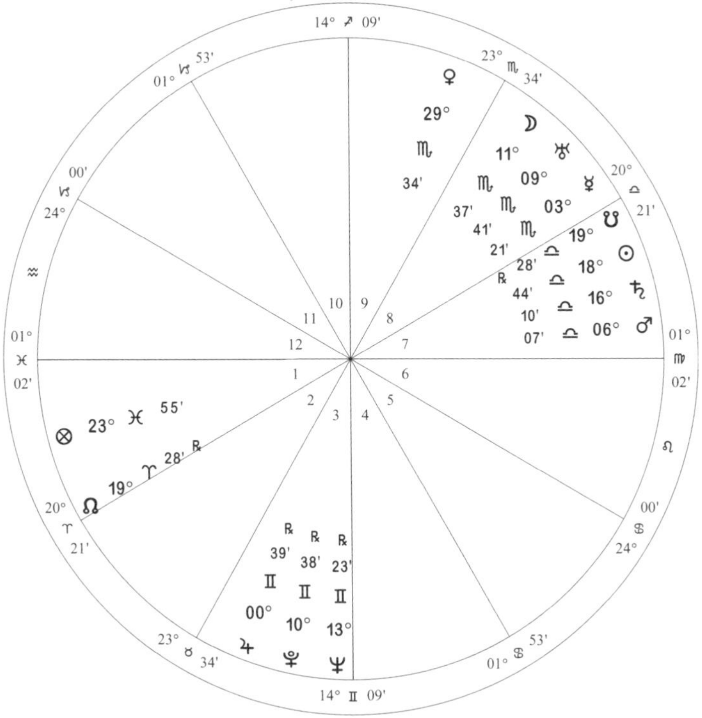

Dorothean Ess. Dig. (No Mut Rec. Points)								
Pl	Ruler	Exalt	Tripl	Term	Face	Detri	Fall	Score
☉	♀	♄	♄	♃	♄	♂	☉ -	- 9 P
☽	♂	--	♀	♃	☉	♀	☽ -	- 9 P
☿	♂	--	♀	♂	♂	♀	☽	- 5 P
♀	♂ m	--	♀ +	♄	♀ +	♀ -	☽	- 1
♂	♀ m	♄	♄	♀	☽	♂ -	☉	- 10 P
♃	☿	☊	♄	☿	♃ +	♃ -	--	- 4
♄	♀	♄ +	♄ +	♃	♄ +	♂	☉	+8
☊	♂	☉	☉	☿	☉	♀	♄	--
⊗	♃	♀	♀	♂	♂	☿	☿	--
As	♃	♀	♀	♀	♄	☿	☿	--
Mc	♃	☋	☉	☿	☽	☿	--	--
☋	♀	♄	♄	☿	♄	♂	☉	--

Hs	Alm. (Pto)
1	♀
2	☉
3	♀
4	☿
5	☽
6	☽
7	☿
8	♄
9	♂
10	♃
11	♀♄
12	♂

Example 11-18b. Eleanor Roosevelt's One-Two Punch 1893

Traditional Medical Astrology.[14] Eleanor's own vitality was very good that year, and so she didn't succumb.

However, when her father died the following year, it must have felt like she just hit rock bottom. Eleanor's 10th year (i.e., year 9) shows an absolutely loaded 8th house in the solar return: South Node right on the cusp of the 8th, and then Mercury, Uranus and the Moon in the SR-8th. Eleanor had the "stranger in a strange land" effect again, with no solar return planet in the same sign as in the nativity, and with Jupiter in the sign opposite its natal location.

A Suicide

None of our example biographies were of people who committed suicide. Sadly, in our world in which teenage and elderly suicide has become one of the leading causes of death, this is not a topic we can ignore.

There is a possible classical model, or at least starting point. In the *Seven Segments of Cardan* translated in part by Lilly, we see the following under the medical section:

> *"39. When Mercury is unfortunate he prejudices the fantasy and inward faculties, and thence threatens madness, etc., but so much the worse if Mars be the Planet that afflicteth him, for then if he be in an earthy sign it threatens the Patient will make away with himself."*

Like any other form of death, we cannot assume that there can be only one astrological explanation. However, the affliction of Mercury would probably not have been the first thought of a modern astrologer as a signature.

Here I present a private case of a gentleman who committed suicide at age 35 some years ago. We'll call him RB. If we first examine his natal chart, we see his 8th house cusp is the baleful fixed star Scheat. We note further the conjunction of Jupiter, ruling his 7th, to the fixed star Vindemiatrix, the widow's star. That makes his marriage partner a widow, but by his actions, or because she is from before he married her? He was engaged at the time of his death, and not to a widow.

We obviously all must die, but we do tend to see suicide as premature death. If we do the hylegical calculation, then RB has the Ascendant as Hyleg, which right away suggests lesser vitality.[15] Lesser vitality is just that: a tendency. Someone with lesser vitality can live into his or her nineties with care.

There is danger of violence in this chart, with the Sun-Moon-Mercury group square natal Mars in Fall. In fact, he did use a gun to commit suicide, but I wouldn't say that this *had* to be suicide. Pluto right at the 12th house cusp *given* the argument of violence *could* be construed as having something to do with self-undoing. Certainly, the pieces were there.

Example 11-19a gives the actual time of suicide. No chart is exclusively one thing, of course, because one person's death is another person's birth. So the question with a death chart is less how it looks like a death as how it relates to the person who has just died. Mars partile trine Mars? Mars was approaching Uranus, but it was nowhere near exact. Saturn was about to change signs into the sign that would be the most difficult for him, with the stellium he had in Libra. But really: nothing is standing out in comparing these charts.

But one consideration here is *which* solar return to examine, because the event of his suicide was just over two weeks before his birthday. Examples 11-19b & c give his solar returns for his birth location in 1979 (the year in which the suicide took place) and 1980 (less than three weeks later). In the 1979 solar return, the ruler of his 7th was in the 12th. He had met a woman at an institution where he was being treated for alcoholism, and he became engaged to her. That symbolism clearly fit. So perhaps did the symbolism of Pluto conjunct the 12th house cusp, although I rather doubt that this is much besides hindsight. The 8th house ruler Mercury was in

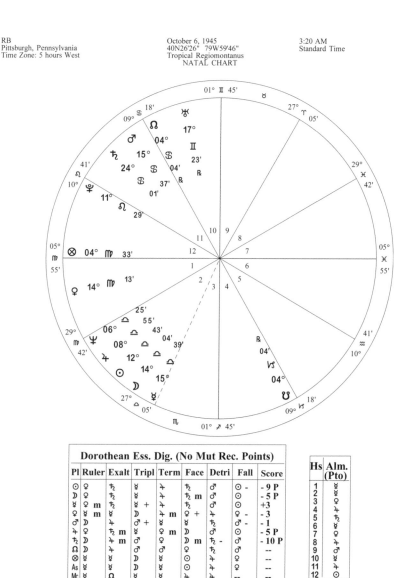

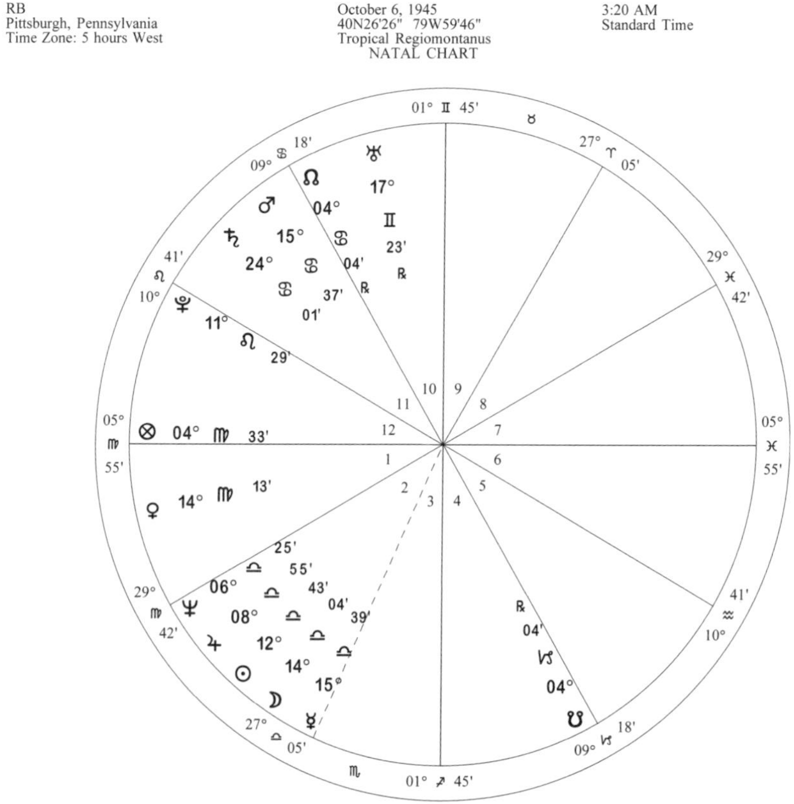
RB
Pittsburgh, Pennsylvania
Time Zone: 5 hours West
October 6, 1945
40N26'26" 79W59'46"
Tropical Regiomontanus
NATAL CHART
3:20 AM
Standard Time

Dorothean Ess. Dig. (No Mut Rec. Points)								
Pl	Ruler	Exalt	Tripl	Term	Face	Detri	Fall	Score
☉	♀	♄	☿	♃	♄	♂	☉ -	- 9 P
☽	♀	♄	☿	♃	♄ m	♂	☉	- 5 P
☿	♀ m	♄	☿ +	♃	♄	♂	☉	+3
♀	☿ m	☿	☽	♃ m	♀ +	♃	♀ -	- 3
♂	☽	♃	♂ +	☿	☿	♄	♂ -	- 1
♃	♀	♄ m	☿	♀ m	☽	♂	☉	- 5 P
♄	☽	♃ m	♂	♀	☽ m	♄ -	♂	- 10 P
☊	☽	♃	♂	♂	♀	♄	♂	--
⊗	☿	☿	☽	☿	☉	♃	♀	--
As	☿	☿	☽	☿	☉	♃	♀	--
Mc	☿	☊	☿	☿	♃	♃	--	--
☋	♄	♂	☽	♀	♃	☽	♃	--

Hs	Alm. (Pto)
1	☿
2	☿
3	♀
4	♃
5	♄
6	☿
7	♀
8	♃
9	♂
10	☿
11	♃
12	☉

Example 11-19. RB nativity

RB's suicide
North Miami, Florida
Time Zone: 5 hours West

September 20, 1980
25N53'23" 80W11'13"
Tropical Regiomontanus
NATAL CHART

2:00 PM
Daylight Saving Time

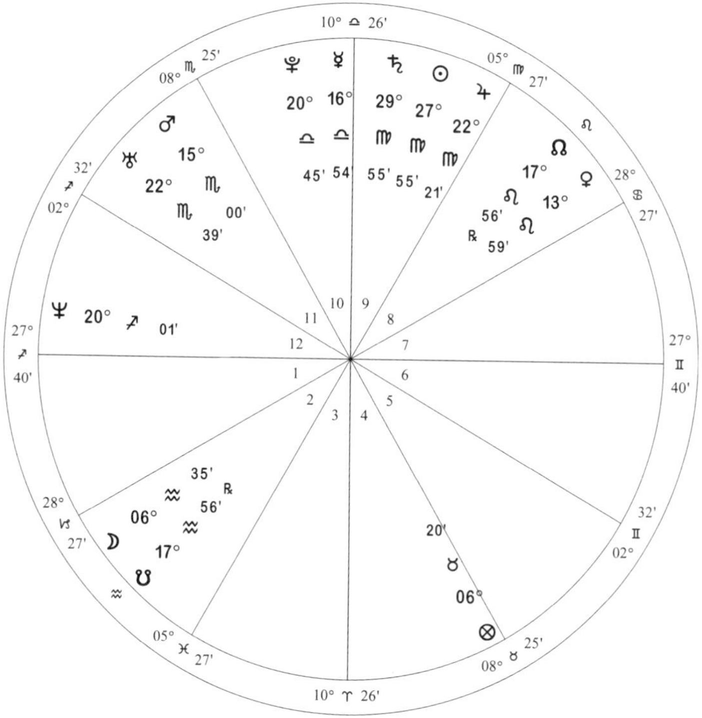

Dorothean Ess. Dig. (No Mut Rec. Points)								
Pl	Ruler	Exalt	Tripl	Term	Face	Detri	Fall	Score
☉	☿	☿	♀ m	♂	☿	♃	♀	- 5 P
☽	♄	--	♄	☿	♀	☉	--	- 5 P
☿	♀	♄ m	♄	♃	♄ m	♂	☉	- 5 P
♀	☉	--	☉ m	♀ +	♃	♄	--	+2
♂	♂ +	--	♀	♀	☉	♀	☽	+5
♃	☿	☿	♀	♄	☿	♃ -	♀	- 10 P
♄	☿	☿ m	♀	♂	☿ m	♃	♀	- 5 P
☊	☉	--	☉	♀	♃	♄	--	--
⊗	♀	☽	♀	♀	☿	♂	--	--
As	♃	☋	☉	♂	♄	☿	--	--
Mc	♀	♄	♄	♀	♄	♂	☉	--
☋	♄	--	♄	♀	☿	☉	--	--

Hs	Alm. (Pto)
1	♃
2	♄
3	♀
4	☉
5	♀
6	☿
7	☿
8	☽
9	☿
10	♄
11	♂
12	♃

Example 11-19a. Suicide, actual time, North Miami

RB
Pittsburgh, Pennsylvania
Time Zone: 5 hours West

October 6, 1979
40N26'26" 79W59'46"
Tropical Regiomontanus
Solar Return for October 6, 1979 in Pittsburgh, Pennsylvania

9:57:05 AM
Daylight Saving Time

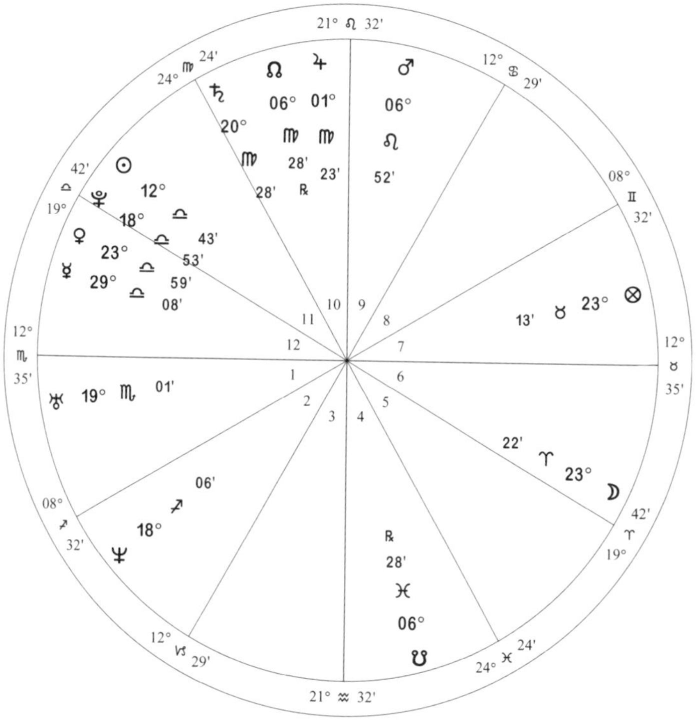

Dorothean Ess. Dig. (No Mut Rec. Points)								
Pl	Ruler	Exalt	Tripl	Term	Face	Detri	Fall	Score
☉	♀	♄	♄	♃	♄	♂	☉ -	- 9 P
☽	♂	☉	☉	♂	♀	♀	♄	- 5 P
☿	♀	♄ m	♄	☊	♃	♂	☉	- 5 P
♀	♀ +	♄	♄ m	☿	♃	♂	☉	+5
♂	☉	--	☉	☿	♄	♄	--	- 5 P
♃	☿	☿	♀	☿	☉	♃ -	♀	- 10 P
♄	☿	☿ m	♀ m	♄ +	☿	♃	♀	+2
☊	☿	☿	♀	☿	☉	♃	♀	--
⊗	♀	☽	♀	♄	♄	♂	--	--
As	♂	--	♀	♃	☉	♀	☽	--
Mc	☉	--	☉	♃	♂	♄	--	--
☋	♃	♀	♀	♀	♄	☿	☿	--

Hs	Alm. (Pto)
1	♂
2	♃
3	♂♄
4	♄
5	♂
6	☉
7	♀
8	☿
9	♃
10	☉
11	☿
12	♄

Example 11-19b. Suicide, birth location, 1979

RB
Pittsburgh, Pennsylvania
Time Zone: 5 hours West

October 5, 1980
40N26'26" 79W59'46"
Tropical Regiomontanus

3:48:50 PM
Daylight Saving Time

Solar Return for October 5, 1980 in Pittsburgh, Pennsylvania

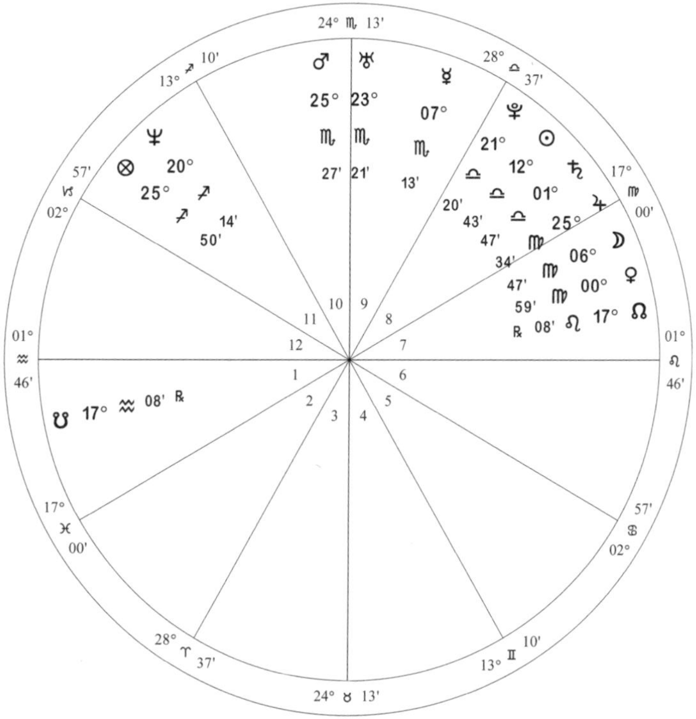

Dorothean Ess. Dig. (No Mut Rec. Points)								
Pl	Ruler	Exalt	Tripl	Term	Face	Detri	Fall	Score
☉	♀	♄	♄	♃	♄	♂	☉ -	- 9 P
☽	☿	☿	♀	☿	☉	♃	♀	- 5 P
☿	♂	--	♀	♃	♂	♀	☽	- 5 P
♀	☿	☿	♀ +	☿	☉	♃	♀ -	- 1
♂	♂ +	--	♀	☿	♀	♀	☽	+5
♃	☿	☿	♀	♂	☿	♃ -	♀	- 10 P
♄	♀	♄ +	♄ +	♄ +	☽	♂	☉	+9
☊	☉	--	☉	♀	♃	♄	--	--
⊗	♃	☋ +	☉	♂	♄	☿	--	--
As	♄	--	♄	♄	♀	☉	--	--
Mc	♂	--	♀	☿	♀	♀	☽	--
☋	♄	--	♄	♀	☿	☉	--	--

Hs	Alm. (Pto)
1	♄
2	♃
3	☉
4	♀
5	☿
6	☽
7	☉
8	☿
9	♄
10	♂
11	♃
12	♀♄

Example 11-19c. Suicide, birth location, 1980

RB
North Miami, Florida
Time Zone: 5 hours West

October 6, 1979
25N53'23" 80W11'13"
Tropical Regiomontanus

9:57:05 AM
Daylight Saving Time

Solar Return for October 6, 1979 in North Miami, Florida

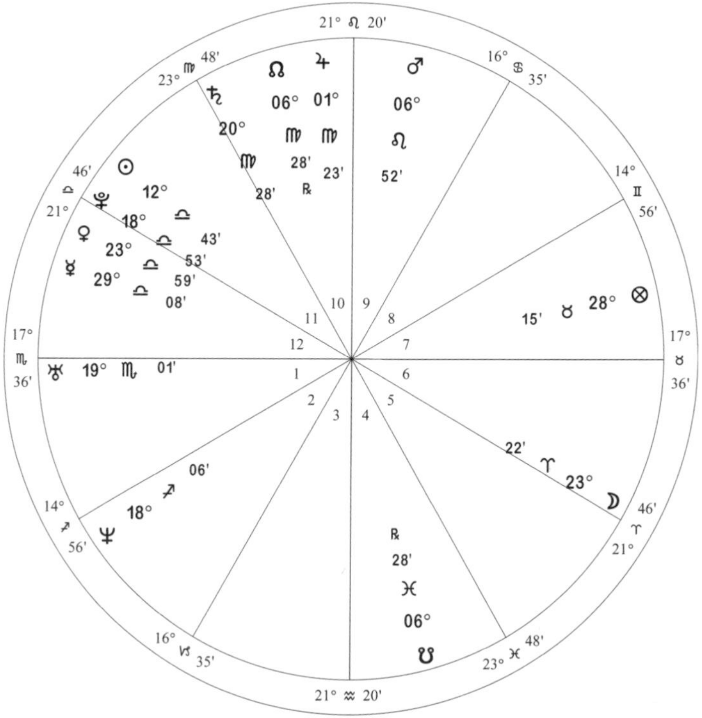

Dorothean Ess. Dig. (No Mut Rec. Points)								
Pl	Ruler	Exalt	Tripl	Term	Face	Detri	Fall	Score
☉	♀	♄	♄	♃	♄	♂	☉ -	- 9 P
☽	♂	☉	☉	♂	♀	♀	♄	- 5 P
☿	♀	♄ m	♄	☊	♃	♂	☉	- 5 P
♀	♀ +	♄	♄ m	☿	♃	♂	☉	+5
♂	☉	--	☉	☿	♄	♄	--	- 5 P
♃	☿	☿	♀	☿	☉	♃ -	♀	- 10 P
♄	☿	☿ m	♀ m	♄ +	☿	♃	♀	+2
☊	☿	☿	♀	☿	☉	♃	♀	--
⊗	♀	☽	♀	♂	♄	♂	--	--
As	♂	--	♀	♀	☉	♀	☽	--
Mc	☉	--	☉	♃	♂	♄	--	--
☋	♃	♀	♀	♀	♄	☿	☿	--

Hs	Alm. (Pto)
1	♂
2	♃
3	♂♄
4	♄
5	♃
6	☉♂
7	♀
8	☿
9	☽
10	☉
11	☿
12	♄

Example 11-19d. Suicide, residence location, 1979

RB
North Miami, Florida
Time Zone: 5 hours West

October 5, 1980
25N53'23" 80W11'13"
Tropical Regiomontanus
Solar Return for October 5, 1980 in North Miami, Florida

3:48:50 PM
Daylight Saving Time

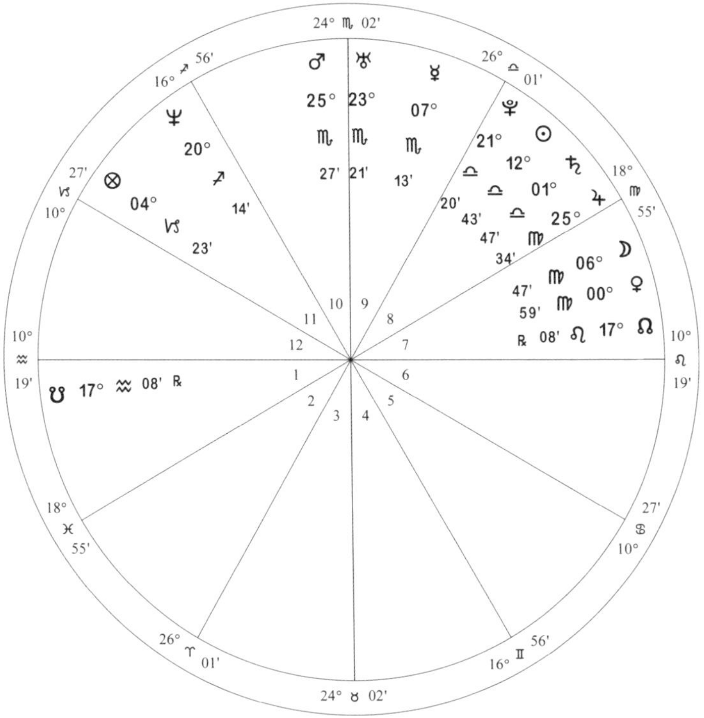

Dorothean Ess. Dig. (No Mut Rec. Points)								
Pl	Ruler	Exalt	Tripl	Term	Face	Detri	Fall	Score
☉	♀	♄	♄	♃	♄	♂	☉ -	- 9 P
☽	☿	☿	♀	☿	☉	♃	♀	- 5 P
☿	♂	--	♀	♃	♂	♀	☽	- 5 P
♀	☿	☿	♀ +	☿	☉	♃	♀ -	- 1
♂	♂ +	--	♀	☿	♀	♀	☽	+5
♃	☿	☿	♀	♂	☿	♃ -	♀	- 10 P
♄	♀	♄ +	♄ +	♄ +	☽	♂	☉	+9
☊	☉	--	☉	♀	♃	♄	--	--
⊗	♄	♂	♀	♀	♃	☽	♃	--
As	♄	--	♄	☿	☿	☉	--	--
Mc	♂	--	♀	☿	♀	♀	☽	--
☋	♄	--	♄	♀	☿	☉	--	--

Hs	Alm. (Pto)
1	♄
2	♃
3	☉
4	♀
5	☿
6	♃
7	☉
8	☿
9	♄
10	♂
11	♃
12	♂♄

Example 11-19e. Suicide, residence location, 1980

the 12th, at the last degree of Libra, not technically afflicted even if suggestive, and still in out-of-sect Triplicity. Libra was the natal sign of Mercury, but the Moon was opposite its natal sign. That Moon in Aries was in a partile opposition to Venus in the 12th, and was also square radix Saturn. To the extent that we could have a classical signature for alcohol addiction, it would have to be the Moon. With the opposition of Moon and Venus in the 6th-12th of this chart square natal Saturn, we would wonder whether the idea of commitment to a relationship was more than he could handle.

In the 1980 solar return, there is a stellium in the 8th, again ruled by Mercury, but Mercury is merely weak here – not afflicted. Neither is the Moon afflicted, but in a sign with Triplicity, and no close aspects to malefics. Venus was in its radix sign, Mars was strong, and Saturn was strong. But that strong Saturn was the ruler of the 1st in the 8th – and in a partile trine to the Ascendant, no less.

So: the 1979 solar return shows the stress, but it is the 1980 solar return that has the 8th house signature. Perhaps that is the explanation of the event occurring in the transitional period.

Examples 11-19d & e give the solar returns for his place of residence, which doesn't give significantly different results. In the solar return for 1979, the physical location moved Pluto off the 12th house cusp, which, given the results, seems a little less descriptive.

Thus, we have seen in our examples that death does look different depending on who dies. And as we might well expect, it is often the survivors with the more distinct patterns. They have to live with the consequences longer.

Chapter 11 Endnotes

1. I owe the terminology to Jane Ridder-Patrick, who in turn got it from a friend.
2. Gadbury, 1661, pp 212-232.
3. As I discussed in Traditional Medical Astrology, a prediction of death in a modern context may be translated as a medical crisis that will not heal itself (if it will) without significant medical intervention. In other words, it should not be taken as an automatic death sentence, but as an admonition to use extreme medical awareness.
4. Gadbury, 1661, pp 227-228
5. Lilly, *Christian Astrology*, p 245.
6. Saunders, 1677, p 15.
7. See Partridge, 1679, 17. Also: Bishop, John, and Richard Kirby. *The Marrow of Astrology the Second Part. Wherein Is Contained, a Table of Houses, Calculated for the Latitude of London: With Tables of Semidiurnal and Seminocturnal Arches. Also Tables of Twilight and Mundane Aspects; and the Whole Doctrine of Nativities, Laid Down in Twenty Genitures, According to the True Intent and Meaning of Ptolomy, Wherein Is Discovered the Errors of Argol, Regiomontanus, and Others. The Like Never before Done in English. By John Bishop, Student in Astrology and Chimistry*. microform. printed for Joseph Streater near Paul's-Wharf in Thames-street and are to be sold by the booksellers in London, London, 1687, p 3
8. In *Traditional Medical Astrology*, I give the method for calculating the Hyleg. Here, the computation shows a weak Hyleg, if there is one at all.
9. Morin (Holden), pp 56-57.
10. Callanan, Thomas. The Astrology of Jean Baptiste Morin, http://www.skyscript.co.uk/morin.html, no year given.
11. Please see Lehman, *Traditional Medical Astrology*, Chapter 4.
12. Here are some sources for Jupiter as ruling fever: Lilly, *Christian Astrology*, p 63; Al-Biruni, p 252; Saunders, *Physic,* p 19. The compiled version for these sources is: Lehman, J. Lee. *The Book of Rulerships*. Atglen, PA: Schiffer Press, 1992.
13. Robert Hand has proposed the more modern-sounding term: planets going on the same journey.
14. Lehman, *TMA*, Chapter 4.
15. Lehman, *TMA*, Chapter 5. This gives both the calculation and a discussion of how to use it.

12

A Life in Solar Returns

A LONG TIME AGO, IN THE GALAXY FAR AWAY KNOWN AS CHAPTER 1, I DISCUSSED THE FACT THAT SOLAR RETURN TECHNIQUE DEVELOPED IN PARALLEL WITH ARIES INGRESS THEORY, BECAUSE BOTH WERE SEEN AS KINDS OF RETURNS: ONE MUNDANE, AND ONE PERSONAL. Before we begin our review, I wish to present one extended example, which ties these two themes together. In addition, this exercise engages us in the real challenge in solar return delineation: just what to say to people, whether friends, family, or clients, about this yearly progress of our lives, as illustrated by our returns.

The human experience of time happens on many levels. We experience the hours in a day. We experience days, weeks, and months. We experience years, decades, and finally, a lifetime. But which of these units of time are the most important? It depends, of course, on the nature of the issue at hand. A politician operates in election cycles; a student operates in however long it will take to get the degree. A farmer operates for the next harvest; an independent contractor on the length of the contract. Even as we have personal cycles, we tend to act as if the present extends indefinitely into the future, no matter how much evidence we have which contradicts this myth.

So just how important is a year in the scheme of human activity? As children, we look forward to our birthdays: we may get a party, some presents. And when I'm eight, then I can do... As we become adults, we still have our birthdays embedded as secular holidays, we may still have a party, and at least we try to do something festive to celebrate. And perhaps most importantly, it's the one time we can be counted upon to reflect on the aging process, and whether our lives are working according to plan.

As astrologers, we know that the return of any body to its natal placement is also a re-setting and re-connecting with the energy of that planet. However, while that body has returned to its natal placement, *the other planets have not!* To use an analogy, the return of a body to its natal placement sets up a vibration with the natal chart. That vibration is a unity, but all the other planetary placements at the time of that planet's return are playing a new harmony compared to it. There is familiarity and difference at the same time, as well as harmony and dissonance. Being creatures of habit, we want that return to be an absolute return, where everything is the same *because then we wouldn't have to do anything about it.* However, more than one sage has said, it's the journey that's the point, and nobody ever learned a thing by staying the same. From this, we understand that the challenge of any return is to embrace the change while celebrating the connection that the return itself represents. The returning planet is the tether to the nativity which is the ground in which change manifests.

For the last nine chapters, we have been immersed in examining different types of solar returns. Now it's time to come back home and examine a *life* – and through it, how successive returns become a pattern that we as astrologers can read.

In chapter 2, we examined the life of Theodore Roosevelt, to see the relationship of solar returns through time: now we will examine his younger cousin Franklin. Also in these last nine chapters, we have used Eleanor as one example, who in many respects was the bridge between these two presidents. Eleanor's father was Theodore's younger brother. Theodore was a Republican; Franklin was a Democrat. Franklin and Eleanor had met through family channels, but they were only distant cousins. The family provided the matrix which allowed them to develop a deeper relationship; the family also provided Franklin with the idea that if "Uncle Ted" (actually his fifth cousin) could be president, so could he. By the time he was in college, Franklin had conceived this idea, and set about consciously applying the model of Uncle Ted to his life's plans. At the age of fifty, in 1932, he accomplished his goal of becoming president. At his side was his friend, Kermit Roosevelt, Theodore's son. Uncle Ted had died in 1919.

So we will examine Franklin's life, from his marriage until his death. And in the process, we will add a dimension that we haven't considered previously: the Aries Ingress. Here's the reason. Franklin consciously identified himself with the goal of becoming president at a fairly early age: early enough to make different life choices than he might have made otherwise. By doing so, he put himself in a position to become a policy-maker, first at the state level, then within the national Democratic Party, then with the country as a whole. As he aligned himself with these constituencies, he began to act outside of himself, he began to influence the larger milieu – and be influenced by it in turn. Not that any of this stifled his ambition, but he realized he could not achieve his goal within a vacuum. In the process, he became an instrument of the body politic: and it is precisely the body politic we study when we do an Aries Ingress for a country capital. Political parties in modern life have become rather like competing dynasties. There is a continuity with a political party which makes it greater than one person – and yet a strong leader can change the direction of a party. The party's history provides a drag (or call it karma, if you like) on what decisions that party can make.

In Franklin's time, the Republican Party had been the dominant political party since Abraham Lincoln and the Civil War in 1861. First the party of abolitionism (the ending of slavery), in the aftermath of the Civil War, the Republican Party then became the party of reconstruction (the reintegration of the South after the Civil War, most often in ways advantageous to the North), and then, the party of Big Business, including the large trusts which were the 19th century equivalent of our modern mega-corporations.

The Democratic Party had so rarely been in power that it had subdivided into three competing factions with little in common:

- The Northeastern/Midwestern Democrats mostly had urban bosses with an equally strong machine that controlled patronage. These were somewhat liberal or progressive, supporting immigrants and ethnic groups in return for party loyalty.
- The Southern Democrats, who were generally conservative and race-baiting, and averse to any improvement in condition for the lower classes.
- The Western Democrats, who saw themselves as the future, and would align with whichever side gave them more clout.

The only Democratic President after the Civil War until the end of the 19th century was Grover Cleveland, who served 1885-1889: one term. By the time that Franklin was coming of age, the Democrats were so used to losing at the national level, that the bulk of their energy was spent in internecine squabbling, and the perception was that the only way a Democrat could be elected would be if the Republicans made a big mistake.

Franklin Roosevelt's Nativity

Let's begin by examining Franklin Roosevelt's natal chart: its strengths and its weaknesses. His chart has a very powerful Moon, and a very debilitated Sun, from a dignity perspective. This described his parents almost perfectly. His mother, Sara Delano, was an overbearing influence until she died. His father was much older than Sara, a widower, and ill most of the time Franklin was growing up. After James Roosevelt died, while Franklin received an inheritance, the bulk of the estate went to Sara – and *under her control, the estate supported Franklin and then his family for most of his adult life*. The 10ᵗʰ house is the mother: and there is that powerful Cancer Moon. Franklin was encouraged to be a Momma's boy.

Not surprisingly with that Moon, Franklin loved the sea, and he loved to sail. His father taught him, and his love of the water would be a source of enjoyment throughout his life. It would affect his career, and be one of the things he passed on to his sons.

The one other early influence was Groton, the preparatory school that opened just one year before Franklin entered. Groton was consciously built on a British school model, with emphasis on athletics as as well as academics, and with truly spartan living conditions, all for the boys of the very wealthy. This was privileged privation. Franklin was not a great athlete, but he tried out for *every* activity, and hardened his body. He spent his young adult years with the muscle tone of an athlete.

Franklin's 3ʳᵈ house is ruled by Mars, so here perhaps we see the influence of Groton. Mars was in Term and retrograde in the 10ᵗʰ house. His athletic ability was not great, but he could look the part, which is one of the meanings of a planet in its own Terms.

Mercury ruled both Ascendant and Midheaven, suggesting the identity of who he was, equated with what he did, and specifically, what he got recognition for doing. His Mercury had in-sect Triplicity. He was curious, and he turned into a great communicator, both through listening and speaking. Notice that the Mercury was partile trine Mars, and partile square Pluto. This was not just the fist in the velvet glove. This man was intensely competitive, but *very* smooth. This also reveals the engine behind his long-standing presidential ambition. FDR was driven, but he wasn't uncouth.

We pick up our story in 1905, when he married Eleanor. His father had already died, and he had completed his degree at Harvard. Continuing to follow his Uncle Ted, he entered Columbia Law School the year before he married. As we enter the stream of events of his life, what do we expect the solar return in question to show us? Do we expect to predict that Franklin would marry in 1905? Or do we ask, *if* Franklin married in 1905, what does it say for the marriage? Or alternatively, why did Franklin not marry *until* 1905, when he "re-met" Eleanor in 1902, after having last seen her as a child?

There are age, cultural, personal *and* astrological answers to these questions, but the first point that I want to emphasize again is this: while we may be looking at the more fate-driven birth location solar returns, *life does not appear to work as a series of proclamations that one must do things at a particular time or not at all*. The unavoidable fate pieces of our lives just as frequently involve others – so the intersection between people and their respective nativities must mesh. Accordingly, the best time may not be that shown in one person's nativity alone.

So mostly, we will be looking at these charts from the standpoint of: *if the Native engages this theme this particular year, how will it work?*

As we said, Franklin "re-met" Eleanor in 1902, so theoretically, he could have married her anytime from then on. *Note to self:* if

NATAL CHART
Franklin D Roosevelt
January 30, 1882
8:45 PM
Hyde Park, Dutchess, NY
41N47'05" 73W56'01"
Local Mean Time
Time Zone: 0 hours West
Tropical Regiomontanus

Day of ☽	Hour of ♄
Last Hr ☽	- 4 mins
Next Hr ♃	+67 mins

FIXED STARS	
♇☌Alcyone	0°59's
☽☌ Murzim	0°42's
⊗☌Alrischa	0°25's
Mc☌Alnilam	0°18's
♂☌Betelgeuse	0°07's
♄☌Hamal	0°04's
♄☌Schedar	0°04'a
⊗☌Mirach	0°37'a

Hs	Alm. (Dor)
1	☿
2	♀♄
3	♂
4	♃
5	♄
6	♄
7	♃
8	☉♂
9	☽
10	☿
11	☽
12	☉

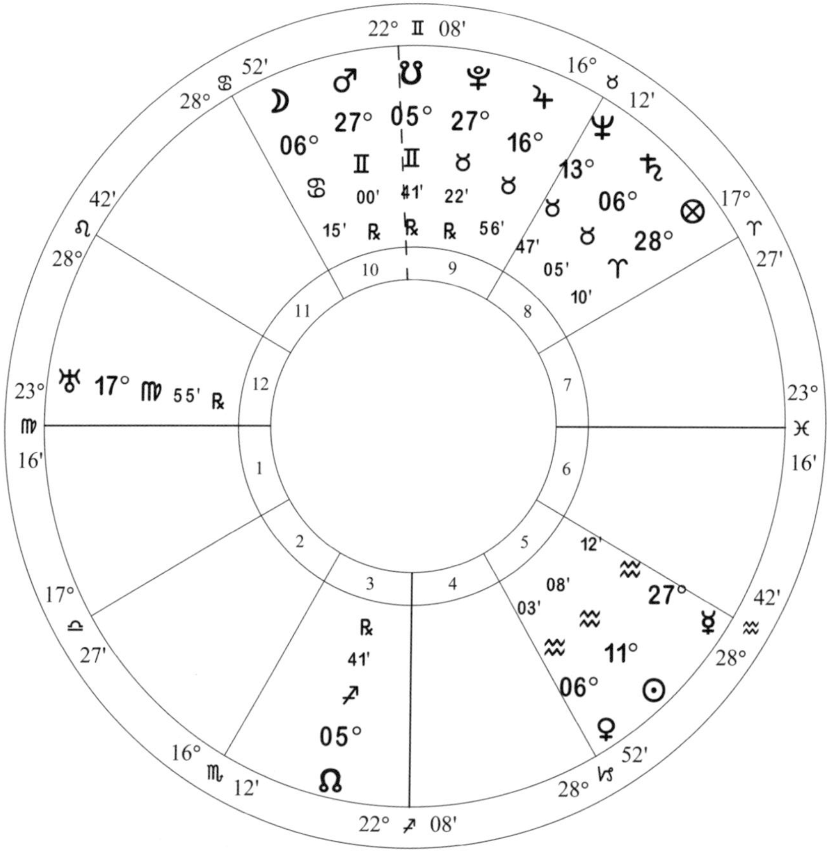

ESSENTIAL DIGNITIES (Dorothean)

Pl	Ruler	Exalt	Tripl	Term	Face	Detri	Fall	Score
☉	♄	--	☿	☿	☿	☉ -	--	- 10 P
☽	☽ +	♃ m	♂	♃	♀	♄	♂	+9
☿	♄	--	☿ +	♂	☽	☉	--	+3
♀	♄ m	--	☿	☿	♀ +	☉	--	+6
♂	☿	☊	☿	♂ +	☉	♃	--	+2
♃	♀	☽ m	☽	♃ +	☽	♂	--	+6
♄	♀ m	☽	☽	♀	☿	♂	--	+0 P
☊	♃	☋	♃	♃	☿	☿	--	--
⊗	♂	☉	♃	♄	♀	♀	♄	--
As	☿	☿	☽	♄	☿	♃	♀	--
Mc	☿	☊	☿	♄	☉	♃	--	--
☋	☿	☊	☿	☿	♃	♃	--	--

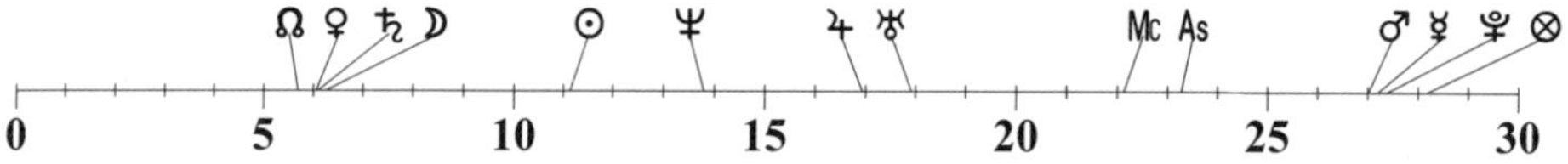

Example 12-1. Franklin Roosevelt's nativity

Franklin was going to marry Eleanor, he needed to know Eleanor. *Note to self:* Franklin was twenty when he "re-met" Eleanor, and thus, already of marriageable age. *Note to self:* Sara Delano Roosevelt, Franklin's mother, opposed the match. Therefore, he was going to have to go against that powerful force in his life. And she *did* throw up obstacles and delays.

1902-1905

In the years 1902-1905, remarkably, Franklin had something conjunct the 7th house cusp *every year*. In 1902, it was the Sun: and he re-met Eleanor. In 1903, it was the South Node: hardly conducive to a successful marriage, or, in his case, any marriage at all. In 1904, it was Neptune. He and Eleanor became formally engaged this year, despite Sara's continued attempts to sabotage the relationship. That sounds more like the young couple sneaking around behind Mom's back.

Finally, with a forceful Mars in Scorpio on the Descendant, Franklin and Eleanor married. Uncle Ted gave the bride away, and if the sitting President garnered most of the attention at the wedding reception, Franklin at least had the opportunity to bask in his ambition close up. It also moved him more closely into his older cousin's circles – to the extent that TR's younger son Kermit became close.

Following Gadbury's solar return rules, having a dignified ruler of the 7th house is an argument of marriage, or an argument of benefit from the marriage partner. It is not, however, an argument that the Native *must* marry – but *if* he does, he will benefit. The Sun is in the 11th house by the Five Degree Rule – making this a year of associations or contacts. Elsewhere, I have discussed the association of the 11th house not only with friends, but with bonding between generations, especially of oligarchs.[1] The symbolism relating to Franklin's determination to follow Uncle Ted's life plan is simply too strong to ignore, as well as so strong as to lead to the question:

Franklin D Roosevelt   January 31, 1905   10:52:51 AM
Hyde Park, Dutchess, NY   41N47'05"   73W56'01"   Standard Time
Time Zone: 5 hours West   Tropical Regiomontanus
Solar Return for January 31, 1905 in Hyde Park, Dutchess, NY

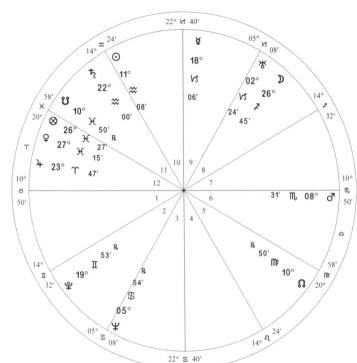

Example 12-2. Franklin Roosevelt's solar return for 1905

Franklin D Roosevelt
Hyde Park, Dutchess, NY
Time Zone: 5 hours West

January 31, 1906
41N47'05" 73W56'01"
Tropical Regiomontanus
Solar Return for January 31, 1906 in Hyde Park, Dutchess, NY

4:38:15 PM
Standard Time

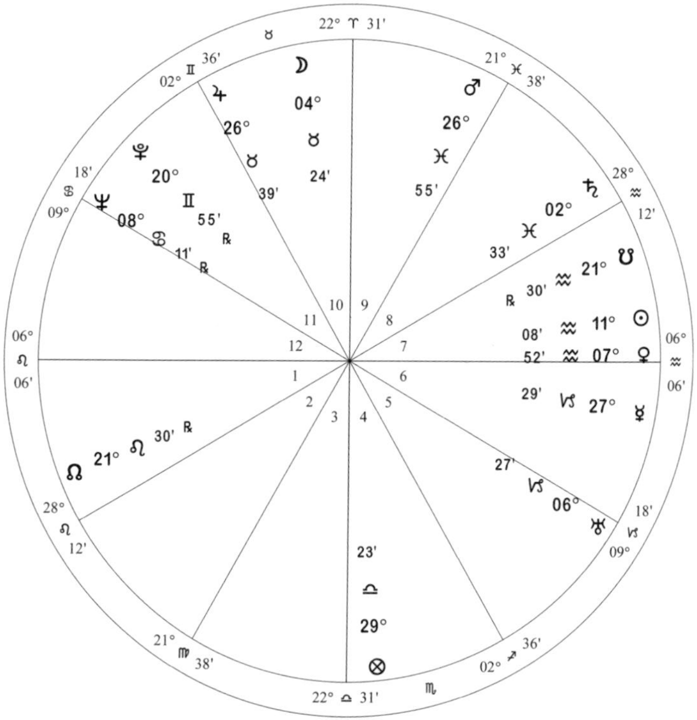

Dorothean Ess. Dig. (No Mut Rec. Points)								
Pl	Ruler	Exalt	Tripl	Term	Face	Detri	Fall	Score
☉	♄	--	♄	☿	☿ m	☉ -	--	- 10 P
☽	♀	☽ +	♀	♀	☿	♂	--	+4
☿	♄	♂	♀	♄	☉ m	☽	♃	- 5 P
♀	♄	--	♄ m	☿	♀ +	☉	--	+1
♂	♃	♀	♀	♄	♂ +	☿	☿	+1
♃	♀	☽	♀	♂	♄	♂	--	- 5 P
♄	♃	♀	♀ m	♀	♄ +	☿	☿	+1
☊	☉	--	☉	♃	♂	♄	--	--
⊗	♀	♄	♄	☊	♃	♂	☉	--
As	☉	--	☉	☿	♄	♄	--	--
Mc	♂	☉	☉	♂	♀	♀	♄	--
☋	♄	--	♄	♃	☽	☉	--	--

Hs	Alm. (Pto)
1	☉
2	☉
3	☿
4	♄
5	♃
6	♄
7	♄
8	♄
9	♃
10	☉♂
11	☿
12	♃

Example 12-3. Franklin Roosevelt's solar return for 1906

was part of the attraction of Eleanor *her* closer relationship to TR?

Franklin had grown up an only child. His half-brother was his father's child from his prior marriage, and James, Jr., was twenty eight years his senior. Eleanor had brothers, but a childhood broken by the death of both parents. Franklin wanted a large family, around six children. With the Sun in the 5th house natally, this would hardly be considered an odd sentiment on his part. They wasted no time starting on the family, while Franklin continued his studies at Columbia Law School. Their first child was born during his 1906 solar return.

The North Node was in the 5th house in Virgo (a barren sign), for his 1905 solar return, when Anna was conceived. Clearly that was not preventative in this case. So this matched Gadbury's second aphorism for having children.

1906

In 1905, the Sun was in the 11th house. In 1906, the Sun was in the 7th. While Mars dignified in Pisces is in the 9th house, showing the progress he was making in law school, the Sun, Mercury and South Node in the 7th shows where Franklin's attention was that year: on his wife. We know now from her journals that Eleanor did not enjoy sex with Franklin, so that may have been part of the meaning of the South Node there, but it was the Venus fecundity which seemed to be taking center stage in Franklin's consciousness anyway.

In the actual year of daughter Anna's birth, 1906, the Moon and Jupiter unimpedited in the 10th are each arguments of the birth of a child. Here the Moon is in Taurus, back in dignity, like the dignified Moon in Cancer in his own nativity. And Jupiter is back in its radix sign, as well as ruling the 5th.

1907

In 1907, their eldest son James was born – and Franklin dropped out of law school and began his career in the law. The Sun is now in the 4th house, along with Mercury and the South Node. For the end of school part, we have Pluto in the 9th house; Mercury ruling it was back in its radix sign. Franklin was eager to go to work – and in his era, it was only necessary to pass the bar exam, not having the law degree wasn't necessary for practice, passing the bar exam was required, which he did.

We had seen Mars in Scorpio as the harbinger of his marriage in 1905 when it conjoined the 7th house cusp. Now we see it in the 2nd and ruling the 2nd. This really does look like an earnest desire on his part to earn some money to support his family. Despite family wealth, Franklin and Eleanor didn't always have enough money themselves to do whatever they wanted. Franklin's mother Sara largely controlled the money, so this can also be seen as Franklin acquiring some level of independence.

How did he get his job? That's where his background was so valuable, because he simply asked around, and eventually landed a job at the prestigious firm of Cater Ledyard & Milburn, where he learned the actual practice of law, something not taught at Columbia. The ruler of the 6th (his job) is in the 9th in Exaltation – he was already part of the Old Boys Network through his undergraduate years at Harvard and his family connections.

As for the birth of his son, the ruler of the 5th was in the 5th – but it was Saturn, only mollified by being in fertile Pisces. I have to say that, while the 4th house Sun does show concerns relating to family, his on-the-job training seems the more important theme for the year.

Franklin D Roosevelt
Hyde Park, Dutchess, NY
Time Zone: 5 hours West

January 31, 1907
41N47'05" 73W56'01"
Tropical Regiomontanus

10:32:52 PM
Standard Time

Solar Return for January 31, 1907 in Hyde Park, Dutchess, NY

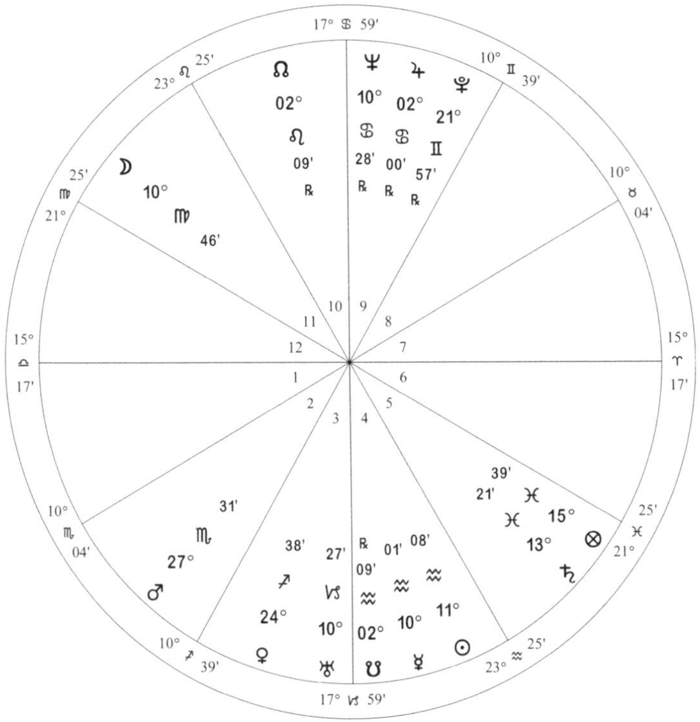

Dorothean Ess. Dig. (No Mut Rec. Points)

Pl	Ruler	Exalt	Tripl	Term	Face	Detri	Fall	Score
☉	♄	--	☿	☿	☿	☉ -	--	- 10 P
☽	☿	☿	☽ +	♀	♀	♃	♀	+3
☿	♄	--	☿ +	☿ +	☿ +	☉	--	+6
♀	♃	☋	♃	♄	♄	☿	--	- 5 P
♂	♂ +	--	♂ +	♄	♀	♀	☽	+8
♃	☽	♃ +	♂	♂	♀	♄	♂	+4
♄	♃	♀	♂	♃	♃	☿	☿	- 5 P
☊	☉	--	♃	♄	♄	♄	--	--
⊗	♃	♀	♂	☿	♃	☿	☿	--
As	♀	♄	☿	♃	♄	♂	☉	--
Mc	☽	♃	♂	☿	☿	♄	♂	--
☋	♄	--	☿	♄	♀	☉	--	--

Hs	Alm. (Pto)
1	♀♄
2	♂
3	♃
4	♂♄
5	♄
6	♃
7	☉♂
8	☽
9	☿
10	☽
11	☉♃
12	☿

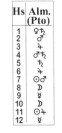

Example 12-4. Franklin Roosevelt's solar return for 1907

Franklin D Roosevelt
Hyde Park, Dutchess, NY
Time Zone: 5 hours West

February 1, 1908
41N47'05" 73W56'01"
Tropical Regiomontanus
Solar Return for February 1, 1908 in Hyde Park, Dutchess, NY

4:24:55 AM
Standard Time

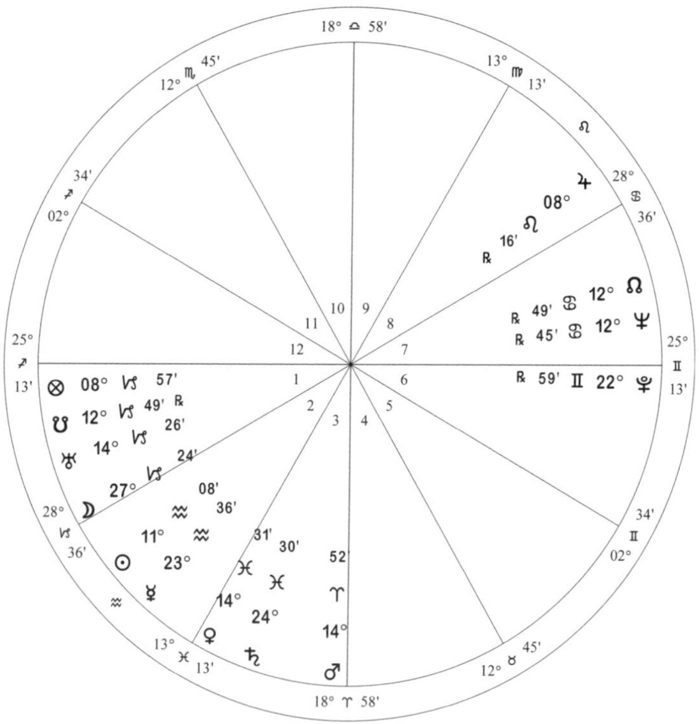

Dorothean Ess. Dig. (No Mut Rec. Points)								
Pl	Ruler	Exalt	Tripl	Term	Face	Detri	Fall	Score
☉	♄	--	☿	☿	☿	☉ -	--	- 10 P
☽	♄	♂	☽ +	♄	☉	☽ -	♃	- 2
☿	♄	--	☿ +	♃ m	☽	☉	--	+3
♀	♃	♀ +	♂	☿	♃	☿	☿	+4
♂	♂ +	☉	♃	☿	☉	♀	♄	+5
♃	☉	--	♃ +	☿ m	♄	♄	--	+3
♄	♃	♀	♂	♂	♂	☿	☿	- 5 P
☊	☽	♃	♂	♃	☿	♄	♂	--
⊗	♄	♂	☽	☿	♃	☽	♃	--
As	♃	☋	♃	♂	♄	☿	--	--
Mc	♀	♄	☿	♃	♄	♂	☉	--
☋	♄	♂	☽	♃	♂	☽	♃	--

Hs	Alm. (Pto)
1	♃
2	♄
3	♃
4	☉♂
5	☽
6	☿
7	☿
8	☽
9	☿
10	♀♄
11	♂
12	♃

Example 12-5. Franklin Roosevelt's solar return for 1908

1908

The year 1908 seemed to be one of those years where life simply continued. There was no addition to the family that year. Franklin continued to learn the tricks of the trade, still a junior lawyer. The only change in that year I can find is that they vacationed in New Jersey instead of Campobello because of concerns over son James developing pneumonia – from which he recovered. The Sun was in the 2nd, and FDR was taking care of business. The Moon in Capricorn at the 2nd house cusp suggests that they were experiencing cash flow, which was probable. Sara was still regularly infusing cash into their living circumstances.

The solar return has at least two features worth noting. First, the South Node in the 1st *could* represent lessened vitality. We don't have any record of Franklin being particularly sick that year. Perhaps the issue is that he was twenty-six: still young enough to throw off many of the more minor problems and to ignore a small downtick in vitality.

The modern astrologer might be concerned about Pluto near the Descendant, ruling his wife. As far as we know, Eleanor suffered no health nor other catastrophic problems in this year. In Chapter 9, we observed that Eleanor's solar return for the year that Franklin developed polio showed the illness very strongly. So it's not that it is impossible to read the spouse in the person's solar return. Notice that Mercury ruling the 7th is in Triplicity – and in its radix sign. Mercury is also trine the 7th house cusp. Eleanor is a strong influence that year, but she is not showing as being happy with that Pluto placement. Why? Most likely, the continuing meddling of her mother-in-law in their lives was definitely a source of dissatisfaction. This has some astrological evidence, in that Saturn ruled FDR's 10th (his mother), and Saturn was square that Pluto and the 7th house cusp.

1909

In 1909, their family expanded again with the birth of Franklin, Jr. Unfortunately, at the end of the Summer season, all three Roosevelt children caught the flu, and Franklin, Jr., died from it before his first birthday. Franklin's chart ruler, Mars, was in the 8th house of death. The house of the death of children is the 12th: the 8th from the 5th. Saturn in Detriment was in that house, a condition of Saturn worse than the radix Saturn. Thus, both malefics were in an 8th house, if the death of children is granted as a theme. Franklin's Sun was in the 11th: he was still trying to learn the ropes at the law office while this tragedy with his son was playing out. The Moon was opposite Mars, a feisty position. The illness and then decline of their son was difficult on both parents, and it is always hard to keep things on an even footing when it's the easiest thing to take out your frustrations on the person closest. Eleanor is shown as strong (Venus in Capricorn ruling the 7th in Triplicity) but volatile (conjunct Uranus).

1910

Eleanor became pregnant again just a couple of months after Franklin Jr.'s death. So in 1910, there was a birth. The 5th house cusp and the Ascendant were both in fertile signs, and the ruler of the 5th was in Taurus. The South Node in the 5th did not prevent a successful birth, and Elliott was actually the longest lived of the Roosevelt children.

So now we ask: when ambitious young men who are already married have the Sun in the 7th house of a solar return, do they focus their attention on their wives? I'm not saying that Franklin ignored Eleanor: I'm sure he didn't, in fact. However, the 7th house rules partnerships and open enemies – and contests. Franklin was already aware that his life plan had the law as a stepping stone to politics. However, unlike his Uncle Ted, Franklin belonged to the minority

Franklin D Roosevelt
Hyde Park, Dutchess, NY
Time Zone: 5 hours West

January 31, 1909
41N47'05" 73W56'01"
Tropical Regiomontanus
Solar Return for January 31, 1909 in Hyde Park, Dutchess, NY

10:06:22 AM
Standard Time

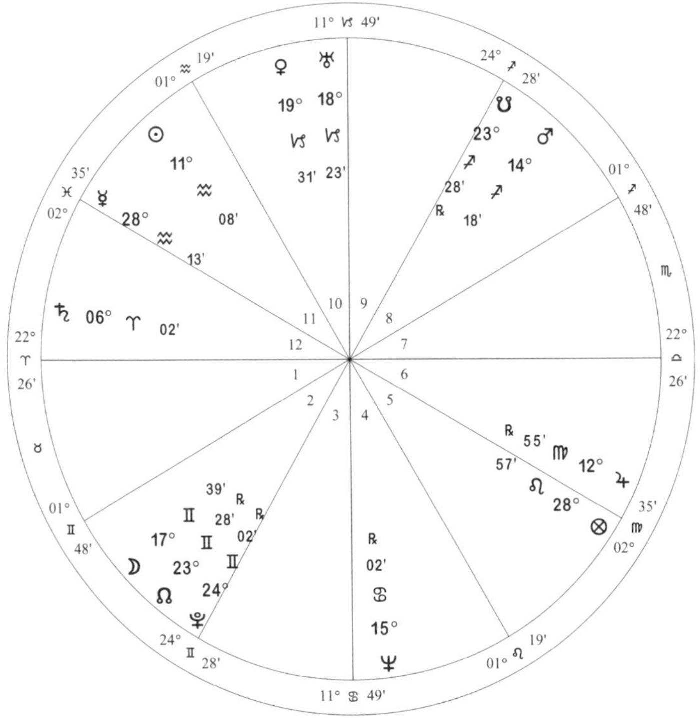

Dorothean Ess. Dig. (No Mut Rec. Points)								
Pl	Ruler	Exalt	Tripl	Term	Face	Detri	Fall	Score
☉	♄	--	♄ m	☿	☿	☉ -	--	- 10 P
☽	☿	☊	♄	♀	♂ m	♃	--	- 5 P
☿	♄	--	♄	♂ m	☽	☉	--	- 5 P
♀	♄	♂	♀ +	♂	♂	☽	♃	+3
♂	♃	☋	☉	☿ m	☽ m	☿	--	- 5 P
♃	☿	☿	♀	♀	♀	♃ -	♀	- 10 P
♄	♂	☉	☉ m	♀	♂	♀	♄ -	- 9 P
☊	☿	☊ +	♄	♄	☉	♃	--	--
⊗	☉	--	☉	♂	♂	♄	--	--
As	♂	☉	☉	♂	♀	♀	♄	--
Mc	♄	♂	♀	☿	♂	☽	♃	--
☋	♃	☋	☉	♄	♄	☿	--	--

Hs	Alm. (Pto)
1	☉♂
2	☿
3	☿♄
4	♃
5	☉
6	☿
7	♄
8	♃
9	♃
10	♂♄
11	♄
12	♀

Example 12-6. Franklin Roosevelt's solar return for 1909

Franklin D Roosevelt
Hyde Park, Dutchess, NY
Time Zone: 5 hours West

January 31, 1910
41N47'05" 73W56'01"
Tropical Regiomontanus

4:02:37 PM
Standard Time

Solar Return for January 31, 1910 in Hyde Park, Dutchess, NY

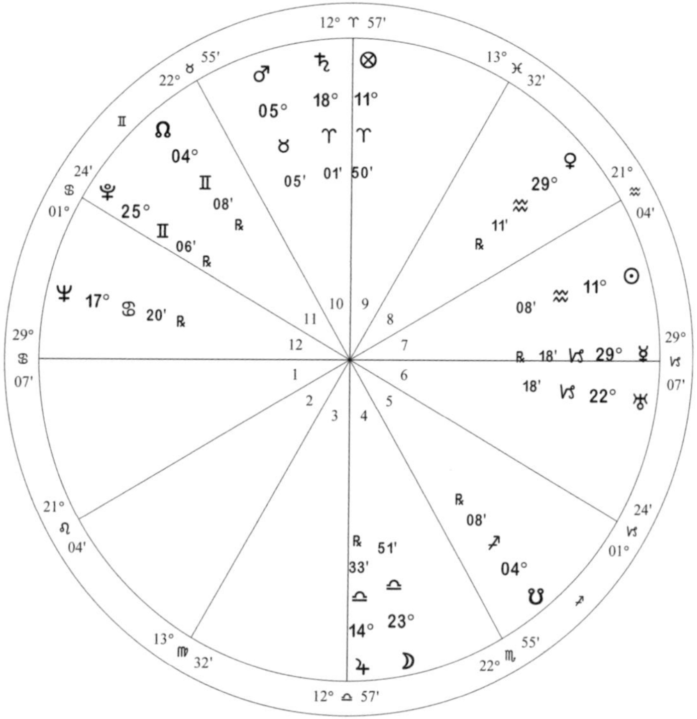

Dorothean Ess. Dig. (No Mut Rec. Points)								
Pl	Ruler	Exalt	Tripl	Term	Face	Detri	Fall	Score
☉	♄	--	♄ m	☿	☿ m	☉ -	--	- 10 P
☽	♀	♄	♄	☿	♃	♂	☉	- 5 P
☿	♄	♂	♀	♄ m	☉ m	☽	♃	- 5 P
♀	♄	--	♄	♂ m	☽	☉	--	- 5 P
♂	♀	☽	♀	♀ m	☿	♂ -	--	- 10 P
♃	♀	♄	♄	♃ +	♄	♂	☉	+2
♄	♂	☉	☉ m	☿ m	☉	♀	♄ -	- 9 P
☊	☿	☊ +	♄	☿	♃	♃	--	--
⊗	♂	☉	☉	♀	☉	♀	♄	--
As	☽	♃	♀	♄	☽	♄	♂	--
Mc	♂	☉	☉	♀	☉	♀	♄	--
☋	♃	☋	☉	♃	☿	☿	--	--

Hs	Alm. (Pto)
1	☽
2	☉
3	☿
4	♄
5	♂
6	♀♄
7	♄
8	♄
9	♃
10	☉
11	♀
12	☽

Example 12-7a. Franklin Roosevelt's solar return for 1910

Sun enters Ari 3-21-1910
Washington, D.C.
Time Zone: 5 hours West

March 21, 1910
38N53'42" 77W02'12"
Tropical Regiomontanus
NATAL CHART

7:02:59 AM
Standard Time

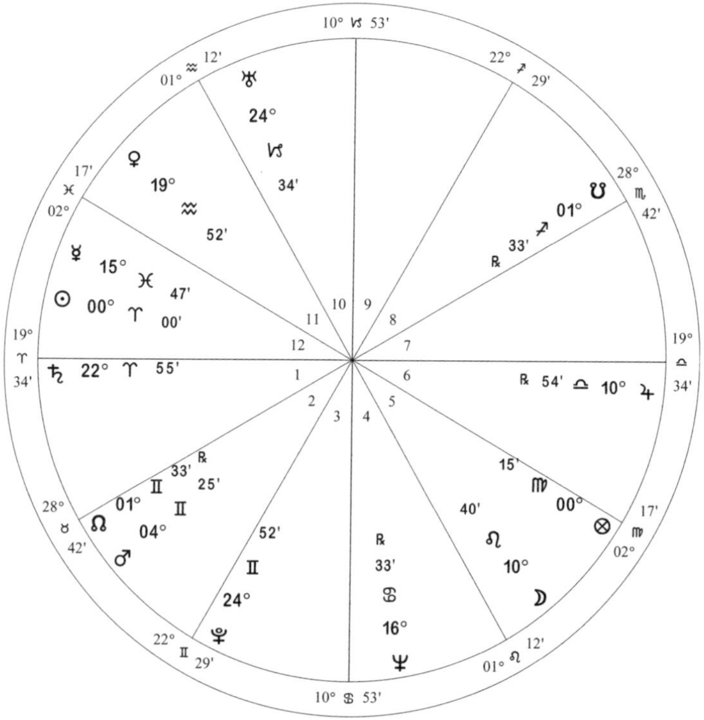

Dorothean Ess. Dig. (No Mut Rec. Points)								
Pl	Ruler	Exalt	Tripl	Term	Face	Detri	Fall	Score
☉	♂	☉ +	☉ +	♃	♂	♀	♄	+7
☽	☉	--	☉	☿	♃	♄	--	- 5 P
☿	♃	♀	♀	☿ +	♃	☿ -	☿ -	- 7
♀	♄	--	♄	♀ +	☿	☉	--	+2
♂	☿	☊	♄	☿	♃	♃	--	- 5 P
♃	♀	♄	♄	♀	♄	♂	☉	- 5 P
♄	♂	☉	☉	♂	♀	♀	♄ -	- 9 P
☊	☿	☊ +	♄	☿	♃	♃	--	--
⊗	☿	☿	♀	☿	☉	♃	♀	--
As	♂	☉	☉	☿	☉	♀	♄	--
Mc	♄	♂	♀	☿	♂	☽	♃	--
☋	♃	☋	☉	♃	☿	☿	--	--

Hs	Alm. (Pto)
1	☉
2	♀
3	☿♄
4	♃
5	☉
6	☿
7	♄
8	♂
9	♃
10	♂♄
11	♄
12	♀

Example 12-7b. Aries Ingress for 1910, Washington, DC

party: opportunities for office would come along less frequently. But Franklin was already putting out the word that he was interested in politics. In 1910, an opportunity opened up for the Democrats in the New York State Senate district where Hyde Park was located. The Democrats figured that, if nothing else, Franklin's family was rich enough to finance the campaign – which Sara did – and Franklin won the election!

In the 1910 solar return, Franklin's Ascendant was at 29 degrees – he was right on the cusp of a change. This was true: he was about to leave the law behind. Furthermore, Mercury was also at twenty nine degrees, and sitting partile conjunct the 7th house cusp. Venus was in its natal sign.

There is also quite an angularity about this 1910 return. Mars, Saturn, Fortuna, Mercury, Jupiter and the Moon – even Uranus is pretty close to angular. Saturn in Aries is one of those marks of a competitor as we have seen. FDR won this election by violating tradition, and driving to all the various towns and hamlets – a new technology that he would master, which was something that became a hallmark of his political career. With all the angularity, this is quite a harbinger of the start of his "public" career.

1910 also marks the start of his legislative career, or perhaps his employment as a politician, because, unlike the federal government, the State government commenced with the new year, which was still under the 1910 return, not 1911.

An elected legislature is generally considered to be the 11th house, a derivation of the king's counselors, and here we see the North Node. Perhaps more importantly, the 11th house ruler Venus is back in its radix sign. Venus was also part of the twenty-nine degree transition cohort. And what better word for transition considering Franklin's first actions as a State Senator! I mentioned in the introduction to this chapter that the Democratic Party in this time was split between several factions. In New York state, the dominant faction was still Tammany Hall, even if Boss Tweed himself was gone. In 1911, the state legislatures still elected national Senators: direct election by the people was not established until two years later, in

1913. To this point, whichever party was in power expected to elect their choice for Senator. The Tammany Hall apparatus was focused on New York City. Franklin was not elected from New York City, and further, he had run for office on a platform emphasizing clean government. Whatever the boss systems could boast for providing needed services for immigrants, clean they were not. Franklin led a revolt which ultimately forced Tammany to nominate a cleaner candidate. The same competitive juices that had encouraged him to fight for election continued to flow as he entered the Statehouse.

Most of the Senate fight occurred after Franklin's 1911 solar return had come into play. And one could note that, taking office on January 1, 1911, he was in that one-month transitional period so hotly discussed by many astrologers. Notice that in both the 1910 and 1911 charts, the 11th house cusp is a fixed sign. This simply indicates that, on matters relating to the legislature itself, he was more than happy to be stubborn and dig in his heels. Being a fixed sign Aquarius anyway, his maximum flexibility was always *before* he made up his mind.

Being 29 in 1911, this was the year of his Saturn return, and Saturn had just entered his natal Saturn sign Taurus at the time of his solar return. A stint in the state legislature was on his Uncle Ted Life Trajectory Plan, and so his check-off list of life's goals was proceeding apace.

It is only in 1910 that Franklin became a public figure. And immediately, he launched into a political fight which had national implications for the Democratic Party. Freshmen state senators generally don't do this! In 1911, that rebellion continued, with SR-Venus ruling his Ascendant partile conjunct radix Mercury, and in its own radix sign. While he did compromise with Tammany Hall ultimately, the gauntlet was thrown down, and he became much more noticeable than your average freshman state senator. In the 1911 chart, Neptune was in the 10th house. He had become the public face of fighting corruption, an image that worked well, as that had been the hallmark of Uncle Ted, so recently president. If Neptune is about deception, then fighting it must surely also have a Neptune component. Having the same last name as his much more popular and famous relative, and also being related to him, provided an extra neptunian glamour when Franklin followed a public path that echoed Uncle Ted. Mercury and Uranus were also angular, with Mars hovering near the 4ᵗʰ house cusp as well. The SR-Moon was trine radix Moon. So this year proceeded on track for Franklin as well.

1910 Aries Ingress

The 1910 Aries Ingress shows Saturn in Aries conjunct the Ascendant, an angry Saturn. The people were restless and angry in this chart. It was precisely the voter backlash against the Republicans that brought the Democrats into power in New York. Since this was not a presidential election year, this Aries Ingress chart did not impact directly on President Taft, *except* through his ability to govern. Now, of course, since Franklin's solar return occurred less than two months before the Aries Ingress, his SR-Saturn position will be quite similar. But it was in the *10ᵗʰ house* of Franklin's chart: he *could* take on this voter anger as a personal badge and slogan – and he did.

His position as a state legislator, relatively low on the political totem pole, meant that he was hardly in a position to be a primary agent of the USA Aries Ingress. But he could catch a wave, so to speak – and he did.

1911

In 1911, the New York state Democratic caucus eventually fielded a compromise candidate that was acceptable to all parties, and now Roosevelt could simply go back to work and learn about

---

From Private to Public Persona

So we must ask: if Franklin became a public figure in 1910, does that mean he is now an agent of change on a national level? He may be, but I believe the answer is situational. Not every state legislator ever becomes part of the national destiny. One simply has to read all the crazy legislation which has been proposed by state legislators over the years to realize that election to state office can be a whimsical process.[2] Few freshman legislators are more than bench-warmers for their first few terms in office, if not their entire careers. But Franklin put himself in the position to confront what he considered a dangerous and unfortunate aspect of the Democratic Party structure. His decision in 1910 put him on a course that still had ramifications in the 1932 presidential campaign.

When a politician raises an issue that either becomes a national trend, or through participation accelerates an existing such process, he or she now potentially becomes a nexus in the national fate. At this point, the Aries Ingress for the country capital kicks in as a factor to be considered with that individual.

Roosevelt's ability to jump into the stream was certainly helped by his patrician status. As his biographer Brands points out, it was the simple fact that Franklin and Eleanor could afford to rent a house (most legislators could only afford to rent a room in a roominghouse) meant that their house became the headquarters for the protest Democrats, thereby making Franklin the *de facto* leader. But enter the stream he did, and so this means we must examine the 1910 Aries Ingress for Washington as yet another factor impacting Franklin in that time period. The one trick we must immediately point out is that the "birthday" of the Aries Ingress is different from the Native's birthday, so there will be some overlaps between years that are different between the two charts.

In 1911, William Howard Taft, a non-reform Republican, was in office. The Democrats had won the House of Representatives in the election that had also brought Franklin Roosevelt to the New York statehouse.

Franklin D Roosevelt
Hyde Park, Dutchess, NY
Time Zone: 5 hours West

January 31, 1911
41N47'05" 73W56'01"
Tropical Regiomontanus
Solar Return for January 31, 1911 in Hyde Park, Dutchess, NY

9:46:43 PM
Standard Time

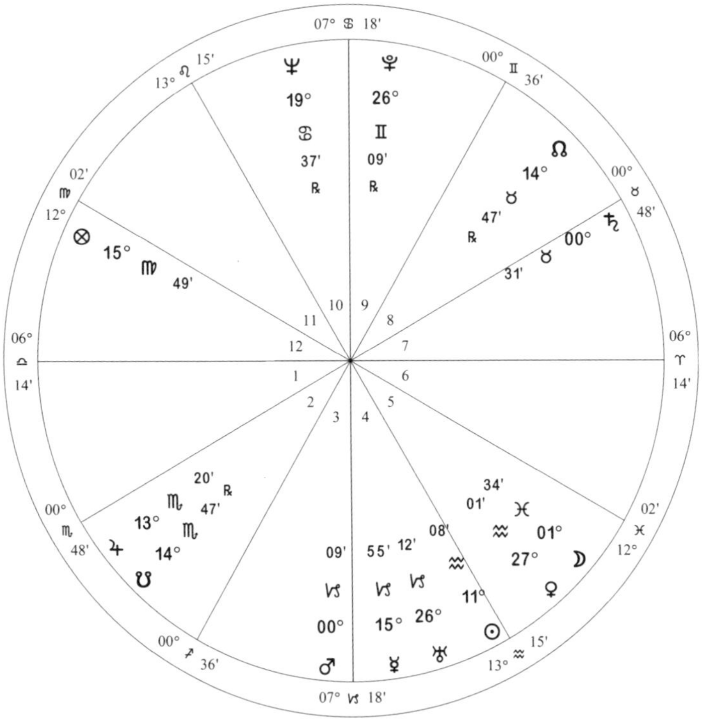

Dorothean Ess. Dig. (No Mut Rec. Points)								
Pl	**Ruler**	**Exalt**	**Tripl**	**Term**	**Face**	**Detri**	**Fall**	**Score**
☉	♄	--	☿	☿	☿	☉ -	--	- 10 P
☽	♃	♀	♂ m	♀	♄	☿	☿	- 5 P
☿	♄	♂	☽	♃	♂	☽	♃	- 5 P
♀	♄ m	--	☿	♂ m	☽	☉	--	- 5 P
♂	♄	♂ +	☽ m	♀ m	♃	☽	♃	+4
♃	♂	--	♂	♃ +	☉	♀	☽	+2
♄	♀ m	☽	☽	♀	☿	♂	--	- 5 P
☊	♀	☽	☽	☿	☽	♂	--	--
⊗	☿	☿	☽	♃	♀	♃	♀	--
As	♀	♄	☿	♀	☽	♂	☉	--
Mc	☽	♃	♂	♃	♀	♄	♂	--
☋	♂	--	♂	♀	☉	♀	☽	--

Hs	Alm. (Pto)
1	♀
2	♂
3	♃
4	♄
5	♄
6	♃
7	♂
8	☽♀
9	☿
10	♃
11	☉
12	☿

Example 12-8a. Franklin Roosevelt's solar return for 1911

Sun enters Ari 3-21-1911
Washington, D.C.
Time Zone: 5 hours West

March 21, 1911
38N53'42" 77W02'12"
Tropical Regiomontanus
NATAL CHART

12:54:27 PM
Standard Time

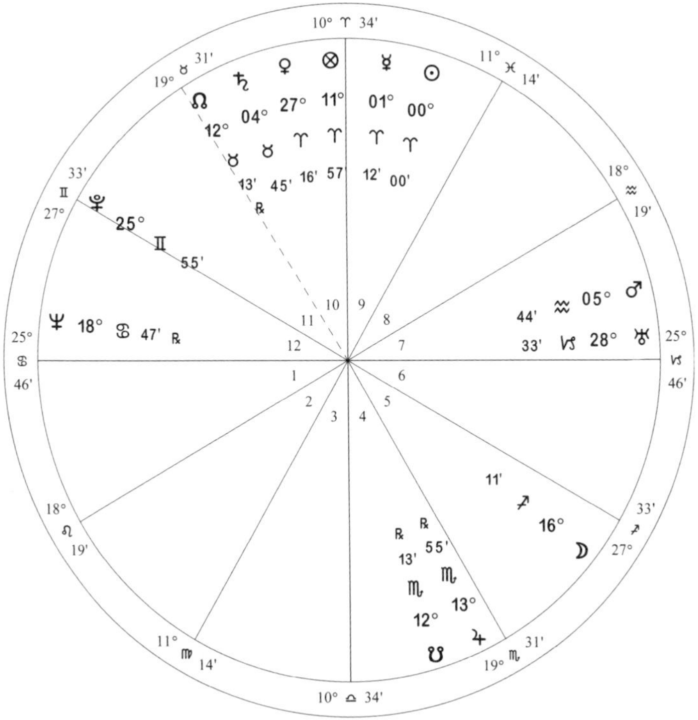

Dorothean Ess. Dig. (No Mut Rec. Points)								
Pl	**Ruler**	**Exalt**	**Tripl**	**Term**	**Face**	**Detri**	**Fall**	**Score**
☉	♂	☉ +	☉ +	♃	♂	♀	♄	+7
☽	♃	☋	☉	☿	☽ +	☿	--	+1
☿	♂	☉	☉	♃	♂	♀	♄	- 5 P
♀	♂	☉	☉	♄ m	♀ +	♀ -	♄	- 4
♂	♄	--	♄	♄	♀	☉	--	- 5 P
♃	♂	--	♀	♃ +	☉	♀	☽	+2
♄	♀	☽	♀	♀ m	☿	♂	--	- 5 P
☊	♀	☽	♀	☿	☽	♂	--	--
⊗	♂	☉	☉	♀	☉	♀	♄	--
As	☽	♃	♀	♀	☽	♄	♂	--
Mc	♂	☉	☉	♀	☉	♀	♄	--
☋	♂	--	♀	♃	☉	♀	☽	--

Hs	Alm. (Pto)
1	☽
2	☉
3	☿
4	♄
5	♂
6	♃
7	♄
8	♄
9	♃
10	☉
11	♀
12	☿

Example 12-8b. Aries Ingress for 1911, Washington, DC

legislation. Once again, his patrician status had gotten him the opportunity – but he still had to take advantage of the opportunity received.

FDR's personal chart was more quiet in 1911. The Sun was just at the 5th house cusp, and the angular planets were Neptune, Mercury and Uranus. We don't know the extent to which he focused his attention more on his children this year. He did achieve some national notice for fighting Tammany Hall, and so the Uranus and Neptune prominence make some sense. But this appears to be a "business as usual" solar return.

1912: Solar Return and Aries Ingress

If 1911 was quiet, that was not so in 1912. The split in the Republican Party that had allowed the Democrats to win in 1910 only got worse in 1912. Uncle Ted had become convinced that the Conservatives of his party were destructive, not merely wrong. After Taft was nominated for a second term at the Republican convention, TR decided to run as an independent. This split in the dominant party allowed the Democrat Woodrow Wilson to be elected. We can see this split in the 1912 Aries Ingress, as the Mars-Pluto conjunction at the MC (the president or presidency), with Neptune in the 10th square the Nodes (and thus at the Bendings) and square the Moon, with the square configuration being in cardinal signs. The cardinality shows a very public split, with TR's and Taft's loss in the election challenging the Republicans to reconfigure themselves before something worse happened.

Franklin's chart for 1912 looked pretty good. Jupiter right on the Ascendant, ruling it, and in dignity, gave him an easy time: and some luck as well. FDR liked Wilson, because he presented the progressive wing of the Democratic Party. So he organized a group of New York Democrats for Wilson before Wilson won the nomination. Thus, he met Wilson, although he didn't have any major role in the campaign.

Franklin D Roosevelt
Hyde Park, Dutchess, NY
Time Zone: 5 hours West

February 1, 1912
41N47'05" 73W56'01"
Tropical Regiomontanus

3:26:54 AM
Standard Time

Solar Return for February 1, 1912 in Hyde Park, Dutchess, NY

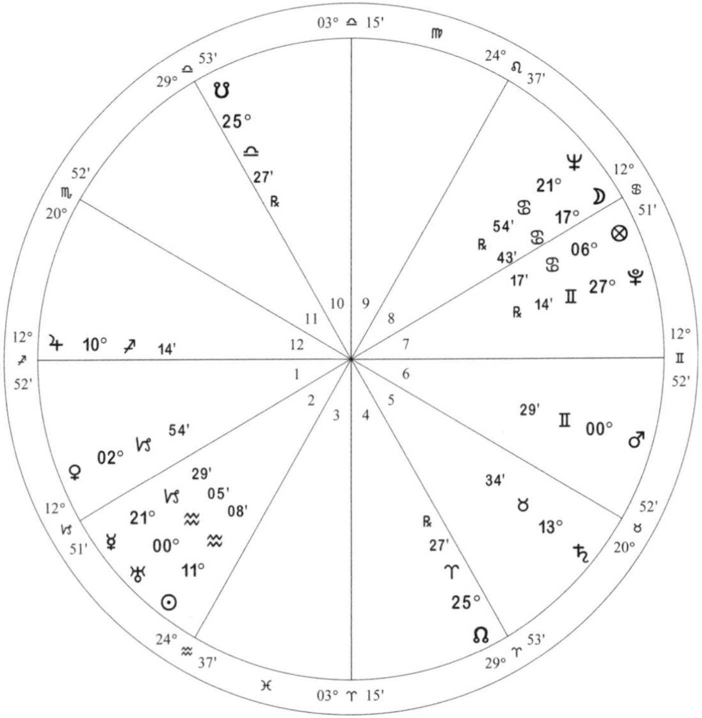

Dorothean Ess. Dig. (No Mut Rec. Points)								
Pl	Ruler	Exalt	Tripl	Term	Face	Detri	Fall	Score
☉	♄	--	☿	☿	☿ m	☉ -	--	- 10 P
☽	☽ +	♃	♂	☿	☿	♄	♂	+5
☿	♄	♂	☽	♂ m	☉ m	☽	♃	- 5 P
♀	♄ m	♂	☽	♀ +	♃	☽	♃	+2
♂	☿	☊	☿	☿ m	♃	♃	--	- 5 P
♃	♃ +	☋	♃ +	♀	☽	☿	--	+8
♄	♀ m	☽	☽	☿	☽	♂	--	- 5 P
☊	♂	☉	♃	♂	♀	♀	♄	--
⊗	☽	♃	♂	♃	♀	♄	♂	--
As	♃	☋	♃	♀	☽	☿	--	--
Mc	♀	♄	☿	♄	☽	♂	☉	--
☋	♀	♄	☿	☊	♃	♂	☉	--

Hs	Alm. (Pto)
1	♃
2	♂♄
3	♄
4	♂
5	♂
6	☽
7	☿
8	♃
9	☉♃
10	♄
11	♀
12	♂

Example 12-9a. Franklin Roosevelt's solar return for 1912

Sun enters Ari 3-20-1912
Washington, D.C.
Time Zone: 5 hours West

March 20, 1912
38N53'42" 77W02'12"
Tropical Regiomontanus
NATAL CHART

6:29:26 PM
Standard Time

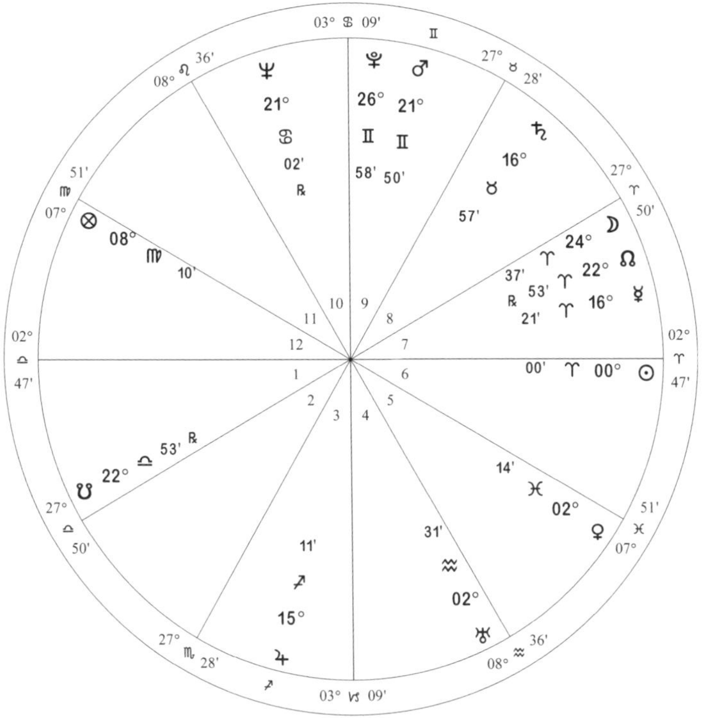

Dorothean Ess. Dig. (No Mut Rec. Points)								
Pl	Ruler	Exalt	Tripl	Term	Face	Detri	Fall	Score
☉	♂	☉ +	♃	♃	♂ m	♀	♄	+4
☽	♂	☉	♃	♂	♀	♀	♄	- 5 P
☿	♂ m	☉	♃	☿ +	☉	♀	♄	+2
♀	♃	♀ +	♂	♀ +	♄	☿	☿	+6
♂	☿ m	☊	☿	♄	☉ m	♃	--	- 5 P
♃	♃ +	☋	♃ +	☿	☽	☿	--	+8
♄	♀	☽	☽	♃	☽	♂	--	- 5 P
☊	♂	☉	♃	♂	♀	♀	♄	--
⊗	☿	☿	☽	♀	☉	♃	♀	--
As	♀	♄	☿	♄	☽	♂	☉	--
Mc	☽	♃	♂	♂	♀	♄	♂	--
☋	♀	♄	☿	☿	♃	♂	☉	--

Hs	Alm. (Pto)
1	♄
2	♀
3	♂
4	♄
5	☿♄
6	♀
7	♂
8	♂
9	☽
10	☽
11	☉
12	☿

Example 12-9b. Aries Ingress for 1912, Washington, DC

Notice that in his 1912 solar return, Venus rules the 10th and is in the 1st in dignity, namely Triplicity. The ruler of the 10th in the 1st dignified means a gift or promotion from a boss figure, a king. Remember that Triplicity itself has a direct association with luck. When Wilson prepared to take office, his problem was that the Democrats had been out of power so long that they literally didn't even have a shadow cabinet: a pool of people who had served in a previous administration who could be tapped to occupy jobs for which they had developed expertise. We have seen this repeatedly in our own era, when the second Bush administration utilized people who had been in the first Bush administration, or the Reagan administration; or when the Obama administration nominated people who had been in the Clinton administration.

Wilson and his team were scrambling, because the Democratic Party simply didn't have enough people with prior background to fill the top federal jobs. The man who would become Secretary of the Navy remembered that there was this nice fellow from New York who liked sailing. He was from North Carolina, so that was also a good geographical balance. So Franklin was nominated to be Assistant Secretary of the Navy because he liked to sail! We would say it was the Jupiter and the ruler of the 10th in the 1st dignified, of course!

For Franklin, just turning thirty, this was a dream come true. He had never intended a permanent legislative career, and Uncle Ted had been Assistant Secretary of the Navy, with Franklin even inheriting TR's old office!

The only downside of 1912 for Franklin was that, over the Summer, he had a recurrence of typhoid fever. Here we see Mars (fever) in the 6th house, partile trine Uranus. Remember that malefics associated with the 6th house are what can cause illness. Here, Venus ruled the 6th house with dignity. A benefic associated with the 6th will tend to mitigate the possibility of disease; here, the disease happened, but it was not a dangerous case.

1913

Franklin didn't take office until after his 1913 solar return occurred, because in 1913, the Inauguration date was still in March. Franklin's chart ruler Mars was in the 11th by the Five Degree Rule: and he was transitioning to a new 11th house position: the staff of the president. His Sun was also there, showing the importance of the affairs of this house for him in this year. That Mars was exalted, so he would perform his duties well, and enhance his reputation as a result. This was the last solar return with Saturn in his radix sign, and Mercury was also in its radix sign.

Before we leave Franklin's 1913 solar return, we should note the meaning of Neptune in the 5th house. One meaning of Neptune is deception; here the deception is that 1913 was when Eleanor hired Lucy Mercer as a social secretary to help her learn Washington's social ropes: and Franklin ultimately had an affair with her, although exactly when it started is unknown. Is this the meaning of the South Node conjunct the Descendant, that Eleanor was being destroyed?

1913 Aries Ingress

The Aries Ingress for 1913 shows a mixed read with respect to the President: the South Node at the MC, but a very dignified Venus in Taurus ruling the MC. This probably shows perfectly this conundrum of Wilson's: the positive mandate of the people, and the reality of staffing problems. The Sun at the IC and ruler of the 9th suggests a bridge between foreign policy and the land: this bridge was not a bridge, but the completion of the Panama Canal, which opened after Wilson triggered an explosion to open up the last segment. Franklin's SR-Ascendant at 2 Aries fit into the pattern of planets around the solar position of the Aries Ingress, pulling him into the developing picture.

Franklin D Roosevelt
Hyde Park, Dutchess, NY
Time Zone: 5 hours West

January 31, 1913
41N47'05" 73W56'01"
Tropical Regiomontanus
Solar Return for January 31, 1913 in Hyde Park, Dutchess, NY

9:19:50 AM
Standard Time

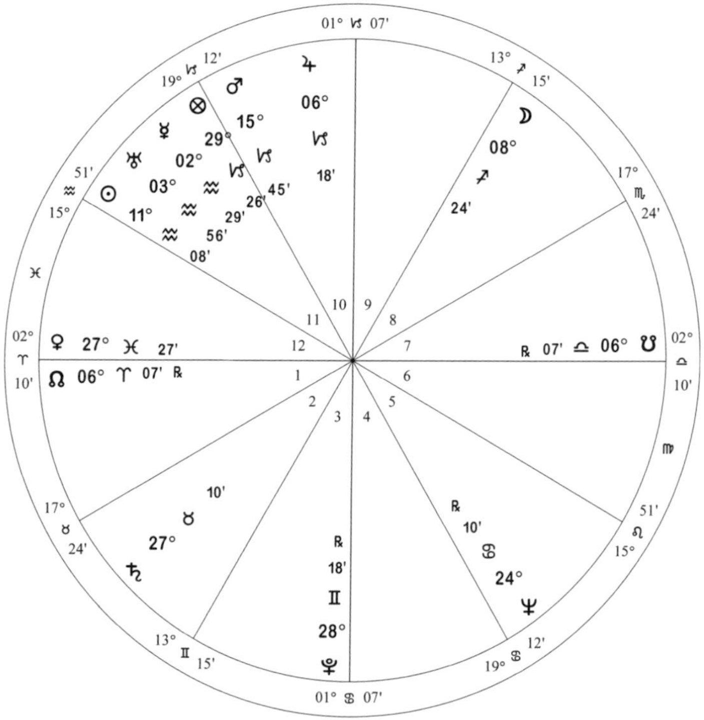

Dorothean Ess. Dig. (No Mut Rec. Points)

Pl	Ruler	Exalt	Tripl	Term	Face	Detri	Fall	Score
☉	♄	--	♄	☿	☿	☉ -	--	- 10 P
☽	♃	☋	☉	♀	☿	☿	--	- 5 P
☿	♄	--	♄	♄	♀	☉	--	- 5 P
♀	♃	♀ +	♀ +	♄	♂	☿	☿	+7
♂	♄	♂ +	♀	♃	♂ +	☽	♃	+5
♃	♄	♂	♀	☿	♃ +	☽	♃ -	- 3
♄	♀	☽	♀	♂	♄ +	♂	--	+1
☊	♂	☉	☉	♀	♂	♀	♄	--
⊗	♄	♂	♀	♄	☉	☽	♃	--
As	♂	☉	☉	♃	♂	♀	♄	--
Mc	♄	♂	♀	♀	♃	☽	♃	--
☋	♀	♄	♄	♀	☽	♂	☉	--

Hs	Alm. (Pto)
1	☉
2	♀
3	☿
4	☽
5	☽
6	☉
7	♄
8	♂
9	♃
10	♀♄
11	♂
12	♄

Example 12-10a. Franklin Roosevelt's solar return for 1913

Sun enters Ari 3-21-1913
Washington, D.C.
Time Zone: 5 hours West

March 21, 1913
38N53'42" 77W02'12"
Tropical Regiomontanus
NATAL CHART

12:18:02 AM
Standard Time

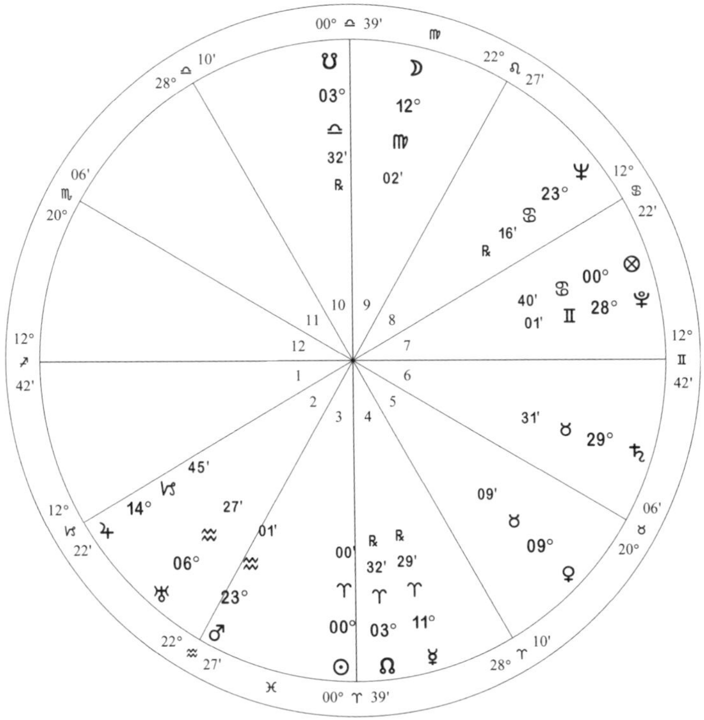

Dorothean Ess. Dig. (No Mut Rec. Points)								
Pl	Ruler	Exalt	Tripl	Term	Face	Detri	Fall	Score
☉	♂	☉ +	♃	♃	♂	♀	♄	+4
☽	☿	☿	☽ +	♀	♀	♃	♀	+3
☿	♂	☉	♃	♀ m	☉	♀	♄	- 5 P
♀	♀ +	☽	☽	☿ m	☿	♂	--	+5
♂	♄	--	☿	♃	☽	☉	--	- 5 P
♃	♄	♂	☽	♃ +	♂	☽	♃ -	- 2
♄	♀	☽	☽	♂	♄ +	♂	--	+1
☊	♂	☉	♃	♃	♂	♀	♄	--
⊗	☽	♃	♂	♂	♀	♄	♂	--
As	♃	☋	♃	♀	☽	☿	--	--
Mc	♀	♄	☿	♄	☽	♂	☉	--
☋	♀	♄	☿	♄	☽	♂	☉	--

Hs	Alm. (Pto)
1	♃
2	♂♄
3	♄
4	♂
5	♂
6	☽
7	☿
8	♃
9	☉♃
10	♄
11	♀
12	♂

Example 12-10b. Aries Ingress for 1913, Washington, DC

Notice, by the way, that Aries Ingresses share the same basic temporal patterns as any other yearly return. So we saw in the 1912 Aries Ingress that the Sun was at the 7th; in 1913, it was at the 4th; in 1914, it was at the Ascendant.

1914

In 1914, the second Franklin Jr. was born. Mars, ruling the 5th house was in fertile Cancer, as was the Ascendant. The 5th house cusp was likewise in a fertile sign. This was all traditional lore, but again we emphasize the fact that his chart was propitious for the birth of a child did not *mandate* the birth of a child – as we shall see.

In the world, 1914 was the "year the Great War came upon us all" – except the United States. Europe had erupted into chaos as the Balkans seemingly disintegrated before everyone's eyes. I have covered this piece of history through the Aries Ingresses in *Astrology of Sustainability*.[3]

Meanwhile, Franklin had focused his attention on winning the primary for Senator from New York, now that direct election had been accomplished. But this was one of his few political failures. He did have some angularity in the chart, but in a sense, it was the *wrong* angularity. Neptune in the 1st house is not the greatest placement unless you are in a Neptune field: and Franklin was not. In fact, he was blindsided by Tammany Hall, a nice payback for his earlier rebellion as a State Senator – and a fine description of Neptune in the 1st. His 1st house ruler, the Moon in Aries, is not so strong as his competition, Saturn in Gemini, which has Triplicity.

1914 Aries Ingress

If we examine the Aries Ingress for 1914, the President (10th) and the people (1st) have the same ruler, Jupiter, with participating Triplicity and located right on the 12th house cusp. But then there is this Pluto at 29 degrees lurking right at the 4th house cusp. This

Franklin D Roosevelt
Hyde Park, Dutchess, NY
Time Zone: 5 hours West

January 31, 1914
41N47'05" 73W56'01"
Tropical Regiomontanus
Solar Return for January 31, 1914 in Hyde Park, Dutchess, NY

3:04:55 PM
Standard Time

Sun enters Ari 3-21-1914
Washington, D.C.
Time Zone: 5 hours West

March 21, 1914
38N53'42" 77W02'12"
Tropical Regiomontanus
NATAL CHART

6:10:48 AM
Standard Time

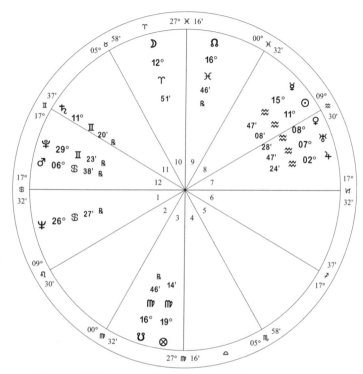

Example 12-11a. Franklin Roosevelt's solar return for 1914

Example 12-11b. Aries Ingress for 1914, Washington, DC

is great symbolism for the American isolationism, first, Wilson's scholarly opinion that war was impossible; and then secondly, that the United States really would be unaffected by the war, and thus able to skip it. Pluto was the giant elephant in the room that everyone ignored.

If FDR, with his solar return, was not in a position to obtain an electional victory, his expertise in his job was getting him attention, even though he wasn't entirely heeded there either. The 10th in his solar return, namely Wilson (this time as his boss) is again Jupiter in Aquarius. Franklin's Moon in Aries was perhaps leading a bit on rearmament, because what he was verifying quantitatively was how unprepared the U.S. Navy was for any action or conflict. His 1st house ruler in the 10th put him quite publicly in front of congressional committees, testifying on these issues. But if he was getting press, that still doesn't mean that he was being heeded.

Meanwhile, with Mars ruling the 5th from the 12th, we would do well to presume that the affair with Lucy was on, that position looking a lot like a man having an affair trying to conceal it from his wife.

1915

In 1915, the isolationism of the United States continued, even as naval warfare between the warring parties escalated. Wilson's position was entrenched, and Roosevelt's position on naval preparedness was a tightrope act. Wilson's own policy on neutrality was tested as the Germans increased their submarine warfare, and passenger ships, sometimes with American passengers, were sunk, such as the *Lusitania*.

And what better symbolism for FDR's awkward situation than Pluto in the 10th, just barely in Cancer, and Saturn conjunct the 10th house cusp? His boss is sorely afflicted by this configuration! FDR himself was Mercury in Aquarius, his radix sign, and in what

Franklin D Roosevelt
Hyde Park, Dutchess, NY
Time Zone: 5 hours West

January 31, 1915
41N47'05" 73W56'01"
Tropical Regiomontanus
Solar Return for January 31, 1915 in Hyde Park, Dutchess, NY

8:59:28 PM
Standard Time

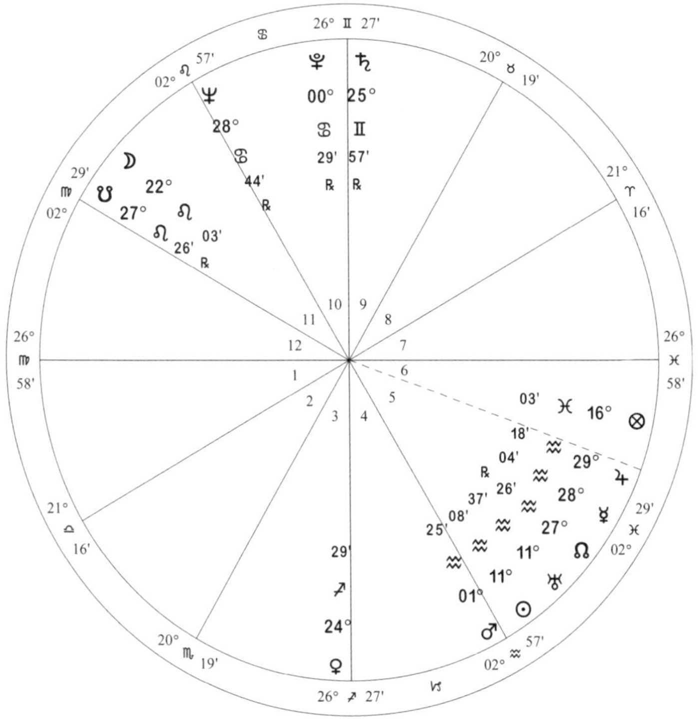

Dorothean Ess. Dig. (No Mut Rec. Points)								
Pl	Ruler	Exalt	Tripl	Term	Face	Detri	Fall	Score
☉	♄	--	☿	☿	☿	☉ -	--	- 10 P
☽	☉	--	♃	♃	♂	♄	--	- 5 P
☿	♄ m	--	☿ +	♂	☽	☉	--	+3
♀	♃	☋	♃	♄	♄	☿	--	- 5 P
♂	♄	--	☿	♄ m	♀	☉	--	- 5 P
♃	♄	--	☿	♂	☽	☉	--	- 5 P
♄	☿ m	☊	☿	♂ m	☉	♃	--	- 5 P
☊	♄	--	☿	♂	☽	☉	--	--
⊗	♃	♀	♂	☿	♃	☿	☿	--
As	☿	☿	☽	♂	☿	♃	♀	--
Mc	☿	☊	☿	♂	☉	♃	--	--
☋	☉	--	♃	♂	♂	♄	--	--

Hs	Alm. (Pto)
1	☿
2	☿♀
3	♂
4	♃
5	♄
6	♀
7	♃
8	♂
9	☽
10	☿
11	☉
12	☿

Example 12-12a. Franklin Roosevelt's solar return for 1915

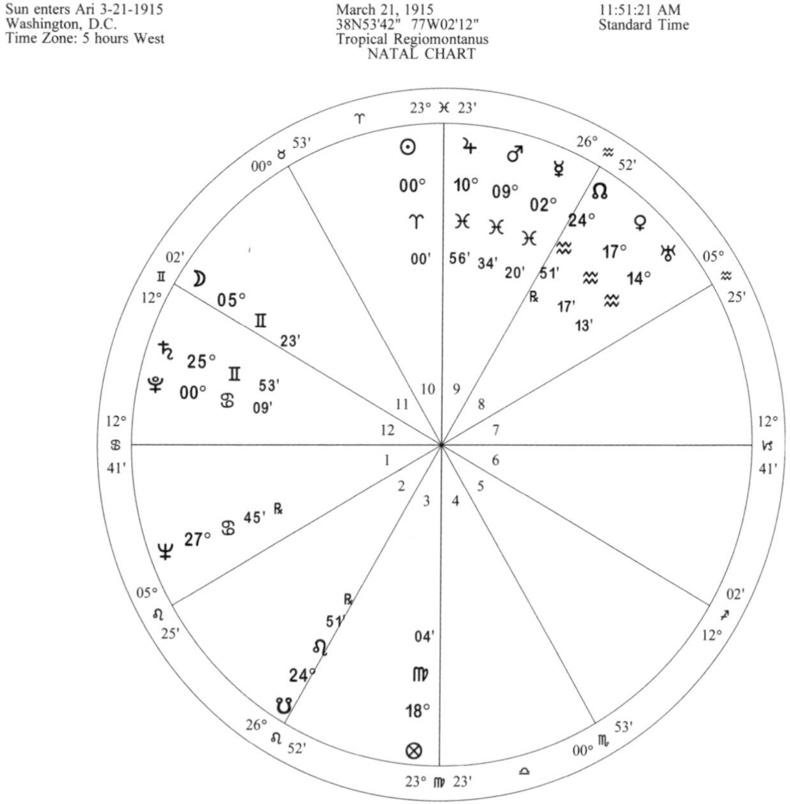
Sun enters Ari 3-21-1915
Washington, D.C.
Time Zone: 5 hours West
March 21, 1915
38N53'42" 77W02'12"
Tropical Regiomontanus
NATAL CHART
11:51:21 AM
Standard Time

Dorothean Ess. Dig. (No Mut Rec. Points)								
Pl	**Ruler**	**Exalt**	**Tripl**	**Term**	**Face**	**Detri**	**Fall**	**Score**
☉	♂	☉ +	☉ +	♃	♂	♀	♄	+7
☽	☿	☊	♄	☿	♃	♃	--	- 5 P
☿	♃	♀	♀	♀	♄	☿ -	☿ -	- 14 P
♀	♄	--	♄	♀ +	☿	☉	--	+2
♂	♃	♀	♀	♃	♄	☿	☿	- 5 P
♃	♃ +	♀	♀	♃ +	♃ +	☿	☿	+8
♄	☿	☊	♄ +	♂	☉	♃	--	+3
☊	♄	--	♄	♃	☽	☉	--	--
⊗	☿	☿	♀	♄	♀	♃	♀	--
As	☽	♃	♀	♃	☿	♄	♂	--
Mc	♃	♀	♀	♂	♂	☿	☿	--
☋	☉	--	☉	♃	♂	♄	--	--

Hs	Alm. (Pto)
1	♃
2	☉
3	☉
4	☿
5	♂
6	♃
7	♂♄
8	♄
9	♄
10	♃
11	♀
12	☿

Example 12-12b. Aries Ingress for 1915, Washington, DC

we might call a positive besiegement: between the North Node and Jupiter, which has participating Triplicity in Aquarius, all in the 5th house. The angularity in his chart is highlighting his boss, not so much him. So this positive besiegement will protect him, even as its succedent placement reduces his influence.

When do we decide to interpret the 10th as honors and achievement, and when do we interpret it as one's boss? The practical answer is situational. When Franklin was a State Senator, while he may have voted mostly with the party, he was essentially his own boss. In a legislative situation in which party membership absolutely determines one's vote, perhaps there is less sense of independence. But when you are an Assistant Secretary of the Navy, just as when you are an employee of a company (not a top-level manager), you are not *making* policy. In these cases, the tendency with the 10th house is to apply a kind of trickle-down theory: if the boss looks comfortable and honorable, and especially if there is a good connection between 1st and 10th, then some of the boss's honor and power will trickle down to the Native. But if the boss looks stressed, or there is a hard aspect between Native and boss, then there will be problems with the boss.

1916

1916 marked the presidential re-election season for Wilson, and now the Republicans were reunited, while the Democrats were hovering on disintegration. From the standpoint of house placement, the Aries Ingress of 1916 resembled Franklin's 1915 return, except that the Saturn-Pluto conjunction was separating. Wilson looked very weak as Mercury in Pisces. There is one difference between Aries Ingresses and solar returns: Aries Ingresses do not always encompass an entire year.

- If the Ascendant for the Aries Ingress is fixed, then only the Aries Ingress applies.

- If the Ascendant is mutable, then both the Aries and Libra Ingresses must be interpreted.
- If the Ascendant is cardinal, then all four must be used.[4]

Wilson did look much stronger in the Autumn. Ironically, he would win election using the slogan, "He kept Us out of War," and then barely a month after his Inauguration in 1917, he joined the Allies cause in war.

Franklin, as a member of the administration, had not only to defend Wilson's policies, but also to aid in his reelection. His solar return for the year shows little in the way of angular planets, with only Jupiter in the 4th – the least public angular house. FDR was quietly seething over the Germans, eager to get into the war, despite Wilson's policy. His 1916 chart is heavily loaded in the 2nd and 8th houses. Now, this *could* have meant a focus on earning money, or debt, or the spouse earning money. But this doesn't exactly apply to his predicament.

Another meaning of the 2nd house refers to the second in a duel – and strangely, I believe that it is from this meaning that we can derive a number of properties and functions that modern astrologers have sometimes equated with the word "values." Let's consider. In a duel, your second is generally your friend. Consider this from your friend's perspective. He (male, in the historical usage) may well see the problem brewing, possibly even more clearly than than his friend, the soon-to-be dueling participant. Being his friend, the second does everything to prepare for what he now sees as the inevitable.

He prepares his friend both psychologically ("you must do what you think is right!") and logistically (by providing the weapons). And so Franklin worked on naval preparedness, even as he chafed that the higher-ups still couldn't bring themselves to go to war. And if, through all this work at naval yards, there were ship- and dock-workers who learned that they owed their jobs to the Democratic Party, well so much the better....

Franklin D Roosevelt
Hyde Park, Dutchess, NY
Time Zone: 5 hours West

February 1, 1916
41N47'05" 73W56'01"
Tropical Regiomontanus
Solar Return for February 1, 1916 in Hyde Park, Dutchess, NY

2:51:54 AM
Standard Time

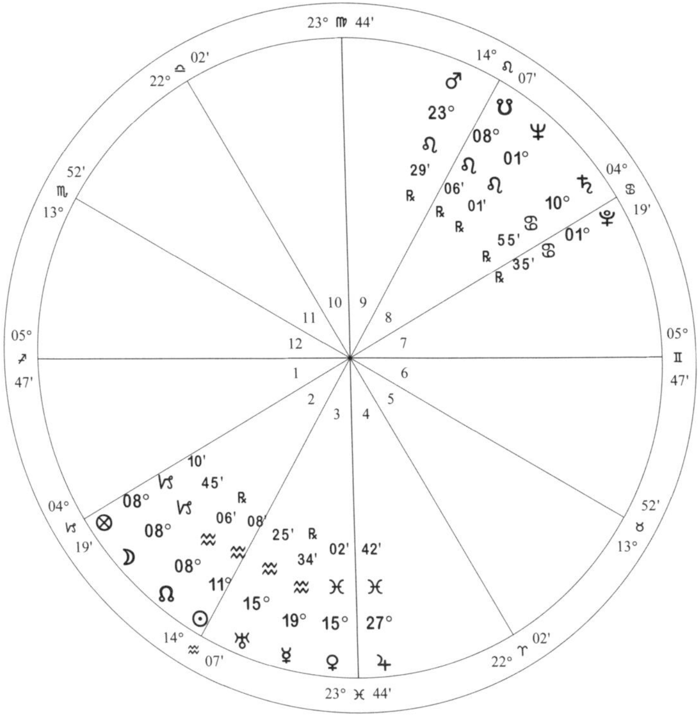

Dorothean Ess. Dig. (No Mut Rec. Points)								
Pl	Ruler	Exalt	Tripl	Term	Face	Detri	Fall	Score
☉	♄	--	☿	☿	☿	☉ -	--	- 10 P
☽	♄ m	♂	☽ +	☿	♃	☽ -	♃	- 2
☿	♄	--	☿ +	♀ m	☿ +	☉	--	+4
♀	♃	♀ +	♂	☿ m	♃	☿	☿	+4
♂	☉	--	♃ m	♃	♂ +	♄	--	+1
♃	♃ +	♀	♂ m	♄ m	♂	☿	☿	+5
♄	☽ m	♃	♂	♃ m	☿	♄ -	♂	- 10 P
☊	♄	--	☿	☿	♀	☉	--	--
⊗	♄	♂	☽	☿	♃	☽	♃	--
As	♃	☋	♃	♃	☿	☿	--	--
Mc	☿	☿	☽	♄	☿	♃	♀	--
☋	☉	--	♃	☿	♄	♄	--	--

Hs	Alm. (Pto)
1	♃
2	♄
3	♄
4	♃
5	♂
6	☽
7	☿
8	☽
9	☉
10	☿
11	☿♀
12	♂

Example 12-13a. Franklin Roosevelt's solar return for 1916

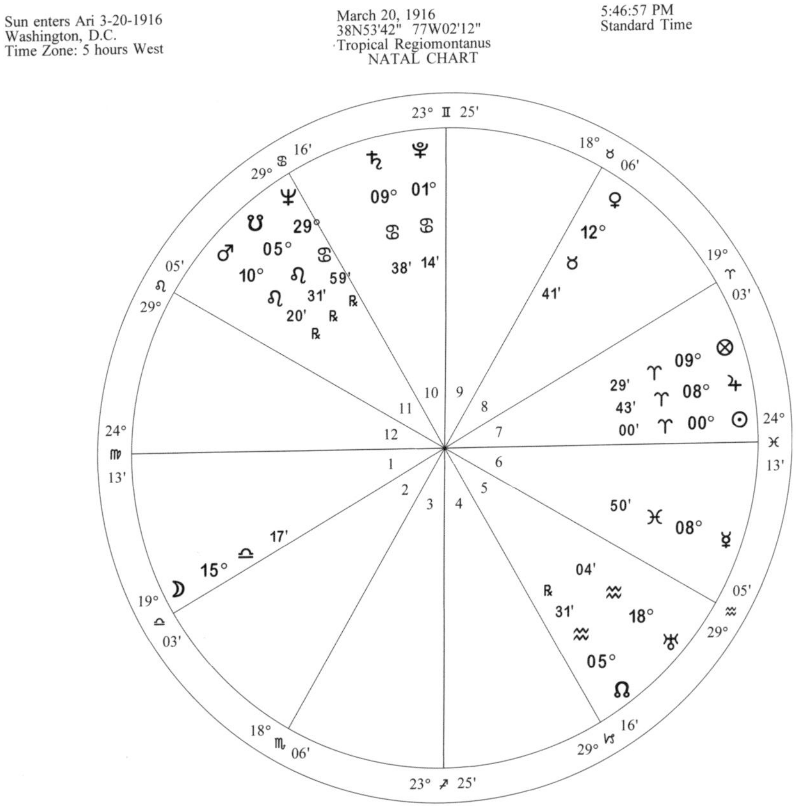
Sun enters Ari 3-20-1916
Washington, D.C.
Time Zone: 5 hours West
March 20, 1916
38N53'42" 77W02'12"
Tropical Regiomontanus
NATAL CHART
5:46:57 PM
Standard Time

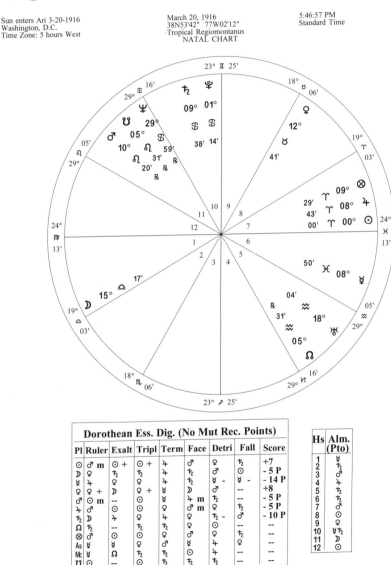

Dorothean Ess. Dig. (No Mut Rec. Points)								
Pl	Ruler	Exalt	Tripl	Term	Face	Detri	Fall	Score
☉	♂ m	☉ +	☉ +	♃	♂	♀	♄	+7
☽	♀	♄	♄	♃	♄	♂	☉	- 5 P
☿	♃	♀	♀	♃	♄	☿ -	☿ -	- 14 P
♀	♀ +	☽	♀ +	☿	☽	♂	--	+8
♂	☉ m	--	☉	☿	♃ m	♄	--	- 5 P
♃	♂	☉	☉	♀	♂ m	♀	♄	- 5 P
♄	☽	♃	♀	♃	♀	♄ -	♂	- 10 P
☊	♄	--	♄	♄	♀	☉	--	--
⊗	♂	☉	☉	♀	♂	♀	♄	--
As	☿	☿	♀	♂	☿	♃	♀	--
Mc	☿	☊	♄	♄	☉	♃	--	--
☋	☉	--	☉	♄	♄	♄	--	--

Hs	Alm. (Pto)
1	☿
2	♄
3	♂
4	♃
5	♄
6	♄
7	♂
8	☉
9	♀
10	☿♄
11	☽
12	☉

Example 12-13b. Aries Ingress for 1916, Washington, DC

So a focus on the 2nd house can literally be a focus on being second or *a* second – and the challenge of acting positively and creatively within that function as a supporting player. FDR's correspondence suggests that he was itching for the U.S.A. to go to war – by this time, he saw it as inevitable. But as a junior official, he had to wait.

In January 1917 (still under Franklin's 1916 solar return), the Germans announced a change in their submarine tactics, which made neutral shipping much more subject to bombardment. The Germans had concluded that the USA would enter the war on the side of the English and French, and that if they could only cut off supplies long enough, they could exhaust those two countries before the USA could get enough personnel and equipment to Europe to make any difference.

1917

After that, Roosevelt didn't have long to wait. Events in Russia and Mexico acted to hasten American entry into the war, which finally occurred in April 1917.

I discussed the Aries Ingress charts for 1917 and 1918 in *Astrology of Sustainability* as they related to the influenza pandemic, which was considerably accelerated by the overcrowding of soldiers and their transport around the world.[5] Here, our focus is more on the war. The notable configuration for that 1917 Aries Ingress was the Venus-Mercury-Mars conjunction in Pisces trine Saturn in Detriment in Cancer, the conjunction being very close to the IC in Washington. Wilson had attempted all along to guide the U.S.A. on moral and rational principles – but here, the 10th house is ruled by Mercury in Pisces: and this wasn't working well, given the poor condition of Mercury.

Roosevelt's natal Ascendant was pretty much opposite that configuration in Pisces: so one can either interpret this as his impatience with the glacial pace of the arrival of war, or with his enthusiasm for supporting his president (Franklin's radix Ascendant

Franklin D Roosevelt
Hyde Park, Dutchess, NY
Time Zone: 5 hours West

January 31, 1917
41N47'05" 73W56'01"
Tropical Regiomontanus
Solar Return for January 31, 1917 in Hyde Park, Dutchess, NY

8:31:48 AM
Standard Time

Sun enters Ari 3-21-1917
Washington, D.C.
Time Zone: 5 hours West

March 20, 1917
38N53'42" 77W02'12"
Tropical Regiomontanus
NATAL CHART

11:37:18 PM
Standard Time

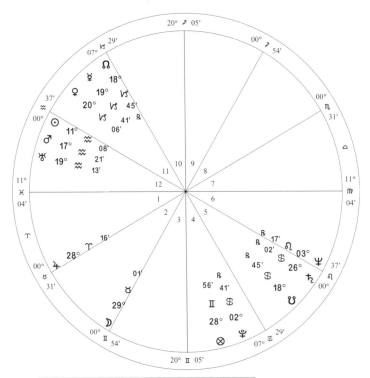

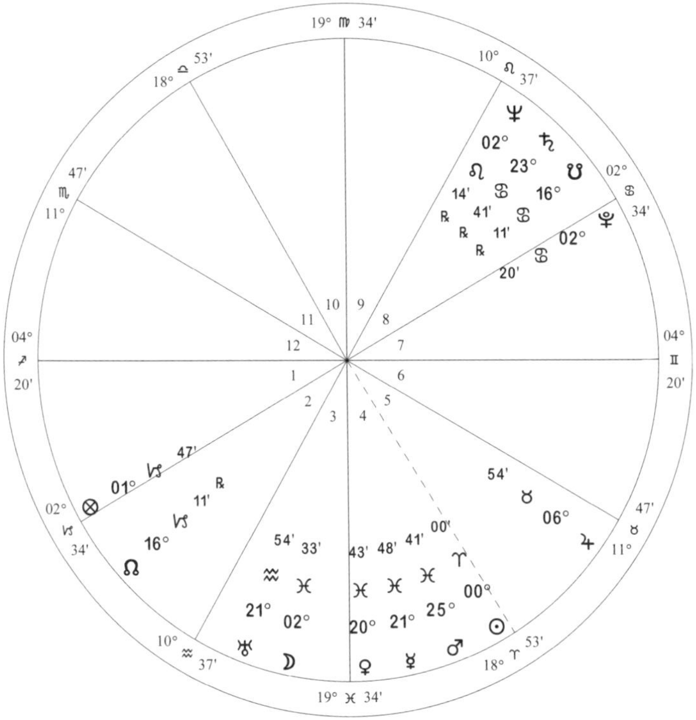

Example 12-14a. Franklin Roosevelt's solar return for 1917

Example 12-14b. Aries Ingress for 1917, Washington, DC

Dorothean Ess. Dig. (No Mut Rec. Points) — Example 12-14a

Pl	Ruler	Exalt	Tripl	Term	Face	Detri	Fall	Score
☉	♄	--	♄	♅	♅	☉ -	--	- 10 P
☽	♀	☽ +	♀	♂	♄ m	♂ m	--	+4
☿	♄	♀	♀	♂ m	☽	☽	♃	- 5 P
♀	♄	♄	♀ +	♂ m	☽	☽	♃	+3
♂	♄	--	♄	♅	☉	☽ m	♄	- 5 P
♃	♀	☉	♀	♀	☽ m	♀	♄	- 5 P
♄	☽	♃	♀	♀	☽ m	♄ -	♂	- 10 P
☊	☽	--	☽	♀	♂	♄	♃	--
⊗	☽	--	☽	♀	♄	♄	♃	--
As	♃	♀	♃	♀	♃	☿	☿	--
Mc	♃	☽	♃	♀	♃	☿	☿	--
☋	☽	♃	☽	♀	♃	♄	♂	--

Hs	Alm. (Pto)
1	♃
2	♃
3	☽
4	☽
5	♄
6	♃
7	☿
8	♂
9	♀
10	♄
11	♄
12	♄

Dorothean Ess. Dig. (No Mut Rec. Points) — Example 12-14b

Pl	Ruler	Exalt	Tripl	Term	Face	Detri	Fall	Score
☉	♂	☉ +	♃	♃	♂	♀	♄	+4
☽	♀	♀	♂	♂	♂	♄ m	♅	- 5 P
☿	♃	♃	♂	♂	♅	♅	♅	- 14 P
♀	♃ m	♀ +	♂	♂	♂	☿	--	+4
♂	♂	☉	♃ +	♂ +	♅	♀	☿	+6
♃	♀ m	☽	☽	☽	☿	♂	--	- 5 P
♄	♃	♃	♂	♀	☽	☽ m	♄ -	- 10 P
☊	♀	♃	♂	♂	♀	♂	♅	--
⊗	♄	♂	☽	♀	☽	☽	♃	--
As	♃	☽	♃	♀	♃	☿	☿	--
Mc	♂	♄	♃	♅	♀	♀	☽	--
☋	☽	♃	☽	♀	♃	♄	♂	--

Hs	Alm. (Pto)
1	♃
2	♂
3	♄
4	♃
5	☉ ♂
6	☽
7	♃
8	☽
9	♃
10	☽
11	♀
12	♄

is close to the MC of the Ingress chart) once Wilson finally got on the war plan.

Ever since FDR became Assistant Secretary of the Navy, he had striven for greater naval preparedness. Now the war was here – and his solar return featured only Pluto unequivocally angular, with Jupiter essentially succedent. But that Jupiter ruled the Ascendant *and* 10th and had Triplicity: Franklin, acting in his role of second, gains influence with his boss.

The problem was the 12th house for this year. Franklin's imitation of Uncle Ted called for him to resign his desk job and join the military. But this was a different war! His attempts to become a hero fell flat, and he had to content himself with Mars in the 12th, watching the war from his position in the administration that would not let him resign and enlist.

1918

By early 1918, the flu pandemic was beginning to affect US troops. As I had indicated in *Astrology of Sustainability*, the real argument of the epidemic occurred in 1917 – when the virus was mutating and multiplying.

With regard to the 1918 Aries Ingress, Mars in the 7th would indicate the involvement of soldiers with the public enemies of the USA. The president shows as Jupiter in Gemini, the ruler of the 10th. Now it may seem strange to see a president in wartime as being in Detriment, especially as the Allies were eventually the victors in the war. Jupiter in Gemini also has Triplicity, but that's not the whole story.

Wilson, scholar-politician and Princeton University President, always attempted to act on principle, however this principle was the Saturn version, given his natal Sun-Saturn opposition. The Saturn version is much more likely to be intransigent – and frankly, tending toward the autocratic, because Saturn believes that there can be only one type of principle, no room for debate, and certainly not special

Franklin D Roosevelt
Hyde Park, Dutchess, NY
Time Zone: 5 hours West

January 31, 1918
41N47'05" 73W56'01"
Tropical Regiomontanus

2:27:43 PM
Standard Time

Solar Return for January 31, 1918 in Hyde Park, Dutchess, NY

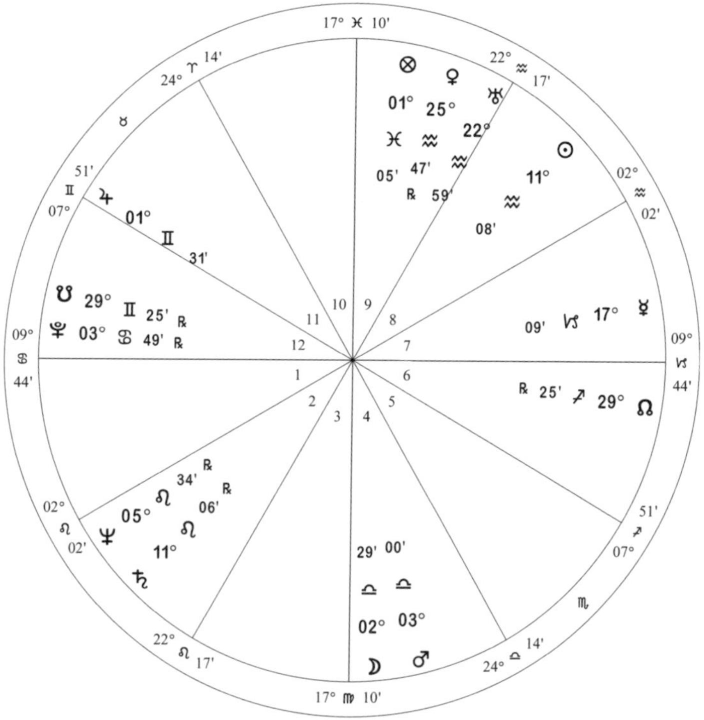

Dorothean Ess. Dig. (No Mut Rec. Points)								
Pl	Ruler	Exalt	Tripl	Term	Face	Detri	Fall	Score
☉	♄ m	--	♄ m	☿	☿	☉ -	--	- 10 P
☽	♀	♄	♄	♄	☽ +	♂	☉	+1
☿	♄	♂	♀	♃ m	♂	☽	♃	- 5 P
♀	♄	--	♄	♂	☽	☉	--	- 5 P
♂	♀	♄	♄	♄	☽	♂ -	☉	- 10 P
♃	☿	☊	♄	☿ m	♃ +	♃ -	--	- 4
♄	☉ m	--	☉ m	☿	♃	♄ -	--	- 10 P
☊	♃	☋	☉	♂	♄	☿	--	--
⊗	♃	♀	♀	♀	♄	☿	☿	--
As	☽	♃	♀	♃	♀	♄	♂	--
Mc	♃	♀	♀	☿	♃	☿	☿	--
☋	☿	☊	♄	♂	☉	♃	--	--

Hs	Alm. (Pto)
1	♃
2	☉
3	☉
4	☿
5	♄
6	♃
7	♄
8	♄
9	♄
10	♃
11	☉♂
12	☿

Example 12-15a. Franklin Roosevelt's solar return for 1918

Sun enters Ari 3-21-1918
Washington, D.C.
Time Zone: 5 hours West

March 21, 1918
38N53'42" 77W02'12"
Tropical Regiomontanus
NATAL CHART

5:25:41 AM
Standard Time

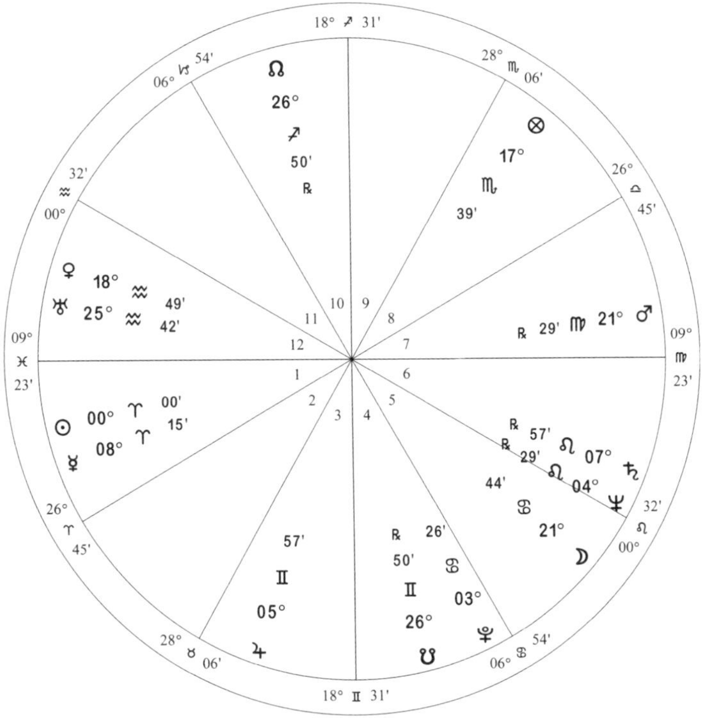

Dorothean Ess. Dig. (No Mut Rec. Points)								
Pl	Ruler	Exalt	Tripl	Term	Face	Detri	Fall	Score
☉	♂	☉ +	♃	♃	♂	♀	♄	+4
☽	☽ +	♃	♂ m	♀	☽ +	♄	♂	+6
☿	♂ m	☉	♃ m	♀	♂ m	♀	♄	- 5 P
♀	♄	--	☿	♀ +	☿	☉	--	+2
♂	☿ m	☿	☽ m	♄	☿ m	♃	♀	- 5 P
♃	☿	☊	☿ m	☿	♃ +	♃ -	--	- 4
♄	☉	--	♃	☿	♄ +	♄ -	--	- 4
☊	♃	☋	♃	♂	♄	☿	--	--
⊗	♂	--	♂	♀	☉	♀	☽	--
As	♃	♀	♂	♃	♄	☿	☿	--
Mc	♃	☋	♃	☿	☽	☿	--	--
☋	☿	☊	☿	♂	☉	♃	--	--

Hs	Alm. (Pto)
1	♃
2	♂
3	☽
4	☿
5	♃
6	☉
7	☿
8	♀
9	♂
10	♃
11	♄
12	♄

Example 12-15b. Aries Ingress for 1918, Washington, DC

circumstances according to the needs of an individual. Brand's comment on the matter was to note how easily the Progressive mind can slip into coercion, and after all the delays, once war was declared, the Wilson Administration imposed censorship, suspended significant components of civil rights, and instituted a draft for the first time, which Wilson insisted was not coercive.[6]

The problem with a planet in Detriment is that it is largely left to its own devices. The harder work on the part of the Native to figure things out may be a benefit ultimately; but it can also introduce some very strange pathways. In Wilson's case, he decided very publicly to call on the 1918 election to be a mandate on his war policies, despite the political wisdom that off-year elections almost always favored the opposition party. The Republicans stormed back and won both houses of Congress, thereby undercutting Wilson's prestige considerably.

Roosevelt's own Moon-Mars conjunction in Libra in his 1918 solar return made him gung-ho enough, as far as the war was concerned. He was actually eager to at least get to the front, even if he couldn't enlist. He would go to England and France to inspect naval facilities. His solar return had Venus in the 9th in her natal sign – and also Uranus right on the 9th house cusp. So his cruise to Europe was on a destroyer sailing on its maiden voyage. But the hardest thing for him was the voyage home, because he had contracted pneumonia, and possibly, the flu itself. He was bedridden the entire voyage back, only to be met by a stretcher, Eleanor and Sara.

Okay, so now about the 7th house. Remember back to Chapter 3 that the basic classical interpretation is that when the ruler of the 7th is a benefic or well fortified, the spouse behaves in a dignified manner, and if not, the reverse? Well... that's in the mind of the beholder. Because Franklin was so ill, they gave Eleanor his suitcase, which she unpacked and found – love letters from Lucy Mercer! Oops! It was Franklin behaving badly, not Eleanor. Eleanor was devastated, and Sara was pretty upset too. So perhaps the better description is that the partner is not going to act in a fashion that the Native likes. Here, the ruler of the 7th house was Saturn in Leo, retrograde and *in a partile opposition to the Sun*. In a three-way conversation, Eleanor evidently offered a divorce, and Sara evidently threatened to cut off all financial support to him if he did become divorced. His political adviser Howe reminded him that divorce was suicide for a politician.

The entente that resulted was that Franklin was to no longer see Lucy (he only adhered to this for a while, not permanently), Eleanor was to have no more conjugal "duties." The marriage was to continue, and to look absolutely normal on the surface. Eleanor gained the freedom to do pretty much what she wanted, as long as appearances were maintained.

Meanwhile, we see President Wilson again as Jupiter in Gemini, but now we are looking more at Franklin's experience of him than his national persona. Wilson's decision about the election would end up reflecting badly on everybody in the administration, because Congress would take out much of their animosity on those lower down than on Wilson. The Moon (Franklin's 1st house ruler) and Jupiter are in a trine, but it's a separating trine. There may have been considerable respect, but metaphorically, it's waning.

There's one final factor to consider this year, and that's the placement of the Sun in the 8th house. One meaning probably related to his illness, which was serious. But the other was that in January 1919 (before his birthday), Uncle Ted died. Considering how much Franklin had looked up to, not to mention patterned his life on TR, this must have been a considerable blow.

Franklin didn't return to Washington until after his 1919 solar return, so he wasn't involved with the 1918 campaign. The landscape had changed considerably.

1919

Wilson was attempting what he considered the high road – a concept he would call Peace without Victory, which was universally

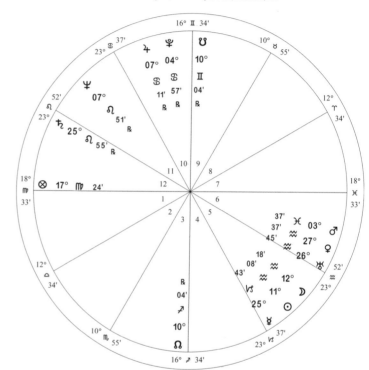

Franklin D Roosevelt
Hyde Park, Dutchess, NY
Time Zone: 5 hours West
January 31, 1919
41N47'05" 73W56'01"
Tropical Regiomontanus
8:16:34 PM
Standard Time
Solar Return for January 31, 1919 in Hyde Park, Dutchess, NY

Dorothean Ess. Dig. (No Mut Rec. Points)

Pl	Ruler	Exalt	Tripl	Term	Face	Detri	Fall	Score
☉	♄ m	--	☿	☿	☿ m	☉ -	--	- 10 P
☽	♄	--	☿ m	♀	☿	☉	--	- 5 P
☿	♄	♂	☽ m	♄	☉ m	☽	♃	- 5 P
♀	♄	--	☿	♂ m	☽	☉	--	- 5 P
♂	♃	♀	♂ +	♀ m	♄ m	☿	☿	+3
♃	☽	♃ +	♂	♃ +	♀	♄	♂	+6
♄	☉ m	--	♃	♂	♂ m	♄ -	--	- 10 P
☊	♃	☋	♃	♀	☽	☿	--	--
⊗	☿	☿	☽	♃	♀	♃	♀	--
As	☿	☿	☽	♄	♀	♃	♀	--
Mc	☿	☊	☿	♀	♂	♃	--	--
☋	☿	☊	☿	♃	♂	♃	--	--

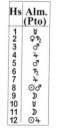

Hs	Alm. (Pto)
1	☿
2	♀♄
3	♂
4	♃
5	♂
6	♄
7	♃
8	☉♂
9	☽
10	☿
11	☽
12	☉♃

Example 12-16a. Franklin Roosevelt's solar return for 1919

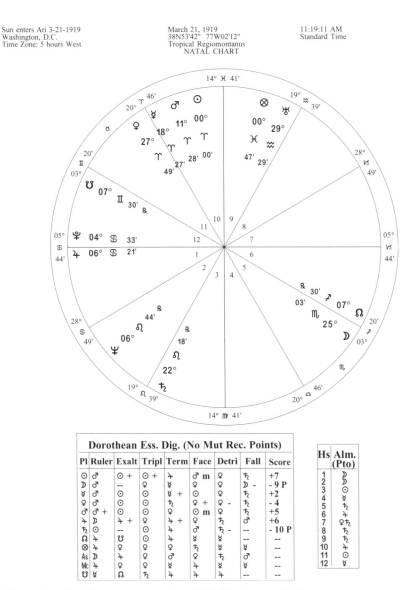

Sun enters Ari 3-21-1919
Washington, D.C.
Time Zone: 5 hours West

March 21, 1919
38N53'42" 77W02'12"
Tropical Regiomontanus
NATAL CHART

11:19:11 AM
Standard Time

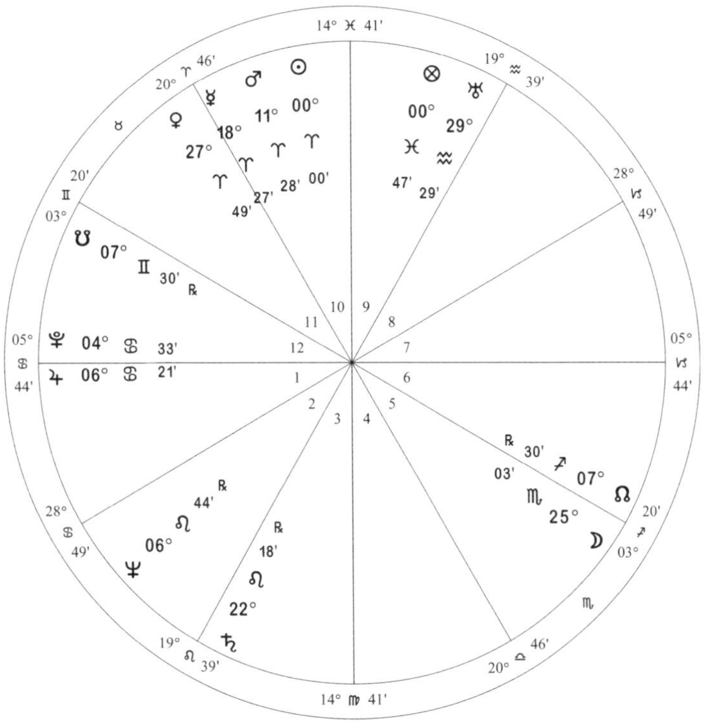

Dorothean Ess. Dig. (No Mut Rec. Points)

Pl	Ruler	Exalt	Tripl	Term	Face	Detri	Fall	Score
☉	♂	☉ +	☉ +	♃	♂ m	♀	♄	+7
☽	♂	--	♀	☿	♀	♀	☽ -	- 9 P
☿	♂	☉	☉	☿ +	☉	♀	♄	+2
♀	♂	☉	☉	♄	♀ +	♀ -	♄	- 4
♂	♂ +	☉	☉	♀	☉ m	♀	♄	+5
♃	☽	♃ +	♀	♃ +	♀	♄	♂	+6
♄	☉	--	☉	♃	♂	♄ -	--	- 10 P
☊	♃	☋	☉	♃	☿	☿	--	--
⊗	♃	♀	♀	♀	♄	☿	☿	--
As	☽	♃	♀	♂	♀	♄	♂	--
Mc	♃	♀	♀	☿	♃	☿	☿	--
☋	☿	☊	♄	♃	♃	♃	--	--

Hs	Alm. (Pto)
1	☽
2	☽
3	☉
4	☿
5	♄
6	♃
7	♀♄
8	♄
9	♄
10	♃
11	☉
12	☿

Example 12-16b. Aries Ingress for 1919, Washington, DC

despised by all the other powers in the war. Right or wrong, Wilson's ideas were politically inexpedient. Meanwhile, he had a Republican Congress that was just itching to dismantle his works, and get the presidency back on the next two-year pass. This was the stress on Wilson when he went to Europe. Franklin was part of the entourage.

The Aries Ingress for 1919 shows Wilson as Jupiter, ruler of the 10th, conjunct Pluto at the Ascendant. Jupiter may have been exalted, but we have already seen that Jupiter is not much of a fighter. And this was the problem. After the military stopped fighting, it was the job of Wilson and his team to finish the job. Wilson was both incredibly idealistic and incredibly religious, which meant he had the bad habit of assuming that God takes sides. The idea of the League of Nations was brilliant – but none of the countries in 1919 really had any interest in ceding power. So persuasive as Wilson tried to be, he was opposing too much: and especially a Republican Congress. After getting the treaty signed, Congress rejected it. And during the year, Wilson became exhausted from campaigning for the League of Nations, and ultimately, had a stroke.

One other national item is worth mentioning: prohibition, which took effect in 1919. Modern astrologers tend to give alcohol and other drugs to Neptune, but the classical choice would be the Moon, which rules all liquids. Here, with an extremely unhappy Moon in Scorpio square *Saturn*, the purchase of alcohol was outlawed. It's worth realizing that this amendment had its primary negative impact (from the user's point of view) on the lower classes. The amendment did not make *possession* of alcohol illegal, only its purchase, so the upper class could afford to stockpile before the amendment took effect. What would ultimately be understood about the amendment during the Great Depression is exactly how much the government was losing in tax revenue! But that dimension wasn't fully appreciated until economic downtimes.

As an underling in the administration, FDR's job was primarily to sell off U.S. military property which had been relocated to Europe. His job is shown from his 1919 solar return. This solar return was a new moon. Franklin's last new moon had occurred at age 18, when he graduated from Groton, and it was also during this period that his father died. In 1919, he was 37. The new moon occurs roughly every nineteen years, but not everyone has one at all. As you may recall from Chapter 2 and scattered references since, stepping out on a new path can be the manifestation of this energy.

So just what represented a new beginning that year? In 1919, the solar return Ascendant was within five degrees of his natal Ascendant, so there was some similarity to his nativity as well. The year 1919 was when Wilson's administration unraveled, with the failure of the ratification of the Treaty of Versailles and Wilson's stroke. Many of the top members of the administration were leaving, even before the election year coming up in 1920.

Franklin had, at this point, spent nine years in politics: roughly half a nodal cycle, just as he experienced a solar return new moon. He began planning to get back into the private sector, but it was awkward, with the number of people who had already left the administration. He wanted to get out, but felt that he couldn't gracefully do so. So he spent the year pushing paper as the administration imploded, shown in his chart by Pluto in the 10th.

1920

Franklin's personal no man's land in the lameduck administration continued into 1920. As soon as Wilson had the stroke, the administration was effectively dead. The 1920 Aries Ingress with the MC ruled by combust Mercury retrograde in Pisces says it all: the president was no longer on the job. Wilson's dream of the League of Nations was dying, and the Moon square Pluto, with Pluto in the 10th, didn't help it.

FDR's 1920 solar return had Saturn on the 10th: a big fat peregrine retrograde Saturn. In addition, the SR-Pluto was partile conjunct his radix Moon, which was Franklin's most dignified planet. The Part of Fortune was very close to that Pluto. So what happened? There was one new wrinkle in 1920: now, women had the vote. So

Franklin D Roosevelt
Hyde Park, Dutchess, NY
Time Zone: 5 hours West

February 1, 1920
41N47'05" 73W56'01"
Tropical Regiomontanus

2:00:12 AM
Standard Time

Solar Return for February 1, 1920 in Hyde Park, Dutchess, NY

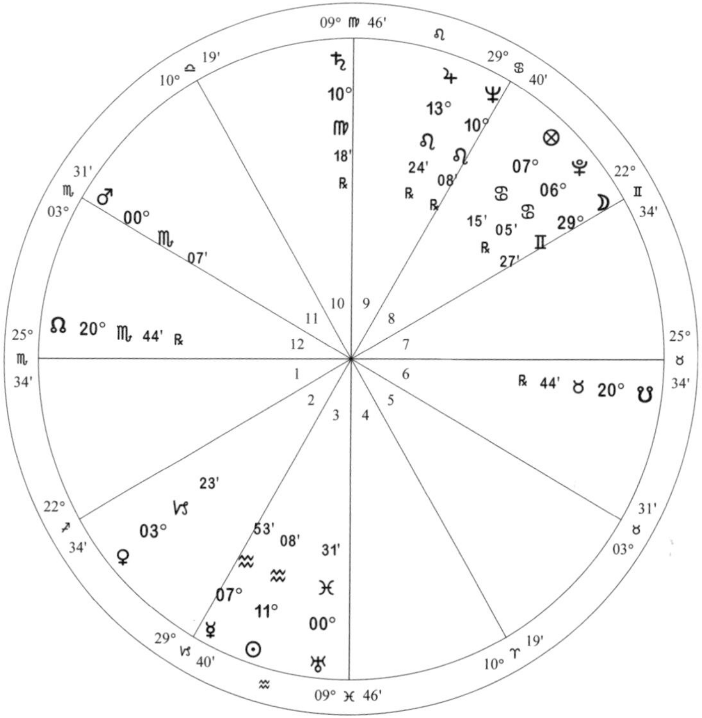

Pl	Ruler	Exalt	Tripl	Term	Face	Detri	Fall	Score
☉	♄	--	☿	☿	☿	☉ -	--	- 10 P
☽	☿	☊	☿	♂	☉	♃	--	- 5 P
☿	♄ m	--	☿ +	☿ +	♀	☉	--	+5
♀	♄	♂	☽	♀ +	♃	☽	♃	+2
♂	♂ +	--	♂ +	♂ +	♂ +	♀	☽	+11
♃	☉	--	♃ +	♀	♃ +	♄	--	+4
♄	☿ m	☿	☽	♀	♀	♃	♀	- 5 P
☊	♂	--	♂	♀	♀	♀	☽	--
⊗	☽	♃	♂	♃	♀	♄	♂	--
As	♂	--	♂	☿	♀	♀	☽	--
Mc	☿	☿	☽	♀	☉	♃	♀	--
☋	♀	☽	☽	♃	♄	♂	--	--

Dorothean Ess. Dig. (No Mut Rec. Points)

Hs	Alm. (Pto)
1	♂
2	♃
3	♄
4	♃
5	☉♂
6	☽♀
7	☽
8	☿
9	☽
10	☿
11	♀
12	♂

Example 12-17a. Franklin Roosevelt's solar return for 1920

Sun enters Ari 3-20-1920
Washington, D.C.
Time Zone: 5 hours West

March 20, 1920
38N53'42" 77W02'12"
Tropical Regiomontanus
NATAL CHART

4:59:21 PM
Standard Time

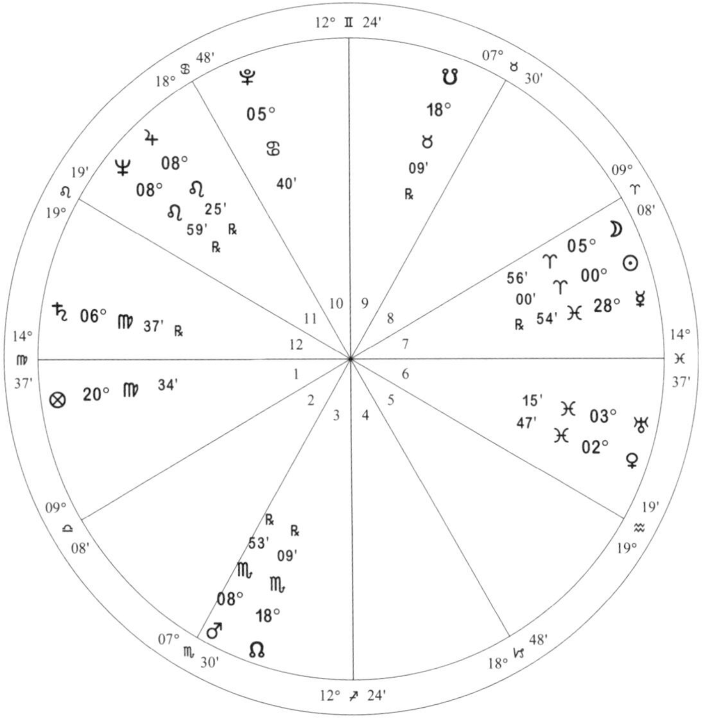

Dorothean Ess. Dig. (No Mut Rec. Points)								
Pl	Ruler	Exalt	Tripl	Term	Face	Detri	Fall	Score
☉	♂	☉ +	☉ +	♃	♂	♀	♄	+7
☽	♂	☉	☉	♃	♂	♀	♄	- 5 P
☿	♃	♀	♀	♄ m	♂	☿ -	☿ -	- 14 P
♀	♃	♀ +	♀ +	♀ +	♄	☿	☿	+9
♂	♂ +	--	♀	♃	♂ +	♀	☽	+6
♃	☉	--	☉	☿	♄	♄	--	- 5 P
♄	☿	☿	♀	☿ m	☉	♃	♀	- 5 P
☊	♂	--	♀	♀	☉	♀	☽	--
⊗	☿	☿	♀	♄	☿	♃	♀	--
As	☿	☿	♀	♃	♀	♃	♀	--
Mc	☿	☊	♄	♃	♂	♃	--	--
☋	♀	☽	♀	♃	☽	♂	--	--

Hs	Alm. (Pto)
1	☿
2	♀♄
3	♂
4	♃
5	♂♄
6	♄
7	♃
8	☉
9	♀
10	☿
11	☽
12	☉

Example 12-17b. Aries Ingress for 1920, Washington, DC

the Democrats decided that a very photogenic man with a nice wife would be a good candidate for vice president. This also amounted to "balancing the ticket," since the presidential candidate was from a different part of the country.

Franklin loved campaigning, and so he and Eleanor traveled all over the country by rail. And this was a good example of winning by losing, given those Saturn and Pluto configurations. Franklin got a great deal of national exposure, mostly positive. In politics, the vice presidential candidate is rarely blamed if the ticket loses. Franklin got to be the good soldier, and he got to be seen and heard. It also had to be far more fun to be out campaigning than attempting to do his job in a headless administration. But he was too level-headed to have any illusions that the ticket had the slightest chance of winning. It didn't.

He understood that, in this era, the Democrats, at least at a national level, were still only capable of winning when the Republicans made a serious error, as had happened in 1912. There was no telling when that next error would occur. For the moment, at the end of 1920, Franklin was set to become a private citizen. He still harbored presidential ambitions that were as strong as ever, but he understood completely that he had to wait, and not peak too soon.

1921

So, in 1921, we will dispense with the Aries Ingresses for a time, and just examine FDR's solar return charts. And frankly, that was enough! This solar return featured Neptune opposite the Sun, manifesting from the 6th to the 12th. Saturn was opposite Mars across the 7th-1st. The Moon in Scorpio in a wide square to the Sun doesn't look entirely happy either. Earlier in the year, the incoming Republican Congress and administration attempted to tar him with a scandal, but Franklin defended himself vigorously, and the charges didn't stick, apparently being understood for the political motivation behind them.

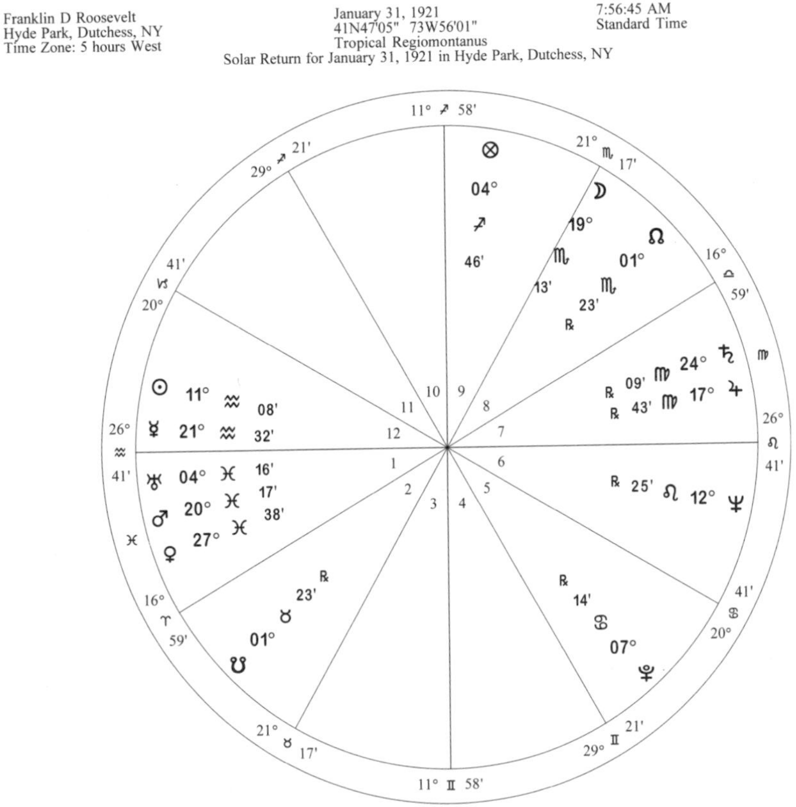
Franklin D Roosevelt
Hyde Park, Dutchess, NY
Time Zone: 5 hours West
January 31, 1921
41N47'05" 73W56'01"
Tropical Regiomontanus
7:56:45 AM
Standard Time
Solar Return for January 31, 1921 in Hyde Park, Dutchess, NY

Dorothean Ess. Dig. (No Mut Rec. Points)								
Pl	Ruler	Exalt	Tripl	Term	Face	Detri	Fall	Score
☉	♄	--	♄	☿	☿	☉ -	--	- 10 P
☽	♂	--	♀	♀	☉	♀	☽ -	- 9 P
☿	♄ m	--	♄	♃	☽	☉	--	- 5 P
♀	♃	♀ +	♀ +	♄	♂	☿	☿	+7
♂	♃	♀	♀	♂ +	♂ +	☿	☿	+3
♃	☿	☿	♀	♃ +	♀	♃ -	♀	- 3
♄	☿ m	☿	♀	♂	☿	♃	♀	- 5 P
☊	♂	--	♀	♂	♂	♀	☽	--
⊗	♃	☋ +	☉	♃	☿	☿	--	--
As	♄	--	♄	♂	☽	☉	--	--
Mc	♃	☋	☉	♀	☽	☿	--	--
☋	♀	☽	♀	♀	☿	♂	--	--

Hs	Alm. (Pto)
1	♄
2	☉
3	♀
4	☿
5	☿
6	☽
7	☉
8	♄
9	♂
10	♃
11	♃
12	♂

Example 12-18. Franklin Roosevelt's solar return for 1921

But that was small potatoes compared to the events of the summer, because this was the year Franklin contracted polio. This happened during the family vacations, and unfortunately, he was originally misdiagnosed, resulting in some weeks of counter-productive treatment for polio. In fact, in this period, adult polio was rare, so most physicians didn't recognize the symptoms: the disease was mostly called infantile paralysis.

This was a great shock to all. In Chapter 9, I discussed Eleanor's chart for this year, which clearly showed the health crisis of her husband. While this crisis was going on, Franklin's political advisor Louis Howe virtually moved in to help with Franklin's treatment. Depression is a common polio symptom, and certainly understandable, since major mobility problems are likely to result, almost overnight. Howe encouraged Franklin to see this medical set-back as not being fatal to his political career. Franklin's mother Sara was convinced that the polio meant that Franklin would retire to Hyde Park as a genteel invalid for the rest of his life. Franklin and Louis had other plans. And Howe, who had been despised by Eleanor, reached out to her, and encouraged her to take a more active political role herself, a role which ultimately developed into becoming Franklin's eyes and ears with the public.

Eventually, Franklin would improve from when he couldn't even grasp a pen to where he had full use of his arms. He learned to walk with braces (which were much heavier and bulkier than they are now), and we shall see that he established a regimen for his therapy that he followed for the rest of his life, when he could. But he never came close to regaining full use of his legs.

1922

At first, the disease really did drive him into the 12th house – out of public view. Eleanor referred to the winter of 1921-1922 as one of the most trying times of her life. Franklin's 1922 solar return does not look as bad as his 1921 one. But this is typical for a catastrophic

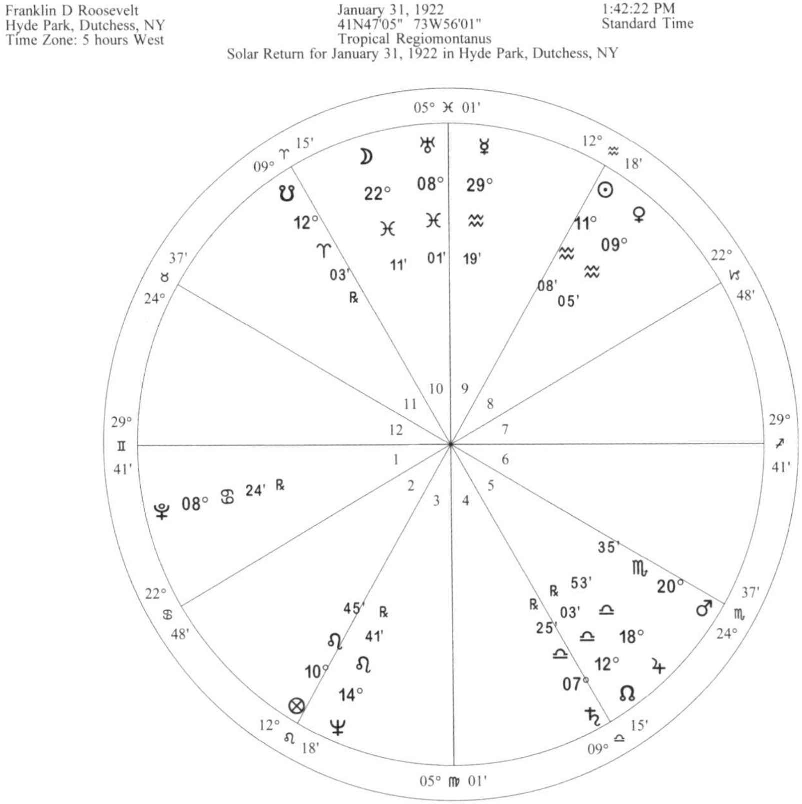
Franklin D Roosevelt
Hyde Park, Dutchess, NY
Time Zone: 5 hours West
January 31, 1922
41N47'05" 73W56'01"
Tropical Regiomontanus
1:42:22 PM
Standard Time
Solar Return for January 31, 1922 in Hyde Park, Dutchess, NY
05° ♓ 01'
05° ♍ 01'
29° ♊ 41'
29° ♐ 41'

Dorothean Ess. Dig. (No Mut Rec. Points)								
Pl	Ruler	Exalt	Tripl	Term	Face	Detri	Fall	Score
☉	♄	--	♄	☿	☿	☉ -	--	- 10 P
☽	♃	♀	♀	♂	♂	☿	☿	- 5 P
☿	♄	--	♄	♂	☽	☉	--	- 5 P
♀	♄ m	--	♄	☿	♀ +	☉	--	+1
♂	♂ +	--	♀	♀	♀	♀	☽	+5
♃	♀	♄	♄	♃ +	♄	♂	☉	+2
♄	♀ m	♄ +	♄ +	♀	☽	♂	☉	+7
☊	♀	♄	♄	♃	♄	♂	☉	--
⊗	☉	--	☉	☿	♃	♄	--	--
As	☿	☊	♄	♂	☉	♃	--	--
Mc	♃	♀	♀	♀	♄	☿	☿	--
☋	♂	☉	☉	♀	☉	♀	♄	--

Hs	Alm. (Pto)
1	☿
2	☽
3	☉
4	☿
5	♀♄
6	♂
7	♃
8	♂
9	♄
10	♀
11	☉
12	♀

Example 12-19. Franklin Roosevelt's solar return for 1922

event: Franklin "hit bottom" in 1921, but getting out from the bottom would be hard work, although technically work on the upswing. But, the 1922 chart had 29 degrees rising, and Mercury, the Ascendant ruler, was also posited at 29 degrees. When the Native has late placements – as FDR did, having Mercury and Mars at 27 degrees, the effect may not be quite as critical, but I do feel that when the chart has substantial representation at 29 degrees, the Native will be called upon to make a difficult transition – and the success of the outcome is not always guaranteed. The proximity of Mercury to the MC may represent Franklin's determination to beat this disease. As we just saw, this Mercury was very close to his natal position, and it was also partile trine the Ascendant.

Mars ruled the 6th in Scorpio, hovering just in the range of the 6th. Remember that a malefic associated with the 6th is an argument of disease, but this is a dignified malefic. Pluto is in the 1st, which I think may represent the dawning awareness that things really have changed. In an era where no provisions were made for the disabled, Franklin rapidly discovered that he literally could not move within corporate America. All of his efforts to physically conquer the disease by conditioning (the Mars in Scorpio) were not enough against polished floors and steps.

1923

It was in 1923 that he really began to address therapy at Warm Springs, Georgia, where the natural heat and buoyancy of the water made hydrotherapy a much more satisfying process. In 1923, Franklin's Sun was at the 6th house cusp. Franklin found an immediate affinity with Warm Springs, GA, and they with him. The Warms Springs resort was decrepit, having been built for a market that never entirely developed. Franklin loved that water, and felt he was making great progress there; the townspeople hoped that this rich Easterner could spur economic development for their area. To me, the Sun so close to the 6th house cusp really shows Franklin

Franklin D Roosevelt
Hyde Park, Dutchess, NY
Time Zone: 5 hours West

January 31, 1923
41N47'05" 73W56'01"
Tropical Regiomontanus

7:33:52 PM
Standard Time

Solar Return for January 31, 1923 in Hyde Park, Dutchess, NY

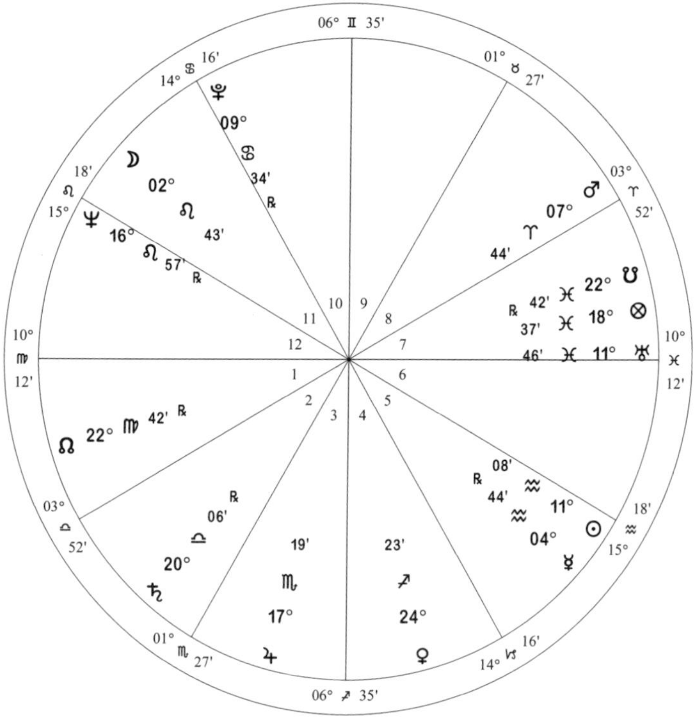

Dorothean Ess. Dig. (No Mut Rec. Points)								
Pl	Ruler	Exalt	Tripl	Term	Face	Detri	Fall	Score
☉	♄	--	☿	☿	☿	☉ -	--	- 10 P
☽	☉	--	♃	♄	♄	♄	--	- 5 P
☿	♄	--	☿ +	♄ m	♀	☉	--	+3
♀	♃	☋	♃	♄	♄	☿	--	- 5 P
♂	♂ +	☉	♃ m	♀	♂ +	♀	♄	+6
♃	♂	--	♂ m	♀	☉	♀	☽	- 5 P
♄	♀	♄ +	☿	☿ m	♃	♂	☉	+4
☊	☿	☿	☽	♄	☿	♃	♀	--
⊗	♃	♀	♂	☿	♃	☿	☿	--
As	☿	☿	☽	♀	♀	♃	♀	--
Mc	☿	☊	☿	☿	♃	♃	--	--
☋	♃	♀	♂	♂	♂	☿	☿	--

Hs	Alm. (Pto)
1	☿
2	♄
3	♂
4	♃
5	♂♄
6	♄
7	♃
8	♂
9	☽♀
10	☿
11	☽
12	☉

Example 12-20. Franklin Roosevelt's solar return for 1923

taking over his own therapy. The ruler of the 6th was dignified, which also argues that we are seeing attention upon health, not declining health. Mercury, ruling the 1st house of health, is in the radix sign, where Mercury has Triplicity, so it looks like Franklin's perception of improvement was accurate.

1924

Roosevelt's 1924 solar return had Mars in Sagittarius in the 1st house, ruling the 6th. While conjunct a very benefic Jupiter in Sagittarius, Mars was in the sign opposite his radix Mars, and Mars was peregrine. This doesn't look like great improvement physically, but neither does it look worse. His 1924 return was very Jupiterian by sign, with Jupiter also ruling the Moon, Venus, and Uranus. Jupiter ruled the 2nd and 4th, so we could get literal here and say that this year was about Franklin working constructively on foundations, or perhaps real estate, since Jupiter was dignified.

In 1924, his quest for improved health continued, but very slowly. He and Louis Howe were also very cognizant that this was an election year, and Franklin's future path needed to be charted. As early as 1922, they had begun a correspondence campaign with New York state Democrats to keep Franklin's name visible, all the while that he declined any offers because of health. Franklin was probably far more realistic than most Democrats about the fact that the Democrats nationally were still unelectable, even if individual Democrats could win on a state level. However, in 1924 most Democrats were somewhat aware that they were more likely testing out the 1928 campaign than seriously expecting to win. Roosevelt became the campaign manager for Al Smith, the Governor of New York. The two of them had a rather rocky history with each other, but the alliance suited them both at this time. Roosevelt addressed the national Democratic Convention to nominate Smith, putting himself once more into the national spotlight, demonstrating that he was not only still a force, but an increasing influence within the party.

I would take that influential speech as quite probably the North Node-MC conjunction. FDR came out of that convention with his reputation enhanced, in the same way that then-Senator Obama emerged from the 2004 Democratic Convention with his reputation enhanced.

When a Solar Return takes Effect

For comparison, let's examine that scenario, which also allows us to reconsider an item we discussed previously in Chapters 1 and 11; namely, when does a solar return take effect? Obama's birthday is August 4; the speech in question took place July 27, 2004, just a few days before. Does this fall under the 2003 or the 2004 solar return? Let's try to sort this out.

The event was a major 10th house event: Obama achieved buzz, and went from being a junior Senator from Illinois to *somebody*. In 2003, the 10th house cusp was ruled by Saturn in Cancer, opposite Obama's radix Saturn by sign. While the Part of Fortune is in the 10th and conjunct Obama's natal Saturn, it's disposed by the debilitated SR-Saturn, as well as Mars in Pisces (Triplicity, but opposite Mercury), Venus in Leo (peregrine), and the Moon in Scorpio (Fall). While that Mars is interesting, I wouldn't count on it in opposition to Mercury to so clearly catch the moment and nuance as he did.

Compare that to his 2004 solar return, just a few days after the speech. Now we have the North Node in the 10th – like Franklin's for 1924. Mars, which rules the MC, was on Obama's natal North Node, and conjunct Obama's natal Uranus. This event has a Uranus nature: a single speech, and his reputation changed overnight. The solar return Sun was angular both years – and of course, he had to get the invitation to speak under the 2003 solar return, so it's not that 2003 could be really bad in any case. So it does look in this example as if the effect of a solar return *can* start before the actual birthday, but how far is not determined here.

Barack Obama
Honolulu, Hawaii
Time Zone: 10 hours West

August 4, 1961
21N18'25" 157W51'30"
Tropical Regiomontanus
NATAL CHART

7:24 PM
Standard Time

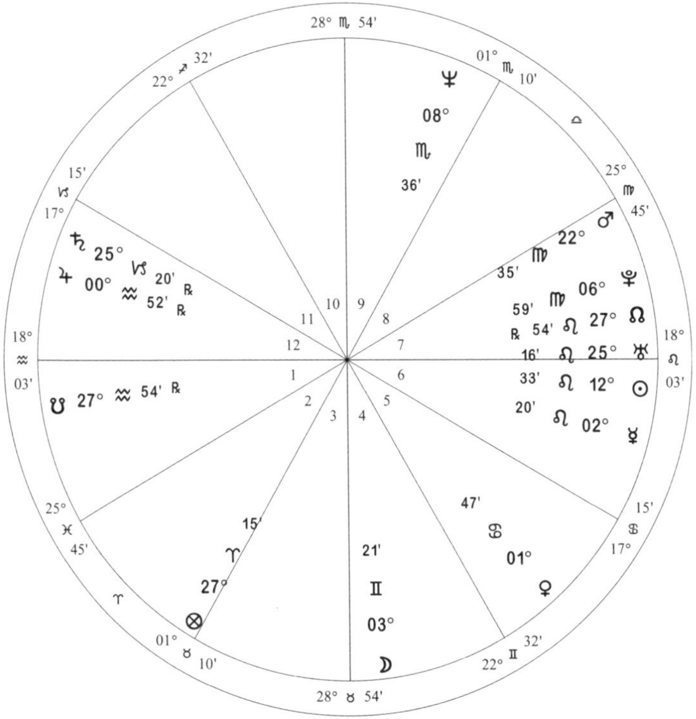

Dorothean Ess. Dig. (No Mut Rec. Points)								
Pl	Ruler	Exalt	Tripl	Term	Face	Detri	Fall	Score
☉	☉ +	--	♃	☿	♃	♄	--	+5
☽	☿	☊	☿	☿	♃	♃	--	- 5 P
☿	☉	--	♃ m	♄	♄	♄	--	- 5 P
♀	☽	♃	♂	♂	♀ +	♄	♂	+1
♂	☿	☿	☽	♄	☿	♃	♀	- 5 P
♃	♄	--	☿ m	♄	♀	☉	--	- 5 P
♄	♄ +	♂	☽	♄ +	☉	☽	♃	+7
☊	☉	--	♃	♂	♂	♄	--	--
⊗	♂	☉	♃	♄	♀	♀	♄	--
As	♄	--	☿	♀	☿	☉	--	--
Mc	♂	--	♂	♄	♀	♀	☽	--
☋	♄	--	☿	♂	☽	☉	--	--

Hs	Alm. (Pto)
1	♄
2	♂
3	☽♀
4	☽
5	☿
6	☽
7	☉
8	☿
9	♂
10	♂
11	♃
12	♂♄

Example 12-21. Barack Obama nativity

Barack Obama
Honolulu, Hawaii
Time Zone: 10 hours West

August 4, 2003
21N18'25" 157W51'30"
Tropical Regiomontanus
Solar Return for August 4, 2003 in Honolulu, Hawaii

10:57:55 PM
Standard Time

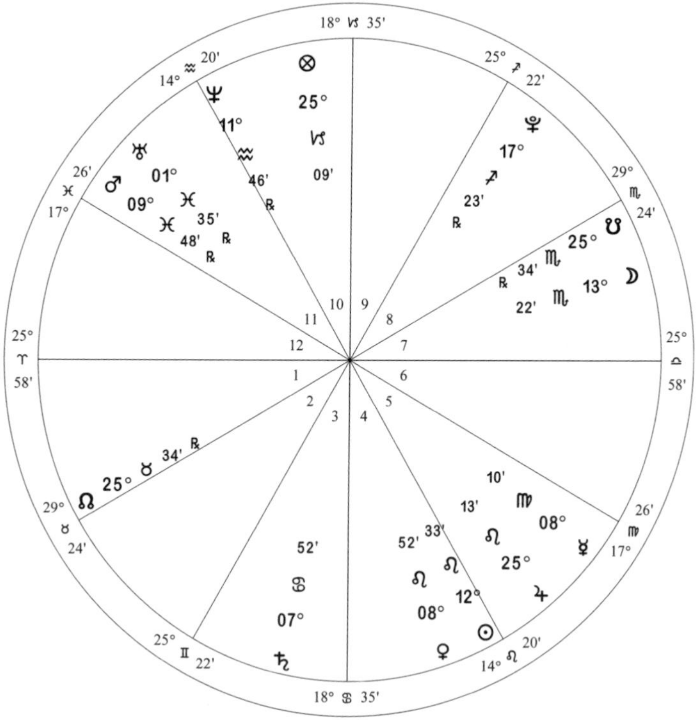

Dorothean Ess. Dig. (No Mut Rec. Points)								
Pl	Ruler	Exalt	Tripl	Term	Face	Detri	Fall	Score
☉	☉ +	--	♃	☿	♃	♄	--	+5
☽	♂	--	♂	♃	☉	♀	☽ -	- 9 P
☿	☿ +	☿ +	☽	♀ m	☉	♃	♀	+9
♀	☉	--	♃	☿ m	♄ m	♄	--	- 5 P
♂	♃	♀	♂ +	♃ m	♄	☿	☿	+3
♃	☉	--	♃ +	♂ m	♂	♄	--	+3
♄	☽	♃	♂	♃	♀ m	♄ -	♂	- 10 P
☊	♀	☽	☽	♄	♄	♂	--	--
⊗	♄	♂	☽	♄	☉	☽	♃	--
As	♂	☉	♃	♂	♀	♀	♄	--
Mc	♄	♂	☽	♃	♂	☽	♃	--
☋	♂	--	♂	☿	♀	♀	☽	--

Hs	Alm. (Pto)
1	♂
2	☽
3	☿
4	☽
5	☉
6	☿
7	♀
8	♂
9	♃
10	♂♄
11	♄
12	♃

Example 12-21a. Barack Obama solar return 2003

Barack Obama
Honolulu, Hawaii
Time Zone: 10 hours West

August 4, 2004
21N18'25" 157W51'30"
Tropical Regiomontanus
Solar Return for August 4, 2004 in Honolulu, Hawaii

4:52:56 AM
Standard Time

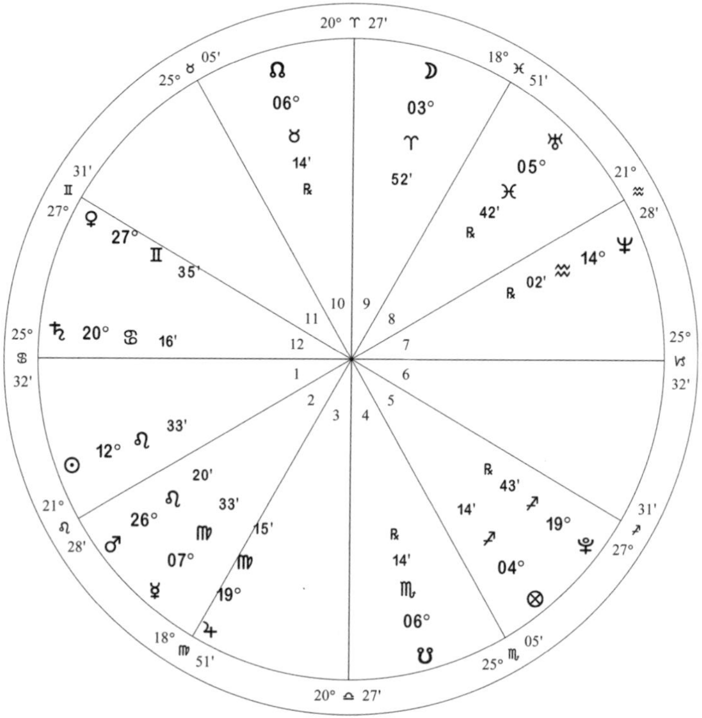

Dorothean Ess. Dig. (No Mut Rec. Points)								
Pl	Ruler	Exalt	Tripl	Term	Face	Detri	Fall	Score
☉	☉ +	--	♃	☿	♃	♄	--	+5
☽	♂	☉	♃ m	♃	♂	♀	♄	- 5 P
☿	☿ +	☿ +	☽	♀	☉	♃	♀	+9
♀	☿	☊	☿	♂	☉	♃	--	- 5 P
♂	☉	--	♃	♂ +	♂ +	♄	--	+3
♃	☿	☿	☽ m	♄	♀	♃ -	♀	- 10 P
♄	☽	♃	♂	♀	☽	♄ -	♂	- 10 P
☊	♀	☽	☽	♀	☿	♂	--	--
⊗	♃	☋ +	♃	♃	☿	☿	--	--
As	☽	♃	♂	♀	☽	♄	♂	--
Mc	♂	☉	♃	☿	♀	♀	♄	--
☋	♂	--	♂	♃	♂	♀	☽	--

Hs	Alm. (Pto)
1	☽
2	☉♃
3	☿
4	☿♀
5	♂
6	♃
7	♄
8	♄
9	♃
10	♂
11	☽
12	☿

Example 12-21b. Barack Obama solar return 2004

Franklin D Roosevelt
Hyde Park, Dutchess, NY
Time Zone: 5 hours West

February 1, 1924
41N47'05" 73W56'01"
Tropical Regiomontanus
Solar Return for February 1, 1924 in Hyde Park, Dutchess, NY

1:27:28 AM
Standard Time

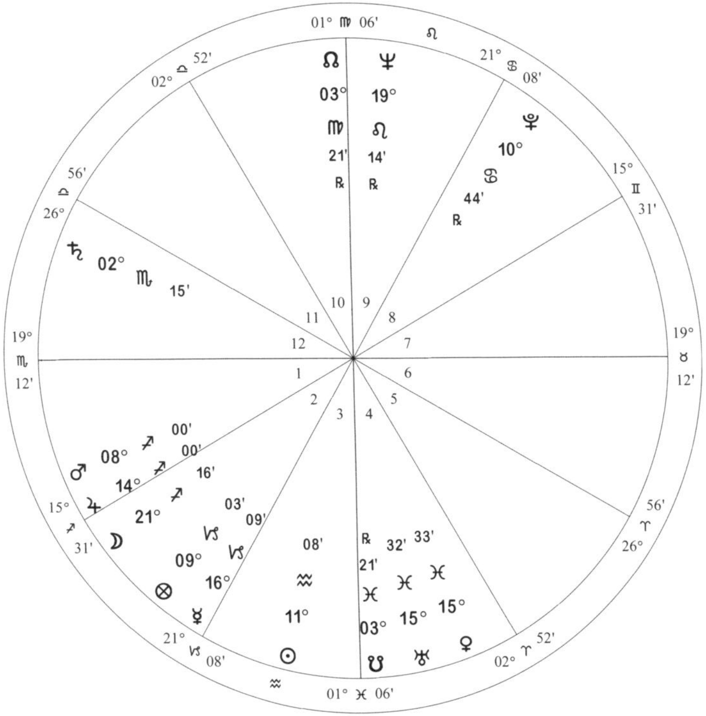

Dorothean Ess. Dig. (No Mut Rec. Points)								
Pl	Ruler	Exalt	Tripl	Term	Face	Detri	Fall	Score
☉	♄	--	☿	☿	☿	☉ -	--	- 10 P
☽	♃	☋	♃	♄	♄	☿	--	- 5 P
☿	♄	♂	☽	♃ m	♂ m	☽	♃	- 5 P
♀	♃	♀ +	♂	☿	♃	☿	☿	+4
♂	♃	☋	♃	♀	☿ m	☿	--	- 5 P
♃	♃ +	☋	♃ +	☿ m	☽	☿	--	+8
♄	♂	--	♂	♂	♂	♀	☽	- 5 P
☊	☿	☿	☽	☿	☉	♃	♀	--
⊗	♄	♂	☽	☿	♃	☽	♃	--
As	♂	--	♂	♀	☉	♀	☽	--
Mc	☿	☿	☽	☿	☉	♃	♀	--
☋	♃	♀	♂	♀	♄	☿	☿	--

Hs	Alm. (Pto)
1	♂
2	♃
3	♂
4	♀
5	♂
6	♂
7	☽
8	☿
9	☽
10	☿
11	♄
12	♀

Example 12-22. Franklin Roosevelt's solar return for 1924

1925: Sunrise Solar Return

In 1925, Franklin already surmised that it was unlikely that 1928 would be the Democrats' year, because he simply could not anticipate any catastrophe that could change what was then the excellent business climate for everybody but the farmers. While the buzz from the 1924 convention could have set him up for 1928, he therefore knew he had to *not* peak too soon.

His 1925 solar return was a sunrise chart with the Sun conjunct the South Node. He had sunrise charts at ages 10 and 43. In Chapter 2, we noted the approximate return of the natal angles at ages 33 and 66; here, the 33 year cycle means that the angle at age 10 is repeated at age 43. There's not much we can glean from his sunrise chart at age 10! I had my first sunrise chart (not as close as this: there's no guarantee that a person will ever have a solar return with the Sun conjunct the Ascendant within a degree or two) in 1974, when I received my Masters degree, which was a big deal for me at the time. Its reoccurrence in 2007 did mark more of a change in direction. But the MA could be considered the beginning of my PhD work, so the image isn't too far off. A sunrise chart represents a birth or change of direction of some sort.

But in Franklin's case, of what? Jupiter ruled his 10th house, and Jupiter was in the 12th house, in Fall. That's actually a pretty good description of Al Smith, the 1924 presidential candidate. It was and is tradition within US political parties that the most recent presidential candidate has a certain standing within the party, even if not officially as its administrative head. This influence is much enhanced if the candidate won, but still present with a loss. Describing the losing candidate of several months prior as debilitated Jupiter is just perfect. Smith and FDR really had been potential rivals for a long time, although whether the word rival is the best fit, or it is simply more descriptive to say that they had different priorities. FDR can be represented here either as Saturn, ruling the Ascendant, or the Sun, rising as we have discussed. Jupiter and Saturn are linked by a sextile: they were officially allies at this time.

Franklin D Roosevelt
Hyde Park, Dutchess, NY
Time Zone: 5 hours West

January 31, 1925
41N47'05" 73W56'01"
Tropical Regiomontanus

7:12:08 AM
Standard Time

Solar Return for January 31, 1925 in Hyde Park, Dutchess, NY

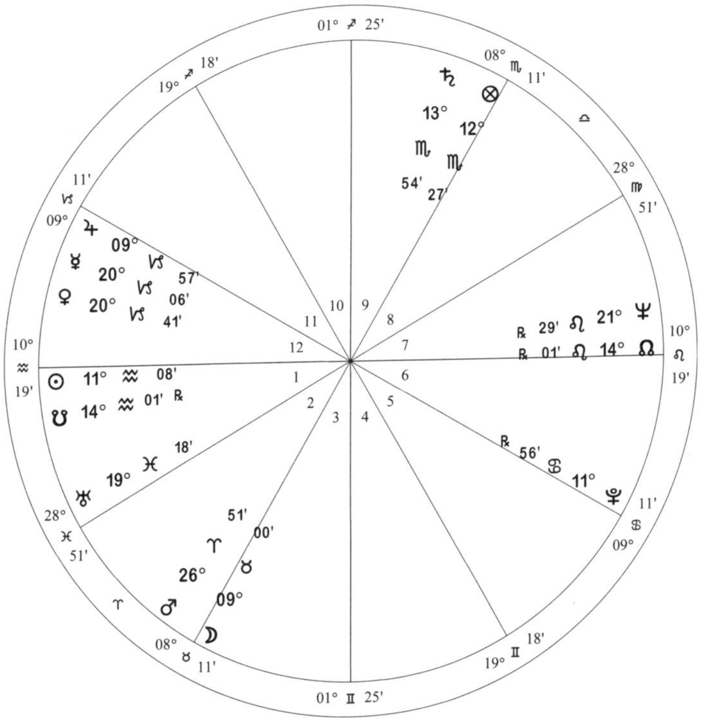

Dorothean Ess. Dig. (No Mut Rec. Points)								
Pl	**Ruler**	**Exalt**	**Tripl**	**Term**	**Face**	**Detri**	**Fall**	**Score**
☉	♄	--	☿	☿	☿ m	☉ -	--	- 10 P
☽	♀	☽ +	☽ +	☿	☿	♂	--	+7
☿	♄	♂	☽	♂	☉ m	☽	♃	- 5 P
♀	♄	♂	☽	♂	☉	☽	♃	- 5 P
♂	♂ +	☉	♃	♄	♀	♀	♄	+5
♃	♄	♂	☽	☿	♃ +	☽	♃ -	- 3
♄	♂	--	♂	♃	☉	♀	☽	- 5 P
☊	☉	--	♃	♀	♃	♄	--	--
⊗	♂	--	♂	♃	☉	♀	☽	--
As	♄	--	☿	☿	☿	☉	--	--
Mc	♃	☋	♃	♃	☿	☿	--	--
☋	♄	--	☿	♀	☿	☉	--	--

Hs	Alm. (Pto)
1	☿
2	♃
3	☽
4	☿
5	☿
6	♃
7	☉
8	☿
9	♂
10	♃
11	♃
12	♄

Example 12-23. Franklin Roosevelt's solar return for 1925

In addition to this being a sunrise chart, Franklin also had the Moon in Taurus, a very powerful placement, trine that Jupiter, sextile Pluto, and sextile by sign his radix Moon. While his recovery had not been as extensive as he had hoped, it is clear that his presidential ambitions were not even slightly dimmed. And make no mistake: he was extremely ambitious. With all the fixed placements in this chart, Franklin understood that he had to wait. However, more than any of the other Democrats of this era, he recognized that the party had to transcend its traditional regional factionalism if it was ever to be anything other than the party that got elected when the Republicans dropped the ball. And recognizing that 1928 would be too soon, he had to figure out what would work as an *eight* year strategy, not a *four* year strategy. Thinking in such a time scale, we can begin to understand the symbolism of the sunrise solar return chart. This truly was the birth of a strategy within his larger goal.

So he spent 1925 making the rounds, calling for party unity, attempting to reduce animosities, and generally doing everything possible to be a loyal Democrat. This was not an easy course, and with the number of fixed squares and oppositions, one would expect this was especially hard. It was, because this was the year of the so-called Scopes Monkey trial, the trial in Tennessee that tested the state law against the teaching of evolution in the schools. William Jennings Bryan, long a leader of progressive issues in the Democratic Party as well as Evangelical in outlook, joined the prosecution, and the trial completely encapsulated the range of difference within the Democratic Party, from the Evangelicals to the secularists.[7]

1926

By 1926, Franklin had shifted his attention to other interests entirely. With the Moon in Virgo in the 4th, in out-of-sect Triplicity, he bought the Warm Springs, GA resort, and began to remodel the facility, marketing it to both vacationers and polio victims. The Moon also ruled the 2nd house. The Moon associated with the 2nd house represents cash flow: the money goes in; the money goes out.

Franklin D Roosevelt
Hyde Park, Dutchess, NY
Time Zone: 5 hours West

January 31, 1926
41N47'05" 73W56'01"
Tropical Regiomontanus
Solar Return for January 31, 1926 in Hyde Park, Dutchess, NY

1:12:57 PM
Standard Time

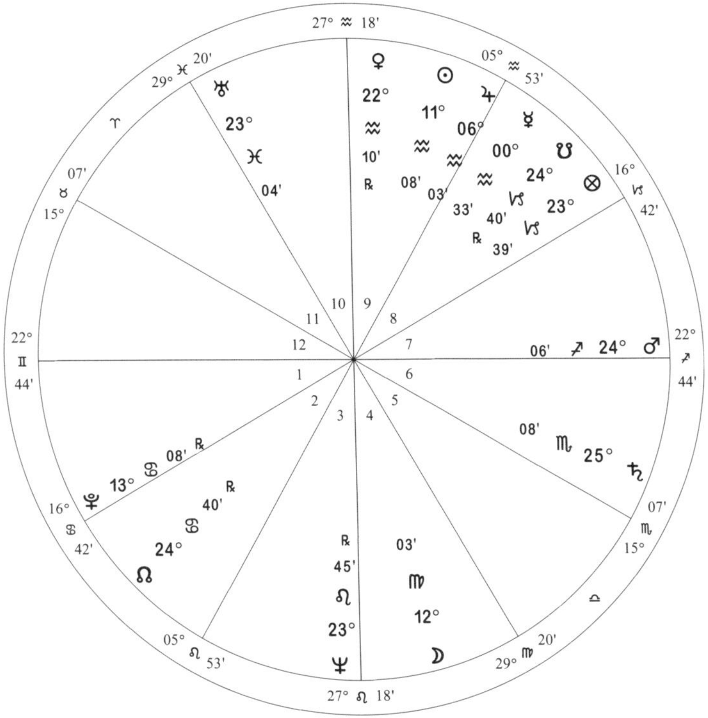

Dorothean Ess. Dig. (No Mut Rec. Points)								
Pl	Ruler	Exalt	Tripl	Term	Face	Detri	Fall	Score
☉	♄	--	♄	☿	☿	☉ -	--	- 10 P
☽	☿	☿	♀	♀	♀ m	♃	♀	- 5 P
☿	♄	--	♄	♄ m	♀	☉	--	- 5 P
♀	♄	--	♄ m	♃	☽ m	☉	--	- 5 P
♂	♃	☋	☉	♄	♄	☿	--	- 5 P
♃	♄	--	♄	☿	♀	☉	--	- 5 P
♄	♂	--	♀ m	☿ m	♀	♀	☽	- 5 P
☊	☽	♃	♀	♀	☽	♄	♂	--
⊗	♄	♂	♀	♂	☉	☽	♃	--
As	☿	☊	♄	♄	☉	♃	--	--
Mc	♄	--	♄	♂	☽	☉	--	--
☋	♄	♂	♀	♂	☉	☽	♃	--

Hs	Alm. (Pto)
1	☿♄
2	☽
3	☉
4	☉
5	☿
6	♂
7	♃
8	♂♄
9	♄
10	♄
11	♃
12	♀

Example 12-24. Franklin Roosevelt's solar return for 1926

The Sun in Aquarius in Detriment ruling the 4th was probably a good description of the property when he bought it, because the property really was run down. We have seen that the Sun in Detriment is not bad for FDR when it represents *him*, but it can be bad for anybody else. For him, the Sun in Aquarius is good, being his own placement; for anyone or anything else, it's a planet in Detriment. But the Sun is in the 9th: a property (Sun rules the 4th) that is a spa (a recreational or travel location, hence the 9th house).

With both Mercury and Venus in radix signs, this whole situation had to engage him in a very pleasant and stimulating way. With Venus partile trine the Ascendant so close to the MC, he would be a good spokesman for his resort. He was. But this also kept him out of politics – for the moment.

1927

As 1927 rolled around, Roosevelt had seen nothing to change his mind about running as the Democratic candidate in 1928. Yet *his* was the name that had the buzz. Of course, he could always defer for health reasons, but he found it better to have a good offense, and so he decided to campaign for Al Smith again. Rather than allow himself to be drafted, he continued to express his unwavering support for Smith.

Like 1926, in 1927, FDR had both Mercury and Venus back in Aquarius, their natal sign. If nothing else, this should indicate that his mind was sharp. Notice that Mercury ruled both Ascendant and MC. But both Mercury and Venus were cadent. Mercury's dignity and the two inferior planets' radix sign placements meant that Franklin didn't have many obstacles to endure from them, but the cadency showed that he was working behind the scenes.

Parenthetically, this looked like a good year for Eleanor, with Jupiter in Pisces conjunct the Descendant – that would be a strong indication for good things from one's spouse. Eleanor was learning politics and public speaking: there was great call for

Franklin D Roosevelt
Hyde Park, Dutchess, NY
Time Zone: 5 hours West

January 31, 1927
41N47'05" 73W56'01"
Tropical Regiomontanus
Solar Return for January 31, 1927 in Hyde Park, Dutchess, NY

7:08:07 PM
Standard Time

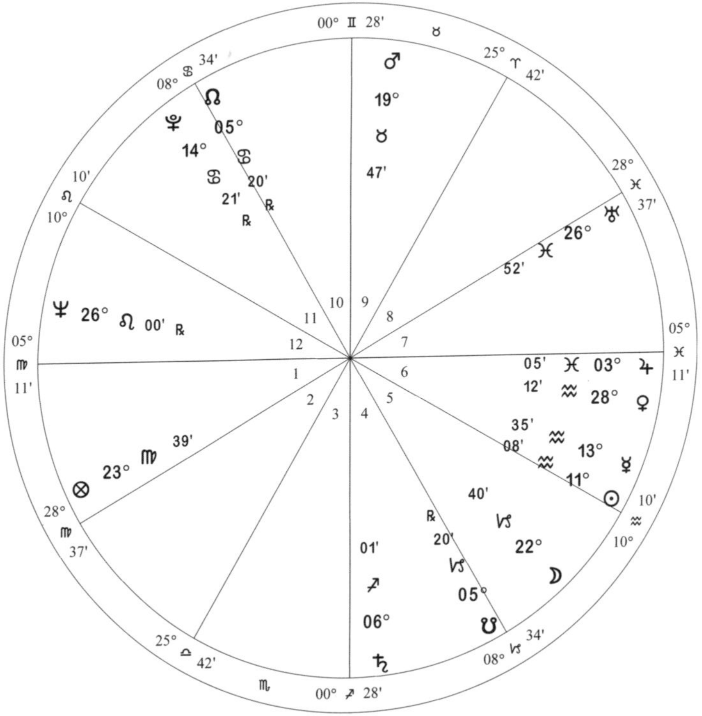

Dorothean Ess. Dig. (No Mut Rec. Points)								
Pl	**Ruler**	**Exalt**	**Tripl**	**Term**	**Face**	**Detri**	**Fall**	**Score**
☉	♄	--	☿	☿	☿	☉ -	--	- 10 P
☽	♄	♂ m	☽ +	♂	☉	☽ -	♃	- 2
☿	♄	--	☿ +	♀	☿ +	☉	--	+4
♀	♄	--	☿	♂	☽	☉	--	- 5 P
♂	♀	☽ m	☽	♃	☽	♂ -	--	- 10 P
♃	♃ +	♀	♂	♀	♄	☿	☿	+5
♄	♃	☋	♃	♃	☿	☿	--	- 5 P
☊	☽	♃	♂	♂	♀	♄	♂	--
⊗	☿	☿	☽	♄	☿	♃	♀	--
As	☿	☿	☽	☿	☉	♃	♀	--
Mc	☿	☊	☿	☿	♃	♃	--	--
☋	♄	♂	☽	♀	♃	☽	♃	--

Hs	Alm. (Pto)
1	☿
2	☿
3	♀
4	♃
5	♄
6	☿
7	♀
8	♃
9	♂
10	☿
11	♃
12	☉

Example 12-25. Franklin Roosevelt's solar return for 1927

women's involvement (at least in auxiliaries) in these early days of the women's vote, and it took Eleanor some time to overcome her natural shyness, but she was participating in New York state politics.

1928

The next presidential election year was 1928. Franklin's strategy was to keep Smith in the spotlight. He served as floor manager at the convention, and his nomination speech was the first time such a speech was broadcast on national radio – thus featuring FDR as much or more than Smith himself, because the tradition at nominating conventions was for the nominees not to attend. Franklin's ruler is Mars, ruler of the SR-Ascendant. Mars is conjunct the 3rd house cusp: it's cadent, but in one of the lesser cadent houses, the 3rd and the 9th, that are not considered as malefic as the 6th and 12th. Mars, however, is exalted – arguably the strongest position possible for a malefic, especially since it is also in Triplicity. By being for Smith, Franklin was getting attention without risking being the top of the ticket, or the second on it, because he and Smith were from the same state. So Franklin basked in the national attention without committing himself or being seen as a loser.

Notice an interesting thing about the Sun. The Sun is ruling the 10th – and of course, this is a solar return. *If the Sun refers to FDR*, then the Sun is simply a significator for him, and whatever dignity or debility it has, is simply its natal state. *But if the Sun represents somebody else*, now the condition of the Sun becomes relevant. There is an interesting parallel idea with this. In all regular Inauguration charts in the USA since the 1930s, the chart *always* has the Sun in Aquarius, and the Sun is *always* conjunct the MC. Why? The 20th Amendment to the Constitution states that the president takes office on January 20th following the election; that amendment was ratified in 1933. So the Sun *must* be in Aquarius. The Constitution itself states that the president takes office at noon.

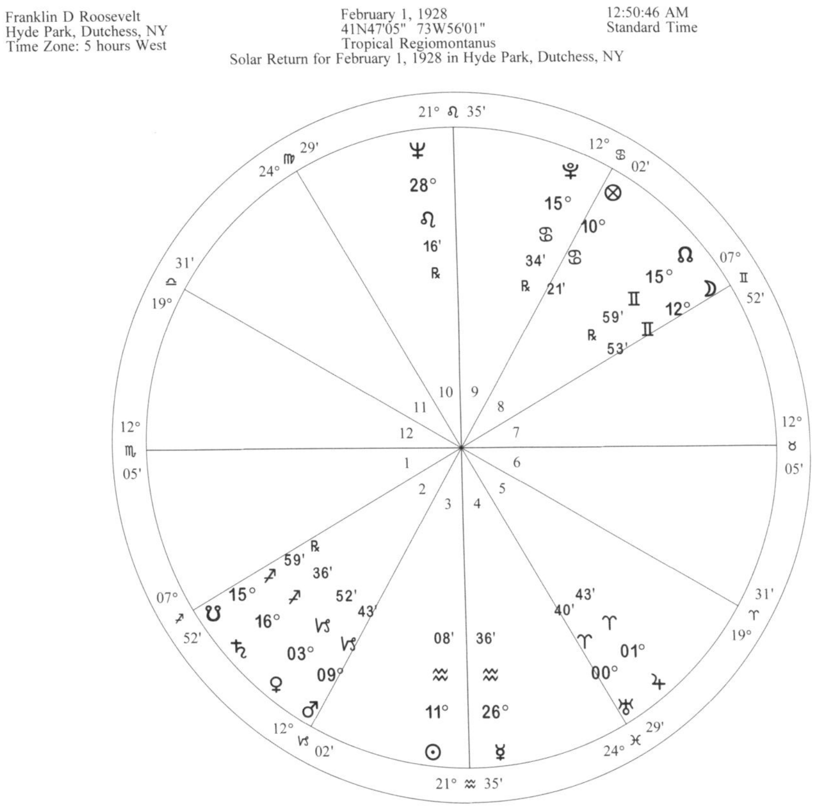
Franklin D Roosevelt
Hyde Park, Dutchess, NY
Time Zone: 5 hours West
February 1, 1928
41N47'05" 73W56'01"
Tropical Regiomontanus
Solar Return for February 1, 1928 in Hyde Park, Dutchess, NY
12:50:46 AM
Standard Time

Dorothean Ess. Dig. (No Mut Rec. Points)

Pl	Ruler	Exalt	Tripl	Term	Face	Detri	Fall	Score
☉	♄	--	☿	☿	☿	☉ -	--	- 10 P
☽	☿	☊	☿	♃	♂	♃	--	- 5 P
☿	♄	--	☿ +	♂ m	☽	☉	--	+3
♀	♄	♂	☽	♀ +	♃	☽	♃	+2
♂	♄	♂ +	☽	☿ m	♃ m	☽	♃	+4
♃	♂	☉	♃ +	♃ +	♂ m	♀	♄	+5
♄	♃	☋	♃	☿	☽	☿	--	- 5 P
☊	☿	☊ +	☿	♀	♂	♃	--	--
⊗	☽	♃	♂	♃	☿	♄	♂	--
As	♂	--	♂	♃	☉	♀	☽	--
Mc	☉	--	♃	♃	♂	♄	--	--
☋	♃	☋	♃	☿	☽	☿	--	--

Hs	Alm. (Pto)
1	♂
2	♃
3	♂♄
4	♄
5	♂
6	☉♂
7	☽
8	☿
9	♃
10	☉♃
11	☿
12	☿♀♄

Example 12-26. Franklin Roosevelt's solar return for 1928

At noon, the Sun is conjunct the MC in standard time. Thus, the conclusion.

But let's follow the logic. The Sun in Detriment therefore is a ruler of all presidents. Does this mean that all presidents are in Detriment? Some of us might argue that! But we may note that the calendar date of the Inauguration is constrained. The Sun can *only* be in Detriment. This is like saying that the Sun can *only* be exalted at the Aries Ingress. When the calendar date is constrained, we cannot apply the dignity of the Sun to the argument of what it represents in any case *where the time is also constrained*. The president takes office at noon according to the Constitution whether the oath of office is properly applied or not. The Sun will always be at the MC at that time. So when the Inaugural Sun in a chart is used for the president, the fact that it's in detriment is ignored, although that doesn't have to apply to anything else the Sun rules in the chart.

So we have a conundrum with FDR's 10th house for 1928. The Sun rules it, and by definition, Franklin's Sun is in Detriment – and yet it is *his* Sun. Having a recapitulation of the natal chart is considered a good thing in a solar return. How can these both be true? In our example here, Al Smith, as shown through the 10th (FDR's "boss," since Roosevelt is his floor manager), is the Sun in Detriment: he's a weak candidate who loses.

But when, a little later in the same solar return, the New York state Democrats nominated Roosevelt for governor, he won, because, applying the 10th house to himself and not to someone else, the 10th in this year is ruled by the Sun in Aquarius, accidentally dignified *in his case alone* by being in the sign of his *natal* Sun. That same 10th house can show both a loss and a victory, because the reading is different depending on whether it refers to the Native or to somebody else. Even more so that year: Smith lost the presidency badly, while Franklin cruised into the governorship against the Republican tide. His strong showing in New York put him as the rising star, while the rout at the presidential level left Smith crumpled.

1929

This, of course, meant that in 1929, Franklin had to go back to work! In those days, the term of office for the governor was two years, not the four years that has become the norm. His job was further complicated by a solid Republican majority in both houses of the state legislature. He began his administration by creating the regular broadcasts that, during his presidency, would be called fireside chats. But he needed some time to perfect his style, and he did it at a state level. But nothing budged the Republicans until the market crashed on Black Thursday, October 1929. Suddenly, the Republican expectation of sweeping Roosevelt away in the 1930 election didn't look quite so likely, as the financial collapse stubbornly refused to go away.

Franklin's solar return at first doesn't look promising. The South Node so close to the MC hinted that his job was not going to be easy, but instead, very exhausting. At the time he began the job, the idea of that would have sounded strange, except for the stress of having to work with a hostile legislature. However, Franklin *himself* looked in good shape, with his Sun in the 1st and Mercury in its radix sign.

But what to do with that South Node? The Western tradition has not maintained an image of the South Node as flushed out as the Indian system, which has classified *Rahu* and *Ketu* as of the nature of planets, and thus having a much more vibrant set of meanings. The South Node is malefic and destructive in the West. But why, and how? Modern delineations have run from karmic, to fatal, to evolutionary, or to simply connections, in the case of cosmobiologists.

The nodal axis astronomically marks the intersection of the plane of the orbit of the Sun-Earth with the orbit of the Earth-Moon. Being a line of intersection (two lines intersect in a point, or two planes in a line in normal geometry), we thus understand that we must consider two words in their meaning: *line* and *intersection*. The

Franklin D Roosevelt
Hyde Park, Dutchess, NY
Time Zone: 5 hours West

January 31, 1929
41N47'05" 73W56'01"
Tropical Regiomontanus
Solar Return for January 31, 1929 in Hyde Park, Dutchess, NY

6:44:36 AM
Standard Time

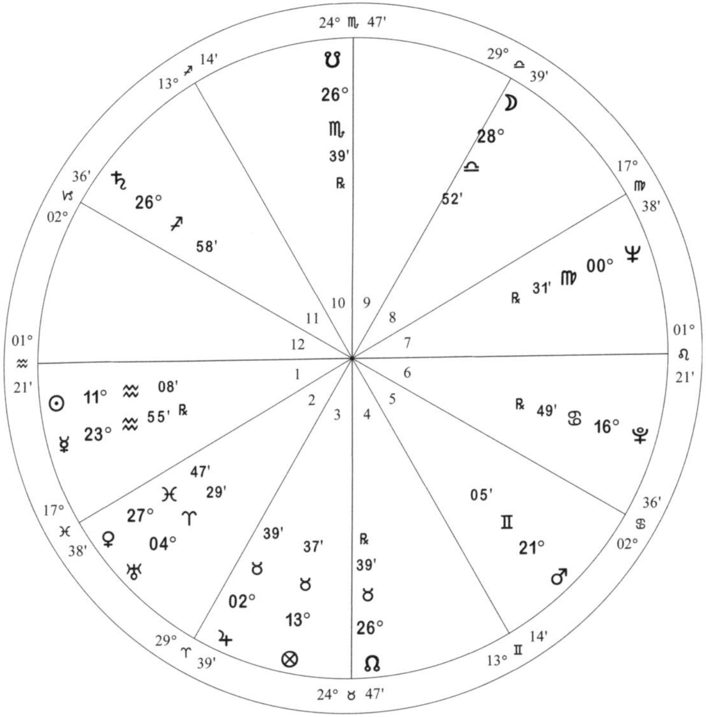

Dorothean Ess. Dig. (No Mut Rec. Points)								
Pl	**Ruler**	**Exalt**	**Tripl**	**Term**	**Face**	**Detri**	**Fall**	**Score**
☉	♄	--	☿	☿	☿	☉ -	--	- 10 P
☽	♀	♄	☿	☊	♃	♂	☉	- 5 P
☿	♄	--	☿ +	♃	☽	☉	--	+3
♀	♃ m	♀ +	♂	♄	♂	☿	☿	+4
♂	☿	☊	☿	♄ m	☉	♃	--	- 5 P
♃	♀ m	☽	☽	♀	☿	♂	--	- 5 P
♄	♃	☋	♃	♂ m	♄ +	☿	--	+1
☊	♀	☽	☽	♂	♄	♂	--	--
⊗	♀	☽	☽	☿	☽	♂	--	--
As	♄	--	☿	♄	♀	☉	--	--
Mc	♂	--	♂	☿	♀	♀	☽	--
☋	♂	--	♂	☿	♀	♀	☽	--

Hs	Alm. (Pto)
1	♄
2	♃
3	♂
4	☽
5	☿
6	☽
7	☉
8	☿
9	♀
10	♂
11	♃
12	♄

Example 12-27. Franklin Roosevelt's solar return for 1929

North Node and the South Node are also known as the Ascending and Descending Nodes. As the zodiacal equivalents of these two points of intersection of this line, one cannot be considered without the other. I do think there are times where benefic and malefic are truly appropriate appellations for each. In medical astrology, the South Node can be a point of destruction. But that is the extreme end of the interpretation. A South Node conjunction to the Ascendant in a surgery may represent a dire outcome, but the South Node conjunct the Ascendant in a solar return does not *have* to be fatal. However, that is not to say that the South Node is not experienced as unpleasant.

Within Western understanding, I think the easiest way to describe the nodes is through the metaphor of the breath. We can use the intake of breath for the North Node, and the outflow of breath for the South Node. Breath, vitality, things – come in at the North Node, and go out at the South Node. The vast majority of people prefer the experience of accumulation to the experience of loss.[8] But no life is stable that only grows and never shrinks: that's a sure definition of a runaway situation which is rapidly working up to a crash.

In practical usage, this idea of loss with the South Node has multiple meanings. In Franklin's case with it conjunct the MC, it was the first time he was a working politician since he contracted polio, and that *had* to be a considerable drain on him. Until October, the complete refusal of the legislature to work with him on anything had to be disheartening. But as the Great Depression developed – and it hardly appeared in full flush overnight – it had to be harrowing to anyone who cared about the average person.

One other point. We saw in the prior year how we had the interesting contrast that, when referring to FDR, the Sun acted primarily as a benefit, because it was, by definition, in its natal sign, but when applied to another, its intrinsic dignity and other qualities would apply. Here, this dual advantage/disadvantage is shown for Eleanor, because the 7th house cusp of the solar return is Leo. Franklin's election as governor put certain restraints upon her, as

far as what independent roles she could play, being the governor's wife. But Franklin benefited from her enormously, both from her being his eyes and ears, and because of the political groundwork she had been laying independently.

By the time that New Year's Day 1930 rolled around, it was not yet clear how universal economic problems were, nor how long they would last. But it was becoming clear that this was not going to be just a blip in the stock market. In fact, to any contemporary who took the trouble to study the developing situation, it rapidly became clear that the market was merely one component of the problem. In *Astrology of Sustainability*, I discussed the droughts that plagued this period: droughts so severe that the result was the Dust Bowl.[9] Remember further that I mentioned that farmers were the one group who hadn't shared in the prior economic boom.

1930

Also, this economic downturn didn't just affect the United States, but had global dimensions as well. The war reparations demanded of Germany by the winning European powers produced hyperinflation in Germany, an inability to pay, and a dependency on these monies by the winning powers. So as 1930 progressed, the Republicans' grip on power loosened as the economic problems continued.

Franklin Roosevelt's success in New York State was building. He continued to practice his radio approach, and in the process, he was able to communicate to the people that he was trying to do everything possible to deflect their misery, while the Republicans were standing in the way.

Franklin's 1930 solar return showed the Sun at the 10th, with Venus there as well, also in the radix sign. This chart actually has quite a bit of dignity: Mars in exaltation and Triplicity, Saturn in rulership, Moon in Triplicity, and Jupiter mixed between Detriment and Triplicity. The Moon in the 10th puts the people of New York in his court (as governor), and he was very effective at getting his

Franklin D Roosevelt
Hyde Park, Dutchess, NY
Time Zone: 5 hours West

January 31, 1930
41N47'05" 73W56'01"
Tropical Regiomontanus

12:27:46 PM
Standard Time

Solar Return for January 31, 1930 in Hyde Park, Dutchess, NY

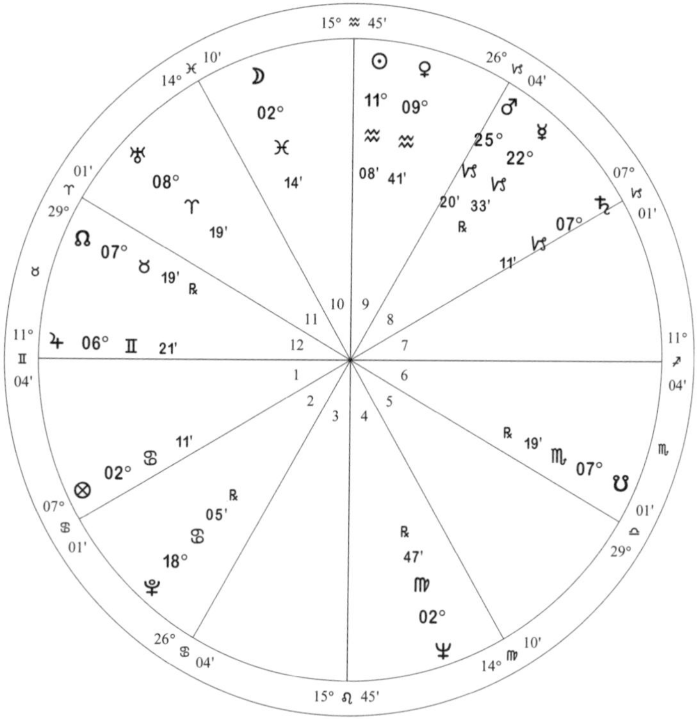

Dorothean Ess. Dig. (No Mut Rec. Points)

Pl	Ruler	Exalt	Tripl	Term	Face	Detri	Fall	Score
☉	♄	--	♄	☿	☿ m	☉ -	--	- 10 P
☽	♃	♀	♀	♀	♄	☿	☿	- 5 P
☿	♄	♂	♀	♂	☉ m	☽	♃	- 5 P
♀	♄	--	♄ m	☿	♀ +	☉	--	+1
♂	♄	♂ +	♀	♄	☉	☽	♃	+4
♃	☿	☊	♄	☿	♃ +	♃ -	--	- 4
♄	♄ +	♂	♀ m	☿	♃	☽	♃	+5
☊	♀	☽	♀	♀	☿	♂	--	--
⊗	☽	♃	♀	♂	♀	♄	♂	--
As	☿	☊	♄	♃	♂	♃	--	--
Mc	♄	--	♄	♀	☿	☉	--	--
☋	♂	--	♀	♃	♂	♀	☽	--

Hs	Alm. (Pto)
1	☿
2	♃
3	☽
4	☉
5	☿
6	♄
7	♃
8	♄
9	♄
10	♄
11	♃
12	☉

Example 12-28. Franklin Roosevelt's solar return for 1930

message to them. He trounced his Republican opponent, and the margin was so large that it really set him up for the presidential election season coming up in 1932. Here, we note that his opponent would precisely fit that mixed message Jupiter, ruler of the 7th, conjunct the 1st house cusp. Your opponent in your court is a very powerful message.

1931

This meant that Franklin was free as early as 1931 to begin to weave together the threads that would enable his nomination in 1932. What was needed in this year was the behind-the-scenes politicking that would put together the necessary two-thirds majority of delegates the following year. And lo! The only angular planet that Franklin had was Neptune! Yet this was an extremely powerful chart, with the Moon-Jupiter partile conjunction, both bodies highly dignified in the house of friendship, square Uranus: Franklin was positioning himself to ride the wave of resentment against the Republicans, in a time where being the outsider was advantageous. Further, this was a recapitulation of the natal Moon sign. As I have mentioned elsewhere, the 11th house includes the concept of the mentor, and of intergenerational ties among the ruling class. This was one of the ways Franklin was putting together his run: by calling in favors from the old Wilson crowd. So he spent 1931 on the phone and making speeches.

One other incidental event for 1931: for the first time in fifteen years, Franklin returned to Europe, a trip necessitated by his mother falling ill with pneumonia while visiting there. Notice Uranus conjunct the 9th house cusp partile squared by the Moon! The Moon was the Almuten of the 10th house, his mother. The square undoubtedly indicated that any such trip was at best an interruption as he planned his ascent to the presidency, and certainly a bother, given his physical condition and the lack of any accommodations specifically for it.

Franklin D Roosevelt
Hyde Park, Dutchess, NY
Time Zone: 5 hours West

January 31, 1931
41N47'05" 73W56'01"
Tropical Regiomontanus
Solar Return for January 31, 1931 in Hyde Park, Dutchess, NY

6:14:26 PM
Standard Time

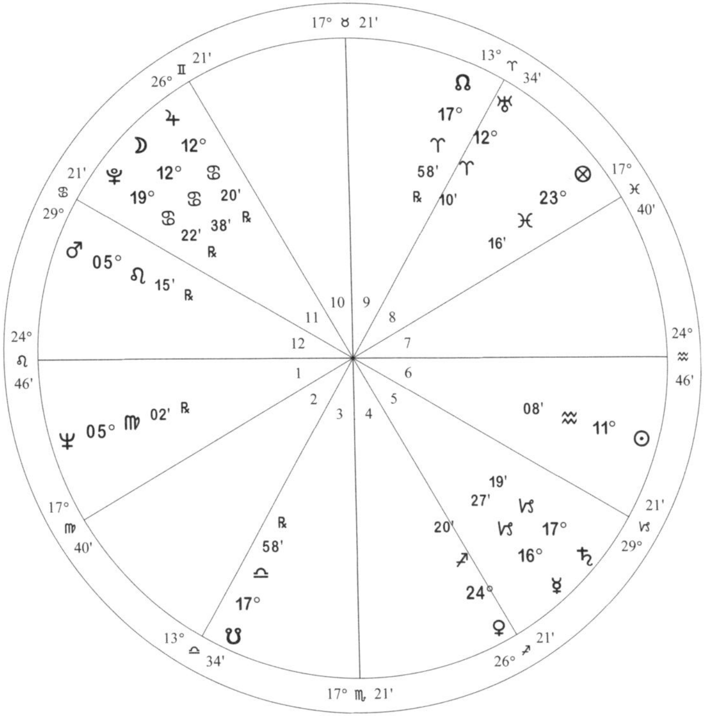

Dorothean Ess. Dig. (No Mut Rec. Points)								
Pl	Ruler	Exalt	Tripl	Term	Face	Detri	Fall	Score
☉	♄	--	☿	☿	☿	☉ -	--	- 10 P
☽	☽ +	♃	♂	♃	☿	♄	♂	+5
☿	♄	♂	☽	♃	♂	☽	♃	- 5 P
♀	♃	☋	♃	♄	♄	☿	--	- 5 P
♂	☉	--	♃ m	♄	♄ m	♄	--	- 5 P
♃	☽	♃ +	♂ m	♃ +	☿	♄	♂	+6
♄	♄ +	♂	☽	♃	♂ m	☽	♃	+5
☊	♂	☉	♃	☿	☉	♀	♄	--
⊗	♃	♀	♂	♂	♂	☿	☿	--
As	☉	--	♃	♃	♂	♄	--	--
Mc	♀	☽	☽	♃	☽	♂	--	--
☋	♀	♄	☿	♃	♄	♂	☉	--

Hs	Alm. (Pto)
1	☉♃
2	☿
3	♀♄
4	♂
5	♃
6	♄
7	♄
8	♃
9	☉♂
10	☽
11	☿
12	☽

Example 12-29. Franklin Roosevelt's solar return for 1931

1932: Solar Return and Aries Ingress

In 1932, the table was set. As we look at the Aries Ingress, the question is: what are we seeing? I have done quite a bit of work on the statistical examination of presidential elections, and the Aries Ingress chart does not work as a predictor of the outcome of the election, if it is examined from the point of view of party in power, and party out of power. A brief consideration shows how this makes sense. For almost the entire year mapped out by this chart, Herbert Hoover was in office. Therefore, to expect to see both the year from March 20th on, plus the result of the election, is asking a bit too much.

The point of this chart is that the fixed angles reveal Hoover's strong and fixed belief that the depression was something which was an international event, and which required only minor economic corrections at home. He believed that it was inappropriate for the US government to address anything related to joblessness, or to the misery of the people who lost their jobs. An engineer by training and disposition, Hoover relied on technical fixes. Now – this looks like fixed signs, with only minor tinkering employed. At first, the image of Hoover may seem surprising: a very strong Venus in Taurus right at the MC. Hoover did not lack for conviction, or for the power to carry out his convictions. The problem was the South Node in the 2nd, with Mercury ruling the 2nd in a partile conjunction with Uranus: the economy was tanked (South Node in the 2nd), and any effort at attempting to control it (through Mercury) would backfire, because the expected ways wouldn't work (ruler of the 2nd conjunct Uranus). The Moon-Neptune conjunction shows the people disillusioned.

What is interesting is that the Venus in Taurus in the Aries Ingress was partile conjunct Franklin's natal Neptune: FDR rode the wave of discontent all the way to the top. Franklin's own 1932 solar return has angular planets again, with Jupiter, Sun, Neptune, and Mars all angular along the MC/IC axis. The angular Sun-Mars partile conjunction is notable, and this SR-Mars is trine its natal sign.

Franklin D Roosevelt
Hyde Park, Dutchess, NY
Time Zone: 5 hours West

February 1, 1932
41N47'05" 73W56'01"
Tropical Regiomontanus
Solar Return for February 1, 1932 in Hyde Park, Dutchess, NY

12:07:01 AM
Standard Time

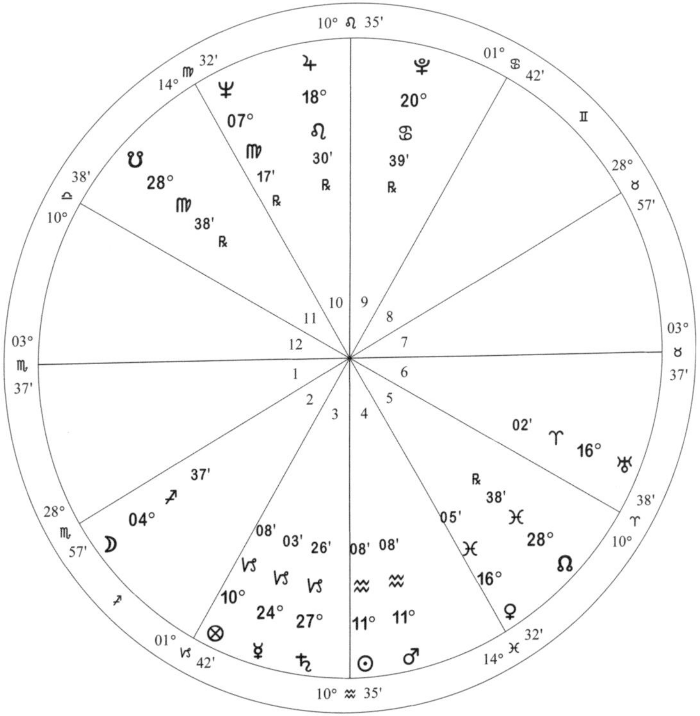

Pl	Ruler	Exalt	Tripl	Term	Face	Detri	Fall	Score
☉	♄	--	☿	☿	☿ m	☉ -	--	- 10 P
☽	♃	☋	♃	♃	☿	☿	--	- 5 P
☿	♄	♂	☽	♂ m	☉ m	☽	♃	- 5 P
♀	♃	♀ +	♂	☿	♃	☿	☿	+4
♂	♄	--	☿	☿ m	☿	☉	--	- 5 P
♃	☉	--	♃ +	♀	♃ +	♄	--	+4
♄	♄ +	♂	☽	♄ +	☉	☽	♃	+7
☊	♃	♀	♂	♄	♂	☿	☿	--
⊗	♄	♂	☽	☿	♂	☽	♃	--
As	♂	--	♂	♂	♂	♀	☽	--
Mc	☉	--	♃	☿	♃	♄	--	--
☋	☿	☿	☽	♂	☿	♃	♀	--

Dorothean Ess. Dig. (No Mut Rec. Points)

Hs	Alm. (Pto)
1	♂
2	♂
3	♄
4	☿
5	♃
6	☉♂
7	☽♀
8	☽
9	☽
10	☉
11	☿
12	♀

Example 12-30a. Franklin Roosevelt's solar return for 1932

Sun enters Ari 3-20-1932
Washington, D.C.
Time Zone: 5 hours West

March 20, 1932
38N53'42" 77W02'12"
Tropical Regiomontanus
NATAL CHART

2:53:37 PM
Standard Time

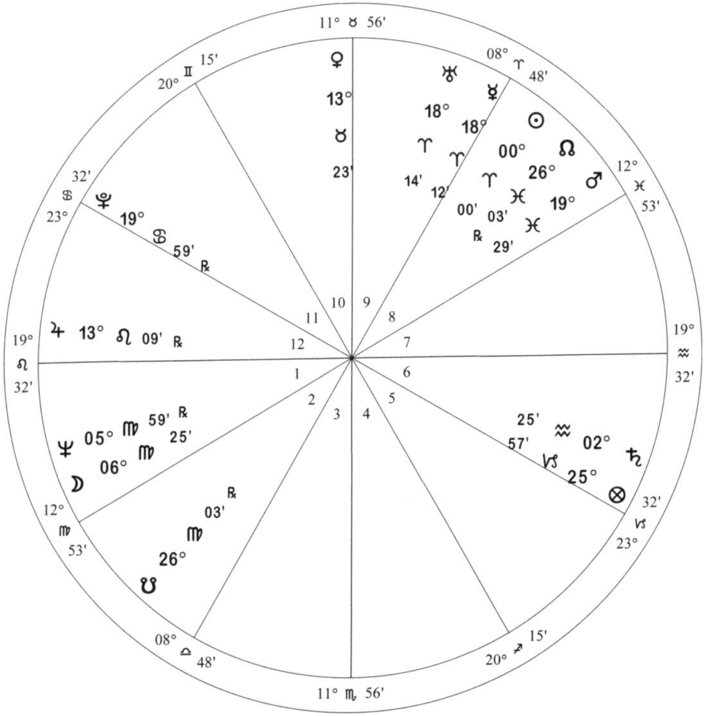

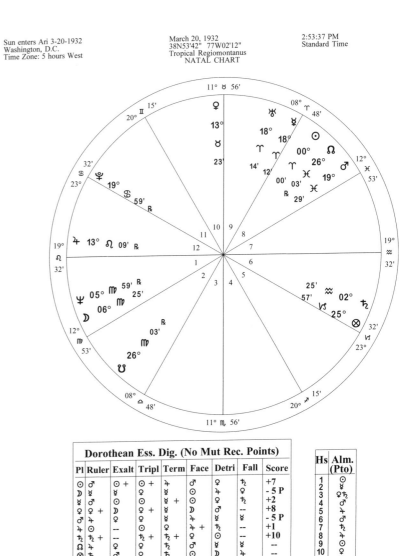

Pl	Ruler	Exalt	Tripl	Term	Face	Detri	Fall	Score
☉	♂	☉ +	☉ +	♃	♂	♀	♄	+7
☽	☿	☿	♀	☿	☉	♃	♀	- 5 P
☿	♂	☉	☉	☿ +	☉	♀	♄	+2
♀	♀ +	☽	♀ +	☿	☽	♂	--	+8
♂	♃	♀	♀	☿	♃	☿	☿	- 5 P
♃	☉	--	☉	♀	♃ +	♄	--	+1
♄	♄ +	--	♄ +	♄ +	♀	☉	--	+10
☊	♃	♀	♀	♄	♂	☿	☿	--
⊗	♄	♂	♀	♄	☉	☽	♃	--
As	☉	--	☉	♃	♃	♄	--	--
Mc	♀	☽	♀	☿	☽	♂	--	--
☋	☿	☿	♀	♂	☿	♃	♀	--

Dorothean Ess. Dig. (No Mut Rec. Points)

Hs	Alm. (Pto)
1	☉
2	☿
3	♀♄
4	♂
5	♃
6	♂
7	♄
8	♃
9	☉
10	♀
11	☿
12	☽

Example 12-30b. Aries Ingress for 1932, Washington, DC

Competition, anyone? In 1928, when FDR was elected governor of New York, the MC was also Leo. Then, Mars ruling the Ascendant was exalted; here, it was conjunct the Sun. Franklin's angles for this year were also all fixed, like the Aries Ingress chart. He wasn't in the mood for compromise.

1933: Solar Return and Aries Ingress

In 1933, there was still a much longer time between election and taking office, as this was the last year the president was inaugurated in March. This meant that there were four months of Hoover being a lame duck, repudiated by the electorate, and still *completely convinced that he understood the depression*. 1932 had shown some lukewarm improvement in the economy that Hoover saw as vindication of his policies; FDR's was the much more radical outlook, and he had no intention of cooperating with Hoover in the interval between election and inauguration. Part of that transition fell under his 1933 solar return.

Notice the shift from the angular emphasis being MC/IC fixed and Ascendant/Descendant cardinal. When Franklin became president, the 10th house ceased to have meaning as anybody "above" him: he became the king. The 10th is his honor and achievement, but his ability to act and move comes through the Ascendant. In 1933, there was another partile aspect: Venus opposite Pluto, not far from those angles. Also notice the Part of Fortune conjunct the MC. With the Moon conjunct Uranus, Franklin was ready to try some new and different things. Meanwhile, the 1933 Aries Ingress had a notable conjunction in the 10th house: South Node and Neptune. The people were ready for an activist president: and Franklin's Mars was ready to act, with its participating Triplicity. Saturn was dignified in Aquarius in the 4th, with the Moon in Capricorn conjunct the IC. Attention was squarely on the domestic situation, even as Hitler was coming to power in Germany. The vast majority of Americans ignored these European currents.

Franklin D Roosevelt
Hyde Park, Dutchess, NY
Time Zone: 5 hours West

January 31, 1933
41N47'05" 73W56'01"
Tropical Regiomontanus

5:45:08 AM
Standard Time

Solar Return for January 31, 1933 in Hyde Park, Dutchess, NY

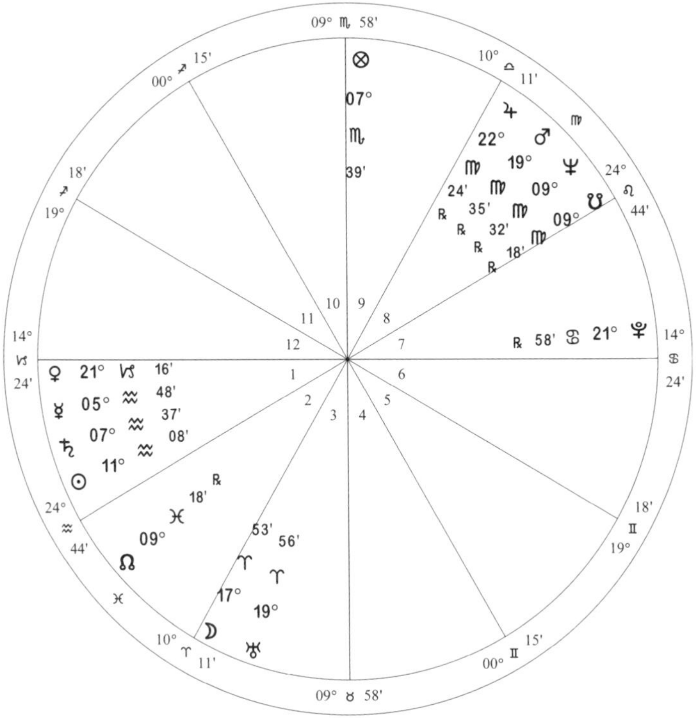

Dorothean Ess. Dig. (No Mut Rec. Points)								
Pl	Ruler	Exalt	Tripl	Term	Face	Detri	Fall	Score
☉	♄	--	☿	☿	☿	☉ -	--	- 10 P
☽	♂	☉	♃ m	☿	☉	♀	♄	- 5 P
☿	♄	--	☿ +	♄ m	♀	☉	--	+3
♀	♄	♂	☽	♂	☉	☽	♃	- 5 P
♂	☿	☿	☽	♄	♀	♃	♀	- 5 P
♃	☿	☿	☽ m	♄	☿	♃ -	♀	- 10 P
♄	♄ +	--	☿	☿ m	♀	☉	--	+5
☊	♃	♀	♂	♃	♄	☿	☿	--
⊗	♂	--	♂	♃	♂	♀	☽	--
As	♄	♂	☽	♃	♂	☽	♃	--
Mc	♂	--	♂	♃	♂	♀	☽	--
☋	☿	☿	☽	♀	☉	♃	♀	--

Hs	Alm. (Pto)
1	♂♄
2	♄
3	☉♂
4	☽
5	☿
6	☿
7	☽
8	☉♃
9	♀
10	♂
11	♃
12	♃

Example 12-31a. Franklin Roosevelt's solar return for 1933

Sun enters Ari 3-21-1933
Washington, D.C.
Time Zone: 5 hours West

March 20, 1933
38N53'42" 77W02'12"
Tropical Regiomontanus
NATAL CHART

8:43:08 PM
Standard Time

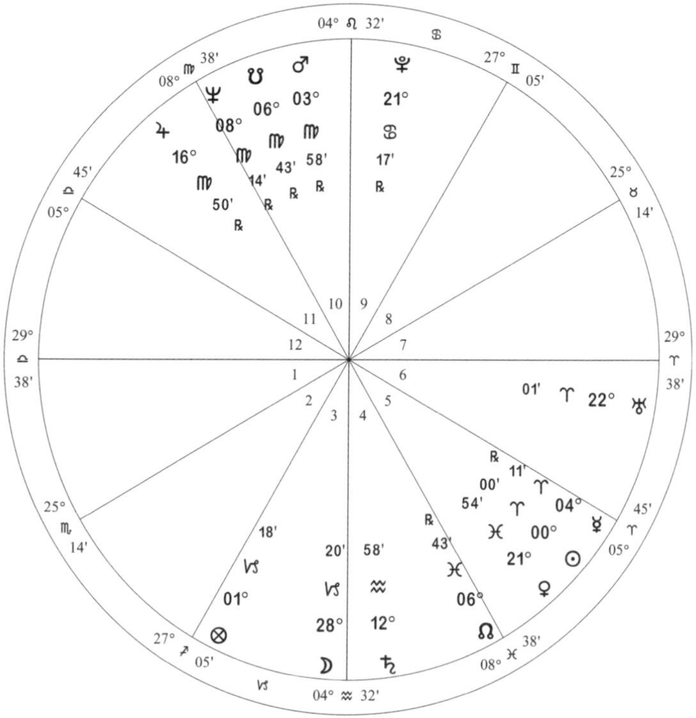

Dorothean Ess. Dig. (No Mut Rec. Points)								
Pl	Ruler	Exalt	Tripl	Term	Face	Detri	Fall	Score
☉	♂	☉ +	♃	♃	♂ m	♀	♄	+4
☽	♄	♂	☽ +	♄	☉	☽ -	♃	- 2
☿	♂ m	☉	♃	♃	♂	♀	♄	- 5 P
♀	♃	♀ +	♂	♂	♂	☿	☿	+4
♂	☿ m	☿	☽	☿	☉ m	♃	♀	- 5 P
♃	☿	☿	☽	♃ +	♀	♃ -	♀	- 3
♄	♄ +	--	☿	♀	☿	☉	--	+5
☊	♃	♀	♂	♀	♄	☿	☿	--
⊗	♄	♂	☽	♀	♃	☽	♃	--
As	♀	♄	☿	☊	♃	♂	☉	--
Mc	☉	--	♃	♄	♄	♄	--	--
☋	☿	☿	☽	☿	☉	♃	♀	--

Hs	Alm. (Pto)
1	♀
2	♂
3	♃
4	♄
5	♃
6	♂
7	♂
8	☽
9	☿
10	☉
11	☿
12	♄

Example 12-31b. Aries Ingress for 1933, Washington, DC

Almost his first act as president was to close the banks, an act which was probably illegal, although Congress later passed a law allowing it. But bold and unprecedented it was. The Moon-Uranus may look a bit reckless, but the Mars in Virgo does not. He was trying to engineer a fix, even if not all his methods were successful. In this case, the bank holiday did largely serve to reduce the run on the banks. Almost simultaneously, he worked on and created legislation on farm relief, government job creation, securities reform, currency reform: fifteen major pieces of legislation in his first one hundred days in office! The New Deal massively changed the relationship of government to the people – and to the economy.

One of FDR's innovations was to increase the number and scope of press briefings. If we were to pick a planet for this, it would have to be Mercury. Here in his 1933 solar return, Mercury was in the 1st house, conjunct Saturn and the Sun, with both Mercury and Saturn dignified. Then, as now, a typical press briefing provided information to the press, either about past or future actions of the administration, or reactions to current events. While information contained in them wasn't always considered directly quotable or attributable, most of it was. FDR created an entirely different type: by enforcing a rule (Saturn) of confidentiality on the press (Mercury), he actually brought them in on what he was *thinking*, even when he hadn't actually reached any decisions. He made them collaborators *to* the process, rather than reporters *of* it. White House reporters had to conceal information from even their editors in order to stay in this privileged circle. FDR would give them little items to officially report: but the background was available only of they policed themselves. The lure of the background process proved irresistable. These rules would serve the military well later on when the country went to war.

The American economy continued to improve – as might be expected from the 1933 Aries Ingress, with Mars ruling the 2nd, and in the 10th, in Virgo, where it has Triplicity. Roosevelt's unprecedented economic powers, granted to him by Congress, may well have accelerated the trend that was already starting before the 1932 election. Whether true or not, the average American seemed to believe that Franklin had a great deal to do with it.

1934: Solar Return and Aries Ingress

In 1934, the Aries Ingress also had a dignified 2nd house ruler, this time Saturn in Aquarius. But some progress also meant that there were a lot of different opinions about where to go from here, with labor unrest on the one side, and calls for socialism, or for various forms of utopianism. The labor situation was a case in point. In an economic downturn, generally unemployment increases because there is excess manufacturing capacity. Excess capacity puts a downward pressure on wages and an upward pressure on unemployment. This would not be an easy situation for workers – except that unions were part of the Democratic constituency. In 1934, we have the labor unions (6th house) ruled by Mercury in Pisces (in Detriment) in the 2nd house of money and wages opposite Neptune in Virgo. Furthermore, the Moon is square both in Gemini, disposed by that Mercury, as is the Neptune. That the labor unions were dissatisfied was obvious: engaging in labor actions during this time was questionable tactics. However, the Mercury in Pisces configuration would not be expected to show good judgment.

With the Part of Fortune conjunct the 10th, one would expect that Franklin's reforms would continue to be passed, and they were. Farm prices came under federal legislation: the ruler of the 4th (the farmers, who worked the land) was in the 1st, and not in the greatest of shape. With Saturn ruling the Ascendant and Saturn so dignified in Aquarius, the idea of an old age pension was being seriously proposed, although Social Security did not pass until 1935.

Comparing the Aries Ingress to FDR's solar return for 1934, the plight of the land and the onset of the drought conditions which would lead to the dust bowl is clearly shown in Roosevelt's chart, demonstrating once again that the old idea of examining the chart of the king is still valid even in a democracy. The configuration

Franklin D Roosevelt
Hyde Park, Dutchess, NY
Time Zone: 5 hours West

January 31, 1934
41N47'05" 73W56'01"
Tropical Regiomontanus
Solar Return for January 31, 1934 in Hyde Park, Dutchess, NY

11:37:29 AM
Standard Time

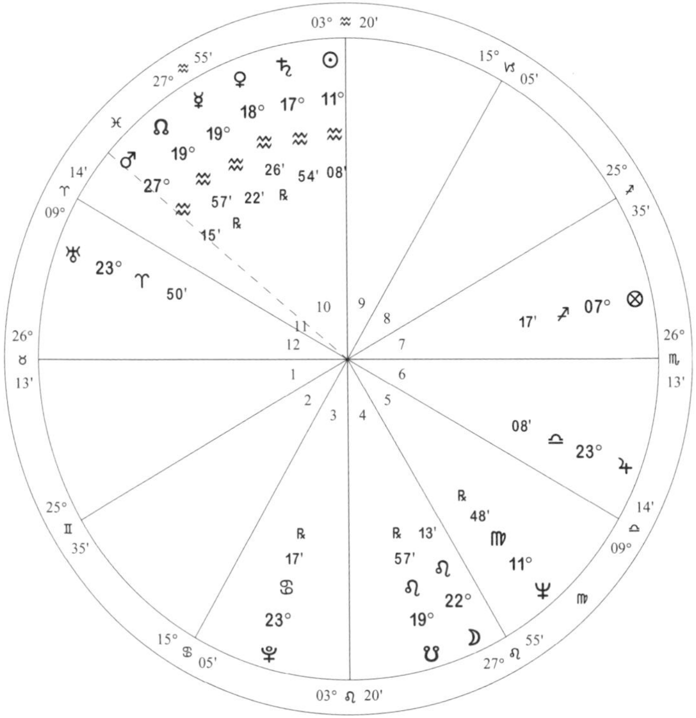

Dorothean Ess. Dig. (No Mut Rec. Points)								
Pl	Ruler	Exalt	Tripl	Term	Face	Detri	Fall	Score
☉	♄	--	♄	☿	☿	☉ -	--	- 10 P
☽	☉	--	☉	♃	♂ m	♄	--	- 5 P
☿	♄	--	♄	♀	☿ +	☉	--	+1
♀	♄	--	♄	♀ +	☿	☉	--	+2
♂	♄	--	♄	♂ +	☽ m	☉	--	+2
♃	♀	♄	♄	☿	♃ +	♂	☉	+1
♄	♄ +	--	♄ +	♀	☿	☉	--	+8
☊	♄	--	♄	♀	☿	☉	--	--
⊗	♃	☋ +	☉	♃	☿	☿	--	--
As	♀	☽	♀	♂	♄	♂	--	--
Mc	♄	--	♄	♄	♀	☉	--	--
☋	☉	--	☉	♃	♃	♄	--	--

Hs	Alm. (Pto)
1	♀
2	☿
3	☽
4	☉
5	☉
6	♀♄
7	♂
8	♃
9	♂♄
10	♄
11	♄
12	☉

Example 12-32a. Franklin Roosevelt's solar return for 1934

Sun enters Ari 3-21-1934
Washington, D.C.
Time Zone: 5 hours West

March 21, 1934
38N53'42" 77W02'12"
Tropical Regiomontanus
NATAL CHART

2:27:57 AM
Standard Time

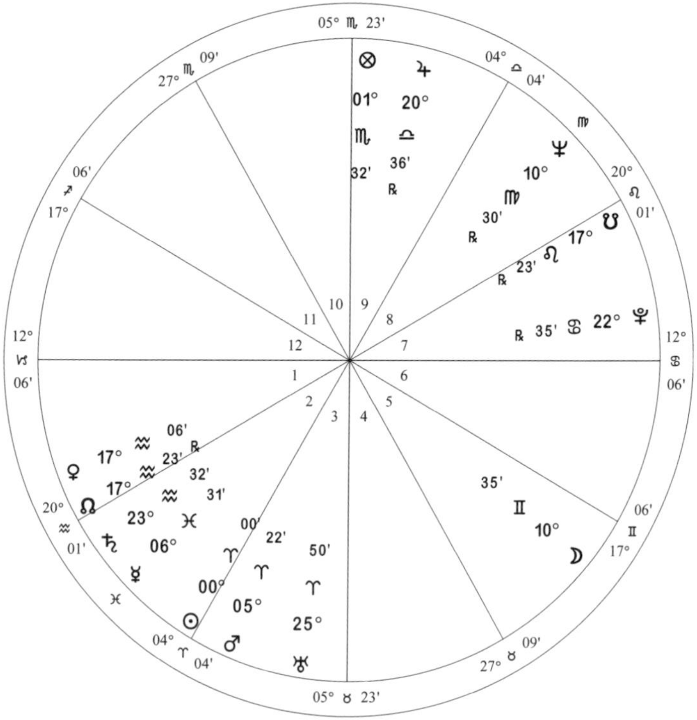

Dorothean Ess. Dig. (No Mut Rec. Points)								
Pl	Ruler	Exalt	Tripl	Term	Face	Detri	Fall	Score
☉	♂	☉ +	♃	♃	♂	♀	♄	+4
☽	☿	☊	☿	♃	♂	♃	--	- 5 P
☿	♃	♀	♂	♀	♄	☿ -	☿ -	- 14 P
♀	♄	--	☿	♀ +	☿	☉	--	+2
♂	♂ +	☉	♃	♃	♂ +	♀	♄	+6
♃	♀	♄	☿	☿	♃ +	♂	☉	+1
♄	♄ +	--	☿	♃	☽	☉	--	+5
☊	♄	--	☿	♀	☿	☉	--	--
⊗	♂	--	♂	♂	♂	♀	☽	--
As	♄	♂	☽	♃	♂	☽	♃	--
Mc	♂	--	♂	♂	♂	♀	☽	--
☋	☉	--	♃	♀	♃	♄	--	--

Hs	Alm. (Pto)
1	♂♄
2	♄
3	♂
4	☽♀
5	☽
6	☿
7	♃
8	☉♃
9	♄
10	♂
11	♂
12	♃

Example 12-32b. Aries Ingress for 1934, Washington, DC

of the land is shown with the Moon and South Node in the 4th, opposite Saturn-Venus-Mercury-North Node in the 10th. This very powerful opposition is the most significant configuration in the chart, showing that this would be a major focus of his energy. In addition to farm relief, there was also a Home Owners Loan Act, to attempt to stimulate housing in a time where most people were extremely reluctant to borrow money to buy a house. I remember in the 1960s when my mother worried about having taken out a loan for our house which was for 20% of the value of the house, after putting down 80%! To Americans, the idea of personal debt was not comfortable at all. With the South Node near the 8th house, banking reform continued, and the United States reformed its use of gold and silver.

The year culminated for Franklin with the pickup of a significant number of Senate seats, providing even more of a mandate for the Democrats.

1935: Solar Return and Aries Ingress

1935 provided a dramatic difference to the last two years. The congressional victories of the previous year should have provided smooth sailing for the New Deal but this was not to be. The Aries Ingress for 1935 shows the South Node partile conjunct the 4th house cusp: the signature I discussed in *Astrology of Sustainability* as representing the dust bowl.[10] As if that wasn't enough, the 12th house featured a Venus-Uranus conjunction: volatility resulting from secret enemies. And the 9th house rulership by Saturn shows Saturn, now in Pisces, acting as a malefic again. The roughly five year period when Saturn is in Capricorn and Aquarius is the only time when a planet has sign rulership in two consecutive signs. As I discussed in *Astrology of Sustainability*, actually the period from Sagittarius to Aquarius is notable this way, because Saturn is the mixed Triplicity ruler of the fire signs., and so has some strength there as well.[11] This means there is one period of roughly eight consecutive years where

Franklin D Roosevelt
Hyde Park, Dutchess, NY
Time Zone: 5 hours West

January 31, 1935
41N47'05" 73W56'01"
Tropical Regiomontanus
Solar Return for January 31, 1935 in Hyde Park, Dutchess, NY

5:26:41 PM
Standard Time

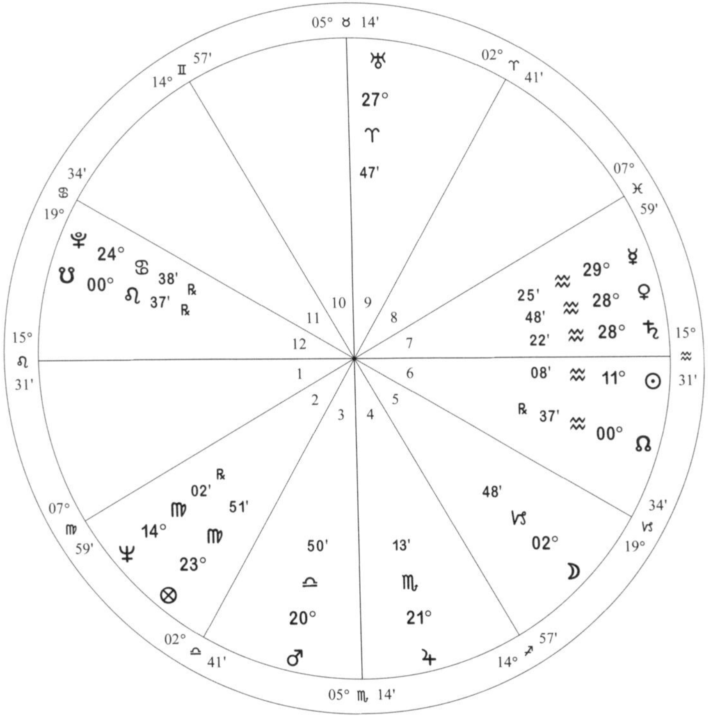

Dorothean Ess. Dig. (No Mut Rec. Points)								
Pl	Ruler	Exalt	Tripl	Term	Face	Detri	Fall	Score
☉	♄	--	☿	☿	☿	☉ -	--	- 10 P
☽	♄	♂	☽ +	♀	♃	☽ -	♃	- 2
☿	♄	--	☿ +	♂ m	☽	☉	--	+3
♀	♄	--	☿	♂	☽	☉	--	- 5 P
♂	♀	♄	☿	☿ m	♃	♂ -	☉	- 10 P
♃	♂	--	♂	☿	♀	♀	☽	- 5 P
♄	♄ +	--	☿	♂	☽	☉	--	+5
☊	♄	--	☿	♄	♀	☉	--	--
⊗	☿	☿	☽	♄	☿	♃	♀	--
As	☉	--	♃	♀	♃	♄	--	--
Mc	♀	☽	☽	♀	☿	♂	--	--
☋	☉	--	♃	♄	♄	♄	--	--

Hs	Alm. (Pto)
1	☉
2	☿
3	♄
4	♂
5	♃
6	♂
7	♄
8	♀
9	♂
10	☽♀
11	☿
12	☽

Example 12-33a. Franklin Roosevelt's solar return for 1935

Sun enters Ari 3-21-1935
Washington, D.C.
Time Zone: 5 hours West

March 21, 1935
38N53'42" 77W02'12"
Tropical Regiomontanus
NATAL CHART

8:17:47 AM
Standard Time

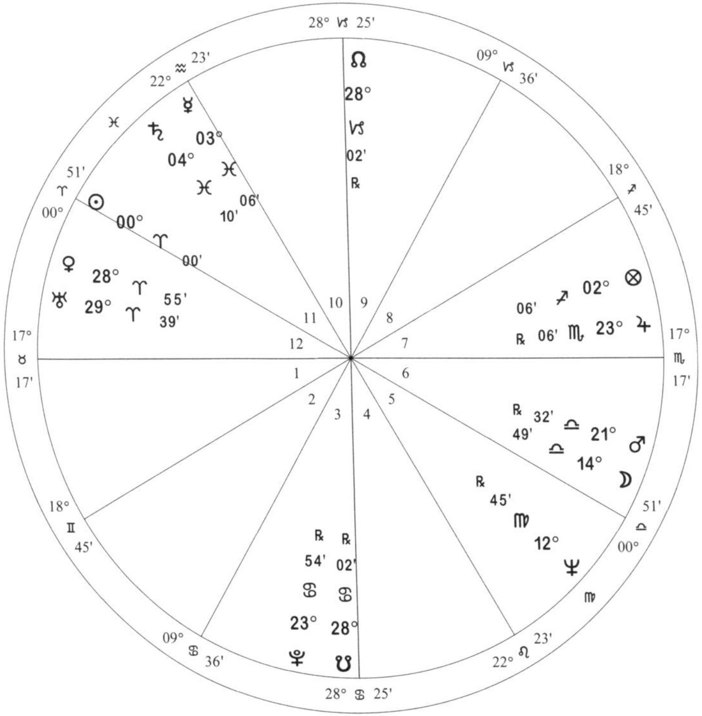

Dorothean Ess. Dig. (No Mut Rec. Points)								
Pl	Ruler	Exalt	Tripl	Term	Face	Detri	Fall	Score
☉	♂	☉ +	☉ +	♃	♂	♀	♄	+7
☽	♀	♄	♄	♃	♄	♂	☉	- 5 P
☿	♃	♀	♀	♀	♄	☿ -	☿ -	- 14 P
♀	♂ m	☉	☉	♄ m	♀ +	♀ -	♄	- 4
♂	♀ m	♄	♄	☿	♃	♂ -	☉	- 10 P
♃	♂	--	♀	☿	♀	♀	☽	- 5 P
♄	♃	♀	♀	♀ m	♄ +	☿	☿	+1
☊	♄	♂	♀	♄	☉	☽	♃	--
⊗	♃	☋ +	☉	♃	☿	☿	--	--
As	♀	☽	♀	♃	☽	♂	--	--
Mc	♄	♂	♀	♄	☉	☽	♃	--
☋	☽	♃	♀	♄	☽	♄	♂	--

Hs	Alm. (Pto)
1	♀
2	☿
3	♃
4	☽
5	☉
6	♄
7	♂
8	♃
9	♄
10	♄
11	♄
12	☉

Example 12-33b. Aries Ingress for 1935, Washington, DC

Saturn has ceased to be problematic. Or is it? The stock market crash of 1929 did occur with Saturn in late Sagittarius. The entry of Saturn into one of its "easy" signs for this magical dignified run actually seems to have loosened the bonds of Saturn – resulting in an overheated Jupiterian enthusiasm which simply crashed of its own weight. Hoover's painfully slow movements followed, then Franklin's radical social tinkering.

But Saturn's Ingress into Pisces is a moment of shock, because suddenly, Saturn ceases to function easily, and turns around into its usual truculent self. In 1935, Saturn ruled the 9th house of the Aries Ingress. While the 9th can rule foreign affairs (which were looking increasingly ominous from FDR's standpoint), the immediate problem was the law, and specifically, the Supreme Court, which began to declare key pieces of the New Deal legislation illegal.

In Roosevelt's solar return for 1935, we see many of these same themes. First, we see the prominence of the 7th house: open enemies. At first, this wouldn't make sense, because the Democrats were so much stronger. But enemies can come from different quarters than simply across the Congressional aisle. The 9th house was ruled by Mars: the very belligerent Mars in Detriment. Franklin's Sun conjunct the Descendant meant that, for the first time in his presidency, he was experiencing sufficient resistance that he had to operate to counter it, not just to move forward with the programs that he considered the Democratic mandate.

1936: Solar Return and Aries Ingress

1936 was the next presidential election year. Voter opinion polling had not reached any level of sophistication at all in the 1930s, but such as there was suggested that 80% of the American populace identified as Republican. The Republican nominee, Alf Landon, was quite confident, but FDR beat him in a landslide. What happened?

Franklin D Roosevelt
Hyde Park, Dutchess, NY
Time Zone: 5 hours West

January 31, 1936
41N47'05" 73W56'01"
Tropical Regiomontanus

11:04:23 PM
Standard Time

Solar Return for January 31, 1936 in Hyde Park, Dutchess, NY

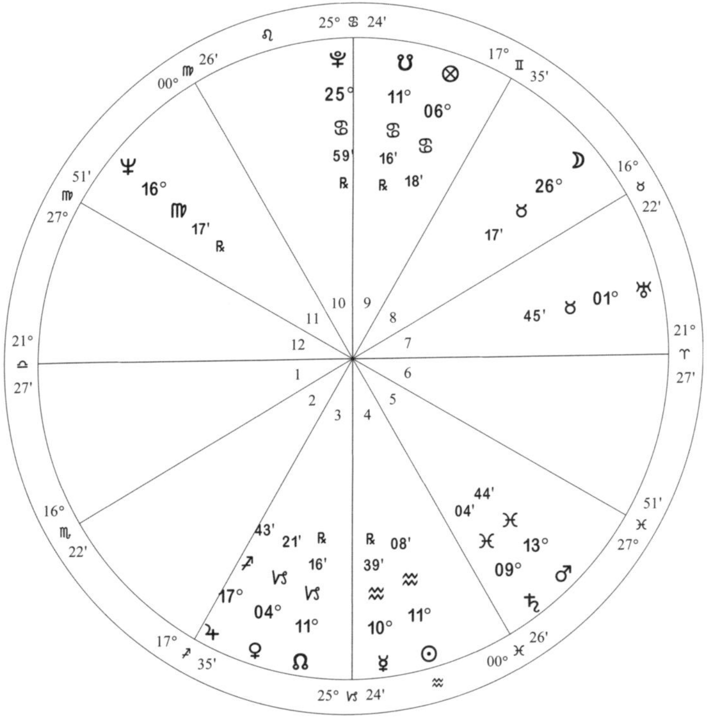

Dorothean Ess. Dig. (No Mut Rec. Points)								
Pl	Ruler	Exalt	Tripl	Term	Face	Detri	Fall	Score
☉	♄	--	☿	☿	☿	☉ -	--	- 10 P
☽	♀	☽ +	☽ +	♂	♄	♂	--	+7
☿	♄	--	☿ +	☿ +	☿ +	☉	--	+6
♀	♄	♂ m	☽	♀ +	♃	☽	♃	+2
♂	♃	♀ m	♂ +	♃	♃	☿	☿	+3
♃	♃ +	☋	♃ +	☿	☽	☿	--	+8
♄	♃	♀	♂	♃	♄ +	☿	☿	+1
☊	♄	♂	☽	☿	♂	☽	♃	--
⊗	☽	♃	♂	♃	♀	♄	♂	--
As	♀	♄	☿	☿	♃	♂	☉	--
Mc	☽	♃	♂	♀	☽	♄	♂	--
☋	☽	♃	♂	♃	☿	♄	♂	--

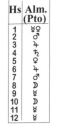

Hs	Alm. (Pto)
1	☿♀
2	♂
3	♃
4	♄
5	♀
6	♃
7	♂
8	☽
9	☿
10	☽
11	☿
12	☿

Example 12-34a. Franklin Roosevelt's solar return for 1936

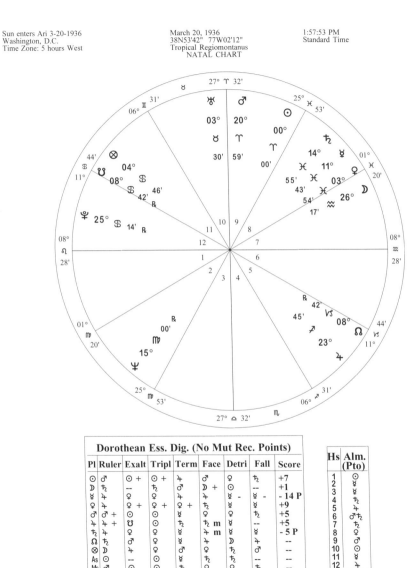

Sun enters Ari 3-20-1936
Washington, D.C.
Time Zone: 5 hours West

March 20, 1936
38N53'42" 77W02'12"
Tropical Regiomontanus
NATAL CHART

1:57:53 PM
Standard Time

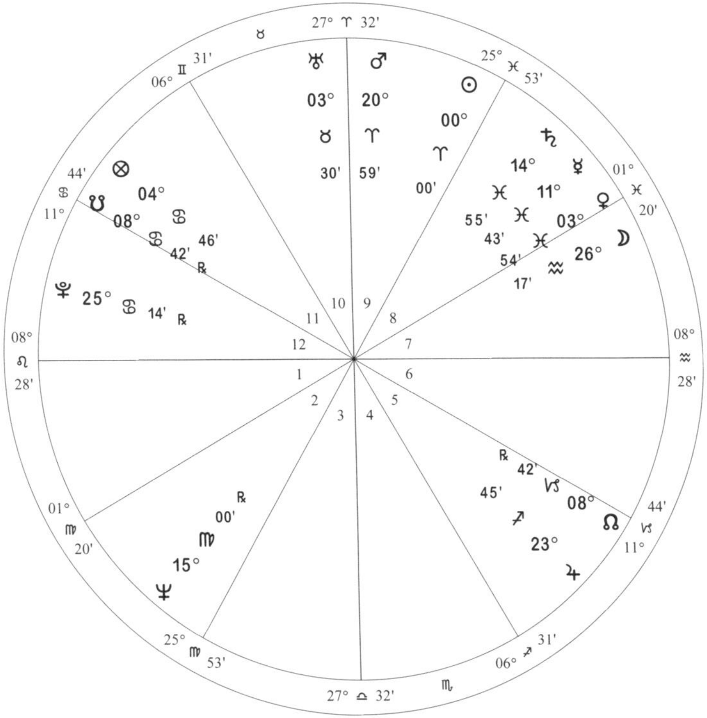

Dorothean Ess. Dig. (No Mut Rec. Points)								
Pl	Ruler	Exalt	Tripl	Term	Face	Detri	Fall	Score
☉	♂	☉ +	☉ +	♃	♂	♀	♄	+7
☽	♄	--	♄	♂	☽ +	☉	--	+1
☿	♃	♀	♀	♃	♃	☿ -	☿ -	- 14 P
♀	♃	♀ +	♀ +	♀ +	♄	☿	☿	+9
♂	♂ +	☉	☉	☿	♀	♀	♄	+5
♃	♃ +	☋	☉	♄	♄ m	☿	--	+5
♄	♃	♀	♀	☿	♃ m	☿	☿	- 5 P
☊	♄	♂	♀	☿	♃	☽	♃	--
⊗	☽	♃	♀	♂	♀	♄	♂	--
As	☉	--	☉	☿	♄	♄	--	--
Mc	♂	☉	☉	♄	♀	♀	♄	--
☋	☽	♃	♀	♃	♀	♄	♂	--

Hs	Alm. (Pto)
1	☉
2	☿
3	☿
4	♄
5	♃
6	♂♄
7	♄
8	♀
9	♂
10	☉
11	☿
12	♃

Example 12-34b. Aries Ingress for 1936, Washington, DC

The Sun rules both the Ascendant (the people) and is Almuten of the 10th – the president. However the people self-identified, the fact was, they identified with what FDR was doing for them. The Sun is trine the Ascendant – again, the people were pretty satisfied with his actions. Where the two are not entirely identified, FDR was Mars in Aries – a very strong position, and barely conjunct the MC and thus with angular strength as well.

It's relatively uncommon to unseat an incumbent president unless there is serious restlessness among the people, as had happened in the prior election. What the polling merely suggested was that the people hadn't changed their historical affiliation with the Republican party: they may have favored the man Roosevelt and his party at the moment, but this had not yet resulted in a paradigm shift.

Franklin's own solar return for 1936 had Pluto partile conjunct the MC. This is actually a good example to demonstrate that Pluto does not necessarily destroy, and it isn't necessarily malefic in the denial sense. What it means is that Franklin was determined to stay in office, and was willing to do everything necessary to assure it. Perhaps this was also indicative of the windfall.

When Franklin began his second term in 1937, he immediately stirred up a hornet's nest. His *bête noire* for his last term had been the Supreme Court, which had invalidated some of the key pieces of his legislation. He devised a way to attack them that was generic, but immediately recognized by everybody for what it was: he proposed adding additional justices at all levels of the federal court system as the sitting justices exceeded a particular age. Critics would call this stacking the court.

1937: Solar Return and Aries Ingress

FDR's proposal to do this fell in the period between his 1937 solar return and the 1937 Aries Ingress. However, the genesis of the idea was no doubt under his 1936 solar return, with that Pluto conjunct the MC. Beware of machination with this configuration. In his 1937 solar return, he was ruled by Venus in Pisces: dignified, but cadent. The Moon was in the 9th house, showing his focus on this issue, but the Moon was peregrine. His bald attempt to gerrymander the Supreme Court fooled no one, annoyed Congress, which wasn't consulted in advance, and was not supported by the people when he attempted to take the case directly to them. While his proposal failed, FDR did get relief. All but two of the Supreme Court justices were appointed by Republicans, thus adhering generally to a Republican viewpoint, thus severely questioning many of Roosevelt's proposals. But one justice, Owen Roberts, apparently noticed Roosevelt's strong showing in 1936 and changed his mind about the constitutionality of the New Deal legislation, reversing a 5-4 majority against FDR, to a 5-4 in favor. The need for stacking disappeared, but so had FDR's aura of invincibility.

Congress is shown by the 11th, and here, Mars was in Scorpio: Congress was looking stronger than Roosevelt. Power sharing would have to happen. But all this happened before the Aries Ingress: at which point, Republicans were getting their knives sharpened. Too bad. The new Aries Ingress for 1937 again showed a strong president, with the Moon in Cancer conjunct and ruling the 10th, and applying to Pluto: the president regained his nerve, and then some. But Congress had not faltered either, being shown by the Sun in Aries, so it remained a formidable force. Jupiter in Capricorn in Fall was conjunct the IC, and the economy was also about to sputter again. Dust storms were still continuing, so the land was still compromised. The Sun was in the 6th: and employment declined in that year, thereby drawing attention to the issue. The South Node was widely conjunct the 9th house cusp from the 9th house. News in foreign affairs was mostly bad, as news of massacres in Spain, Ethiopia, and China brought dismay – but the very thought of intervention by the U.S. remained unthinkable.

FDR's 1937 solar return also shows the issues of the year beautifully. With Venus in Pisces ruling the 10th, his leadership

Franklin D Roosevelt
Hyde Park, Dutchess, NY
Time Zone: 5 hours West

January 31, 1937
41N47'05" 73W56'01"
Tropical Regiomontanus
Solar Return for January 31, 1937 in Hyde Park, Dutchess, NY

5:01:19 AM
Standard Time

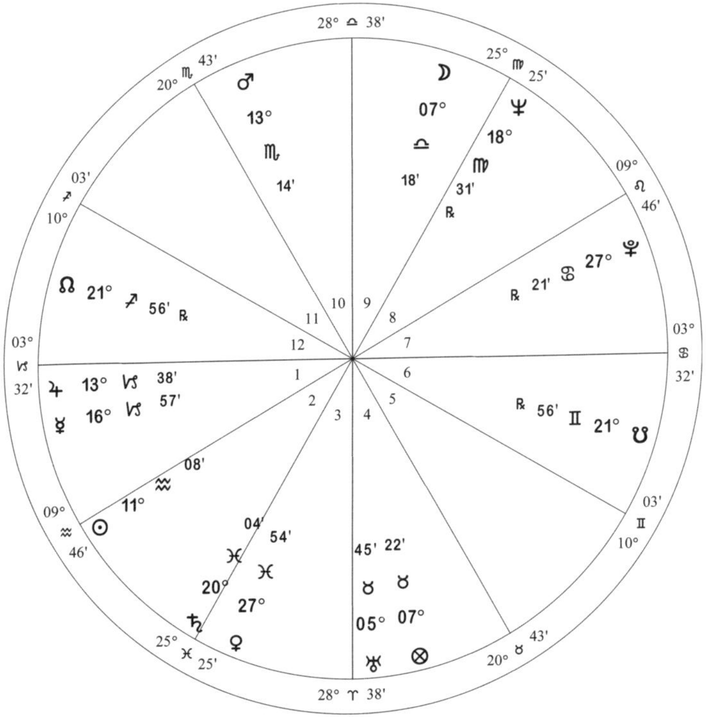

Dorothean Ess. Dig. (No Mut Rec. Points)								
Pl	Ruler	Exalt	Tripl	Term	Face	Detri	Fall	Score
☉	♄	--	☿	☿	☿	☉ -	--	- 10 P
☽	♀	♄	☿ m	♀	☽ +	♂	☉	+1
☿	♄	♂	☽ m	♃	♂	☽	♃	- 5 P
♀	♃	♀ +	♂	♄	♂	☿	☿	+4
♂	♂ +	--	♂ +	♃	☉	♀	☽	+8
♃	♄ m	♂	☽	♃ +	♂	☽	♃ -	- 2
♄	♃ m	♀	♂	♂	♂	☿	☿	- 5 P
☊	♃	☋	♃	♄	♄	☿	--	--
⊗	♀	☽	☽	♀	☿	♂	--	--
As	♄	♂	☽	♀	♃	☽	♃	--
Mc	♀	♄	☿	☊	♃	♂	☉	--
☋	☿	☊	☿	♄	☉	♃	--	--

Hs	Alm. (Pto)
1	♄
2	☿♄
3	♂
4	♂
5	☽
6	☿
7	☽
8	☉
9	☿
10	♀
11	♂
12	♃

Example 12-35a. Franklin Roosevelt's solar return for 1937

Sun enters Ari 3-21-1937
Washington, D.C.
Time Zone: 5 hours West

March 20, 1937
38N53'42" 77W02'12"
Tropical Regiomontanus
NATAL CHART

7:45:06 PM
Standard Time

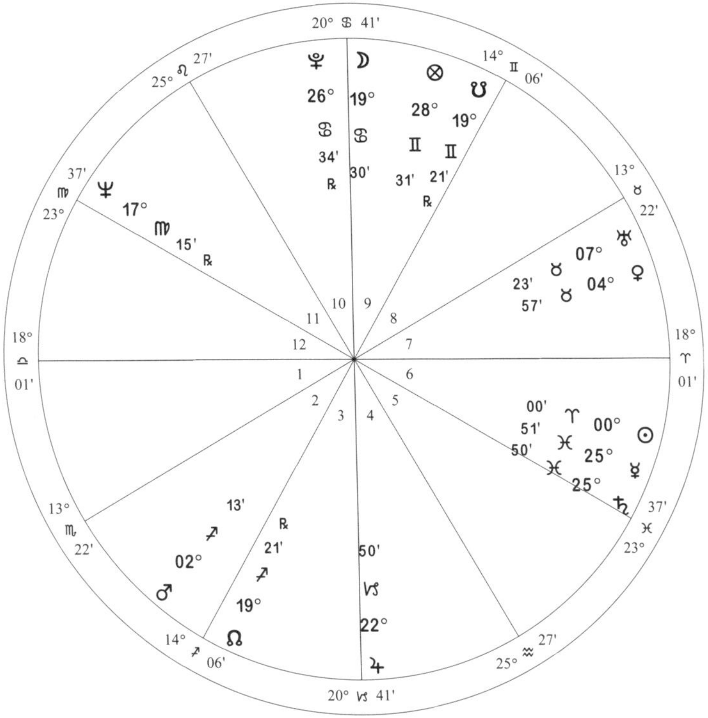

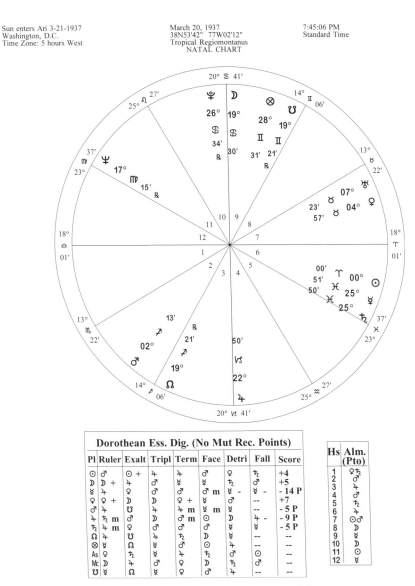

Dorothean Ess. Dig. (No Mut Rec. Points)								
Pl	Ruler	Exalt	Tripl	Term	Face	Detri	Fall	Score
☉	♂	☉ +	♃	♃	♂	♀	♄	+4
☽	☽ +	♃	♂	☿	☿	♄	♂	+5
☿	♃	♀	♂	♂	♂ m	☿ -	☿ -	- 14 P
♀	♀ +	☽	☽	♀ +	☿	♂	--	+7
♂	♃	☋	♃	♃ m	☿ m	☿	--	- 5 P
♃	♄ m	♂	☽	♂ m	☉	☽	♃ -	- 9 P
♄	♃ m	♀	♂	♂	♂	☿	☿	- 5 P
☊	♃	☋	♃	♄	☽	☿	--	--
⊗	☿	☊	☿	♂	☉	♃	--	--
As	♀	♄	☿	♃	♄	♂	☉	--
Mc	☽	♃	♂	♀	☽	♄	♂	--
☋	☿	☊	☿	♀	♂	♃	--	--

Hs	Alm. (Pto)
1	♀♄
2	♂
3	♃
4	♂
5	♄
6	♃
7	☉♂
8	☽
9	☿
10	☽
11	☉
12	☿

Example 12-35b. Aries Ingress for 1937, Washington, DC

remains intact. The Sun in the 2nd shows the focus on economic issues. The Moon in the 9th shows his interest in foreign affairs, but his ambivalence about doing anything about it: it's a peregrine Libra Moon, so he has yet to lock in a policy. The South Node in the 6th shows the unemployment situation. It shows one additional matter, too. Mars in Scorpio may have ruled Congress (the 11th house) – but it was in the 10th, and it ruled the 4th. Ignoring the advice of conventional economists, FDR decided that the newest dip was the result of big businesses attempting to evade the consequences of the terms of the New Deal. So he proposed a massive public works program that would fortify U.S. *infrastructure* – a 4th house concept if ever there was one.

1938: Solar Return and Aries Ingress

1938 would be a showdown of these interests in Congress. Business interests opposed the minimum wage and maximum hours that FDR wanted to pass, and part of that opposition came from Southern Democrats, who saw economic advantage in their deflated labor costs relative to the rest of the country. The Aries Ingress shows an unhappy Congress, with the Moon in Scorpio in the 11th. Neptune sat right on the 9th house: whatever was going on in foreign countries, we didn't want to know about it. And there was a lot going on: this period would later be called the time of appeasement, as Hitler was moving ahead by threatening the war that he would start the following year. But mostly, the focus was at home, as can be seen by the clustering of almost everything else at the bottom of the chart. This chart has a great deal of debility: the Moon, as we have just seen, but also Venus in Aries, ruling the president, Saturn in Aries, and Mars in Taurus, ruling Congress. This configuration does not bode well for a quiet, polite time. Both rulers of the people, the Moon and the ruler of the Ascendant, are debilitated: meaning, they are getting restless again. Congress was showing itself as combative. Why not? By their reckoning, Franklin was in his second, and thus, final term. So now they could think of themselves as having longer tenure than he would, and thus, that their interests might well be different, especially going into a congressional election year, and then into the election of 1940. Franklin was likewise smoldering. While he analyzed the new economic drop as caused by big business trying to usurp more, the conservatives blamed progressive taxation. He began to wonder if the entire New Deal was at stake, especially since he could envision conservatives in his own party being as eager to dismantle it as the Republicans, once he was out of office, regardless of which party won the presidency.

Venus in Aries can be downright dangerous. FDR decided to campaign against anti-New Deal Democrats in the South who were up against pro-New Deal Democrats during the primaries. But compared to Mars, Venus was cadent. And also, superiors tend to beat inferiors in contests. FDR's attempted purge mostly failed – and Republicans picked up seats as well in the by-year election. The latter was a well-known phenomenon: you might recall we discussed this with Wilson's political mistake in calling the 1918 by-year election a mandate on his policies. Franklin hadn't stated the case as baldly as Wilson, but his fate was similar, except that the Democrats kept their majorities in Congress. But this new Democratic majority would not be so favorable to their perceived lame duck leader.

While the Aries Ingress for 1938 spells out the issues beautifully, at first, Franklin's 1938 solar return doesn't look like what we would expect. It's another New Moon chart, his first since age 37 – and the last one he would experience. His previous New Moon year, he was in the middle of the Wilson years: ironically, in 1919, when he was part of the administration dealing with the tactical errors of Wilson – just as he was about to commit similar tactical errors of his own! In 1918, Wilson felt as strongly about Peace without Victory as in 1938 Roosevelt would feel about the New Deal. In 1919, a young Roosevelt was attempting to learn his lessons about party loyalty; in 1938 an older Roosevelt was trying to enforce not party loyalty, but programmatic loyalty. It wasn't working. But a view of FDR's chart for

Franklin D Roosevelt
Hyde Park, Dutchess, NY
Time Zone: 5 hours West

January 31, 1938
41N47'05" 73W56'01"
Tropical Regiomontanus
Solar Return for January 31, 1938 in Hyde Park, Dutchess, NY

10:52:49 AM
Standard Time

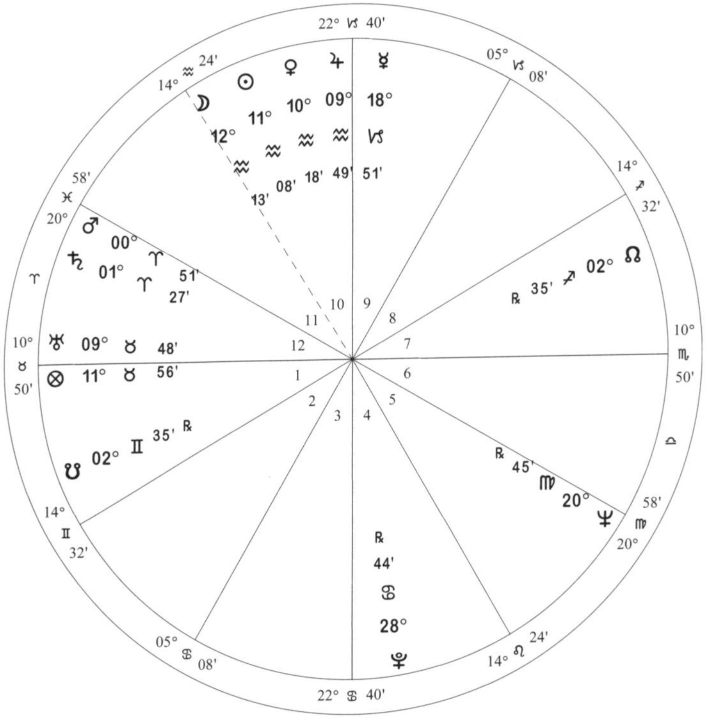

Dorothean Ess. Dig. (No Mut Rec. Points)								
Pl	Ruler	Exalt	Tripl	Term	Face	Detri	Fall	Score
☉	♄	--	♄ m	☿	☿	☉ -	--	- 10 P
☽	♄	--	♄	♀	☿	☉	--	- 5 P
☿	♄	♂	♀	♃ m	♂	☽	♃	- 5 P
♀	♄	--	♄	☿	☿	☉	--	- 5 P
♂	♂ +	☉	☉	♃	♂ +	♀	♄	+6
♃	♄	--	♄	☿ m	♀	☉	--	- 5 P
♄	♂	☉	☉ m	♃	♂	♀	♄ -	- 9 P
☊	♃	☋	☉	♃	☿	☿	--	--
⊗	♀	☽	♀	☿	☽	♂	--	--
As	♀	☽	♀	☿	☽	♂	--	--
Mc	♄	♂	♀	♂	☉	☽	♃	--
☋	☿	☊	♄	☿	♃	♃	--	--

Hs	Alm. (Pto)
1	♀
2	☿
3	☽
4	☽
5	☉
6	☿
7	♂
8	♃
9	♀♄
10	♂
11	♄
12	♃

Example 12-36a. Franklin Roosevelt's solar return for 1938

Sun enters Ari 3-21-1938
Washington, D.C.
Time Zone: 5 hours West

March 21, 1938
38N53'42" 77W02'12"
Tropical Regiomontanus
NATAL CHART

1:43:07 AM
Standard Time

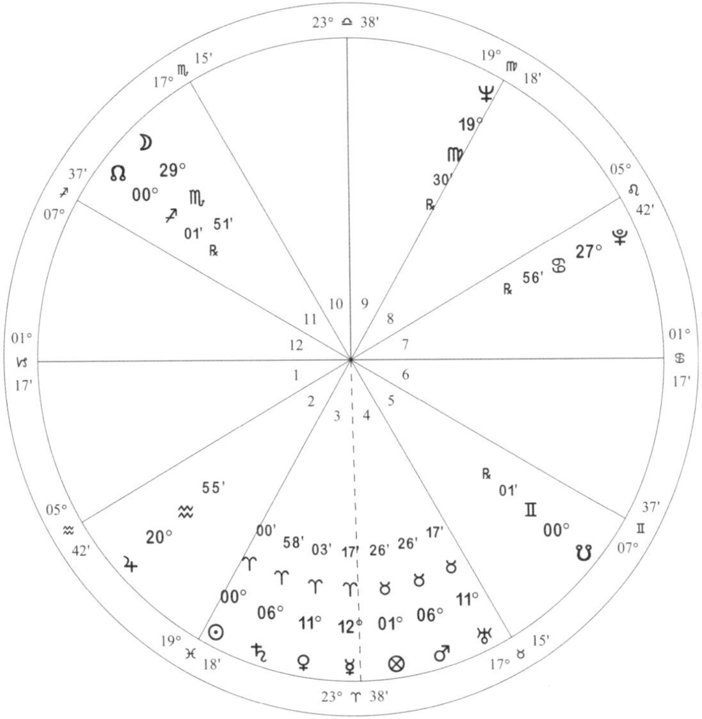

Dorothean Ess. Dig. (No Mut Rec. Points)								
Pl	Ruler	Exalt	Tripl	Term	Face	Detri	Fall	Score
☉	♂	☉ +	♃	♃	♂	♀	♄	+4
☽	♂	--	♂ m	♄	♀	♀	☽ -	- 9 P
☿	♂	☉	♃ m	♀	☉	♀	♄	- 5 P
♀	♂ m	☉	♃	♀ +	☉	♀ -	♄	- 3
♂	♀ m	☽	☽ m	♀	☿	♂ -	--	- 10 P
♃	♄	--	☿ m	♃ +	☽	☉	--	+2
♄	♂	☉	♃	♀	♂	♀	♄ -	- 9 P
☊	♃	☋	♃	♃	☿	☿	--	--
⊗	♀	☽	☽	♀	☿	♂	--	--
As	♄	♂	☽	♀	♃	☽	♃	--
Mc	♀	♄	☿	☿	♃	♂	☉	--
☋	☿	☊	☿	☿	♃	♃	--	--

Hs	Alm. (Pto)
1	♄
2	♄
3	♃
4	♂
5	☽
6	☿
7	☽
8	☉
9	☿
10	☿♀
11	♂
12	♃

Example 12-36b. Aries Ingress for 1938, Washington, DC

1938 shows an inordinate amount of fixed. Through the Ascendant, he was Venus, just like in the Aries Ingress – except that here, it was a combust peregrine Venus that only had angularity and a conjunction to Jupiter going for it. Franklin's ineffectiveness is clear enough from this chart: but what was equally obvious was his determination to hang on to power. Whatever the biographers may say, I believe this was the year that he began to consider staying on for an unprecedented third term. In fact, there was already some speculation about the possibility. FDR's vice president was a conservative Southerner, so FDR would have to find a strong New Dealer who he thought could win. But I believe the New Moon, appearing as it did in the middle of a difficult fight, meant that Roosevelt felt he needed to stay in place longer, or his entire policy would be in jeopardy. It does appear that, by the end of 1939, he had reached the decision to stay in office if he could. Whether he decided earlier is open to discussion, because no evidence of his decision process remains.

1939: Solar Return and Aries Ingress

While events in Germany in 1938 were disturbing, it wasn't until 1939 that they attracted much attention in the U.S. With the strong isolationist bent that was the majority position still, Mars took over from Neptune as the planet conjunct the cusp of the 9th in the Aries Ingress. War was in the offing whether the United States was participating or not. The president was given by Saturn in Aries in the 12th. As Yogi Berra said, "Déjà vu, all over again." There was Roosevelt in Wilson's administration, wanting war, and preparing for it. Here was Roosevelt, ahead of the curve in realizing that war was probably inevitable, and making the same arguments for defense preparedness that the Wilson Administration used, before they ran under the slogan, "He kept us out of war!" as FDR soon would run under much the same circumstances. The difference was that Roosevelt favored war, but knew his opinions were in the minority, where Wilson had not favored war.

While Roosevelt may have had the good sense to keep his opinions to himself, no matter how difficult that was, the U.S. was on the verge of change. The 29 degree rising with Pluto in a partile square from the 4th shows that the isolationist majority was cracking in 1939. It was in 1939 that the Aries Ingress was a New Moon – one year after FDR's. This New Moon occurred in the 12th house, out of people's immediate awareness – and the Sun was in a partile square to Mars. Under the circumstances, Roosevelt's call for a military build-up for prudence's sake, was going to be perceived as the right position, even if the rest of his opinions were carefully kept close to his chest.

Roosevelt's solar return for 1939 shows his hands still tied. The Moon was in the 11th house: his eyes were on Congress, and the Moon was in a partile square to Neptune, showing dissatisfaction still running strong. The South Node was in the 10th in a partile conjunction to fixed Uranus, making it a tedious and stressful year, where the pressure was probably close to the breaking point at all times. A fixed Uranus is especially difficult, because fixed is so contrary to the nature of this planet. The Sun was conjunct the Descendant, showing that Roosevelt had to spend more time than usual considering his enemies: and in this time period, these were his political enemies, not foreign powers. The outbreak of war in Europe at least had the effect of moving public opinion to notice that Roosevelt had predicted it, while the isolationists had denied the possibility of it. When he finally got Congress to defeat the arms embargo, it meant that U.S. industry could now increase its production by producing war matériel for Great Britain and the Allies, while officially remaining neutral.

What we see in this series of comparisons of the Aries Ingress with FDR's solar returns is a curious phenomenon. Some of the slower planet configurations by house are showing up in FDR's chart a year before they appear in the Aries Ingress of the United States. For example, in 1939, Roosevelt had the South Node and Uranus in his 10th. In 1940, these same two factors would be in the

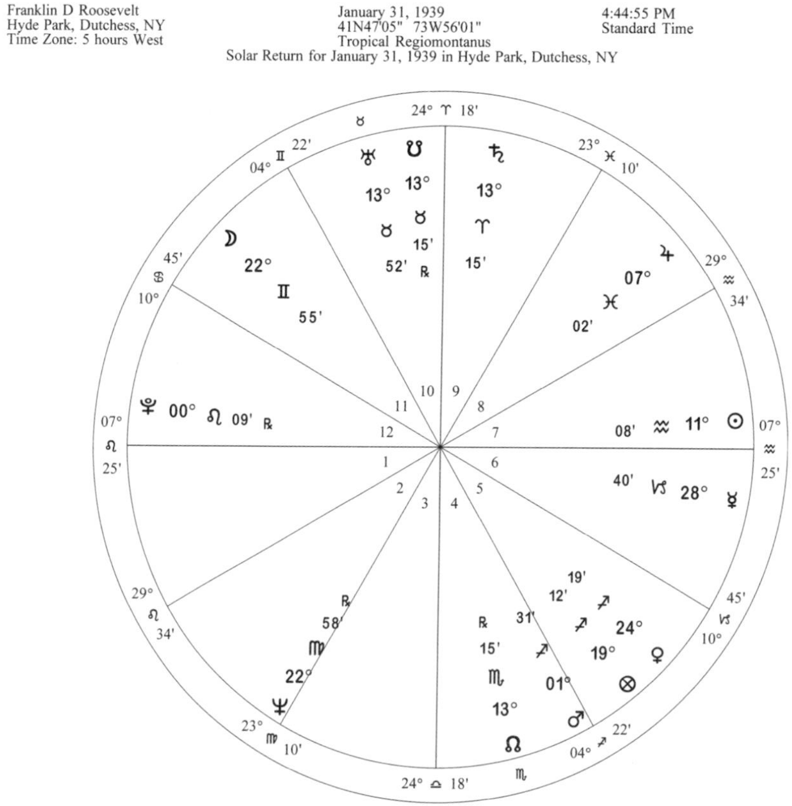
Franklin D Roosevelt
Hyde Park, Dutchess, NY
Time Zone: 5 hours West
January 31, 1939
41N47'05" 73W56'01"
Tropical Regiomontanus
4:44:55 PM
Standard Time
Solar Return for January 31, 1939 in Hyde Park, Dutchess, NY

Dorothean Ess. Dig. (No Mut Rec. Points)

Pl	Ruler	Exalt	Tripl	Term	Face	Detri	Fall	Score
☉	♄	--	♄ m	☿	☿ m	☉ -	--	- 10 P
☽	☿	☊	♄	♄	☉	♃	--	- 5 P
☿	♄	♂	♀	♄	☉ m	☽	♃	- 5 P
♀	♃	☋	☉	♄ m	♄	☿	--	- 5 P
♂	♃	☋	☉	♃	☿	☿	--	- 5 P
♃	♃ +	♀	♀	♀	♄	☿	☿	+5
♄	♂	☉	☉ m	♀ m	☉	♀	♄ -	- 9 P
☊	♂	--	♀	♃	☉	♀	☽	--
⊗	♃	☋ +	☉	♄	☽	☿	--	--
As	☉	--	☉	☿	♄	♄	--	--
Mc	♂	☉	☉	♂	♀	♀	♄	--
☋	♀	☽	♀	☿	☽	♂	--	--

Hs	Alm. (Pto)
1	☉
2	☉
3	☿
4	♄
5	♃
6	♂♄
7	♄
8	♄
9	♃
10	☉♂
11	☿
12	♃

Example 12-37a. Franklin Roosevelt's solar return for 1939

10th house of the Aries Ingress. In 1940, he had Pluto in the 10th, making him perhaps politically belligerent with respect to winning the nomination and election for the third time. But in 1941, Pluto is in the 10th in the Aries Ingress, the year the United States joined the war. It is as if Franklin's ideas and desires were running a year ahead of when the country caught up to him: quite literally.

1940: Solar Return and Aries Ingress

But before we get ahead of ourselves, 1940 dawned with Europe at war, the United States gearing up as an armament manufacturer, but with an official policy of neutrality. And yes, it was a presidential year and FDR had every intention of running. His birthday in 1940, two months earlier than the Aries Ingress, had, as we mentioned above, Pluto in the 10th. This was not the look of a president winding down his term to go off into the sunset. His Ascendant ruler was Venus, dignified in Pisces by both Exaltation and Triplicity: his charm and strength had returned after what for him was an unfortunate time of weakness.

And the 7th house showed the unmistakable backdrop of a war the United States as a whole still hoped to avoid. All three classical malefics joined together in warlike Aries to remind FDR and everybody else that maneuvering to stay out of war was not going to be easy. His State of the Union address called for an increase in military expenditures, again, for prudence's sake.

Roosevelt's Sun – he himself – was in the 4th: staying out of the war, focused at home, even if he tried to find ways to help Britain unofficially. In this 4th house period, for the first time, he didn't address the Democratic nominating committee in person, and he contrived to make his renomination look like a draft, and not his personal decision.

The 1940 Aries Ingress, as we have seen, recapitulates a couple of themes from FDR's solar return of 1939. Here is a very busy and frustrating year for the president – as it had to be, given the gap

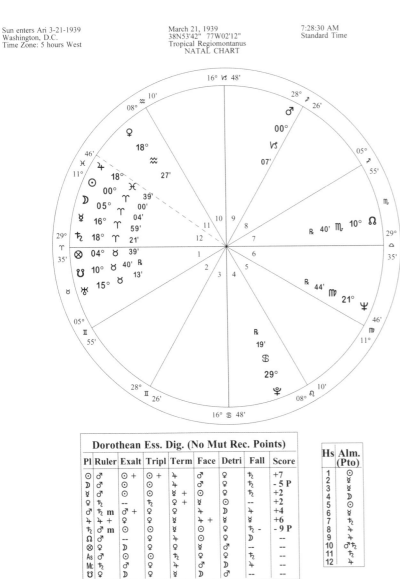

Sun enters Ari 3-21-1939
Washington, D.C.
Time Zone: 5 hours West

March 21, 1939
38N53'42" 77W02'12"
Tropical Regiomontanus
NATAL CHART

7:28:30 AM
Standard Time

	Dorothean Ess. Dig. (No Mut Rec. Points)							
Pl	Ruler	Exalt	Tripl	Term	Face	Detri	Fall	Score
☉	♂	☉ +	☉ +	♃	♂	♀	♄	+7
☽	♂	☉	☉	♃	♂	♀	♄	- 5 P
☿	♂	☉	☉	☿ +	☿	♀	☉	+2
♀	♄	--	♄	♀ +	♀ +	☉	--	+2
♂	♄ m	♂ +	♀	♀	♃ +	♀	♃	+4
♃	♃ +	♃	☉	♃	♃ +	☿	♀	+6
♄	♂ m	☉	☉	☿	☿	☉	♄ -	- 9 P
☊	♀	♀	♀	♃	♀	♂	--	--
⊗	♀	--	♀	♀	☿	♂	♀	--
☋	♀	♀	♀	♃	♀	♂	--	--
As	♂	☉	☉	♄	♀	♀	♄	--
Mc	♄	♂	♀	♀	☿	☽	♃	--
☋	♀	☽	☽	☿	♀	♂	♂	--

Hs	Alm. (Pto)
1	☿
2	☿
3	☿ ♀
4	☽ ☉
5	☉
6	☿ ♄ ♀
7	♃
8	♃
9	♃
10	♂ ♄
11	♄
12	♃

Example 12-37b. Aries Ingress for 1939, Washington, DC

between his private opinion and his public actions. While Pluto was in his solar return 10th, in the Aries Ingress, it was Pluto conjunct the 1st. It is interesting that one of the major attacks of Wendell Wilkie, the Republican nominee, was regarding *power* – a somewhat coded wording of concern over Franklin's decision to run for a third term, but a perfect Pluto word. But that Pluto was partile trine the Aries Ingress Sun, the Almuten of the 10th house. The power that would triumph was Roosevelt's.

Undoubtedly, that angular Pluto position was weakening America's isolationism, just as Roosevelt was finding new and innovative ways to support Britain militarily without actually engaging the United States in the fight. But it was his statement just on the eve of the election that no American would fight in the war that gained him the presidency one more time. After the election, he expanded U.S. aid to Britain through the proposal for the Lend-Lease program. And herein we examine one last element of his 1940 solar return: the Moon in Scorpio in the 2nd. As I mentioned before, a Moon in Scorpio is seldom a happy position. Here, the focus is on money – which was the crux of the issue that he had faced in this election year just past. Roosevelt had accepted the Keynesian economic argument that the recovery had faltered in 1939 because he had tried to balance the budget too soon: that by cutting spending, jobs had been lost in a period where consumption was remaining low, as everyone was worried about the economic conditions of 1930 returning. His policies regarding rearmament and selling arms to Europe were already ramping up industrial production, which was beginning to reduce the 14% unemployment of 1939 – still less than the 20% unemployment when he took office. The Lend-Lease program was difficult to sell in Congress, because many saw it as expanding the U.S. role in the war. With Moon in Scorpio disposed by Mars in Aries: was there any question this was true? But it would help the U.S. economy by increasing production still more, thereby continuing the decrease in unemployment.

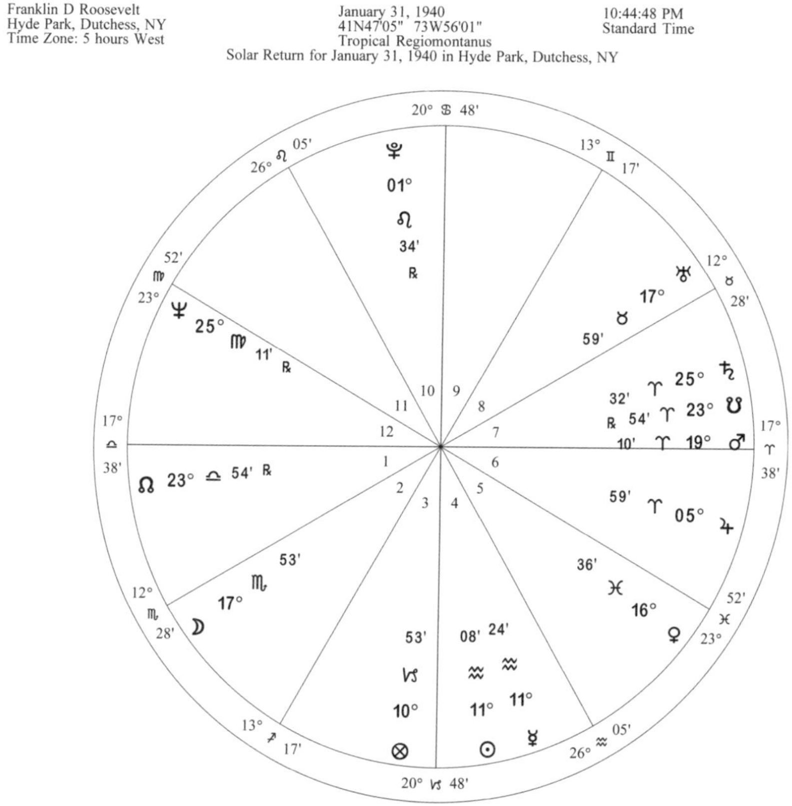
Franklin D Roosevelt
Hyde Park, Dutchess, NY
Time Zone: 5 hours West
January 31, 1940
41N47'05" 73W56'01"
Tropical Regiomontanus
10:44:48 PM
Standard Time
Solar Return for January 31, 1940 in Hyde Park, Dutchess, NY

Dorothean Ess. Dig. (No Mut Rec. Points)								
Pl	Ruler	Exalt	Tripl	Term	Face	Detri	Fall	Score
☉	♄	--	☿	☿	☿	☉ -	--	- 10 P
☽	♂	--	♂	♀	☉	♀	☽ -	- 9 P
☿	♄	--	☿ +	☿ +	☿ +	☉	--	+6
♀	♃	♀ +	♂	☿	♃	☿	☿	+4
♂	♂ +	☉	♃	☿	☉	♀	♄	+5
♃	♂	☉	♃ +	♃ +	♂	♀	♄	+5
♄	♂	☉	♃	♂	♀	♀	♄ -	- 9 P
☊	♀	♄	☿	☿	♃	♂	☉	--
⊗	♄	♂	☽	☿	♂	☽	♃	--
As	♀	♄	☿	♃	♄	♂	☉	--
Mc	☽	♃	♂	♀	☽	♄	♂	--
☋	♂	☉	♃	♂	♀	♀	♄	--

Hs	Alm. (Pto)
1	♀♄
2	♂
3	♃
4	♂
5	♄
6	♃
7	☉♂
8	☽
9	☿
10	☽
11	☉
12	☿

Example 12-38a. Franklin Roosevelt's solar return for 1940

Sun enters Ari 3-20-1940
Washington, D.C.
Time Zone: 5 hours West

March 20, 1940
38N53'42" 77W02'12"
Tropical Regiomontanus
NATAL CHART

1:23:46 PM
Standard Time

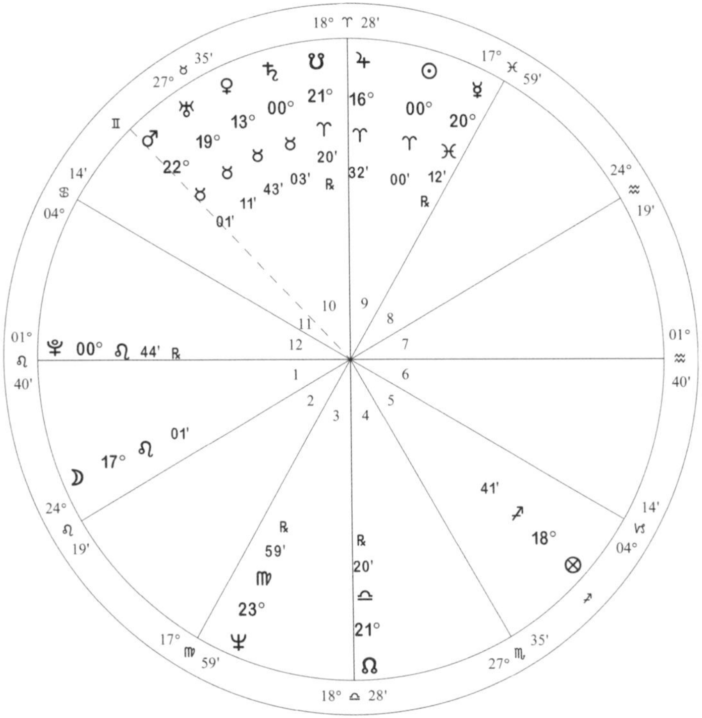

Dorothean Ess. Dig. (No Mut Rec. Points)								
Pl	Ruler	Exalt	Tripl	Term	Face	Detri	Fall	Score
☉	♂	☉ +	☉ +	♃	♂	♀	♄	+7
☽	☉	--	☉	♀	♃	♄	--	- 5 P
☿	♃	♀	♀	♂	♂	☿ -	☿ -	- 14 P
♀	♀ +	☽	♀ +	☿	☽	♂	--	+8
♂	♀	☽	♀	♄	♄	♂ -	--	- 10 P
♃	♂	☉	☉	☿	☉	♀	♄	- 5 P
♄	♀	☽	♀	♀	☿	♂	--	- 5 P
☊	♀	♄	♄	☿	♃	♂	☉	--
⊗	♃	☋ +	☉	☿	☽	☿	--	--
As	☉	--	☉	♄	♄	♄	--	--
Mc	♂	☉	☉	☿	☉	♀	♄	--
☋	♂	☉	☉	♂	♀	♀	♄	--

Hs	Alm. (Pto)
1	☉
2	☉
3	☿
4	♄
5	♂
6	♀♄
7	♄
8	♄
9	♃
10	☉
11	♀
12	☽

Example 12-38b. Aries Ingress for 1940, Washington, DC

1941: Solar Return and Aries Ingress

Roosevelt would need his 1941 solar return to push the idea through Congress, which happened in February. This solar return featured the return of Jupiter and Saturn to their natal sign positions, a mark of how age 59 falls roughly at the second Saturn return and the fifth Jupiter return. Here, in 1941, at their conjunction, they formed the basis for this portion of Tecumseh's curse: that during the period when the Jupiter-Saturn conjunction occurred in the Earth signs, any president elected under that configuration would die in office.[12] But as we may note, this observation did not mandate that the death would occur in the same term of office in which the conjunction occurred.

His 10th house ruler, Venus, was angular in the 1st house in Capricorn, a sign of her Triplicity. The Sun was in the 2nd: this would still be a year of emphasizing economic recovery even as Roosevelt edged the U.S. onto a war footing. Mars was sitting quietly in the 12th house: this could not be his emphasis. We shall return to this, and the Neptune in the 9th house, in a few short months.

The Aries Ingress showed the Moon in Capricorn conjunct the IC, with Mars in Capricorn in the 4th. The focus of attention in the Spring of 1941 was strictly at home, even if the munitions industry was leading industrial production at this time. The president was strong-willed and willing to take risks, shown by Pluto in the 10th. But the 10th was ruled by that Moon in Capricorn, which, with its mix of dignity and debility, meant that FDR had to tread lightly. He was not going to get everything he wanted.

So, with Neptune in the 9th, he resorted to deception, extending patrols out into the Atlantic, while denying that this amounted to creating convoys. He redefined Greenland as part of North America, thus bringing it under the Monroe Doctrine. He arranged for the creation of Defense Savings Bonds and Stamps that were really war bonds. He declared a national emergency after the first U.S. ship was sunk by a German U-boat – and yet the country was not at war.

Roosevelt continued his foreign policy initiatives with Britain and Russia as he circled closer to war, while denying to the American people that he was doing so. War would wait only until December, when yet another version of that Neptune in the 9th house in his chart manifested: the surprise attack of the Japanese on Pearl Harbor on December 7, 1941, that formally brought the U.S. into the war. The thing was: FDR recognized that a two-front war, i.e., Asia and Europe, would be profoundly harder to fight than a one-front one. He preferred Europe, because he considered it the more immediate threat. All his efforts had gone to bringing the U.S. into war against Germany first. On that count, he failed.

In the midst of all this activity, on September 7, 1941, his mother died. The 29 degrees on the 8th house cusp with Pluto there may have marked the transition, but this was one year in which that sad event could not be seen as the dominant one. It is interesting that Uranus was in the 5th house: the 8th from the 10th, the mother's death. Sara died quite suddenly from a massive stroke, although her health had been failing for some time.

How much did Roosevelt know in advance of Pearl Harbor? As the American and British intelligence had cracked the codes being used in Japanese diplomatic cables, they knew quite a lot, but not everything. In early November 1941, they knew that November 25th was a deadline for diplomatic initiatives before what sounded like the commencement of a military campaign. They knew that there had been a recent coup in Japan that brought a general into the Prime Ministership in place of a civilian government. When November 25th rolled around, Roosevelt convened what would become his war cabinet to discuss the likelihood of a sneak attack. But at Pearl Harbor? That prospect wasn't mentioned, with Roosevelt evidently believing the Philippines to be the likely target. While he may have felt the need to wait for Japan to strike first in order to get the U.S. people engaged as a result, he apparently hadn't expected a disaster of the magnitude that Pearl Harbor represented. Nonetheless, the U.S. quickly found itself at war with Japan. Within days, Germany

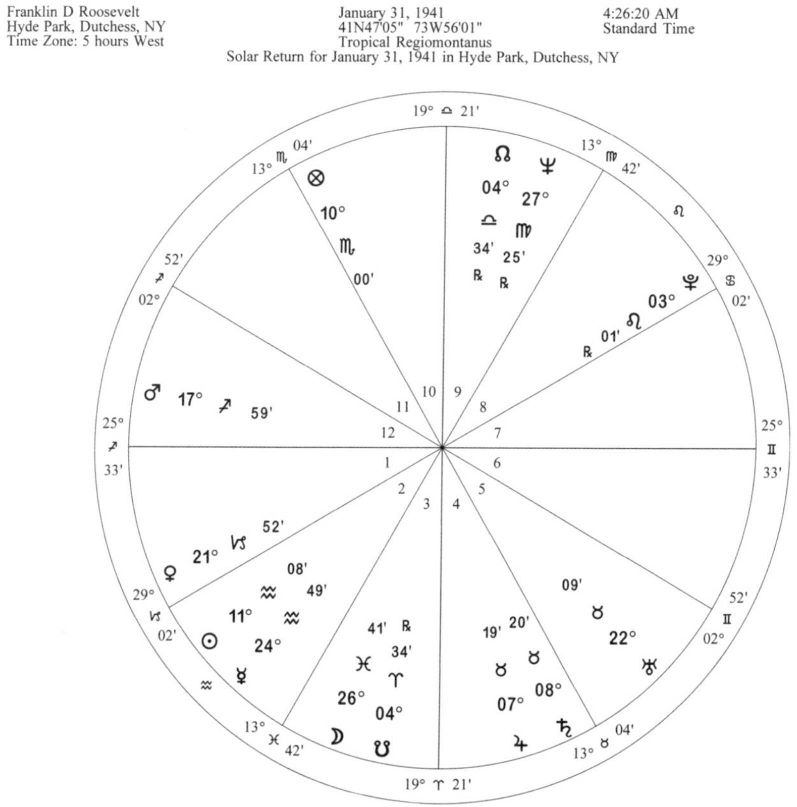
Franklin D Roosevelt
Hyde Park, Dutchess, NY
Time Zone: 5 hours West
January 31, 1941
41N47'05" 73W56'01"
Tropical Regiomontanus
4:26:20 AM
Standard Time
Solar Return for January 31, 1941 in Hyde Park, Dutchess, NY

Dorothean Ess. Dig. (No Mut Rec. Points)

Pl	Ruler	Exalt	Tripl	Term	Face	Detri	Fall	Score
☉	♄	--	☿	☿	☿	☉ -	--	- 10 P
☽	♃	♀	♂	♄	♂ m	☿	☿	- 5 P
☿	♄	--	☿ +	♃	☽	☉	--	+3
♀	♄ m	♂	☽	♂	☉	☽	♃	- 5 P
♂	♃	☋	♃	☿	☽ m	☿	--	- 5 P
♃	♀	☽	☽	♀	☿	♂	--	- 5 P
♄	♀ m	☽	☽	☿	☿	♂	--	- 5 P
☊	♀	♄	☿	♄	☽	♂	☉	--
⊗	♂	--	♂	♃	☉	♀	☽	--
As	♃	☋	♃	♂	♄	☿	--	--
Mc	♀	♄	☿	☿	♄	♂	☉	--
☋	♂	☉	♃	♃	♂	♀	♄	--

Hs	Alm. (Pto)
1	♃
2	♄
3	♃
4	☉♂
5	☽
6	☿
7	☿
8	☽
9	☿
10	☿♀♄
11	♂
12	♃

Example 12-39a. Franklin Roosevelt's solar return for 1941

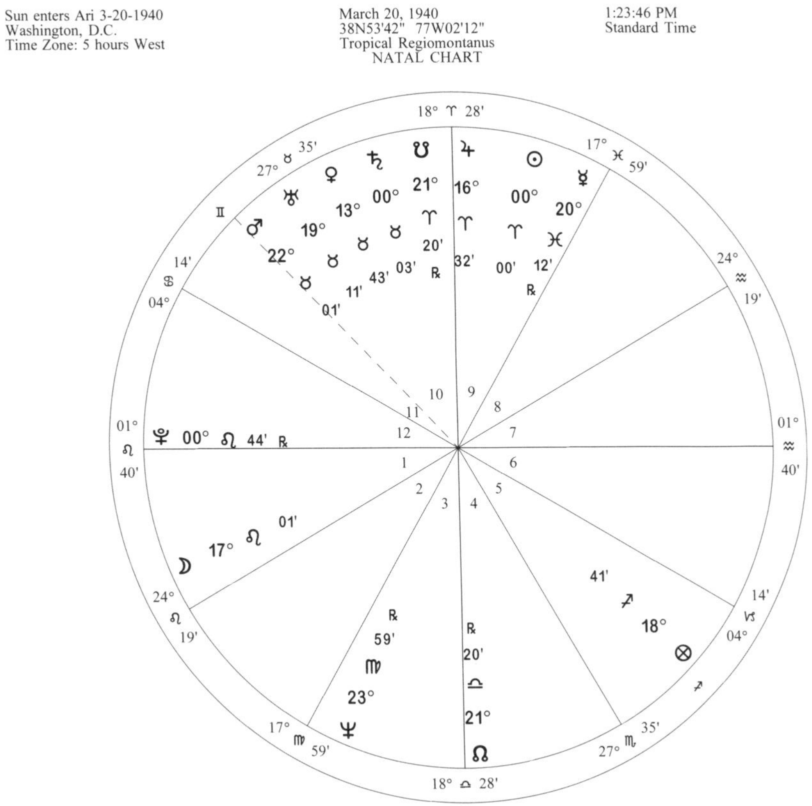
Sun enters Ari 3-20-1940
Washington, D.C.
Time Zone: 5 hours West
March 20, 1940
38N53'42" 77W02'12"
Tropical Regiomontanus
NATAL CHART
1:23:46 PM
Standard Time

Dorothean Ess. Dig. (No Mut Rec. Points)								
Pl	Ruler	Exalt	Tripl	Term	Face	Detri	Fall	Score
☉	♂	☉ +	☉ +	♃	♂	♀	♄	+7
☽	☉	--	☉	♀	♃	♄	--	- 5 P
☿	♃	♀	♀	♂	♂	☿ -	☿ -	- 14 P
♀	♀ +	☽	♀ +	☿	☽	♂	--	+8
♂	♀	☽	♀	♄	♄	♂ -	--	- 10 P
♃	♂	☉	☉	☿	☉	♀	♄	- 5 P
♄	♀	☽	♀	♀	☿	♂	--	- 5 P
☊	♀	♄	♄	☿	♃	♂	☉	--
⊗	♃	☋ +	☉	☿	☽	☿	--	--
As	☉	--	☉	♄	♄	♄	--	--
Mc	♂	☉	☉	☿	☉	♀	♄	--
☋	♂	☉	☉	♂	♀	♀	♄	--

Hs	Alm. (Pto)
1	☉
2	☉
3	☿
4	♄
5	♂
6	♀♄
7	♄
8	♄
9	♃
10	☉
11	♀
12	☽

Example 12-39b. Aries Ingress for 1941, Washington, DC

through interlocking treaties declared war on the U.S. Roosevelt had his war. From mid-December until his next birthday, he was caught up in planning and some skirmishes in Asia. The first U.S. troops would arrive in Europe on January 26, 1942.

1942: Solar Return and Aries Ingress

In 1942, the war proceeded, but the outcome was by no means clear. It took a while for the U.S. to stage in Europe. In Asia, the massive equipment losses at Pearl Harbor still impacted the American ability to effectively fight in the field. By the end of the year, American and British forces were landing in North Africa, and fuel rationing was occurring in the U.S. But the ramping up of wartime production had effectively eroded the Great Depression, even if rationing and the dislocation of troops hardly produced a normal economy. The Great Depression would be declared officially ended at the end of 1943.

Roosevelt's solar return for age sixty showed angularity in the 1st and 4th. The presence of three malefics in the 1st wasn't so much evil for his vitality as indicative of the subject of his concerns. Mercury, Venus, and Saturn were all in their natal signs. Because of these recapitulations of their natal placements, FDR was simply doing what came naturally, even if it wasn't grabbing the big headlines. This is another example of a very fixed chart, but with the twenty-nine degrees rising of a transitional circumstance. This was a year of doing what it took.

The 1942 Aries Ingress for Washington, DC showed no angularity at all. Yet the Moon in Taurus showed a year where things were being accomplished, simply not resolved. This was not the year that everyone remembers as pivotal. The British lost Singapore, but the Americans scored victories with Coral Sea and Midway, especially through destroying the Japanese carriers. Republicans picked up seats, but no majority, in the congressional elections.

Franklin D Roosevelt
Hyde Park, Dutchess, NY
Time Zone: 5 hours West

January 31, 1942
41N47'05" 73W56'01"
Tropical Regiomontanus

10:22:24 AM
Standard Time

Solar Return for January 31, 1942 in Hyde Park, Dutchess, NY

Sun enters Ari 3-21-1942
Washington, D.C.
Time Zone: 5 hours West

March 21, 1942
38N53'42" 77W02'12"
Tropical Regiomontanus
NATAL CHART

2:10:40 AM
War Time

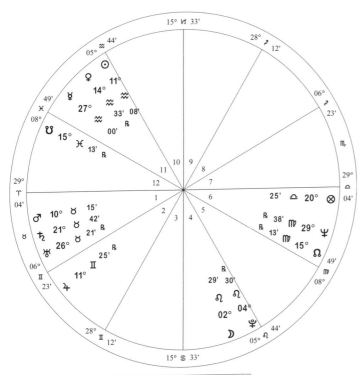

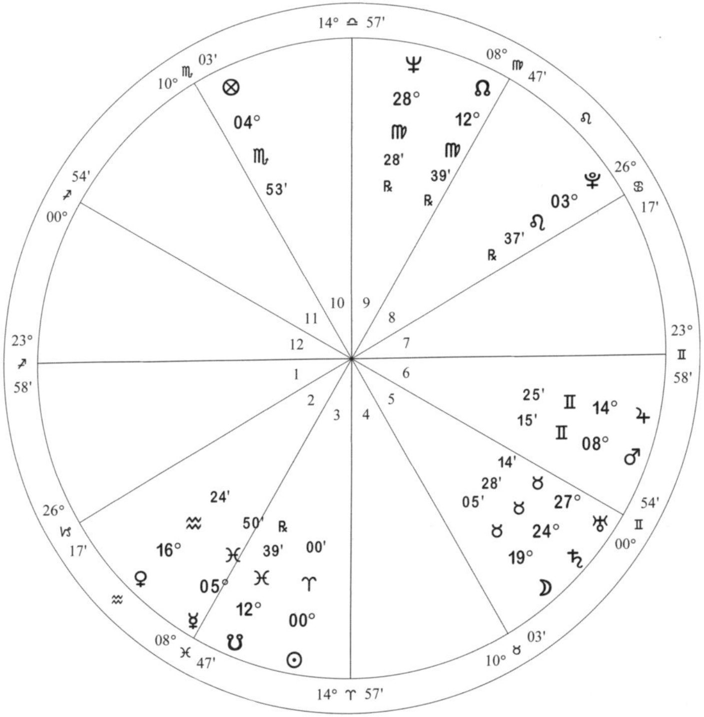

Example 12-40a. Franklin Roosevelt's solar return for 1942

Dorothean Ess. Dig. (No Mut Rec. Points)										**Hs**	**Alm. (Pto)**
Pl	Ruler	Exalt	Tripl	Term	Face	Detri	Fall	Score			
☉	♄	--	♄	☿	☿	☉ -	--	- 10 P		1	☉
☽	♄	--	☉	♄ m	♄	☉	--	- 5 P		2	☿
☿	♄	--	♄ m	☿ m	☽	☉ -	--	- 5 P		3	♄
♀	♄ m	--	♄ m	♂ +	☿	♂	--	+2		4	♃
♂	♀	☽	♀	♀ +	☽	♂ -	--	- 10 P		5	♀
♃	♀	☊	♀	♃ +	♃ +	♂	--	- 3		6	☿
♄	♀ m	--	♀ m	♃	♄ +	♂	--	+1		7	♄
☊	♀	--	♀	☿	♃	♂	--	--		8	♀
⊗	♀	--	☿	☿	♃	♂	--	--		9	♃
As	♂	☉	♃	♀	☿	♀	♄	--		10	♂
Mc	♄	♂	♀	♃	♂	☽	♃	--		11	♄
☋	♃	--	♀	♀	☿	☿	--	--		12	

Example 12-40b. Aries Ingress for 1942, Washington, DC

Dorothean Ess. Dig. (No Mut Rec. Points)										**Hs**	**Alm. (Pto)**
Pl	Ruler	Exalt	Tripl	Term	Face	Detri	Fall	Score			
☉	♂	☉ +	♃	♃	♂	♀	♄	+4		1	☉
☽	♂	☽ +	☽ +	♃	☽ +	♄	--	+8		2	♃
☿	♃ m	♀	♃	♂ m	♃	♃	☿ -	- 14 P		3	♃
♀	♄	--	♄	☿	☽	♂	--	+2		4	☉ ♂
♂	♃	☊	♃	♃ m	♃	♀	--	- 5 P		5	☿
♃	☿ m	--	♄	♃ +	♂ m	♃ -	--	- 10 P		6	♀
♄	♀	☽	♀	♄ +	♃ +	♂	--	+3		7	♄
☊	♃	--	♄	☽	♃	☿	♃	--		8	☽
⊗	♂	--	♃	♀	☿	♀	☽	--		9	☽
As	♄	☋	☿	♀	♃	☉	♀	--		10	♀ ♄
Mc	♀	♄	☿	♃	♀	♂	♄	--		11	♀
☋	♀	--	♀	♀	☿	♂	--	--		12	♃

1943: Solar Return and Aries Ingress

In 1943, FDR's solar return had the slowly approaching Sun-Pluto opposition angular. With the Sun in the 7th house, he was consumed with war issues. It was in 1943, before the 1943 Aries Ingress, that Roosevelt appointed Dwight Eisenhower as the European commander: this proved an auspicious choice, with the 10th house being Aries, ruled by Mars exalted.

The Aries Ingress for 1943 likewise showed some angularity, just as FDR's solar return did. But not everything was going well. This was still the era in which the U.S. had not been able to field long-range fighters to protect their bombers, so that the successful completion of twenty-five bombing missions by the *Memphis Belle* was still considered exceptional. U.S. forces were not winning every battle they fought, and General Rommel was proving to be the brilliant general he was in Africa. The Virgo Moon in the 6th was still showing the importance of the build-up of equipment. Still, the invasion of Italy began, as Allied soldiers would fight their way slowly through Europe, declaring victory in Italy in 1943.

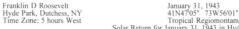

Franklin D Roosevelt
Hyde Park, Dutchess, NY
Time Zone: 5 hours West

January 31, 1943
41N47'05" 73W56'01"
Tropical Regiomontanus

5:18:09 PM
War Time

Solar Return for January 31, 1943 in Hyde Park, Dutchess, NY

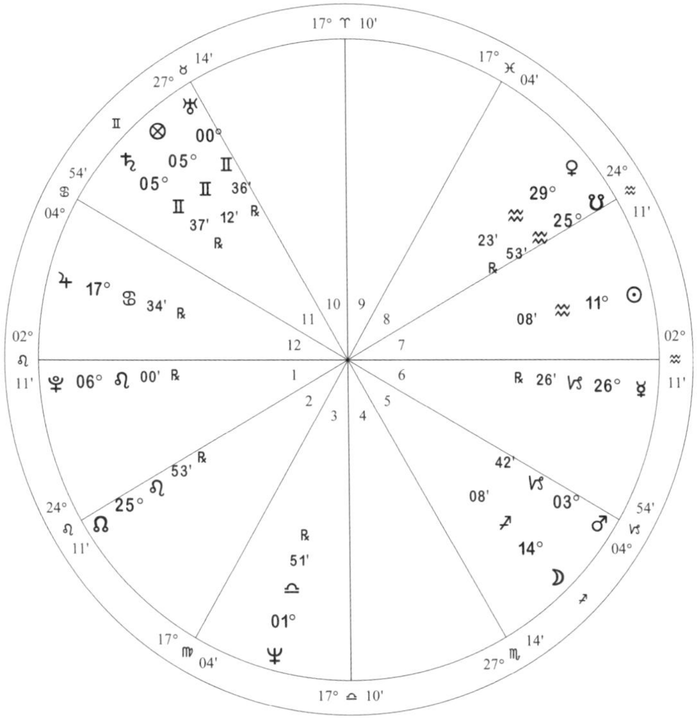

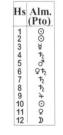

Dorothean Ess. Dig. (No Mut Rec. Points)								
Pl	Ruler	Exalt	Tripl	Term	Face	Detri	Fall	Score
☉	♄	--	♄	☿	☿ m	☉ -	--	- 10 P
☽	♃ m	☋	☉	☿	☽ +	☿	--	+1
☿	♄ m	♂	♀	♄ m	☉ m	☽	♃	- 5 P
♀	♄	--	♄	♂ m	☽	☉	--	- 5 P
♂	♄	♂ +	♀	♀ m	♃	☽	♃	+4
♃	☽ m	♃ +	♀	☿	☿	♄	♂	+4
♄	☿ m	☊	♄ +	☿ m	♃	♃	--	+3
☊	☉	--	☉	♂	♂	♄	--	--
⊗	☿	☊	♄	☿	♃	♃	--	--
As	☉	--	☉	♄	♄	♄	--	--
Mc	♂	☉	☉	☿	☉	♀	♄	--
☋	♄	--	♄	♂	☽	☉	--	--

Hs	Alm. (Pto)
1	☉
2	☉
3	☿
4	♄
5	♂
6	♀♄
7	♄
8	♄
9	♃
10	☉
11	♀
12	☽

Example 12-41a. Franklin Roosevelt's solar return for 1943

Sun enters Ari 3-21-1943
Washington, D.C.
Time Zone: 5 hours West

March 21, 1943
38N53'42" 77W02'12"
Tropical Regiomontanus
NATAL CHART

8:02:38 AM
War Time

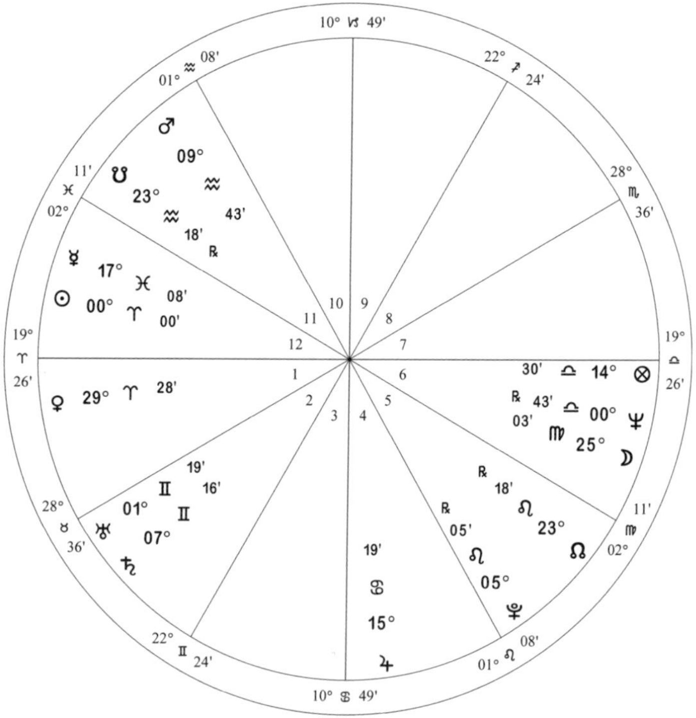

Dorothean Ess. Dig. (No Mut Rec. Points)								
Pl	**Ruler**	**Exalt**	**Tripl**	**Term**	**Face**	**Detri**	**Fall**	**Score**
☉	♂	☉ +	☉ +	♃	♂	♀	♄	+7
☽	☿	☿	♀	♂	☿	♃	♀	- 5 P
☿	♃	♀	♀	☿ +	♃ m	☿ -	☿ -	- 7
♀	♂	☉	☉	♄	♀ +	♀ -	♄	- 4
♂	♄	--	♄	☿	♀	☉	--	- 5 P
♃	☽	♃ +	♀	☿	☿ m	♄	♂	+4
♄	☿	☊	♄ +	♃	♃	♃	--	+3
☊	☉	--	☉	♃	♂	♄	--	--
⊗	♀	♄	♄	♃	♄	♂	☉	--
As	♂	☉	☉	☿	☉	♀	♄	--
Mc	♄	♂	♀	☿	♂	☽	♃	--
☋	♄	--	♄	♃	☽	☉	--	--

Hs	Alm. (Pto)
1	☉
2	♀
3	☿♄
4	♃
5	☉
6	☿
7	♄
8	♂
9	♃
10	♂♄
11	♄
12	♀

Example 12-41b. Aries Ingress for 1943, Washington, DC

1944: Solar Return and Aries Ingress

Roosevelt's 1944 solar return showed a shift to angularity as represented by the MC/IC axis, which suggests more public success. The Part of Fortune partile conjunct the MC does suggest success, especially as both are ruled by a highly dignified Moon in Taurus. And this was in fact the case, with D-Day and its invasion of Nazi-occupied France becoming a major push to end the war in Europe. Not only that, without a peep of protest, he won yet another term as president in 1944. By December, most of the remaining Japanese fleet was destroyed at the Battle of Leyte Gulf. Still, Pluto was continuing its progress toward opposition to his Sun. In November 1944, just a couple days after the election, Pluto would station retrograde at 10 Leo, as close as it ever got to his Sun in his lifetime.

In 1944, Neptune conjunct the Ascendant no doubt impacted his health. This is the first time that any health issues seem to enter FDR's presidency, because, apart from his post-polio issues, the only mention of any health problems prior to this were sinus conditions. In his 1943 solar return, with Pluto rising and Mars conjunct the 6th, he contracted influenza following his overseas trip to Teheran and elsewhere. In March 1944, hypertension and a heart condition were diagnosed. A working vacation was arranged, but Roosevelt was not going to take time off during a war. The discovery of gallstones (developed the prior year with Mars conjunct the 6th house cusp?) led to a low fat diet and weight loss. Throughout this illness, he showed little interest in discussing his condition with his doctors. Granted, this was not unusual at the time, but one also wonders about whether there was some denial going on, or simply too much obsession with the war. However, his weight loss continued, despite a diet of eggnog which was prescribed. He had lost his sense of taste, and relatives noted his changed and deteriorated condition during the Christmas holidays.

Possibly the last major agenda item under his 1944 solar return was the briefing where he was made aware of the progress toward

Franklin D Roosevelt
Hyde Park, Dutchess, NY
Time Zone: 5 hours West

January 31, 1944
41N47'05" 73W56'01"
Tropical Regiomontanus
Solar Return for January 31, 1944 in Hyde Park, Dutchess, NY

10:58:37 PM
War Time

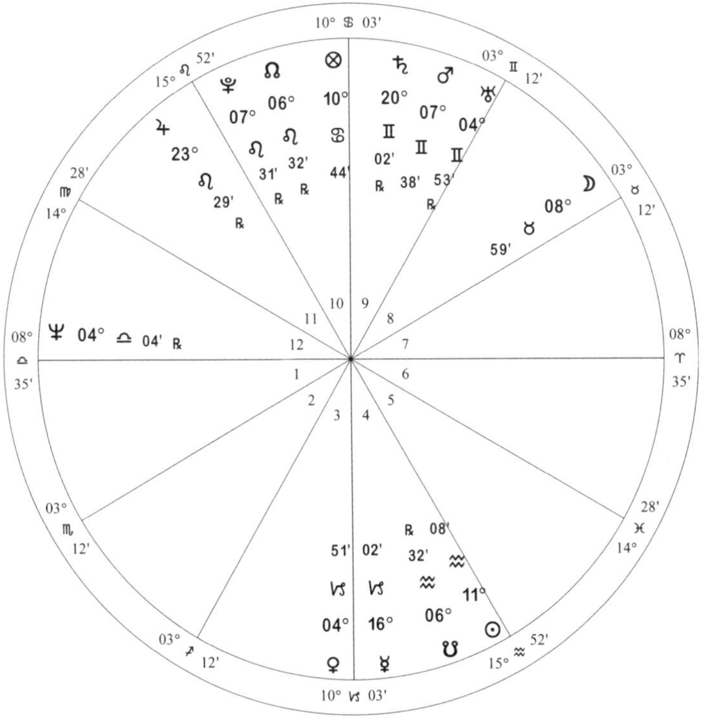

Dorothean Ess. Dig. (No Mut Rec. Points)								
Pl	Ruler	Exalt	Tripl	Term	Face	Detri	Fall	Score
☉	♄	--	☿	☿	☿	☉ -	--	- 10 P
☽	♀	☽ +	☽ +	☿	☿	♂	--	+7
☿	♄ m	♂	☽	♃	♂	☽	♃	- 5 P
♀	♄	♂	☽	♀ +	♃	☽	♃	+2
♂	☿	☊	☿	♃	♃ m	♃	--	- 5 P
♃	☉	--	♃ +	♃ +	♂ m	♄	--	+5
♄	☿ m	☊	☿	♀	☉	♃	--	- 5 P
☊	☉	--	♃	☿	♄	♄	--	--
⊗	☽	♃	♂	♃	☿	♄	♂	--
As	♀	♄	☿	♀	☽	♂	☉	--
Mc	☽	♃	♂	♃	☿	♄	♂	--
☋	♄	--	☿	☿	♀	☉	--	--

Hs	Alm. (Pto)
1	♀
2	♂
3	♃
4	♂♄
5	♄
6	♃
7	♂
8	☽♀
9	☿
10	♃
11	☉
12	☿

Example 12-42a. Franklin Roosevelt's solar return for 1944

Sun enters Ari 3-20-1944
Washington, D.C.
Time Zone: 5 hours West

March 20, 1944
38N53'42" 77W02'12"
Tropical Regiomontanus
NATAL CHART

1:48:38 PM
War Time

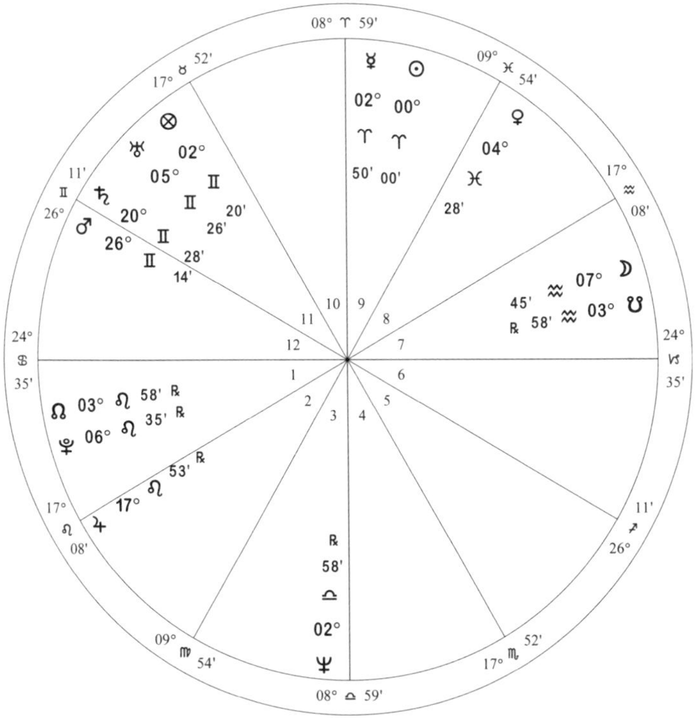

Dorothean Ess. Dig. (No Mut Rec. Points)								
Pl	Ruler	Exalt	Tripl	Term	Face	Detri	Fall	Score
☉	♂	☉ +	☉ +	♃	♂ m	♀	♄	+7
☽	♄	--	♄	☿	♀	☉	--	- 5 P
☿	♂ m	☉	☉	♃	♂	♀	♄	- 5 P
♀	♃	♀ +	♀ +	♀ +	♄	☿	☿	+9
♂	☿ m	☊	♄	♂ +	☉ m	♃	--	+2
♃	☉	--	☉	♀	♃ +	♄	--	+1
♄	☿	☊	♄ +	♀	☉	♃	--	+3
☊	☉	--	☉	♄	♄	♄	--	--
⊗	☿	☊	♄	☿	♃	♃	--	--
As	☽	♃	♀	♀	☽	♄	♂	--
Mc	♂	☉	☉	♀	♂	♀	♄	--
☋	♄	--	♄	♄	♀	☉	--	--

Hs	Alm. (Pto)
1	☽
2	☉
3	☿
4	♀♄
5	♂
6	♃
7	♂
8	♄
9	♃
10	☉
11	♀
12	☿

Example 12-42b. Aries Ingress for 1944, Washington, DC

the implementation of the atomic bomb. The briefing told him that the bomb would not be ready until Summer at the earliest, so, if it were to factor in the ending of the war or post-war considerations, that would be the most optimistic timing.

The 1944 Aries Ingress had Mars ruling the MC – still the war leader, but this Mars was in the 12th house. Mars, in fact, was within a degree of Roosevelt's radix Mars, so there's no doubt of the symbolism. Was its placement in the 12th house showing his time away from Washington designed to help him recover his health? The Sun in the 9th applying to the trine to Pluto shows the approaching success of foreign ventures.

1945: Solar Return and Aries Ingress

Despite his illness of the prior year, Roosevelt agreed to the Yalta Conference in February 1945: maybe the best climate in old Russia, but still, not the most welcoming of conditions. Photographs from this conference show his weight loss. On the agenda were the final push into Germany, and the post-war structure of Europe, both topics of great concern to FDR.

The conference ended with a public communiqué and a private understanding. The private understanding was an agreement that within several months of the end of the European conflict, the Soviet Union would enter the war against Japan. We will consider the significance of this agreement later.

The Yalta Conference occurred shortly after Franklin's 1945 solar return. Here, we see a configuration he had not had since he was eight years old: Neptune conjunct the MC within five degrees. We also see the North Node conjunct the 8th house cusp, and the Moon ruling the 8th applying to Jupiter ruling the 1st in what would be an argument of death were this a horary about that topic. Is the Neptune on the MC a sign of the loosening of his power?

Venus, ruling the 10th, was dignified in Pisces: he would go out at the top of his game, just a month before Victory in Europe.

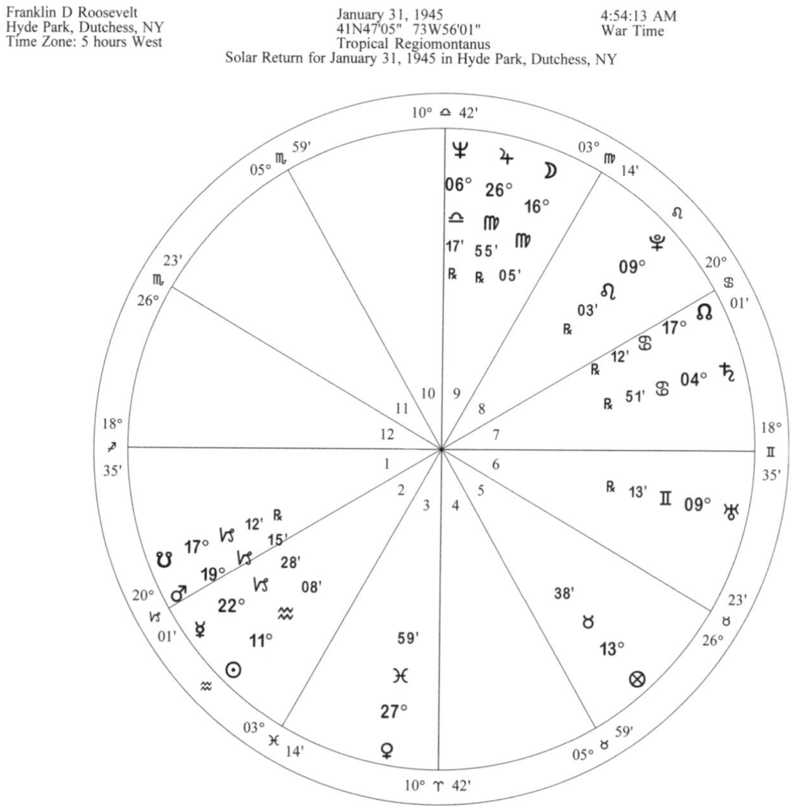
Franklin D Roosevelt
Hyde Park, Dutchess, NY
Time Zone: 5 hours West
January 31, 1945
41N47'05" 73W56'01"
Tropical Regiomontanus
4:54:13 AM
War Time
Solar Return for January 31, 1945 in Hyde Park, Dutchess, NY
10° ♎ 42'
10° ♈ 42'
18° ♐ 35'
18° ♊ 35'

Dorothean Ess. Dig. (No Mut Rec. Points)								
Pl	Ruler	Exalt	Tripl	Term	Face	Detri	Fall	Score
☉	♄	--	☿	☿	☿ m	☉ -	--	- 10 P
☽	☿	☿	☽ +	♃	♀	♃	♀	+3
☿	♄	♂	☽	♂	☉ m	☽	♃	- 5 P
♀	♃	♀ +	♂	♄	♂	☿	☿	+4
♂	♄	♂ +	☽	♂ +	♂ +	☽	♃	+7
♃	☿	☿	☽	♂	☿	♃ -	♀	- 10 P
♄	☽	♃	♂	♂	♀	♄ -	♂	- 10 P
☊	☽	♃	♂	☿	☿	♄	♂	--
⊗	♀	☽	☽	☿	☽	♂	--	--
As	♃	☋	♃	☿	☽	☿	--	--
Mc	♀	♄	☿	♀	♄	♂	☉	--
☋	♄	♂	☽	♃	♂	☽	♃	--

Hs	Alm. (Pto)
1	♃
2	♂
3	♀
4	☉♂
5	☽♀
6	☽
7	☿
8	☽
9	☿
10	♀
11	♂
12	♂

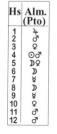

Example 12-43a. Franklin Roosevelt's solar return for 1945

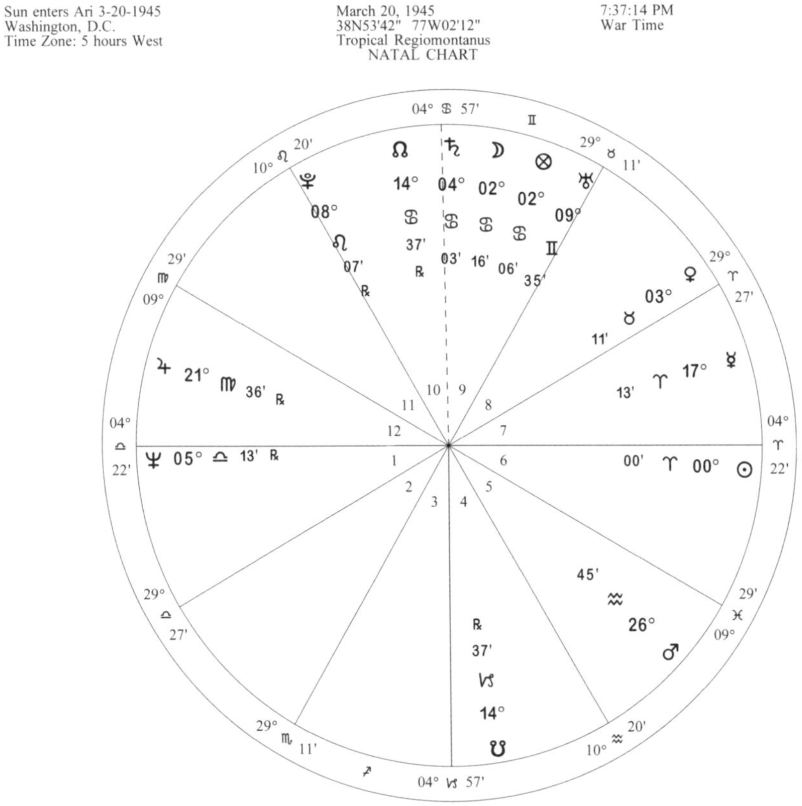
Sun enters Ari 3-20-1945
Washington, D.C.
Time Zone: 5 hours West
March 20, 1945
38N53'42" 77W02'12"
Tropical Regiomontanus
NATAL CHART
7:37:14 PM
War Time

Dorothean Ess. Dig. (No Mut Rec. Points)

Pl	Ruler	Exalt	Tripl	Term	Face	Detri	Fall	Score
☉	♂	☉ +	♃	♃	♂	♀	♄	+4
☽	☽ +	♃	♂	♂	♀	♄	♂	+5
☿	♂	☉	♃	☿ +	☉	♀	♄	+2
♀	♀ +	☽	☽	♀ +	☿	♂	--	+7
♂	♄	--	☿	♂ +	☽	☉	--	+2
♃	☿	☿	☽	♄	☿	♃ -	♀	- 10 P
♄	☽	♃	♂	♂	♀	♄ -	♂	- 10 P
☊	☽	♃	♂	☿	☿	♄	♂	--
⊗	☽	♃	♂	♂	♀	♄	♂	--
As	♀	♄	☿	♄	☽	♂	☉	--
Mc	☽	♃	♂	♂	♀	♄	♂	--
☋	♄	♂	☽	♃	♂	☽	♃	--

Hs	Alm. (Pto)
1	♄
2	♀
3	♂
4	♄
5	☿
6	♃
7	♂
8	♂
9	☽
10	☽
11	☉
12	☿

Example 12-43b. Aries Ingress for 1945, Washington, DC

During the Yalta conference, a change in his pulse, not to mention his fatigue, indicated that the left ventricle of his heart was failing. His final address to Congress after he returned from Yalta was conducted from his wheelchair for the first time.

And at this point, the Aries Ingress for 1945 kicked in. This chart showed his fate far more clearly than his nativity. Saturn in Cancer (detriment) was partile conjunct the MC. Neptune was conjunct the Ascendant. And perhaps most poignantly, it was a sunset chart.

The Moon in Cancer, in a partile conjunction with the Part of Fortune, applied to the Saturn-MC conjunction. Venus in Taurus ruled 1st and was in the 8th. The King is dead. Long live the King.

Just before noon on April 12, 1945, at his regular retreat in Warm Springs, Georgia, Franklin Roosevelt collapsed and lost consciousness in the presence of Lucy Mercer Rutherford and others. A cerebral hemorrhage was diagnosed. He was declared dead at 3:35 pm CWT.[12]

We have seen in this study of forty one years of Franklin Roosevelt's life how both the solar returns and Aries Ingresses applied, because of his very public status. We also can see how sequential solar returns create patterns, and how some of these patterns recur for all of us at particular ages.

In the final chapter, we shall summarize some of the most important factors in analyzing any solar return, or a series of them.

Chapter 12 Endnotes

1. Lehman, J. Lee. *The Eleventh House*. Learning with Lee CD Series #15. Lehman Associates: Malabar, FL.
2. The New York Times columnist Gail Collins enjoys documenting many of the most extreme peccadillos.
3. Lehman, *Astrology of Sustainability*, pp 154-159.
4. See Lehman, 2011, *Astrology of Sustainability*, footnote 63 on page 53.
5. Lehman, 2011, *Astrology of Sustanability*, pp 160-167.
6. Brands, Traitor to his Class, p 111.

7. In our current time period, we often assume that Evangelicals are intrinsically conservative. Actually, this is only a recent trend. Through much of the 19th century, Evangelicals were far more likely to be Democrats, and to generally push for liberal causes, except that they favored prohibition and were anti-evolution. It was after Bryan's death that many Evangelicals and Fundamentalists concluded that the body politic was so completely sinful that they should just stay out of politics entirely. It was only in the 1970s and later that a strong appeal to this group was made by Republican strategists. See, for example, Cherny, Robert W., and Oscar Handlin. A Righteous Cause : The Life of William Jennings Bryan. Library of American Biography. Boston: Little, Brown, 1985.

8. I discussed the meaning of the nodal axis more extensively in *Classical Astrology for Modern Living*, Chapter 10

9. Lehman, *Astrology of Sustainability*, pp 172-175.

10. Lehman, *Astrology of Sustainability*, pp 172-175.

11. Lehman, *Astrology of Sustainability*, see Table 8-3 on p 243.

12. See Lehman, *Astrology of Sustainability*, p33, and the surrounding pages, for a greater understanding of how this observation fits into historical and astrological context.

12. Brands, 2008, p 812.

13
Conclusions

ESPECIALLY NOW THAT WE HAVE HAD THE CHANCE TO EXAMINE SUCH A STRETCH OF FRANKLIN ROOSEVELT'S LIFE, WE ARE IN A GOOD POSITION TO REVIEW OUR METHOD, AND POINT OUT THE MOST IMPORTANT IDEAS FOR HOW TO DELINEATE SOLAR RETURNS.

Throughout this book, we have examined how solar returns work together as a sequence. We have seen how there are rules and interpretations to examine the different houses of the solar return chart to delineate different themes in the year as a whole. But beyond the specific rules, we have followed a series of general procedures in any one year to put that year into context:

The return of any planet to its natal sign brings a resonance with that planet that makes its application feel very comfortable in that year. In other words, if the natal Mercury is in Taurus, any year that SR-Mercury is in Taurus will feel intellectually comfortable. We should add that this issue of resonance probably falls off in importance as the person ages. Younger people tend to be both physically more resilient and emotionally/intellectually more vulnerable, so that may well be why the resonance will seem more important to, say, a Michelle Kwan during her competitive years, than to Franklin Roosevelt during his presidency.

The house positions of both Sun and Moon seem to show a lot about the focus of the Native in that year. Angular placement of the Sun really does argue for a more public experience.

The Sun has certain unique properties in a solar return *precisely because* it is the planet that by definition must be in its radix sign. So, if the Sun is in Aquarius as it was for Franklin Roosevelt, when it refers to him, that sign cannot be interpreted as in Detriment, because when the Sun is representing the Native, it *must* be in Aquarius, as in this case, because it's a return. So when the Sun shows something about Roosevelt himself, the Sun is a positive influence, being in its radix sign. However, the people in the solar return shown by any house with Leo on the cusp would be interpreted as being in Detriment.

Unless a radix planet is in Detriment or Fall, having a planet in dignity is a positive influence in that solar return.

The solar return, here shown almost exclusively for the birth location, is interpreted as a chart in its own right, but it is also referenced to the nativity in order to see resonance patterns, whether by sign recapitulation, or aspect resonances.

As a practical matter, I find horary rules to be a very useful adjunct – more powerfully so than in regular nativity delineation. Perhaps it's the fact that a solar return only lasts a year, which makes its shorter time frame more similar to that of a typical horary.

What can solar returns tell us about the process of life? This touches upon the human experience of time. On the one hand, time is a completely theoretical construct. On the other hand, we experience our lives relative to larger cycles defined by our earthly existence. I *know*, sitting here writing this in July, that in early August, temperatures will tend to be slightly warmer than they are now, and then the temperature will start to drop as we move toward winter. I *know* that the temperature is usually warmer during the day than at night. I *know* that, given the area that I live in, there may be a pronounced wet and rainy season. If I have any relation to the land at all, I *know* there is a certain appropriate time of year to plant any crop that I wish to grow.

The three cycles most embedded in our lives are the diurnal one, the lunar one, and the seasonal cycle, with the lunar and solar cycles jockeying for the second and third positions, depending on the nature of the society. Not only our bodies, but those of other animals and plants, are built around chemical changes which mediate the circadian rhythm, the daily cycle of sleep, eating, and metabolism. Not only our bodies, but those of other animals and plants, are built around chemical changes which mediate the lunation rhythm, with the lunar cycles timing the human estrous cycle, or the quality of many kinds of sushi. Even plants have functions that change with the phases of the moon.

The solar cycle was, perhaps, one of the greatest and earliest human scientific discoveries, as we came to understand how the seasons repeated. This knowledge in the temperate and polar regions, taught us how to survive, given annual changes in food type availability, and was absolutely critical to the invention of agriculture.

A lifetime for a human being is a harder unit to measure, because we don't know how much time we have. But as civilization becomes more complex, so does the ability to plan. For better or for worse, we become capable of planning out over multiple years. We learn to anticipate college, graduate school, vocational training, military service, or a job, all in terms of years to complete before the next step is taken. In all of this, a year is a very meaningful unit of time, and one's age a useful indicator of one's status in life.

And thus, we come back to the utility of the solar return. Human civilization drives us to plan in years, and thus, years become an increasingly useful marker of time. The ability to plan in years is the ability to understand our connection to the future, and to the past. While it may be the marker of our spiritual connection to *be here now*, and experience life in the moment, *now* doesn't get you a meal in the middle of winter in traditional Norway if you didn't plan for it!

One cannot make a plan for an entire Saturn cycle except in its barebones outline. When Franklin Roosevelt decided that he wanted to be president like Uncle Ted, *did* he or *could* he pick the year it would happen? It is clear that he used his Uncle Ted's biography as a general guide to steps he needed to take to achieve his goal. But he could not plan his life on a yearly basis, because he understood that there are things that can happen in any one year that temporarily accelerate or decelerate the life plan. As it was, Theodore Roosevelt became president at an age eight years younger than Franklin. But he was elected as vice president, not president, and had McKinley lived, he would have been "eligible" to run for president only at the end of McKinley's hypothetical term of office – *eight years later*. But would Franklin have seen his life as a failure if he had been yet four more years older when he became president? He would have seen it as the exigencies of life.

It is in the realm of prediction of these exigencies that the solar return exists. Transits are in the moment. The "moment" for a Pluto transit may actually last years, but between aspects, that planet is not speaking at all in this system. Do I never experience Pluto between Pluto transits? The solar return shows this annual cycle. It is thus a planning cycle, a way to navigate between and through the years. Interpreted as a full chart, and not as a derivative one, in any year different planets rise to prominence, and then possibly fall away the next year. It tells us both when we can be on track, and when circumstances are likely to knock us off track.

We can return now to the question of location. As an author, of course it was much simpler not to have to attempt to figure out where my subjects were on their birthdays. *But that's not a reason for a methodology choice.* As we discussed in Chapter 1, the use of the locational return is going to be most effective when it is done in an invocational way: where the conditions are designed to "fix" that location into one's consciousness for the year. Consciously traveling to a location, and engaging in rituals could make a difference in keeping the memory of that place for a year. But perhaps the person who doesn't celebrate the location of the birthday will not embed the location.

The celebration of the art of relocating for the solar return first began to grab the astrological imagination in the general era of prosperity following the end of World War II. It was promulgated by a generation used to seeing life as a series of opportunities, and that shunned any belief in limitations. I demonstrated in *Astrology of Sustainability* that in the era of Pluto in Capricorn, and then Aquarius, the belief in no limits is no longer viable to us for some period to come. The belief of the Pluto in Leo generation that the sky was the limit is cracking badly today. This is not to say that relocating for a solar return is no longer viable: it is simply to acknowledge that the degree of choice we experience in our lives depends on our societal and economic circumstances. It is well to have "tricks of the trade" for those people who, through economically superior circumstances, really can experience life as primarily choice-driven. But when we are working with people challenged by job loss, incomes plummeting, adult children who cannot afford to move out, and the high cost of aging parents with health problems, fate-based systems may be the more appropriate method of analysis.

We have also seen how the belief in choice can create its own demons. When it became fashionable to reconceptualize the idea that our attitudes can affect our disease circumstances, the rationale was to take patients out of the victimization that they might otherwise experience, and move them into a position of greater power and control. However, that theory applied to the extreme could result in yet a new victimization, as patients were held responsible for having disease at all, thus getting bacteria, viruses, not to mention environmental toxicity, off the hook. Causation may happen on many levels.

By now, we've been through enough examples to see the workings of the solar return throughout the life. We've seen that, even though our consciousness can extend past single years, that each year brings different experiences, opportunities, and challenges.

Even in the most rigidly fate-based systems, there still are choices until very close to the end of one's life. As I am writing this, I have just been working with a gentleman who has had four surgeries for brain cancer, and is looking at the possibility of a fifth. He is a Sun Cancer, with Pluto applying by opposition to the Sun, which will become exact next year. When we followed Franklin Roosevelt through the late 1930s and into the 1940s, his sequential solar returns showed an inexorable progress of Pluto toward his Sun-Pluto opposition: FDR died just before the aspect became exact. This is not to imply that the only possible meaning of a hard aspect of Pluto to the Sun is death: but it would be foolish to presume that that could not be a possibility, either.

However, as I examine the sequence of solar returns for my client, I see that his 2007 solar return, the year before the condition was diagnosed, is already showing supreme health stress, with the ruler of the 6th house in *Cancer* (yes, the sign does correlate *somewhat* to the disease), within a degree of the 7th house cusp (the Portals of Death, to use a Hellenistic phrase), as well as being combust, peregrine and retrograde. This is a common observation: a really bad health year from the standpoint of the solar return occurring a year before the symptoms become manifest.

Not that the year of diagnosis tends to be any better. In my client's case, the *Annus horribilis* of the developing cancer (which appears to be environmental toxicity, indicated by a Saturn-Neptune opposition) was followed by two years of angular difficult placements: the cancer manifested with visible symptoms, and he went through the four surgeries. Then, with Pluto partile conjunct his IC, the least visible of the angles, no outward signs manifested, except a few anomalous symptoms, which led him to a new set of tests in his next solar return, for the current year, which has the South Node on the Portals of Death, and the Moon opposite Pluto and square Saturn, all applying. Next year, it's Mars on the Portals of Death, with Pluto partile opposite the Sun, and the Moon in Scorpio in the 8th house. After that, it's smooth sailing. Can he survive? It won't be easy, and I'd have to say the odds are against him. But I can truly tell him that *if* he can survive through 2012, he will have some years of relief.

What is the lesson? In following the consecutive solar returns, first of Theodore Roosevelt, then Franklin Roosevelt, we saw that the very structure of sequential solar returns shows that there will be changes from year to year. Each successive year, the Sun "moves" roughly a quadrant. Jupiter moves roughly a sign. The other planets move faster or slower, but the result is that the solar return chart *will* look different from year to year. So even under the slow-developing transit like the aspects of Pluto or Neptune, each successive return will tell a different story about that developing aspect, not to mention all the other components of the return.

Given this degree of reshuffling, it's actually unusual to have so unrelenting a series of solar returns as my client has from 2007-2012. So this alone is enough to mandate the need to sit up and take notice when it does happen. But this also shows how unusual it is to have a run like Michelle Kwan's, occurring precisely during the peak of her physical abilities. Such a run either ten years earlier or later would not have done her any such good, but it does make us appreciate the astrological reasoning behind why her success over such a time period in amateur athletics was and will continue to be such a rare accomplishment.

When you think about it, it's hard to follow the same path for a series of sequential years. School years change; teachers change; supervisors change; companies restructure and change; children grow. Our experience of life in the day-to-day is continuity; but the longer the time interval, the more that change becomes obvious.

If there were no change, there would be little point to studying astrology. At its best, astrology is the map of the dialogue that we each experience with the universe, which is manifested as change, which, in turn, evokes still more dialogue, and still more change. Life is change; death is stillness. Personally, I prefer to use what maps I can find to help navigate. Solar returns are one such map.

Synopsis of Classical Concepts Necessary
to Understand Solar Returns

There are several basic concepts from traditional astrology which are absolutely crucial to the understanding of classical solar return method. In **Essential Dignities**[1] and **Classical Astrology for Modern Living**[2] I described these concepts fully. However, for those new to classical astrology, this can serve as an introduction to these critical components of the classical method.

Essential and Accidental Dignities

Classical astrology recognizes five essential dignities, and a whole series of accidental ones. The essential dignities are:

- Sign, 5 points of dignity
- Exaltation, 4 points of dignity
- Triplicity, 3 points of dignity
- Term, 2 points of dignity
- Face, 1 point of dignity

Having said that, there are several different methods for the determination of Triplicities and Terms. My preferred Table of

Dignities is shown in Appendix C. This is a synthesis of the traditional sign, exaltation and Face rulers, the Dorothean Triplicities, and the Chaldean Terms. Put another way, this Table differs from Lilly's only in the Triplicities.

The three dignities Sign, Exaltation and Triplicity are called the Major Dignities; Term and Face are the Minor Dignities. This expresses something about the importance of the assessment represented by dignity: it is a method of calculating the strength of a planet, functionally defined as the ability of the planet to get what it wants.

A planet in its own Sign (as Mars in Aries) when it represents a Significator, symbolizes a person able to charge out and get what she or he wants. That person is ready and able to do what it takes to accomplish the goal. A planet in its own Exaltation (as Sun in Aries) when it represents a Significator, shows a person who gets things done by having someone else do it for them. A planet in its own Triplicity (as Jupiter in Aries at night) when it represents a Significator, gives someone who gets his or her desires by being in the right place at the right time – by luck, in other words.

A planet in its own Term (as Mercury at sixteen degrees of Aries)

when it represents a Significator, gives a person who looks the part, but may not have any skill at all in the matter at hand. Still, having the appearance of competency, the person may yet pull it off. A planet in its own Face (as Venus at twenty two degrees of Aries) when it represents a Significator, gives someone fearful about the whole process. As a result, while this really isn't much of a dignity, the person's attention is focused! A planet with dignity only by Face is barely saved from being peregrine.

When a planet has no dignity at all by any of the five means (and this includes both the in-sect and out-of-sect Triplicity rulers), then that planet is ***peregrine***. A peregrine planet in horary represents someone incapable of effecting a result. These people get distracted and wander off the mark. As a result, seldom does an affirmative outcome actually move to fruition if the Significators are peregrine. In natal, a peregrine planet seldom gets results by being able to go directly from point A to point B.

A planet in ***Detriment*** or ***Fall*** (also shown in Appendix C) is a planet that is beginning the race several steps behind everyone else. For a planet in this state to get what it wants, the person signified has to come up with a novel solution – attempting to accomplish the matter in what would appear to be the most straightforward way will guarantee failure. Because most people are reluctant to actually engage in that level of creativity, the debility frequently stops the person from accomplishing the goal.

Accidental Dignity

The accidental dignities and debilities are shown in Table A-1. They can be divided into several generic types:

- House placement (i.e., angular, succedent, cadent)
- Motion (swift, slow, direct, retrograde)
- Oriental and Occidental
- Moon increasing or decreasing in Light
- Closeness to the Sun
- Aspects to malefic and benefic planets
- Conjunctions with fixed stars and the Nodes

Table A-1. Accidental Dignities & Debilities. Source: Lilly, *Christian Astrology*, p 115.

Accidental Dignities		***Accidental Debilities***	
In the M.C. or Ascendant	5	In the 12th House	-5
In the 7th, 4th & 11th Houses	4	In the 8th & 6th Houses	-2
In the 2nd & 5th Houses	3	Retrograde	-5
In the 9th House	2	Slow in Motion	-2
In the 3rd House	1	♄ ♃ ♂ Occidental	-2
Direct (except ☉ & ☽)	4	♀ ☿ Oriental	-2
Swift in Motion	2	☽ decreasing in light	-2
♄ ♃ ♂ Oriental	2	Combust of the ☉	-5
♀ ☿ Occidental	2	Under the ☉ Beams	-4
☽ increasing in light, or Occidental	2	Partile ☌ with ♄ or ♂	-5
Free from combustion & ☉ Beams	5	Partile ☌ with ☋	-4
Cazimi	5	Besieged of ♄ or ♂	-5
Partile ☌ with ♃ or ♀	5	Partile ☍ with ♄ or ♂	-4
Partile ☌ with ☊	4	Partile □ with ♄ or ♂	-3
Partile △ with ♃ or ♀	4	In ☌ or within	
Partile ✶ with ♃ or ♀	3	5° of Caput Algol	-5
In ☌ with *Cor Leonis*	6		
In ☌ with Spica	5		

The accidental dignities are tallied separately from the essential dignities. One of the frustrations of this system is that it's not entirely clear that all categories of dignity or debility are really equivalent. For example, is being Direct *really* equivalent in strength to being conjunct Spica? I would say, no!

Essential versus Accidental Dignity

The classical beginner often wastes valuable time trying to weigh this conundrum: which of the two is more important? In other words, what do you do when a planet is essentially dignified, but accidentally debilitated, or *vice versa*? The answer is: you cannot make this determination based on the points.

In my experience, having a Significator conjunct one of the especially strong fixed stars, like Spica or Algol, is sufficient to affect the outcome of the situation. It's very rare for a Significator conjunct Spica to not succeed; it's very hard for a Significator conjunct Algol not to fail.

Each class of accidental dignity rates somewhat differently. An easy aspect to the benefics is probably less helpful than hard aspects to the malefics are harmful. Aid from another or from a circumstance (the fundamental meaning of a sextile or trine to a benefic) is seldom enough to turn a no into a yes, *although if you are considering a scenario where the help of another really could be that critical, then this may turn your reading*. For example, if you are asking about a job, and your Significator will trine Jupiter, and Jupiter is not otherwise a Significator in this Question, this could be that Jupiter represents a person with some social standing or authority who comes to your defense. Perhaps the boss you would be working for is a friend of someone who has been a mentor to you, and happens to mention your application. However, this possible boon to your situation is only likely to occur if that benefic is in turn dignified, so essential dignity comes to the fore once more.

The hard aspects to the malefics have somewhat the reverse interpretation. Here, the prospective employer mentions your name to someone who speaks against you, whether from personal knowledge, or simply maliciousness. However, if the malefic is dignified by at least major essential dignity, the effect is much lessened, if not completely eliminated.

Notice that both benefics and malefics essentially debilitated are planets behaving badly: they are unpredictable in their effects.

The house placement of Significators is actually somewhat simpler than the table of accidental dignities implies: the important issue is whether a planet is Cadent, because that may make it more difficult for it to express itself. Angular is strongest, but there's less of a differential between angular and succedent than either of those two and cadent.

Swift or increasing in Light are descriptive of the parties involved. Similarly, the issue of cazimi, combustion, or beams is more a part of the story than an assessment of strength.

The Part of Fortune

Good comes from the Part of Fortune, if it has dignity from its dispositor(s). Figure A-1 shows its method of calculation.

Figure A-1. Methods of calculating the Part of Fortune.

Modern:

Fortuna, Day & Night	= Ascendant + ☽ - ☉
Spirit, Day & Night	= Ascendant + ☉ - ☽

Ancient:

Fortuna, Day	= Ascendant + ☽ - ☉
Fortuna, Night	= Ascendant + ☉ - ☽
Spirit, Night	= Ascendant + ☽ - ☉
Spirit, Day	= Ascendant + ☉ - ☽

The Part of Fortune, being a calculated point, has no essential dignity, apart from that "given" to it by its dispositors. When the dispositors are well dignified, then an aspect of a Significator to the Part of Fortune (points are considered passive; hence, they *do not aspect planets*, although they can receive aspects) provides a material benefit to that Significator.

Antiscia and Contra-antiscia

This technique, which goes back to Hellenistic astrology, involves drawing a line between 0 degrees Cancer and 0 degrees Capricorn. We have just split the zodiac along the axis of the Solstices. Now we wish to examine what degrees of the zodiac are symmetrical with respect to this line. But why should we care?

29 degrees Gemini and one degree Cancer are equal in distance to 0 degrees Cancer – they are each one degree away. The day is longest (by definition) when the Sun is at zero Cancer. The Sun at 29 degrees Gemini and one degree Cancer have days of equal length, and nights of equal length. (When I say equal, I mean within the observational capacity of the ancient Greeks!) Both have days just slightly shorter than the longest possible day. This relationship of having days of equal length is referred to as being *antiscial* to each other, or as being in *Antiscion*.

Various pairs of Signs are related to each other by antiscion as shown in Table A-2.

Table A-2. Antiscial & Contra-antiscial Signs.

Antiscial signs	Contra-antiscial signs
♈ ♍	♈ ♓
♉ ♌	♉ ♒
♊ ♋	♊ ♑
♎ ♓	♎ ♍
♏ ♒	♏ ♌
♐ ♑	♐ ♋

The sign and degree exactly opposite the antiscial degree of a planet is called its *Contra-antiscion*.

Planets in antiscial or contra-antiscial relationship were considered to be related to each other as if they were in aspect: a relationship by antiscion was considered analogous to a conjunction; a contra-antiscial relationship was considered analogous to an opposition. The orb to use is unknown, because none of the sources spelled it out.

Mutual Reception

In an earlier work, I spent an entire chapter on mutual reception.[3] For our purposes here, I want to summarize two concepts; interested readers are referred to my previous work for more detail.

First, the concept that planets in mutual reception somehow "swap positions" (e.g., if the Moon is in Capricorn and Saturn is in Cancer, this can be read as if the Moon were in Cancer and Saturn in Capricorn) can be definitively traced to a modern misunderstanding of an ambiguous translation of Ptolemy. It is simply not true.

Planets in mutual reception retain their own dignities – or lack thereof. What the mutual reception does is guarantee that each of the planets will attempt to come to the aid of the other. How good or how welcome that aid would be is dependent on the intrinsic dignity of the planets involved.

Consider, for example, Mars in Capricorn and Saturn in Cancer in a night chart. This doesn't look quite like a reception at all, but Mars is in Saturn's sign, while Saturn is in Mars' Triplicity. This is a perfectly good reception, but consider the difference from Mars' and Saturn's points of view. Saturn gets help from Mars – Mars in Capricorn exalted, so this is definitely the kind of help that anyone could value. Saturn has a good ally here. But Mars – the help comes from a Saturn in Detriment. This represents the kind of help that maybe Mars would rather do without! But Mars is stuck with it, so now the help becomes a hindrance.

The second major concept concerning receptions is the difference between strong and weak reception. Strong reception is when the dignities used for the reception are Sign, Exaltation, or Triplicity, as with our example above. Weak reception is when the dignities involved are Term and Face. Weak reception can be virtually ignored, because the link is simply not that strong. This, incidentally, illustrates a weakness in the point system of dignity: a planet with dignities by Term and Face ($+2 +1 = +3$) is *not* as strong as a planet in Triplicity ($+3$). There is a bigger gap between the strong and weak dignities, and hence receptions, than there actually is within each of the two groups.

Applying and Separating

It's worth reminding the reader of the importance of distinguishing between applying and separating aspects. This is a concept that can be virtually ignored in Natal, but it is crucial in Horary, mundane, and electional. A separating aspect represents an event in the past. An applying aspect represents an event in the future. It's that simple.

Appendix A Endnotes
1. 1989. Whitford Press: West Chester, PA.
2. 1996. Whitford Press: West Chester, PA.
3. *CAML*, Chapter 11.

B
Glossary

A or AA Data: The reference is to the Rodden Rating system developed by Lois Rodden (1928-2003), and these two particular categories define birth data that is considered accurate. AA data is generally birth certificate, birth record, or a family record. "A" data is quoted from the person, family member or close associate.

Accidental Dignity: This is a mix of conditions, all of which relate to the strength of a planet being increased (or decreased, with accidental debility) because of the planet's placement, apart from its tropical zodiacal position. The kinds of factors in the tables of accidental dignity include: house placement, whether oriental or occidental, in conjunction to fixed stars, aspects to benefics or malefics, closeness to the Sun, and speed. [SEE APPENDIX A]

Air: The element in Hellenistic philosophy that is hot and wet; except cold to the Stoics.

Almuten/Almutem: There are five Essential Dignities for any degree of the zodiac: the rulership (+5), exaltation (+4), triplicity (+3), term (+2), and face (+1). If you take a particular house cusp, find the planet which rules each of the five essential dignities of the position, and assign the points to each planet, then the planet with the highest point value is the Almuten. For example: for 8 Aries 15 in a day chart: Mars is the ruler (+5), the Sun rules the exaltation (+4), the triplicity (+3) and the face (+1) = +8, and Venus the terms (+2): the Sun is Almuten. Arabic sources give the word as "Almutem," but by the 17th Century, the word was consistently being translated and used as "Almuten." See Appendix C for a Table of Dignities.

Almuten of the Profession: This is a compound Almuten, consisting of summing the essential dignity points for the four angles.

Antiscion: "Some of the learned in this Art do hold that the Antiscions of the Planets be equivalent unto a Sextile or a Trine-aspect, especially if they were beneficial Planets; and their Contrantiscions to be of the nature of Quadrate or Opposition. How to know the Antiscions is no more than this; first, know the Antiscions of the signs, which is no more but a sign being equally distant with another from Cancer and Capricorn the two Tropicks; as Gemini hath its Antiscion in Cancer, Taurus in Leo, Aries in Virgo, Pisces in Libra, Aquarius in Scorpio, and Capricorn in Sagittary; for when the Sun is in 1° of Gemini, he is as far from the Tropick point of Cancer as when he is in 29° of Cancer; and in the 5° of Taurus, as when the 25° of Leo, &c.... The Contrantiscion is known thus; look in what sign, degree and minute your Antiscion falls, and your contrantiscion will be in the same degree and minute as your opposite sign to your Antiscion." [Ramesey, 1653, pp 76-77]

Apoklima: A Greek word for the 12th house from a house or sign. So the 12th house is *apoklima* the 1st house, and the 5th house is *apoklima* the 6th house.

Application, "is when two Planets approach each other, either by Body or Aspect; and this may be three several ways: First, when both Planets are direct, for Example, Jupiter in 11 deg. of Aries, and Mars in 9 degrees of Aries, both of them direct; here Mars applies to a conjunction of Jupiter.

"The second is when two Stars are Retrograde, and apply to each other by a Retrograde motion; thus Jupiter in 9 degrees of Aries. Retrograde, and Mars in 11 degrees of the same Sign Retrograde also, here Mars applies to the body of Jupiter by Retrograde motion.

"Thirdly, when one Planet is Retrograde in more degrees of a Sign, and another direct in fewer; as suppose Mars in 12 degrees of Aries Retrograde, and Venus in 10 degrees of Aries, here Mars applies to Venus and Venus applies to Mars, and this kind of application is of great force and efficacy in all manner of Astrological Resolutions; but this must be remembered also, that a Superior Planet cannot apply to an Inferior one, unless he be Retrograde." [Partridge, 1679, p 19]

Beholding: This word has shifted somewhat over time, but it refers to two planets which are either in ptolemaic aspect (conjunction, opposition, trine, square or sextile) or antiscial, or contrantiscial relationship.

The Bendings: The points square the Nodal axis. If a planet square the Nodes is zodiacally between the North Node and the South Node (i.e., start counting at the North Node), then it is at the Northern Bending; if between the South Node and the North Node, it is at the Southern Bending.

Besieging: "This I think needs no Explanation, for every Souldier understands it; as suppose Saturn in 10 deg. Jupiter in 1 deg. and Mars in 13 deg. of Leo; here Jupiter is besieged by Saturn and Mars." [Partridge, 1679, p 22]

Cazimi: "...When a Planet is in the heart of the Sun; that is, not distant from him above 17 min. as Mars in 10 deg. 30 min. of Aries, the Sun in 10 deg. 15 min. of Aries; here Mars is in Cazimi." [Partridge, 1679, p 21] Bonatti adds that the planet must be similarly conjunct in latitude as well as longitude.

Chronocrators: Planets that have a rulership over a particular time interval.

Co-Almuten: When two or three planets have the same points of dignity in a particular degree. **See Almuten.**

Compound Almuten: The almuten of a planet or point is computed by examining the zodiacal degree of the position and calculating the points of the planets that rule that degree. For example, 16 Aries 15 is computed as: Mars +5 points for rulership; Sun +4 points for exaltation; Sun, Jupiter and Saturn each +3 points for Triplicity (this is the Medieval style; the Lilly style would be to only count the in-sect Triplicity ruler), Mercury +2 points for Term, and Sun +1 point for Face. In a compound almuten, multiple points are used, and this computation for a single point is repeated for the zodiacal placement of each position. In the ancient system there is no generic term for this process, only names are given to the particular type of compound almuten, such as Ruler of the Geniture, Killing Planet, Almuten of the Profession, etc.

Combustion: "A Planet is Combust when he is not distant from the Sun 8 deg. 30 min. either before or after him; for Example, Jupiter in 10 deg. of Aries, the Sun in 14 deg. and Mars in 18, here both Jupiter and Mars are Combust; and observe that a Planet going to Combustion is more afflicted than when departing from it." [Partridge, 1679, p 21]

Decans/decanates: The division of each of the zodiacal signs into 3 units of 10° each. The so-called Chaldean decanates are the essential dignity known as the Face.

Epicycle: In the ptolemaic cosmology, epicycles were circular components of a planetary orbit, which were combined to compute retrograde periods.

Essential Dignity: Essential dignity was a system for assessing the strength of a planet by its placement in the zodiac alone. There were five essential dignities: by sign, Exaltation, Triplicity, Term, and Face. A planet with dignity can act or do as it wants, whereas a planet without dignity has difficulty getting from Point A to Point B except by a very circuitous route. [SEE APPENDIX A]

Face: One of the minor dignities, also called Chaldean decanates. The faces are 10° slices of the signs, marked by planetary rulers falling in the sequence known as the Chaldean order. The Face is given +1 point.

Five Degree (5°) Rule: Consider the movement of the planets diurnally. For example, the Sun rises by going from the 1st House to the 12th House. A planet on the 12th House side of the Ascendant may be said to be angular if it is within 5° of the Ascendant: this is the so-called 5° rule. Depending on the source, this may actually entail anywhere from 2° to 7-8°, and whether the House moved into is Angular, Succedent, or Cadent (largest for Angular; smallest for Cadent). Generally, Medieval sources give 7° for angular cusps, 5° for succedent cusps, and 3° for cadent cusps. The five degree rule goes back at least to the early Arabic period.[1]

Handing Over: In Hellenistic astrology, this is the process of when a radix planet passes rulership to a planet in the profection, a system for moving the Ascendant one sign per year or other time interval. Thus, if the natal ascendant is in Cancer, then the Moon (ruling Cancer) hands over to the Sun (ruling Leo) after the first year of life.

Hyleg: The Giver of Life; the planet or point computed which is necessary for length of life calculations. Also called the Apheta or Prorogator.

Hylegical points: Those points which are commonly computed to be the Hyleg: the Sun, Moon, Part of Fortune, and Ascendant.

Imbecilic: a planet retrograde or combust.

Interrogatory Astrology: Those branches of astrology that relate to the answering of questions and interpreting events: horary, electional, and event interpretation.

Joys: This word was used two ways, which can lead to some confusion. One use was as a synonym for "exaltation." The second was an indicator of which house would be the top choice for a given planet. The joys by house are: Mercury = 1st House, Moon = 3rd House, Venus = 5th House, Mars = 6th House, Sun = 9th House, Jupiter = 11th House, and Saturn = 12th House.

Lord of the Year: A system for assigning a primary ruler for an Aries Ingress or solar return. The methods of computation vary.

Mixed Reception: Most mutual receptions are seen between essential dignity of the same type, as each planet is in the other's rulership. A mixed reception occurs when the type of essential dignity is different, as planet A is in planet B's exaltation, and planet B is in planet A's Triplicity.

Occidental: "When a Planet or Star sets after the Sun is down." [Partridge, 1679, p 22]

Oriental: "When a Planet riseth before the Sun." [Partridge, 1679, p 22]

Partile: Within the same degree number. Notice that this is not an orb size. The Moon at 6 Leo 01 is partile Mars at 6 Leo 59, while the Moon in the same place, and Mars at 5 Leo 59 is within a degree, but not partile. Any aspect may be called either partile, or plactic, for those that are not partile.

Peregrine: "A Planet is Peregrine when he is in a Sign and degree where he hath no Essential dignity, as Mars in 26 degrees of Gemini is Peregrine, because he hath no dignity there, &c." [Partridge, 1679, p 21]

Planets on the Same Journey: One planet ruling two houses.

Profections: A system for moving the chart one house per year. Also used for smaller subdivisions of time.

Reception "When two Planets are in each other's dignities, as the Sun in Aries, and Mars in Leo, here is a Reception by House, it may be also by Exaltation, Triplicity, Term and Face." [Partridge, 1679, p 20-21]

Rendering: When a dispositor of an imbecilic planet also aspects it; and the dispositor is also dignified.

Sect: Whether diurnal or nocturnal. The primary sect of a chart is whether the chart itself is by day or night. A night chart has the Sun posited in the 1st through 6th Houses; a day chart has the Sun in the 12th through 7th Houses: right on the Ascendant-Descendant is anyone's guess! In addition, planets were considered to have intrinsic sect (Sun, Jupiter and Saturn: diurnal; Moon, Venus and Mars: nocturnal; Mercury: mixed); signs had intrinsic sect (Masculine = diurnal, Feminine = nocturnal), and planets had sect placement, according to whether they were diurnally or nocturnally placed in the chart in question.

Sect Light: The Sun, for a day chart; the Moon for a night chart.

Separation: "When two Planets have been in Conjunction or Aspect and are going from it as Jupiter in 6 degrees of Aries and Mars in 7 degrees; here Mars separates himself from Jupiter; but yet he is not quite separated from him till they are distant from each other 8 degrees 30 minutes, which is the moiety of both their Orbs; what their Orbs and Aspects are." [Partridge, 1679, p 19-20]

Sidereal year: Based on the return of the Sun to a particular star position.

Siting stones: A physical method for computing units of time in the solar cycle, using the return of the Sun to the same place from year to year

Term: One of the five essential dignities. The Term ruler was said to be "of the body" of that planet, so if the Ascendant is in the Terms of Saturn, it would represent a person serious, older, in a saturnine profession, etc. - primarily physical or outward appearance. The Term was given +2 points, and is considered a minor dignity.

Triplicity: One of the five essential dignities. Triplicities run by element, so there is one set of rulers for the fire signs, another for earth, etc. Triplicity is worth +3 points on the scale of essential dignities. The trick is that there are three different systems. Two of them utilize a day, night, and mixed ruler; the third, which was in common use by English astrologers in the 17th Century, used only day and night. Among the most obvious differences between the two that will be seen in this work is Jupiter being the mixed Triplicity ruler of Air: thus, for a year with Jupiter In Aquarius, Jupiter will often be the most dignified planet, and will virtually always be a contender for use because of the dignity.

Tropical Year: based on the definition of the beginning of Spring as a particular zodiacal degree, such as 0 Aries.

Under the Sun's Beams: "a Planet is said to be under the Sun's beams, till he is full 17 degrees distant from him." [Partridge, 1679, p 21]

Via Combusta: zone from 15 Libra to 15 Scorpio. Considered a dangerous area of the sky.

Void of Course: "is when a Planet is separated from one, and doth not apply to any other while he is in that Sign, and it is most observable in the Moon." [Partridge, 1679, p 21]

Glossary Endnote

1. Dykes, Benjamin N. *Persian Nativities. Volume I: Masha'allah and Abu 'Ali.* Minneapolis, MN: Cazimi Press, 2009, p. 15, from Māshā'Allāh: *The Book of Aristotle.*

C

Table of Essential Dignities*

	Ruler	Exalt.	Triplicity			Terms					Faces		
			Day	Night	Mix†						0-10	10-20	20-30
♈	♂ D	☉ 19	☉	♃	♄	0 ♃ 6	6 ♀ 14	14 ☿ 21	21 ♂ 26	26 ♄ 30	♂	☉	♀
♉	♀ N	☽ 3	♀	☽	♂	0 ♀ 8	8 ☿ 15	15 ♃ 22	22 ♄ 26	26 ♂ 30	☿	☽	♄
♊	☿ D	☊ 3	♄	☿	♃	0 ☿ 7	7 ♃ 14	14 ♀ 21	21 ♄ 25	25 ♂ 30	♃	♂	☉
♋	☽ DN	♃ 15	♀**	♂	☽	0 ♂ 6	6 ♃ 13	13 ☿ 20	20 ♀ 27	27 ♄ 30	♀	☿	☽
♌	☉ DN		☉	♃	♄	0 ♄ 6	6 ☿ 13	13 ♀ 19	19 ♃ 25	25 ♂ 30	♄	♃	♂
♍	☿ N	☿ 15	♀	☽	♂	0 ☿ 7	7 ♀ 13	13 ♃ 18	18 ♄ 24	24 ♂ 30	☉	♀	☿
♎	♀ D	♄ 21	♄	☿	♃	0 ♄ 6	6 ♀ 11	11 ♃ 19	19 ☿ 24	24 ♂ 30	☽	♄	♃
♏	♂ N		♀**	♂	☽	0 ♂ 6	6 ♃ 14	14 ♀ 21	21 ☿ 27	27 ♄ 30	♂	☉	♀
♐	♃ D	☋ 3	☉	♃	♄	0 ♃ 8	8 ♀ 14	14 ☿ 19	19 ♄ 25	25 ♂ 30	☿	☽	♄
♑	♄ N	♂ 28	♀	☽	♂	0 ♀ 6	6 ☿ 12	12 ♃ 19	19 ♂ 25	25 ♄ 30	♃	♂	☉
♒	♄ D		♄	☿	♃	0 ♄ 6	6 ☿ 12	12 ♀ 20	20 ♃ 25	25 ♂ 30	♀	☿	☽
♓	♃ N	♀ 27	♀**	♂	☽	0 ♀ 8	8 ♃ 14	14 ☿ 20	20 ♂ 26	26 ♄ 30	♄	♃	♂

† Also called Participating Triplicity
* Dorothean Triplicities and so-called Ptolemaic or Chaldean Terms.
** Lilly gives both day and night in the water signs to Mars.
Font used is ET AStro, compliments of Esoteric Tehnologies Pty, Ltd

D

Lifetime Events for Individuals Cited

Aldrin, Buzz
Data: 20 January 1930, 2:17 pm EST, Glen Ridge NJ. Quoted BC/BR. Rodden Rating: AA.
Age 21: graduated third in class at West Point, June 1951 **[Chapter 7]**
Age 22: transferred to combat flight duty in Korean War, flying 66 combat missions **[Chapter 4]**
Age 24: Marriage to Joan 29 December 1954 **[Chapter 3]**
Age 36: Gemini 12 pilot, launched 11 November 1966
Age 38: mother apparently committed suicide with an overdose **[Chapter 11]**
Age 39: Apollo 11 mission to the Moon, launched 16 July 1969, 9:32 am, Cape Canaveral, FL Landed 20 July 1969 4:17 pm EDT. Stepped out 10:56 pm EDT. **[Chapter 4]**
Age 40: extra-marital affair
Age 41: began position as Commandant, USAF Test Pilot School at Edwards Air Force Base; treated for depression October 1971 **[Chapter 8]**
Age 42: retired from Air Force 1 March 1972; moved to California 3 June 1972
Age 43: book, *Return to Earth*, published Fall 1973
Age 44: father died, 28 December 1974
Age 45: divorced; began alcoholism treatment 7 August 1975; second marriage 31 December 1975 **[Chapters 3, 9]**
Age 47: divorced; July 1977 went to work as a Cadillac salesman
Age 48: October 1978: stopped drinking **[Chapter 9]**
Age 55: met future wife Lois Driggs, 4 October 1985
Age 58: third marriage to Lois Driggs, 14 February 1988 **[Chapter 3]**
Age 59: wife Lois's family savings and loan business seized by government; stock value worthless overnight; Lois worked to develop the business side so Buzz could go on the speaking circuit **[Chapter 4]**
Age 66: sci-fi book, *Encounter with Tiber*, published 1996 (co-author); visited the site of the *Titanic* in a small submarine
Age 68: popularizing Spaceshare concept of civilian space travel, and Starbooster company to develop rocket and other designs
Age 79: book, *Magnificent Desolation*, published Jun 2009
Age 81: Filed for divorce, 2011 **[Chapter 3]**

Angelou, Maya
Data: 4 April 1928, 2:10 pm CST, St. Louis, MO. Quoted BC/BR. Rodden Rating: AA.
Age 3: her parents end marriage: she and brother sent to Stamps, Arkansas to paternal grandparents
Age 7: father takes both children back to live with her mother in St. Louis, where Maya was raped by a friend of her mother's. When the rapist was killed after the trial by persons unknown, she barely spoke for six years, feeling responsible. Both children returned to Stamps. **[Chapter 6]**
Age 14: she and brother moved to San Francisco to live with mother (1942)
Age 15: stabbed by father's girlfriend in a quarrel (1943)
Age 17: gives birth to boy who was the product of a one-night stand (1945) **[Chapter 5]**
Age 26: principal dancer in *Porgy and Bess* European touring company (1955)
Age 32: co-organizer, Cultural association for Women of African Heritage (CAWAH) (January 1961)

Age 33: starred as the White Queen in Jean Genet's *The Blacks* Off-Broadway (opened October 1961)

Age 34: moved to Ghana (Summer, 1962) **[Chapter 6]**

Age 36: returned to USA to work with Malcolm X with the Organization of Afro-American Unity (February 1965). Malcolm X assassinated 21 February 1965

Birthday Age 40: she had been asked by Martin Luther King to organize Poor People March on Washington, and she had said she would begin work after her birthday - King was assassinated on her birthday; wrote ten-part series on NET (PBS), *Blacks, Blues, Black!* Asked by a publisher to begin writing her autobiography

Age 44: starred in *Look Away* on Broadway (premiered 7 Jan 1973); received Tony nomination

Age 45: married Paul de Feu (December 1973)

Age 48: Played Ngo Buto in miniseries *Roots* (premiered 23 January 1977); received Emmy nomination

Age 52-53: Divorced 1981

Age 53: accepted Reynolds Professorship at Wake Forest University in Winston-Salem, NC, which became a lifetime endowed position

Age 64: became first poet to participate in presidential inauguration since Robert Frost in 1961 (20 January 1993)

Age 70: directed *Down the Delta* (1998)

Age 72: awarded Presidential Medal of Freedom (February 2011) **[Chapter 8]**

Austen, Jane

Data: 16 December 1775, 11:45 pm LMT, Steveston, England. From memory: Rodden Rating: A.

Age 7: boarding school in Oxford, which she loathed, later in the year to be relocated to Southhampton, where she and her sister contracted what was probably typhus

Age 9: attended Abbey School in Reading, over the Summer; stayed until end of 1786

Age 12: began writing

Age 15: first novel written; *History of England* (a satire) completed 26 November 1791

Age 19: given a writing desk by her father for her birthday, her first literary effort was to create the scandalous character of *Lady Susan*,

Age 20: brief flirtation with Thomas Lefroy, cut off by his family, December 1795

Age 21: completed what would become *Pride and Prejudice*, August 1797

Age 22: revised *Sense and Sensibility*, mid 1798; began *Northanger Abbey*

Age 25: family moved to Bath, announced December 1800; completed May 1801 **[Chapter 6]**

Age 26: received proposal of marriage; first accepted and then declined, early December 1802

Age 29: father died 21 January 1805, 10:20 pm, Bath **[Chapter 11]**

Age 33: Jane, sister Cassandra and her mother move to Chawton July 1809, to a cottage owned by one of Jane's brothers **[Chapter 6]**

Age 35: *Sense and Sensibility* published, late October 1811; Jane received £100 from the first edition

Age 37: *Pride and Prejudice* published, January 1813. Jane received an advance of £110 for the publication rights.

Age 38: writing *Emma*; *Mansfield Park* published, May 1814, which was freshly written (*Sense and Sensibility* and *Pride and Prejudice* had been written years before)

Age 40: *Emma* published December 1815, and *Mansfield Park* second edition by different publisher. Proceeds of each offset each other as 2nd edition *Mansfield Park* was not successful; began writing *The Elliotts*, completed 16 August 1816, which was posthumously published under the title *Persuasion*.

Age 41: died 18 June 1817, 4:30 am, Winchester **[Chapter 11]**

Curie, Marie

Data: 7 November 1867, 10:36 am, Warsaw, Poland. Quoted BC/BR. Rodden Rating: AA.

Age 6: oldest sister Zosia died of typhus at age 14, 31 January 1874

Age 10: mother died of tuberculosis, 9 May 1878; entered Russian-speaking gymnasium, Fall 1878

Age 15: finished first in her class at gymnasium, 12 June 1883

Age 23: October 1891, arrived in Paris to begin study the the Sorbonne after tutoring, governess jobs, and at least one failed romance **[Chapter 7]**

Age 25: Spring 1893: license (degree) in physics, ranking first **[Chapter 7]**

Age 26: Spring 1894: license (degree) in mathematics, ranking second; met Pierre Curie **[Chapters 3, 7]**

Age 27: married Pierre Curie, 26 July 1895

Age 29: daughter Irène born 12 September 1897; Pierre's mother died 2 weeks later; Pierre's father then came to live with them

Age 30: began work on "Bequerel rays" as she began work on her doctorate; discovered polonium and reported on it, using the word "radioactivity" for the first time, July 1898

Age 31: began work on finding second element 11 November 1898, where within a month they had the first evidence for radium, which Marie then spent 3 years isolating in sufficient quantity to fully analyze chemically

Age 32: named first female faculty member of École normale supérieure at Sèvres **[Chapter 4]**

Age 34: father died, 14 May 1902; established atomic weight of radium as 225, July 1902

Age 35: received doctorate June 1903; miscarried August 1903, and ill much of the rest of the year, possibly with anemia [Chapter 7]

Age 36: won Nobel Prize along with Pierre and Bequerel [Chapter 8]

Age 37: daughter Eve born 6 December 1904

Age 38: husband Pierre died 19 April 1906. She continued and even expanded their laboratory, but after a break for mourning [Chapters 3, 4]

Age 42: begins sexual affair with Paul Langevin, an old friend of Pierre's, July 1910

Age 43: rejected by the Academy of Science for membership 24 January 1911; story goes public about her affair, 4 November 1911

Age 44: received Nobel Prize in Chemistry; announced by Reuters on her birthday, 7 November 1911; hospitalized 29 December 1911 for a kidney ailment [Chapter 8]

Age 46: her radium standard was registered with the Bureau of Weights and Measures as the international standard

Age 47: volunteered in medical radiography during World War I

Age 53: had developed cataracts, about 1920; by this time, her laboratories were expanding as she arranged private funding

Age 54: inducted into the Academy of Medicine, February 1922

Age 66: died, of aplastic anemia, 4 July 1934

Fleming, Peggy

Data: 27 July 1948, 3:39 pm PDT, San Jose, CA. Quoted BC/BR. Rodden Rating: AA.

Age 9: began skating (1957)

Age 11: moved to Pasadena, CA

Age 12: coach died on Sabena crash, which killed US Olympic skating team (1961)

Age 15: US Champion (1964)

Age 16: US Champion and World Bronze (1965)

Age 17: US Champion and World Champion (1966); father died [Chapters 8, 11]

Age 18: US Champion and World Champion (1967) [Chapter 8]

Age 19: US Champion, World and Olympic Gold Medalist; turned pro (1968) [Chapter 8]

Age 21: married 13 June 1970

Age 28: son Andy 30 January 1977 [Chapter 5]

Age 40: son Todd 18 September 1988 [Chapter 5]

Age 43: mother died (1992)

Age 48: Coach Carlo Fassi died at World Championships (1997)

Age 49: diagnosed with and treated for breast cancer (operation 12 February 1998, midnight, Los Gatos, CA) [See also Traditional Medical Astrology, pp 249-251.]

Godwin Shelley, Mary

Data: 30 August 1797, 11:20 pm, London, England. Quoted BC/BR. Rodden Rating: AA.

Age 0: Mother (Mary Wollstonecraft) died 11 days after giving birth to Mary

Age 4: father remarried, Mary Jane Clairmont (21 December 1801)

Age 5: brother William Jr born (28 March 1803)

Age 14: sent to Scotland by father, June 1812

Age 15: returned to London from Scotland, June 1813

Age 16: met Percy March 1814; reconnected with Shelley 5 May 1814, declared her love 26 June 1814, then ran away with Percy Shelley at dawn (5 am) 28 July 1814, accompanied by half-sister Claire Clairmont; remained on Continent 6 weeks before returning, penniless [Chapter 3]

Age 17: miscarried, 22 February 1815, back in England; became pregnant again almost immediately

Age 18: son William born 24 January 1816; second trip to Switzerland with Percy and Claire to meet Byron; June was the time of the genesis of Frankenstein [Chapter 5]

Age 19: half-sister Fanny Imlay committed suicide with laudanum, 10 October 1816; Percy and Mary married 30 December 1816 [Chapter 3]

Age 20: daughter, Clara, 2 September 1817; Frankenstein published anonymously 1 January 1818; left for Italy 12 March 1818

Age 21: daughter Clara died September 1818 in Venice; son William died June 1819 in Rome

Age 22: son Percy Florence born 12 November 1819; writing extremely productive in this time

Age 24: miscarried, with considerable blood loss 16 June 1822; Percy drowned sailing off coast of Livorno on a journey begun 8 July 1822 [Chapters 3, 5, 11]

Age 25: Valperga published 19 February 1823; left Genoa for England 23 July 1823; retains custody of son Percy Florence, but with allowance and economic control by husband's father Timothy, who detested Mary, her husband, and their ideas – and this clout was used to block Mary from publishing posthumous works of Percy's; Mary continued writing, but published anonymously as long as Timothy was alive [Chapter 6]

Age 28: The Last Man published 23 January 1826: not a commercial success, but considered an early work of science fiction

Age 29: Percy's older son Charles by Harriet died 14 September 1826, making Percy Florence the heir to the Shelley fortune, and restoring Mary's allowance from Timothy; began publishing book reviews, still anonymously

Age 35: half brother William Godwin Jr. Died of cholera, September 1832

Age 38: father William Godwin died just after 7 pm 7 April 1836, London [Chapter 11]

Age 39: Faulkner published February 1837

Age 42: Shelley's poems published under Mary's editorship, November 1839
Age 46: Father-in-law Sir Timothy Shelley dies, 24 April 1844, with her son as heir, and allowing her to live comfortably from then on
Age 53: died 1 February 1851, probably of a brain tumor **[Chapter 11]**

Hamill, Dorothy

Data: 26 July 1956, 9:18 pm CST Chicago, IL. Quoted BC/BR. Rodden Rating: AA.
Age 0: family moved from Chicago to Greenwich, CT
Age 8: began skating
Age 12: US Novice Champion (1969)
Age 15: US 4ᵗʰ (1972)
Age 16: US Silver (1973)
Age 17: US Champion and World Silver (1974) **[Chapter 8]**
Age 18: US Champion and World Silver (1975) **[Chapter 8]**
Age 19: US Champion, Olympics Champion and World Champion (1976) **[Chapter 8]**
Age 23: bought own house in Pacific Palisades section of Los Angeles (1980)
Age 25: mother treated for breast cancer; marriage to Dean Martin 8 January 1982, Los Angeles **[Chapter 3]**
Age 26: major theft of jewelry ($300,000) at a hotel 23 December 1982 **[Chapter 10]**; friend Karen Carpenter died 4 February 1983
Age 27: Won Emmy for *Romeo and Juliet*; divorce 1 June 1984 **[Chapter 3]**
Age 30: 2ⁿᵈ marriage to Kenneth Forsythe 5 March 1987, sunset, Anchorage, Alaska; first husband Dean Paul Martin dies in a plane crash 21 March 1987 **[Chapters 3, 11]**
Age 32: daughter Alexandra born September 1988 **[Chapter 5]**
Age 36: bought Ice Capades with husband and one other investor, Spring 1993 **[Chapter 4]**
Age 37: broke rib, 5 January 1994 **[Chapter 9]**
Age 38: announced retirement 18 December 1994; sold Ice Capades to Family Channel February 1995 **[Chapter 4]**
Age 39: announced separation 21 August 1995; filed for bankruptcy 30 March 1996 **[Chapter 3, 4]**
Age 40: fought for and received custody of daughter; returned to professional skating
Age 42: father died, September 1998; injury on 19 September 1998 with bruised collarbone, ultimately resulting in diagnosis of osteoarthritis; joined Champions on Ice **[Chapter 9]**
Age 51: diagnosed and treated for breast cancer
Age 53: 3ʳᵈ marriage to John MacColl, 21 November 2009, Baltimore, MD **[Chapter 3]**

Hamilton, Scott

Data: 28 August 1958, 9:00 am EST, Toledo, OH. From memory. Rodden Rating: A. Note: Scott was adopted.
Age 2: stopped growing. Began round of interminable medical examinations, special diets, etc. [See also *Traditional Medical Astrology*, pp 246-249.]
Age 9: starts skating; resumes normal diet; growth problem goes away without ever being diagnosed
Age 18: adopted mother died of cancer, and maternal grandfather died three months later
Age 19: US Bronze; 11ᵗʰ in Worlds (1ˢᵗ senior placement, 1978)
Age 21: US Bronze; 5ᵗʰ in Olympics (1980)
Age 22: US Champion and World Champion (1981) **[Chapter 8]**
Age 23: US Champion and World Champion (1982) **[Chapter 8]**
Age 24: US Champion and World Champion (1983) **[Chapter 8]**
Age 25: US Champion, World and Olympic Gold Medalist; turned pro (1984) **[Chapter 8]**
Age 34: mastered the back flip **[Chapter 10]**; maternal grandmother died (1993)
Age 35: father died during Olympics (1994) **[Chapter 11]**
Age 38: diagnosed and treated for testicular cancer (1997). Operation: 24 June 1997, 6:30 am, Cleveland, OH)
Age 44: married
Age 45: child, Aidan, 16 September 2003 **[Chapter 9]**
Age 46: diagnosed and treated for non-cancerous brain tumor near pituitary, November 2004 **[Chapter 9]**
Age 49: child, Maxx, 21 January 2008
Age 51: surgery for benign brain tumor **[Chapter 9]**
Age 52: surgery to repair artery apparently nicked in brain tumor surgery **[Chapter 9]**

King, Jr., Martin Luther

Data: 15 January 1929, 12:00 pm CST, Atlanta, GA. From memory. Rodden Rating: A
Age 12: Grandmother died; family moved within Atlanta, 18 May 1941
Age 19: ordained minister 25 February 1948; graduated B.A., Morehouse College 8 June 1948 **[Chapter 7]**
Age 22: received Bachelor of Divinity, Crozer Seminary 8 May 1951
Age 23: meets Coretta Scott, January 1952
Age 24: married 18 June 1953, Marion, AL
Age 25: accepts pastorship at Dexter Avenue Baptist Church in Montgomery, AL (officially installed 31 October 1954) **[Chapter 7]**
Age 26: received doctorate in systematic theology, Boston University School of Theology, 5 June 1955; daughter Yolanda born 17 November; elected head

of Montgomery Improvement Association, 5 December 1955 after Rosa Parks was arrested **[Chapter 7]**

Age 27: bus boycott led to conviction under an anti-boycott statute; the US Supreme Court declared the bus segregation laws unconstitutional 13 November 1956

Age 28: became head of Southern Leaders Conference (became SCLC), 14 Feb 1957; son Martin Luther King III born, 23 Oct 1957

Age 29: stabbed in Harlem, 20 September 1958

Age 31: moved to Atlanta, 1 February 1960; Greensboro, NC lunch counter sit-in begins **[Chapter 6]**

Age 32: son Dexter Scott born 30 January 1961; Albany Movement May-August

Age 34: daughter Bernice Albertine born, 28 March 1963; April - September: Birmingham campaign; "I have a dream" speech at the March on Washington, 28 August 1963 **[Chapter 10]**

Age 35: Civil Rights Act of 1964 signed 2 July; received Nobel Peace prize 10 December 1964 **[Chapter 8]**

Age 36: Selma, AL campaign. Selma to Montgomery March concludes with speech by King, 25 March 1965; federal Voting Rights Act passed 1965; Watts riots, Los Angeles, Summer 1965; Chicago campaign started

Age 37: Stokely Carmichael coins the expression "Black Power" during the continuation of James Meredith's march through Mississippi, as the Black movement splits into subgroups with different priorities, June 1966 **[Chapter 8]**

Age 38: gave first anti-[Vietnam]-war speech, 4 April 1967, although he had earlier expressed specific anti-war views, 1967; launched Poor People's Campaign, 4 December 1967

Age 39: assassinated while in Memphis supporting a sanitation strike, 4 April 1968

Kwan, Michelle

Data: 7 July 1980, 10:05 am PDT, Los Angeles, CA. Quoted BC/BR. Rodden Rating: AA. Note that an earlier chart with a different time and Torrance, CA as the birth location is extant.

Age 13: US Silver; finished 8th at Worlds, in her first appearance there; preserving slots for American women for the following year (1994)

Age 15: US Champion and World Champion (1996) **[Chapter 8]**

Age 17: US Champion, Olympic Silver, and World Champion (1998); suffered stress fracture and toe injury during the 1997-1998 season **[Chapter 8]**

Age 18: US Champion and World Silver (1999) **[Chapter 8]**

Age 19: US Champion and World Champion (2000) **[Chapter 8]**

Age 20: US Champion and World Champion (2001) **[Chapter 8]**

Age 21: US Champion and Olympic Bronze (2002) **[Chapter 8]**

Age 22: US Champion (2003) **[Chapter 8]**

Age 23: US Champion (2004) **[Chapter 8]**

Age 24: US Champion (2005) **[Chapter 8]**

Age 25: hip and abdominal injuries precluded her quest for the 2006 Olympics **[Chapters 8, 9]**

Age 26: arthroscopic surgery to repair labrum (hip) injury (2006) **[Chapter 9]**

Age 28: received B.A. Degree **[Chapter 7]**

Lacoste, René

Data: 2 July 1904, 4:51 am GMT, Paris, France. Quoted BC/BR. Rodden Rating: AA

Age 15: takes up tennis

Age 19: runner-up at Wimbledon

Age 20: winner of French Open and Wimbledon, singles and doubles (1925), before birthday); ranked Number 1 in the World

Age 22: winner of US Open, French Open (1927); ranked Number 1 in the World

Age 23: winner of US Open, Wimbledon (1928), met future wife (1927)

Age 24: winner of French Open (1929); retired for health reasons

Age 26: oldest son Bernard born 22 June 1931

Age 29: founded clothing company **[Chapter 4]**

Age 40: daughter Catherine born 27 June 1945

Age 41: death of mother, Marie-Madelaine Larrieulet

Age 47: clothing company introduced color shirts, which his son said was what really increased sales

Age 58-59: patents steel tennis racquet, and turns the clothing firm over to his son Bernard to run **[Chapter 10]**

Age 92: died **[Chapter 11]**

Pasteur, Louis

Data: 27 December 1822, 2:00 am, Dole, France. Quoted BC/BR. Rodden Rating: AA

Age 3: moved to Marnoz, when grandmother gave mother her house, 1826

Age 15: went to Paris to study at collège Saint-Louis - lasted less than one term **[Chapter 7]**

Age 17: Baccalauréat in Letters (Arts), August 1840; continued in October for science, with job as substitute teacher **[Chapter 7]**

Age 18: failed exam for Baccalauréat August 1841; had to take another year **[Chapter 7]**

Age 19: passed exam for Baccalauréat in science August 1842; returned to entrance exam for École normale and passed the first test, but decided on another year of studying before taking the second set

Age 20: admitted to École normale in Paris **[Chapter 7]**

Age 23: September 1846, remained at École normale as a graduate assistant after passing the physics exam **[Chapter 7]**

Age 24: August 1847: defended his thesis for his Doctorate of Science **[Chapter 7]**

Age 25: Mother died of stroke, 21 May 1848; discovered isomer of tartaric acid using crystallography in part. This was a major career moment. Only job he could get in Autumn was in Dijon in a secondary school. **[Chapter 11]**

Age 26: accepted acting professorship of chemistry in Strasbourg, January 1849. Married 29 May 1849 to Marie Laurent, the daughter of the Rector of the University of Strasbourg.**[Chapter 6]**

Age 27: daughter Jeanne born April 1850

Age 28: son born 8 November 1851

Age 29, toured German and Italian industrial facilities to discover issues related to tartaric acid production, Summer 1852

Age 30, won 1,500 franc prize from Society of Pharmacy of Paris for preparing racemic acid from tartaric acid; named Chevalier de la Légion d'honneur; daughter Cécile born 1 October 1853 **[Chapter 8]**

Age 31: promoted to Professor of Chemistry and Dean of Faculty of Sciences at Lille, September 1854

Age 34: discovered lactic acid yeast fermentation, published April 1857; rejected for membership in the Academy of Sciences; promoted to administrator and director of scientific studies at École normale in Paris, October 1857 **[Chapters 6, 8, 10]**

Age 35: daughter Marie-Louise born, 19 July 1858

Age 36: awarded prize for experimental physiology by Academy of Sciences, 1859; daughter Jeanne died of typhoid, 10 September 1859 7 pm Arbois **[Chapter 8]**

Age 37: published monograph on alcoholic fermentation, establishing that yeast did the fermentation, not that fermentation brought about the yeast, 1860

Age 38: developed experiments which refuted spontaneous generation of microbes

Age 39: elected to the Academy of Sciences to succeed a mentor who had died, 8 December 1862; earlier in the year, received their Alhumbert Prize for his spontaneous generation work, which brought 2500 francs **[Chapter 8]**

Age 40: daughter Camille born, July 1863; appointed to a chair at École des Beaux-Arts

Age 42: father died 15 June 1865; daughter Camille died of a liver tumor, 11 September 1865

Age 43: daughter Cécile died of typhoid, 23 May 1866; volume *Etudes sur le vin* published

Age 44: appointed professor at the Sorbonne, 24 October 1867, but the French emperor created a laboratory of physiological chemistry for him, relieving him of previous administrative and teaching duties

Age 45: attack of hemiplagia (stroke), 19 October 1868. Didn't walk again until

following January, but remained conscious throughout. **[Chapter 9]**

Age 47: appointed to the Senate 27 July 1870 for his work on silkworm parasites

Age 57: eldest sister Virginie died 30 July 1880; discovered that osteomyelitis was caused by staphylococcus

Age 58: Pasteur succeeds Littré to seat in Académie française, 1881; outdoor experiment confirms Pasteur's attenuation protocols for anthrax vaccination of sheep **[Chapter 8]**

Age 62: treats Joseph Meister with attenuated rabies 6 July 1885 - 1st successful treatment for rabies

Age 64: Institute Pasteur begun construction after a subscription had been raised of 2.5 million francs, as a research institute and rabies treatment facility, 1887; second stroke with aphasia 23 October 1887 morning

Age 65: Institut Pasteur officially opens, 14 November 1888 12:30 pm **[Chapter 4]**

Age 71: suffered possibly another stroke, but bedridden for three months, 1 November 1894 **[Chapter 9]**

Age 72: died 28 September 1895, 4:20 pm, after another stroke with aphasia

Roosevelt, Eleanor
Data: 11 October 1884, 11:00 am, New York, NY. BC/BR in hand. Rodden Rating: AA

Age 2, survived shipwreck of *Britannic* **[Chapter 11]**

Age 4: brother, Elliott Jr. born; died at age 3, scarlet fever and diphtheria

Age 6: brother, Hall Roosevelt born, 28 June 1891

Age 8: Mother died, 7 December 1892, diphtheria **[Chapter 11]**

Age 9: Father died, 13 August 1894 **[Chapter 11]**

Age 15: attended Allenswood finishing school outside London

Age 20: Marriage, 17 March 1905 **[Chapter 3]**

Age 21: Child, Anna, born 3 May 1906 **[Chapter 5]**

Age 23: Child, James, born, 23 December 1907 **[Chapter 5]**

Age 24: Child, Franklin Jr., born March 1909; dies 7 months later of flu **[Chapter 5]**

Age 25: Child, Elliott, born, 23 September 1910

Age 26: moved to Albany (FDR elected State Senator) 1 January 1911 **[Chapter 6]**

Age 30: Child, Franklin Jr., born 17 August 1914

Age 30-31: hired Lucy Mercer as her personal secretary: Lucy would become FDR's mistress

Age 31: Child, John, born, 13 March 1916

Age 33: discovers FDR's affair with Lucy Mercer, September 1918. Sexual relations cease. **[Chapter 3]**

Age 36: Husband contracts polio, diagnosed 25 August 1921 **[Chapter 9]**

Age 37: begins rise into New York State Democratic Party politics, advocating minimum wages, shorter work weak, and health insurance
Age 41: Arrested for picketing at a women's labor strike, 1926 **[Chapter 10]**
Age 42: Resigned from her Democratic Party posts when FDR elected New York governor
Age 43: Meets Lorena Hickock, September 1928
Age 48: Husband elected President, 1932; relationship with Hickock deepens, probably becoming sexual around 30 October 1932[1] **[Chapter 3]**
Age 52: Keynote speaker at No-Foreign-War Crusade, 1937
Age 54: Resigns from Daughters of the American Revolution over discriminatory practices, 1939 **[Chapter 10]**
Age 56: Brother Hall died 25 September 1941, alcoholism
Age 60: Husband died, 12 April 1945
Age 61: Elected Chairperson of UN Commission on Human Rights, 29 April 1946. Served until Eisenhower Administration
Age 76: appointed UN delegate, 1961
Age 78: died 7 November 1962, 6:15 pm, New York, tuberculosis, which she had contracted in her teens **[Chapter 11]**

Roosevelt, Franklin

Data: 30 January 1882, 8:45 pm, Hyde Park, NY. BC/BR in hand. Rodden Rating: AA
Age 18: graduated Groton Spring 1900; enrolled at Harvard; Father died, 8 December 1900
Age 21: became engaged to Eleanor, November 1903
Age 23: married 17 March 1905, with Eleanor's Uncle Theodore, then President, giving her away
Age 28: elected State Senator, first election won, November 1910
Age 30: typhoid recurrence
Age 31: appointed Assistant Secretary of the Navy; met Lucy Mercer
Age 32: lost nomination for (federal) Senate seat in New York
Age 36: Eleanor discovered his infidelity with Lucy
Age 38: nominated for vice president, lost; November 1920
Age 39: contracted polio, Summer 1921
Age 46: elected governor of New York, November 1928
Age 48: re-elected governor by a landslide, November 1930
Age 50: elected president of the USA, November 1932
Age 51: took office; closed banks in a bank holiday to stabilize the industry; gained control from Congress to cut pensions, pass currency reform, pass public job creation, Securities Act; 1933
Age 52: congressional by-year election returns greater majority for Democrats in confirmation of his New Deal policies, 1934

Age 53: Supreme Court declares key legislation in New Deal unconstitutional, 1935
Age 54: re-elected president in a landslide, November 1936
Age 56: Republicans and conservative Democrats gain seats, but Democrats maintain control of Congress, November 1938
Age 58: FDR is the first president to run for and win a third term in office, November 1940
Age 59: Pearl Harbor brings the USA into World War II, 7 December 1941
Age 60: Democrats lost seats, but not their majority, in the congressional elections, November 1942
Age 62: re-elected to 4th term as president, November 1944
Age 63: died 12 April 1945, Warm Springs, GA 3:35 pm.

Roosevelt, Theodore

Data: 27 October 1858, 7:45 pm, New York, NY. Biography. Rodden Rating: B[2]
Age 19: met his first wife this year **[Chapter 3]**; father died 9 February 1878
Age 21: became engaged to Alice Lee, January 1880
Age 22: married Alice Lee on his birthday, 1880; enrolled in Columbia Law School (never matriculated)
Age 23: he entered the New York State Assembly as its youngest member, January 1882
Age 25: death of *both* wife and mother on February 14, 1884 **[Chapter 11]**; "retires" to North Dakota cattle ranching
Age 28: loses election for mayor of New York, November 1886; married Edith Carrow 2 December 1886 in London; suffered major financial loss on his North Dakota cattle ranch because of the very hard winter of 1886-1887; son Theodore Jr. born September 1887 **[Chapter 3]**
Age 29: Edith miscarries July 1888 about ten days after TR got a concussion playing polo
Age 30: campaigns for Harrison for president, who won through the Electoral College. Harrison then appointed him to the Civil Service Commission.; son Kermit born **[Chapter 4]**
Age 32: daughter Ethel born
Age: 35: brother Elliott (father of Eleanor Roosevelt) died Summer 1894; son Archie born April 1894
Age 36: appointed a Police Commissioner of New York City (one of four), and shortly, President of the Commission, 1895, where he undertook a vigorous campaign against corruption **[Chapter 4]**
Age 38: appointed Assistant Secretary of the Navy under McKinley Administration; begins to agitate for US intervention in Cuba **[Chapter 4]**
Age 39: US declared war on Cuba; TR resigned Navy post to go into active service; 1898

Age 40: elected Governor of New York, November 1898

Age 42: elected Vice President, November 1900; became President 14 September 1901, following the assassination of William McKinley

Age 46: elected president in a landslide; announced immediately afterwards that he would not run again, November 1904

Age 50: embarked on a year-long hunting "scientific" expedition through Africa with son Kermit after presidency concluded, March 1909

Age 52: drawn back into politics over dissatisfaction with Taft and Democratic gains in congressional elections, November 1910; Robert La Follette started encouraging TR to join the third party, the Progressives

Age 53: Roosevelt introduced as alternate candidate to Taft for Republican nomination, which splits the party; Roosevelt lost nomination, but decided to run on Third Party ticket; shot on 14 October 1912 at close range, but gave his speech anyway

Age 54: lost presidential bid, November 1912

Age 55: 9 December 1913 embarked on South American trip on which he nearly died after a leg injury and the development of malaria; it was only his son Kermit who managed to get him out alive **[Chapter 11]**

Age 59: leg surgery to treat Amazonian wound, February 1918; son Quentin killed in action in World War I; July 1918

Age 60: diagnosed with inflammatory rheumatism November 1918; died 6 January 1919 4:15 am Oyster Bay, NY diagnosed as coronary thrombosis **[Chapter 11]**

Shelley, Percy Bysshe

Data: 4 August 1792, 10:00 pm, Horsham, England. From memory. Rodden Rating: A

Age 17: matriculated Oxford College (10 April 1810) **[Chapter 7]**

Age 18: expelled from Oxford 25 March 1811 because of his published pamphlet, *The Necessity of Atheism* **[Chapter 7]**

Age 19: eloped with Harriet Westerbrook (August 1811); "met" William Godwin through correspondence (early January 1812) **[Chapter 3]**

Age 20: victim of an armed break-in that could well have been an assassination attempt (26 February 1813) **[Chapter 10]**; daughter, Eliza Ianthe born (June 1813 - 16 June 1876)

Age 21: ran away with Mary Godwin at dawn (5 am) 28 July 1814 remained on Continent 6 weeks before returning, penniless; continued to live with Mary outside London; wrote *Alastor*

Age 22: son Charles Shelley born to Harriet (November 1814 - 1826); grandfather died, leaving Percy the direct heir of the Shelley estate 6 January 1815, with a financial settlement with his father **[Chapters 3, 4]**

Age 23: son William born 24 January 1816; second trip to Switzerland with Mary and Claire to meet Byron

Age 24: Harriet committed suicide late November 1816; Percy and Mary married 30 December 1816; lost custody of his two children by Harriet **[Chapter 3]**

Age 25: daughter, Clara, 2 September 1817; left for Italy 12 March 1818

Age 26: daughter Clara died September 1818 in Venice; son William died June 1819 in Rome

Age 27: son Percy Florence born 12 November 1819; writing extremely productive in this time

Age 29: Percy drowned sailing off coast of Livorno on a journey begun 8 July 1822 **[Chapter 11]**

Life Events Endnotes

1. Roosevelt, Eleanor, Lorena A. Hickok, and Rodger Streitmatter. *Empty without You : The Intimate Letters of Eleanor Roosevelt and Lorena Hickok.* New York: Free Press, 1998, pp 8-9. My interpretation of Streitmatter's citation of Hickock's biography of ER.

2. Rodden database gives source notes as follows: "LMR quotes Stefan Lorant, "The Life and Times of Theodore Roosevelt" (1959, p.19)

Yoe Stein writes "Because the maternal grandmother of the President, Mrs Bulloch, felt impelled the next day to write every detail of such an event to her married daughter in Philadelphia, the circumstances attending Teddy Roosevelt's birth are no mystery. She wrote,"When the different servants were flying about for doctors and for Susan Newberry, the nurse, I was almost the whole time alone with Mittie. Anna had taken Bamie over to Lizzie Ellis'. I send for her but she was too unwell to come - I could not bear the idea of having no female friend with me so sent for Mrs. Roosevelt (Grandmother of the President, his father's mother) and she came over. Mittie continued to get worse and worse until a quarter to eight in the evening when the birth took place." Source: http://www.astro.com/astro-databank/Roosevelt%2C_Teddy

E

Classical Solar Return Aphorisms

THE PROBLEM WITH APHORISMS IS THAT THEY ARE, WELL, APHORISTIC. Few ancient writers produced technical manuals that were comprehensive, specific, and organized in a systematic way. It was too easy to extract ideas from example charts, and only generally list them by some organizing principle, like house. This tends to result in a lot of undigested material. In this Appendix, I have compiled the aphorisms of several of the later classical writers on solar returns, so that it is possible to see the overlaps in method. These are presented in Tables One and Two, arguments for a good and bad year.

Table 1. Arguments for a Good Year from the solar return

Arguments of a good solar year	Cardan	Morin[1]	Gadbury[2]
"When the Ascendant of a Revolution is the same with that of the Person's Nativity, something promised in the geniture happens. but much more certainly if the Moon shall be also in her place of the geniture, or the Lord of the Ascendant in a place partially behold the same house of the Radix."[3] [Gadbury adds that the Ascendant sextile or trine also has the same effect]	✓		✓

Arguments of a good solar year	Cardan	Morin[1]	Gadbury[2]
Multiple factors in the same sign, or in those sextile or trine to the Radix positions			✓
The Radix Ascendant Ruler well posited from a good house			✓
Ascendant of the revolution in the place of the Moon, and the Radix Moon, while the Revolution Moon is in the same sign as the Radix Moon, and aspecting fortunes (the Moon sign and approximate degree repeats every nineteen years, but there's no guarantee that it will be well aspected)		✓	✓
Part of Fortune in a good place in the revolutional figure			✓
Ruler of the revolutional 2nd in the 1st brings financial gain			✓
A planet that is peregrine in the Radix 2nd house, but posited in the 1st of the revolution brings financial gain from an unexpected person or place			✓
If the Ruler of the revolutional Ascendant applies to the Ruler of the 2nd, then there is financial gain through work			✓

Arguments of a good solar year	Cardan	Morin[1]	Gadbury[2]
"The Lord of the Ascendant, and *Luna* with *Mercury* well placed in the Revolution, inclines the Native to study, and to learn languages, &c. With *Saturn*, he is sober and austere. With *Jupiter*, just honest, and of a good behavior. With *Mars*, confident, bold, sometimes rash and furious. With the Sun, he is imperious and lofty, but prudent. With *Venus*, wanton and pleasant, and much frequenting Womens Companies. This is to be understood as well in their Sextiles and Trines as in their Conjunctions."[4]			✓
The house of the revolutionary Part of Fortune shows the type of financial gain, provided that the Part of Fortune and its dispositor are fortified.			✓
A radix peregrine planet in the revolutional 2nd house dignified shows financial gain from a direction where it is usually blocked			✓
Saturn in the 8th house dignified gives financial benefits from wills and legacies			✓
Revolutionary Ruler of the 2nd and Part of Fortune in the 2nd well dignified brings riches			✓
Revolutionary Ruler of the 10th and Part of Fortune in the 10th well dignified brings riches from office, profession, promotion, or honor, or from the Native's mother			✓
Revolutionary Ruler of the 9th and Part of Fortune in the 9th well dignified brings riches from longer trips, learning, or the Church			✓
Revolutionary Ruler of the 12th and Part of Fortune in the 12th well dignified brings riches from one's secret enemies, from large animals, or from adversity			✓

Arguments of a good solar year	Cardan	Morin[1]	Gadbury[2]
If the sign on the revolutionary 5th is the sign of radix Venus or Jupiter, the Native could have children this year			✓
Venus, Jupiter, the Moon, and the North Node in fruitful (*i.e.*, the water) signs in the revolutional 5th can bring children.		✓	✓
Venus, Jupiter, the Moon, and the North Node in easy aspect to the Ruler of the revolutional 5th can bring children			✓
Ruler of revolutionary 1st, 6th, Sun and Moon dignified and in easy aspect indicate a healthy year			✓
Ruler of the revolutionary 1st and 7th conjunct, sextile, or trine from the 5th, 7th or 11th denotes the possibility of marriage			✓
If the radix Venus is disposed by Jupiter, and revolutionary Jupiter is disposed by Venus; or revolutionary Venus is in the place of radix Jupiter, then marriage is possible			✓
The Rulers of both the radix and revolution in the 7th denotes marriage			✓
Revolutionary Part of Fortune, Lord of the Year, or North Node in the 9th means profits from travels			✓
Revolutionary Ascendant in the sign of the radix MC gives a renewal to the career		✓	✓
Revolutionary Jupiter, Venus, or North Node in the 10th means the Native thrives in the career			✓
Same planet Ruler of 1st and 10th with dignity gives preferment		✓	
Significant journeys with revolutionary Sun and Moon in the 9th, one ruling the 1st and the other, the 10th		✓	

Table 2. Arguments for a Bad Year from the solar return.

Arguments of a difficult solar year	Cardan	Morin	Gadbury[5]
"When the Dragon's Tail in a Nativity unfortunately beholds the Lord of the Ascendant and in a Revolution the Moon shall be joined therewith, and the Lord of the House of Death being then in the place of an infortune in the Radix, shall likewise behold it, the Party that year will die."[6]	✓		✓
"When the Infortunes are strong in the Radix, and the Moon applies to a powerful fixed Star of the Nature of Mars in a Revolution, the Party will be apt to commit man-slaughter that year, or be in danger about it."[7]	✓		
"If in a Revolution the Lord of the Geniture Retrograde (if he be one of the Inferiors), begins to be under the Sun beams, or (if he be one of the Superiors) if he be afflicted by an Infortune, you may expect some danger of your life that year."[8]	✓		
"When in a Person's Revolution whose only significator of life was debilitated in the Radix, the Fortunes shall be combust in any house but the Ascendant, and the Infortunes being above the Earth, shall behold the Sun, Ascendant, and Moon, or the Moon be under the Earth, such person without any ill direction may die that year."[9]	✓		
"If a Geniture be weak as to life, and three Planets be joined in a Revolution, there is imminent danger of some eminent disease, especially if they happen in the sixth house."[10]	✓		
"When the Moon is joined with Saturn in a Revolution, and he casts a square to the Ascendant, such person shall that year suffer in his body by reason of a disease of his mind."[11]	✓		

Arguments of a difficult solar year	Cardan	Morin	Gadbury[5]
"When the Moon agreeing with Saturn in the Radix, or being with any other Planet in his dignities, if she happen in a Revolution (after the age of forty years) to be corporally joined with Saturn in the same latitude, or being full of light shall be in opposition to him and in contrary latitude from the sixth house to the eighth, the Native will undoubtedly fall into some strange disease and die thereof."[12]	✓		
"When the houses of the Ascendant or Moon in the Radix shall be in square or opposition to the Infortunes in a Revolution, the Native will suffer much trouble, but if the Moon be in conjunction with them, then he shall do much mischief to other people, but if besides this the Infortunes are Lords of inimical places, He shall both do damage to others and suffer much himself. "[13]	✓		
"Fatal will that year be to the Native's health, when in the Revolution many of the Hylegicals come to bad places of the Figure, or to the Aspects of the Infortunes. "[14]	✓		
"If any Planet be afflicted in an annual revolution, the effects will appear when he shall apply by body, square or opposition to the Planet that is Lord of the sign wherein he is."[15]	✓		
"Diseases are for the most part of the nature of the Lord of the sixth house, or the Planet therein posited as well in Revolutions as Nativities."[16]	✓		✓
Multiple factors in signs square or opposite to the Radix positions			✓
Revolution 1st has a malefic, or a malefic beholds the cusp			✓
If the Ruler of the revolutional Ascendant separates from the Ruler of the 2nd, then there is financial loss through work			✓

Arguments of a difficult solar year	Cardan	Morin	Gadbury[5]
Infortune in the revolutional 2nd brings financial loss			✓
Saturn Ruler of the revolutional 3rd in the Ascendant brings problems with siblings and cousins			✓
Infortunes behold the Ascendant			✓
Revolutionary Mars conjunct Radix Mercury brings losses and dangers		✓	✓
Ruler of revolutionary Ascendant combust, unless the Ruler is also essentially dignified, but the loss is worse if essentially debilitated			✓
The Lights conjoined in the 4th or 7th gives the death of a parent			✓
Ruler of the revolutionary Ascendant retrograde in the 8th can bring sickness unto death[17]			✓
Ruler of the revolution conjunct the South Node brings much sickness and danger from it			✓
The revolutionary Moon conjunct Saturn, which is in hard aspect to the Ascendant, then the Native is dangerously sick in body and mind			✓
All the revolutionary planets weak, Cadent, and poorly dignified			✓
The revolutionary Ascendant conjunct Radix Mars, with revolutionary Mars in hard aspect to the Ascendant and not cadent, then dangers, quarrels, wounds and acute diseases			✓
An eclipse near the degree of the Sun, Moon or Ascendant portends death			✓
Moon in hard aspect and mutual reception with fortunes			✓
Sun square or opposite radix Ascendant degree or ruler brings troubles and dangers			✓
Sun in the revolutional 12th brings conspiracies against the Native			✓

Arguments of a difficult solar year	Cardan	Morin	Gadbury[5]
Saturn and Mars conjunct in the revolutional 10th brings the death of the mother, and loss of honor			✓
Revolutional Moon or Ruler of the Ascendant in hard aspect to malefics brings loss and detriment, especially if either malefic is Ruler of the 7th or 12th			✓
If Mercury is Lord of the Year and combust, then there are problems with buying, selling, accounting, and writing			✓
Malefics in the revolutionary 12th bring triumphs to one's enemies		✓	✓
Aries on the revolutionary Ascendant brings fear of a violent death			✓
Taurus on the revolutionary Ascendant brings sickness			✓
Libra on the revolutionary Ascendant brings the possibility of sickness through gluttony			✓
The radix Ruler of the Ascendant poorly aspected denotes disease			✓
The revolutionary Moon afflicted by malefics or combust denotes disease			✓
The Moon unfortunate at birth, and the revolutionary Mars in the place of radix Mars or Saturn denotes evil to the Native			✓
Malefics in the revolutional 1st bring sickness, and especially if the malefic is Lord of the Year			✓
Saturn in Leo hard aspect Mars, or Mars in Sagittarius hard aspect Saturn can denote falls from a horse			✓
The Lord of the Ascendant, and the Moon badly placed in the Revolution, with squares and oppositions from other planets denotes the bad qualities of the aspecting planet predominating			✓
Revolutional Part of Fortune in bad aspect to dispositor brings financial loss			✓

Arguments of a difficult solar year	Cardan	Morin	Gadbury[5]
Revolutionary Saturn retrograde in the 4th house gives problems with inheritance of land, or land generally			✓
Revolutionary Ruler of the 2nd and Part of Fortune in the 2nd poorly dignified brings loss			✓
Revolutionary Ruler of the 10th and Part of Fortune in the 10th poorly dignified brings loss from office, profession, promotion, or honor, or from the Native's mother			✓
Revolutionary Ruler of the 9th and Part of Fortune in the 9th poorly dignified brings loss from longer trips, learning, or the Church			✓
Revolutionary Ruler of the 12th and Part of Fortune in the 12th poorly dignified brings loss from one's secret enemies, from large animals, or from adversity			✓
Afflictions to the 4th house of a revolutional chart will show afflictions to the father, and possibly to land. This can also be seen through afflictions of the Sun by Saturn.			✓
Mercury afflicting the Ruler of the revolutional 4th can result in problems with land titles, or legal maneuvering			✓
Saturn, Mars or South Node in the 5th brings problems with children			✓
Venus ruling the revolutional 5th in square or opposition to Mars brings lasciviousness, but probably not a permanent relationship			✓
Malefics in the revolutional 6th house can indicate disease			✓
Malefics afflicting the Ruler of the 6th house can indicate disease			✓

Arguments of a difficult solar year	Cardan	Morin	Gadbury[5]
Ruler of the revolutional Ascendant square or opposite the ruler of the 6th can indicate disease			✓
Angular revolutionary Sun and Moon in opposition can indicate eye disease			✓
Revolutionary Ruler of 8th in square or opposition to Ascendant Ruler is danger of death			✓
Revolutionary Ruler of the 9th in the 12th gives scant profit to journeys taken			✓
Revolutionary Ruler of 8th in 1st is a danger of death			✓
Revolutionary Ruler of the Ascendant in the 8th afflicted by malefics is danger of death		✓	✓
Ruler of the radix 4th or 8th square or opposite Revolutionary Ruler of Ascendant is danger of death		✓	✓
Revolutionary Sun and Saturn in opposition to each other across the 2nd and 8th is grave danger of death			✓
Benefics in the revolutionary 12th denote powerful enemies			✓
Radix 8th house Ruler as Ruler of Ascendant means danger of death		✓	
Sun in the radix 12th brings dangers		✓	
Radix Ruler of the 11th in the 12th gives harm from false friends		✓	
Revolutionary Ruler of the 12th at the 8th house cusp is an argument of death		✓	

Appendix E Endnotes

1. Morin (Holden), Chapter 7.
2. Gadbury, John, 1661, pp 212-232.
3. Aphorism 5 in Cardan (Lilly)
4. Gadbury, *Genethlialogia*, p 218.
5. Gadbury, John, 1661, pp 212-232.
6. Cardan (Lilly), Aphorism 2.
7. Cardan (Lilly), Aphorism 3.
8. Cardan (Lilly), Aphorism 6.
9. Cardan (Lilly), Aphorism 8.
10. Cardan (Lilly), Aphorism 9.
11. Cardan (Lilly), Aphorism 12.
12. Cardan (Lilly), Aphorism 14.
13. Cardan (Lilly), Aphorism 15.
14. Cardan (Lilly), Aphorism 17.
15. Cardan (Lilly), Aphorism 18.
16. Cardan (Lilly), Aphorism 19.
17. As I discussed in *Traditional Medical Astrology*, a prediction of death in a modern context may be translated as a medical crisis that will not heal itself (if it will) without significant medical intervention. In other words, it should not be taken as an automatic death sentence, but as an admonition to use extreme medical caution.

F

Solar Return Placements for Examples Used

Solar Return Sun

In 1st house: M Curie 1899 Chapter 4, T Roosevelt 1901 Chapter 2, M Curie 1903 Chapter 8, T Roosevelt 1905 Chapter 2, F Roosevelt 1925 Chapter 12, F Roosevelt 1929 Chapter 12, F Roosevelt 1933 Chapter 12, ML King 1963 Chapter 10, P Fleming 1967 Chapter 8, D Hamill 1974 Chapter 8, D Hamill 1982 Chapter 10, S Hamilton 1982 Chapter 8, M Kwan 2004, Chapter 8, M Kwan 2008 Chapter 7, B Aldrin 2011 Chapter 3

In 2nd house: L Pasteur 1839 Chapter 7, T Roosevelt 1847 Chapter 11, L Pasteur 1847 Chapter 11, T Roosevelt 1888 Chapter 4, F Roosevelt 1908 Chapter 12, M Curie 1911 Chapter 8, F Roosevelt 1912 Chapter 12, T Roosevelt 1913 Chapter 11, F Roosevelt 1916 Chapter 12, E Roosevelt 1932 Chapter 3, F Roosevelt 1937 Chapter 12, F Roosevelt 1941 Chapter 12, F Roosevelt 1945 Chapter 12, ML King 1948 Chapter 7, B. Aldrin 1949 Chapter 7, JL Lehman 1973 locational Chapter 2, P Fleming 1975 Chapter 5, D Hamill 1986 Chapter 3 and Chapter 11

In 3rd house: J Morin 1656 Chapter 11, J Austen 1800 Chapter 6, J Austen 1804 Chapter 11, M Shelley 1822 Chapter 6, M Curie 1890 Chapter 7, M Curie 1894 Chapter 3, T Roosevelt 1896 Chapter 4, T Roosevelt 1900 Chapter 2, E Roosevelt 1907 Chapter 5, F Roosevelt 1920 Chapter 12, F Roosevelt 1924 Chapter 12, F Roosevelt 1928 Chapter 12, ML King 1960 Chapter 6, ML King 1964 Chapter 8, B Aldrin 1969 Chapter 4, JL Lehman 1973 Chapter 2, P Fleming 1987 Chapter 5, D Hamill 1994 Chapter 4

In 4th house: J Austen 1808 Chapter 6, J Austen 1816 Chapter 11, L Pasteur 1842 Chapter 7, L Pasteur 1846 Chapter 7, E Roosevelt 1886 Chapter 11, M Curie 1902 Chapter 7, T Roosevelt 1904 Chapter 2, F Roosevelt 1907 Chapter 12, T Roosevelt 1908 Chapter 2, F Roosevelt 1911 Chapter 12, M Gandhi 1913 Chapter 6, F Roosevelt 1932 Chapter 12, F Roosevelt 1936 Chapter 12, F Roosevelt 1940 Chapter 12, F Roosevelt 1944 Chapter 12, B Aldrin 1948 Chapter 7, B Aldrin 1952 Chapter 4, P Fleming 1966 Chapter 8, D Hamill 1973 Chapter 8, B Aldrin 1989 Chapter 4, M Kwan 1995 Chapter 8, M Kwan 1999 Chapter 8

In 5th house: P Shelley 1821 Chapter 11, L Pasteur 1887 Chapter 4, M Curie 1893 Chapter 7, F Roosevelt 1915 Chapter 12, F Roosevelt 1919 Chapter 12, F Roosevelt 1923 Chapter 12, ML King 1955 Chapter 7, B Aldrin 1968 Chapter 11, D Hamill 1981 Chapter 3, S Hamilton 1981 Chapter 8, M Kwan 2003 Chapter 8

In 6th house: M Shelley 1813 Chapter 3, L Pasteur 1837 Chapter 7, L Pasteur 1841 Chapter 7, M Shelley 1859 Chapter 11, T Roosevelt 1899 Chapter 2, T Roosevelt 1903 Chapter 2, M Curie 1905 Chapters 3 & 4, E Roosevelt 1906 Chapter 5, T Roosevelt 1907 Chapter 2, E Roosevelt 1910 Chapter 6, F Roosevelt 1927 Chapter 12, F Roosevelt 1931 Chapter 12, F Roosevelt 1935 Chapter 12, B Aldrin 1947 Chapter 7, M Angelou 1962 Chapter 6, S Hamilton 1993 Chapter 11, JL Lehman 2005 Chapter 11

In 7th house: P Shelley 1812 Chapter 10, M Shelley 1821 Chapters 3, 5 & 11, L Pasteur 1845 Chapter 7, F Roosevelt 1906 Chapter 12, F Roosevelt 1910 Chapter 12, T Roosevelt 1911 Chapter 11, T Roosevelt 1918 Chapter 11, F Roosevelt 1939 Chapter 12, F Roosevelt 1943 Chapter 12, M Angelou 1945 Chapter 5, B Aldrin 1951 Chapter 7, P Fleming 1965 Chapters 8 & 11, P Fleming 1986 Chapter 5, B Aldrin 1988 Chapter 3, M Kwan 1998 Chapter 8

In 8th house: P Shelley 1816 Chapter 3, T Roosevelt 1886 Chapter 3, M Curie 1892 Chapter 7, F Roosevelt 1914 Chapter 12, F Roosevelt 1918 Chapter 12, F Roosevelt 1922 Chapter 12, ML King 1950 Chapter 7, ML King 1954 Chapter 7, S Hamilton 1980 Chapter 8, Suicide 1980 Chapter 11, M Kwan 2002 Chapter 8, D Hamill 2009 Chapter 3

In 9th house: P Shelley 1811 Chapters 3 & 7, M Shelley 1816 Chapters 3 & 5, T Roosevelt 1894 Chapter 4, T Roosevelt 1898 Chapter 2, E Roosevelt 1905 Chapter 5, E Roosevelt 1909 Chapter 5, F Roosevelt 1926 Chapter 12, F Roosevelt 1930 Chapter 12, E Roosevelt 1938 Chapter 10, B Aldrin 1971 Chapter 8, B Aldrin 1975 Chapter 3, D Hamill 1988 Chapter 5, D Hamill 1992 Chapter 4

In 10th house: T Roosevelt 1877 Chapter 11, T Roosevelt 1902 Chapter 2, F Roosevelt 1905 Chapter 12, T Roosevelt 1906 Chapter 2, E Roosevelt 1917 Chapter 3, F Roosevelt 1934 Chapter 12, F Roosevelt 1938 Chapter 12, ML King 1966 Chapter 8, D Hamill 1975 Chapter 8, S Hamilton 1983 Chapter 8, R Lacoste 1996 Chapter 11, M Kwan 1997 Chapter 8, M Kwan 2001 Chapter 8, M Kwan 2005 Chapter 8, M Angelou 2010 Chapter 8

In 11th house: J Morin 1649 Chapter 11, M Shelley 1815 Chapter 5, L Pasteur 1840 Chapter 7, L Pasteur 1848 Chapter 6, E Roosevelt 1892 Chapter 11, F Roosevelt 1909 Chapter 12, F Roosevelt 1913 Chapter 12, T Roosevelt 1918 Chapter 11, E Roosevelt 1925 Chapter 10, F Roosevelt 1942 Chapter 12, B Aldrin 1950 Chapter 7, B Aldrin 1954 Chapter 3, E Roosevelt 1962 Chapter 11, P Fleming 1976 Chapter 5, Suicide 1979 Chapter 11, D Hamill 1983 Chapter 3, D Hamill 1987 Chapter 5

In 12th house: P Shelley 1810 Chapter 7, P Shelley 1814 Chapters 3 & 4, L Pasteur 1852 Chapter 8, L Pasteur 1856 Chapters 6, 8 & 10, M Curie 1891 Chapter 7, E Roosevelt 1904 Chapter 3, E Roosevelt 1908 Chapter 5, F Roosevelt 1917 Chapter 12, F Roosevelt 1921 Chapter 12, R Lacoste 1933 Chapter 4, M Angelou 1935 Chapter 6, ML King 1949 Chapter 7, R Lacoste 1962 Chapter 10, P Fleming 1988 Chapter 5, D Hamill 1995 Chapters 3 & 4, M Kwan 1996 Chapter 8, M Kwan 2000 Chapter 8, S Hamilton 2003 Chapter 5

Solar Return Moon

In 1st house: P Shelley 1816 Chapter 3, M Shelley 1816 Chapters 3 & 5, T Roosevelt 1905 Chapter 2, F Roosevelt 1908 Chapter 12, T Roosevelt 1913 Chapter 11, M Angelou 1935 Chapter 6, ML King 1954 Chapter 7, M Kwan 1998 Chapter 8, M Kwan 1999 Chapter 8, S Hamilton 2003 Chapter 5

In 2nd house: J Morin 1656 Chapter 11, L Pasteur 1842 Chapter 7, M Curie 1891 Chapter 7, T Roosevelt 1898 Chapter 2, E Roosevelt 1904 Chapter 3, E Roosevelt 1905 Chapter 5, F Roosevelt 1909 Chapter 12, F Roosevelt 1916 Chapter 12, F Roosevelt 1917 Chapter 12, F Roosevelt 1924 Chapter 12, F Roosevelt 1932 Chapter 12, F Roosevelt 1940 Chapter 12, B Aldrin 1952 Chapter 4, B Aldrin 1968 Chapter 11, D Hamill 1973 Chapter 8, S Hamilton 1980 Chapter 8, D Hamill 1981 Chapter 3, D Hamill 1988 Chapter 5

In 3rd house: J Morin 1649 Chapter 11, J Austen 1800 Chapter 6, J Austen 1808 Chapter 6, P Shelley 1810 Chapter 7, J Austen 1816 Chapter 11, M Shelley 1859 Chapter 11, M Curie 1892 Chapter 7, M Curie 1899 Chapter 4, T Roosevelt 1906 Chapter 2, F Roosevelt 1925 Chapter 12, F Roosevelt 1933 Chapter 12, F Roosevelt 1941 Chapter 12, ML King 1955 Chapter 7, P Fleming 1986 Chapter 5

In 4th house: P Shelley 1811 Chapters 3 & 7, T Roosevelt 1899 Chapter 2, E Roosevelt 1906 Chapter 5, T Roosevelt 1907 Chapter 2, F Roosevelt 1910 Chapter 12, F Roosevelt 1918 Chapter 12, F Roosevelt 1926 Chapter 12, R Lacoste 1933 Chapter 4, F Roosevelt 1934 Chapter 12, F Roosevelt 1942 Chapter 12,, M Angelou 1945 Chapter 5, ML King 1948 Chapter 7, ML King 1964 Chapter 8, B Aldrin 1969 Chapter 4, Suicide 1970 Chapter 11, D Hamill 1974 Chapter 8, S Hamilton 1981 Chapter 8, D Hamill 1982 Chapter 10, P Fleming 1987 Chapter 5, R Lacoste 1996 Chapter 11, M Kwan 2000 Chapter 8, M Kwan 2008 Chapter 7

In 5th house: M Curie 1893 Chapter 7, T Roosevelt 1900 Chapter 2, E Roosevelt 1907 Chapter 5, T Roosevelt 1908 Chapter 2, F Roosevelt 1911 Chapter 12, M Gandhi 1913 Chapter 6, F Roosevelt 1919 Chapter 12, F Roosevelt 1927 Chapter 12, F Roosevelt 1935 Chapter 12, E Roosevelt 1938 Chapter 10, F Roosevelt 1943 Chapter 12, E Roosevelt 1962 Chapter 11, S Hamilton 1982 Chapter 8, P Fleming 1988 Chapter 5, M Kwan 2001 Chapter 8

In 6th house: L Pasteur 1837 Chapter 7, L Pasteur 1845 Chapter 7, L Pasteur 1852 Chapter 8, M Curie 1894 Chapter 3, M Curie 1902 Chapter 7, B Aldrin 1947 Chapter 7, ML King 1949 Chapter 7, B Aldrin 1954 Chapter 3, M Angelou 1962 Chapter 6, B Aldrin 1971 Chapter 8, Suicide 1979 Chapter

11, D Hamill 1975 Chapter 8, D Hamill 1983 Chapter 3, M Angelou 2010 Chapter 8

In 7th house: P Shelley 1812 Chapter 10, M Shelley 1813 Chapter 3, P Shelley 1821 Chapter 11, M Shelley 1821 Chapters 3, 5 & 11, T Roosevelt 1877 Chapter 11, T Roosevelt 1901 Chapter 2, ML King 1950 Chapter 7, P Fleming 1965 Chapters 8 & 11, ML King 1966 Chapter 8, JL Lehman 1973 relocated Chapter 2, Suicide 1980 Chapter 11, S Hamilton 1983 Chapter 8, M Kwan 1995 Chapter 8, M Kwan 2002 Chapter 8, M Kwan 2003 Chapter 8, B Aldrin 2011 Chapter 3

In 8th house: L Pasteur 1846 Chapter 7, T Roosevelt 1886 Chapter 3, E Roosevelt 1892 Chapter 11, T Roosevelt 1894 Chapter 4, M Curie 1903 Chapter 8, F Roosevelt 1905 Chapter 12, E Roosevelt 1908 Chapter 5, M Curie 1911 Chapter 8, F Roosevelt 1912 Chapter 12, F Roosevelt 1913 Chapter 12, F Roosevelt 1920 Chapter 12, F Roosevelt 1921 Chapter 12, F Roosevelt 1928 Chapter 12, F Roosevelt 1929 Chapter 12, E Roosevelt 1932 Chapter 3, F Roosevelt 1936 Chapter 12, F Roosevelt 1944 Chapter 12, B Aldrin 1948 Chapter 7, P Fleming 1966 Chapter 8, JL Lehman 1973 Chapter 2, B Aldrin 1988 Chapter 3, D Hamill 1992 Chapter 4, JL Lehman 2005 Chapter 11

In 9th house: J Austen 1804 Chapter 11, P Shelley 1814 Chapters 3 & 4, M Shelley 1822 Chapter 6, T Roosevelt 1902 Chapter 2, E Roosevelt 1909 Chapter 5, E Roosevelt 1917 Chapter 3, T Roosevelt 1918 Chapter 11, E Roosevelt 1925 Chapter 10, F Roosevelt 1937 Chapter 12, F Roosevelt 1945 Chapter 12, ML King 1963 Chapter 10, S Hamilton 1992 Chapter 10, M Kwan 1996 Chapter 8

In 10th house: M Shelley 1815 Chapter 5, L Pasteur 1839 Chapter 7, T Roosevelt 1847 Chapter 11, L Pasteur 1847 Chapter 11, E Roosevelt 1886 Chapter 11, L Pasteur 1887 Chapter 4, T Roosevelt 1903 Chapter 2, F Roosevelt 1906 Chapter 12, E Roosevelt 1910 Chapter 6, T Roosevelt 1911 Chapter 11, F Roosevelt 1914 Chapter 12, F Roosevelt 1922 Chapter 12, F Roosevelt 1930 Chapter 12, F Roosevelt 1938 Chapter 12, B Aldrin 1949 Chapter 7, ML King 1960 Chapter 6, P Fleming 1967 Chapter 8, P Fleming 1975 Chapter 5, B Aldrin 1989 Chapter 4, M Kwan 2004 Chapter 8, D Hamill 2009 Chapter 3

In 11th house: T Roosevelt 1888 Chapter 4, T Roosevelt 1896 Chapter 4, T Roosevelt 1904 Chapter 2, M Curie 1905 Chapters 3 & 4, F Roosevelt 1907 Chapter 12, F Roosevelt 1915 Chapter 12, F Roosevelt 1923 Chapter 12, F Roosevelt 1931 Chapter 12, F Roosevelt 1939 Chapter 12, B Aldrin

1950 Chapter 7, P Fleming 1976 Chapter 5, D Hamill 1986 Chapters 3 & 11, S Hamilton 1993 Chapter 11, D Hamill 1994 Chapter 4, M Kwan 1997 Chapter 8, M Kwan 2005 Chapter 8

In 12th house: L Pasteur 1840 Chapter 7, L Pasteur 1841 Chapter 7, L Pasteur 1848 Chapter 6, L Pasteur 1856, Chapters 6, 8 & 10, M Curie 1890 Chapter 7, B Aldrin 1951 Chapter 7, R Lacoste 1962 Chapter 10, B Aldrin 1975 Chapter 5, D Hamill 1987 Chapter 5, D Hamill 1995 Chapters 3 & 4

Solar Return Moon

In Aries: P Shelley 1814 Chapters 3 & 4, L Pasteur 1846 Chapter 7, E Roosevelt 1886 Chapter 11, T Roosevelt 1898 Chapter 2, E Roosevelt 1905 Chapter 5, F Roosevelt 1914 Chapter 12, F Roosevelt 1933 Chapter 12, M Angelou 1962 Chapter 6, E Roosevelt 1962 Chapter 11, P Fleming 1967 Chapter 8, P Fleming 1975 Chapter 5, Suicide 1979 Chapter 11, P Fleming 1986 Chapter 5, D Hamill 1986 Chapters 3 & 11, M Kwan 1996 Chapter 8

In Taurus: L Pasteur 1887 Chapter 4, T Roosevelt 1901 Chapter 2, F Roosevelt 1906 Chapter 12, E Roosevelt 1908 Chapter 5, F Roosevelt 1917 Chapter 12, F Roosevelt 1925 Chapter 12, M Angelou 1935 Chapter 6, F Roosevelt 1936 Chapter 12, F Roosevelt 1944 Chapter 12, B Aldrin 1947 Chapter 7, Suicide 1971 Chapter 11, B Aldrin 1975 Chapter 3, S Hamilton 1983 Chapter 8, M Kwan 1999 Chapter 8

In Gemini: J Austen 1804 Chapter 11, L Pasteur 1841 Chapter 7, M Shelley 1859 Chapter 11, M Curie 1892 Chapter 7, M Curie 1903 Chapter 8, T Roosevelt 1904 Chapter 2, F Roosevelt 1909 Chapter 12, M Curie 1911 Chapter 8, F Roosevelt 1920 Chapter 12, F Roosevelt 1928 Chapter 12, E Roosevelt 1938 Chapter 10, F Roosevelt 1939 Chapter 12, ML King 1954 Chapter 7, D Hamill 1973 Chapter 8, D Hamill 1981 Chapter 3, D Hamill 1992 Chapter 4, M Kwan 2002 Chapter 8

In Cancer: J Morin 1649 Chapter 11, P Shelley 1812 Chapter 10, T Roosevelt 1847 Chapter 11, L Pasteur 1852 Chapter 8, T Roosevelt 1877 Chapter 11, T Roosevelt 1888 Chapter 4, E Roosevelt 1892 Chapter 11, T Roosevelt 1896 Chapter 4, T Roosevelt 1907 Chapter 2, F Roosevelt 1912 Chapter 12, B Aldrin 1951 Chapter 7, R Lacoste 1962 Chapter 10, P Fleming 1965 Chapters 8 & 11, B Aldrin 1989 Chapter 4, M Kwan 2005 Chapter 8

In Leo: M Shelley 1815 Chapter 5, T Roosevelt 1899 Chapter 2, E Roosevelt 1906 Chapter 5, F Roosevelt 1915 Chapter 12, T Roosevelt 1918 Chapter

11, F Roosevelt 1923 Chapter 12, E Roosevelt 1925 Chapter 10, F Roosevelt 1934 Chapter 12, F Roosevelt 1943 Chapter 12, ML King 1949 Chapter 7, B Aldrin 1954 Chapter 3, ML King 1960 Chapter 6, P Fleming 1976 Chapter 5, S Hamilton 1981 Chapter 8, D Hamill 1987 Chapter 5, D Hamill 1995 Chapters 3 & 4, M Kwan 1997 Chapter 8, B Aldrin 2011 Chapter 3

In Virgo: L Pasteur 1839 Chapter 7, L Pasteur 1847 Chapter 11, M Curie 1890 Chapter 7, F Roosevelt 1907 Chapter 12, E Roosevelt 1917 Chapter 3, F Roosevelt 1926 Chapter 12, F Roosevelt 1945 Chapter 12, Suicide 1980 Chapter 11, P Fleming 1987 Chapter 5, S Hamilton 1992 Chapter 10, S Hamilton 2003 Chapter 5, M Kwan 2008 Chapter 7

In Libra: P Shelley 1810 Chapter 7, M Shelley 1821 Chapters 3 & 5 & 11, M Curie 1893 Chapter 7, T Roosevelt 1894 Chapter 4, T Roosevelt 1902 Chapter 2, E Roosevelt 1909 Chapter 5, F Roosevelt 1910 Chapter 12, T Roosevelt 1913 Chapter 11, F Roosevelt 1918 Chapter 12, F Roosevelt 1929 Chapter 12, R Lacoste 1933 Chapter 4, F Roosevelt 1937 Chapter 12, B Aldrin 1949 Chapter 7, ML King 1955 Chapter 7, ML King 1963 Chapter 10, B Aldrin 1968 Chapter 11, D Hamill 1982 Chapter 10, M Kwan 2000 Chapter 8, D Hamill 2009 Chapter 3

In Scorpio: M Shelley 1813 Chapter 3, J Austen 1816 Chapter 11, P Shelley 1821 Chapter 11, L Pasteur 1842 Chapter 7, T Roosevelt 1886 Chapter 3, T Roosevelt 1905 Chapter 2, M Gandhi 1913 Chapter 6, F Roosevelt 1921 Chapter 12, F Roosevelt 1940 Chapter 12, , B Aldrin 1952 Chapter 4, ML King 1966 Chapter 8, B Aldrin 1971 Chapter 8, D Hamill 1974 Chapter 8, M Kwan 1995 Chapter 8, M Kwan 2003 Chapter 8, JL Lehman 2005 Chapter 11

In Sagittarius: J Austen 1808 Chapter 6, M Shelley 1816 Chapters 3 & 5, L Pasteur 1837 Chapter 7, L Pasteur 1845 Chapter 7, L Pasteur 1856 Chapters 6, 8 & 10, T Roosevelt 1900 Chapter 2, E Roosevelt 1904 Chapter 3, F Roosevelt 1905 Chapter 12, T Roosevelt 1908 Chapter 2, F Roosevelt 1913 Chapter 12, F Roosevelt 1924 Chapter 12, F Roosevelt 1932 Chapter 12, F Roosevelt 1943 Chapter 12, ML King 1950 Chapter 7, P Fleming 1966 Chapter 8, Suicide 1970 Chapter 11, S Hamilton 1982 Chapter 8, M Kwan 1998 Chapter 8, M Angelou 2010 Chapter 8

In Capricorn: J Austen 1800 Chapter 6, P Shelley 1816 Chapter 3, L Pasteur 1848 Chapter 6, M Curie 1891 Chapter 7, M Curie 1899 Chapter 4, E Roosevelt 1907 Chapter 5, F Roosevelt 1908 Chapter 12, T Roosevelt 1911 Chapter 11, F Roosevelt 1916 Chapter 12, F Roosevelt 1927 Chapter 12, F Roosevelt 1935 Chapter 12, M Angelou 1945 Chapter 5, B Aldrin 1947

Chapter 7, D Hamill 1988 Chapter 5, P Fleming 1988 Chapter 5, S Hamilton 1993 Chapter 11, R Lacoste 1996 Chapter 11

In Aquarius: J Morin 1656 Chapter 11, L Pasteur 1840 Chapter 7, M Curie 1894 Chapter 3, M Curie 1902 Chapter 7, T Roosevelt 1903 Chapter 2, E Roosevelt 1910 Chapter 6, F Roosevelt 1919 Chapter 12, F Roosevelt 1938 Chapter 12, B Aldrin 1950 Chapter 7, ML King 1964 Chapter 4, JL Lehman 1973 Chapter 2, B Aldrin 1988 Chapter 3, M Kwan 2001 Chapter 8

In Pisces: P Shelley 1811 Chapters 3 & 7, M Shelley 1822 Chapter 6, M Curie 1905 Chapters 3 & 4, T Roosevelt 1906 Chapter 2, F Roosevelt 1911 Chapter 12, F Roosevelt 1922 Chapter 12, F Roosevelt 1930 Chapter 12, E Roosevelt 1932 Chapter 3, F Roosevelt 1941 Chapter 12, ML King 1948 Chapter 7, D Hamill 1975 Chapter 8, S Hamilton 1980 Chapter 8, D Hamill 1983 Chapter 3, D Hamill 1994 Chapter 4, M Kwan 2004 Chapter 8

Solar Return Ascendant

In Aries: M Shelley 1813 Chapter 3, F Roosevelt 1909 Chapter 12, T Roosevelt 1911 Chapter 11, F Roosevelt 1913 Chapter 12, F Roosevelt 1942 Chapter 12, B Aldrin 1950 Chapter 7, P Fleming 1966 Chapter 8, D Hamill 1981 Chapter 3, M Kwan 1995 Chapter 8, M Kwan 1999 Chapter 8

In Taurus: J Morin 1649 Chapter 11, P Shelley 1821 Chapter 11, T Roosevelt 1899 Chapter 2, T Roosevelt 1903 Chapter 2, F Roosevelt 1905 Chapter 12, E Roosevelt 1906 Chapter 5, T Roosevelt 1907 Chapter 2, E Roosevelt 1910 Chapter 6, F Roosevelt 1934 Chapter 12, M Angelou 1935 Chapter 6, F Roosevelt 1938 Chapter 12, ML King 1966 Chapter 8, D Hamill 1973 Chapter 8, B Aldrin 1975 Chapter 3

In Gemini: M Curie 1905 Chapters 3 & 4, MK Gandhi 1913 Chapter 6, F Roosevelt 1922 Chapter 12, F Roosevelt 1926 Chapter 12, F Roosevelt 1930 Chapter 12, ML King 1950 Chapter 7, ML King 1954 Chapter 7, B Aldrin 1971 Chapter 8, S Hamilton 1981 Chapter 8, P Fleming 1987 Chapter 5, D Hamill 1994 Chapter 4, M Kwan 2008 Chapter 7

In Cancer: M Shelley 1822 Chapter 6, L Pasteur 1837 Chapter 7, L Pasteur 1841 Chapter 7, L Pasteur 1845 Chapter 7, E Roosevelt 1886 Chapter 11, M Curie 1893 Chapter 7, F Roosevelt 1910 Chapter 12, F Roosevelt 1914 Chapter 12, F Roosevelt 1918 Chapter 12, R Lacoste 1933 Chapter 4, B Aldrin 1951 Chapter 7, R Lacoste 1962 Chapter 10, P Fleming 1967 Chapter 8, JL Lehman 1973 Chapter 2, P Fleming 1975 Chapter 5, D Hamill 1982

Chapter 10, D Hamill 1986 Chapters 3 & 11, B Aldrin 1988 Chapter 3, M Kwan 1996 Chapter 8, M Kwan 2000 Chapter 8, M Kwan 2004 Chapter 8, M Angelou 2010 Chapter 8

In Leo: P Shelley 1814 Chapters 3 & 4, L Pasteur 1887 Chapter 4, T Roosevelt 1896 Chapter 4, T Roosevelt 1900 Chapter 2, M Curie 1902 Chapter 7, T Roosevelt 1904 Chapter 2, F Roosevelt 1906 Chapter 12, E Roosevelt 1907 Chapter 5, T Roosevelt 1908 Chapter 2, F Roosevelt 1931 Chapter 12, E Roosevelt 1932 Chapter 3, F Roosevelt 1935 Chapter 12, F Roosevelt 1939 Chapter 12, F Roosevelt 1943 Chapter 12, B Aldrin 1947 Chapter 7, ML King 1955 Chapter 7, JL Lehman 1973 relocated Chapter 2, D Hamill 1974 Chapter 8, S Hamilton 1982 Chapter 8, P Fleming 1988 Chapter 5, D Hamill 1995 Chapters 3 & 4

In Virgo: J Austen 1808 Chapter 6, P Shelley 1810 Chapter 7, J Austen 1816 Chapter 11, L Pasteur 1842 Chapter 7, L Pasteur 1846 Chapter 7, T Roosevelt 1888 Chapter 4, M Curie 1890 Chapter 7, M Curie 1894 Chapter 3, F Roosevelt 1915 Chapter 12, F Roosevelt 1919 Chapter 12, F Roosevelt 1923 Chapter 12, F Roosevelt 1927 Chapter 12, M Angelou 1945 Chapter 5, B Aldrin 1968 Chapter 11, Suicide 1970 Chapter 11, P Fleming 1976 Chapter 5, D Hamill 1983 Chapter 3, D Hamill 1987 Chapter 5, B Aldrin 1989 Chapter 4, R Lacoste 1996 Chapter 11, M Kwan 2001 Chapter 8, S Hamilton 2003 Chapter 5, M Kwan 2005 Chapter 8

In Libra: J Austen 1800 Chapter 6, J Austen 1804 Chapter 11, M Shelley 1815 Chapter 5, T Roosevelt 1847 Chapter 11, T Roosevelt 1901 Chapter 2, M Curie 1903 Chapter 8, T Roosevelt 1905 Chapter 2, F Roosevelt 1907 Chapter 12, E Roosevelt 1908 Chapter 5, F Roosevelt 1911 Chapter 12, M Curie 1911 Chapter 8, T Roosevelt 1913 Chapter 11, F Roosevelt 1936 Chapter 12, F Roosevelt 1940 Chapter 12, F Roosevelt 1944 Chapter 12, B Aldrin 1948 Chapter 7, B Aldrin 1952 Chapter 4, ML King 1964 Chapter 8, D Hamill 1975 Chapter 8, S Hamilton 1983 Chapter 8, M Kwan 1997 Chapter 8

In Scorpio: P Shelley 1811 Chapters 3 & 7, L Pasteur 1839 Chapter 7, L Pasteur 1847 Chapter 11, M Curie 1891 Chapter 7, M Curie 1899 Chapter 4, E Roosevelt 1904 Chapter 3, T Roosevelt 1918 Chapter 11, F Roosevelt 1920 Chapter 12, E Roosevelt 1925 Chapter 10, F Roosevelt 1928 Chapter 12, F Roosevelt 1932 Chapter 12, ML King 1948 Chapter 7 ML King 1960 Chapter 6, M Angelou 1962 Chapter 6, E Roosevelt 1962 Chapter 11, B Aldrin 1969 Chapter 4, Suicide 1979 Chapter 11, D Hamill 1988 Chapter 5, D Hamill 1992 Chapter 4

In Sagittarius: J Morin 1656 Chapter 11, M Shelley 1816 Chapters 3 & 5, T Roosevelt 1877 Chapter 11, E Roosevelt 1892 Chapter 11, T Roosevelt 1906 Chapter 2, F Roosevelt 1908 Chapter 12, F Roosevelt 1912 Chapter 12, F Roosevelt 1916 Chapter 12, E Roosevelt 1917 Chapter 3, F Roosevelt 1941 Chapter 12, F Roosevelt 1945 Chapter 12, B Aldrin 1949 Chapter 7, Suicide 1971 Chapter 11, S Hamilton 1992 Chapter 10, M Kwan 1998 Chapter 8, M Kwan 2002 Chapter 8, D Hamill 2009 Chapter 3

In Capricorn: P Shelley 1812 Chapter 10, P Shelley 1816 Chapter 3, L Pasteur 1852 Chapter 8, L Pasteur 1856 Chapters 6, 8, & 10, T Roosevelt 1898 Chapter 2, T Roosevelt 1902 Chapter 2, E Roosevelt 1905 Chapter 5, E Roosevelt 1909 Chapter 5, F Roosevelt 1933 Chapter 12, F Roosevelt 1937 Chapter 12, E Roosevelt 1938 Chapter 10, M L King 1963 Chapter 10, P Fleming, 1965 Chapters 8 & 11, S Hamilton 1980 Chapter 8, P Fleming 1986 Chapter 5, B Aldrin 2011 Chapter 3

In Aquarius: M Shelley 1821 Chapters 3, 5 & 11, L Pasteur 1848 Chapter 6, M Curie 1892 Chapter 7, T Roosevelt 1894 Chapter 4, F Roosevelt 1921 Chapter 12, F Roosevelt, 1925 Chapter 12, F Roosevelt, 1929 Chapter 12, ML King 1949 Chapter 7, Suicide 1980 Chapter 11,

In Pisces: L Pasteur 1840 Chapter 7, M Shelley 1859 Chapter 11, T Roosevelt 1886 Chapter 3, F Roosevelt 1917 Chapter 12. B Aldrin 1954 Chapter 3, S Hamilton 1993 Chapter 11, M Kwan 2003 Chapter 8, J L Lehman, 2005 Chapter 11

Solar Return Sun conjunct Ascendant: L Pasteur 1856 Chapters 6 & 8 & 10, M Curie 1891 Chapter 7, T Roosevelt 1901 Chapter 2, E Roosevelt 1908 Chapter 5, F Roosevelt, 1925 Chapter 12, P Fleming 1967 Chapter 8, D Hamill 1974 Chapter 8, M Kwan 2000 Chapter 8, S Hamilton 2003 Chapter 5

Solar Return Moon conjunct Ascendant: M Angelou 1935 Chapter 6, M Kwan 1998 Chapter 8, S Hamilton 2003 Chapter 5

Solar Return Mercury conjunct Ascendant: L Pasteur 1856 Chapters 6 & 8 & 10, M Curie 1891 Chapter 7, M Kwan 2000 Chapter 8, M Kwan 2008 Chapter 7, B Aldrin 2011 Chapter 3

Solar Return Venus conjunct Ascendant: T Roosevelt 1847 Chapter 11, L Pasteur 1847 Chapter 11, T Roosevelt 1877 Chapter 11, E Roosevelt 1925 Chapter 10, S Hamilton 1982 Chapter 8, S Hamilton 2003 Chapter 5

Solar Return Mars conjunct Ascendant: P Shelley 1814 Chapters 3 & 4, T Roosevelt 1900 Chapter 2, B Aldrin 1969 Chapter 4, Suicide 1970 Chapter 11, M Kwan 1997 Chapter 8, M Kwan 2000 Chapter 8

Solar Return Jupiter conjunct Ascendant: M Curie 1905 Chapters 3 & 4, F Roosevelt 1912 Chapter 12, B Aldrin 1968 Chapter 11, Suicide 1971 Chapter 11

Solar Return Saturn conjunct Ascendant: E Roosevelt 1886 Chapter 11, B Aldrin 1947 Chapter 7, S Hamilton 1983 Chapter 8

Solar Return Uranus conjunct Ascendant: M Shelley 1816 Chapters 3 & 5, F Roosevelt 1938 Chapter 12

Solar Return Neptune conjunct Ascendant: B Aldrin 1948 Chapter 7

Solar Return Pluto conjunct Ascendant: M K Gandhi 1913 Chapter 6, R Lacoste 1933 Chapter 4, F Roosevelt 1943 Chapter 12, ML King 1955 Chapter 7, D Hamill 1975 Chapter 8, S Hamilton 1983 Chapter 8, M Kwan 2002 Chapter 8, B Aldrin 2011, Chapter 3

Solar Return North Node conjunct Ascendant: F Roosevelt 1913 Chapter 12, D Hamill 1982 Chapter 10

Solar Return Sun conjunct Descendant: L Pasteur 1845 Chapter 7, T Roosevelt 1907 Chapter 2, F Roosevelt 1939 Chapter 12, B Aldrin 1951 Chapter 7, JL Lehman 2005 Chapter 11

Solar Return Moon conjunct Descendant: ML King 1950 Chapter 7, M Kwan 2002 Chapter 8

Solar Return Mercury conjunct Descendant: L Pasteur 1837 Chapter 7, L Pasteur 1845, Chapter 7, F Roosevelt 1910 Chapter 12, P Fleming 1986 Chapter 5

Solar Return Venus conjunct Descendant: F Roosevelt 1906 Chapter 12, M Angelou 1962 Chapter 6, S Hamilton 1980 Chapter 8, M Kwan 1998 Chapter 8

Solar Return Mars conjunct Descendant: L Pasteur 1837 Chapter 7, F Roosevelt 1905 Chapter 12, F Roosevelt 1926 Chapter 12, F Roosevelt 1940 Chapter 12, S Hamilton 2003 Chapter 5, D Hamill 2009 Chapter 3

Solar Return Jupiter conjunct Descendant: E Roosevelt 1917 Chapter 3, F Roosevelt 1927 Chapter 12, B Aldrin 1952 Chapter 4, JL Lehman 1973 location Chapter 2, D Hamill 1981 Chapter 3

Solar Return Saturn conjunct Descendant: L Pasteur 1856 Chapter 6 & 8 & 10, T Roosevelt 1904 Chapter 2, D Hamill 1981 Chapter 3

Solar Return Uranus conjunct Descendant: F Roosevelt 1923 Chapter 12

Solar Return Neptune conjunct Descendant: B Aldrin 1950 Chapter 7, B Aldrin 1971 Chapter 8, D Hamill 1986 Chapters 3 & 11, M Kwan 1996 Chapter 8

Solar Return Pluto conjunct Descendant: F Roosevelt 1908 Chapter 12

Solar Return North Node conjunct Descendant: J Austen 1800 Chapter 6, T Roosevelt 1886 Chapter 3, F Roosevelt 1925 Chapter 12, M Angelou 2010 Chapter 8

Solar Return Sun conjunct MC: P Shelley 1811 Chapters 3 & 7, T Roosevelt 1898 Chapter 2, T Roosevelt 1902 Chapter 2, F Roosevelt 1930 Chapter 12, F Roosevelt 1934 Chapter 12, ML King 1966 Chapter 8, B Aldrin 1975 Chapter 3, M Kwan 1997 Chapter 8

Solar Return Moon conjunct MC: J Austen 1804 Chapter 11, T Roosevelt 1847 Chapter 11, E Roosevelt 1886 Chapter 11, L Pasteur 1887 Chapter 4, B Aldrin 1949 Chapter 7, P Fleming 1967 Chapter 8, M Kwan 1996 Chapter 8, M Kwan 2004 Chapter 8

Solar Return Mercury conjunct MC: T Roosevelt 1894 Chapter 4, T Roosevelt 1898 Chapter 2, E Roosevelt 1917 Chapter 3

Solar Return Venus conjunct MC: no examples within orb

Solar Return Mars conjunct MC: T Roosevelt 1886 Chapter 3, ML King 1948 Chapter 7, Suicide 1980 Chapter 11,

Solar Return Jupiter conjunct MC: P Shelley 1816 Chapter 3, L Pasteur 1846 Chapter 7, M Kwan 2001 Chapter 8

Solar Return Saturn conjunct MC: M Shelley 1813 Chapter 3, F Roosevelt 1915 Chapter 12, F Roosevelt 1920 Chapter 12

Solar Return Uranus conjunct MC: P Shelley 1812 Chapter 10, E Roosevelt 1910 Chapter 6, F Roosevelt 1922 Chapter 12, Suicide 1980 Chapter 11, M Angelou 2010 Chapter 8

Solar Return Neptune conjunct MC: B Aldrin 1949 Chapter 7

Solar Return Pluto conjunct MC: T Roosevelt 1913 Chapter 11, F Roosevelt 1915 Chapter 12, F Roosevelt 1936 Chapter 12, JL Lehman 2005 Chapter 11

Solar Return North Node conjunct MC: J Austen 1816 Chapter 11, M Curie 1890 Chapter 7, F Roosevelt 1924 Chapter 12, D Hamill 1983 Chapter 3

Solar Return Sun conjunct IC: J Austen 1808 Chapter 6, M Shelley 1822 Chapter 6, T Roosevelt 1900 Chapter 2, M Curie 1902 Chapter 7, F Roosevelt 1932 Chapter 12, ML King 1964 Chapter 8, M Kwan 1995 Chapter 8

Solar Return Moon conjunct IC: M Shelley 1859 Chapter 11, M Curie 1892 Chapter 7, M Kwan 2000 Chapter 8

Solar Return Mercury conjunct IC: M Shelley 1822 Chapter 6, T Roosevelt 1904 Chapter 2, B Aldrin 1969 Chapter 4, JL Lehman 1973 natal Chapter 2

Solar Return Venus conjunct IC: L Pasteur 1887 Chapter 4, M Curie 1890 Chapter 7, M Curie 1902 Chapter 7, F Roosevelt 1915 Chapter 12

Solar Return Mars conjunct IC: J Austen 1816 Chapter 11, F Roosevelt 1932 Chapter 12, R Lacoste 1933 Chapter 4, ML King 1964 Chapter 8, M Kwan 2008 Chapter 7

Solar Return Jupiter conjunct IC: M Curie 1891 Chapter 7, F Roosevelt 1910 Chapter 12, F Roosevelt 1916 Chapter 12, P Fleming 1966 Chapter 8, S Hamilton 1982 Chapter 8

Solar Return Saturn conjunct IC: T Roosevelt 1896 Chapter 4, M Curie 1903 Chapter 8, ML King 1955 Chapter 7, M Kwan 2008 Chapter 7

Solar Return Uranus conjunct IC: T Roosevelt 1896 Chapter 4, JL Lehman 1973 location Chapter 2, D Hamill 2009 Chapter 3

Solar Return Neptune conjunct IC: L Pasteur 1847 Chapter 11, M Curie 1892 Chapter 7, , F Roosevelt 1909 Chapter 12, E Roosevelt 1910 Chapter 6, F Roosevelt 1926 Chapter 12, B Aldrin 1968 Chapter 11, D Hamill 1983 Chapter 3

Solar Return Pluto conjunct IC: M Curie 1892 Chapter 7, F Roosevelt 1913 Chapter 12, M Angelou 1935 Chapter 6, P Fleming 1988 Chapter 5

Solar Return North Node conjunct IC: E Roosevelt 1906 Chapter 5, T Roosevelt 1907 Chapter 2F Roosevelt 1929 Chapter 12, M Kwan 1996 Chapter 8

Solar Return is New Moon (within 8 degrees): J Austen 1808 Chapter 6, L Pasteur 1848 Chapter 6, T Roosevelt 1886 Chapter 3, T Roosevelt 1905 Chapter 2, F Roosevelt 1919 Chapter 12, F Roosevelt 1938 Chapter 12, Rene Lacoste 1962 Chapter 10, M Angelou 1962 Chapter 6, P Fleming 1965 Chapter 8, P Fleming 1965 Chapter 11, S Hamilton 1992 Chapter 10, D Hamill 1995 Chapter 3, D Hamill 1995 Chapters 3 & 4

Solar Return is Full Moon (within 8 degrees): J Austen 1804 Chapter 11, M Shelley 1822 Chapter 6, L Pasteur 1852 Chapter 8, E Roosevelt 1905 Chapter 5, F Roosevelt 1923 Chapter 12, F Roosevelt 1942 Chapter 12, R Lacoste 1996 Chapter 11.

Solar Return Moon is Void of Course: J Austen 1804 Chapter 11, L Pasteur 1839 Chapter 7, M Curie 1894 Chapter 3, F Roosevelt 1908 Chapter 12, F Roosevelt 1920 Chapter 12, F Roosevelt 1929 Chapter 12, F Roosevelt 1938 Chapter 12, B Aldrin 1950 Chapter 7, P Fleming 1967 Chapter 8, D Hamill 1982 Chapter 10, P Fleming 1986 Chapter 5, D Hamill 1992 Chapter 4

References

Abu, Ma'shar. (2010). *On Solar Revolutions*. Minneapolis, MN, Cazimi Press.

Al-Biruni, M. i. A. and R. R. Wright (1934). *The Book of Instruction in the Elements of the Art of Astrology*. London, Luzac & Co.

Aldrin, B. and K. Abraham (2009). *Magnificent Desolation : The Long Journey Home from the Moon*. New York, Harmony Books.

Angelou, M. (1970). *I Know Why the Caged Bird Sings*. New York, Random House.

Angelou, M. (1974). *Gather Together in My Name*. New York, Random House.

Angelou, M. (1986). *All God's Children Need Traveling Shoes*. New York, Random House.

Barker, S. (1984). *The Signs of the Times : the Neptune factor and America's destiny*. St. Paul, Minn., U.S.A., Llewellyn Publications.

Bell, L. (2005). *Cycles of light: Exploring the Mysteries of Solar Returns*. London, Centre for Psychological Astrology Press.

Bonatti, G. and J. Cardan (1986). *The astrologer's guide*. London, Regulus Publishing Co., Ltd.

Bradley, D. A. (1948). *Solar and Lunar Returns*. St. Paul, Minn., Llewellyn Publications.

Brady, B. (1992). *The Eagle and the Lark: A Textbook of Predictive Astrology*. York Beach, Me., S. Weiser.

Brands, H. W. (1997). *T. R.: The Last Romantic*. New York, NY, Basic Books.

Brands, H. W. (2008). *Traitor to His Class: The Privileged Life and Radical Presidency of Franklin Delano Roosevelt*. New York, Doubleday.

Curry, P. (1989). *Prophecy and Power: Astrology in Early Modern England*. Princeton, N.J., Princeton University Press.

Davison, R. C. (1990). *Cycles of Destiny. Understanding Return Charts*. Wellingborough, Aquarian.

Debré, P. (1998). *Louis Pasteur*. Baltimore, Johns Hopkins University Press.

Discepolo, C. (2007). *Transits and Solar Returns*. Napoli, Ricerca '90.

Eshelman, J. A. (1985). *Interpreting Solar Returns*. San Diego, Calif., ACS Publications.

Ewbank, V. & J. Wickenburg. (1973). *When Your Sun Returns*. Seattle, self-published.

Fleming, P. and P. Kaminsky (1999). *The Long Program: Skating toward Life's Victories*. New York, Pocket Books.

Gadbury, J. (1659). *The Nativity of the late King Charls Astrologically and Faithfully Performed*. London, James Cottrel.

Gadbury, J. (1661). *Genethlialogia, or, The doctrine of nativities containing the whole art of directions and annual revolutions, whereby any man (even of an ordinary capacity) may be enabled to discover the most remarkable and occult accidents of his life ... : also tables for calculating the planets places for any time, either past, present, or to come : together with the doctrine of horarie questions, which (in the absence of a nativity) is sufficient to inform any one of all manner of contingencies necessary to be known*. London, Printed for William Miller ...

Gadbury, J. (1680). *The nativity of the most valiant and puissant monarch, Lewis the fourteenth, king of France and Navarre astronomically and astrologically handled*. London, s.n.

Gauquelin, M. and F. Gauquelin (1972). *Birth and Planetary Data Gathered since 1949 Coordonnées natales et planétaires rassemblées depuis 1949. Series C, volume 1, Profession - heredity, Results of series A & B, Profession - hérédité, Résultats des séries A & B*. Paris, Laboratoire d'étude des relations entre rythmes cosmiques et psychophysiologiques.

Gillespie, M., R. J. Butler, et al. (2008). *Maya Angelou: A Glorious Celebration*. New York, Doubleday.

Godwin, J., C. Chanel, et al. (1995). *The Hermetic Brotherhood of Luxor: Initiatic and Historical Documents of an Order of Practical Occultism*. York Beach, ME, S. Weiser.

Gottfried, T. (1997). *Eleanor Roosevelt : First Lady of the Twentieth Century*. New York, Franklin Watts.

Hamill, D. and D. Amelon (2007). *A Skating Life*. New York, Hyperion.

Hamilton, S. and L. Benet (2000). *Landing it*. New York; Maidstone, Pinnacle ; Amalgamated Book Services.

Holden, J. H. (2008). *Five Medieval Astrologers*. Scottsdale, AZ, American Federation of Astrologers.

Johnson, K. P. (1994). *The Masters Revealed: Madam Blavatsky and the Myth of the Great White Lodge*. Albany, State University of New York Press.

Juste, D. (2007). *Les Alchandreana Primitifs: Étude sur les Plus Anciens traités astrologiques latins d'origine arabe (Xe siècle)*. Leiden, Brill.

King, M. L. and C. Carson (1998). *The Autobiography of Martin Luther King, Jr*. New York, Intellectual Properties Management in association with Warner Books.

Kirby, B. and J. Stubbs (1990). *Interpreting Solar and Lunar Returns:*

A Psychological Approach. Shaftesbury, Element.

Lehman, J. L. (1996). *Classical Astrology for Modern Living : From Ptolemy to Psychology & Back Again*. Atglen, Pa., Schiffer Publishing.

Lehman, J. L. (2002). *Martial Art of Horary Astrology*. Atglen, PA, Schiffer Publishing.

Lehman, J. L. (2011). *Astrology of Sustainability: The Challenge of Pluto in Capricorn*. Atglen, PA, Schiffer Publishing.

Lehman, J.L. (2011) *Traditional Medical Astrology*. Atglen, PA, Schiffer Publishing.

Lilly, W. (1647). *Christian astrology modestly treated of in three books : the first containing the use of an ephemeris, the erecting of a scheam of heaven, nature of the twelve signs of the zodiack, of the planets, with a most easie introduction to the whole art of astrology : the second, by a most methodicall way, instructeth the student how to judge or resolve all manner of questions contingent unto man, viz., of health, sicknesse, riches, marriage ... : the third contains an exact method whereby to judge upon nativities*. London, Printed by.

Louis, A. (2008). *The Art of Forecasting Using Solar Returns*. Bournemouth, The Wessex Astrologer.

Masha'allah (2009). *Six Astrological Treatises by Masha'allah*. Tempe, AZ, American Federation of Astrologers.

McCullough, N. (1999). *Solar Returns: Formulas & Analyses*. Ingleside, TX, Namac Pub.

Merriman, R. A. (2000). *The "New" Solar Return Book of Prediction*. W. Bloomfield, MI, Seek-It Publications.

Morin, J. B. (1661). *Astrologia Gallica Principiis & Rationibus Propriis Stabilita*. Hagae-Comitis, ex typographia Adriani Vlacq.

Morin, J. B. (2002, 2003). *Astrologia Gallica: book twenty-three, Revolutions*. Tempe, AZ, American Federation of Astrologers.

Partridge, J. (1679). *Mikropanastron, or, An astrological vade mecum briefly teaching the whole art of astrology, viz. questions, nativities, with all its parts, and the whole doctrine of elections, never so comprised, nor compiled before, so that the young student may learn as much here as in the great volumes of Guido, Haly or Origanus.* London, Printed for William Bromwich ...

Pearce, A. J. (1879, 1970). *The Text-book of Astrology.* Washington, DC, American Federation of Astrologers.

Penfield, M. H. (1996). *Solar Returns in Your Face.* Tempe, AZ, American Federation of Astrologers.

Quinn, S. (1995). *Marie Curie: A Life.* New York, Simon & Schuster.

Rashid, R. and R. Morelon (1996). *Encyclopedia of the History of Arabic Science.* London ; New York, Routledge.

Rochberg, F. (1998). *Babylonian Horoscopes.* Philadelphia, American Philosophical Society.

Rochberg-Halton, F. (1992). "Calendars: Ancient Near East." *The Anchor Bible Dictionary.* D. N. Freedman. New York, Doubleday: 810-814.

Roosevelt, E., L. A. Hickok, et al. (1998). *Empty Without You : the Intimate Letters of Eleanor Roosevelt and Lorena Hickok.* New York, Free Press.

Rose, D. (1984). *Easy Predictions with Solar Returns.* Lynchburg, VA, Mercury Hour.

Saunders, R. (1677). *The Astrological Judgment and Practice of Physick, deduced from the Position of the Heavens at the Decumbiture of the Sick Person, &c.* London, Thomas Sawbridge.

Shea, M. F. (1998). *Planets in Solar Returns: Yearly Cycles of Transformation and Growth.* Glenelg, MD, Twin Stars, Unlimited.

Sobel, D. (1995). *Longitude: The True Story of a Lone Genius Who Solved the Greatest Scientific Problem of his Time.* New York, Walker.

St. Clair, W. (1989). *The Godwins and the Shelleys: The Biography of a Family.* New York, Norton.

Teal, C. (1999). *Predicting Events with Astrology.* St. Paul, MN, Llewellyn Publications.

Tiberius, O. O. (1995). *Three Books on Nativities.* Berkeley Springs, WV, Golden Hind Press.

Volguine, A. (1976). *The Technique of Solar Returns.* New York, ASI Publishers.

Wainstock, D. (1996). *The Decision to Drop the Atomic Bomb.* Westport, Conn., Praeger.

Index